This unique work is the first in a series of publications dedicated to the condition of the air forces of the Red Army prior to the Nazi invasion of 22 June 1941.

The author describes in detail the composition and the capabilities of the Soviet aviation alignment in the Baltic Special Military District, as well as the training of flight crews and technical personnel; the number and quality of the materiel; the condition of the logistics structures, as well as the operational and tactical plans of both Soviet and German Command; and their reconnaissance operations.

By using data from Soviet and German archive documents, a chronology is recreated (along with the details) of the air battles in the skies over the Baltic region on the first day of the Great Patriotic War.

The photographs, as well as biographies, are presented of all the commanders of the divisions, regiments and of the command headquarters of the Baltic Special Military District.

More than 300 unique photographs of Soviet and German aircraft are presented (together with those of their pilots) from the Soviet and German Archives, as well as from private collections. The camouflage, markings and insignia of aircraft that participated in the air battle are recreated, and maps illustrating the bases belonging to the two warring sides (both original and those recreated from archive documents) are presented.

In Soviet historiography, these events have been afforded insufficient attention and, in fact, right up until 1991, not one serious work on this topic had been published. Actually, the first large-scale research undertaken following the collapse of the USSR in the 1990s was conducted by D.B. Khazanov. In his monographs, the events of the first few days of the war are finally researched using an enormous amount of non-fiction literature (including foreign literature), as well as the relatively small amount of archive documents that had been published up until that time; however, owing to the fact that access to archive documents in that period was still very restricted, there were a great number of incidents that went undisclosed in these works and, as a whole, the course of events was examined in general terms (although overall, it was very objective).

Unfortunately, the lack of historiography has enabled some opportunistic authors in recent years to publish several works of pseudo-research, in which disreputable attempts have been made to misrepresent the achievements of the pilots and commanders of the air forces of the Red Army – thus the publication of objective research (based on archive documents) is long overdue; however, it is only in the last few years – with the large-scale de-classification of the archives and the new opportunities in document processing – that conducting work of this scale has proved possible. Naturally, this publication does not lay claim to a 100 percent disclosure of this topic, but despite the shortcomings inherent in similar works, it does enable history enthusiasts to follow stage by stage the condition of the Red Army Air Force; their preparations to counter aggression on the part of fascist Germany; and the battle in the air on the first day of the Great Patriotic War.

Mikhail Valeryevich Timin was born on 30 July 1979 in the city of Ulyanovsk, in the Union of Soviet Socialist Republics (USSR). He attained a higher education – graduating from Ulyanovsk State Technical University – and currently lives in Moscow, Russia. Married with two sons, he is a researcher specialising in the history of the Air Forces of the USSR and is the author of approximately 50 publications in the following journals: *Aviatsiya i Kosmonavtika*, *AviaMaster*, *AviaPark* and *FlyPast*, as well as on the internet portal warspot.ru. For more than 10 years, he has been engaged in researching documents on Soviet military aviation in the Russian Archives: The Central Archive of the Ministry of Defence of the Russian Federation (in Podolsk), The Russian State Military Archive (Moscow) and The Russian State Documentary Film and Photo Archive (in Krasnogorsk).

AIR BATTLES OVER THE BALTIC 1941

The Air War on 22 June 1941 – The Battle for Stalin's Baltic Region

Mikhail Timin

Translated by Kevin Bridge

Helion & Company

Helion & Company Limited
Unit 8 Amherst Business Centre
Budbrooke Road
Warwick
CV34 5WE
England
Tel. 01926 499 619
Fax 0121 711 4075
Email: info@helion.co.uk
Website: www.helion.co.uk
Twitter: @helionbooks
Visit our blog http://blog.helion.co.uk/

Published by Helion & Company 2018
Designed and typeset by Mach 3 Solutions Ltd (www.mach3solutions.co.uk)
Cover designed by Paul Hewitt, Battlefield Design (www.battlefield-design.co.uk)
Printed by Gutenberg Press Limited, Tarxien, Malta

ISBN 978-1-911512-56-1

British Library Cataloguing-in-Publication Data.
A catalogue record for this book is available from the British Library.

For details of other military history titles published by Helion & Company Limited contact the above address, or visit our website: http://www.helion.co.uk.

We always welcome receiving book proposals from prospective authors.

Contents

List of Maps

In colour section.

List of Tables

Preface to the English edition

On the eve of the 75th anniversary of the outbreak of the Great Patriotic War any illumination of all the twists and turns of the air war on 22 June 1941 is highly symbolic. In Soviet historiography these events have been afforded surprisingly little attention, and in fact over the past 50 years right up until 1991 not one serious work on this topic has been published. Actually, the first large-scale research to be undertaken in the '90s in the last century was carried out by D.V. Khazanov. In his monographs the events of the first few days of the war are researched using an enormous amount of non-fiction literature including foreign literature, as well as the relatively small number of archival documents that had been published up until that time. However owing to the fact that access to the archive documents back then was still very restricted there were a great number of incidents that went undisclosed in these works, and as a whole the course of events was examined in general terms and the research was relatively limited, although overall it was very objective.

Thus the publication of objective research based on archive documents is long overdue. However it is only in the last few years, with the large-scale declassification of the archives and the new opportunities in document processing, that conducting work of this scale has proved possible. Naturally this publication does not lay claim to 100 percent disclosure of this topic, but despite the shortcomings inherent in similar works it does enable history enthusiasts to follow stage by stage the condition of the Red Army Air Force, their preparations to counter aggression on the part of fascist Germany, and the battle in the air on the first day of the Great Patriotic War.

Acknowledgements

The author would like to thank the following for their assistance in the writing of this publication: Aleksey Isayev, Miroslav Morozov, Aleksandr Novichenko, Konstantin Strelbitskiy, Sergey Chekunov, Yuriy Svoyskiy, Sergey Cherepanov, Oleg Kiselev, Sergey Buldygin, Aleksey Pekarsh, Sergey Pshirkov, Dmitriy Volodin, Gennady Sloutskiy, Aleksey Vasetskiy, Ilya Grinberg, Adndrey Mikhaylov, Dmitriy Karlenko, Miroslav Vavrzhinskiy, Anton Potapov, and Gedeminas Kulikauskas

The photographs reproduced in this book are from the Author's collection, and from the Central Archive of the Ministry of Defence of the Russian Federation, the Russian State Documentary Film and Photo Archive, and also from the collections owned by the following contributors: Aleksey Vasetskiy, Ilya Grinberg, Adndrey Mikhaylov, Dmitriy Karlenko, Miroslav Vavrzhinskiy, Anton Potapov, and Gedeminas Kulikauskas. They were also drawn from online sources. The following artists produced work for this publication: Vladimir Kamskiy, Igor Zlobin, Aleksandr Kazakov, and Aleksey Valyayev-Zaytsev.

1

The Soviet Aviation alignment in the Baltic Region on the eve of the Great Patriotic War

1.1 The Formation of the Soviet Aviation Alignment in the Baltic Region, and the Composition and the Condition of the Air Forces of the Baltic Special Military District in 1940

The arrival of Soviet Aviation in the territory of the Baltic States – Lithuania, Latvia, and Estonia – occurred just one and a half years prior to the outbreak of the Great Patriotic War, and moreover initially this occurred within the confines of agreements concerning mutual assistance reached with the governments of these republics. In accordance with these agreements a limited contingent of Soviet forces would be deployed on the territory of each of these states, including air forces.

The first to be redeployed into Lithuania back at the end of 1939 was the 10th Fighter Air Regiment. Then, right at the beginning of the year, the 21st Fighter Air Regiment was relocated to Latvia, while in Estonia the 35th High-Speed Bomber Air Regiment together with the 38th Fighter Air Regiment from the Leningrad Military District was redeployed to Estonian territory as part of the Special Red Army Air Force Group, as were the 15th Fighter Air Regiment from the Belarussian Special Military District and the 7th Long-Range Bomber Air Regiment from Special Purpose Air Army 2. After the end of the Soviet–Finnish war in April 1940 the 148th Fighter Air Regiment from the Leningrad Military District were relocated to the Baltic Region, and the 31st and 54th High-Speed Bomber Air Regiments from the Belarussian Special Military District were relocated in May of that year. The alignment of Soviet air forces was only completed with the succession of the Baltic States into the USSR in the summer and autumn of 1940, when the 31st Fighter Air Regiment, the 5th Light Ground Attack Air Regiment from the Belarussian Special Military District and the 42nd Fighter Air Regiment from the Kaliningrad Military District were redeployed to Lithuania, while the 40th and the 46th High-Speed Bomber Air Regiments from the Belarussian Special Military District, the 9th High-Speed Bomber Air Regiment and the 49th Fighter Air Regiment from the Leningrad Military District were redeployed to Latvia. The directorate of the 4th Mixed Air Division, as well as the 50th and 63rd High-Speed Bomber Air Regiments from the Leningrad Military District were sent to Estonia.

By way of a decree from the People's Commissariat for Defence No. 0/4/104732 dated 25 July 1940 the composition and the disposition of Soviet aviation units in the newly formed Baltic Special Military District were reinforced. In total by the end of October 1940 in Latvia and Lithuania the 7th and 8th Mixed Air Divisions had been deployed in the first echelon. The 148th Fighter Air Regiment based at Leipaja, the 10th Fighter Air Regiment and 46th High-Speed Bomber Air Regiment in Siauliai, the 9th High-Speed Bomber Air Regiment in Panevezys and the 31st High-Speed Bomber Air Regiment in Vaijnode came under the 7th Mixed Air Division. The 15th and 31st Fighter Air Regiments in Kaunas, the 42nd Fighter Air Regiment and the 54th High-Speed Bomber Air Regiment in Vilnius and the 61st Ground Attack Air Regiment (which had been reformed from the 5th Light Ground Attack Air Regiment) in Kedainiai came under the 8th Mixed Air Division.

The 6th Mixed Air Division was formed in the second echelon, with the 40th High-Speed Bomber Air Regiment in Vindava, the 7th Long-Range' Bomber Air Regiment in Mitava,* the 29th Fighter Air Regiment in Riga, and the 49th Fighter Air Regiment in Daugavpils. Apart from that the following units were separate: the 1st Transport Bomber Air Regiment* which had been redeployed to Velikiye Luki from the Northern Caucasus Military District and the reformed 312th Reconnaissance Air Regiment, and the 2nd, 3rd, 10th, 11th, and 16th Air Observation Squadrons. A short time later the 65th Air Observation Squadron in Estonia and the 22nd, 24th, and 29th Air Observation Squadrons of the Baltic Territorial Corps were added to the Air Force line-up for this military district.

The idiosyncratic third echelon was comprised of the 4th Mixed Air Division in Estonia. This division was transferred from the Air Forces of the Leningrad Military District in September 1940. The line-up consisted of the 35th High-Speed Bomber Air Regiment in Tartu, the 50th High-Speed Bomber Air Regiment in Ungru, the 38th Fighter Air Regiment and the 63rd High-Speed Bomber Air Regiment in Tallinn. One feature of the deployment of the 4th Mixed Air Division was that it could be used either against fascist Germany or against Finland.

In accordance with decree No. 0220 issued by the People's Commissariat for Defence and dated 13 September 1940, Air Force departments were set up within the 8th and 11th Army's headquarters that had deployed to the Baltic Region.

All the regiments in the Air Forces of the Baltic Special Military District, with the exception of the 312th Reconnaissance Air Regiment were regular units and had been formed in 1938–39.

In fighter aviation out of eight regiments, seven of them—the 10th, 15th, 21st, 31st, 38th, 42nd, and 49th Fighter Air Regiments—were products of the reorganisation of the Red Army Air Force from a 'squadron' to a 'regimental' system and were formed in 1938–39 on the basis of separate fighter squadrons. The only regiment to be formed in 1940 was the 148th Fighter Air Regiment. This regiment was a product of sorts of the mobilisation seen during the Soviet–Finnish War period and in fact the regiment was also a regular unit, in as much as it was formed of four squadrons that had been drawn as a whole from the 16th and 34th Fighter Air Regiments of the 57th Air Brigade, of the Air Forces of the Moscow Military District.

All of the bomber air regiments were also formed in 1938–39. Interestingly a proportion of the bomber regiments, specifically the 35th, 50th, and 54th High-Speed Bomber Air Regiments that came under the Air Forces of the Baltic Special Military District were originally formed as high-speed bomber air squadrons, whose personnel had assimilated the first bombers to enter service with the Red Army Air Force, the SB, in 1936–37. Other units converted onto the SB from other aircraft types in 1939–40. Thus the 9th High-Speed Bomber Air Regiment (this was previously the 9th Heavy Bomber Air Regiment) operated the TB-3, the 46th High-Speed Bomber Air Regiment (this was previously the 1st Light Bomber Air Regiment) respectively operated the R-5, and the 63rd High-Speed Bomber Air Regiment (this had previously been the 3rd Light Bomber Air Regiment) only began to receive SB bombers in place of the R-5 and R-Zet in August 1940. A peculiarity of the formation of the 40th High-Speed Bomber Air Regiment was that it was formed in July 1939 in Shatalovo on the basis of the remaining personnel and materiel from the

* In the winter of 1940–41 the 1st Heavy Bomber Air Regiment and the 7th Long-Range Bomber Air Regiment were transferred to come under the Long-Range Bomber Aviation (LRA) units.

56th High-Speed Bomber Air Regiment that had been sent to Mongolia to play its role in combat operations at Khalkhin-Gol.

The 5th Light Ground Attack Air Regiment, which was the one in this military district, was formed in 1938 on the basis of the squadrons in the 114th 'Gomel' Light Ground Attack Brigade, Belarussian Military District, which operated the R-5SSS. In September 1940, in connection with the unit's reformation with new personnel and materiel it was renamed the 61st Ground Attack Air Regiment and the majority of the personnel were transferred away. To make up the numbers several pilots were transferred from fighter regiments within the districts, together with graduates from flying schools.

The 312th Reconnaissance Air Regiment was created on the basis of the 4th Long-Range Reconnaissance squadron, the 36th and 43rd Battlefield Reconnaissance Squadrons, and liaison sections from aerial gunnery divisions were converted to form the corps air squadrons.

What then were the formations and units in the Air Forces of the Baltic Special Military District, their personnel, command, and materiel? In order to answer this question it would be pertinent to remind the reader briefly of the events taking place in the Soviet Air Force on the threshold of the 1930s–1940s.

The reform of the Soviet air forces in 1938, and as a consequence the transfer from a squadron to a regimental administrative system, required several thousand pilots and navigators to be taken out of flying schools immediately without the latter having completed the full programme of study. As a consequence of this, in 1938 around 6,000 pilots who had amassed 20–30 flying hours (in all in 1938 some 6,017 pilots and 1,654 observers were taken out of flying schools) arrived to augment these units, and moreover they had only amassed 7–10 hours solo flying as a proportion of this total figure. The situation seems truly exceptional when the actual figures for this augmentation are taken into account. Thus, if at the beginning of 1938 there were around 5,000 pilots in the front line Air Force units, then in the autumn their numbers had increased to a little more than double that figure—up to 11,122 individuals.

How this looked in practice can be deduced by looking at the example of several regiments that formed part of the Air Forces of the Baltic Special Military District.

The 50th High-Speed Bomber Air Regiment was formed on 15 April 1938 on the basis of the 4th, 5th, and 6th High-Speed Bomber Air Squadrons and the 147th High-Speed Bomber Air Brigade in Siverskiy. By June 1939 some 45 young pilots had been drafted in and converted onto the SB by the regular personnel on the regiment.

The 10th Fighter Air Regiment was formed on 25 April 1938 in Bobruysk. The personnel were selected from the 30th, 33rd, 45th, 56th, 57th, and 105th Fighter Squadrons. Once it had been formed, the regiment came under the 56th Fighter Air Brigade. Some 44 young pilots who had arrived from the flying schools were commissioned between 15 May 1938 and 3 August 1938. In total as of 1 October 1938 there were 59 personnel listed in the regiment (of these only 15 were regular pilots). In accordance with an order from the commander of the 56th Fighter Air Brigade in May 1939 eight personnel were selected from the regiment and were posted to the People's Republic of Mongolia 'to combat the Japanese Samurai.'

The 31st Fighter Air Regiment began to be formed on 10 May 1938 in Bryansk on the basis of the well-known 83rd Air Brigade of the air forces of the Belarussian Special Military District, and had been fully formed by 13 August 1938. The regular personnel came from the 107th and 61st Fighter Squadrons, and for the most part they were graduates from the flying schools who completed their training in 1937, although the commanders of these squadrons had combat experience in Spain and in China. The situation was much worse with the regular pilots. The Falcons had very little experience of solo flying on the I-16. According to the unit's historical log-book: 'Some 52 young pilots from the various flying schools had not been pressed into service at these schools to assimilate the I-16.'

The twists and turns that took place in the Red Army air forces can be followed with some accuracy using the example of the 31st Fighter Air Regiment and the difficulties encountered in the formation of the aviation regiments between 1938–1939 can be understood. The entire gravity of the situation can only be acknowledged following a comparison of the information concerning the overall number of new arrivals into the units of newly qualified pilots, with their level of training, against individual pilots. Thus, one of those new arrivals into the 31st Fighter Air Regiment, a young pilot who had just graduated from the Stalingrad Higher Aviation Academy, was Lieutenant L.D. Goryachko who amassed 32 hrs 49 mins (in 305 flights). Of those:

- Introductory flights with an instructor accounted for: 9 hrs 58 mins (in 103 flights), of which: 3 hrs 33 mins (32 flights) had been in a U-2, while 6 hrs 25 mins (in 71 flights) had been in the UTI-4;
- Check flights with an instructor in the U-2 accounted for: 5 hrs 3 mins (in 35 flights);
- Solo flights accounted for 17 hrs 47 mins (in 169 flights) of which: 7 hrs 33 mins (in 63 flights) were in the U-2, while 3 hrs 27 mins (in 32 flights) were in the UT-1, and 4 hrs 33 mins (in 53 flights) were in the UTI-4, while **2 hrs 14 mins (in 21 flights) had been in the I-16.**

Undoubtedly the future Major-General of Aviation was very fortunate in that he came into the regiment at the beginning of 1939 and had almost a year and a half for additional training before the outbreak of war. However with only 21 flights in an I-16 (it works out that on average each flight lasted for 6 mins 28 secs and even taking into account the 53 flights on the UTI-4, which on average lasted for 5 mins 15 secs, it is clear that his time was spent exclusively on take-off and landing practice) he would have had little chance of surviving the forthcoming war.

The situation for Junior Lieutenant S.A. Yevtushenko, who graduated from the Borisogleb Higher Aviation Academy in 1938, was slightly better. He had amassed 10 hrs 20 mins (in 44 flights) on the I-16 whilst at the academy.

Given these graphic examples it is not difficult to imagine how complex a task the training of some 40–50 'semi-trained pilots' coming into the regiments with such a miserly number of hours on combat aircraft from the flying schools was for the commanders of these regiments, as these pilots had to be practically retrained to fly a combat aircraft!

Despite the seriousness of the task of assimilating such a complicated aircraft to fly as the I-16 with, to put it mildly, poorly trained personnel, the commanders of the 31st Fighter Air Regiment, albeit with difficulty, succeeded in getting these newly-qualified men of 'Stalin's Falcons' airborne. This task had been completed, on the whole, by the end of 1938. In all in 1938 the regiment's pilots had amassed 4,340 hrs and practised aerial gunnery 602 times (of these 249 or 44.7 percent hit the target).

However this was achieved at a high price in the truest sense of the word: 'In 1938 the unit had an incredibly high accident rate as well as incurring other incidents in flight. In the training year 1938 overall there were: three fatal accidents, five accidents, and 35 other incidents—crashes, emergency landings, and losses of orientation.' This result was entirely predictable given the weakness in the level of training among the pilots who had just joined the regiments and also that far from all the regular pilots were admitted to an instructor's position, which undoubtedly required special skills.

In 1939 the regiment's pilots continued to hone their combat training, and moreover the enhancement of qualifications among the personnel had a positive effect on the accident rate, which gradually reduced. From 1 January 1939 to 1 November 1939 the regiment amassed 4,067 hrs (with 8,873 landings) and practised aerial gunnery 252 times (of these 127 or 50 percent hit the target). Furthermore there were five accidents, 12 crashes, and three emergency landings in this period.

Table 1 Emergency incidents in the 31st Fighter Air Regiment in 1938

Nature of the incident	Responsibility for these incidents		
	Personnel	Materiel	Technicians
Fatal accidents	2 (67%)	1 (33%)	
Accidents	4 (80%)		1 (20%)
Crashes	20 (57%)		15 (43%)
Emergency landings	3 (75%)		1 (25%)
Losses of orientation	6 (100%)		

In November 1939 two squadrons with the best-trained pilots from the 31st and the 21st Fighter Air Regiments that had been sent to Latvia, were transferred, and in turn two squadrons from the latter took in younger pilots.

Despite the events that occurred the combat training within these units was already gathering pace and in 1940 the 31st Fighter Air Regiment surpassed all other fighter regiments that were based in the European part of the USSR in terms of their level of combat training: 'From 1 January 1940–15 November 1940 the regiment amassed 6,794 hrs of daytime flying, of these 6,092 were on the I-15 and the I-16 and 701 hrs were flown in training aircraft. They opened fire 1,540 times, of which 932 hit the target.'

Events in the other Red Army Air Force units unfolded in much the same way. By the beginning of 1940, despite the periodic rotation of personnel and the deployment of units to different theatres of operations as local conflicts began, the commanders succeeded in turning their 'semi-trained pilots' into fully fledged pilots, who between 1938 and 1939 developed their piloting techniques and assimilated combat aircraft as a whole.

Today it is quite difficult to come to the conclusion, first and foremost because of the lack of evidence, that the process of the formation, breaking in, and training of these units could decisively have been completed any quicker if the young pilots who were sent to readily formed units had been able to complete the full flying training programme at their flying schools. The same could be said if the Red Army Air Force were in a better state of combat readiness by the outbreak of the Great Patriotic War.

The leadership of the Red Army Air Force, having placed the training of new pilots on the shoulders of the commanders of front line units, and squadrons together with their deputies and aides, made a serious miscalculation in terms of the timescales for this experiment, which as a result dragged on for over a year. Moreover despite the fact that in parallel with the formation of these units the command was successful in organising the training of new pilots the youngsters had really only just started their combat training. This played a fateful role during the fighting at Khalkhin-Gol at the beginning of which the well-trained Japanese pilots, though were outnumbered, inflicted a series of defeats on the young pilots of the 22nd and 70th Fighter Air Regiments. Nevertheless the majority of the aviation regiments by mid 1939 were combat ready in favourable weather conditions when flying as a squadron, while the regular pilots were prepared to fly in inclement weather conditions, day and night, and at high altitude. In practically all these units highly achievable prerequisites were drawn up for the final completion by 1940 of the processes of combat training and of creating really effective tools for conducting air combat from these 'half finished' air regiments.

Unfortunately the events that unfolded in 1940 did not allow a full implementation of these measures to enable combat training of all the Red Army Air Force units to reach a high level. There were many reasons behind this and they are all very serious.

At the end of 1939 the Soviet–Finnish War broke out and dozens of regiments and squadrons were sent to the Karelian peninsula. In total, owing to the conflict that lasted for three and a half months, a significant number of units and formations were taken out of the combat training process.

These units were not able to return to their permanent bases and to regroup since between the end of May and the beginning of June the deployment of aviation units to the borders began in connection with the operations surrounding the succession of the Baltic States to the USSR. Soviet forces were deployed here from 17–21 June 1940, as well as to the succession of Bessarabia and Bukovina between 28 June–1 July. Following these events many units were redeployed once again and were based in these newly acquired territories.

Apart from that a limited contingent of Soviet forces back at the end of 1939 were located in Estonia: this was the so-called Special Air Group made up of the 35th and 52nd High-Speed Bomber Air Regiments, the 7th and 53rd Long-Range Bomber Air Regiments, and the 15th and 38th Fighter Air Regiments. The directorate of the 18th Air Brigade was located in Latvia, as was the 31st High-Speed Bomber Air Regiment, the 21st and 148th Fighter Air Regiments, and in Lithuania the 10th Fighter Air Regiment and the 54th High-Speed Bomber Air Regiment. The location of adjacent states in this area had a negative effect on the level of combat training in these aviation regiments.

First and foremost these units were forced to equip and construct airfields, weapons ranges, firing ranges, facilities for combat training classes, as well as accommodation for personnel etc.

Secondly there were inevitably difficulties in supplying units with fuel and engine lubricants, ammunition and so on, since the supplies for all of the above came from the USSR.

The aviation units that arrived after the succession of the Baltic States into the USSR also encountered similar problems to the regiments already based there, and were forced to spend time building a material base, accommodating their personnel and so on. Naturally these circumstances could not fail to have an effect on the condition of these same aviation units and their combat readiness reduced sharply.

A report on the results of combat training in the Air Forces of the Baltic Special Military District for 1940 describes the emerging situation impassively.

The 35th High-Speed Bomber Air Regiment: the regiment was redeployed from SIVERSKIY airfield (in the Leningrad Military District) to SINALEPP airfield (near HAAPSALU in ESTONIA) and played an active part in the fighting up until the end of the war.

In the winter SINALEPP airfield was one of the best airfields in ESTONIA but in summer it was very restricted. It would become waterlogged after the lightest of rainfall and apart from that there were subterranean water flows through the middle of the airfield, which meant that even in the dry summer weather this location never dried out.

On 14 August 1940 the regiment was redeployed to the permanent airfield in TARTU, which is located in the north-eastern part of the city.

The size of TARTU airfield, up until the moment the regiment arrived, meant it was not possible to conduct routine combat training. At the present time the airfield is undergoing an expansion, which will finally be completed by the end of November of this year.

The regiment's personnel are billeted in TARTU, and are scattered around the entire city, which increases the notice period for crews to respond to a scramble.

There is only one building for combat training classes per squadron and they are not fitted out, there are no instruments or visual aids available for these classes at all. The study materials provided by personnel are inadequate. The regiment does not have a range of its own, and uses the ranges belonging to the Leningrad Military District as well as the newly equipped range on Hiiumma Island.

The 50th Red Banner High-Speed Bomber Air Regiment: this regiment was redeployed to field airfields from the outset of the war with FINLAND close to the front line and played an active part in the fighting right up until the end of the war.

The permanent base for this regiment up until 24 October was the SIVERSKIY airfield, where the personnel completed an academic year of combat training, that is to say the regiment was in the best position with a fantastic airfield and well-equipped training facilities.

On 24 October 1940 the regiment was redeployed to UNGRU airfield (near HAAPSALU in the Estonian Soviet Socialist Republic). Construction of this airfield has not been completed, there are only three starting areas and no turf, as a result of which it is impossible to fly in rainy conditions.

The personnel are billeted in HAAPSALU which is located six kilometres from the airfield and the living quarters around the airfield are inadequate to accommodate even junior specialists, let alone personnel.

The only training classrooms available are in the town itself.

The regiment is able to use the range on Hiiumma Island, there are no firing ranges around the airfield but there is a firing range that was once fully fitted out some 8–12 kilometres from the airfield, which can be used initially.

The 63rd High-Speed Bomber Air Regiment. This regiment played an active role in the fighting in the war with FINLAND and for the entire academic year was based at KRASNOGVARDEYSK airfield (in the Leningrad Military District). The permanent base for this regiment is KUUSIKU airfield, which is not ready at the present time, facilities for personnel are inadequate and the regiment has been redeployed temporarily to TALLINN airfield.

The regiment has converted to the SB from the SSS aircraft in this academic year. Conversion of aircrew onto this new materiel has been the principal task during the course of this academic year.

During the course of 1940 the regiment was redeployed from one airfield to another six times. In the summer the combat training was carried out in camp conditions.

With their redeployment to the territory of the Estonian Soviet Socialist Republic (ESSR) conditions for the regiment deteriorated.

The 38th Fighter Air Regiment. At the beginning of hostilities in the war with Finland this regiment was redeployed from PSKOV to KLOOGA airfield (in the PALDISKI region, ESSR) from where it was to play an active part in the fighting up until the end of the war.

The regiment was based up until June at KLOOGA airfield, which owing to severely limited resources, the airfield frequently becoming waterlogged, and the poor condition of the ground led to delays in the roll-out of flying training.

On 17 June the regiment was redeployed to TALLINN airfield, which following expansion and additional development was then ready for day and night flying operations.

The classrooms are being fitted out, the personnel are billeted here and there, but they live in very satisfactory conditions.

The regiment has the use of an artillery range on which it conducts bombing and strafing of ground targets.

The 40th High-Speed Bomber Air Regiment. This regiment has been based at VINDAVA airfield since June 1940. Up until 18 June the regiment was based at SHATALOVO airfield. For the most part the regiment was brought up to full strength with young pilots from the flying schools in December of that year. The poor condition of VINDAVA airfield delayed normal flying operations.

The accommodation for the regiment's personnel is satisfactory, classrooms and shooting galleries are provided but there is no high-quality furniture, no 'Batchler' and a complete lack of sports equipment.

The 21st Fighter Air Regiment. The regiment has been based on LATVIAN territory since January 1940. On 13 August 1940 it was redeployed to RIGA airfield, which is suitable for day and night flying operations. The accommodation for regimental command is in the city itself, some distance from the airfield, which lengthens the timescales for the regiment to prepare to respond to a scramble.

The 49th Red Banner Fighter Air Regiment. The regiment was redeployed from PSKOV to DVINSK airfield on 22 September and for the most part is made up of young personnel. Up until 13 March 1940 the regiment took part in the war with Finland. In the course of June and July the regiment did not fly owing to a lack of fuel. One squadron has not had any materiel since 15 September. The personnel are accommodated in the city itself at a distance of seven kilometres from the airfield, which affects their combat readiness...

The 46th High-Speed Bomber Air Regiment. This regiment is based at SHAVLI airfield, which is suitable for day and night flying operations. The personnel are housed in the town itself, at a distance of four kilometres from the airfield. There are no classrooms.

The 31st High-Speed Bomber Air Regiment. This regiment has been based on VAIJNODE airfield since July 1940: The airfield is suitable for normal flying operations. The personnel are housed in newly constructed regimental command accommodation close to the airfield. There are classrooms but they are not fitted out, there is no furniture, training instrumentation, or textbooks...

The 9th High-Speed Bomber Air Regiment. This regiment has been based at PONEVEZH airfield since 2 September 1940. Owing to its small size the airfield is only suitable for daytime flying operations but is undergoing expansion. From 18 June up until 2 September the regiment was located at RIGA airfield. The personnel are housed in the city at a distance of five kilometres from the airfield. The regiment has not been provided with classroom facilities, and there is a complete lack of furniture in the four classrooms that are available.

The 148th Fighter Air Regiment. This regiment is based on LIEPAJA airfield. The condition of the airfield is satisfactory but it becomes waterlogged after light rain and the regiment has not flown for some time owing to the condition of the airfield. The personnel are housed in the town at a distance of seven kilometres from the airfield. There are no classroom facilities available.

The 54th Red Banner High-Speed Bomber Air Regiment. This regiment is based on Vilno airfield. Up until 11 March 1940 the regiment was active in the war with Finland. After the end of the war it was redeployed to MOGILEV. The regiment commenced combat training on 15 April 1940. During the course of 1940 the regiment was redeployed seven times, which delayed the organisation of combat training. The regiment has not been provided with classroom facilities...

> **The 61st Ground Attack Air Regiment.** The regiment is based on KEDAINIAI. Up until 15 March 1940 the regiment operated from PONEVEZH airfield, and KEDAINIAI airfield was not suitable for normal regimental operations, the new airfield has only just been completed. The regiment is in the process of formation and conversion onto their new materiel—the I-153. The accommodation for regimental personnel is unsatisfactory, they are scattered around the city and there are no classrooms or shooting ranges…
>
> **The 15th Fighter Air Regiment.** This regiment was actively engaged in the war with Finland up until 12 March 1940. Upon cessation of hostilities the regiment remained in ESTONIA, and was based on VALLI airfield (on DAGO island). At the end of August the regiment was redeployed to KOVNO airfield. Only two classrooms are available for this regiment but they are not fitted out and there is no furniture…
>
> **The 42nd Fighter Air Regiment.** The regiment has been based on VILNO airfield since June 1940. The regiment arrived from VELIKIYE LUKI in the Kaliningrad Military District. The lack of textbooks, classrooms, as well as inexperienced personnel, together with the lack of materiel all delayed the course of combat training.

Another negative factor, as strange as it may seem, was political in nature. The point being that the personnel in the Red Army units billeted in the territory of the Baltic States were actively, so to speak, offering assistance to the workers and the peasants of these countries in their political struggle for the victory of socialism, and for their liberation from the yoke of the landowners and capitalists. Moreover at the beginning of June 1940 nobody could have predicted how the political and military leadership of the Baltic States would behave and events could develop in line with any scenario, up to and including combat operations to neutralise their national armies.

Parallel to the foreign policy factors in the heart of the Red Army air forces in the spring of 1940, the deployment process for Red Army air forces was launched, in accordance with Decree No. 92ss issued by the Committee for Defence under the Council of People's Deputies and dated 26 February 1940. Within the confines of this decree, Directives issued by the People's Commissariat for Defence on the formation of 35 new aviation regiments were signed on 20 February of that year. In the course of implementing these measures the regular Air Force units were stripped of their personnel to form the new regiments, and for the majority of them this was akin to total annihilation. Trained pilots were deployed to their new postings in significant numbers and not without difficulty. Regiments that were located in the European part of the USSR were to suffer heavily, such as the aforementioned 31st Fighter Air Regiment, which lost 51 pilots from their number, or practically 2/3 of their personnel. Correspondingly, newly trained pilots, who had graduated from accelerated programmes at flying schools arrived to replace them, exactly as their predecessors had done, and the regimental command were forced to begin the process of training over again. It is likely that many of the commanders of aviation units at that time had a feeling of 'déjà-vu' in this situation. It has to be said that the quality of the training did nevertheless improve for many pilots in comparison with the 1938–1939 graduates, as now practically all of them had amassed 40–50 flying hours, and each of the pilots had 8–12 hrs in a combat aircraft. Even so this practice was insufficient, and with the lack of additional training, sending pilots to fly independent sorties in combat aircraft was very risky. Apart from that combat training had not been fully developed at the aviation colleges, and naturally this set of circumstances did not improve the situation at hand. Sending these units and their pilots with their level of training to the Baltic region was considered prohibitive, and just before the units were deployed the least experienced pilots were replaced with regular pilots from other units. By way of an example this was precisely how Lieutenant A.A. Dmitriev, one of the best aces in the Red Army Air Force for 1941, who was transferred with a group of other pilots from the 33rd Fighter Air Regiment, came to be in the 15th Fighter Air Regiment.

The extent to which the administrative and mobilisation measures carried out in the Red Army air forces were a serious test can be judged by the following statistical data: the Red Army Air Force formed 43 fighter and 44 bomber air regiments between 1 April 1938 and 10 May 1940. By way of a comparison the period from 1938 until 10 May 1940 also saw a relatively significant increase in the number of units in the *Luftwaffe*—in all 16 fighter and 15 bomber air groups were formed.

Table 2 A comparison of the number of units in the Red Army Air Force and the *Luftwaffe* across different time periods

Red Army Air Force	**1 April 1938**	**1 Oct 1939**	**10 May 1940**	***Luftwaffe***	**26 Sept 1938**	**1 Sept 1939**	**10 May 1940**
Fighter Air Regiment	35	55	78	JG	23	19	29
Combined Air Regiment	1	6	3	ZG	–	10	11
Heavy Bomber Air Regiment	12	4	4	KGzbV	–	11	9
Long-Range Bomber Air Regiment	–	36	52	KG	30	31	46
High-Speed Bomber Air Regiment	–	36	52				
Light Bomber Air Regiment	27	7	7	StG	8	9	10
Light Ground Attack Air Regiment	12	13	13	Ii/LG2	1	1	1

Moreover if the numerical strengths in the newly formed units were compared, it emerges that if the Germans needed around 1,350 fighter and 750 bomber crews, then the Red Army Air Force needed three to four times more as 3,225 and 3,300 crews were needed respectively. If the *Luftwaffe* were satisfied with this number, then for the Red Army Air Force this was just the beginning of the process.

In accordance with decree No. 1344-524ss dated 25 July 1940, issued by the Council of People's Deputies of the USSR and entitled 'ON THE STRUCTURE OF THE RED ARMY AIR FORCE', some 48 new fighter and bomber air regiments needed to be formed in the course of 1940 along with 12 new directorates for the air divisions. At the same time the existing regiments merged into air divisions, some 38 directorates in total. Apart from that the formation of two heavy bomber, 10 reconnaissance, 58 corps air squadrons, and six medical air squadrons was planned. Following the implementation of the above measures the numerical strength of the Red Army Air Force should have increased to 60,248, and the number of pilots was to increase to 5,500. Thus in total in 1940 the number of pilots in Red Army Air Force front line units was to increase in the course of a year to 12,000 with all that this entailed, such as employing regular pilots in front line units to train the new graduates for which it was necessary to transfer the experienced personnel to new formations. A consequence of this was that the level of training in regular units, that had been built up at a great cost between 1938–1939, depreciated.

All these processes needed to be repeated:

Employing pilots from front line units to train recent graduates
The transfer of experienced flight crews to new formations
Employing regular pilots as instructors.

Naturally the consequence of all this was an unavoidable depreciation in the level of training in regular units that had been built up at such a great cost between 1938–1939.

A reorganisation of the brigade directorates into divisional directorates did not pass without consequences, in that the level of combat readiness among the formations headquarters was reduced. Thus, a report on the results of combat training in the Air Forces of the Baltic Special Military District for 1940 notes:

> The Directorate of the 4th Air Division. The divisional headquarters arrived from Krasnogvardeysk on 4 September 1940 (part of the Air Forces of the Leningrad Military District) and is currently deployed in Tallinn. This headquarters is not at full strength. The divisional headquarters is six commanders short, which means it has not been possible to pull the headquarters together to form a leadership apparatus and to implement the management of combat training in the divisional units to its fullest extent.
>
> The Directorate of the 6th Air Division. The divisional headquarters was formed on the basis of the headquarters of the 18th Air Brigade. This headquarters is not at full strength.
>
> This headquarters has not been pulled together fully as an operational management body owing to a lack of time. Determination and decisiveness are not evident in the management of combat training, requiring some cajoling as well as reminders.
>
> The Directorate of the 7th Air Division. At the time of its formation the divisional headquarters was located in SHAVLI (in the Lithuanian Soviet Socialist Republic) but was redeployed to LIEPAJA on 16 October; the headquarters has not been at full strength up until the present time.
>
> This unit has not pulled together fully as a management body and management of combat training is not running smoothly.
>
> The Directorate of the 8th Air Division. The divisional headquarters was formed in September 1940. The divisional headquarters has yet to be made up to full strength.
>
> This headquarters has not been pulled together, and the management of combat training is not conducted with any determination or decisiveness.

However in the second half of 1940 the Air Forces of the Baltic Special Military District were very lucky and avoided these organisational measures: not one new unit, be it fighter or bomber aviation unit, was formed within the Baltic Special Military District at all (one exception was the formation of the 312th Reconnaissance Air Regiment as well as corps squadrons). Nevertheless some of the experienced flight crews were given command posts within the newly formed units in other districts. Almost all the regiments surrendered around 10–15 command personnel each to this, and in return they received graduates from flying schools by way of augmentation. In total in the second half of 1940 and the beginning of 1941 some 273 young pilots joined the air forces of the Baltic Special Military District, of these 182 were fighter pilots and 91 were bomber pilots (there were fighter pilots who were destined to serve in the 61st Ground Attack Air Regiment). It was thanks to this successful confluence of circumstances that at the end of 1940 a combat capable cohort of some 50–60 regular pilots remained in practically every regiment in the air forces of the Baltic Special Military District.

Table 3 The availability and distribution of pilots in the district's units in terms of length of service, and their numbers as of 1 January 1941

	The total number of pilots	In their second year of service or more	In their first year of service
The 10th Fighter Air Regiment	83	56 (67%)	27 (33%)
The 15th Fighter Air Regiment	72	52 (72%)	20 (28%)
The 21st Fighter Air Regiment	77	52 (68%)	25 (32%)
The 31st Fighter Air Regiment	75	55 (73%)	20 (27%)
The 38th Fighter Air Regiment	69	55 (80%)	14 (20%)
The 42nd Fighter Air Regiment	73	73 (100%)	– (0%)
The 49th Fighter Air Regiment	81	61 (75%)	20 (25%)
The 148th Fighter Air Regiment	75	55 (73%)	20 (27%)
The 61st Fighter Air Regiment	81	56 (69%)	25 (31%)
The total number in Fighter and Ground Attack Air Regiments	**686**	**515 (75%)**	**171 (25%)**
The 9th Mixed Air Brigade	65	27 (42%)	38* (58%)
The 31st High-Speed Bomber Air Regiment	78	58 (74%)	20 (26%)
The 35th High-Speed Bomber Air Regiment	50	46 (92%)	4 (8%)
The 40th High-Speed Bomber Air Regiment	77	52 (68%)	25 (32%)
The 46th High-Speed Bomber Air Regiment	55	51 (93%)	4 (7%)
The 50th High- Speed Bomber Air Regiment	65	50 (77%)	15 (23%)
The 54th High- Speed Bomber Air Regiment	77	42 (55%)	35** (45%)
The 63rd High- Speed Bomber Air Regiment	61	– (0%)	61*** (100%)
The 312th Reconnaissance Air Regiment	32	– (0%)	32**** (100%)
The total number in High-Speed Bomber and Reconnaissance Air Regiments	**560**	**326 (58%)**	**234 (42%)**

Notes
* This takes into account the academic year, since the personnel would have converted onto the SB from the TB-3
** This takes into account the academic year, since the personnel were transferred from the 61st Fighter Air Regiment and converted onto the SB from the R-5SSS.
**** This takes into account the academic year, since the personnel converted onto the Yak-2 aircraft.

1.2 Combat Training in 1940

As a whole, owing to the availability of a considerable number of regular pilots, the level of training in the aviation units of the air forces of the Special Baltic Military District looked reasonably optimistic according to the 'Summary of Combat Training in Air Force Units' produced by the 1st Directorate of the Chief Directorate of the Red Army air forces at the beginning of January 1941:

> The 10th Fighter Air Regiment—this regiment consists of 56 crews who are capable of conducting daylight combat sorties at medium altitudes flying in a formation of nine aircraft, and 18 crews who are trained for nocturnal operations. Some 46 crews are able to fly at high altitudes of H–7,000 m.

The 15th Fighter Air Regiment are trained to conduct daylight combat sorties at altitudes of up to 7,000 m and consists of 55 crews, of which 48 are capable of operating at altitudes in excess of 7,000 m. Twelve crews have been trained on night operations, including nine in the Night Squadron.

The 21st Fighter Air Regiment—this regiment, consisting of 52 crews—is trained to conduct daylight combat sorties in favourable weather conditions at altitudes of up to H–9,000 m. Eleven crews have been trained for nocturnal operations.

The 31st Fighter Air Regiment—this regiment—consisting of 55 crews, is trained to conduct daylight combat sorties at medium altitudes in favourable weather conditions. Twenty-five crews have been trained for nocturnal operations and 13 pilots have been trained to fly at altitudes of over 7,000 m.

The 38th Fighter Air Regiment is combat capable. This regiment is able to conduct daylight combat sorties employing 45 crews in average weather conditions up to an altitude of H–6,000 m. the regiment is capable of operating with individual crews and flights up to H–8,000 m. Twelve crews are trained for nocturnal operations.

The 42nd Fighter Air Regiment conducts daylight combat sorties at medium altitudes in favourable weather conditions. Fifteen crews have been trained for nocturnal operations. Thirty-five pilots are capable of operating at an altitude of 7,000 m.

The 49th Fighter Air Regiment—this regiment, consisting of 58 crews is trained for daylight combat sorties at altitudes of H–5,000 m. Twenty-one crews have been trained for nocturnal operations.

The 148th Fighter Air Regiment—some 53 crews in this regiment are trained to conduct daylight combat sorties in favourable weather conditions flying in a formation of nine aircraft. Thirty-four crews are trained to operate at altitudes of H–7,000 m. None of the crews in the regiment are trained for nocturnal operations.

The 9th High-Speed Bomber Air Regiment is trained to conduct daylight combat sorties at medium altitudes in favourable weather conditions flying in a formation of nine aircraft, and consists of 51 crews, of which none are trained for nocturnal operations.

The 31st High-Speed Bomber Air Regiment is trained to conduct daylight combat sorties at medium altitudes in inclement weather conditions flying in a formation of nine aircraft with 45 crews. Nine crews are trained to conduct nocturnal operations with individual aircraft.

The 35th High-Speed Bomber Air Regiment is capable of conducting daylight combat operations at medium altitudes in average weather conditions. Twenty-four crews are capable of conducting nocturnal combat sorties in average weather conditions.

The 40th High-Speed Bomber Air Regiment is capable of conducting daylight combat sorties in average weather conditions at medium altitudes with 55 crews. Ten crews are trained for nocturnal combat operations in average weather conditions, and crews who have completed the programme of high altitude training are on a rest period lasting seven months.

The 46th High-Speed Bomber Air Regiment's crews are trained to conduct daylight combat operations at medium altitudes with 43 crews flying in a formation of nine aircraft in average weather conditions. Fourteen crews are trained to conduct nocturnal combat operations with individual aircraft.

The 50th High-Speed Bomber Air Regiment conducts daylight combat operations in uncomplicated weather conditions at high altitudes employing five squadrons, nocturnal operations are carried out flying in sections with 17 crews.

The 54th High-Speed Bomber Air Regiment is able to operate in the day in favourable weather conditions at medium altitudes with 53 crews, some 17 crews are able to fly in sections on nocturnal operations.

The 63rd High-Speed Bomber Air Regiment is able to operate in the day in favourable weather conditions at medium altitudes with 38 crews, six crews are able to fly at night in individual aircraft.

The 61st Ground Attack Air Regiment—this regiment has converted onto new materiel. The flight crews have begun to assimilate new materiel in accordance with the conversion programme. The regiment is not ready to undertake combat operations.*

The 312th Reconnaissance Air Regiment—this regiment is in the process of being formed.*

The overall state of combat training in the Air Forces of the Baltic Special Military District in 1940 was set out in the 'Report on the results of combat training in the Air Forces of the Baltic Special Military District for 1940', see Tables 4, 5 and 6.

Table 4 The total flying hours among Air Force units in the district (from 1 January to 25 October 1940)

Total flying	Hours	Landings		Hours	Landings
4th Air Division			**6th Air Division**		
35th High-Speed Bomber Air Regiment	4,214	3,417	The 40th High-Speed Bomber Air Regiment	6,113	6,308
50th High-Speed Bomber Air Regiment	5,958	6,266	The 7th Long- Range Bomber Air Regiment	2,638	3,374
63rd High-Speed Bomber Air Regiment	4,350	9,341	The 21st Fighter Air Regiment	2,608	6,206
38th Fighter Air Regiment	4,320	5,660	The 49th Fighter Air Regiment	3,233	9,557
Total	18,842	24,684	Total	14,592	25,445
7th Air Division			**6th Air Division**		
The 46th High-Speed Bomber Air Regiment	4,222	6,046	The 54th High-Speed Bomber Air Regiment	5,236	3,168
The 31st High-Speed Bomber Air Regiment	4,996	3,291	The 61st Ground Attack Air Regiment	4,126	8,637
The 9th High-Speed Bomber Air Regiment	5,889	10,299	The 15th Fighter Air Regiment	2,695	4,377
The 148th Fighter Air Regiment	2,796	3,780	The 31st Fighter Air Regiment	5,715*	10,253
The 10th Fighter Air Regiment	3,560	5,654	The 42nd Fighter Air Regiment	5,572	11,190
Total	21,463	29,070		23,344	37,625
Total for the Air Forces of the District					

Note
* According to other sources the personnel of the 31st Fighter Air Regiment amassed 6,794 flying hours

* Attention is drawn to the almost complete lack of combat capability among the ground attack and reconnaissance aviation within the district, this however is due to the materiel not being delivered in time. Moreover if the 61st Ground Attack Air Regiment received their allocated I-153s, the 312th Reconnaissance Air Regiment did not receive the Yak-2s they had been promised, not in 1940, or even in 1941. The district's Air Observation Squadron was in an analogous position, since the augmentation of the squadron with materiel was delayed and the introduction of the UPB could only get underway in 1941, after the 61st Ground Attack Air Regiment had handed these units their ageing R-5SSS ground attack aircraft.

The very high value for the flying hours amassed by some units—of between 5,000–7,000 hrs—which equates to approximately 80–100 hrs per crew(!)—has to be noted. Considering however that the better half of the regiments in the district—the 31st, 35th, 50th, 54th, 63rd, (the 3rd Squadron), the 46th (2nd Squadron), 9th (a composite squadron) Bomber Air Regiments, and the 15th, 38th, 49th, 148th Fighter Air Regiments had participated in the 'Winter War' with Finland, a considerable proportion of the personnel had amassed an even greater number of hours in combat.

This first and foremost concerns the 49th Fighter Air Regiment, whose pilots carried out 4,466 combat sorties (amassing 4,097 hrs), fought 60 air battles, and shot down 28 enemy aircraft (according to other data this figure is 19). Many pilots in the regiment had completed 100 or more combat sorties in the space of three and a half months.

The 38th Fighter Air Regiment carried out 2,288 combat sorties (amassing 2,541 hours) and recorded seven combat victories.

The 50th High-Speed Bomber Air Regiment carried out 2,321 combat sorties (amassing 2,735 hrs).

The 35th High-Speed Bomber Air Regiment carried out 1,709 combat sorties (including 74 night sorties) and dropped 851 tonnes of bombs.

The 31st High-Speed Bomber Air Regiment carried out 967 combat sorties (amassing 2,620 hours).

Other regiments did not operate so intensively, and yet they could nevertheless boast of their participation in combat:

The 148th Fighter Air Regiment carried out 910 combat sorties (amassing 1,120 hours) and recording three enemy aircraft shot down.

The 63rd High -peed Bomber Air Regiment carried out 603 combat sorties, of which 445 were at night (amassing 850 hours).

The 15th Fighter Air Regiment carried out 514 combat sorties (amassing 433.5 hours), and recording one enemy aircraft shot down.

Table 5 Bomber training in the Air Force units of the Baltic Special Military District as of 25 October 1940

	Bombing raids carried out	Bombing raids completed successfully	Average number of bombing raids per navigator
4th Air Division			
The 35th High-Speed Bomber Air Regiment	6	6	
The 50th High-Speed Bomber Air Regiment	535	369	9.0
The 63rd High- Speed Bomber Air Regiment	203	142	4.0
The 38th Fighter Air Regiment	127	118	2.5
Total	871	635	6.0
The 6th Air Division			
The 40th High-Speed Bomber Air Regiment	585	493	9.0
The 7th Long-Range Bomber Air Regiment	335	225	5.0
The 21st Fighter Air Regiment	0	0	
The 49th Fighter Air Regiment	0	0	
Total	920	718	8.0

	Bombing raids carried out	Bombing raids completed successfully	Average number of bombing raids per navigator
The 7th Air Division			
The 46th High-Speed Bomber Air Regiment	295	195	4.0
The 31st High-Speed Bomber Air Regiment	15	8	
The 9th High- Speed Bomber Air Regiment	367	230	
The 148th Fighter Air Regiment	115	44	
The 10th Fighter Air Regiment	17	12	4.7
Total	809	489	4.0
The 8th Air Division			
The 54th High-Speed Bomber Air Regiment	889	855	15.0
The 61st Ground Attack Air Regiment	195	184	
The 15th Fighter Air Regiment	334	244	7.0
The 31st Fighter Air Regiment	0	0	
The 42nd Fighter Air Regiment	216	110	3.0
Total	1,634	1,393	5.5
Total for the Air Forces of the Military District	4,234	3,235	7.0

For fighter air regiments this relates to dive bombing

Table 6 Air battles conducted by Air Force units of the Baltic Special Military District as of 25 October 1940

	Individual air battles		Group air battles		Average number of air battles per pilot	
	Carried out	Completed successfully	Carried out	Completed successfully	Individual	Group
The 4th Air Division						
The 35th High-Speed Bomber Air Regiment						
The 50th High-Speed Bomber Air Regiment			1	1		
The 63rd High-Speed Bomber Air Regiment						
The 38th Fighter Air Regiment	544	414	58	36	11.0	4.0
Total	544	414	59	37		
The 6th Air Division						
The 40th High-Speed Bomber Air Regiment			5	5		
The 7th Long-Range Bomber Air Regiment						
The 21st Fighter Air Regiment	226	210	52	52	4.0	1.0
The 49th Fighter Air Regiment	232	232	3	3	3.0	
Total	458	442	60	60		

	Individual air battles		Group air battles		Average number of air battles per pilot	
	Carried out	Completed successfully	Carried out	Completed successfully	Individual	Group
The 7th Air Division						
The 46th High-Speed Bomber Air Regiment						
The 31st High-Speed Bomber Air Regiment						
The 9th High-Speed Bomber Air Regiment	3	3	4	4	0.9	3.0
The 148th Fighter Air Regiment	98	97	1	1	1.5	
The 10th Fighter Air Regiment	1,075	1,031	559	522	18.5	9.5
Total	1,176	1,131	564	527		
The 8th Air Division						
The 54th High-Speed Bomber Air Regiment						
The 61st Ground Attack Air Regiment						
The 15th Fighter Air Regiment	936	715	102	102	13.0	3.0
The 31st Fighter Air Regiment	876	859	110	108	10.5	1.5
The 42nd Fighter Air Regiment	670	665	136	138	9.0	1.5
Total	2,482	2,239	348	348		
Total for the Air Forces of the Military District	4,660	4,226	1,031	972		

Despite the relatively positive overall indicators from the Directorate of Combat Training the statistics listed above cannot fail to impact combat training itself. An analysis of the whole spectrum of documents concerning combat training reveals not only positive incidents, but also brings a number of serious problems to light. Thus the Act on the Results of an Audit of the Condition and Training of the Air Forces of the Baltic Special Military District, which was carried out by way of an inspection of the air forces of the Red Army in the period from 6 January–6 February 1941, lists a number of shortcomings, specifically relating to the weak aerial gunnery and bombing training prevalent in practically all units without exception:

> In the fighter regiments insufficient attention is paid to aerial gunnery training, and the crews rarely fire at drogues ... the principal reasons behind the unsatisfactory aerial gunnery training in the fighter regiments lies in the insufficient training of crews in firing at drogues and at ground targets, the unsatisfactory state of the drogues, and the reluctance to employ gun cameras, as well as insufficient ground school training.

The section concerning the combat training in the **31st Fighter Air Regiment** notes: 'On average each pilot has completed 14 aerial gunnery missions firing on a drogue (this relates to the whole of 1940). The principal disadvantage in conducting air combat and aerial gunnery lies in failing to employ gun cameras. The regiment has 72 gun cameras and they are all faulty.'

Naturally, one or two missions for each pilot firing on a drogue in the course of a month is hardly an outstanding result, but unfortunately the training in other units was worse:

The 21st Fighter Air Regiment: 'As far as aerial gunnery training is concerned pilots with two years service have transferred to carrying out a 3rd objective. The past few months have seen few missions in which pilots have been firing on drones due to inclement weather conditions, and no ground attack missions have been carried out owing to the lack of a firing range...'

The 42nd Fighter Air Regiment: 'From June to December 1940 the regiment converted onto the I-153 from the I-15bis. In connection with assimilation of the I-153 the regiment has not engaged in combat training ... aerial gunnery and air combat missions have not been conducted since November, nor have there been any ground attack missions since April 1940...'

The 38th Fighter Air Regiment: 'Some 12 pilots from the 19th Combat Training Course for Fighter Aviation FA-41 were tested on their aerial gunnery skills and the following results were attained: EXCELLENT–five pilots, GOOD–1 pilot, FAILED TO COMPLETE–6 pilots. The principal shortcomings in terms of aerial gunnery training are as follows:

a) The absence of gun cameras;
b) The lack of ground-based training apparatus;
c) The frequent loss of drogues

An assessment of aerial gunnery training revealed that the regiment was at a low level although in terms of their training crews should be able to fire at a level corresponding to excellent or good. The regiment does have some excellent gunners (Yuppa, Kochetkov, Shepetov, Belous amongst others...) who would be able to pass on their experience of gunnery to the other pilots.'

The 49th Fighter Air Regiment: 'The Crews carried out exercises 13–19 in the aerial gunnery programme in their second year. Of the four pilots who engaged in aerial-gunnery from the 1st Squadron, only one completed exercise 13 with a score of 'GOOD'. Gun cameras were very rarely used.'

The 148th Fighter Air Regiment: 'In the course of 1940 some 195 individual firings on drogues were carried out, of which 74 hit the target, the regiment did not fire on the drogues in flight formation. Twelve of the pilots were checked for their aerial gunnery skills whilst firing on drogues, of those: 1–GOOD, 6–MEDIOCRE, and 5–UNSATISFACTORY. Some 62 individual firings on fixed targets were conducted in the course of 1940, of which 71 hit the target, while 97 firings were conducted in flight formation, all of which hit the target...'

The 15th Fighter Air Regiment: 'Some 360 firings were carried out by way of aerial gunnery training, of which 262 hit the target. The majority of the pilots were on exercise 28 in the Combat Training Course for Fighter Aviation FA-41. Some 165 firings were conducted as a flight, of which 130 hit the target. Some 158 individual firings were carried out on fixed targets, of which 81 hit the target. Some 74 firings were conducted as a flight, of which 40 hit the target. The number of hits per pilot was 12 (this is for the whole of 1940). Forty gun cameras were delivered in the December, although only nine had actually been fitted to aircraft.'

> **The 10th Fighter Air Regiment:** A check was carried out of the pilot's competency in terms of aerial-gunnery and 10 flights attained a score of mediocre for firing on drogues, whilst a single flight attained a score of excellent (the Flight Commander was Berzin); one flight attained a score of excellent, one flight attained a score of mediocre, while seven flights attained a score of unsatisfactory…

Bomber units did nothing to embellish the report either:

> The aerial gunnery training in the bomber air regiments that were assessed was found to be satisfactory. The drogues were found to be in an unsatisfactory condition, especially in the 54th and 9th High-Speed Bomber Air Regiments. The training of both gunner/radio-operators and gunners was found to be exceptionally poor. These crews are not trained in the tactics of air combat. Gun cameras are not employed in their training either.

Moreover even the units that had come through the war were, according to the commission's reports, deserving of an unbiased assessment. Thus the following was written of the 50th High-Speed Bomber Air Regiment: 'Ground strafing training for gunner/radio-operators using ShKAS machine guns is unsatisfactory … The overall assessment for the regiment as a whole is unsatisfactory…'

In the remainder of the regiments it was acknowledged that the situation was only slightly better:

> The 31st High-Speed Bomber Air Regiment: 'The state of aerial gunnery training for the regiment as a whole is unsatisfactory. On the plus side the 1st Squadron attained an assessment of good, while on the minus side the 2nd Squadron were assessed as unsatisfactory. The drogues are maintained in good order.'
>
> The 9th High-Speed Bomber Air Regiment: '1. Aerial gunnery training is unsatisfactory. In the course of inspection testing out of the eight crews seven of them trailed tangled drogues, and only one crew conducted a firing in accordance with exercise 6 of the Aerial Gunnery Training Course 40 … without completing the exercise…'
>
> The 40th High-Speed Bomber Air Regiment: 'The state of aerial-gunnery training for the regular pilots is SATISFACTORY.'
>
> The 46th High-Speed Bomber Air Regiment: 'The overall assessment is SATISFACTORY.'

In this same act the situation with regard to bombing training in Air Force units is characterised as follows:

> Bombing training has been slow to evolve even in bomber air regiments. The 9th and 40th High-Speed Bomber Air Regiments have not conducted any bombing missions for a protracted period of time. The 31st High-Speed Bomber Air Regiment have conducted just 21 bombing missions from medium altitudes in the course of the last year and six photo-bombing missions. The number of bombing missions per navigator during 1940 and into January 1941 across all the regiments, apart from the 50th, ranges from 0.4 to 4. The principal reason behind such a low number of bombing missions lies in the lack of bombing ranges. The ranges that are available are not equipped, even though two of them are able to offer both day and night bombing practice from any altitude (specifically this refers to the DAGO and VILNO islands). There is a shortage of P-40 bombs across all the regiments as well as the explosives to go with them. Apart from that one of the reasons that is impacting on the

> development of bombing training is the lack of sufficient perseverance on the part of divisional and regimental commanders.
>
> In the 46th High-Speed Bomber Air Regiment out of the 11 crews who underwent inspection testing only nine hit the target, and out of the 28 crews in the 50th High-Speed Bomber Air Regiment only 15 hit the target.
>
> The fighter regiments conducted very little bombing … neither the technical staff or the aircrew had assimilated the technique of attaching the bombs to the underside of the aircraft. Bombing training as a whole in the Air Force units serving in this district is unsatisfactory, with the exception of those personnel who have been trained to a satisfactory level.

On the minus side the 9th High-Speed Bomber Air Regiment, which had only recently converted onto the SB bomber, stood out:

> The regiment was given time to make use of the divisional range from 14 October 1940. The regiment does not have a range of its own. From May 1940 onwards the regiment did not conduct any bombing, with the exception of crews flying individual periodic sorties and a single scramble to conduct a bombing run against personnel. Bombing training is poor.

Unfortunately even the crews from the seasoned regiments failed to excel in their training, the report notes the following shortcomings:

> The 31st High-Speed Bomber Air Regiment: A group of 10 navigators, up to and including flight navigators, took part in the inspection bombing. Owing to the weather the bombing was carried out at altitudes of between 600–2,000 m. Of the 10 who dropped the bombs five of them excelled, and another five did not complete the exercise.
>
> In the period from 1 June to January 1941 the regiment carried out just 21 bombings in total from medium altitudes, as well as six with using photo-bombs. The average number of bombings per navigator over the six months was 0.4. As a result of the low level of bombing training in the course of 1940 the navigators were not able to maintain their skills in bombing and bombing training is in an unsatisfactory state.

The navigators of the 50th High-Speed Bomber Air Regiment made a slightly better account of themselves:

> Some 28 crews took part in the inspection testing and the overall assessment of the regiment in terms of bombing training is satisfactory.
>
> The shortcomings in terms of conducting bombing runs are as follows:
>
> a) Failure to comply with the specific requirements in terms of their heading, making unnecessary approaches, dropping bombs from an altitude of less than 100 m, and not keeping a tally of the number of bombs used in a salvo.
> b) The discipline required when making an approach to the target on the bombing range is lacking; one flight in the 3rd Air Squadron altered the direction of their bombing run, while another flight in the 5th Air Squadron commenced their bombing run when the 3rd Air Squadron were still using the range, and moreover the bombing was conducted on intersecting combat headings.

Things were a little better in the 54th High-Speed Bomber Air Regiment, however following their relocation to Vilnius the regiment would very rarely engage in bombing missions owing to the lack of a bombing range:

> In the course of 1940 the regiment had 82 bombing missions in hand. Of these 55 (or 67 percent) were sucessful. The average number of bombing runs per navigator was 1.1. Bombing runs were only conducted from low and medium altitudes.
>
> 2. There were two incidents of FAB-50 bombs being dropped outside of the bombing range.
>
> THE OVERALL ASSESSMENT OF BOMBING TRAINING IS UNSATISFACTORY.

At the beginning of 1941 the Deputy Head of the Directorate of Combat Training of the Chief Directorate of Red Army Air Force Colonel Titov noted the most blatant incidents in a report on the state of the combat and aerial gunnery training service in the Red Army Air Force:

> 1. Experience in terms of combat and training practice demonstrates the weakness in bombing and aerial-gunnery training in Red Army Air Force units.
>
> a) Bombing accuracy is poor. The results of the bombing raids carried out by the high-speed bomber air regiments, is assessed as being less than mediocre.
> b) The proportion of bombing runs and aerial gunnery per crew is very low (seven to eight bombing runs, and firings per year).
> c) Knowledge among personnel of the theory of bombing and of aerial gunnery, together with knowledge of the procedures both in the air and on the ground is exceptionally poor.
> d) The principal personnel in the Air Force units—the flight, squadron, and regimental commanders—are not adept at resolving issues concerning aerial gunnery, since these subjects are not covered sufficiently at higher education institutions.
> e) The higher education institutions do not envisage live aerial gunnery or bombing practice for pilots, from whom the future commanders of the various units will be drawn, and as a result their theoretical knowledge (for fighter pilots 30 hrs are allocated to bombing, and 90 hrs to aerialgunnery, while for bomber pilots the figures are 80 hrs of bombing, and 67 hrs of aerial gunnery) is not consolidated.
> f) There are no qualified specialists in aerial gunnery and bombing in the units themselves, who could assist the commander of a unit to organise and closely supervise this activity. The reason for this is that not one of the Red Army Air Force higher education institutions offers a specialisation in gunnery training. There is nobody serving in these regiments who is responsible for the state of aerial gunnery, while at divisional (as well as at corps and district) level nobody knows who is responsible for the condition of the ranges, shooting galleries, and classrooms, or for the condition and the appropriate training of serving personnel in aerial gunnery and aerial bombing. The reason for this is that the designation of responsibilities between the combat training department, and navigators, and weapons engineers has yet to take place.
> g) There is no required tally of the results of aerial bombing and aerial gunnery in these units. The shooting galleries, ranges, and classrooms are often in a state of disrepair, since there is nobody available to take care of them.

This was echoed by the head of the 6th Department of the Combat Training Directorate of the Principal Directorate of the Red Army Air Force Lieutenant-Colonel Glakhenshausen:

> In connection with this all measures must now be taken to enhance the accuracy of aerial bombing and aerial gunnery. This can be achieved by eradicating a series of shortcomings of an organisational, technical, and methodological nature.
>
> Owing to the lack of the required leadership in terms of aerial gunnery training the theoretical and practical training of aircrew serving in Red Army Air Force units is superficial. The results for aerial-bombing in the course of 1940 are lower than mediocre, out of the total number of aerial gunnery missions only 70% were successful. The limited totals for aerial gunnery and bombing missions per crew over the course of a year (four aerial gunnery missions and seven to eight bombing missions), gives rise to circumstances in which aircrew are not able to cope with their workload in the air. This is the reason why instances of material failures in flight, as well as bombs being dropped outside of the bombing ranges (there were 143 cases of this in the course of 1940) and so on are common. Nobody is there to summarise their experience and as such the errors that are happening are not being eradicated as they should be, and are being repeated year on year.

The appendix to the memorandum notes that in 1940 in the units of the Baltic Special Military District the average number of aerial gunnery missions per pilot was 12 per year (of these eight were to fire at a drogue and four were to fire at ground targets). These figures, although they represented the highest result among the units of the air forces of the western border districts, came nowhere near the optimal 30 aerial gunnery missions firing on a drogue per year per crew, and were much lower than in the air forces of the Far Eastern Front and the Zabaykal Special Military District. Here these figures would reach 40 (26 at a drogue and 14 at ground targets) and 24 (13 at a drogue and 11 at ground targets) aerial gunnery missions per year per pilot respectively.

The situation was worse for bombing, and on average the figure was 5.5 exercises carried out per crew per year. The bomber air regiments of the air forces of the Special Military District remained outsiders in this 'socialist competition' even in terms of this vector, sharing last place with the Air Forces of the Northern Caucasian Military District, the Siberian Military District, and the Caucasian Military District. By way of a comparison the Air Forces of the Far Eastern Front carried out—if this were calculated per crew—26 bombing missions per year, but even here the optimal figure was still thought to be 30 missions.

> Summing up we note that despite the fact that the pilots in the best regiments in the Air Forces of the Baltic Special Military District (the 31st Fighter Air Regiment and the 54th High-Speed Bomber Air Regiment) carried out on average 14 aerial gunnery and 15 bombing missions respectively per crew, the overall condition of aerial gunnery and bombing training within the units in this district was mediocre, and even those regiments that achieved acceptable results overall showed considerable loopholes in terms of the organisation of combat training as well as lengthy breaks of up to several months, in the course of which crews would not be involved in aerial gunnery or aerial bombing at all.
>
> The lack of regular practice in skills such as aerial gunnery and bombing considerably reduced the combat capability of these units, and this drawback could lead to a low level of effectiveness during the course of combat operations.

Another 'weak point' in aviation training in this district lay in the training of navigators, and the Act on the inspection did not hold back in this regard:

> In the fighter regiments personnel are not capable of carrying out calculations on the interception, pursuit, and escort of bombers. None of the aircrew in any of the fighter regiments are trained in resolving navigational issues, calculating an approximation of heading, or of

> distance. In certain regiments (such as the 31st Fighter Air Regiment) the flight area is not studied in detail and aerial maps do not show raised state borders. Squadron navigators in the fighter regiments do not receive the prerequisite instruction in guidelines and procedures from the regimental navigators concerning the navigational training for fighter pilots, while the divisional staff navigators do not control the course of training within fighter units.

The navigator training in high-speed bomber air regiments was considered satisfactory, but even this was not without its shortcomings:

> Navigator training in the bomber air regiments that underwent inspection is at a satisfactory level. Squadron commanders and their deputies (in the 50th, 9th, and 54th high-speed bomber air regiments) lag behind in terms of their navigator training. Squadron navigators do not know how to carry out calculations on the timing of sunset and sunrise in accordance with the navigator's handbook when their targets are located in a different time zone. Regimental groups of squadron navigators very rarely study this. In recent times the bomber air regiments have demonstrated a poor level of training in cross-country flying. Few aircraft in this district are fitted with a fixed-loop radio compass, or if they are fitted with one it is not used. There are no non-directional radio beacons available. Many of the navigators have not assimilated the issues of tactical navigation. The bomber air regiments are poorly supplied with aerial maps. Only the one regiment has 'Batchlers'. Even the most basic equipment for training navigators to measure the drift angle or to carry out the required navigational calculations for their bombing runs is absent in these regiments.
>
> The time service is poorly organised. The navigators have not sufficiently assimilated the service manual.

Discipline in radio communication was traditionally poor, or to put it more accurately, it was completely lacking. Moreover this was linked, as strange as it may seem, not to the lack of radio sets, but actually to a reluctance among personnel, and this was at all levels, to use radio technology:

> The overall training for seasoned gunners/radio-operators for flight operations is satisfactory, theoretical training is unsatisfactory. In the 40th, 9th, 46th, 63rd, and 54th High-Speed Bomber Air Regiments 25 percent of the young gunner/radio-operators who arrived at the school in November, are still not ready to fly since their progress is slow. There are no training classes in communication in these regiments (the 40th, 46th, and 54th High-Speed Bomber Air Regiments) and the training process for communication is progressing at a very low level. The ground based radio sets designed to train gunners/radio-operators are not used.
>
> Regimental, divisional, and district headquarters do not use radio communication at all, despite their alert posture, and the establishment of radio-networks over the course of several months.
>
> In fighter units the pilots' knowledge of the RSI-3 receiver is poor. In certain regiments there is no provision in the training plan for assimilation of the new receivers (particularly in the 42nd Fighter Air Regiment). Command posts have not made arrangements for the aircraft to be controlled by radio. Microphones for portable radio sets, monitoring receivers, and warning systems are not tolerated in the command posts. Exercises in radio communication are not included in the package of training flights. Signal acquisition from target identifying panels is not generated either. This situation with respect to communication testifies to the fact that the commanders in the fighter regiments underestimate the use of radios in fighter aircraft to enable them to be controlled in flight. Order No. 44, which was given by the Commander of the Baltic Special Military District for the year 1940, is not being carried out.

> Training for signal companies is satisfactory, but the chiefs of staff do not allocate sufficient time to their work across all the regiments. As a result planning for combat training within these companies is poorly managed. The resultant orders issued by the regiments do not mention combat training for these companies. The radio-operators in the signals companies are not capable of operating the microphone (particularly in the 38th Fighter Air Regiment). The 11AK portable radio sets have not undergone testing in the garrisons to check if the microphone works, while in the 38th Fighter Air Regiment this equipment was not functioning at all during inspection testing. The signals companies are often redirected to stand guard, how is that for fulfilling the requirements of decree No. 0360 issued by the People's Commissariat for Defence and dated 20 December 1940, which stipulates that the signals troops be released and relieved to carry out duties other than those they are intended for. The base commanders do not pay sufficient attention to ensuring the signals companies are supplied with equipment. The supply of spare parts for aircraft radio sets is equally thin on the ground.

Probably the only thing the personnel of the Air Forces of the Baltic Special Military District had to really boast about were their excellent individual flying skills and their formation flying. In practically all the regiments the exercises in aircraft handling were passed with results that were 'good' or 'excellent': 'The check that was carried out during the inspection of the flying skills of the senior personnel in the fighter and bomber regiments demonstrated training that was rated as good or excellent.'

1.3 The Materiel

If the plusses and minuses of the situation that had arisen over the staffing of aviation regiments with personnel and their training still warranted discussion, then the issues concerning the availability and the condition of the aircraft and engine fleet in the air forces of the Baltic Special Military District, which was in fact a wider problem in the Red Army Air Force as a whole, could be summed up in one word, it was—to put it mildly—dreadful.

The Workers' and Peasants' Red Army Air Force, particularly on the threshold of the Second World War, was in acute need of modern aircraft and power plants. Following the 'breakthrough', however, in the mid-1930s when the I-15, I-16, and SB took to the skies, a deep stagnation had set in that had not been successfully overcome. The work that had started on a whole spectrum of new aircraft between 1936–1938 had not reached a logical conclusion right up to the start of the Second World War. Polikarpov's new designs remained at the prototype stage: the I-180 fighter, the VIT ground attack aircraft, and the SPB dive bomber. Work on the introduction into service of the DB-3 long-range bomber was progressing very slowly and the TB-7 heavy bomber was undergoing protracted development. Yatsenko's I-28 fighter had not entered series production even though in 1940 this aircraft had been listed on the plan for entry into service as the Air Force expanded. Despite the attention from the country's leadership the programme to manufacture the 'Ivanov' multi-role aircraft was faltering and it was only in 1940 that production of the BB-1, otherwise known as the Su-2, had begun, that is to say four years after the specification had been issued. Work on the project to manufacture an armoured ground attack aircraft the BSh-2 (the future Il-2) had ground to a halt, and development work on this aircraft had begun back at the beginning of 1938. Rhythmic production of these 'flying tanks' only began between May–June 1941.

At the time of the transfer to a regimental system at the beginning of 1938 a considerable percentage of the materiel at the disposal of the Red Army Air Force was comprised of obsolete aircraft such as the R-5, R-5SSS, R-ZET, R-6, TB-3, the type 4 and 5 I-16s, and the I-15, which needed to be replaced as soon as possible. The leadership of the Air Force were well aware of this but no modern aircraft, which were ready to be put into production, had been developed and manufactured. As a result the newly formed regiments inherited materiel from the disbanded squadrons.

For the most part this situation had arisen because of a serious crisis in the development and manufacture of new, powerful aero engines. Any new 'breakthrough' in aeronautical engineering would require engines with an output in excess of 1,000 h.p. The engine manufacturers however had not been able to put the M-62, M-63, M-70, M-87, M-88, M-89, M-105, and AM-35 engines with an output ranging from 1,000–1,400 h.p., into production or achieve sustainable operation for some considerable time. This was in spite of the fact that these aero engines were already listed in the manufacturing programme for the year 1938 and that the designers of these aircraft were focused on their flight performance characteristics at the design stage.

Given this situation the only thing to do was to rely on the work to modify the I-15, I-16, DB-3, and SB, which had already proved themselves relatively well. These aircraft had less powerful M-25V, M-87, and M-103 engines that were nevertheless already in production. Unfortunately, however, achieving any significant improvements in terms of the characteristics of modified aircraft fitted with these engines proved unsuccessful. For example at the design stage a design speed of 520 km/hr was anticipated for the type 10 I-16 fitted with a 775 h.p. M-25V engine, however the speed remained that of the previous model, and the reliability of these new engines left something to be desired. The situation was almost the same with the SB aircraft, but the M-87 engines, which were used in the development of the DB-3, were never refined to achieve stable operation and as a consequence the aircraft that employed these engines were not manufactured in 1938.

Naturally, work to modify these aircraft never ceased, but it was only in 1939 that the opportunity arose to make use of the new, powerful M-62, M-63, M-87, M-88, M-103A, M-105, and AM-35A engines after which the process of modification of the new versions of the I-16, I-153 (which more or less continued the development lineage and was for the most part an extensive modification of the I-15/I-15bis) as well as the SB, and DB-3 moved forward much more efficiently. In May 1939 the aircraft manufacturing programme for 1938–1940 was affirmed. That is to say the development process for 'new'* designs as well as the next stage in the modification of 'old' designs began at practically the same time. Naturally, the design, manufacture and testing of the 'newest' designs required considerable time and therefore putting the modified versions of the 'old' aircraft types into production became a matter of life and death. The Air Force needed to be re-equipped as soon as possible, since in the spring of 1939 the political environment became more and more heated, and there was a very real taste of war in the air.

Design and manufacturing shortcomings together with the exceptionally low reliability of the new engines once again played a decisive role in the manufacturing and modification of these aircraft. The M-62, M-87, M-105, AM-35, and specifically the M-63 and the M-88, which had been developed over a long period of time and which entered production only after an enormous amount of work, turned out to be so 'crude' that an enormous number of design shortcomings and defects had to be eradicated. In the course of operations factory brigades were constantly refining these engines at the front line units themselves. This work however did not have the desired effect and after a number of accidents and catastrophes flights in aircraft employing the M-63 and

* Aircraft that were classed as 'new' or the 'newest' designs is a term that refers in historical publications to MiG-3, Yak-1, LaGG-3, Pe-2, Il-2, Su-2, and Er-2 aircraft, production of which only commenced at the end of 1940 and the beginning of 1941. Therefore the term 'older' or 'obsolete' aircraft traditionally refers to I-15, I-15bis, SB, DB-3, TB-3, R-5, R-ZET, and R-10 aircraft, which were developed between the end of the 1920s–mid 1930s.

M-88 engines were banned in September 1940, and flights in aircraft employing M-62 and M-87 engines were restricted. According to an 'ANALYSIS OF THE ACCIDENT RATE FOR 1940 AS A RESULT OF THE MANUFACTURING AND DESIGN SHORTCOMINGS IN THE MATERIEL' this is how the situation looked as far as the condition of the engine fleet in the Red Army Air Force was concerned in 1940:

M-63 ENGINES
In total there were 156 accidents involving engines, which caused:
Fatal accidents with I-16 aircraft, 3
Fatal accidents with I-153 aircraft, 1
Accidents with I-16 aircraft, 6
Accidents with I-153 aircraft, 3
Number of pilots killed, 4
The principal reasons behind these accidents were:

1. Failure of the master cylinder rod bushing

M-62 ENGINES
In total there were 286 accidents involving engines, which caused:
Accidents with I-16 aircraft, 2
Accidents with I-153 aircraft, 14
The principal reasons behind these accidents were:

1. Failure of the master cylinder rod bushing
2. The connecting rods breaking off

M-25V ENGINES
In total there were 173 accidents involving engines, which caused:
Fatal accidents with I-16 aircraft, 1
Accidents involving I-16 aircraft, 3
Accidents involving I-15bis aircraft, 5
Number of pilots killed, 1
The principal reasons behind these accidents were:

1. Failure of the master cylinder rod bushing
2. Failure of the supercharger
3. Burn-out and scoring of the pistons

M-100 and M-103 ENGINES
In total there were 220 accidents involving engines, which caused:
Aircraft accidents, 6
The principal reasons behind these accidents were:

1. Bearing failure in the supercharger
2. Failure of the reduction gearing, and the retaining pins in the rear bearing on the reduction gear shaft shearing off
3. Burn-out and scoring of the valves

M-87 ENGINES
In total there were 194 accidents involving engines, which caused:
Aircraft accidents: 1
The principal reasons behind this accident were:

1. A failure of the high-speed bearing in the supercharger

2. Burnout and failure of a piston
3. The formation of shoulders in the cylinders

M-88 ENGINES

In total there were 116 accidents involving engines
The principal reasons behind these accidents were:

1. Failure of the 1st gear in the supercharger
2. Burnout and failure of a piston
3. The formation of shoulders in the cylinders.

Owing to the disastrous situation with powerful engines the new modifications of the I-16—which were designated types 18, 24, 27, 28, 29— SB bombers of the 201st and 221st series, the DB-3B, and the I-153 only began in fact to enter service with Air Force units in any numbers from the second half of 1939 onwards and by the outbreak of the Second World War they represented a considerable proportion of the total number of aircraft.

A very tense situation developed in fighter aviation. During the course of the modification of the I-16 fighter aviation first and foremost was counting on the modification fitted with an M-63 engine, and it was decided that the M-62 engines could for the most part be retrofitted to type 5 and 10 I-16s that were already in service. Therefore just 177 examples of the new I-16s fitted with M-62 type 18 engines were manufactured in 1939, while for type 27s the figure was even lower: 59 examples, after which production was transferred to aircraft fitted with M-63 engines. However neither the plans for the modification of the old 'Ishaks' or the manufacture of new modified variants was ever realised to its fullest extent.

The principal consumers of the M-62 engines were to have been the early series I-16s, which it was proposed, would be modified to become type 18s. On 10 September 1939 the Military Council of the Workers' and Peasants' Red Army Air Force affirmed a plan that proposed the retrofitting of 750 examples of type 10 I-16s and 1,000 examples of type 5 I-16s with M-62 engines. Moreover the type 5 was also to be fitted with additional synchronised ShKAS machine guns.

However this work was protracted and very labour intensive. In fact in the course of a year up until 7 July 1940 some 283 M-62s had been delivered to aviation units in various districts, while the number of engines actually fitted was minuscule: by this date M-62s had been fitted to 31 type 10 I-16s (of these 28 examples were in the Moscow Military District and three in the Leningrad Military District). In the course of this work however it was decided not to fit the new engines onto the type 5 I-16s in view of the wear on the latter, and in accordance with decree No. 225ss dated 8 July 1940 and issued by the Committee for Defence under the Council of People's Deputies of the USSR, only 750 type 10 I-16s were earmarked for modification.

Even this work however was not carried through to the end. Up until 20 September 1940 a further 42 I-16s had been modified in a similar way. As we have seen above reliable operation of the M-62 engines was not achieved on the type 5 I-16s and as such it was decided that further work on the modification of the early series I-16s be stopped. As a result of a decree issued by the Committee for Defence dated 11 October 1940 all the work on the retrofitting of I-16s with M-25A and M-25V engines and M-62s was stopped.

Thus neither the 1,750 nor even 750 of the early series I-16s were ever modified to type 18 standard and the regular fighter air regiments were forced to continue operating the morally, and often even physically obsolete types 5, 10, and 17 I-16s.

Owing to even greater difficulties with the M-63 engines, and reliable operation of this engine was never achieved right up until the end of production, the manufacture of types 24, 28 and 29 I-16s was slowed down. In 1939 only 155 type 24 and 16 type 28 I-16s were manufactured. Later in 1940 production was resumed but by the end of August of that year and owing to the ban on operating aircraft with M-63 engines the release of I-16s from the factories was stopped. In October 1940 a considerable number of fighter aircraft that had not been accepted into service owing to defects with their M-63 power plants had accumulated at the various factories—628 examples in fact. By way of a temporary measure aimed at enhancing the reliability of these engines it was proposed that the output of the M-63s be amended to that of the M-62s, by reducing the revolutions per minute and the pressurisation.

Owing to the lack of deliveries of the I-16 aircraft the equipping of 14 fighter air regiments, which had been formed in the second half of 1940, with this aircraft was aborted. These regiments did receive these aircraft but not in anything like the numbers that were supposed to be delivered, and only on the eve of 1941. These same regiments only commenced their combat training in the spring of 1941. This failure in the production of the 'Ishaks' however was not the only difficulty. What arguably could be called the principal disappointment in terms of the modified I-16s was that even with the M-63 engines the stipulated 500 km/hr speed was never achieved and the maximum speed stabilised at around 460–470 km/hr. The reliability of the new engines left something to be desired and the frequent manufacturing defects on aircraft that had only been in series production for one year led to a situation in which for practically the entire second half of 1939 and 1940 the factory brigades, together with Air Force technicians were busy eradicating the many defects in these 'modified' aircraft, including in the most difficult conditions during the 'Winter War' with Finland.

Practically all the fighter regiments that were equipped with the later series of I-16s in 1940 were unable to conduct full-scale combat training owing to the ban on operating aircraft fitted with M-63 engines, and the newly formed units were not able to bring the young pilots up to speed.

Outwardly a report written by the Commander of the 57th Air Brigade of the air forces of the Moscow Military District, Colonel Sbytov illustrates the difficult situation concerning the modified fighters (it was this same unit that was one of the first to be re-equipped with the modified I-16s):

> Dear Comrade Stalin!
> I am obliged to approach you to bring this small memorandum to your attention. Repeated attempts at resolving the issue through the Air Force and party channels have not produced results.
>
> The position concerning flying, the condition of the materiel, and combat readiness is such, that this cannot be tolerated, although neither the People's Commissariat for the Aviation Industry or the Air Force Directorate are proposing any decisive measures.
>
> The design and manufacturing defects in the I-16 and I-153 aircraft fitted with the M-63 and M-62 engines do not enable the Air Force units to remain at a permanent state of readiness, and are seriously affecting the realisation of the plan for combat training.
>
> These same issues concerning design and manufacturing defects in aircraft and engines have continued over the course of several years and are not being eradicated by the manufacturing plants.
>
> Owing to the fact of these serious shortcomings in aircraft and engines, this materiel is not able to operate in service without failures, and pilots do not have the confidence that the aircraft will perform well in the air.
>
> The principal defects are:
>
> 1. Failure of the master cylinder rod bushing
> 2. The situation with respect to other engine components is also lamentable.

> The piston rings should operate for 300 hrs, but they are failing after only 25–30 hrs and technicians are forced to remove the cylinders and change the piston rings on three to four occasions every 100 hrs of operating time.
>
> The MF-9P magneto was designed for the M-25 engine, but these are being fitted onto M-63 engines, where it is unable to operate beyond 25 hrs. The 'AEE' factory is now producing a new magneto, however this is unsuitable, since on installation it blocks the oil storage tank.
>
> The operation of the AK-25-4-DF carburettor is poor. The float mechanism freezes on a regular basis, the reason for this has yet to be determined.
>
> Overall as far as the M-62 and M-63 engines and the I-16 and I-153 aircraft are concerned the number of defects is such that after each normal day of flying operations up to 20% of the aircraft is defective.
>
> After these aircraft were delivered to front line units, they were returned to the factory. At the present time they are overrun with an enormous number of different brigades aimed at eradicating these defects.
>
> I am not able to describe every outrage that is taking place in this memorandum, but one thing is clear, without a solution to these issues from the state the employees of the People's Commissariat for the Aviation Industry, who are afraid of taking the blame, will hush this up; they want to take the edge off this issue, and the Air Force Military Acceptance Committee, which is responsible for all this negligence will commit the same criminal act in relation to the People's Commissariat for the Aviation Industry.
>
> Member of the All-Union Communist Party of Bolsheviks N. Sbytov 14 September 1940.

Unfortunately despite this and similar reports and messages written by Colonel Sbytov the situation with respect to the condition of these aircraft and of the M-62 and M-63 engines did not undergo any profound changes right up until 22 June 1941.

Against the backdrop of problems with the entry of the modified I-16s into production, and also the influence of the successful debut of the I-15 fighter in Spain in the autumn of 1936, and the concepts for a manoeuvrable fighter that were weighing on the minds of the designers and of the military, production of a modified I-15 aircraft was arranged at Factory No.1 in Moscow, starting from 1938 onwards. Back on 14 December 1936 N.N. Polikarpov approached the People's Commissariat for Heavy Industry in a letter, in which he set out the requirement for just such a fighter:

> We need to set to work immediately on the development of an enhanced, manoeuvrable fighter … Recent events have shown that the role of a manoeuvrable fighter is unwavering, and that it is not possible to conduct air combat without such an aircraft. The creation of a completely modern manoeuvrable fighter is possible, and our provisional estimates of a maximum speed of 430 km/hr with an M-25V engine whilst retaining or even enhancing the aircraft's manoeuvrability point to this. In view of this it would be expedient to include the design and manufacture of a modern fighter based on the I-15 in the production programme for Factory No. 21 for 1937.

As a result at the beginning of 1937 a specification was drawn up for the modification of the I-15, in accordance with which the I-15bis fighter was created. According to the design calculations this aircraft should have been able to develop a maximum speed of 430 km/hr, however whilst still in the course of testing it became clear that even with the installation of a more powerful M-25V engine it would not be possible to achieve any serious enhancements in the aircraft's flight performance characteristics. The speed characteristics remained those of the I-15, and the horizontal manoeuvrability had even deteriorated. Specialists, who tested the aircraft, noted immediately that the aircraft did not meet the contemporary requirements for, and in fact was worse than the predecessors to the I-15, which was manufactured between 1934–1935. The combat evaluation flights undertaken in 1937 demonstrated the complete failure of the I-15bis as a fighter:

> On 19 September 1937 whilst attacking a TB-7 aircraft at an altitude of 2,500–3,000 m from a position above and behind the aircraft the I-15bis lost its altitude advantage, lagging behind the four-engine bomber. This latter circumstance was assessed as 'the fighter's complete lack of combat readiness'. Apart from the suddenness of an attack it offers no advantages in air combat with I-15 and I-16 aircraft and is only able to break off combat on its own initiative with great difficulty ... all the advantages in combat that the I-16 had ... the I-15 has the advantage in terms of rate of climb and manoeuvrability, while the I-15bis is only able to break off combat in a dive by virtue of its powerful M-25V engine.

Despite such unflattering opinions from the experts, production of this new fighter commenced right at the end of 1937 at one of the finest aircraft factories in the USSR, Factory No. 1. Specifically in the programme of deployment for 1938 it was proposed that there should be one, or on very rare occasions, two squadrons of I-15bis aircraft in each fighter air regiment. However judging by the way the new units were formed, some of these new regiments nevertheless were equipped solely with the 'Bis'. For example the 42nd Fighter Air Regiment was equipped with I-15bis fighters during the 'Winter War', which were fitted with external tanks, and which operated as escorting fighters. This however was forced upon them as the I-15bis as a rule served as a stand in for the I-16 while the regiments were being formed, since Factory Nos. 21 and 153 could not keep up with the deliveries of the latter. By the second phase of the Spanish Civil War it became clear that the biplane era was already a thing of the past, but after the complete fiasco that the I-15bis pilots suffered in Mongolia the squadrons equipped with these fighters began rapidly to be re-equipped with its younger brother the I-153. This aircraft appeared as a further development of the manoeuvrable I-15/I-15bis biplane line, and was the pinnacle of Polikarpov's biplane lineage. Its entry into service with the air forces of the Red Army right at the height of the battle of Khalkhin-Gol and its relatively successful operations in combat inspired a new impulse for what seemed like a fading concept. The relatively successful and rapid introduction of this aircraft into series production was without doubt, the work of the collective at Factory No.1, whose workers succeeded in organising the mass production of this new aircraft in the shortest possible time. One positive aspect was that from the outset a decision was taken to use the M-62 engine for the 'Chaika', which was less powerful, but more reliable than the M-63. Production of the M-62, to supply factory No. 1, was arranged at the Moscow Engine Manufacturing Plant No. 24 along with the M-17 and M-34 engines. It was thanks to this specific set of circumstances that in 1939 some 1,011 examples of the I-153 were manufactured, while in 1940 some 2,362 aircraft were produced, which was two and a half times more than the I-16, of which in the same year only 1,607 examples were manufactured.

In many ways it was due to the rhythmic work of Factory No.1 in the course of the Soviet-Finnish War with acute timescales and a lack of the new I-16s, which were so urgently needed, that the units began to be re-equipped with the new 'Chaikas'. From the beginning of 1940 units began to arrive at the front line that were equipped solely with 'Chaikas'. By way of an example the 148th Fighter Air Regiment received I-153s as it was being formed, and the 15th Fighter Air Regiment was re-equipped with the I-15bis and type 5 I-16s just prior to their deployment to the front line. In the 38th and 49th Fighter Air Regiments meanwhile the squadrons re-equipped with the 'Chaika' from the I-15bis and early I-16s in the course of combat operations.

The ever-growing production of the I-153 and the relatively successful use of the 'Chaikas' in combat (moreover the aircraft made a very good account of itself not only as a classic fighter but also as a fighter-bomber) evidently served as an impulse and when it came to the spring deployment of

1940 the formation of new regiments equipped solely with I-153s was planned. It is paradoxical, but this ambiguous decision, specifically the same could be said of the continued production of morally obsolete and slow aircraft (the 'Chaikas' could only develop a maximum speed of 425 km/hr) was taken against a backdrop of a dreadful hysteria over the speed of future aircraft that were undergoing development, and the fact that speed was specified as the principal consideration in their design. It was this characteristic that would determine whether the aircraft entered series production or not.

Nevertheless it was very clear to the majority of specialists that the recent successes were in the main due to the weaknesses in the opposing Finnish Air Force, and not the exceptional capabilities of the I-153. Given all its shortcomings the later series I-16s were much better suited to the role of a fighter than the 'Chaika'. The later series 'Ishaks' held an advantage in speed over the I-153 of approximately 40–50 km/hr, which enabled them to intercept the majority of bombers and reconnaissance aircraft then in service in the Air Forces of possible enemies.

In many contemporary publications the authors try to find in the I-153 'Chaika' if not the exceptional qualities of a fighter aircraft but at least the individual qualities of a kind that enabled this aircraft to engage both bombers, and the fastest modern fighters of the *Luftwaffe* in combat successfully. These qualities usually relate to an excellent horizontal manoeuvrability or an air-cooled radial engine with a low sensitivity to bullets and shrapnel getting inside it. However these considerations often overlook the following: any fighter, which is not capable of imposing its will on an enemy, and in the case of the I-153 this often occurred by virtue of its openly poor speed characteristics, is only capable of repelling enemy attacks, and becomes a passive participant. It was the capability of German fighters to catch up with an enemy and also to break off combat, which is no less important, that afforded German pilots a principal advantage over Soviet fighters for practically the entire four years of the war.

Equipping the majority of the fighter air regiments of the Red Army Air Force in 1940 with I-153s cannot be called an optimal decision. Without a doubt this was a decision that was forced due to problems that arose with the production of the modified I-16. Nevertheless the capabilities of the I-153 as a light, strike aircraft are worthy of quite high praise, especially when the relatively serious training of pilots in dive bombing techniques is taken into consideration, as well as the fact that pilots in a whole series of regiments had practical experience of operating the 'Chaika' as a ground attack aircraft in combat conditions during the 'Winter War'. To a large extent, up until the large-scale arrival of Il-2, Ar-2, and Pe-2 aircraft in front line units the I-153 and I-15bis fighters were probably the only aircraft in the Red Army Air Force that were capable of providing effective support to troops on the battlefield.

Unfortunately the technical condition of the 'Chaikas' left something to be desired, and in this sense the I-153 was no different to the I-16, or the I-15bis. According to the same 'ANALYSIS OF THE ACCIDENT RATE FOR 1940 AS A RESULT OF THE MANUFACTURING AND DESIGN SHORTCOMINGS IN THE MATERIEL':

THE I-16 AIRCRAFT

In total there were 1,407 failures (incidents) which occurred for a variety of reasons, and which caused:
Fatal accidents, 2
Accidents, 5
Number of pilots killed,: 2
The principal reasons behind this were:

1. The throttle levers breaking off
2. A failure of the bulkheads in the oil storage tank
3. Fractures in the 5th assembly in the engine mountings
4. A failure in the 4th rib assembly in the centre wing section

THE I-153 AIRCRAFT
IN TOTAL THERE WERE 735 FAILURES (INCIDENTS) WHICH OCCURRED FOR A VARIETY OF REASONS, AND WHICH CAUSED:
FATAL ACCIDENTS, 4
ACCIDENTS, 17
NUMBER OF PILOTS KILLED, 4
The principal reasons behind this were:

1. A failure in the pipes for the fuel pressure gauge
2. A failure in the side undercarriage bracing struts
3. Fractures and failures in the eyelets for the stabiliser struts
4. Deformation in the forward stabiliser spar
5. A failure of the eyelets and the incidence wires

THE I-15BIS AIRCRAFT
IN TOTAL THERE WERE 173 FAILURES (INCIDENTS) WHICH OCCURRED FOR A VARIETY OF REASONS, AND WHICH CAUSED:
FATAL ACCIDENTS, 3
ACCIDENTS, 3
NUMBER OF PILOTS KILLED, 3
The principal reasons behind this were:

1. A failure in the undercarriage half-axles
2. A failure of the foot pedals
3. A failure in the bulkheads and leaks in the fuel tanks
4. Fractures in the attachment assemblies connecting the stabiliser to the fin

... Factory No. 1 issued 72 reports concerning modifications and the eradication of various manufacturing defects with the I-153 aircraft alone.

Out of the 72 manufacturing defects the brigades at Factory No. 1 were only obliged to eradicate six, the rest of the work being done by personnel at the various military units. Unfortunately this work was not completed in full: as a report by the Head of the 2nd Directorate of the Principal Directorate of the Air Force, Troyan dated 17 February 1941 to the Deputy Head of the Principal Directorate of the Red Army Air Force Lieutenant-General Astakhov shows, many of these defects had not been eradicated by the beginning of 1941:

I am obliged to report that much of the work that has not been completed, and which was specified in the reports concerning the I-153 aircraft has now been postponed by factory No.1.

This work should have been completed by the factory brigades. However the factory has recently been putting off sending the brigades to these Districts. Thus by way of an example a brigade was formed at a factory in the Baltic Special Military District three months ago and has still not been sent to the plant.

The situation with respect to spare parts being dispatched in accordance with these reports is also unsatisfactory, and this work needs to be carried out by the front line units themselves. According to many of the reports these spare parts have still not been forwarded.

These circumstances slow down the normal operation of the I-153 aircraft In Red Army Air Force Units and do not protect the units from accidents.

I would ask you to instruct factory No. 1 to:

1. Carry out all the work on the I-153 aircraft by 1 May 1941, after sending the brigades to the Baltic Special Military District and to the Western Special Military District as soon as possible.
2. Send the spare parts that are outstanding to the Red Army Air Force units in accordance with all the reports by 15 March 1941.

Unfortunately this work was still not completed by 22 June 1941, although the brigade at Factory No. 1 spent the entire time at the various units of the air forces of the Baltic Special Military District.

Thus the very modest flight performance characteristics, together with the many design and manufacturing defects and the negative experience operating the modified fighters fitted with the M-62 and M-63 engines in front line units to put it mildly did not give any cause for optimism. In the spring of 1940 a decision was taken to cease production of the I-16 and I-153 to make way for the production of more 'modern' aircraft designs. It is difficult to describe this as a balanced and considered decision, since as a consequence of its execution the plan to deliver these aircraft to the newly formed units in the second half of 1940 and to replace the life-expired and morally obsolete type 5 I-16s in front line units with the more modern I-16s and I-153s were at an end.

Considering the breakdown in the work to modernise the 'old' aircraft, this gave the leadership of the People's Commissariat for the Aviation Industry food for thought since on cessation of production of the I-16 and I-153 these factories were supposed to commence production of the completely 'new' aircraft designs. If the attempts at a relatively simple modification of the production fighters had fallen through, then what could be expected of the these new aircraft that were entering production, all the more so when the problem surrounding the reliability of the engines and the culture of low productivity at the manufacturing plants had not been eradicated.

As was mentioned above the bomber units in the Red Army Air Force by the outbreak of the Second World War comprised a large number of light bomber air regiments, in which obsolete light bombers such as the R-5 and the R-ZET were listed on the inventory, as well as heavy bomber air regiments, which were equipped with just as obsolete a machine in the shape of the TB-3. Thus as of 1 April 1939 there were 59 bomber air regiments: of those: 30 were high-speed bomber air regiments, seven were long-range bomber air regiments, 11 were light bomber air regiments, and a further 11 were heavy bomber air regiments. Owing to the fact that production of the corresponding 'new' aircraft types had failed to get underway, it was decided that the light bomber air regiments and the heavy bomber air regiments would be re-equipped with the SB and DB-3 respectively. These measures however only got underway in spring 1939, and had not been completed either by the summer of 1939, nor even of 1940. By way of an example the 63rd High-Speed Bomber Air Regiment and the 4th Mixed Air Division swapped their archaic R-5 and R-ZET aircraft for SB bombers in the summer of 1940, and moreover they did not receive the standard number of combat aircraft.

Production of the high-speed SB bombers, which it was subsequently decided would replace the obsolete R-5, R-ZET, and TB-3 in Air Force units, began back in 1936. Factory nos. 22 and 125 found it hard to assimilate production of this completely new aircraft design. Apart from that Engine Manufacturing Plant No. 26 was not able to assimilate the manufacture under licence of Hispano-Suiza engines for some considerable time, which were designated M-100 in the Soviet Union. In fact the manufacture of engines only commenced after a great deal of work in 1936, and moreover the quality of these engines was very poor, and the service life just 50 hrs. For example in the course of the Spanish Civil War a great number of engine defects were recorded in the aircraft that were sent to Spain. The following is taken from a report by Military Technician 2nd class Petrov:

> The engine situation is worse. They are failing on a regular basis. Of the nine we have [here he is referring to nine SB bomber aircraft] six engines had to be removed immediately. I know that at the factories that are producing these engines they are struggling with the joint between the casing and the block, but this joint ruptures anyway ... the engines rattle furiously ... on one occasion a serious knocking set in ... we thought the teeth on the reduction gear had sheared. I removed the cover, and the reduction gear but found nothing, and yet the engine would howl at low revs and shake violently. On another occasion all the mixture control levers and the brackets broke. One engine began to allow water to seep through the joint connecting the cylinder casing to the block, the cylinders in the M-100 engines leak. The coupling in the magneto breaks on a regular basis, causing failures in the ignition ... to sum up the engine needs work as it fails regularly. We were forced to send three of our engines to Barcelona to the *Hispano* plant since they were giving out a metallic knocking noise, and we were not able to find the reason for this on site.

Moreover the situation did not improve a great deal in the interim, for example in 1938 some 169 M-100 engines were sent to the SAF-9 factory in Barcelona for repair.

While the Soviet specialists brought the SB aircraft and their engines up to an acceptable standard, high-speed monoplanes arrived to replace the biplane fighters. By spring 1937 the newest German Bf 109B fighters had arrived in Spain, and the SB with its top speed of 393 km/hr at an altitude of 5,000 m was not able to get away from these aircraft, while the relatively light armament with its limited field of fire coupled with the lack of self-sealing tanks afforded crews little chance of success in air combat. The fitting of M-100A engines rated at 860 hp enabled an increase in speed of up to 419–423 km/hr, which, in actual fact did not improve the situation. Although this significantly improved parameter did enable the service life of the M-100A engines to be increased up to 200 hrs. The enemy did not stand still either and the advent of the powerful 'Messerschmitt-109' C and D variants with their enhanced firepower, and which were armed with four machine guns, made the lives of the Soviet bomber crews even more difficult.

A further modification of the SB led at the end of 1938 to aircraft fitted with M-103 engines rated at 960 h.p., which had variable-pitch propellers, the so-called 96 series aircraft. This however was not accompanied by a significant enhancement of their performance characteristics. Progress however in terms of fighter development amongst potential enemies continued, and the Bf 109E-1/3 entered service with the *Luftwaffe*. This aircraft was fitted with DB 601A engines rated at 1,050 h.p., and flew 150 km/hr faster than the SB, and furthermore the E-3 was fitted with two 20 mm MG-FF 'Oerlikon' guns. In the air forces of other countries around the world a great number of new fighter designs appeared as well, and the high-speed bomber would not be able to get away from these aircraft due to their speed. Thus, in the summer of 1939 Ki-27 fighters serving with the Japanese Army Aviation would catch up with and destroy the 'Tupolev' aircraft, despite the fact that they were only armed with two rifle-calibre, synchronised machine guns. Six months later during the 'Winter War' the relatively archaic Dutch-built Finnish 'Fokker' DXXI fighters shot down SB aircraft without any difficulties. In fact, it became clear before the outbreak of the Second World War that the units equipped with the SB could only operate with fighter cover against the relatively modern air forces, and this actually happened during the final battles in the Spanish Civil War and in the course of armed combat in Mongolia. A further modification of the SB and the advent of 201 series aircraft in the summer of 1939, which were fitted with a ducted radiator did not raise the aircraft to a qualitatively new level. The designers were only able to achieve a maximum speed of just 409 km/hr, which was even worse than the production 96 series aircraft. The aircraft were very vulnerable because the system for filling the tanks with spent gases was not developed to a condition in which it could become operational, and this system was not used in front line units. The old turrets were left on the aircraft, with their limited field of fire and so on. In fact the only positive aspect was the enhanced visibility for the pilot, which overall of course was insufficient.

A decision was taken in the wake of this failed modernisation on 29 July 1939 to replace production of the SB at Factory No. 22 with the 'Polikarpov' dive bomber the SPB. Apart from that it was around the same time that a decree was issued to commence production at Factory No. 1 of another competitor to the SB in the shape of the 'Yakovlev' Yak-2. However owing to the fact that production of the SPB was protracted, and was subsequently cancelled altogether, production and modernisation of the SB continued. By November 1939 testing of the lead aircraft of the 221st series had already been completed, and some progress was achieved in the course of this testing in the speed characteristics of this aircraft.

The maximum speed was 445 km/hr, although some of the changes that were desperately needed such as filling the tanks with carbon dioxide gas, and fitting of the modernised MV-3 and MV-2 turrets etc. were only introduced into the design of this aircraft in the first half of 1940, while these changes were not applied to the majority of the aircraft produced up until that point. It was for these reasons that in May 1940 another decision was taken to cease production of the 'Tupolev' veteran. Nevertheless owing to the fact that the factories were not ready to manufacture the new Ar-2 and Pe-2 bombers and problems with rolling out production of Yak-2 and its modification the Yak-4 (in 1940 some 150 aircraft were produced at Factory Nos. 1 and 81), production of the SB continued. This is despite the fact that a relatively significant number of shortcomings and defects were observed even in 1940 in aircraft that had been in production over the course of four years.

LIST OF THE PRINCIPAL DESIGN AND MANUFACTURING DEFECTS IN VARIOUS AIRCRAFT

The SB aircraft.

1. The dive bombers have an insufficient reserve of strength.

   Deformations were observed in the outer skin of aircraft that went on to become dive bombers, as well as shearing and weakening of the rivets used to attach the outer skin to the wing and centre-section spars.

2. Aircraft from 1st–54th series manufactured at Factory No. 22 and aircraft from the 1st–5th series manufactured at Factory No. 125 have insufficient weight balancing in the ailerons. In 1940 two aircraft of these series crashed due to the onset of a flutter type vibration.

   According to the conclusion drawn up by the Central Aero and Hydrodynamics Institute operation of these aircraft at more than 265 km/hr of indicated air speed does not guarantee flight safety.

3. The pipes and expansion tanks in the cooling system are not protected at all from the effects of corrosion, and as such they fail after a few months of operation.

   Despite the number of complaints Factory nos. 22 and 125 have not done anything to date to enhance the resilience of the material used to manufacture the pipes and tanks to the effects of corrosion.

4. In later series aircraft the hydraulic hoses are fitted not with a steel, but a copper lined braiding. Hoses with a copper lined braiding are not strong enough and fail easily.

5. Aircraft manufactured in 1936, 1937, 1938, and 1939 are not fitted with equipment to fill the tanks with carbon dioxide. Factory nos. 22 and 125 have still not initiated work to install carbon dioxide tanks.

6. Aircraft manufactured at Factory No 22 from the 254th–297th series onwards are fitted with a system to fill the tanks with spent gases. This system does not make provision for screening condensation and as such is not used.

The factory has also not started work to date on a modification to this system, which would see condensation tanks being added.

7. In the majority of aircraft manufactured between 1936–1937 the replacement of the riveted tanks has not taken place. The vast majority of the rivet tanks are defective owing to leaks in the riveted joints and need to be replaced.
8. On aircraft manufactured between 1936–1937 the replacement of the valves on the undercarriage legs has not been completed. Owing to a lack of the new design of undercarriage legs, Red Army Air Force units and technical colleges are forced to operate aircraft with valves on their undercarriage legs, on which the riveted joints are out of tolerance.
9. The reserve of strength in the beading on the tyres, on the 900 x 800 mm wheels, insufficient.

Since Factory No. 22 was working at full production and had a large capacity for manufacturing the SB, 1940 saw the largest number of these aircraft produced, as a result of which it was possible to replenish the losses incurred at Khalkhin-Gol and in the Soviet-Finnish War as well as supplying the high-speed bomber air regiments that were formed in autumn 1940 with new aircraft. However owing to the fact that it was not possible to achieve any significant enhancement in flight performance characteristics as a result of the modifications, even after the fitting of the M-105 engines production of the SB was nevertheless stopped at the end of 1940. This was despite the fact that the new bomber designs had yet to undergo state, or even operational testing.

In the end the cessation of production of the SB along with the absence of production of the 'newest designs' of aircraft disrupted the equipping of the high-speed bomber air regiments, newly formed in autumn 1940 and the re-equipping of the light bomber air regiments. Practically all these regiments received an insignificant number of SB aircraft and they were they unable to conduct full-scale combat training, but were not even able to convert their regular light bomber air regiment personnel or allow their new pilots to graduate to the new high-speed bomber air regiments.

An even more complicated situation arose with the DB-3 long-range bombers. After starting off on a high note with his 'loop' in a TsKB-26 aircraft in the summer of 1936, in order to enable the design to enter production and achieve technical reliability Ilyushin had two years to get the aircraft 'into shape'. The main problem was caused by the Gnome-Rhone 14K 'Mistral-Major' engines, which in the Soviet Union were designated M-85 and which, despite the best efforts of Factory No. 29, could not be made to operate normally. This was in spite of the fact that a large number of indigenous French components were used in their manufacture. The maximum service life for these engines was just 50 hrs in total, and moreover they would often fall short even of this. The same problems arose with the modernisation of the M-86s. Apart from that the aircraft themselves had a great many defects and the Design Bureau, along with the collectives from Factory Nos. 38 and 18 spent almost the whole of 1938 on their eradication. As a result it was only with a great deal of work that these two factories managed to hand over just 394 DB-3 aircraft to the Military Acceptance Committee by 1 January 1939, and of these only 244 aircraft found their way to Air Force units. From the beginning of 1939 these factories had transferred to the production of aircraft with the next modification of the Gnome-Rhone—the M-87 engine rated at 950 h.p. The service life of this engine could be increased up to 100 hrs. Nevertheless the reliability problems experienced with these engines were not eradicated. As such in 1939 there were 150 incidents of engine failure in the M-86 and M-87 engines in front line units, which were accompanied by accidents, failures, and even fatal accidents with these aircraft.

Owing to the small number of aircraft that had been manufactured only five long-range bomber air regiments were fully equipped by 1 January 1939 and a further three had begun their conversion. In an attempt at a further modification of the aircraft the DB-3f was designed and manufactured in 1939. This aircraft differed significantly from the DB-3 and first and foremost these differences were technological. The Soviet factories, influenced by the American experience transferred to the moulded template method of production and in connection with this practically the entire structure of the DB-3's airframe needed to be redesigned. Apart from that a new navigator's cockpit was fitted to the aircraft, and all the tanks were initially self-sealing and were fitted with a carbon dioxide boost system. M-88 engines rated at 1,100 h.p. were also fitted.

Without a doubt the move to new technology, which involved the widespread use of pressing and other innovations, which simplified production considerably, served as an impulse for the further development of this aircraft. However for some reason, in parallel with the all-metal modification the Design Bureau also began to develop a design for the DB-3f that had a wooden fuselage, which it was envisaged would be put into series production in 1940. Furthermore for some reason an increase in speed of up to 500 km/hr was anticipated from this wooden aircraft, whilst retaining the range and payload. This miracle of course did not happen and even the all-metal aircraft were not capable of achieving the specified parameters. The main stumbling block again was the engines, which stubbornly refused to operate reliably. Following fruitless attempts to bring the M-88 up to an acceptable condition—and the engine was not accepted into service even in 1939—it was decided that the first aircraft would be fitted with M-87B engines, which had already been fitted to the DB-3. It was with these engines that the aircraft did produce a speed of 445 km/hr during state testing in September 1939, and moreover with a whole 'raft' of defects and shortcomings. However owing to a variety of circumstances no repeat tests were carried out following the eradication of these issues!

The Red Army Air Force, which was expanding at breakneck speed, required an enormous number of long-range bombers, but there were simply no alternatives to the DB-3f. In the end the factories began to manufacture the new bombers, moreover with both types of engines and of course with the entire set of defects that had not been corrected, which led almost immediately to the aircraft and engines failing en masse. The military acceptance committee did not accept a single DB-3f aircraft in the course of 1939. In spring 1940 when the Design Bureau and the factories were feverishly trying to eradicate the design defects, the aircraft that had been manufactured were all but taken apart and put back together again several times. The situation concerning the M-88 engines however only deteriorated. A DB-3f fitted with M-88 engines, which was presented for state testing in April 1940 managed to achieve just 425 km/hr, that is to say 20 km/hr less than with the less powerful engines, and what is more the range reduced by 500 km. This aircraft was subject to harsh criticism and again failed to pass state testing. After this acceptance of these aircraft fitted with M-88 engines ceased, and right up until 1941 it was only the aircraft fitted with M-87B engines that were sent to front line units.

It is paradoxical, but it is nevertheless a fact that for the whole of 1940 three factories produced an aircraft that had failed to complete state testing. In total 1,106 DB-3f aircraft were manufactured. It would have been naïve to expect these aircraft to operate normally in front line units, and naturally, the introduction of the new aircraft into service was followed by an endless stream of complaints and reproaches. The documents coldly set out the facts, again the 'LIST OF THE PRINCIPAL DESIGN AND MANUFACTURING DEFECTS IN VARIOUS AIRCRAFT' states:

THE DB-3 AIRCRAFT

In total there were 1,886 failures (incidents) that occurred for a variety of reasons, and which caused:

Fatal accidents, 1

Accidents, 1

Number of pilots killed, 3

The principal reasons behind these were:

1. Leaks in the fuel tanks
2. Failures in the undercarriage locks
3. Failures in the pipes for the oil supply system
4. The retaining rings on the brake wheel flange shifting
5. Failures in the mass balance brackets on the elevators

On 6 August 1940 decree No. 340ss was issued by the Committee for Defence concerning the situation with respect to series production of the M-88. At the same time all flights in aircraft fitted with M-88 engines were banned. However owing to the lack of alternative engines it was decided again to work on eradicating the defects, and by 13 November, in accordance with decree No. 422ss issued by the Committee for Defence, it was decided that production of the M-88 engine would continue:

> In connection with the conclusion to the work to eradicate the defects in the M-88 engines and the satisfactory results that have been obtained in the course of testing ... the People's Commissariat for the Aviation Industry is permitted to resume series production of M-88 engines at Factory No. 29.

In the end, having grown tired of trying to achieve satisfactory results from the DB-3f, in autumn 1940 a highly logical decision was reached that production of this aircraft was to case in 1941 in favour of the 'Ilyushin' DB-4, which was to be produced at Factory No. 39 and the 'Yermolayev' Er-2 at Factory No. 18. It was decided that production of the DB-3f would be retained at Factory No. 126, and it was planned to manufacture just 350 aircraft at this location.

As a result of the lack of regular deliveries of DB-3f aircraft and the mass of design and manufacturing defects in this new bomber the plan to equip the long-range bomber air regiments that were newly formed in 1940 and to re-equip the regular units was disrupted. Apart from that as a result of the ban on operating the aircraft fitted with M-88 engines the situation became such that many of the regular, as well as the newly formed long-range bomber units were not able to commence combat training in the second half of 1940.

Bomber aviation in the Red Army Air Force had not received any of the reliable, modified, 'old' aircraft types neither by the outbreak of the Second World War, nor in the entire course of 1940. In their heyday, between 1936–1937 when the SB and DB-3 aircraft could claim to be first-class bombers, they did suffer from a number of teething difficulties, including unreliable engines. Between 1938–1941, however, even when they were fitted with M-103, M-105, M-87, and M-88 engines, they represented relatively mediocre aircraft, and furthermore they had a number of design shortcomings and manufacturing defects, which could not be eradicated right up until the end of production. The large-scale production of these aircraft between 1939–1940 enabled front line units to be saturated with them, although this occurred for the most part due to the fact that there was a shortage in the Red Army Air Force of new, advanced bomber aircraft, which would have been capable of replacing the SB and DB-3f in service.

If aircraft were serving in fighter and bomber aviation that were worthy of modification, then in light bomber, ground attack and reconnaissance aviation there was to a great extent nothing available with which to modernise the fleet. The R-5 aircraft family had become hopelessly obsolete, and the resources for upgrading onto the R-ZET had been exhausted back in 1936. The R-10 turned out not to be very successful, first and foremost due to the poor forward and downward visibility but also the divided seating arrangement for the crew. The 'Ivanov' programme, as mentioned above, was hopelessly protracted and the enormous fleet of rapidly deteriorating light bombers and ground attack aircraft made of wood and canvas required immediate replacement.

The lack of a modern, short-range bomber in the Red Army Air Force fleet served as a basis and in 1938 a decision was taken to re-equip the light bomber air regiments as well as some of the light ground attack air regiments with the SB. Unfortunately the problems listed above with the production of the SB did not permit this to be achieved within acceptable timescales, and if between 1938–1939 it was possible to call this an optimal decision of sorts then by 1940 it did not correspond to the situation that was unfolding. The only way to rescue the situation was to equip these regiments with Su-2 light bombers, production of which commenced in 1940. Indeed in general terms equipping a light bomber air regiment with these aircraft, as units that had operated single-engine, short-range bombers for some time, would have been the right thing to do, and undoubtedly would have facilitated a rapid assimilation of this 'new' aircraft in front line units. Re-equipping however some of the light bomber air regiments if only with a few of the 'new' aircraft did not work out. The introduction of the Su-2 was very difficult, owing to technical difficulties and the many defects with this aircraft, and even if a decision had been taken to equip light bomber air regiments with these aircraft, this would not have been possible:

> Between January and April 1940 the BB-1 aircraft underwent joint testing with the more powerful M-88 engines. During the course of this testing the aircraft had to make four emergency landings owing to poor workmanship in the engine propeller group—the aircraft underwent four engine changes.
>
> The lack of workmanship in the engine propeller group comprised:
>
> a) An excessively high oil temperature
> b) The lack of reliability in the engine due to the pistons overheating and the cranking mechanism becoming jammed...
>
> The BB-1 aircraft fitted with an M-88 engine, even though it is required by the Red Army Air Force, cannot be accepted for normal operations in front line units owing to the poor workmanship in the engine ... gradual work to introduce this aircraft could lead to it becoming obsolete in the process of its manufacture and refinement.

It did not prove possible to rely on the stable operation of the M-88 engine and even the variant fitted with an M-87 engine was only introduced into series production after an enormous amount of work.

Thus, for very specific reasons the process of converting the light bomber air regiments onto the SB was actually frozen, and plans to convert onto the Su-2 did not happen either. It was therefore decided at the beginning of 1941 to re-equip many of these units with Il-2 ground attack aircraft, but only until the latter received the I-15bis and I-153s.

In general terms the very fact of the acceptance into service in 1940 of a single-engine, short-range bomber that was not capable of dive bombing and which had very modest flight performance characteristics does seem quite strange. At the same time it could be said that the concept of a similar aircraft had by that time reached a dead end. Taking everything into consideration this decision is defined not as one based on the requirements of the time but one born of the inertia surrounding the 'Ivanov' programme. A reasonably logical decision in that situation would have been to equip the corps squadrons with Su-2s. However according to the re-equipment programme for the Air Force all the Su-2s that had already been manufactured were to be used to equip the 11 short-range bomber air regiments that were formed between 1940–1941, while the air observation squadrons were to be equipped with Yak-2s.

In many ways the situation in ground attack aviation was analogous. In fact following the acceptance into service with the Red Army Air Force in the first half of the 1930s of the LSh-5 and R-5SSS no other new aircraft of this same class entered series production right up until 1941, with the exception of the DI-6sh, which was only partially successful. In essence, ground attack aviation in the middle of the 1930s and right up until the summer of 1941 was searching for a specialised ground attack aircraft. The gamble with the BSh-1 (which in America was known as the V-11 'Vultee') had not worked, and production of this aircraft could only commence in 1939, when the aircraft did not meet the requirements of a modern ground attack platform. In total around 50 of the aircraft that were manufactured were never used, and were handed over to the Civilian Air Fleet.

Work on the 'Ilysuhin' BSh-2 was also protracted and Air Force command used the R-5SSS and DI-6 as well as I-15bis aircraft as an urgent replacement, although they had been obsolete for some time. These aircraft began to be taken out of service with fighter regiments in the summer of 1939. In a sense this eased the situation, but the handover process for the '*Bis*' aircraft and subsequently the 'Chaikas' was very slow owing to problems with the delivery of modernised fighters to the fighter air regiments. It was only possible to equip ground attack regiments with these aircraft by the end of 1940. Moreover it was these same units in the western districts that were the last to receive the 'new' materiel. That same 61st Ground Attack Air Regiment of the Air Forces of the Baltic Special Military District only set about the assimilation of the I-15bis/I-153s right at the end of 1940.

The lack of production of modern ground attack aircraft led to ground attack aviation units being equipped with obsolete I-15bis and I-153 aircraft between 1939–1940, although even this decision was delayed. As a result the combat training of a significant part of the ground attack aviation units in these new aircraft only commenced in 1941 and by the outbreak of the Great Patriotic War was in its early stages.

Reconnaissance aviation, despite the apparent abundance of reconnaissance aircraft in the Red Army Air Force such as the R-5, R-ZET, R-10, and SB was in the worst possible condition and exclusively received aircraft that were left over from other units. Work for the most part on future reconnaissance aircraft at the end of the 1930s did not lead to the production of modern types.

The next attempt at creating a reconnaissance aircraft of a specific design in 1939 was relatively successful. This aircraft was the BB-22 (which was redesignated the Yak-2) and entered series production and was accepted into service. Production of 500 of these 'Yakovlev' aircraft was envisaged in the course of 1940 and initially it was planned to equip the four short-range bomber air regiments, which were newly formed in the spring of 1940. Subsequently, in accordance with the plans made at the time, in the autumn of 1940 the Yak-2 entered service with eight newly formed reconnaissance regiments and with 40 corps reconnaissance squadrons for which the plan for the production of this aircraft was expanded to 1,300 examples. However this aircraft suffered from such a high number of design shortcomings and manufacturing defects that work to eradicate these defects actually continued for the entire course of 1940, and despite the achievement of specific results and the entry into production of an enhanced version the BB-22bis (this was actually a Yak-4), a firm conclusion was reached at the end of the year that the Yak-2 aircraft that had been manufactured at Factory Nos. 1 and 81 were not reliable and combat capable in the configuration in which they were tested.

Specifically, back the end of the summer of 1940 following the removal of the Yak-2 from production at Factory No. 1 in favour of Factory No. 81 it was very clear that the production of an enormous number of 'Yakovlev' bombers would be aborted in 1941. In the meantime following combat testing and the build up of experience in operating the first series production aircraft a veritable squall of complaints and claims aimed at the reconnaissance capabilities of the BB-22 started to arrive from the Principal Directorate of the Air Force. Thus a memorandum written by Colonel Titov and dated 15 January 1941 to the Head of the Principal Directorate of the Air Force Lieutenant-General Rychagov remarks on the unsuitability of these aircraft as reconnaissance machines in no uncertain terms:

> The materiel with which it is intended to re-equip our reconnaissance aviation units such as the BB-22 (Yak-4) is completely incapable of performing the role of a reconnaissance aircraft in terms of its flight performance characteristics and the complete lack of photographic equipment. As a result it will be much more difficult to provide the proper training for our reconnaissance crews.

A report on the shortcomings in terms of combat training for reconnaissance aviation in the winter period between 1940–41 was even more categorical:

> I consider it necessary to withdraw the Yak-4 aircraft from reconnaissance regiments owing to the fact that it cannot be fitted with camera equipment. Reconnaissance units should be equipped with SB aircraft in the near future and parallel to this the question of creating a modern reconnaissance aircraft by 1942 should be raised.

The final blow for the Yak-2 and the Yak-4 was dealt by the relatively successful testing and the start of series production of the Pe-2, which was superior to the Yaks on all counts and on 11 February 1941, in accordance with a decree issued by the Council of People's Deputies production of the Yak-4 was stopped.

However this decision did nothing at all to ease the situation in reconnaissance units that continued to operate a volatile mix of different obsolete and life-expired aircraft, and some of the squadrons and regiments were left without any materiel at all. Following a number of meetings in March 1941 a decision was taken to re-equip the reconnaissance air regiments based in the European part of the USSR with the Pe-2 in the third and fourth quarters of 1941. Prior to receiving their 'Peshkas', however, these units were to be equipped with the SB to enable them at least to commence combat training. It was decided that all the 'Yakovlev' aircraft that had been produced already were to be concentrated in the 314th and 316th Reconnaissance Air Regiments.

Against a backdrop of the prospects of the entry into service of modern, short-range reconnaissance and observation aircraft looking bleak, at that same time in March 1941 a decision was taken to equip the majority of the air observation squadrons with the SB, which it was proposed would be withdrawn from bomber units after the latter had been re-equipped with the Pe-2. This decision, like no other before it, underlined the entire gravity of the situation. In no way would it have been possible for the SB to become a fully-fledged short-range reconnaissance aircraft, or even an observation aircraft for that matter. There were however no other aircraft available that could be drawn from anywhere else.

After equipping regiments and squadrons either with old or worn out aircraft, or with new aircraft that were unsuitable for performing the role of a reconnaissance aircraft it would have been strange to expect a high degree of performance in combat from these units. Furthermore this decision brought with it another huge problem. The point being that according to the deployment programme for the Red Army Air Force for 1941 the SB aircraft that had been withdrawn from service with high-speed bomber air regiments were to enter service with aviation technical colleges. However after the decision had been taken to transfer the SB to the air observation squadrons the graduation of the specific number of bomber pilots from these institutions that was stipulated in the plan for 1941 was under threat. The reason for this was that these students would not have any aircraft on which to train, and the flying schools and colleges that were training crews on the SB were only 56 percent equipped at the beginning of March of that year. How the authorities were to replace the SB in the technical colleges is not known—no answer to this question was found in the documents.

Another tight spot was the lack of long-range reconnaissance units in reconnaissance aviation. The Red Army Air Force did not have any purpose-built strategic reconnaissance aircraft and were not able to carry out long-range reconnaissance raids to serve the interests of the People's Commissariat for the Aviation Industry and the General Headquarters. Issues concerning the availability of similar aircraft technology and long-range aviation units were regularly discussed, but right up until the outbreak of war no decisions had even been taken concerning the production of these aircraft or the formation of the corresponding units.

The equipping of reconnaissance aviation units with SB aircraft at the end of 1940 and the beginning of 1941 was naturally forced upon the leadership, since attempts to produce purpose-built reconnaissance and observation aircraft in the USSR had fallen through, and in the first half of 1941 not one reconnaissance aircraft was manufactured. The issue of setting up production of reconnaissance aircraft was put off until the end of 1941.

The condition of the materiel in the Air Forces of the Baltic Special Military District could serve as an illustration of the difficult position that had arisen in the Red Army Air Force. In total as of 1 January 1941 there were 1,195 combat aircraft in the air regiments and squadrons serving in this district. Of these:

512 were fighters (of which there were 310 I-153s, 155 I-16s and 56 I-15bis aircraft);
468 SB and USB bombers (in field conditions the training cockpit was changed for a combat example):
 47 were DB-3 bombers;
 90 were ground attack aircraft
 78 were short-range reconnaissance and observation aircraft
Apart from that there were 186 training, transport, and liaison aircraft

Combat aircraft:
447 were SBs (of which 414 were serviceable) and 21 were USBs (of which 17 were serviceable);
47 were DB-3s (of which 46 were serviceable);
368 were I-153s (of which 326 were serviceable), and all of them were fitted with M-62 engines;
110 were I-16s fitted with M-25 and M-25V engines (of these 127 were serviceable), and of these nine were type 17s and four were type 10s;
14 were I-16s fitted with M-62 engines (of which 13 were serviceable);
31 were I-16s fitted with M-63 engines (of these 16 were type 24s and 15 were type 28s);
79 were I-15bis aircraft;
Four were R-5s;
40 were R-5SSS aircraft (of these 24 were about to be handed over to the air observation squadrons from the 61st Ground Attack Air Regiment);
Five were Xe-126s;
Seven were Hawker Harts (of which four were serviceable);
10 were SV-5s (of which eight were serviceable);
12 were ANBO-41s.

Auxiliary and training aircraft:
75 were U-2s (of which 65 were serviceable);
28 were UTI-4s (of which 25 were serviceable);
24 were UT-1s (of which 20 were serviceable);
Eight were UT-2s;

Three were S-2s;
10 were ANBO-51s;
Four were PTO-4s;
Three were KOD-2s (all of which were serviceable);
Three were KOD-1s (of which one was serviceable);
Three were PONs;
Two were Dragon Rapides;
One was a DC-2;
One was a Lockheed 14;
One was a Bücker Brans (which was unserviceable);
One was a Miles;
One was an AVRO (which was unserviceable).

At first glance the availability of 1,195 combat aircraft in service with the air forces of this district would appear to be most impressive, but a detailed look at the breakdown of these aircraft by type immediately dispels the qualitative indicator. For example the principal fighter aircraft in the Air Force units of the Baltic Special Military District by the winter of 1940–41 was the I-153 and in total there were 301 of these aircraft listed as operational. The 148th, 15th, and 38th Fighter Air Regiments were equipped solely with the 'Chaika', as were the 1st and 3rd squadrons of the 49th Fighter Air Regiment. One further regiment, the 42nd Fighter Air Regiment, had re-equipped with the I-153 and the I-15bis by the beginning of the autumn. Naturally a fighter with a maximum speed of 425 km/hr cannot be called modern, despite the fact that the majority of these aircraft were manufactured in 1940.

Given a normal training environment in 1941 the units of the Baltic Special Military District, which were equipped with I-153s, could have formed a significant force capable if not of slowing down the advance of the *Wehrmacht's* motorised units, then at least of inflicting palpable losses on them. In the context of this discussion however about the condition of fighter aviation in the Air Forces of the Baltic Special Military District itself, we note that the positive aspects of the I-153 as a strike aircraft, and the satisfactory training of pilots as fighter-bomber crews came to nothing owing to the fact that the units equipped with these aircraft, in accordance with the deployment programme, were to be re-equipped with MiG-3, Yak-1, and LaGG-3 aircraft in 1941.

The second most numerous fight aircraft was the type 5 I-16, with 96 examples. The early 'Ishaks' were very much life-expired and were only valid as combat training aircraft, these aircraft equipped three squadrons each in the 10th and 31st Fighter Air Regiments, apart from that there was an 'accumulation' of type 5 I-16s in service with all four squadrons of the 21st Fighter Air Regiment. In honourable third place is the 'fearsome' I-15bis with 56 examples. Up until September 1940 the 42nd Fighter Air Regiment was equipped solely with this aircraft, which was obsolete in all respects. In the 4th Air Squadron of the 10th Fighter Air Regiment, the 1st Air Squadron of the 31st Fighter Air Regiment, the 'bis' remained in service up until January–February 1941. There were less than five dozen of the more or less modern later type I-16 fighters in service with the units in this district. The 21st and 49th Fighter Air Regiments were partially equipped with these aircraft. A total of 17 type 24 I-16s and 15 type 28 I-16s entered service with the 21st Fighter Air Regiment in the spring of 1940. Apart from that back at the time of the 'Winter War' with Finland the 49th Fighter Air Regiment began to operate type 18 I-16s after receiving one and a half dozen of these aircraft, along with the I-153.

No new I-16s were found to re-equip the regular units in the air forces of the Baltic Special Military District. This circumstance was clearly linked to the cessation of series production of the I-16 and the decision to commence production of the I-200 (MiG-1), I-301 (LaGG-3), and I-26 (Yak-1) fighters. As a result of this in the bowels of the Principal Directorate of the Air Forces of the

Baltic Special Military District it was planned to commence re-equipment of the regular regiments of the Air Forces of the Baltic Special Military District and at the same time avoid the later types of I-16, by re-equipping with MiG and Yak aircraft straight away. To put it artistically a bird in the hand is worth two in the bush, so to speak. In accordance with the deployment programme for the new materiel, which was signed on 15 August 1940, two regiments of the Air Forces of the Baltic Special Military District were to receive new aircraft before the end of the year: the 31st Fighter Air Regiment was equipped with the I-200 fighters, and the 21st Fighter Air Regiment with the I-26.

After the programme for 1940 had fallen through, a new re-equipment programme was drawn up in accordance with which in 1941 the MiG-3 aircraft were to be deployed as follows: in the first quarter or the 31st Fighter Air Regiment would receive their aircraft, while in the second quarter it would be the turn of the 10th, 15th, and 21st Fighter Air Regiments, and in the third quarter it would be the 42nd and 148th, and lastly the fourth quarter would see the pilots of the 38th Fighter Air Regiment receiving their new materiel in the shape of the Yak-1, together with the 49th Fighter Air Regiment, which would receive LaGG-3 fighters.

Thus at the beginning of 1941 there were no modern fighters in the air forces of this district, while the modified I-16s, which with a certain stretch of the imagination could be called 'replacements' for the modern aircraft, amounted to less than 50 examples, which accounted for less than 10 percent of the total number of fighters in the district.

Ground attack aviation in the Baltic Special Military District was limited to a single regiment, the 61st Ground Attack Air Regiment, which by that same year 1939 did not have any 'new' I-15bis ground attack aircraft in service. It was only right at the end of 1940 that one of the latter received the I-153. Naturally it is not possible to talk of combat readiness in relation to these units at all and the pilots had only just begun to assimilate what was for them a new aircraft. Moreover the paradox of the situation was that according to the re-equipment programme for 1941 the 61st Fighter Air Regiment by the second quarter was to have converted onto the Il-2. There is no doubt that the pilots serving in this regiment were just not able to assimilate the 'Chaika' fully before they converted again onto the Il-2.

The principal, and indeed the only aircraft type in the bomber regiments in this district was the SB (that is if the DB-3s serving in the 7th Long-Range Air Regiment, which back in November 1940 it was decreed would be handed over for long-range bomber aviation were excluded). The district's bomber regiments, with the exception of the 63rd High-Speed Bomber Air Regiment had a great deal of experience in operating the 'Tupolev' bomber, including in combat. Interestingly it was actually the 63rd High-Speed Bomber Air Regiment that continued to operate the SB in accordance with the plan, while the seven other bomber air regiments were to re-equip onto the Pe-2.

The plan envisaged that the first to convert would be the 50th High-Speed Bomber Air Regiment in the second quarter. Subsequently in the third quarter it was proposed that the 9th High-Speed Bomber Air Regiment would convert onto the Pe-2, while the fourth quarter would see the 31st, 35th, 40th, 46th, and 54th High-Speed Bomber Air Regiments receive their 'Peshkas'.

Apart from that in order to train the crews in dive bombing it was planned to re-equip one squadron each from the 46th and 54th High-Speed Bomber Air Regiment with Ar-2 dive bombers by 1 March 1941.

Nevertheless for the majority of the year 1941, in the event of the outbreak of hostilities, all bomber aviation units in the Baltic Special Military District had to rely on the 'trusty old' SB, although there were certain points of difference. The point being that the majority of the bomber regiments in the district (with the exception of the 9th, 31st, and 63rd High-Speed Bomber Air Regiments, in which 99 percent of the aircraft were 221 series machines) had a varied cocktail of SBs of a variety of series in service. These ranged from the earliest models fitted with M-100A engines and nose-mounted radiators to the new 221 series aircraft, and moreover as a rule these aircraft would be alternated in the order of battle—and often a single section would consist of aircraft of a different series and year of manufacture to one another. Naturally in a real combat environment this would have a disastrous effect on the speed of the group as a whole. These problems were revealed as part of the combat experience gained at Khalkhin-Gol but had not been resolved in front line units right up until the outbreak of the Great Patriotic War.

Probably the worst situation in the air forces in this district was the one that had unfolded in reconnaissance aviation, which consisted of a single reconnaissance air regiment, a few corps air squadrons (which were lent to aerial gunnery corps) and individual aviation detachments. In fact up until the re-equipping of the 61st Ground Attack Air Regiment and the transfer of R-5SSS to the air observation squadrons these units did not have any combat aircraft and were not able to conduct full-scale combat training. Nevertheless even the transfer of obsolete ground attack aircraft did not enable a solution to the problem. Firstly, the fitting of a radio set and a camera to each airframe was the minimum requirement in order to convert the R-5SSS to a reconnaissance and observation aircraft. This naturally entailed receipt of this equipment from the factories and warehouses, which was just not realistic right up until the outbreak of war. The second, and the most important reason was that the aircraft were so worn out that they could only be returned to further operations following extensive work.

By way of an example this is how the air observation squadrons in the Air Forces of the Baltic Special Military District looked according to a report into the condition of the materiel in May 1941:

> **The 112th Air Observation Squadron.** This squadron, which consists of 12 crews, is capable of conducting daylight combat operations at medium altitudes, and four crews are able to conduct night operations. Owing to the lack of serviceable materiel the combat aircraft in this unit are not combat capable.
>
> **The 10th Air Observation Squadron.** This squadron, which consists of 16 crews, is capable of conducting daylight combat operations at medium altitudes and in favourable weather conditions, and four crews are able to conduct night operations. Owing to a shortage of serviceable materiel (out of the eight SSS aircraft seven are unserviceable) the combat aircraft in this squadron are not combat capable.
>
> **The 11th Air Observation Squadron.** This squadron, which consists of 20 crews, is capable of conducting daylight combat operations at medium altitudes in favourable weather conditions, and three crews are able to conduct night operations. Owing to a shortage of serviceable materiel (out of the seven SSS aircraft six were unserviceable) the combat aircraft in this squadron are not combat capable.
>
> **The 16th Air Observation Squadron.** This squadron, which consists of six crews, is capable of conducting daylight combat operations to correct artillery fire, as well as liaison and reconnaissance at medium altitudes and favourable weather conditions. Owing to a lack of serviceable materiel this squadron is not combat capable.
>
> **The 65th Air Observation Squadron.** This squadron consists of 16 crews and is capable of conducting daylight combat operations at medium altitudes in favourable weather conditions. Owing to a lack of serviceable materiel this squadron is not combat capable.
>
> **The 2nd Aerial Photographic Detachment.** This detachment consists of five crews and is capable of conducting day and night aerial photographic operations at medium altitudes

in unfavourable weather conditions. Owing to the lack of serviceable materiel in terms of combat aircraft this detachment is unserviceable.

In fact five squadrons out of nine, plus the 2nd Air Detachment, were not combat capable owing to the lack of serviceable materiel.

The 312th Reconnaissance Air Regiment by the first quarter of 1941 was to have received Yak-2 reconnaissance aircraft by way of augmentation. Three of the squadron commanders even succeeded in converting to the 'Yakovlev' aircraft in December 1940 at the Air Force Scientific Research Institute but the regiment was never to receive these aircraft. Thus, there were no reconnaissance aircraft in the unit in 1940, and it was not possible to conduct combat training. After this, as it finally became clear that the prospects for the delivery of the Yaks looked bleak, a decision was taken to equip this regiment with Pe-2 aircraft at the end of 1941. Up until the moment the 'Peshkas' entered service with the regiment still had to assimilate the SB, which up until that point had been in the process of withdrawal from bomber units. Unfortunately this process, with respect to the 312th Reconnaissance Air Regiment was seriously delayed. It was only at the end of March that the regiment received three SB aircraft and one USB, subsequently between April–May this same number of aircraft were received. Only at the end of May was a radical decision taken—namely to transfer five SB aircraft each from the 35th, 46th, 50th, and 54th High-Speed Bomber Air Regiments. For a variety of reasons this process was protracted, and in the end it was only in the middle of June that 15 SBs were transferred from the 35th, 46th, and 54th High-Speed Bomber Air Regiments.

It therefore follows that the availability of three dozen reconnaissance aircraft in the air observation squadrons of the Baltic Territorial Aerial Gunnery Corps should be treated with some scepticism. The presence of disparate aircraft types, such as a Stampe-et-Vertongen SV-5, Henschel Hs 126B, and a Hawker Hart in the Aerial Photographic Detachment No. 41 did not bode well for subsequent operations. The reason for this was that Soviet industry did not manufacture spare parts for these aircraft and in the event of their being used intensively these aircraft would probably have disappeared from the scene rather quickly, owing to technical difficulties.

Again we note that the leadership of the Red Army Air Force were fully aware of the situation that was unfolding, and in accordance with the re-equipment programme all the air observation squadrons were to receive new materiel in the 3rd–4th quarters of 1941. However for some reason aside from the Su-2 short-range reconnaissance aircraft, which was fitting for the air observation squadrons, according to the plan the territorial corps squadrons were to re-equip with the SB, and all the rest with the Yak-4. Subsequently in March 1941 this decision was amended and from then on all the air observation squadrons in this district were compelled to re-equip with the SB.

It was not only the reconnaissance units but also many of the bomber air regiments and fighter air regiments which suffered from the wear and tear on their old machines, and significant resources on the part of the maintenance personnel were spent purely on maintaining the 'vintage' aircraft in an airworthy condition. At the beginning of 1941 the condition of the materiel was characterised in the report as follows:

The 50th Bomber Air Regiment:

1. This regiment is equipped with SBs, 46, USBs, five, and U-2s, nine.
2. On 1 February 1941 the following were serviceable: SBs, 31, USBs, four, and U-2s, five. Unserviceable aircraft were as follows: SBs, 15
3. the service life of the aircraft is 79 percent and that of the engines 48 percent. The situation with respect to the service life of the engines is poor.

...

7. This regiment is equipped with 1st series SB aircraft. The materiel is old and in poor condition.

The 46th High-Speed Bomber Air Regiment:

As of 23 January 1941 this regiment had:

a) SB aircraft, 63, of which USBs, 2
b) Serviceable, 57, and unserviceable, six.

The regiment is not able to restore the unserviceable aircraft by themselves owing to a lack of serviceable engines and consumable spare parts. The two unserviceable aircraft have been in this condition for two months.

2. The service life of the engines is 84.5 percent, and that of the aircraft 55.8 percent.

The 21st Fighter Air Regiment:

1. Type 5 I-16 fighters fitted with M-25 engines in total 33, of which unserviceable nine, in the workshops undergoing an intermediate overhaul, eight, undergoing general repair, one

   The remaining service life of the aircraft: for the type 5, 10, and 17 I-16s, 56 percent.
   For the type 24 and 28 I-16s, 96 percent.
   For the M-25 engines, 72 percent, and for the M-63 engines, 84 percent
2. The condition of the materiel: 33 I-16 aircraft fitted with M-25 engines have been operating very reliably since 1936–1937 and the maximum flying hours they have amassed amounts to 290 hrs. Of these aircraft 21 need to undergo an intermediate overhaul. Thirty-one I-16s fitted with M-63 engines were delivered in November 1940. Of these 13 aircraft are operational. Eighteen aircraft have been assembled but have not been degreased, although there are no plans to fly these aircraft.

   The condition of the I-16 aircraft fitted with M-63 engines is good. The condition of the 21 aircraft fitted with M-25 engines is unsatisfactory.

The 10th Fighter Air Regiment:

'The remaining service life for the I-16s is 40 percent, and for the I-15s, 75 percent.

The remaining service life for the M-25 engines is 79 percent, and for the M-25V engines, 66 percent.

The aircraft have been operational since 1936–1937 and have amassed between 140–280 flying hours.'

The 31st Fighter Air Regiment:

The remaining service life for the aircraft is 27 percent. The remaining service life for the engines is 21 percent. The I-16 aircraft fitted with M-25 engines have been operating since 1936–1937 and have amassed between 200–280 hrs. The remaining service life for the I-15bis aircraft is 58 percent, while that of the engines for these aircraft is 51 percent.

[Interestingly even the regiments that received their new aircraft still did not represent a shining example in terms of their technical condition and moreover these aircraft had been operating for around a year. For the most part this was due to the low level of reliability in the new engines, which was at 50–100 percent, however many engines did not even reach that figure.]

The 9th High-Speed Bomber Air Regiment:

'1. As of 19 January 1941 the regiment had: SBs, 58 (of these two were training aircraft and a further two were undergoing repair). The service life for the aircraft was at 82 percent, while that of the engines was 37 percent.

The low percentage for the remaining service life threatens to disrupt the regiment's combat training.'

The 148th Fighter Air Regiment:

'As of 28 January 1941 the 148th Fighter Air Regiment had: I-153s fitted with M-62 engines, 70, of these 11 were unserviceable.

The remaining service life for the aircraft was 84 percent, while for the engines this figure was 55 percent. The aircraft are stored in the open air.'

The 49th Fighter Air Regiment:

This regiment had: I-15s fitted with M-62 engines, 39, of which seven were unserviceable, type 18 I-16s fitted with M-62s, 14, of which two were unserviceable. The remaining service life for the combat aircraft was at 77 percent. The remaining service life for the engines amongst the combat aircraft was at 57 percent. The I-16 aircraft fitted with M-62 engines amassed between 40–60 flying hours in January 1940, and the condition of these aircraft is good. The I-153 aircraft fitted with M-62 engines that were delivered between 1939–1940, have amassed between 30–150 hrs.

The regiment's materiel continues to be stored in the open air.

The 38th Fighter Air Regiment:

'In total this regiment has: I-153s fitted with M-62 engines, 58, of which 13 were unserviceable. The remaining service life for the aircraft is at 80 percent, while for the engines this figure is at 45 percent. The I-153 aircraft, which were delivered in November 1939, have amassed between 50–100 flying hours.'

Taking the facts listed above into account, and despite there being almost 1,200 aircraft in service, it has to be said that in terms of the plan for the provision of materiel the situation the Air Forces of the Baltic Special Military District found themselves in was catastrophic. In fact by the beginning of 1941 there were no modern aircraft in service with the various units in this district, and many units were operating aircraft manufactured between 1936–1937 while other aircraft types such as long-range bombers were completely absent.

The situation was more or less the same for the air forces of the other surrounding districts. It is also worth noting that right from the beginning of 1940 modified type 24, 28, and 29 I-16s, as well as series 221 SBs, and DB-3fs began to enter service with Air Force units in significant numbers. This marked a turning point in this situation, and provided some hope that the Red Army Air Force would at last convert onto modified aircraft.

These measures, however, did not come to fruition. The principal reason for this was the expansion that took place in 1940, for which 35 new air regiments were formed in the spring of that year, and a further 48 began to be formed in the summer of 1940. The newly manufactured aircraft were for the most part used to equip these units. Apart from that the production of 'modified' aircraft had fallen through. As a result of this the majority of units that were formed between the summer and autumn of 1940 did not receive any combat aircraft right up until 1941, since the latter were being developed at the factories and were not able to start fulfilling the plan for combat training.

Following the problem with the production of 'modified' aircraft back at the beginning of 1940 a conclusive decision was taken to cease their production in favour of the principally new aircraft designs, the I-126, I-200, I-301, BB-1, BB-22, BSh-2, PB-100, and so on.

The Soviet technical and military leadership, which by all accounts were influenced by the way that the French Air Force and the British Expeditionary Corps had been overcome at lightning speed, as well as reports concerning the condition of the German aviation industry, decided on the production of 'new' aircraft types even before they had completed state testing. However the People's Commissariat for the Aviation Industry in 1940 were not able to deliver the mass production of 'new' aircraft types, and only managed to manufacture small batches of MiG-1, and Yak-1 fighters, and Ar-2 dive bombers. Apart from that a number of Yak-2 and Su-2 short-range bombers were manufactured from previous projects. Furthermore 'traditionally' the first aircraft to emerge from the factory had a large number of design and manufacturing defects, required significant development, and would not be able to enter service with the Air Force. In connection with the fact that production of the 'old' aircraft types had been stopped, the obsolete models could not be replaced in the regular regiments either with modified examples, or with the 'newest' aircraft for that matter. Accordingly the re-equipment programme for 1940 to convert the Air Force onto the 'new' materiel was finally aborted. Not one of the front line regiments had been converted and the personnel were not able to commence assimilation of these modern aircraft.

In contrast to the Red Army Air Force, German industry succeeded in providing the *Luftwaffe* by the outbreak of the Second World War with modern aircraft and engines. By 1 September 1939 practically all the German tactical fighter aviation groups had been re-equipped with the 'newest' Bf-109E-1/3s (they were fitted with the DB 601A engine rated at 1,050 h.p.), while the dive bomber units had re-equipped with the Ju-87B (which was fitted with a Jumo-211Da engine rated at 1,200 h.p.) and the bomber groups with the Do 17Z and the He 111P/H (these were fitted with the BRAMO 323P engine rated at 1,000 h.p. and the Db 601A and Jumo 211 A-1 of 1,050 and 1,075 h.p. each respectively). More than 50 percent of the reconnaissance aviation units were equipped with long-range reconnaissance Do 17Ps and short-range Hs 126 B-1 reconnaissance machines. The 'capacity' that the Germans created continued to expand and in the following year the production range of combat aircraft was renewed. By the spring of 1940 the fighter units had received Bf 109E-4/E-7 (powered by a DB 601N rated at 1,200 h.p.) en masse and the bomber units had begun actively to convert onto the newest Ju-88A-1 (powered by a Jumo-211B engine rated at 1,200 h.p.).

Incidentally it has to be noted that things were far from ideal for the Germans either, and as such the specific delay in the production tempo for the Ju-88A-1 bombers and the long-range Bf 110 fighters was only overcome in 1940. It was for this reason that the majority of heavy fighter groups entered into the Second World War with only the 'vintage' Bf 109Ds in service that had been freed up following the re-equipping of the fighter air groups. Nevertheless the German designers and manufacturers were able to take the idea for a heavy twin-engine fighter to large-scale mass production back in 1940. For the Soviet aviation industry at that time however these aircraft were termed 'too complex' and right up until 22 June 1941 no aircraft like this entered service with the Red Army Air Force. The Soviet air forces did not have any aircraft that were analogous to the Ju-88A bomber at all right up until 1942 when the first Tu-2s began to enter service with bomber units in small numbers.

Subsequently in the autumn of 1940 the *Luftwaffe* began to re-equip with the Bf 109F-1/2 (powered by a DB 601N engine rated at 1,200 h.p.) and the Ju-88A-5 (powered by a Jumo-211 engine rated at 1,200 h.p.) while Red Army Air Force units continued to operate 'veterans' such as the type 5, 10, and 17 I-16s, the I-15bis, R-5, R-ZET, and SB (up until the 221 series aircraft) as well as the early series DB-3s. Despite their positive merits and qualities however these belonged to a bygone era and required immediate replacement. The materiel of the Red Army Air Force in fact remained at the level it had occupied in the mid-1930s, and naturally was not able to compete on a par with the technology of the *Luftwaffe*.

Thus a highly disagreeable conclusion has to be made: owing to the shortcomings in the work of the Soviet aviation industry, and the frequent formation of new aviation units, the Red Army Air Force was not able to re-equip in 1940, not with the new aircraft types such as the MiG-3, Yak-1, LaGG-3, Pe-2, Su-2, and Il-2 or even on to the modified I-16s and I-153s fitted with M-62/63, 221 series SBs, and DB-3fs fitted with M-88 engines. The modification of the so-called 'old aircraft types' between 1938–1940, was only partially completed, and achieving reliable operation of the aircraft and particularly the engines did not prove possible in the majority of cases.

Even after having been granted, as a result of the famous pact, a period of grace lasting a year and a half the Soviet aviation industry was still not able to succeed in closing the gap with the German aviation industry and indeed the opposite actually happened, in that the gap actually increased. The modification programme for 'old' aircraft types was stopped and the programme to manufacture 'new' aircraft was just getting started. Moreover the prospects of a breakthrough in this situation were bleak. The worst aspect though was that by the time mass production of the 'modified' and 'new' aircraft had commenced, their flight performance characteristics did not correspond to the requirements of the times at all.

Along with this it should be noted that the situation which arose regarding the materiel in 1940 could have proved catastrophic were it not for two aircraft, the manufacturing of which was entrusted to two of the most influential aircraft manufacturing plants in the USSR.

This situation was eased somewhat thanks to the mass production by Factory No. 1 of I-153 aircraft between 1939–1940, and by Factory No. 22 of 221 series SBs. In fact with the help of these aircraft the Red Army Air Force command succeeded in patching up some deficiencies in their plans for re-equipping the air force, as they equipped fighter and ground attack regiments with the 'Chaikas' and reconnaissance and light bomber regiments with the SB, which were 'new' aircraft that the industry was not able to produce. Naturally though it was not possible to solve all the issues in this way and if the ground attack regiments could be re-equipped with the remaining I-15bis aircraft or even these same I-153s that were left over after the re-equipping of fighter air regiments, then the long-range bomber aviation units could be re-equipped thanks to the DB-3fs produced at Factory Nos. 18 and 39, which had not completed state testing, and were technically unreliable. The reconnaissance aviation units however still did not have modern aircraft and were forced to be content with their obsolete machines, and the same obsolete aircraft that were freed up following the re-equipping of bomber and ground attack regiments.

1.4 The Condition of the Logistical Forces, and of the Network of Airfields

A further weak link in the Air Forces of the Baltic Special Military District was the provision of airfields and the condition of the supply services—the airbases, ranges, airfield maintenance companies and so on. The relatively limited number of airfields that there were in the district in 1940—of 15 permanent airfields and 11 operational—which significantly reduced the manoeuvrability of the Soviet alignment and created a sense of overcrowding in terms of bases for armed forces. A series of airfields served as bases for two to three units each. The situation with respect to the airfields was exacerbated by the fact that the poor technology that the ground-based supply services had meant that it was not possible for a single airbase to service more than two regimental airfields, and as such dispersing a unit over more than two sites did not prove possible either, without damaging combat readiness.

A report on the course of combat training in 1940 notes: 'Almost all the airfields in the district that were constructed in 1940 have no grass surface and as such they would only be suitable for very limited operations, particularly in the spring and autumn.'

According to an audit report:

> There are 15 permanent and 11 operational airfields in this district for winter operations. As of 1 February 1941 all the permanent airfields were suitable for operations in the course of January, and there were no interruptions in the flying owing to the airfields not having been adequately prepared. Of the 11 operational airfields only 10 are suitable for operations.

Almost immediately following the accession of the Baltic States measures were taken to correct the situation at hand, and the construction and reconstruction of 62 airfields got underway in this district. The results, however, were disappointing. The Baltic States were not able to cope with this enormous task on their own and the construction of 44 operational airfields was put off until the following year:

> The execution of the task to construct airfields in the Baltic Special Military District has all but ground to a halt. The shortcomings in terms of airfield construction were as follows: construction of assets in districts such as Odessa and the Baltic districts was carried out without any blueprints or estimation of costs. The search for suitable sites was conducted purely on their external characteristics, without any diligent study. As a result the sites that were chosen in many cases were unsuitable for use as operational airfields and landing sites and the district commanders were subsequently forced to turn them down. This led to a pointless waste of state funds and a delay in the fulfilment of the plan to construct these sites.
>
> In reality the transfer of land, the setting of timescales for the demolition of existing structures and the clearance of vegetation was for the airfield department within the Air Forces of the Baltic Special Military District conducted without the consent of the governments of the various republics, and on occasion solely as instructed by the base commanders. In accordance with the corresponding timescales the individual landowners demolished the existing structures and cleared crops that had yet to ripen themselves. Subsequently a series of sites set aside in this way for the construction of airfields turned out to be unsuitable and were returned to the peasantry, who would request compensation for the losses they had incurred…
>
> The 5th Directorate did not posses precise data on which to plan the provision of building materials around the various districts, and as such their allocation was done using a rule of thumb. Thus for October 1940 some 40 wagons of cement were due to be sent to the station at Riga for the Air Forces of the Baltic Special Military District, when according to the requisition only 12 wagons of cement were required…
>
> In total a sum of 17,770,000 Roubles were spent on the construction of airfields in 1940, but not one airfield or landing site was handed over. This situation occurred due to the fact that the subsequent construction of these airfields, after the rifle divisions had occupied themselves with the construction of battalion defence areas in the border districts, was carried out for the most part by the airfield engineering battalions. In total there were only five airfield engineering battalions in the district itself. Their disposition within the district was as follows: as of 15 March 1940 the vehicle repair programme was 21.8 percent complete, the tractor repair programme was 25 percent complete, and the programme for the repair of road building and special purpose vehicles was 30 percent complete. The supply of airfield engineering battalions in the Baltic Special Military District with spare parts was on average 25 percent of consumption, and for tractors and road building vehicles this figure was at 10 percent.
>
> Aside from these battalions construction was carried out by the personnel at the various airbases and by the local population. This was clearly insufficient. The situation with respect to airfield construction was critical.

The condition of combat training at the airbases was also giving cause for concern:

The divisional and regimental aviation headquarters are not engaged in combat training, neither do they have oversight of it. For the most part training takes place on the basis of the airbase training courses for the year 1939–1940. Tactical logistics training for the base commanders is at a low level. The textbooks are insufficient. A large number of the newly promoted leadership cadres at these airfields do not have any specific training, and they are not being trained in this specialist field.

At the present time the airbases fully support the flying operations of the aviation regiments and on the basis of the position they find themselves in, and of their available funds, they are able to support operations carried out by aviation regiments operating from two airfields.

The principal airfields are provided with storage facilities in which to store equipment and armament, with the exception of Airfields Nos. 206 (in Siauliai) and 25 (in Kaunas) where some of the ammunition is stored under tarpaulins. Construction of warehousing facilities is not envisaged on operational airfields.

The level of understaffing with respect to drivers is considerable.

The staffing levels in the airfield maintenance companies serving the bomber and fighter regiments (consisting of between 74–94 individuals) does not ensure normal operations with respect to guard duty and as such young aircraft specialists are being drafted in for this, as well as liaison brigades, and airfield operations brigades.

The airfield operations brigades themselves are not fully equipped with tractors. There are supposed to be 73 tractors in these brigades around the various districts but in fact there are 28 and as such base commanders are forced to make up the shortfall by taking tractors away from the mechanised transport companies.

Work to improve the situation with respect to the network of airfields for the air forces of the Baltic Special Military District, which began across a large number of sites simultaneously in 1940 and employed the skills of the personnel in this district, was not successful. For example out of the 49 operational airfields earmarked for construction and reconstruction the majority were unfinished and were not suitable for operations. Thus, owing to the lack of airfields that were capable of supporting operations all year round the combat training of the various units became more difficult. Apart from that relocating airfields became much more difficult in a combat scenario.

The airbases and other logistics units serving the air forces were equipped with materiel and manned by personnel that corresponded almost to a peacetime footing. One significant disadvantage was the partial shortage of special purpose equipment and machinery. In addition the personnel serving in these units were constantly diverted away from conducting their service duties and directed onto various fatigue duties, first and foremost the construction of new airfields, but also of parks, community areas, and so on.

As of 12 April 1940 the line-up for the logistics services was as follows:

The 4th Mixed Air Division—airbases Nos. 20, 35, 44, and 123;
The 6th Mixed Air Division—airbases Nos. 118, 138, 201, 208, and 312;
The 7th Mixed Air Division—airbases Nos. 13, 116, 119, 127, and 206 as well as individual airfield maintenance companies Nos. 30, and 31.
The 8th Mixed Air Division—airbases Nos. 25, 110, 140, 204, and 213 as well as individual airfield maintenance companies Nos. 32, 33, and 34.

Conclusions

Despite what at first glance appeared to be relatively ideal qualitative figures in terms of combat training and numerical strength, the actual state of combat readiness in the Air Forces of the Baltic

Special Military District specifically for conducting combat operations was relatively low. This for the most part happened for the reasons listed above, principal among which are:

The constant deployment of aviation units during the course of 1940 in connection with different events (the Soviet-Finnish War, relocating to the Baltic States and so on), some regiments had been redeployed 10 times;

The basing of aviation units in the Baltic region on unprepared airfields (as well as the lack of adequately equipped ranges, firing ranges, classrooms and so on);

The Red Army's organisational and mobilisation measures between 1938–1940, which required considerable rotation of personnel and their replacement with poorly trained graduates from flying schools;

The difficulties experienced with combat training particularly in relation to aerial gunnery, bombing, and navigator training;

The lack of modern, and technically reliable materiel.

One idiosyncrasy of the events that took place in the air forces of the Baltic Special Military District, in contrast to the air forces of the Western and Central Districts and the southern districts was that some of these factors, a strange as it may seem, actually did have positive aspects to them.

Thus the fact for example that many of the units did not receive modified aircraft that were in fact technically unreliable enabled combat training to be undertaken routinely and a relatively high number of flying hours to be amassed.

One definite plus was the reinforcement of the regiments that were sent to the Baltic region with regular pilots from units that remained within the territory of the USSR. This meant that these units could to a great extent retain their well-trained personnel who had a relatively high level of competence—a far cry from the very recent students—graduates of flying schools who had served in regiments in other districts.

Naturally enough the greatest success that was achieved in combat training in 1940 amongst the fighter regiments was that attained by the 31st Fighter Air Regiment, which were equipped with type 5 I-16s and I-15bis fighters and which did not participate in the Soviet-Finnish War and was actually redeployed to Kaunas after a final resolution to the 'Baltic question'.

One of the finest bomber regiments was the 40th High-Speed Bomber Regiment, which did not fight in Finland, or in the resolution to the 'Baltic question,' or in any other conflicts, but which quietly got on with combat training.

Another positive decision were the reshuffles that took place in the higher levels of Air Force command in this district. In May 1941 Major-General of Aviation Aleksey Pavlovich Ionov took up his post as commander of the air forces of the Baltic Special Military District. Prior to this he had been Deputy Commander, but in fact from the winter of 1940–1941 he had been acting Commander. The former commander and twice Hero of the Soviet Union Lieutenant-General of Aviation Grigoriy Panteleyevich Kravchenko had been posted to undertake various refresher courses for command personnel under the General Headquarters Academy on 23 November 1940.

A.P. Ionov was a very experienced commander, and a hero pilot of the First World War, he was the only pilot amongst the Soviet aviation commanders to have started his military career as a military pilot, and most importantly, he was a very educated man. Considering his influence on the events of the first days of the war, it is absolutely imperative that the reader be enlightened as to the biography of this extraordinary military figure.

Aleksey Pavlovich Ionov was born on 8 (or 21 by the Orthodox Calendar) February 1894 in the village of Zuevskaya in the province of Yaroslavl into a middle-class peasant family. Between 1902–1912 Aleksey studied at various education institutions in turn, after which he found work in the Principal Bureau of Weights and Measures in St. Petersburg, where he worked as a technician (a battery tester) for the two years prior to the First World War.

In September 1914 Ionov volunteered for service as a rank and file 'hunter' at the Military Aviation School in Gatchina. On 24 September 1915 he passed the exam for the rank of pilot and three days later he was sent into the line of duty.

From 28 October 1915 Military Pilot A.P. Ionov fought on the Western Front as part of the 4th Army Aviation Detachment.

By way of Decree No. 635 issued by 4th Army headquarters and dated 5 June 1916 he was awarded the St. George Cross 4th class, and on 27 June 1916 he was promoted to the rank of Senior Non-Commissioned Officer. The citation stated:

> For aerial reconnaissance on 15, 18, 23 March 1916 and on 23 April 1916, whilst flying his aircraft he came under machine gun, and rifle fire as well as the constant threat of shrapnel from enemy anti-aircraft artillery and yet he kept his composure, maintaining a clearly defined course, pouring scorn on the obvious danger and acting as a shining example of fearlessness and selflessness. It is thanks to this that Ionov's reconnaissance mission was a success, and provided a distinct advantage, since the extremely difficult task that had been laid upon his shoulders was completed perfectly.

By way of Decree No. 684 issued by the 4th Army headquarters and dated 13 September 1916 he was awarded the St. George Cross 3rd class. The citation stated:

> For armed reconnaissance and air combat. On 5 July 1916 during a reconnaissance mission he engaged three German 'Albatross' aircraft in combat on three separate occasions, forcing one of them to break off combat, after which Ionov's aircraft was riddled with bullets but he continued with exemplary courage and composure to complete his sortie. By completing the extremely difficult task he acted as a shining example of a rare selflessness, as well as of fearlessness, and composure. His mission was a success and provided a distinct advantage, since the very difficult task that had been laid upon his shoulders was taken to a perfect conclusion.

On 29 October 1916 he was awarded the St. George Cross 2nd class by way of Decree No. 3659 issued by 4th Army command. The citation stated: 'For a series of combat sorties undertaken on 11, 17, 21, 23, and 27 August 1916 and 12, 14, 15, 16, and 18 September 1916.'

Finally for his deed of arms: 'For a series of aerial reconnaissance missions and battle honours' he was by way of Army Order No. 1164 dated 11 January 1917 found worthy of an Officer's rank, and he was promoted to the rank of Ensign.

In January 1917 the 4th Aviation Detachment, part of the 4th Air Army was redeployed to the Romanian front, where I.P. Ionov continued to win his battle honours. For this he was made Commander of the detachment and was awarded the St. George's Weapon and the Order of Stanislav 3rd class with swords and bow.

The great October socialist revolution all but put an end to this young pilot's career. After taking leave in December 1917 A.P. Ionov did not return to his unit owing to these well-known events, and in January 1918 he was demobbed by the district Military Commissar, after which he lived with his parents in the village of Zuevskaya.

On 10 October however Aleksey Pavlovich was called up for service with the Workers' and Peasants' Red Army and was posted to the Workers' and Peasants' Red Army Military Air Fleet. In January 1919 after becoming seriously ill he was hospitalised and on 28 January 1919 he was medically retired from the Army by the commission under the Military Academy of Medicine.

On his return to his village he was mobilised into civilian work and from 15 March 1919 he worked as a teacher of specific subjects in a vocational school. From 18 September 1920–October 1923 he worked in the Workers' Union for Education in Poshekhonye, where he was acting district head of vocational education. There is little accurate data concerning this period of Ionov's life, although it would appear that a life without flying was not for him. He appeared before the medical commission several times and finally in 1924 he retuned to military aviation.

From 22 March 1924 A.P. Ionov served as a flying instructor in the Workers' and Peasants' Red Army Military Air Fleet Directorate training squadron. From July 1924 he was made a pilot in the 'Ultimatum' detachment and after the detachment was made into a squadron he was made Director of the flying school.

In May 1932 he became Deputy Commander of the 3rd Air Brigade for combat training and from 3 January 1933 he was made Commander of the 200th Light Bomber Air Brigade in Krasnogvardeysk although he had left to go and study at the Air Force Academy of Military Aviation by the end of the year. After graduating from the operation's faculty of the N.E. Zhukovskiy Workers' and Peasants' Red Army Military Aviation Academy in 1935 he was made Commander of the 455th (107th) Air Brigade. For his success in combat training in 1936 he was awarded the Order of the Red Star.

In August 1938, on leaving the brigade he received a posting to the 1st Directorate of the Principal Directorate of the Workers' and Peasants' Red Army Air Force as the Chairman of the 'Commission for the Study and Prevention of Accidents' in the Workers' and Peasants' Red Army Air Force, and as such he was awarded the rank of Brigade Commander. In December he became the Chairman of the Central Commission of the Directorate for Combat Training in the Workers' and Peasants' Red Army Air Force. From 23 November 1939 he was made Deputy Chairman of 4th Directorate (the Higher Education Establishment) of the Principal Directorate of the Workers' and Peasants' Red Army Air Force.

Ahead of the Soviet-Finnish War on 15 November 1939 he was given a posting as the Director of the 14th Army headquarters.

On 15 April 1940 he was awarded the rank of Divisional Commander and on 4 June 1940 he was awarded the rank of Major-General of Aviation, while on 13 July 1940 he was made Deputy Commander of the Air Forces of the Baltic Special Military District and in fact he was acting Commander of air forces. On 10 May 1941 he was appointed Commander of the Air Forces of the Baltic Special Military District.

A.P. Ionov was a very experienced pilot, and as of 1 February 1937 he had personally amassed 2,123 hrs. Aside from his combat experience in the First World War he did complete one combat sortie in the Soviet-Finnish War.

Again we note that in contrast to the majority of the Soviet Air Force Command General A.P. Ionov had completed every stage of the service ladder from pilot to commander of the Air Forces of a given district, having spent around a quarter of century in the Air Force. He was given a comprehensive education including a higher military education. He had combat experience as both a rank and file pilot and as commander of a detachment in the First World War as well as experience of leading the Army Air Force headquarters in the winter of 1939–1940.

He matched up well in terms of certain qualities to the Headquarters Director as well as the Commander of the Operations Directorate of the Headquarters of the Air Forces of the Baltic Special Military District, both of whom had a higher military education and were experienced headquarters staff.

On 12 April 1941 Brigade Commander Stepan Stepanovich Krupin was made Headquarters Commander.

Stepan Stepanovich was an experienced headquarters operative. He fought in the Civil War and spent 15 years in artillery, his final position was as Regimental Commander. He subsequently went to study at the aviation department of the main faculty of the M. Frunze Academy. Following completion of this programme he went on to become first the Head of the Operations Department of the 87th Air Brigade and then Director of the Combat Training Department of the Air Forces of the Kiev Special Military District, and finally Deputy Director of the Air Forces of the Kiev Special Military District Headquarters. He fought in the Soviet-Finnish War and after the conclusion of this war on 21 March 1940 he was awarded the rank of Brigade Commander. In March 1941 he was posted to the position of the Headquarters Director of the 75th Mixed Air Division, but just a month later he was made the Headquarters Director of the Air Forces of the Baltic Special Military District.

The Director of the Operations Department of the Air Force headquarters was Colonel Arseniy Yakovlevich Rasskazov.

Arseniy Yakovlevich fought in the Civil War and went on to continue serving in rifle units, and his final position was as a Commander's Aide in a rifle regiment. In 1934 he graduated from the M. Frunze Academy and subsequently became Director of the Operations Department in the 253rd and 100th Air Brigades. In 1937 he was made Director of the Operations Department of the air forces of the Special Red Banner Far Eastern Army. Subsequently he was made Director of the 2nd Department of the Special Red Banner Far Eastern Army headquarters, and the Director of Logistics in the air forces of the 1st Red Banner Army. At the end of 1938 he became the Assistant Director of headquarters, firstly of the 19th and then the 68th Air Brigades. In March 1939 he was made Director of the 71st Air Brigade. He fought in the Soviet-Finnish War and was Director of the Special Air Group in Estonia. From September 1940 onwards he was Deputy Headquarters Director (the Director of the Operations Department) of the Air Forces of the Baltic Special Military District.

The divisional and regimental commanders of the Air Forces of the Baltic Special Military District were likewise highly experienced pilots and leaders, and the majority of them were well suited to their positions. True to form for example out of the 17 regimental commanders five went on to become generals, and the commander of the 50th High-Speed Bomber Air Regiment Colonel Agaltsov became Marshall of Aviation.

The regular personnel in the various units in the division had a very strong background. Many of the commanders served in the air forces for 10 or more years and had an enormous amount of flying experience between them. For example the squadron commanders in the 10th, and 21st Fighter Air Regiments had amassed the following tally of flying hours on the I-16 alone: Captain Pavel Fyodorovich Bushma 393 hrs, Captain Valentin Petrovich Borovoy 319 hrs, Captain Aleksandr Borisovich Isayev 282 hrs, Senior Lieutenant Grigoriy Aleksandrovich Zaytsev 250 hrs, Captain Mikhail Mikhaylovich Kuzmin 286 hrs, Captain Sergey Nikitovich Glushin 311 hrs, and Captain Ivan Maksimovich Nestoyanov 378 hrs. For the regular commanders in the 15th and 148th Fighter Air Regiments the average number of flying hours across all aircraft types was approximately 400 hrs. Moreover for the squadron commanders and their deputies, as a rule, the total number of flying hours was more than 500. The Commander of the 15th Fighter Air Regiment Major Vladimir Lukich Bobrok had amassed a total of 800 hours across all types of aircraft, while the Deputy Regimental Commander to the Battalion Commissar Aleksey Terentyev Yudayev had amassed 500 hrs. For the squadron commanders Captains Mikhail Vasilyevich Kuznetsov and Vasily Andreyevich Churinov this figure was 600 and 730 hrs respectively. For the deputy squadron commanders Senior Lieutenant Andrey Andreyevich Shemyakov 720 hrs, and Senior Lieutenant Arseniy Alekseyevich Dmitriev 450 hrs, while for Viktor Andreyevich Voronov 720 hrs, and Aleksandr Yefimovich Vasin 515 hrs, and for Pavel Timofeyevich Tarasov 671 hrs. In the 148th Fighter Air Regiment the number of hours was even higher among the commanders, for Regimental Commander Major Georgiy Nikolayevich Zaytsev the figure was at 1,860 hrs, for Squadron Commander Captain Yakov Yegorovich Titayev 1,450 hrs, for Deputy Squadron Commanders Senior Lieutenant Ivan Petrovich Rybin 1,650 hrs, and Senior Lieutenant Grigoriy Fyodorvich Yelfimov 1,300 hrs, while for Leonid Dmitrievich Smirnov 1,000 hrs, and for Mikhail Pavlovich Nekrasov 703 hrs.

The commanders in the bomber air regiments were no less experienced either. For example the 40th High-Speed Bomber Air Regiment had a cadre of commanders who were all experienced. The number of hours the squadron commanders had amassed in the SB were as follows: Captain L.S. Govorunov 300 hrs, Captain A.G. Rogov 441 hrs, Captain G.D. Izosimov 400 hrs, Captain V.B. Malofeyev 460 hrs, Captain V.A. Pankov 353 hrs. As of 1 May 1941 the Commander of the 9th High-Speed Bomber Air Regiment Major N.I. Skitev had amassed 293 hrs on the SB, while for the Squadron Commander Captain V.N. Lukin this figure was 326 hrs on the SB, for Major M.M. Ananin 210 hrs, Captain N.I. Ulasayev 243 hrs, Captain I.P. Korotkov 255 hrs, and for Captain M.A. Krivtsov 268 hrs.

Many of the commanders listed above acquired their combat experience during the course of conflicts in Spain, China, Khalkhin-Gol, and the Soviet-Finnish War. Practically every regiment had a few commanders each who fought in that conflict. They trained their personnel relatively successfully and the young pilots went on to become true aces.

By way of an example 47 pilots in the 9th High-Speed Bomber Air Regiment had amassed on average 150 hrs on the SB. In the 40th High-Speed Bomber Air Regiment the rank and file pilots also maintained this figure at a high level, on average the commanders of the 46 crews that made up the regiment had amassed 170 hrs in the SB.

For 45 pilots in the 21st Fighter Air Regiment the average number of flying hours amassed on the SB was 170 hrs, while for 46 regular pilots in the 10th Fighter Air Regiment the figure was 165 hrs, which doesn't include the hours incurred at the flying schools. (During the course of the Great Patriotic War 14 individuals from the 10th Fighter Air Regiment recorded five or more victories each, that is to say almost one in four became an ace).

The availability of a highly trained cadre of command personnel and a large number of regular pilots in the divisional units afforded the Air Forces of the Baltic Special Military District significant leeway in comparison to the air forces of other districts. This created a meaningful foundation for the units in this district to emerge in first place in terms of combat training in the Red Army Air Force.

Thus despite all the issues listed above in terms of combat training, the aircraft and engine fleet, and the logistical infrastructure and so on, the aviation units in the Baltic Special Military District had every chance of attaining full combat capability by the outbreak of the Great Patriotic War. In the author's opinion this would only have required the regular units to be left as they were, and for the 10th, 21st, 31st, and 49th Fighter Air Regiments to be equipped with later series I-16s, the 312th Reconnaissance Air Regiment to be equipped with SBs, and for combat training to commence as soon as possible.

The Squadron Commander of the 21st Fighter Air Regiment Captain S.N. Gushchin gives an order to the Flight Commander Junior Lieutenant S.F. Andreyev. This photograph was taken in the winter of 1939–1940 in Riga.

Pilots from the 21st Fighter Air Regiment, standing on the far left is V.M. Nasonov, subsequently he would become a Major-General of Aviation.

The Commander of the 4th Squadron, 38th Fighter Air Regiment Captain V.G. Kashtanov issues an order to his Junior Lieutenant G.L. Lobach, this photograph was taken in the winter of 1939–1940 in Tallinn.

Pilots from the 38th Fighter Air Regiment Senior Lieutenant N.I. Shepetov, and Lieutenant V.A. Belous taken against the backdrop of an I-153 aircraft.

Officers of the 148th Fighter Air Regiment. The spring of 1940 in Liepaja.

Squadron Adjutant of the 15th Fighter Air Regiment Senior Lieutenant A.A. Dmitriyev standing next to a type 5 I-16 aircraft, this photograph was taken in 1939 in Belorussia.

The Deputy Squadron Commander of the 15th Fighter Air Regiment Senior Lieutenant T.D. Kuzmin, this photograph was taken in 1939 in Belorussia.

The Deputy Squadron Commander of the 15th Fighter Air Regiment Lieutenant N.F. Kurykin, this photograph was taken in 1939 in Belorussia.

A Soviet Commander poses for a photograph next to a Lithuanian Gloster Gladiator, and Hawker Hart aircraft, Riga, 1940.

Twice Hero of the Soviet Union Lieutenant-General Kravchenko Grigoriy Panteleyevich, the First Commander of the Air Forces of the Baltic Special Military District.

He was born on 10 October 1912 in the village of Golubovka in the Novomoskovsk district of the Dniepropetrovsk region. He joined the Worker's and Peasant's Red Army from 1931 and in 1932 he graduated from the B.M. Myasnikov 1st Military Pilots' School. He was retained following his graduation at the school as an instructor. From 1933 onwards he served in the 403rd Fighter Air Brigade. From the summer of 1934 he was engaged in flight test work in a separate, special purpose fighter squadron. He rose from Junior Pilot, Senior Pilot, Flight Commander, and Senior Lieutenant. For his outstanding personal successes in assimilating military aviation technology he was awarded the 'Badge of Honour' on 25 May 1936.

He participated in armed combat in China from 13 March 1938 to 24 August 1938, he rose from Flight Commander, to Detachment Commander, and finally Squadron Commander. The following is taken from the report on his government tour of duty: 'He completed 78 sorties, and conducted eight air battles, shooting down either individually or as part of a group three bombers, and three I-96s.' He was awarded the Orders of the Red Banner (on 14 November 1938), and the Order of Lenin (on 22 February 1939). He was awarded the title of Hero of the Soviet Union. He took part in the Soviet-Japanese conflict on the River Khalkhin-Gol. He arrived on 2 June 1939 as part of a group led by Sushkevich from a position as a pilot at the Scientific Research Institute of the Workers' and Peasants' Red Army Air Force. He rose from Major to Commander's Aide, to Commander of the 22nd Fighter Air Regiment.

From his recommendation for the title of Hero of the Soviet Union (August 1939): 'He completed several dozen combat sorties in I-16 aircraft and undertook eight air battles, in which he shot down three enemy aircraft on his own, and four as part of a group.'

He was awarded the title of Twice Hero of the Soviet Union on 29 August 1939.

He participated in the Red Army's march into Belorussia, and into Western Ukraine and Western Belorussia.

He became the Head of the Fighter Aviation Department of the Combat Training Directorate of the Red Army Air Force.

He participated in the Soviet-Finnish War, and was the Commander of a Special Aviation Group in Estonia, he was awarded the Order of the Red Banner on 19 January 1940. He was awarded the title of Brigade Commander on 1 February 1940, and Divisional Commander on 11 April 1940.

He was made Head of Fighter Aviation for the Flight-Technical Inspectorate of the 1st Directorate of the Chief Directorate of the Red Army Air Force on 29 April 1940.

He was made the Commander of the Air Forces of the Baltic Special Military District on 19 July 1940, and Lieutenant-General of Aviation on 4 June 1940.

From November 1940 he underwent training on development courses for the Supreme Commander's Staff under the Red Army's General Staff Academy.

He was made Commander of the 64th Fighter Air Division on 27 March 1941 but he did not take up this post as he was still studying at the Supreme Commander's Staff Development Courses under the Red Army's General Staff Academy and on 29 April 1941 he was enlisted in the General Staff Academy.

He participated in the Great Patriotic War. As Commander of the 11th Mixed Air Division (between 22 June–20 November 1941), Commander of the Air Forces of the 3rd Army (between 22 November 1941–March 1942), and the Commander of the 8th Aviation Strike Group, Supreme Command Headquarters (between March–May 1942), and Commander of the 215th Fighter Air Division (from 23 March 1942). He was killed in the course of air combat on 23 February 1943.

He was awarded the Order of the Patriotic War 1st Class on 18 March 1943.

The First Chief of Staff of the Air Forces of the Baltic Special Military District Major-General of Aviation Sergey Pavlovich Sinyakov.

The Commander of the Air Forces of the Baltic Special Military District Major-General of Aviation Aleksey Pavlovich Ionov.

The Chief of Staff of the Air Forces of the Baltic Special Military District Brigade Commander Stepen Stepanovich Krupin.

The Head of the Operations Department of the Headquarters of the Baltic Special Military District Colonel Arseniy Yakovlevich Rasskazov.

The First Commander of the 4th Mixed Air Division Major-General Ivan Gavrilovich Pyatykhin.

He was born on 25 October 1904 in the village of Popasnaya in the Khabarovsk region to a worker's family. He was Russian. He obtained a secondary education.

He joined the Workers' and Peasants' Red Army in 1922 and served in the Cavalry, where he was a Platoon Commander. In 1925 he graduated from Ivanovo-Voznesensk School for the Workers' and Peasants' Red Army's Command Personnel. He was a member of the All-Union Communist Party (of Bolsheviks) from 1925 onwards.

In 1929 he was transferred to the Air Force.

He participated in the battles on the China-Eastern Railway as a pilot-observer in the 25th Separate Air Detachment.

In 1930 he graduated from the 3rd Military School for pilots and navigators in Orenburg.

From March 1932 he was an Assistant Director, Chief of Staff of the 69th Separate Reconnaissance Aviation Detachment.

In 1934 he graduated from Khabarovsk Military Pilots' School.

From January 1935 he was the Commander of the 35th Operational Air Squadron of the 18th Heavy Bomber Air Brigade.

In 1937 he graduated from the Higher Technical School in Lipetsk.

From November 1937 he was Commander of the 3rd High-Speed Bomber Air Regiment, and from April 1938 he was Commander of the 58th High-Speed Bomber Air Regiment, and from November 1938 of the 15th High-Speed Bomber Air Brigade of the Leningrad Military District.

He participated in the Soviet-Finnish War. He was Commander of the 15th High-Speed Bomber Air Brigade (the 2nd and 24th High-Speed Bomber Air Brigades) of the Air Forces of the 13th Army of the North-Western Front. He completed 25 combat sorties. He was awarded the Order of the Red Banner.

He was competent in his command of his brigade, which with successful bombing raids on the areas around Viipuri, Keksgolm, Sortavala inflicted a huge blow on the enemy. The brigade lost 16 aircraft in combat, and six in accidents, and fatal accidents.

On 7 February 1940 Colonel Pyatykhin Ivan Gavrilovich was awarded the title of Hero of the Soviet Union.

He was awarded the 'Golden Star' medal No 290.

From April 1940 he was the Commander of the Air Forces of the 14th Army.

On 4 June 1940 Pyatykhin was awarded the military rank of Major-General of Aviation.

From July 1940 he was the Commander of the 1st Mixed Air Division, and from August 1940 of the 4th Mixed Air Division, and from March 1941 of the 75th Mixed Air Division of the Baltic Special Military District.

He participated in the Great Patriotic War. Between June–July 1941 he commanded the 75th Mixed Air Division of the North-Western Front.

Between July 1941–July 1942 he commanded the Air Forces of the Orlovsk, and then the Southern-Ural Military Districts.

From 22 July 1942 Major-General of Aviation Pyatykhin commanded the 15th Air Army. From November 1943 he commanded the Air Forces of the Khabarovsk Military District.

On 11 May 1944 he was awarded the military rank of Lieutenant-General of Aviation.

From March 1946 he commanded the Air Forces of the Kiev, and then from July 1946 the Arkhangel Military Districts. From 1947 he was a Deputy Commander of the Front Line Unit of the 6th Air Army in the Turkestan Military District. From October 1948 he was part of the reserves.

He died on 22 May 197. He is buried in the Vvedensk cemetery.

He became a Hero of the Soviet Union on 7 February 1940. He was awarded the Orders of Lenin, was three times Laureate of the Orders of the Red Banner, and the orders of Kutuzov 2nd class, as well as medals, and a foreign award.

The Commander of the 6th Mixed Air Army Colonel Ivan Loginovich Fyodorov

He was born on 29 January 1902, in the village of Tsybulevo, in the Yelizavetinsk district of the Odessa region.

He joined the Red Army on 20 June 1921, as a red army soldier. From August 1921 he became a student of the Joint Military School for Red Sergeants in Kharkov. In September 1924 he was made a Commander of a platoon of the 296th Rifle Regiment, 99th Rifle Division. From September 1925 he was a student of the Leningrad School of Military Theory of the Red Army Air Force and from May 1926 of the A.F. Myasnikov 1st Military Pilots' School. From October 1927 he was a Junior Pilot of the 43rd Air Squadron, of the Air Forces of the Belorussian Military District, he later became a Flight Commander and a Commander of an aviation detachment in this same squadron. From November 1932 he was a student attending development courses for Command Personnel under the Zhukovskiy Military Aviation Academy of the Workers' and Peasants' Red Army Air Force. In May 1933 he was made a Commander of the detachment of the 4th Air Squadron of the Air Forces of the Belorussian Military District. From May 1934 the Commander of the 91st Separate Mechanised Aviation Detachment. In October 1935 he was made Commander of the 46th Air Squadron of the Air Forces of the Belorussian Military District. From March 1936 he attended courses in higher tactical flying organised by the Air Forces of the Workers' and Peasants' Red Army Air Force (in Lipetsk). On 25 May 1936 for outstanding successes in combat, and political training, and safety he was awarded the Order of Lenin. In November 1936 he was made Commander of the 11th High-Speed Bomber Air Squadron in the Air Forces of the Belorussian Military District. From 28 November 1937 he was Commander of the 49th High-Speed Bomber Brigade, and on 7 May 1938, he was Acting Commander of the High-Speed Bomber Air Brigade (in 1939 this brigade was posted to Latvia).

He participated in the Soviet-Finnish War. He carried out 17 combat sorties, and was awarded the Order of the Red Banner. On 8 August 1940 he was made Commander of the 6th Mixed Air Division of the Air Forces of the Baltic Special Military District.

He participated in the Great Patriotic War. From 11 August 1940 he was acting Commander of the Air Forces of the 48th Army, and in that same month he was made Commander of the Air Forces of the 34th Army of the North-Western Front. On 10 October 1940 he was made Head of the 14th Higher Aviation School (specialising in initial training). In March 1942 he was made Commander of the 63 rd Bomber Air Regiment of the Air Forces of the Transcaucasian Military District. From 10 October 1942 he was acting Commander of the 132nd Bomber Air Division (he was made Commander on 4 February 1944) and on 28 May 1943 he was made Major-General of Aviation. In October 1947 he was made Commander of the 5th Guard's Bomber Air Corps. From December 1951 he attended courses at the Higher Aviation Academy under the K.E. Voroshilov Higher Military Academy. From October 1952 he was made Assistant Commander of the 26th Air Army. On 22 May 1957 he was pulled back to the reserves. He died on 8 August 1970.

He was awarded the Order of Lenin twice, and the Order of the Red Banner, and the Orders of Suvorov 2nd class, and two Orders of Kutuzov 2nd class, as well as the Order of the Patriotic War 1st class, and other medals, as well as a foreign order, and medals.

The Commander of the 7th Mixed Air Division Pavel Maksimovich Petrov

He was born on 14 March 1902 in the village of Itsepina, He was a Red Army soldier serving in the 12th Fighter Aviation Detachment of the Western Front. From April 1919 he was an officer of the special department of the 2nd Brigade, 7th Army on the Petrograd Front. From April to November 1920 he attended electrician's courses under the Directorate of Artillery for the Kronstadt fortress. From November 1920 he was on an extended period of leave.

From June 1921 he was a Red Army soldier at the Higher School of Pilots and Observers of the Petrograd Military District. From June 1923 he was a student of the Military Technical School of the K.E. Voroshilov Workers' and Peasants' Red Army Air Force. From December 1923 he was made a mechanic and enrolled at the 2nd Higher Military Pilots' School of the Moscow Military District in Lipetsk. From April 1924 he was a Senior Mechanic and enrolled at the 1st Separate Fighter Aviation Squadron of the Leningrad Military District. From December 1925 he was a student at the A.F. Myasnikov 1st Military Pilots' School. After completion of his studies in August 1927 he was retained at the school as a flying instructor. He subsequently became a Flight Commander, then a Squadron Commissar, and then a Detachment Commander. From July 1933 he was a Commander and a Squadron Commissar at the 1st Military Pilots' School. From January 1936 he was a student at the Lipetsk Higher School of Tactical Flying of the Air Forces of the Worker's and Peasant's Red Army Air Force. In January 1937 he was made Commander and Commissar of the 56th High-Speed Bomber Air Squadron of the Air Forces of the North-Caucasian Military District. From June 1938 he was the Head of the 1st Aviation Training Centre of the North-Caucasian Military District. From December 1938 he was Deputy Head of the Chkalovsk Higher Aviation College. From 8 August 1939 he was Commander of the 45th High-Speed Bomber Air Regiment, General Aviation 2, he became a Colonel on 9 November 1939. From November 1939 he was a student attending four month long courses under the Zhukovskiy Military Aviation Academy of the Workers' and Peasants' Red Army Air Force. On 11 February 1940 he was made Commander of the 164th Reserve Air Regiment. He was made Commander of the 44th Fighter Air Division on 19 July 1940 (but did not take up this post). On 8 August 1940 he took up a post of Commander of the 7th Mixed Air Division of the Air Forces of the Baltic Special Military District.

He participated in the Great Patriotic War. On 3 March 1942 Colonel P.M. Petrov was appointed as acting Commander of the Air Forces of the 3rd Strike Army on the Kalinin Front. From 16 June 1942 he became the Commander of the 6th Anti-Aircraft Artillery Brigade. On 15 October 1943 he was made Commander of the 327th Night Bomber Air Division. On 12 December 1945 he was made Commander of the 314th Night Bomber Air Division. On 14 July 1945 he was pensioned off due to poor health. He died in 1968.

He was awarded the Orders of Lenin, the Red Banner, the Red Star, as well as a variety of medals.

The Head of the Air Force Directorate of the 27th Army Colonel Vasiliy Andreyevich Gushchin

He was born on 23 December 1901 in the village of Klipunovo, in the Rzhev district of the Kalinin region.

He joined the Red Army on 19 September 1919 as a volunteer. He was a clerk, and administrator of a technical squadron of the Separate Cavalry Brigade on the Western Front. From July 1920 he was the Head of the Operational Signals Technology Department of the 15th Cavalry Division. On 15 August 1921 he was taken prisoner by the Poles. In September 1921 he voluntarily joined the 3rd Rifle Division of the Volunteer Army under S.N. Bulak-Balakhovich that was formed entirely of prisoners of war and was recruited as an apprentice clerk. In November he escaped from his imprisonment, and after he returned back to his Motherland as a deserter he was put under surveillance under a special department of the 16th Army on the Western Front. In December 1920 as a member of a labour army he was sent to serve under the Directorate of Labour for the work units on the Turkestan Front. From November 1922 as a Red Army soldier in a convoy brigade under the forces of the State Political Directorate on the Turkestan Front, and in January 1923 he was demobbed. From February 1923 he was the Secretary of the Military Committee of the Air Force Headquarters of the Turkestan Front. From August 1923 he was a student of the Eyegorev School of Military Theory of the Air Fleet. From July 1924 he was a student of the A.F. Myasnikov 1st Military Pilots' School. In March 1926 he was a Junior Pilot at the 43rd Separate Artillery Correction Air Detachment of the Air Forces of the Western Military District. From July 1928 he was an instructor at the 2nd Military Flying School of the named after the Ososaviakhim of the USSR, he later became a Flight and a Detachment Commander. From October 1933 he was a student of the Development Courses for the Supreme Commander's Staff under the Zhukovskiy Military Aviation Academy of the Workers' and Peasants' Red Army Air Force. In December 1934 he was made Commander of the 7th Ground Attack Air Squadron, 114th Light Ground Attack Air Brigade of the Air Forces of the Belorussian Military District, and he was a Major. From September 1937 he was made acting Commander of the 52nd Light Ground Attack Air Brigade (65th Light Ground Attack Air Brigade), as a Colonel. On 17 September 1939 he was made Commander of the Air Forces of the Bobruysk Army Group (in the Air Forces of the 4th Army). He participated in the entry of the Red Army into Western Belorussia. In June 1940 he participated in the entry into Lithuania, as a Commander of the 11th Army. On 8 August 1940 he was made Commander of the 8th Mixed Air Division. On 27 May 1941 he was made Commander of the Directorate of the Air Forces of the 27th Army.

He participated in the Great Patriotic War, as acting Commander of the 8th Mixed Air Division. At the beginning of July 1941 he joined the Command of the Air Forces of the 27th Army of the North-Western Front (from December this was known as the 4th Army). On 27 May 1942 he was made Deputy Commander of the 6th Air Defence System Fighter Air Corps.

On 23 August 1942 he was made Commander of the 298th Fighter Air Division of the Air Defence System, in the Eastern, and subsequently the Transcaucasian Air Defence System Fronts. He became a Major-General of Aviation on 1 September 1943.

On 31 December 1945 he was made Commander of the 298th Air Defence System Fighter Air Division, of the North-Western District of the Air Defence System. From April 1948 he was a student studying Higher Aviation Courses at the K.E. Voroshilov Higher Military Academy. On 24 June 1949 he retired. He died on 26 November 1958.

He was awarded the Orders of Lenin, and was twice awarded the Order of the Red Banner 1st Class, as well as a variety of medals.

The Commander of the 9th High-Speed Bomber Air Regiment Mikhail Ivanovich Skitev

He was born on 3 June 1908 in Moscow.

He joined the Red Army on 10 November 1930, serving as a Red Army soldier in the 3rd Aviation Brigade. On 15 November he became a student of the School of Military Theory of the Air Forces of the Red Army in Leningrad. From 12 March 1931 he was a student at the Separate Fighter Air Detachment 100th Aviation Brigade, and in 1932 he passed the pilot's exams via distance learning. Subsequently from 28 June 1933 he became a Junior Pilot, and a Flight Commander of the 4th Separate Fighter Air Detachment. On 16 October 1934 he was made a Detachment Commander of the 1st Light Bomber Air Squadron, and Senior Lieutenant on 14 March 1936. From 31 July 1936 he was made Detachment Commander of the 4th High-Speed Bomber Air Squadron, and subsequently from 29 March 1937 he was made a inspector of piloting techniques, and a Captain on 21 February 1938. On 15 April 1938 he was made Commander of the 3rd Squadron, 35th High-Speed Bomber Air Regiment.

He participated in the entry of the Red Army into Western Belorussia.

He participated in the Soviet-Finnish War.

He was made a Major (on 1 February 1940), and from 20 June 1940 he was made Deputy Commander of the 35th High-Speed Bomber Air Regiment. On 10 November 1940 he was made Commander of the 9th High-Speed Bomber Air Regiment.

He participated in the Great Patriotic War

On 17 November 1942 he was killed in an accident.

He was awarded the Orders of Lenin, and the Badge of Honour.

The Commander of the 31st High-Speed Bomber Air Regiment Lieutenant-Colonel Fyodor Ivanovich Dobysh

He was born on 5 March 1906 in the Mogilev region, Cherikov district, in the village of Kokhanovo.

He joined the Red Army on 15 October 1928, and was a student of the Regimental School of the Belorussian Military District, and then in October 1929 he was a student of the United Belorussian Military School. From 2 June 1931 he was made platoon commander of the 98th Rifle Regiment. From 15 May 1932 he was a student attending courses for combined military and political commanders at the United Military School named after the All-Russian Central Executive Committee. From 15 November 1932 he was made Company Commander of the 98th Rifle Regiment. From 15 February 1933 he was a student attending the 2nd Higher Aviation School named after the *Osoaviakhim*. On 17 December 1934 he was made Flight Commander of the 4th Long-Range Reconnaissance Air Squadron. From 27 July 1935 onwards he was a Detachment Commander in the 11th Air Squadron.

From November 1937 onwards until April 1938 he was on a Government assignment in China. For his successful completion of this government assignment he was awarded the Order of the Red Banner, and the rank of Major (on 29 April 1938).

On 29 July 1938 he was made Assistant Commander of the 31st High-Speed Bomber Air Regiment, from 23 December 1939 he took up command of the 31st High-Speed Bomber Air Regiment.

He participated in the Soviet-Finnish War, and was awarded the Order of Lenin.

He participated in the Great Patriotic War.

He was made a Colonel (on 27 January 1942) and on 12 September 1942 he was made a Commander of the 236th Bomber Air Division (from 18 March 1943 this was transformed into the 1st Bomber Air Division), and Major-General of Aviation (on 1 March 1946). From 11 June 1946 he was made Commander of the 5th Ground Attack Air Corps. From 6 January 1950 he was a student attending higher aviation courses at the K.E. Voroshilov Higher Military Academy. On 22 October 1951 he was made Assistant Commander of the 57th Air Army. From 22 March 1952 he was made Deputy Commander of the 24th Air Army. On 16 December 1955 he was made Commander of the 57th Air Army, and Lieutenant-General (from 26 November 1956). From 22 November 1960 he was made the Commander of the 50th Rocket Army, and a Colonel-General (on 27 April 1962). On 13 July 1972 he retired. He died on 29 November 1980.

He was awarded the Order of Lenin four times, and the Order of the Red Banner, as well as the Orders of Suvorov 2nd class, and Kutuzov 2nd class, together with the Orders of the Patriotic War 1st class, and the Red Star, as well as medals, and also foreign orders, and medals.

The Commander of the 35th High-Speed Bomber Air Regiment Pyotr Mikhaylovich Podmogilniy

He was born on 09 June 1905 in the Kustanaysk district, in the town of Alekseyevka.

He joined the Red Army on 7 December 1927, and was a student of the Artillery School of the Red Banner Baltic Fleet, in the chemistry school. From July 1928 he was a sergeant chemist on board the battleship the 'Paris Commune'. In January 1929 he became a student of the School of Military Theory of the Air Forces of the Red Army in Leningrad. From November 1929 he was a student at the I.V. Stalin Military Naval Pilots' and Observers' School, in Eysk. In June 1931 he was made acting captain serving in the 6th Heavy Bomber Air Regiment, and subsequently he took up a position as captain and then acting detachment commander. On 20 November 1934 he was made Detachment Commander of the 6th Heavy Bomber Air Squadron. From July 1935 he was a Detachment Commander in the 60th Fighter Air Squadron. In July 1937 he attended the Lipetsk aviation development courses organised by the Air Forces of the Red Army.

From 4 November 1938 he was made an Assistant Commander of the 14th Reconnaissance Air Regiment. From 28 March 1939 he was made Assistant Commander of the 3rd Light Bomber Air Regiment, and was a Major from 03 April 1939. On 27 March 1941 he was made a Commander of the 35th High-Speed Bomber Air Regiment.

He participated in the Great Patriotic War.

On 2 November 1942 he was made Squadron Commander of the 815th Long-Range Air Regiment. From 30 March 1943 he was made a Commander of the 8th Separate Long-Range Aerial Reconnaissance Squadron. From 07 July 1943 he was made acting Deputy Commander of the 280th Bomber Air Division, and a Colonel from 26 October 1944. From 12 February 1945 he was made Commander of the 280th Ground Attack Air Division. From 23 October 1946 he was made an Assistant Commander for Flying Training and Air Combat in the 9th Ground Attack Air Division of the Naval Air Forces. On 19 April 1949 he was retired to the reserves.

He was awarded the Order of Lenin, and the Order of the Red Banner twice, as well as the Orders of the Patriotic War 1st Class, and the Red Star, and other medals.

The Commander of the 40th High-Speed Bomber Air Regiment Ivan Yevseyevich Mogilevskiy

He was born on 12 July 1904 in the Minsk region, Lyuban district in the village of Tal.

He joined the Red Army on 23 February 1921 and he was a Red Army soldier in the 64th Rifle Regiment, and the 8th Rifle Division. From 25 May 1921 he was a student at the Minsk Riflemen's Courses for Red Army Commanders. On 23 March 1923 he was made Commander of a section of the 97th Rifle Regiment, 33rd Rifle Division. From 06 January 1924 he was a student at the V.I. Lenin Higher Military School. On 29 June 1924 he was made a Platoon Commander of the 97th Rifle Regiment, 33rd Rifle Division. From 7 October 1926 he attended courses at the Joint Military School in Minsk. On 1 September 1928 he was made Platoon Commander of the 11th Rifle Regiment, 37th Rifle Division. From 29 November 1931 he attended courses at the Command Faculty at the Zhukovsky Military Aviation Academy. On 31 December 1934 he was made Assistant Chief of Staff of the 9th Light Ground Attack Air Regiment. From 7 April 1935 he attended courses at the Myasnikov 1st Military Pilots' School. On 26 October 1935 he returned to his duties as Assistant Chief of Staff of the 9th Light Ground Attack Air Regiment, he was made a Captain on 14 March 1936, a Major on 12 December 1938, and on 8 September 1938 he was made Chief of Staff of the 14th Light Ground Attack Air Squadro. He served as a Major from 17 February 1939. From September 1939 he was a Commander of the 40th High-Speed Bomber Air Regiment.

He participated in the Great Patriotic War, and on 1 July 1941 he failed to return from a sortie.

The Commander of the 46th High-Speed Bomber Air Regiment Major Mikhail Ivanovich Senkov

He was born on 1 October 1904, in the Vitebsk Region, Vysochansk district, in the village of Tsarbuli.

He joined the Red Army from November 1926, and was a Red Army soldier serving in the 17th Air Fleet, later he commanded a section and became Junior Specialist in Chemical and Bacterial Defence. From December 1928 he attended courses at the School of Military Theory of the Red Army Air Force in Leningrad. From May 1930 he was a student at the 2nd Higher Aviation School. In November 1931 he was made Junior Pilot of the 52nd Air Squadron. From December 1932 he was an aircraft commander in the 34th Heavy Bomber Air Squadron. In June 1935 he was made Commander of a detachment of the 33rd Heavy Bomber Air Regiment and was Senior Lieutenant from 14 March 1936. From January 1937 he was an inspector of piloting technique at the 30th Heavy Bomber Air Squadron, and a Captain from 12 February 1938. From July 1938 he was made acting Squadron Commander in the 10th Light Bomber Air Regiment, on 29 August 1938 he was made Commander of the 1st Long Range Bomber Air Regiment (the 46th High-Speed Bomber Air Regiment), and a Major from 4 September 1939.

The Commander of the 50th High-Speed Bomber Air Regiment Filipp Aleksandrovich Agaltsov

He was born on 21 January 1900 in the Tula Region, Yefremovskiy district in the village of Soldatskoe.

He joined the Red Army from 15 July 1919 and participated in the Civil War, he was a machine-gunner in the 1st Separate Communist Battalion. From July 1920 he was the Commander of a machine gun section in the 487th Rifle Regiment, 24th Rifle Division. From January 1923 he was a Political Instructor of a company in the 72nd Rifle Regiment. In May 1923 he was a student at the Kiev Military Political School. From July 1925 he was the Political Instructor of a regimental school and the Secretary of a Party Office in the 7th Artillery Regiment, 7th Rifle Division. From October 1929 he attended courses at the Military Political Academy of the Worker's and Peasants' Red Army Air Force. In April 1932 he was made Commissar of the 9th Fighter Air Squadron. From April 1933 he was a Commissar of the 35th Heavy Bomber Air Regiment. In 1934 he completed a pilot's course at the Myasnikov 1st Military Pilots' School. In April 1935 he was made Deputy Commander of the political department in the 114th Aviation Brigade.

From May 1937 until November 1938 he participated in the national revolutionary war in Spain as a Commissar in the Spanish Air Force, part of the Republican Army. He was awarded the orders of Lenin and of the Red Star.

In August 1941 he was made the Head of the Tambov School of Military Aviation Specialists. From March 1943 he commanded the 292nd Ground Attack Air Division (from 05 February 1944 this became the 9th Guard's Ground Attack Air Division). At the end of 1944 Major-General of Aviation F.A. Agaltsov was made Commander of the 1st Polish Mixed Air Division. From December 1945 he commanded the 4th Ground Attack Air Corps. In February 1947 he was made Commander of the 16th Air Army. From July 1949 he was acting 1st Deputy of the and from April 1953 he was Deputy Commander in Chief of the Armed Forces of the USSR. From May 1956 he was Inspector-General of the Air Force's Principal Inspectorate of the Ministry of Defence of the USSR. From February 1958 he was Deputy Commander in Chief of Air Force Training. In April 1962 he was made Commander of Air Force Long Range Aviation. From 20 January 1969 he was at the disposal of the Commander in Chief of the Air Force. From 25 March 1970 he was retired to the reserves. On 21 December 1970 by way of a Decree from the Politburo Central Committee of the Communist Party of the USSR the order concerning his retirement to the reserves was cancelled and in January 1971 he was made an Inspector and an Adviser to the Group of General Inspectors of the Ministry of Defence of the USSR. In February 1978 he was awarded the title of Hero of the Soviet Union. He died on 29 June 1980.

He was awarded the Order of Lenin four times, as well as the Order of the Red Banner five times, and the orders of Suvorov 2nd class, and Kutuzov 2nd class, the Order of the Patriotic War 1st class, and the Order of the Red Star, together with medals, and other foreign orders, and medals.

The Commander of the 54th High-Speed Bomber Air Regiment Ivan Mikhaylovich Skiba

He was born on 20 February 1910 in Leningrad.

He joined the Workers' and Peasants' Red Army in 25 January 1929 as a student of the Military School of Aviation Technicians. From 30 November 1929 he was a student of the 2nd Military Aviation School for Pilots named after the *Osoaviakhim* of the USSR. On 4 July 1931 he was made a Junior Pilot of the 47th Fighter Aviation Division in the Air Forces of the Ukrainian Military District. From 30 April 1932 he was acting Flight Commander of the 35th Fighter Aviation Division of the Air Forces of the Ukrainian Military District, and subsequently from 11 July 1933 he was made a Commander of a Detachment. On 17 March 1934 he was made Commander of the 76th Fighter Aviation Division in the Air Forces of the Ukrainian Military District. From February 1935 he was acting commander of the 21st Fighter Air Squadron, 101st Air Brigade of the Air Forces of the Transbaikal Military District.

He participated in the battles close to Lake Buir Nuur in 1936 and was Commander of the Fighter Detachment of the Special Purpose Air Squadron.

From 15 February 1937 he attended aviation development courses at the Lipetsk organised by the Air Forces of the Workers' and Peasants' Red Army Air Force, he was made a Captain on 27 August 1937. On 22 November 1937 he was made a Commander of the 105th Fighter Air Squadron, 142 Fighter Air Brigade. From 7 May 1938 he was acting Commander of the 4th Fighter Air Regiment. From June 1938 he was acting Commander of the 15th Fighter Air Regiment, he was made Commander of this regiment on 22 February 1939, becoming a Major on 31 October 1938.

He participated in the entry of the Red Army into Western Belorussia and Western Ukraine.

He participated in the Soviet-Finnish War, and was awarded the Order of the Red Banner on 22 February 1941.

He participated in the Great Patriotic War. From June 1942 he was Deputy Commander of the 263rd Fighter Air Division, and in June was Commander of the 263rd Fighter Air Division. From autumn 1942 he was Deputy Commander of the 274th Fighter Air Division (this subsequently became the 4th Guard's Fighter Air Division), and a Colonel on 2 July 1944. He was killed in an aircraft accident in a Yak-3 on 20 May 1946.

He was awarded the Order of the Red Banner three times, and the Order of the Patriotic War 1st class.

The Commander of the 63rd High-Speed Bomber Air Regiment Pyotr Vasilyevich Novikov

He was born on 23 June 1901 in Vitebsk Region, Gorodok district, in the village of Maksura.

He joined the Red Army on 20 September 1920, he was a Red Army soldier in the 15th Reserve Rifle Regiment. From October 1920 he was a machine gunner in the 252nd Rifle Regiment. In March 1922 he became a student of the Military Infantry School. From October 1925 he was a Platoon Commander in the 98th Rifle Regiment. In November 1928 he was a trainee at the 4th Special Aviation Detachment. From August 1929 he attended lectures at the 3rd Military Aviation School. In September 1930 he was an Air Observer in the 43rd Light Bomber Air Squadron. From November 1931 he attended lectures at the 3rd Military Aviation School. In April 1932 he was Head of the Armament Service in the 43rd Light Bomber Air Squadron. From May 1935 he attended lectures at the Myasnikov 1st Military Aviation School.

In October 1935 he was made Commander of the 5th Light Bomber Air Regiment detachment, becoming a Captain on 14 March 1936. From February 1938 he attended lectures as part of further training courses in aerial tactics held in Lipetsk, becoming a Major on 15 April 1938. From October 1938 he was made Deputy Commander of the 3rd Light Bomber Air Regiment. On 28 March 1939 he was made Commander of the 3rd Light Bomber Air Regiment (63rd High-Speed Bomber Air Regiment), becoming a Colonel on 30 April 1941.

He fought in the Great Patriotic War.

The Commander of the 61st Ground Attack Air Regiment Sergey Nikolayevich Mamushkin

He was born on 21 September 1906 in Leningrad.

He joined the Red Army in 1928, and was a student of the Red Army Air Force's School of Military Theory in Leningrad. In December 1928 he became a student of the Myasnikov 1st Military Pilots' School.

In January 1930 he became a Junior Pilot in the 31st Air Squadron. In November 1931 he became an instructor in the 8th Military Pilots' School, and subsequently from July 1933 a Flight Commander. From April 1934 he was a Detachment Commander in the 14th Light Ground Attack Air Squadron and on 23 April 1938 he was made Squadron Commander of the 3rd Light Ground Attack Air Regiment, becoming a Major on 17 February 1939. From 19 March 1940 he was Acting Commander of the 91st Fighter Air Regiment, and from 25 April 1940 he was confirmed as Commander of the 91st Fighter Air Regiment. On 19 November 1940 he was made Commander of the 61st Ground Attack Air Regiment.

He fought in the Great Patriotic War.

He was made a Lieutenant-Colonel on 31 July 1941, and a Colonel on 19 December 1941. On 13 May 1942 he became the head of the Commandant's Office at the Headquarters of Air Corridor No. 1. On 20 April 1943 he was made head of the Department for Ferry Flights at the Air Force Directorate of the Moscow Military District. On 27 April 1943 he was made Acting Deputy Head of the Moscow Military District Air Force Department. On 30 December 1945 he was made Commander of the 9th Reserve Air Brigade, and on 12 July 1946 he was retired to the reserves.

He was awarded the Order of the Red Banner, and other medals.

The Commander of the 10th Fighter Air Regiment Major Konstantin Pavlovich Derevnin

He was born on 5 December 1905 in Saratov.

He joined the Workers' and Peasants' Red Army on 25 November 1925, he was a Red Army soldier, serving in the 2nd Motorised Regiment, which subsequently became the 59th Rifle Regiment. On 1 March 1926 he became a student of the Red Army Air Force's School of Military Theory in Leningrad. From 15 March 1927 he became a student of the 2nd Military Pilots' School named after the USSR's *Osoaviakhim*. From 15 December 1928 he became a Junior Lieutenant in the 40th Light Bomber Air Squadron. From 21 March 1929 he became a Senior Pilot in the 10th Separate Reconnaissance Air Detachment in the Moscow Military District. In October 1931 he was made Commander of a detachment of the 38th Light Bomber Air Regiment in the Air Forces of the Moscow Military District, becoming a Captain on 14 March 1936. From 19 March 1936 he attended lectures as part of the further aviation training courses in Lipetsk organised by the Air Forces of the Workers' and Peasants' Red Army Air Force. From 15 February 1937 he was made a Commander of the 20th Fighter Air Squadron. On 9 July 1937 he was made Commander of the 22nd Fighter Air Squadron, becoming a Major on 29 April 1938. On 29 August 1938 he was made Commander of the 10th Fighter Air Regiment.

He fought in the Great Patriotic War. On 4 November 1941 he was made Commander of the 773rd Fighter Air Regiment (this was formed as the 273rd Fighter Air Regiment). From 14 August 1946 he was made Deputy Head of the Military Training Department and the Head of the Air Gunnery Service in the White Sea Military District, becoming a Lieutenant-Colonel on 10 December 1946. From 30 January 1952 he was made Head of the Aerial Gunnery Service in the 22nd Air Army. He was retired to the reserves on 9 March 1954.

He was twice awarded the Order of the Red Banner, as well as the Order of the Red Star, as well as other medals.

The Commander of the 15th Fighter Air Regiment, Major Bobrik Vladimir Lukich

He was born on 20 February 1910 in Leningrad.

He joined the Workers' and Peasants' Red Army on 25 January 1929, and was a student of the 2nd Military Aviation Technicians' School. From 30 November 1929 he was a student of the 2nd Military Pilots' School named after the USSR's *Osoaviakhim*. From 4 July 1931 he was a Junior Pilot in the 47th Fighter Air Detachment in the Ukrainian Military District. From 30 April 1932 he was made Acting Flight Commander of the 35th Fighter Air Detachment, Ukrainian Military District, and subsequently on 11 July 1933 he was made Detachment Commander. On 17 March 1934 he was made Commander of the 21st Fighter Air Squadron, 101st Air Brigade in the Air Forces of the Zabaykalsk Military District. He fought in the battles for Buir Lake in 1936, as Commander of the Fighter Detachment of the Special Purpose Air Squadron.

From 15 February 1937 he attended lectures as part of the Further Aviation Training Courses at Lipetsk organised by the Air Forces of the Workers' and Peasants' Red Army Air Force, becoming a Captain on 27 August 1937.

On 22 November 1937 he was made a Commander of the 105th Fighter Air Squadron, 142nd Fighter Air Brigade. From 7 July 1938 he was Acting Commander of the 4th Fighter Air Regiment. From June 1938 he was Acting Commander of the 15th Fighter Air Regiment, being confirmed as Regimental Commander on 22 February 1939, and becoming a Major on 31 October 1938.

He was a participant in the march of Soviet forces into Western Europe and Western Ukraine.

He fought in the Soviet-Finnish War and was awarded the Order of the Red Banner on 22 February 1941.

He fought in the Great Patriotic War. From June 1942 he became the Deputy Commander of the 263rd Fighter Air Division, and in July he was made Commander of the 263rd Fighter Air Division. From autumn 1942 he was Deputy Commander of the 274th Fighter Air Division (subsequently the 4th Guard's Fighter Air Division), becoming a Colonel on 2 July 1944.

He was killed in an accident with a Yak-3 aircraft on 20 May 1946.

He was awarded the Order of the Red Banner three times, as well as the Order of the Patriotic War, 1st class.

The Commander of the 21st Fighter Air Regiment Nikolai Ivanovich Miroshnichenko

He was born on 25 October 1899 on Solyoniy farm in the Proletarsk district, Rostov region.

He joined the Workers' and Peasants' Red Army on 3 March 1927, and was a trainee of the 243rd Rifle Regiment and was withdrawn to the reserves in March 1929. On 15 May 1932 he was a student of the 3rd Military Aviation School for Pilots and Observers (in Orenburg). From December 1933 he attended courses at the Section Commander's Courses under the Myasnikov 1st Military Pilots' School.

From July 1934 he was a Flight Commander and a Detachment Commander of the 34th Fighter Air Squadron, 56th Fighter Air Brigade, and a Lieutenant from 14 March 1936.

He was a participant in the armed combat in Spain between 20 October 1936 until 7 April 1937 as a pilot of the I-15, and in air combat he shot down four enemy aircraft on his own, and a further three as part of a group. He was awarded the Order of the Red Banner (on 2 January 1937 and 17 July 1937).

On 19 July 1937 he was made Commander of the 20th Fighter Air Squadron of the Special Red Banner Army of the Far East. From 25 August 1938 he was a Commander of the 3rd Fighter Air Regiment, and a Major from 2 November 1938. On 31 October 1940 he was made Commander of the 21st Fighter Air Regiment.

He participated in the Great Patriotic War. In air combat he shot down one enemy aircraft on his own, and one in a group.

On 13 August 1942 he was made Squadron Commander of the Kachinsk Military Aviation College and from 25 April 1945 he was an Assistant to the Head of flying training at the college and was made a Lieutenant-Colonel on 10 June 1944. On 5 August 1946 he was made Deputy Head of the Armavir Military Aviation College for flying training, and was made a Colonel on 16 May 1949. From September 1950 he attended Development Training for Commanders, and Heads of Department of the Aviation Divisions under the Red Banner Military Aviation Academy. On 22 October 1951 he was made Commander of the 138th Fighter Air Division, and a Major-General of Aviation on 31 May 1954. From 21 April 1955 he was the Head of the training department and the Higher Education Establishment of the Air Forces of the Volga Military District. He was retired to the reserves on 30 May 1959.

He was awarded the Order of the Red Banner three times, as well as other medals.

The Commander of the 31 st Fighter Air Regiment Major Pavel Ilyich Putkivo

He was born in 1911 in Dniepropetrovsk, in the town of Dmitrovka.

He joined the Workers' and Peasants' Red Army in 1931 and was a student of the 7th Higher Aviation College (in Stalingrad). From 21 December 1933 he was a Junior Pilot in the 40th Fighter Air Squadron, 83rd Fighter Air Brigade in the Belorussian Military District, as a Lieutenant.

He participated in the fighting in Spain from November 1936 until 27 May 1937. He amassed around 170 combat hours and shot down three enemy aircraft on his own, and two as part of a group, on 25 March 1937 he was injured during an enemy air raid on his airfield and he was as a result of his injuries sent immediately back to the USSR. He was awarded the Order of the Red Banner twice (on 2 January 1937 and 17 July 1937).

On 7 May 1938 he was made acting Commander of the 21st Fighter Air Regiment and on 28 March 1939 he was made Regimental Commander, and was given the rank of Major (on 19 April 1939).

From 27 November 1939 he was made Commander of the 31st Fighter Air Regiment.

He participated in the Great Patriotic War. From 26 August 1941 he served in the 402nd Fighter Air Regiment. He shot down two enemy aircraft on his own, and one as part of a group, and was awarded the Order of Lenin (on 16 April 1942) and on 26 August 1941 he was seriously injured (his arm was amputated).

Following his recovery from 24 June 1942 he served the rest of his service in the 10th Flying Training Air Regiment (as a Deputy Squadron Commander). He died on 9 July 1942 in a fatal crash in a UT-2.

The Commander of the 38th Fighter Air Regiment Boris Arsenyevich Sidnev

He was born on 24 March 1911 in Simbirsk.

He joined the Red Army from January 1931 and was a student of the 8th Military Flying School. From January 1932 he was transferred as a pilot to the 36th Air Squadron of the Air Forces of the Ukrainian Military District. From August 1933 he attended courses at the I.V. Stalin Military Aviation Pilots' School. From November 1933 he was a Junior Pilot in the 70th Heavy Bomber Air Regiment, 18th Heavy Bomber Air Brigade in the Air Forces of the Ukrainian Military District. From 23 September 1935 he was the captain of an aircraft in the 71st Heavy Bomber Air Squadron, 18th Heavy Bomber Air Brigade. From June 1936 he was the commander of an aircraft in the Directorate of the 18th Heavy Bomber Air Brigade. From 15 February 1937 he was a pilot and inspector at the Directorate of the 13th Airborne Brigade. From May he was acting commander of the 15th Reconnaissance Air Squadron. On 17 August 1938 he was made

Inspector of piloting techniques in the 69th Fighter Air Regiment. From 25 October 1938 he was a Senior inspector of piloting techniques in the 69th Fighter Air Regiment. In December 1939 he attended Development Courses for in aviation organised by the Worker's and Peasant's Red Army Air Force. On 26 June 1940 he was made Commander of the 38th Fighter Air Regiment.

He participated in the Great Patriotic War. In August 1941 he was made Commander of the 6th Mixed Air Division, and a Colonel (on 18 September 1941). From December 1941 he was made Commander of the Air Forces of the 28th Army. On 6 July 1942 he took up command of the 268th Fighter Air Division (from 18 March 1943 he was he took up command of the 6th Guard's Fighter Air Regiment), and was made Major-General of Aviation on 17 March 1943. On 22 December 1943 he took up command of the 13th Fighter Air Corps. For his capable leadership of the Corps, personal courage, and bravery Major-General of Aviation B.A. Sidnev on 29 May 1945 was awarded the title of Hero of the Soviet Union.

From March 1946 he attended courses at the K.E. Voroshilov Higher Military Academy. In February 1948 he was made Deputy Commander of the Air Forces of the Moscow Military District. From December 1948 he was acting of an Assistant Commander of the Front Line unit of the 14th Air Army. From June 1949 he was Assistant Commander of the 24th Air Army. From March 1952 he was Commander of the 48th Air Army, and was made Lieutenant-General (on 3 August 1953), and Major-General of Aviation (from 7 May 1960). In April 1961 he retired.

He was awarded the Order of Lenin twice, and the Order of the Red Banner twice, he was awarded the Order of Suvorov 2nd class, and the Order of the Patriotic War 1st class, as well as the Red Star, and other medals.

The Commander of the 42nd Fighter Air Regiment Konstantin Emelyanovich Belousov

He was born on 15 December 1905 in Novosibirsk.

He joined the Workers' and Peasants' Red Army from October 1926 and he spent his service in front line Air Force units as a pilot, and Flight Commander. On 28 November 1938 he was made Commander of a Detachment of the 8th Light Ground Attack Air Squadron. From 17 April 1937 he was a Commander of the 8th Light Ground Attack Air Squadron. From 3 September 1938 he was made Commander of the 2nd Light Ground Attack Air Regiment. He participated in the fighting near Lake Khasan and was awarded the Order of the Red Banner (on 25 October 1938), and Major (from 2 November 1938).

From 25 May April 1940 he attended Operational and Tactical Supreme Commander's Development Courses under the Zhukovskiy Military Aviation School. On 20 June 1940 he was made Commander of the 42nd Fighter Air Regiment.

He participated in the Great Patriotic War and on 22 June 1941 he was injured and was hospitalised in Daugavpils. He was taken prisoner in hospital on 27 June 1941. He was held in Kgf.Lg. 2 d.Lw. He tried to escape several times but was unsuccessful. He died in the prisoner of war camp after May 1944.

The Commander of the 49th Fighter Air Regiment Major Pyotr Ivanovich Nedelin

He was born on 27 November 1910 in the village of Ryabinki, Yeletsk district, Orlovsk region.

He joined the Workers' and Peasants' Red Army from 1 July 1931 and was a student at the Leningrad Military Infantry School for the Retraining of Reserve Commanders. From December 1931 he was a student of the School of Military Theory in the Air Forces of the Workers' and Peasants' Red Army Air Force in Leningrad. From June 1932 he was a student at the 14th Higher Aviation School (in Engels). From 13 December 1933 he was a Junior Pilot of the 1st Fighter Air Squadron. From October 1934 he was a Senior Pilot in the 13th Fighter Air Squadron. On 8 January 1936 he was made flight Commander in the 13th Fighter Air Squadron and was given the rank of Lieutenant.

On 19 July 1937 he was made a Flight Commander and a Flying Instructor specialising in Air Combat and Aerobatics at the 8th Higher Aviation School in Odessa, he was also awarded the rank of Senior Lieutenant.

He participated in the fighting in Spain from 10 June 1938 to 4 October 1938 and was a Squadron Commander on I-16s. The following is an extract from the report on his government tour of duty: 'He has amassed either in general flying or in combat 60 hours, and has completed 20 combat sorties, shooting down three *'Messerschmitts'* and a *'Fiat'* and was not shot down himself. He was awarded the Order of Lenin on 22 February 1939. He has completed two forced landings and has been injured in the course of these.'

He was awarded the rank of Major on 19 April 1939. From 19 July 1939 he was made an Assistant Commander of the 49th Fighter Air Regiment. On 26 April 1940 he was made Commander of the 49th Fighter Air Regiment.

He participated in the Soviet-Finnish War and completed 39 combat sorties and amassing 47 hrs overall.

He was awarded the Order of the Red Star (on 26 January 1940).

He participated in the Great Patriotic War and on 21 January 1942 he was seriously wounded during an emergency landing, and was sent to hospital. From 28 April 1942 he was a Senior Inspector of Piloting Techniques at the Flying Training Formation, and Augmentation Directorate of the Principal Directorate for Fighter Aviation within the country's Air Defence System, and was made a Lieutenant-Colonel on 2 November 1942. From 8 July 1943 he was a Senior Pilot and an Inspector of piloting techniques of the 6th Department of the Directorate of the Air Forces of the Western Front in the Air Defence System. On 31 August 1943 he was the Head of the Combat Training Department of the Air Forces of the Western Front within the Air Defence System and he was made a Colonel on 20 April 1944. From 27 April 1945 he was the Head of the Combat Training Department in the 1st Fighter Air Army within the Air Defence System as a Colonel. In air combat he shot down two enemy aircraft as part of a group. On 9 September 1945 he was made a Commander of the 122nd Fighter Air Division in the Air Defence System. From 11 October 1948 he attended development courses for the Supreme Commanders at the Military Aviation Academy. From 8 June 1949 he was made Deputy Commander of the 56th Fighter Air Corps of the Air Defence System and Major-General of Aviation on 11 May 1949. On 21 October 1949 he was made Commander of the 56th Fighter Air Corps of the Air Defence System. On 27 April 1953 he attended courses at the Aviation Faculty of the K.E. Voroshilov Higher Military Academy. From 14 August 1954 he was the Deputy Commander of Fighter Aviation of the Special Leningrad Army of the Air Defence System. From 5 January 1956 he was the Commander of Fighter Aviation in the North-Caucasian Army of the Air Defence System. On 6 December 1957 he was made Deputy Commander of the North-Caucasian Army of the Air Defence System. On 19 May 1959 he was made a Military Air Defence System specialist in the Romanian Army. From 15 August 1961 he was the Air Defence System representative at the Principal Command of the United Armed Forces within the Romanian Army, and was made a Lieutenant-General on 9 May 1961. On 13 March 1962 he was made Chief of Staff of Air Defence System Aviation. On 21 December 1965 he was retired to the reserves. He died on 11 June 1994.

He was awarded the Order of Lenin twice, the Order of the Red Banner, and the Order of the Red Star, and the Patriotic War 1st and 2nd classes, as well as other medals.

The Commander of the 148th Fighter Air Regiment Georgiy Nikolayevich Zaytsev

He was born on 28 February 1910 in Simferopol, Crimean Autonomous Soviet Socialist Republics. He joined the Red Army from July 1928 and voluntarily enrolled as a student at the 2nd Military Pilots' School named after the *Osoaviakhim* of the USSR. On completion of his studies in October 1930 he was retained at the school and spent his service as a flying instructor, flight commander, and detachment commander. In February 1938 he was made Detachment Commander of the 67th Fighter Air Squadron of the Air Forces of the Moscow Military District. In May 1938 he was made acting Assistant Squadron Commander of the 16th Fighter Air Regiment. On 29 November 1939 he was made Squadron Commander of the 34th Fighter Air Regiment. On 12 October 1940 he was made Assistant Commander of the 148th Fighter Air Regiment.

He participated in the Soviet-Finnish War from 1939–1940 and personally undertook 23 combat sorties. On 11 April 1940 he took up command of the 148th Fighter Air Regiment.

He participated in the Great Patriotic War. In March 1943 he was made Deputy Commander of the 287th Fight er Air Division. In October 1944 he took up command of the 185th Fighter Air Division and was made a Colonel (on 26 October 1944). In June 1946 he was made Deputy Commander of the 4th Guard's Fighter Air Division. On 24 June 1947 he took up command of this same division. From April 1948 he was a Commander in the 330th Fighter Air Division. On 27 November 1948 he was retired to the reserves.

He was awarded the Order of Lenin, as well as the Order of the Red Banner twice, and the Orders of the Patriotic War 1st class, and other medals.

The Commander of the 312th Reconnaissance Air Regiment Major Ivan Vasilyevich Georgiev

He was born on 7 November 1902 in the Pskov region, Ostrovsk district in the village of Shelguny.

He joined the Red Army from July 1924, he was a Red Army soldier and a Junior Commander in the 167th Rifle Regiment, 56th Rifle Division. From October 1925 he was a student of the Leningrad School of Military Theory of the Air Forces of the Red Army. From November 1926 he was a student of the 2nd Higher Aviation School. In June 1928 he was a Junior Pilot in the 43rd Air Squadron, later becoming a Senior Pilot and Flight Commander. From June 1933 he was made a Detachment Commander in the 5th Air Squadron. In December 1935 he attended the Lipetsk aviation development courses organised by the Air Forces of the Red Army. In December 1936 he was made a Commander of the 12th High-Speed Bomber Air Squadron, of the 49th Air Brigade. From 25 January 1938 he was acting Commander of the 39th High-Speed Bomber Air Regiment. For his successes in combat training he was awarded the Order of the Red Star on 22 February 1938. In June 1938 he was made Commander of the 39th High-Speed Bomber Air Regiment, he was made a Major.

He participated in the entry of the Red Army into Western Belorussia in September 1939.

He participated in the Soviet-Finnish War

In May 1940 he was made Deputy Commander of the 66th Air Brigade. From August 1940 he was made Commander of the 312th Reconnaissance Air Regiment.

He participated in the Great Patriotic War.

From October 1941 he was made Commander of the 312th Ground Attack Air Regiment. In December 1941 he was made Commander of the 23rd Heavy Bomber Air Division (from March 1942 this became the 53rd Long Range Air Division), and he was made a Colonel. In April 1943 he was made Commander of the 5th Long-Range Air Corps and Lieutenant-General of Aviation on 18 September 1943. In February 1945 he was made Commander of the 9th Guard's Bomber Air Corps. From July 1946 he was made Commander of the 19th in North Korea. From December 1949 onwards he held the position of Commander of the 81st Guard's Bomber Air Corps. He died on 13 November 1950.

He was awarded the Order of Lenin, and the Order of the Red Banner three times, as well as the orders of Kutuzov 1st class, and Suvorov 2nd class, and the Order of the Red Star, and other medals.

A triumvirate of aircraft that enabled serious claims to be made for air superiority during the Spanish Civil War; The type 5 I-16s designed by N.N. Polikarpov, and the high-speed SB bomber designed by A.N. Tupolyov.

The unsuccessful aircraft designed by N.N. Polikarpov: the I-180 fighter, the VIT-2 ground attack aircraft, and the SBP dive bomber. These advanced aircraft were almost refined enough to enable them to enter series production but were simply never manufactured and never became combat aircraft.

A DB-3 long-range bomber (fitted with two M-85s) this photograph was taken from a report on state testing.

The TB-7 heavy bomber (with four AM-34FRN engines and one M-100), this photograph is taken from a report on state testing on 5 November 1937. The way the prototype differs from the production machines can be clearly seen, the production examples went into combat in August 1941.

The prototype I-28 fighter (designed by Yatsensko).

A Bb1 (Su-2) short-range bomber, this photograph is taken from a report on state testing on 13 May 1940.

The BSh-2 ground attack aircraft (twin-engine variant), this photograph is taken from a report on state testing on 11 May 1940.

A type 10 I-16 the first and obviously unsuccessful modernisation of the I-16.

An I-15bis fighter, a further development of the I-15/1-15bis, which was so clearly unsuccessful, this aircraft was already obsolete by the time it was being manufactured, but in spite of this was still produced in huge numbers.

An I-153 aircraft, a further development of the I-15/I-15bis. This aircraft was a lifeline for the fighter and ground attack aviation arms of the Red Army Air Force between 1939–1941.

A modernised SB, fitted with M-100 engines and VISh-2 fixed pitch propellers and prototype MV-3 and MV-2 turrets. This photograph is taken from a report on state testing on 10 June 1937.

A significant modernisation of the SB was the 201 series aircraft. The way in which the engine gondolas have changed is clearly visible. Nevertheless despite the enhanced aerodynamics the speed characteristics of this modification deteriorated in comparison with the 96 series machines.

A significant modernisation of the DB-3 (and what is actually a newly constructed DB-3F aircraft fitted with two M-88 engines). This photograph is taken from a report on state testing on 28 May 1940.

The American 'Valti' V-11, which under the designator BSh-1 was due to become the principal ground attack, and light-bomber aircraft in the Red Army Air Force between 1938–1939. In the end however these aircraft were manufactured in small numbers and all of them were handed over to the Civilian Air Fleet.

The BB-22 (Yak-22) short-range. This aircraft was to have become the principal reconnaissance aircraft serving in the Air Forces of the Workers' and Peasants' Red Army Air Force, but owing to structural and production problems it was produced in small numbers and it only entered service with two reconnaissance, and one short-range bomber regiment.

Aircraft prototypes: the I-200 (which subsequently became the MiG-1/3), the I-301 (the LaGG-3), I-26 (the Yak-1), and the VI-100 (which was subsequently to be rebuilt as a bomber known as the PB-100, or the Pe-2). The decision to accept these aircraft into series production was taken without state testing having been completed, which led in the end to the plans to produce these aircraft being disrupted.

Photograph taken of an accident that occurred on 4 January 1941. The pilot from the 4th Squadron, 15th Fighter Air Regiment Junior Lieutenant V.I. Yermolayev crashed his I-15bis on landing (the aircraft bore the factory No. 5553, and was fitted with an M-25V engine No. 1912605).

2

A Chronicle of Events in 1941

Introduction

All the hopes for a bright future were not destined to be realised, however, and back on 5 November 1940 a decision was taken to by way of decree No. 2265-977SS 'ON THE AIR FORCES OF THE RED ARMY', issued by the Council of People's Commissars, in accordance with which the Red Army Air Force was to be expanded for the third time in four years. Moreover the number of units was expanded by almost a third, in 1941 it was proposed that 100 new air regiments be formed, as well as 25 aviation division directorates, five aviation corps directorates, and in total by the end of the year there were to be 343 regiments, and 79 air division directorates in the Red Army Air Force. Furthermore the number of personnel was not increased in proportion, and it was planned by the end of the year to increase the number of pilots to 60,000 individuals. Some of them were not destined to be sent to augment the units themselves, but were held as reserve pilots. It would not be entirely correct to think of the reform of the Red Army Air Force planned for 1941 as ill-conceived. This was far from an act of Providence but a relatively considered measure; clearly in its development, however, not all the aspects of the situation which had by that time unfolded in the Red Army Air Force were taken into consideration in sufficient measure. Firstly there were the two waves of expansion in 1940, in accordance with which the formation of 93 new air regiments, 32 fighter regiments, 51 bomber regiments, and 10 reconnaissance regiments, as well as 62 air observation squadrons, and 50 aviation division directorates commenced. Secondly the problem of the training of personnel, both in flying schools and in Air Force units had not been solved. Thirdly was the issue of the catastrophic situation with respect to the materiel in terms of engines and aircraft.

In fact this new expansion in 1941 began against a backdrop of the failure of administrative measures in 1940 and not only was it designed to fulfil its purpose, but also to eradicate the shortcomings of the previous year. In connection with this decree No. 2265-977SS issued by the Council of People's Commissars as well as subsequent decrees, first and foremost in a decree issued by the Council of People's Commissars and the Central Committee of the All-Union Communist Party (of Bolsheviks) dated 25 February 1941 and in a decree issued by the Council of People's Commissars No. 0020 dated 11 March 1941 contained quite strict instructions, in accordance with which it was planned that an overarching objective that had been set would be met by the end of 1941, specifically this was:

The formation of new units and formations;
The training of 32,500 pilots, 15,000 navigators, 16,000 air gunners, 16,000 aircraft technicians and aircraft mechanics, and 22,000 junior aviation specialists;
An enhancement in the quality of combat training in Red Army Air Force front line units;
Conversion onto the 'new' aircraft types.

For this the following measures were proposed:

1. In order to recruit the required number of pilots, navigators, gunner/radio operators and technicians a decision was taken to form 32 new aviation and technical aviation colleges, 30 basic aviation training schools, and to expand the existing technical colleges.
   A new system was developed for training pilots, which consisted of two stages. The first would be a so-called basic aviation training school, where students would train to fly the U-2 and the UT-2 (the total number of flying hours would be 30). The second was a specific military pilots school, where students would learn to fly combat aircraft, amassing 24 hrs on fighters and 20 hrs on bombers.

2. Conduct identical combat training for all aircrew in Red Army Air Force front line units including the new recruits joining from flying schools in 1940 and who have not undergone a course in combat training. It was envisaged that two stages of training would be implemented:

   The first stage would be to train crews, sections, and squadrons in daylight combat operations in good weather.
   This stage would involve aircrew who had graduated from flying schools at the end of 1940, as well as aircrew who had not been trained in combat operations as a crew, or as a flight, or squadron.
   A secondment in front line and reserve air regiments should be arranged in the initial period for all aircrew who have graduated from flying schools, with the aim of developing the following:
   For fighter aircrew, aerial gunnery, air combat, high altitude and group flying;
   For bomber aircrew—apart from the above—working together as a crew and bombing;
   The total number of flying hours for the training as a whole should be set at 70 hrs, of these:
   30 hrs is to be allocated to the secondment and 40 hrs to developing combat training as a flight and as a squadron.

   The second stage is combat training as a flight, squadron, and as a regiment in inclement weather conditions in daylight, and as a flight and a squadron by night.
   All the aircrew who have already undergone daylight combat training as a flight and as a squadron in favourable weather conditions are to undergo this stage of the training.
   The total number of flying hours for this entire stage of training should be set at 70 hrs per crew.
   The overall standard for sorties per pilot and per crew for both stages of training should be set at 160 hrs, of these: combat training–140 hrs and for joint exercises with ground forces and tactical flying training–20 hrs.

3. The roll-out of large-scale airfield construction. This measure envisages the construction not only of new airfields, but the reconstruction of existing airfields. The main highlight was the decision to construct 240 concrete runways, which enabled combat training to be conducted all year round without stopping for the muddy periods in autumn and spring.

4. Transfer to a new arrangement for the aviation logistics forces, which envisaged a rejection of an airbase being directly subordinate to each air regiment, in favour of the roll-out of a territorial system, consisting of so-called airfield regions.

5. Draw up a timetable for the re-equipping of aviation units, which clearly sets out a pattern for receiving the 'new' materiel and for the influx of personnel.

6. Develop measures and a plan for the training of personnel on new aircraft within the units themselves:

    1. In order to reduce the timescales for the training of aircrew and technical personnel on new aircraft types it is considered imperative that this training be conducted in the units themselves going forward. With this aim in mind experienced pilots and engineers need to be posted to these districts to provide practical flying training for the new aircraft types, as well as in their operation.
    2. A month prior to a regiment receiving their new aircraft assign two or three new aircraft to train the command personnel in these units, who are up to speed, and to enable the rest of the aircrew and technical personnel in the regiment to train to fly these aircraft and to operate them.
    3. Set a timetable for training on new aircraft types of between eight to 10 flying hours per pilot. Within this timescale pilots should be trained in operating the aircraft confidently on flights around the airfield.
    4. With the aim of a more detailed study of the new aircraft and engine types, send the aircrew and technicians to the manufacturing plants from each of the air regiments based on the following:
       Fifteen technicians
       Five aircrew, this delegation should consist of a regimental commander and four squadron commanders.
    5. Simultaneously to the training in the units themselves conduct training of aircrew from front line units, and first and foremost train divisional and regimental commanders under the Air Force Scientific-Research Institute in the new aircraft types. This training should be undertaken on the basis of all the command cadres across the regiments being trained in the first and second quarters of 1941.

No doubt considerable work was undertaken and very constructive measures were put in place, however so many shortcomings in terms of planning come to light even on cursory inspection, that one is forced to consider the likelihood of their realisation.

Firstly, and quite obviously, is the fact that in making the decision not all the lessons of the previous organisational and mobilisation measures, particularly the expansion of the units, which was conducted 'from scratch' in 1940 were taken into consideration. Nevertheless on the basis of the experience of 1938–1939 it was understood that the process from the moment the decree is signed to the creation of a unit requires a minimum of 9–12 months. Moreover by that time the unit is only just beginning to pull together, and it is only then that the personnel begin to undertake combat training.

Secondly to anticipate success on the part of the aviation industry in the assimilation of the 'newest' aircraft and engines, when one considers the fact that this same industry was only just coming to terms with their incompetence in modifying 'old' aircraft types, was at the very least, naïve. That is to say that the units could not count on the rapid arrival of materiel for the newly formed units in the foreseeable future, even with a trained cadre of personnel. This issue was particularly acute for the 22 newly formed fighter air regiments, which were to receive long-range twin-engine escort fighters, the production of which had not only failed to start, but the aircraft had not yet undergone testing.

Thirdly, any graduate of a higher education institution with a specialisation in construction would say straight away that from the beginning of the design for a new construction project to the signing of the act of acceptance of the newly built project requires a relatively long period of time. Even in ideal conditions the construction of over 500 airfields and 240 concrete runways in a single season is an almost impossible task, even with the head of state paying close attention to this issue.

Fourthly, the graduation of pilots from flying schools in 1941 in peacetime was due to take place nine months after the start of their studies. That is to say the majority of the young pilots would not be able to join their units and start combat training before the second half of the year.

It has to be noted also that any disruption in the execution of any of the points in the plan would mean that all the other components of the programme to reform the Red Army Air Force would remain unfulfilled.

The conclusion, which is completely obvious, is that the decision, which was taken in accordance with decree no. 2265-977SS and which was issued by the Council for People's Commissars, and the subsequent directives and orders, did not address the situation that had arisen in full. The deadlines had been underestimated and as such were self-defeating.

Apart from that in realising the plan to expand and re-equip such a complicated mechanism as the air forces, the People's Commissariat for Defence, the General Headquarters, and the Principal Directorate of the Air Force had for some reason built ideal conditions into these plans from the very beginning, as if to factor out the threat from a western neighbour. In fact the Red Army Air Force, including those military districts that bordered Germany and her allies, had been transformed into one large training unit, which was to bring the pilots who had not been fully trained in the flying schools up to speed, and to convert the entire personnel onto the 'newest', but technically inadequate aircraft types. It was possible that the Red Army Air Force command was operating under directives of some kind from the leadership of the USSR in connection with political agreements with Germany, or some other considerations were in place, of which the author is not aware. Nevertheless no agreements could replace elementary vigilance and common sense and almost all the units and formations in the Air Force had been transferred onto a footing in which they were not combat ready over a relatively long period of time, and if a conflict were to break out they would not be capable of providing close support to the Red Army.

Subsequent events in 1941 unfolded in strict accordance with the decrees issued by the Council of People's Commissars and the Central Committee for the All-Union Communist Party (of Bolsheviks) and by the start of 1941 the Red Army Air Force caught by 'double tsunamis', the first of which was in the name of the 'expansion of the Red Army Air Force' and the second in the name of 're-equipping units with the new materiel'. It was for these reasons that the Soviet air forces were not able to gain full combat readiness right up until the start of the Great Patriotic War.

In fact the winter 1940–1941 became for the Air Forces of the Baltic Special Military District, as for the entire Red Army Air Force as a whole, the 'point of no return' after which subsequent events would not be as successful.

2.1 Combat Training, Re-equipping onto a New Materiel, and the Roll-out of New Units

The year 1941 had began with a training process that had been planned back in the autumn of the previous year and which was designed to introduce the graduates arriving at front line units from the flying schools into operations.

As has already been mentioned above the regiments in the Air Forces of the Baltic Special Military District in the autumn of 1940 had only brushed up against the 'wave' of expansion in the Red Army Air Force. Nevertheless between 15–20 young pilots arrived at each regiment, who had graduated from flying schools on an accelerated programme. It has to be said that 'aces' were graduating from the flying schools throughout 1940, who had amassed eight to 12 flying hours each in I-15, I-15bis, and SB aircraft. This was slightly more than the graduates of 1938–1939, but even so is completely insufficient to train a pilot fully (in total the average flying hours amassed by graduates that year across all types of aircraft, both independently and with an instructor, amounted to between 40–50 hrs).

The situation prevalent in previous years, when young students at flying schools had successfully been taught, albeit with some difficulty, to take-off, fly a 'box pattern' over the airfield, and land, was repeated. These pilots were not taught complex aerobatic manoeuvres, or formation flying, or cross-country flying, or even aerial gunnery techniques. Indeed it was left to the front line units to teach the graduates of 1940, as well as their predecessors from 1938–1939 to 'really' fly an aircraft.

One can imagine the 'joy' that would have been felt by the regimental command at the arrival of these students. The recent expansion however had been of some use, in that the commanders acquired considerable experience in training pilots and steadily began to teach the young pilots to fly. Training was refined and began with a check of piloting techniques. Naturally it was not possible to entrust these new pilots with combat aircraft, first and foremost owing to considerations over their own safety, so the young pilots cautiously took to the skies in the U-2. Subsequent training was planned according to a 'standard' pattern, after the U-2 the pilots would transfer onto their transitional aircraft such as the USB, I-15bis, or the UTI-4, and only then would they be transferred onto the SB, I-153, and I-16 combat aircraft. In order to administer the process of 'completing the training' five I-15bis aircraft from the 42nd Fighter Air Regiment and the 61st Ground Attack Air Regiments were transferred to regiments equipped with I-153s. Regiments equipped with I-16s received additional UTI-4s, while training cockpits were fitted to the SBs in the bomber regiments.

The process of training young pilots in the units themselves required a very large number of training flights as well as the efforts of the regimental and squadron commanders, who in fact became flying instructors. Thus in the regiments in which these students began their training, the flying hours amassed in training aircraft for January was as follows:

- The 15th Fighter Air Regiment: flying hours on the U-2 were 65 hrs, and 580 landings, while for the I-15bis this figure was 33 hrs, and 302 landings
- The 21st Fighter Air Regiment: the flying hours amassed on the UTI-4 were 36 hrs, and 286 landings.
- The 38th Fighter Air Regiment: the flying hours on the U-2 were 33 hrs, and 235 landings, while for the UTI-4 this figure was 50 hrs, and 499 landings.
- The 49th Fighter Air Regiment: the number of flying hours for the UTI-4 was 40 hrs, and 416 landings.
- The 148th Fighter Air Regiment: the number of flying hours on the U-2 was 35 hrs, and 298 landings, while for the UTI-4 this figure was 50 hrs, and 499 landings.
- The 9th High-Speed Bomber Air Regiment: the number of flying hours for the USB was 31 hrs, and 185 landings.
- The 31st High-Speed Bomber Air Regiment: the number of flying hours on the USB was 19 hrs, and 185 landings.
- The 35th High-Speed Bomber Air Regiment: the number of flying hours on the U-2 was 209 hrs, and 440 landings.

In order to 'unify', so to speak, this process of introducing the students to operations, as a rule, the line-up for the regiments in which the students were being trained included one or two squadrons, and it was in these squadrons that the training took place.

The resumption of combat training in many units following the new year break in January 1941 was accompanied by a whole series of accidents and incidents in flight.

Despite the fact that the number of incidents caused by the materiel far outweighed those attributed to any other reason, the district command focused on the poor discipline and training among the aircrew, which was after all not very objective.

Meanwhile at the very end of 1940 the process of converting aircrew onto the 'new' aircraft types in the fighter units of the Red Army Air Force finally began, and for the Air Forces of the Baltic Special Military District this aircraft was the MiG-1. In accordance with the plan, the first unit entrusted with assimilating the newest technology was the personnel of the 31st Fighter Air Regiment and this is completely logical, since this regiment was the best in the district in terms of their combat training results in 1940 and all things considered the regiment looked like it was going to retain this position in 1941. Specifically amongst the front line units in the Red Army Air Force it was this same 31st Fighter Air Regiment that became the first to receive the new Mikoyan fighters and on the eve of the coming year 1941 on 29 and 30 December 1940 some 29 MiG-1s were sent from Factory No. 1 to Kaunas, becoming a new year gift of a kind.

Aside from the acceptance and assembly of the newest fighters in January, the command of the 31st Fighter Air Regiment also continued to introduce the young pilots to operations. This regiment was among the leaders in this field, having trained four pilots independently on the I-16 in December 1940. In January half of the new pilots—10 individuals from the 20 who arrived had already flown the I-16—and apart from that the entire personnel of the 1st squadron that previously operated the I-15bis were all trained on the I-16. Naturally the proposed re-equipping and conversion did not make the task of introducing the new pilots to operations any easier, so the young pilots were concentrated around the 1st and 3rd Squadrons and continued to train on the I-16, while a decision was taken to train the regular pilots of the 2nd and 4th Squadrons on the MiG-1 to begin with.

The 29 MiG-1s that arrived at this unit were manufactured by work brigades at Factory No. 1 with the help of the regiment's technical staff. The leadership of the 31st Fighter Air Regiment even managed to complete eight familiarisation flights in the MiG-1 in January, amassing five hours of flying time. A brigade made up of specialists from the Air Force Scientific Research Institute led by Colonel M.I. Martselyuk arrived in Kaunas to assist in the assimilation of this new aircraft.

From the memoirs of N.I. Petrov, a pilot in the 3rd squadron:

> Test-pilots arrived and flew the aircraft around the airfield, led by Test-Pilot Stefanovskiy,* who in conversation explained the specifics of the piloting techniques used to fly the MiG-1, what we should be careful of etc. This aircraft was one of the first to enter service with our regiment, so nobody had any experience of flying this aircraft in front line units. The piloting instructions for this aircraft were subsequently amended and many of the paragraphs were crossed out and changed.

Veselovskiy, a pilot in the 1st Squadron wrote almost the same in his memoirs:

> A test-pilot arrived in March from Moscow and completed a demonstration flight. The fighter gained speed rapidly and displayed its best qualities at the design altitude of 7,000 m. The first pilots allowed to fly this aircraft solo were those from the divisional directorate, then the

* According to Air Force Scientific Research Institute documents, the leader of the group that arrived in the Baltic Special Military District was Colonel M.I. Martselyuk, together with flying instructor Senior Lieutenant Leonid Mikhaylovich Kuvshinov.

> Commander of the Putkivo regiment and the squadron commanders. The task was made all the more complicated by the fact that there was no two-seat, dual control aircraft, pilots flew this aircraft for the first time on their own.

At the end of the month the regiment handed over 27 type 5 I-16 aircraft to other units and to flying schools, and on 27 January 31 MiG-1s were sent to the unit from Factory No.1. Taking into account that these regiments were almost completely re-equipped with this aircraft the regimental command were seriously considering refining the piloting techniques for the MiG-1 with the personnel of the 2nd and 4th squadrons before 15 February. This task had been put before them by way of a decree on combat training for the month of February.

Overall the start of the year was entirely predictable: In winter conditions, and overburdened as they were with introducing the young pilots to operations, by no means were all the commanders able to arrange combat training as they were supposed to. As a result, many of the units flew very few hours and did not engage in combat training at all. It was probably only the 50th High-Speed Bomber Air Regiment that was engaging in combat training at an acceptable level, although the 61st Ground Attack Air Regiment were gaining a foothold in terms of the number of hours. The personnel in this regiment trained intensively on the I-153.

February began with much promise—the 31st Fighter Air Regiment began to pass their pilots out on the MiG-1. To begin with everything went relatively smoothly and the considerable experience gained by the technical personnel and the assistance offered by the brigade from the Air Force Scientific Research Institute began to tell. Experienced specialists were able to benchmark the way the conversion process was organised. From a report written by Senior Lieutenant Kuvshinov:

1. By the time the conversion began the 8th Mixed Air Division had received 30 MiG-1 and MiG-3 aircraft from Factory No. 1, and the factory brigades assembled and adjusted these aircraft, a short time later a further 30 aircraft arrived and 60 aircraft were assembled.

2. Prior to our arrival the leadership of the 8th Mixed Air Division had studied the materiel of the MiG-1, after which a commission was set up, in which Colonel Martselyuk participated, after receiving reports from the technical personnel.

   Apart from that lectures were conducted with aircrew, in the course of which all the issues concerning the piloting techniques and operation of the materiel both in the air and on the ground were carefully explained.

   Colonel Martselyuk conducted the lectures with the leadership cadres together with factory technician Semyonov (these lectures lasted between 12–15 hrs) as well as with the flight commanders and junior pilots (these lectures lasted four hours).

   The learning materials for the materiel diagrams, wallcharts etc.) were sufficient.

3. The pattern for the conversion was as follows: I would do three check flights doing 'circuits' with each student and one at pilotage level in a UTI-4 aircraft and if the pilot met all the criteria then after they had passed all their tests on their knowledge of the materiel of the MiG-1 they would be sent on a solo flight, or if they did not match up a pilot would not be allowed to fly solo until they had reached the required level in terms of their pilotage techniques on the I-16 (only one individual was not allowed to proceed onto a solo flight in the MiG-1 due to a lack of proficiency in the I-16).

   Ahead of a solo flight in the MiG-1 all the pilots under the supervision of Martselyuk underwent solo training on the I-16 flying a 'circuit' (this took place over five or six flights).

Colonel Martselyuk was in charge of whether the students passed or not, my function was in checking their pilotage techniques in the I-16 and giving my conclusion as to whether they should proceed onto a solo flight in the MiG-1.

This conversion process began on 20 February and concluded on 1 March.

The conversion programme, which had been drawn up by the institute met all the requirements, but on the basis of a decree issued by the People's Commissar concerning a ban on performing Immelman turns, barrel rolls, half rolls, and loops the flying component of the programme had to be reduced and aside from the 'circuit' training a further two or three flights were permitted to an area in the MiG-1 in order to carry out shallow and steep turns, combat turns, and spirals (a spin was banned).

Some 20 individuals from the leadership of the three regiments were converted onto this aircraft, including a divisional inspector of pilotage technique, and an inspector from the Baltic Special Military District.

Apart from that under observation of the leader of the group Colonel Martselyuk, and in consultation with him, the squadron commanders passed more than 30 flight commanders and junior specialists out on the MiG-1 on 1 March.

My personal conclusions.

In conclusion I can say that the MiG-1 and MiG-3 aircraft in terms of their flight performance characteristics can be assimilated by aircrew who have attained a score of 'good' for their pilotage techniques in the I-16, that is to say for those who are able to fly the above mentioned aircraft confidently and intelligently.

The technical staff do not encounter any particular difficulties in assimilating and operating this aircraft either. In connection with the flight-testing of the factory aircraft I flew to an area in the MiG-3 to test the full range of pilotage techniques and came to the conclusion that pilotage in this aircraft, owing to its considerable weight, speed when performing aerobatics, and the way it spins heavily around the longitudinal axis, need to be conducted at a slower pace, that is to say cautiously, so as to reduce pilot fatigue. The load on the pilot is felt much more acutely in the MiG-3. The controls ideally need to be replaced.

Senior Lieutenant Kuvshinov.

In total by the end of the month 46 pilots had flown a solo in the MiG-1 in the 31st Fighter Air Regiment, and had amassed 53 flying hours across 496 flights.

However, despite the glowing reports by the Air Force Scientific Research Institute specialists and divisional command the portfolio of defects in these aircraft, that came to light during their assembly, test flying and operation made for an exhaustive list. The main defects were: poor operation of the spark plugs, cracks in the engine casing, the undercarriage retracting by itself, failures in the oil cooler assemblies and so on. The brigade at Factory No. 1 set about eradicating the defects almost immediately after completing the assembly of these aircraft.

All things considered it was under the very influence of the relatively successful assimilation of the MiGs in the 31st Fighter Air Regiment that district Air Force command decided, without waiting for the second quarter, to commence the re-equipping of the 15th Fighter Air Regiment. For this the regiment was sent eight I-16s and five MiG-1s from the 31st Fighter Air Regiment, after which regimental command also began to train the personnel in the 1st and 2nd Squadrons intensively, and as a result by the end of the month 15 pilots had flown this new aircraft solo. The total number of flying hours the 15th Fighter Air Regiment amassed on the MiG-1 was 12 hrs, across 125 flights, and on the UTI-4 and I-16 transitional aircraft they amassed 27 hrs, across 351 flights, and 86 hrs across 559 flights respectively.

In February the conversion began for pilots of the 46th and 54th High-Speed Bomber Air Regiments onto the Ar-2 aircraft. This took place at the Air Force Scientific Research Institute itself and in total one pilot, navigator, and technician from each of the units was converted onto this aircraft, after which they would ferry one Ar-2 each back to their units.

The rest of the regiments continued the passing out of the young pilots and if in January this passed without any lives being lost, then in February in the 38th Fighter Air Regiment a catastrophe occurred with an I-153 aircraft. On 24 February Lieutenant D.M. Bykovets, a pilot in the 2nd Squadron, was killed. The engine in his I-153 caught fire during flight owing to a technical problem and unfortunately the pilot was not able to bail out by parachute but tried to return to the airfield and land. The conclusion of the commission was that the pilot had lost consciousness due to smoke entering the cockpit and the uncontrolled aircraft hit the ground without returning to the airfield. Tallinn was some two and a half kilometres away. Undoubtedly this happened because the pilot was not sufficiently experienced, as he had made 17 flights (lasting one hour thirty minutes) in the 'Chaika' and he had flown just four hours with his unit prior to that fateful day.

As a whole the results for combat training had increased somewhat in comparison with January and again it was the personnel of the 50th High-Speed Bomber Air Regiment who took the lead, carrying out on average two aerial gunnery and bombing missions each per crew. Nevertheless the learning progressed without any real pressure, and the flying hours even decreased somewhat in comparison with January.

Despite the combat training progressing at such a slow pace and the relatively low flying hours there were several accidents and three fatal accidents in February. Apart from the tragedy mentioned above in the 38th Fighter Air Regiment, the other emergency incidents fell to the regular pilots.

On 1 February Lieutenant Ya.P. Kolbasyuk from the 4th Squadron, 10th Fighter Air Regiment was killed. The conclusion of the committee was that the I-15bis had entered a flat spin at an altitude of 4,000 m and the pilot was not able to pull the aircraft out of this spin, and in attempting to bail out by parachute he had hit the aircraft and was killed.

On 8 February a fatal accident occurred with an R-5 from the 65th Air Observation Squadron as a result of an error that occurred during group flying training. Whilst the group of aircraft were flying as a flight, one of the aircraft, in avoiding a collision with one of the wingmen during a manoeuvre to reshuffle the formation at low altitude, hit the ground and broke up. The crew, consisting of pilot Senior Lieutenant P.M. Semerunin and pilot and observer Senior Lieutenant I.I. Rudnev were killed. The R-5 was beyond economic repair.

On 14 February only a miracle prevented a fatal accident in the 42nd Fighter Air Regiment. Whilst performing a manoeuvre in mid air the two aircraft flown by Flight Commander Junior Lieutenant A.I. Yershov and pilot Junior Lieutenant N.A. Salnikov collided, fortunately both pilots were able to land their damaged aircraft on the airfield.

In March the new materiel continued to enter service with the units of the Air Forces of the Baltic Special Military District. In total up until the end of the month a further 34 MiG-3s and two MiG-1s had been assembled in Kaunas, which meant that two thirds of the 15th Fighter Air Regiment could be equipped with these aircraft. Apart from that two MiG-1s and one MiG-3 were transferred to the 10th Fighter Air Regiment to enable the conversion of personnel to be administered.

The process of assimilation of this new materiel was in full swing. In the third month of 1941 the pilots of the 31st Fighter Air Regiment had amassed a further 79 hrs in the MiG-1 and MiG-3 aircraft (this was achieved across 434 flights), and four pilots each were passed out on this aircraft from the 1st and 3rd Squadrons. Thus some 54 pilots had completed a solo flight in the MiG-1 and MiG-3 aircraft in this unit. The pilots of the 15th Fighter Air Regiment were also trying not to lag behind their colleagues and by the end of the month they had even outstripped them in terms of their flying hours: 82 hrs across 367 flights. In the 15th Fighter Air Regiment by the end of the month 26 pilots had completed a solo flight in the MiG-1 and MiG-3s, and apart from that a further 31 pilots had flown solos in the I-16. Thus the brigade led by Colonel Martselyuk having completed their task honourably, departed from Kaunas.

At the end of March the bomber units in the district also began to receive new aircraft, and the crews of the 46th High-Speed Bomber Air Regiment ferried 11 new Ar-2s to Siauliai.

Unfortunately the sharply increasing intensiveness of the flying in these new aircraft as well as the lack of experienced instructors from the Air Force Scientific Research Institute led to a large number of incidents in flight. Thus in the 31st Fighter Air Regiment some 14 incidents occurred in the space of a month, and in the 15th Fighter Air Regiment some 13 incidents, four emergency landings, and one accident. It turned out that this new aircraft had a capricious disposition, and there was no trace of the glowing remarks made during the first month of assimilation. The main problem were the 16 failures in the outer wing panel that occurred on landing due to pilot error and the nine failures in the tail wheel skid that were due to the landing surfaces on the airfields not having been prepared properly.

Even the experienced pilots could not always cope with these new aircraft. On 17 March the Commander of the 2nd Squadron, 15th Fighter Air Regiment Captain A.P. Sorgin was due to ferry a MiG-1 aircraft from the forward airfield at Potsunay to the regiment's base at Kaunas. He had already completed 21 flights in the MiG-1 and he had amassed a total of 540 hrs on different types of aircraft. Captain Sorgin had not taken account of the strength of the wind on take-off, as a result of which he drifted off course on take-off and crashed into a U-2 aircraft that was standing on the apron. As a result both the MiG-1 and the U-2 had to be repaired and the veteran of the Soviet-Finnish War, and one of the most experienced pilots of the 15th Fighter Air Regiment was tried and dismissed from his position as Squadron Commander. 'Flight Commander of the 401st Fighter Air Regiment Captain Sorgin died from the injuries he sustained in air combat on 5 July 1941.'

What then could be said of the less-experienced pilots—the majority of these incidents occurred because of poor pilotage techniques, which multiplied the insufficient tactical-technical qualities of these new aircraft and engines.

This was how a veteran of the unit H.I. Petrov viewed the problems with the assimilation of the MiGs:

> For example the insufficient engine acceleration time, when the pilot opens the throttles and the engine does not immediately increase its speed, this takes around eight seconds and as such there were many incidents when the pilot had to 'take up the slack' on landing, and undershoot because the engine did not respond. Students have undershot on landing or the aircraft has pulled up during the flare. They are able to go around again but in some cases pilots have bounced the wheels on the ground three times. This is all a failure of design. The main mistake that pilots make in flying the MiG-1 lies in not maintaining their course on take-off. Pilots have not made the switch immediately from the M-25 to the AM-35, with one and a half times more power.

Aside from the issues surrounding refining piloting techniques the situation with regard to the technical condition of the new aircraft became much more acute in March, and by the end of the month the situation had really become critical. A large number of incidents involving leaks in the oil and water coolers came to light, together with failures in the flexible tachometer shafts, cracking in the engine crankcases, the undercarriage retraction system not working, as well as the synchronising systems for the machine guns failing. The AM-35A engines needed to be retrofitted with new Seliverstov mechanical four-link chains and the pressure regulating valves and oil drip pans needed to be replaced. The supercharger control system needed to be redesigned on all the aircraft as well as the oil and water systems. A serious situation arose with respect to the spark plugs: replacing the Z-EMT spark plugs with SV-19 examples had made the situation worse, so the SV-19s had to be changed back to the Z-EMTs. Difficulties experienced with the operation of the engine propeller group and the armament exacerbated an extraordinarily uncomfortable location of various small hatches and filler points, and also the fact that the engine cowlings were a very bad fit and required considerable time (between 30 mins–1 hr 30 mins) for removal and installation. The documents note that on some occasions it was not possible to close the 'Dzus' locks, without the use of a wooden mallet!

The brigades from Factory Nos. 1 and 24 that were working in Kaunas (and consisted of two brigades made up of 20 people) were unfortunately far from able always to correct all the design shortcomings in the aircraft, and the way the work was organised did not correspond to the serious nature of the task. Thus a military representative, Alekseyev, who visited the 31st Fighter Air Regiment from Factory No. 24 reported: 'At the time of my visit the brigade from factory No. 24 were fitting four-link chains ... on 50 percent of the aircraft and this is now idle awaiting delivery of a new batch of components ... the brigade from Factory No.1 arrived before us but have not started work yet because the components have yet to arrive from their manufacturing plant.'

In general terms the situation with respect to the technical condition of these newest aircraft grew ever worse and on 2 April 1941 there were 17 MiG-1 and MiG-3 aircraft awaiting repair for various reasons in both regiments and the situation was not showing any signs of an improvement.

In March the 40th High-Speed Bomber Air Regiment was the leader in conducting combat training, and the personnel from this regiment delivered a fairytale series of 475 bombing training missions and 319 aerial gunnery sorties firing at a drone! Furthermore the number of flying hours increased sharply.

The intensity of combat training increased sharply and the number of flying hours caused a spate of accidents and incidents.

One of the leaders in terms of the number of flying hours at that time was the 61st Ground Attack Air Regiment, and the personnel in this regiment continued to assimilate the I-153, although the training on the 'Chaika' also needed to be taken seriously:

> When landing the I-153 aircraft on frozen ground pilots were not able to hold the aircraft back from slewing to the side at the end of the landing roll and the side panels on seven aircraft have been broken in this way. These turns at the end of a landing roll only happen because the pilots have landed with a drift and have not been motivated mentally to be ready to counter the turn at the end of the landing roll if the airfield has a hard surface.

In the 21st Fighter Air Regiment the pilots ended up falling victim to inclement weather:

> On 29 March four emergency landings were made in I-16 aircraft. During the course of a sortie at high altitude the airfield became blanketed in fog. Two aircraft landed at JELGAVA airfield, and one aircraft landed back at its home base through the fog and another landed inshore on the ice. The aircraft landed safely. These aircraft were sent into the air without taking into account the possibility of fog in the area around the airfield, which the meteorological data had indicated.

Two accidents happened in the 38th Fighter Air Regiment due to a failure of the materiel, and one that was due to the carelessness of the crew and another similar incident occurred involving pilots from the 10th Fighter Air Regiment.

In bomber regiments these incidents were less by an order of magnitude—just four cases.

According to the conclusions formulated by the Baltic Special Military District Command, although this is not emphasised in the document, a relatively clear picture was drawn of the difficulties that the personnel in these units faced almost immediately as they converted onto this new materiel. This was only the beginning of the most difficult process of assimilating new materiel in the front line Air Force units themselves:

1. The incidents in flight during March occurred in the main in fighter units including 50 incidents that occurred with the MiG-1 and MiG-3 aircraft. The majority of these incidents occurred due to the failure of the side panels and the tail wheel skid.

   The problems with the panels occurred because of a lack of methodological training and a lack of mental preparation on the part of the pilots for the process of landing.

   The failures in the tail wheel skid occurred because pilots were not sufficiently well trained in operating from a frozen runway in springtime conditions.

2. Some of these incidents occurred due to unintelligent and careless operation of the materiel by aircrew. As before discipline in the air is again at a low level. The requirement for personnel and for their training remains a point of difference for the work of the leadership in terms of their implementation of the required military discipline and in ensuring flying operations pass without incident.

In the meantime the first warning bell had rung at the start of the year for the leadership of the Red Army Air Force in that the production of the new aircraft types was clearly not progressing at the tempo they had counted upon previously. The plan for the first quarter for fighter production across all the factories of the People's Commissariat for the Aviation Industry was only 55 percent complete, and in terms of the Pe-2 and Su-2 bombers it was only 71 percent complete. Only 66 percent of the production plan had been fulfilled for the long-range DB-3f bombers, which had been in production for the whole of the previous year.

The leadership of the Air Force had realised back in March that they would not receive their new materiel, which was required to re-equip the units themselves, in the given timescales or to the quality required. In fact the entire plan for re-equipment was under threat. It has to be noted that the command reacted to this relatively quickly and implemented measures. Thus the insufficient production of the LaGG-3 aircraft it was decided could be balanced by the MiG-3, and the missing Yak-4 reconnaissance aircraft, as we have seen above, were replaced by SBs.

The planned subsequent development of this re-equipment and combat training programme was interrupted by the expansion of the new units and formations in 1941. For the Air Forces of the Baltic Special Military District directive No. Org/3/520435 issued by the People's Commissar for Defence and dated 24 January 1941 served as the signal for the start of the organisational and mobilisation measures. In accordance with this document a 57th Fighter Air Regiment directorate was to be formed under standard document No. 15/11 as part of the district's line-up, and another five fighter regiments (from the 236th–240th regiments) were to be formed in accordance with standard document No. 15/21, as well the 241st Ground Attack Air Regiment in accordance with standard document No. 15/20. Work to put this formation together was to commence on 1 April 1941 and the formation was to be staffed with graduates from flying schools as well as regular personnel from the Air Forces of the Baltic Special Military District. Simultaneous to the formation of the new units the composition of the existing formations was also changed: the 7th Mixed Air Division and the 49th Fighter Air Regiment were also withdrawn from the line-up of the 6th Mixed Air Division but at the same time the 148th Fighter Air Regiment, and the 31st High-Speed Bomber Air Regiment and the 239th Fighter Air Regiment, which had been formed a short time prior to this in Ezere were added. The 42nd Fighter Air Regiment and the 54th High-Speed

Bomber Air Regiment in Vilnius were withdrawn from the line-up of the 8th Mixed Air Division while the 10th Fighter Air Regiment in Siauliai as well as the 240th Fighter Air Regiment, the 42nd Fighter Air Regiment, and the 54th High-Speed Bomber Air Regiment that were formed only a short time before in Raseiniai. Along with the 236th Fighter Air Regiment which was still in the process of being formed in Alytus, the 237th Fighter Air Regiment in Orany and the 238th Fighter Air Regiment in Vilnius became part of the 57th Fighter Air Division. Thus four formations: the 6th, 7th, 8th Mixed Air Divisions and the 57th Fighter Air Division were to form the first echelon of the Air Forces of the Baltic Special Military District, the position in relation to the composition of the 4th Mixed Air Division had not changed.

However by 17 February 1941 a new directive No. Org/3/52/104 had been sent to the headquarters of the Baltic Special Military District, in accordance with which the composition and disposition of these units had changed again. Thus the 10th Fighter Air Division was again handed back to the 7th Mixed Air Division, and apart from that, the deployment of the new 238th Fighter Air Regiment and the 241st Ground Attack Air Regiment had changed from Vilnius to Panevezys and from Tyrelkai to Jelgava, and the 49th Fighter Air Regiment respectively was withdrawn from the 7th Mixed Air Division and transferred to the 57th Mixed Air Division. This formation, along with the 238th Fighter Air Regiment also lost the 236th Fighter Air Regiment, which was transferred to the 8th Mixed Air Division. It was after these same measures had been implemented that the Air Forces of the Baltic Special Military District took on the shape in which it would greet 22 June 1941. According to this new distribution of forces four divisions were lined up along the border, the 4th Mixed Air Division represented a reserve for this division of a kind, since it was located 30 kilometres from the main forces.

Moving forward a little we can say that on 27 March a directive was signed concerning the formation of the 27th Army within the Baltic Special Military District, and an Air Force department was set up in the 27th Army's headquarters. On that same day Major-General A.P. Andreyev was made the Director of the Headquarters Department of the Air Forces of the 8th Army. The Directors of the Air Forces departments of the 11th and 27th Army headquarters were named on 27 May, these were Major-General V.A. Chumakov and Colonel V.A. Gushchin (who at that time was the Commander of the 8th Mixed Air Division. (He took up this position in July 1941, after which the newly appointed Divisional Commander Colonel N.S. Toropchin arrived).

It should be noted that the Army Air Force departments as they existed at that time were not able to effect an efficient leadership of the combat operations of the formations or even of the units themselves, since the structure of the department was such that they were only able to control combat training as well as the condition of the units and formations that were subordinate to them. The composition of the department was such that aside from the Air Force Director (who was actually the head of the department) administrative personnel, and the head of the production department there were only two departments: the first being the operations and reconnaissance department and the second being the combat training department, which contained only 17 positions. Out of these there were only four in the operations and reconnaissance department: the director and three adjutants, two for the operational side and one for the reconnaissance side. In the combat training department, if the technician, mechanic, engine specialist, and the gunner/radio-operator are excluded there were only seven positions: the director of the department, an operations engineer, a pilot's competency adjutant, a communications training adjutant, a navigational training adjutant, a logistics training adjutant, and a weapons training adjutant. Without a fully-fledged headquarters and their own means of communication the Air Force departments were just a regulatory organ of a kind and were not able to organise an effective leadership for the operations conducted by units and formations in a combat environment.

In accordance with these directives the formation of several new regiments, for some unknown reason, was to be conducted along the border regions; moreover in accordance with the plans for the provision of cover, in the event of conflict these units were to be pulled back to the rear. The author has yet to find an answer in the documents to the question of why such a strange alignment was chosen for their formation, it is possible that the leadership of the Red Army Air Force did have some compelling reasons for this, but the author has not yet managed to decipher this reasoning.

These circumstances however did not have anywhere near the influence on the situation that the decision to form new units at the expense of the Air Force personnel in the district had:

> The newly formed units are to be staffed by aircrew and technical personnel drawn from graduates who have completed the flying schools and aviation units within the district, by special order of the Head of the Principal Directorate of the Red Army Air Force. The rank and file and junior officers are to be drawn from the district's own resources.

Put simply the regular regiments in the district had to send between 20–30 of their personnel at the rank of squadron commander, and their deputies, as well as flight commanders to each of these regiments. In an unequivocal sense these measures entailed the transfer of around 200 experienced fighter pilots of the 460 that were serving in existing regiments by 1 January. Despite the fact that no new bomber aviation units had been formed in this district, some of the regular personnel still had to be sent to new formations in other districts, and the regular units could expect to receive young pilots in return.

As a result of these transformations a cohort of 35–40 experienced pilots were to remain in regular units, while graduates from the flying schools were expected to take the place of the other regular pilots, and the command personnel in these regiments were expected to train them. The formation of these new units, and their training, as well as that of the older units, to an acceptable standard was to be completed by the end of 1941.

One interesting element of the organisational and mobilisation measures was the introduction of changes in the plan for re-equipping the Red Army Air Force in 1941. In accordance with this plan the regiments that had been formed in the Air Forces of the Baltic Special Military District were to be re-equipped with the newest technology in 1941. Furthermore the 236th and 240th Fighter Air Regiments it was proposed would be equipped with the MiG-3 in the third(!) quarter, and the 238th and 239th Fighter Air Regiments were to receive LaGG-3 aircraft in the same timescale, while in the final fourth quarter the 237th Fighter Air Regiment, and the 241st Ground Attack Air Regiment were to receive LaGG-3 aircraft.

The list of tasks put before the leadership of all these units, both the newly formed and the practically reformed regular units was given its final revision at this point and the main points were set as follows:

> Formation, reformation and breaking in of assigned units;
> The graduation and training of young personnel;
> Conversion onto the new materiel;
> To conduct combat training in accordance with the plan for Combat Training Course 41.

Considering the problems that have been identified above with the technical condition of the new aircraft and the poor training of young pilots, these tasks would appear to be challenging, even for regular units. Furthermore as often happens in life, along with the bigger problems a whole series of small and completely unexpected problems also occur. For the 31st and 50th Fighter Air Regiment this concerned the most highly-trained pilots departing in the MiG-1s and MiG-3s to fly to Moscow to train for and participate in an enormous aviation parade planned for 1 May 1941 in Moscow. In total 50 of the most highly-trained pilots left from the two regiments.

In the end pilots from other districts refused to take part in the parade and on 11 April the pilots were sent to their home bases, but they were taken out of combat training for two weeks.

In their absence of the majority of the personnel in the 31st Fighter Air Regiment an extraordinary event took place in Kaunas. On that day four MiG-3s of the 31st Fighter Air Regiment and three I-153s of the 15th Fighter Air Regiment were scrambled to intercept an intruding aircraft. One of the MiGs turned back almost immediately owing to a problem with the radiator and the I-153s lagged behind at an altitude of 8,000 m, while three aircraft piloted by Lieutenant Aksyutin, and Junior Lieutenants Akimov and Yevtushenko tried to force the intruder to land. The subsequent events are described in some detail in the logbook:

> THE DIRECTOR OF THE PRINCIPAL DIRECTORATE OF THE RED ARMY AIR FORCE LIEUTENANT-GENERAL OF AVIATION COMRADE ZHIGARYEV:
>
> On 10 April 1941 at 1125 at an altitude of between 6,000–7,000 m in the skies around Kaunas airfield an unidentified aircraft was spotted, proceeding on a heading of 300–315 degrees.
>
> The duty flight from the 31st Fighter Air Regiment scrambled in the space of two to three minutes: the pilots were Junior Lieutenant AKIMOV, Lieutenant AKSYUTIN, and Junior Lieutenant YEVTUSHENKO.
>
> Whilst climbing Lieutenant AKSYUTIN noticed a MiG-3 in a spin to the right of him at a distance of around 500 m and at an altitude of between 8,000–8,500 m, which then disappeared from view. He continued to gain altitude in order to track this foreign aircraft. At an altitude of 11,000 m AKSYUTIN attacked this strange aircraft from ahead and to the left, and fired two warning bursts from his synchronised Beryozkin guns (his ShKAS machine guns did not work, and even his Beryozkin guns gave out after two short bursts).
>
> The intruder aircraft turned after this to the west, AKSYUTIN's aircraft followed off to starboard on a parallel heading at an interval of 300–400 m. Furthermore AKSYUTIN could clearly see the swastika on the rudder and the white cross on the fuselage. According to AKSYUTIN the aircraft's livery was dark-grey on the top, and pale pink underneath. The canopies on this German aircraft were white so they had probably frozen up.
>
> Furthermore the air speed was 240 km/hr (on the instruments). In an attempt to force the German aircraft to descend and land AKSYUTIN made a left turn around the aircraft with a bank angle of around 30 degrees and as he approached the tail of the German aircraft, attempting to complete his turn more rapidly, he overloaded the stick and entered a spin to port. After completing one rotation AKSYUTIN pulled out into a dive, but as he was trying to reduce his loss of altitude, he again overloaded the stick and entered another spin, this time to starboard.
>
> He exited out of the spin late by applying opposite rudder for two rotations. What is more the stick was in the central position and the engine was on full power. The aircraft did not recover from the spin and after around another five to six rotations AKSYUTIN pushed the stick forward sharply. At that moment he was thrown from the aircraft (at an altitude of between 6,000–7,000 m). AKSYUTIN used his parachute and landed close to the village of Survelishkis around one and a half to two kilometres from where the aircraft crashed. The aircraft burst into flames on impact and burned out—all that remained was a small part of the fuselage and the tail fin (the control surfaces were removed by the local population and the fire brigade). The undercarriage was in the retracted position.
>
> A second aircraft flown by Junior Lieutenant AKIMOV approached the German aircraft at an altitude of 10,000 m, from a position 300 m behind the aircraft and 200 m below it.

At an altitude of 9,000 m AKIMOV noticed to the left of the German aircraft a MiG-3, which whilst in a climb tore away from the German aircraft and entered a dive, after which it disappeared from view. As it turned out later, this was AKSYUTIN's aircraft.

The approach of AKIMOV's aircraft to the German aircraft was slow; in an attempt to speed up this approach AKIMOV performed zoom climbs and in one of these manoeuvres, losing speed, he entered a spin (to starboard), and after recovering from the spin (with some g-force) he entered a spin to port. AKIMOV was able to recover from this spin, taking into account the mistake he had made when pulling out of his previous manoeuvre, at an altitude of 6,000 m. As he pulled out of his dive he noticed that the port undercarriage leg had been forced to deploy, he lowered the starboard undercarriage and landed.

The third aircraft, flown by Junior Lieutenant YEVTUSHENKO entered a spin in a climb somewhere close to Kedainiai.

YEVTUSHENKO's aircraft was spotted by Lieutenant AKSYUTIN as it was caught in its spin (AKSYUTIN was at an altitude of 8,000 m and noticed the spinning aircraft in plain view from a distance of between 500–600 m away).

The local peasants, witnesses, and regimental personnel standing in Kedainiai saw the aircraft (YEVTUSHENKO's) rotating (in a spin), which at an altitude of approximately 1,000–2,000 m stopped, and the aircraft entered a dive and hit the ground with the engine still running, close to the village of Labunovo. Moreover the engine penetrated deep into the ground (between two to two and a half metres).

Judging by the way the remains of the aircraft were distributed it was possible to conclude that the aircraft hit the ground in a dive.

It was clear that YEVTUSHENKO had not made any attempt to bail out of the aircraft since the straps were found to be fastened, and he still had his hand on the stick.

Expert medical analysis suggested that YEVTUSHENKO was killed as he hit the ground, however the possibility of him having fainted cannot be ruled out, since his oxygen mask was found close to his helmet after the impact, and was pulled towards him. The oxygen tank was open.

The reason why YEVTUSHENKO's aircraft entered a spin was probably the same reason that AKSYUTIN's and AKIMOV's aircraft entered a spin, that is a loss of airspeed due to pilot error. The lack of training in high altitude flight and a lack of knowledge of how the aircraft behaved in a spin at these same altitudes served as the reason why these aircraft did not recover from the spin, or from their subsequent dives, in good time. (Junior Lieutenant YEVTUSHENKO had flown just one hour 40 minutes in the MiG-3, he had not assimilated the MiG-3 and he had never flown at altitude in any aircraft).

CONCLUSIONS:

1. The reasons why all three aircraft entered a spin were as follows:
   a. Pilot error in the MiG-3 at high altitudes (the pilots flew these aircraft in the same way at high altitude as they did at low and medium altitudes).
   b. A lack of training in piloting the MiG-3 at medium altitudes.
   c. A lack of a solid grounding in the theory of high altitude flight (steep changes in attitude, how the aircraft behaves in a dogfight, and steep bank angles when turning).

      Not using the correct spin recovery procedure (pushing the stick forward, feet on the pedals, and full power).

2. The most likely reason for the catastrophe that occurred with Junior Lieutenant YEVTUSHENKO's aircraft, apart from the reasons given above, was his loss of consciousness at high altitude (around 8,000–9,000 m), which was caused by a complete

> lack of high altitude training, which was made all the worse by g-forces from the spin with the engine on full throttle. It is possible that comrade YEVTUSHENKO came to at an altitude of around 1,000–1,500 m and recovered from the spin but could not recover from the dive due to insufficient altitude.

Reports on these extraordinary events do provide some details of the pilot's characteristics:

> Lieutenant Aksyutin had graduated in 1935, and had amassed 424 flying hrs in the MiG-3, across 25 flights. He had flown at an altitude of 7,200 m without oxygen and 8,100 m and 11,000 m with oxygen.
>
> Junior Lieutenant Akimov graduated in 1938 and had amassed 237 flying hours. He had completed 25 landings in the MiG-3, and had flown at an altitude of 6,500 m without oxygen, and 9,300 and 10,200 m with oxygen.
>
> Junior Lieutenant YEVTUSHENKO had graduated in 1938, and had amassed 160 flying hours on the MiG-3 aircraft across 14 flights, he had not flown at altitude in this aircraft or out to the combat zone.
>
> Conclusions as to the reasons why these MiG-3 aircraft entered a spin at high altitudes:
>
> The low number of flying hours on these aircraft. Piloting errors at high altitudes. A lack of knowledge of how the MiG-3 behaved at high altitude.

It has to be said that one important element, which remained so to speak in the shadow of this tragedy, was that when Aksyutin tried to open fire his ShKAS machine guns did not fire at all, and his Beryozkin guns gave out almost immediately. Furthermore, this had been noted previously while the calibration of these guns was being adjusted. No measures were taken to address this, and almost no mention remains of this important problem in the documents. It was these same circumstances that were to play a tragic role in the first air battles on 22 June 1941.

Interestingly this was not the first incident and two days prior to the tragedy at Kaunas on 8 April a similar episode occurred in Siauliai. On that day fighters were scrambled to intercept a foreign I-16 aircraft that was being flown by Deputy Commander of the 10th Fighter Air Regiment Captain A.I. Serenko. In an attempt to track the intruder at an altitude of around 8,500 m the tips of the pilot's hands and toes froze ('Serenko did not take-off in his flying gear, but just wore a helmet'), he lost orientation and on finding it again he made an emergency wheels-up landing close to the town of Ostrov. His aircraft was damaged.

After the episode concerning the attempt to intercept the German reconnaissance aircraft on 10 April came to light the problem with the defective operation of the machine guns again required the attention of Factory No. 1. During the course of April–May some 240 new ammunition boxes were sent to Kaunas for the ShKAS machine guns. Alongside this work, 35 fuselage tanks were reconditioned and 88 aircraft had their radiator ducts refurbished and the fuel cocks were replaced.

No sooner had work on this issue begun then a new problem came to light, such as mass delamination of the outer skin on the leading edge of the wing that emerged on many aircraft at the end of April and the beginning of May. In the 31st Fighter Air Regiment cracking appeared in the laminate on 10 MiG-1s, 19 MiG-3s, while in the 15th Fighter Air Regiment this was noticed on three MiG-1s, and 47 MiG-3s.

As a result of this multitude of defects flights in these new aircraft were stopped, with the exception of interceptor sorties, and none of the pilots in the 31st or the 15th Fighter Air Regiments completed any flights in the MiG-1s or the MiG-3s. in fact the entire compliment was in for repair right up until the second half of May, and the majority of the pilots were in Moscow.

Of some comfort was the fact that pilots from the 10th Fighter Air Regiment began to fly the MiG-1 and MiG-3 aircraft under the guidance of instructors from the 31st Fighter Air Regiment.

They amassed 3 hrs 26 mins in the MiG-1 and MiG-3 across 28 flights. In total 13 pilots (other sources give a figure of eight pilots) took to the skies in the MiG-1 and MiG-3 aircraft in this unit.

If the pilots of the 15th and 31st Fighter Air Regiments were prevented from conducting full-scale combat training by preparations for the parade and the problems with the materiel then the personnel in other regiments were grounded by the muddy season in the spring, and almost all of the airfields in this district were unsuitable for flying operations during this period.

It was for these reasons that the only unit capable of conducting combat training in April with a high degree of intensity were the units in the 4th Mixed Air Division. The figures at the end of the month showed that the 38th Fighter Air Regiment had gained the upper hand among the fighter regiments. The 38th Fighter Air Regiment's pilots had completed the training for the young pilots in combat aircraft and the regular pilots had progressed to conducting instrument and night flights in the U-2. The remainder of the regiments with the exception of the 40th High-Speed Bomber Air Regiment and the 148th Fighter Air Regiment were not able to attain the levels they had achieved the previous month. Despite the reduction in the demands on the pilots a relatively high number of incidents occurred.

Despite these unpleasant incidents by the end of April the majority of regiments were able to progress their aircrew, who had joined the regiment in the autumn of 1940, onto the training materiel, and were able to train the young pilots on combat aircraft. It was true however that almost none of these pilots had undertaken any combat training and were not included formally on the tally of combat kills.

May 1941 was very busy. Firstly thanks to the fine weather the intensity of combat training increased sharply. The number of flying hours across almost all of the regiments exceeded 500 hrs, and in some cases it even exceeded 1,000 hrs. The number of aerial gunnery, bombing missions, and cross-country flying also increased, as well as mock air battles. Among the bomber regiments the 40th and 31st High-Speed Bomber Air Regiments in the 6th Mixed Air Division were in the lead, while the 9th and 46th High-Speed Bomber Air Regiments in the 7th Mixed Air Division, the 54th High-Speed Bomber Air Regiment in the 57th Mixed Air Division, the 35th and 50th High-Speed Bomber Air Regiments in the 4th Mixed Air Division in contrast reduced the intensity of their combat training. Not to mention the 38th Fighter Air Regiment which maintained the upper hand as the leader of the fighter regiments by an even greater margin. The number of flying hours for the pilots of this regiment on combat aircraft alone was 686 hrs across 1,856 flights. Aside from the continual training of the pilots who had graduated in 1940 on I-153 aircraft the regiment began to train the sergeant pilots who had graduated in 1941. Another important component of the training was the training of the unit's command personnel on the I-16 transit aircraft, with the aim of developing piloting techniques given the subsequent conversion onto the Yak-1.

The bomber regiments commenced intensive dive bombing training. For example the pilots of the 50th High-Speed Bomber Air Regiment completed a 501 dive bombing training dives in the course of a month, and the 31st High-Speed Bomber Air Regiment completed 318, and the 40th High-Speed Bomber Air Regiment 203. The personnel of the 46th High-Speed Bomber Air Regiment, aside from the 150 training dives they completed in the SB and a further 252 they completed in an Ar-2, were able to complete five dive bombing attacks in the Ar-2.

The arrival of the 'new' materiel continued, and at the end of the month 20 MiG-3s arrived in Siauliai, while the 54th High-Speed Bomber Air Regiment received 11 Ar-2s.

The excellent take-off and landing as well as pilotage characteristics of the Ar-2 aircraft enabled the commanders of the 46th and 54th High-Speed Bomber Air Regiments to train the regular pilots in the new aircraft. Fifteen of them took to the skies in the 54th High-Speed Bomber Air Regiment, while in the 46th High-Speed Bomber Air Regiment not only did 36 veterans of the regiment take to the skies in the newest dive bomber but also three sergeant pilots who had only just arrived, having graduated in 1941.

In the course of operations with the AR-2 however a large number of 'teething troubles' came to light: a high water and oil temperature in the engine propeller group, failures in the water and oil coolers due to an insufficient reserve of strength, and so on.

The main problem was the mass of defects and cracks in the engine mounts. At the beginning of June the district requested new engine mounts for the Ar-2s from Factory No. 22, that is to say these assemblies needed to be changed on practically all these aircraft. A brigade travelled to the Baltic Special Military District from Factory No. 22, who were to carry out the repairs on all the aircraft in the two regiments.

The difficult situation with respect to the technical condition of these new MiG-1, MiG-3, and Ar-2 aircraft actually led to disruption of the conversion process. The pilots of the 46th High-Speed Bomber Air Regiment, who had converted during April and the beginning of May onto the Ar-2 had by the end of the month attained excellent results in terms of their combat training. In June however they were forced to reduce the tempo of their training due to a large percentage of the materiel being out of action. In the case of the 15th and 31st Fighter Air Regiments the lack of a significant period of training for the aircrew due to the preparation for the parade had a negative effect. Having commenced training at the end of January, by the first of June the pilots were marking time since following their return from Moscow they were forced to start to work to restore their take-off and landing skills. Naturally, since combat training and first and foremost aerial gunnery was still some time away the pilots found themselves back where they had been three months previously. At best they were engaged in flying 'circuits', as well as performing shallow and steep turns, combat turns and spirals.

Nevertheless the commanders of the 15th and 31st Fighter Air Regiments continued to train their personnel on these 'newest' aircraft. After having commenced the training of the 1940 graduates, who commenced intensive training on the UTI-4 and the I-16 in May. Thus, the personnel of the 15th Fighter Air Regiment amassed 46 hrs (across 356 flights) on the UTI-4, and on the I-16 they amassed 79 hrs (across 560 flights) respectively. The 31st Fighter Air Regiment however amassed 43 hrs on the UTI-4 (across 360 flights), and 155 hrs (across 641 flights) on the I-16. The regiments were only able to commence flying the MiG-1 and MiG-3 only at the very end of the month, and as such they only amassed a miserly number of hours, for the 31st Fighter Air Regiment this figure was 22 hrs (across 154 flights) while for the 15th Fighter Air Regiment this figure was less: 4 hrs 22 mins (across 46 flights). In order to maintain their skills in aerial gunnery and air combat the regular pilots were forced to undertake the corresponding drills in the I-16 and I-153.

The downtime between April–May could not fail to have an effect on the state of the training for pilots. Following the enforced break in flights underdeveloped piloting techniques began to make themselves known.

An increase in the number of flights led very predictably to an increase in incidents in flight during May, and moreover the pilots were far from at fault in this case. Some of the aircraft in the Air Forces of the Baltic Special Military District, as we have seen many times above, were significantly worn out, and the M-62 and M-63 engines failed so often that they presented an undue risk to the safety of the pilots.

The training of the sergeant pilots that had already commenced also led to an increase in the number of incidents in flight.

When summing up the results of these past five months of 1941 it should be noted that the actions by the command and the formations of the Air Forces of the Baltic Special Military District are without doubt deserving of a positive evaluation. Despite all the various types of difficulties listed above the commanders at all levels succeeded in implementing a series of the most difficult measures:

> To enable the pilots who had graduated in 1940 to train in the I-16 and I-153 and SB as well as starting to train the sergeant pilots who had graduated in 1941;
> Achieve in addition to the above satisfactory results in terms of the combat training of regular pilots in those units that were not involved in the conversion process onto the MiG-3, by the beginning of June;
> Train the entire cadre of regular pilots in the 31st Fighter Air Regiment (54 pilots) on the new materiel as well as half of the 15th Fighter Air Regiment (consisting of 26 'long-serving' pilots) and some of the pilots in their second year of service on the 10th Fighter Air Regiment (for various reasons this fluctuated from eight to 13). Enable the regular pilots of the 46th and 54th High-Speed Bomber Air Regiments to assimilate the Ar-2 and to commence their dive-bombing training.

The gap in assimilation of the MiG-1 and MiG-3 was not the fault of the district command but was due to design defects and the poor technical condition of the new aircraft and was a consequence of the decision taken by the Principal Directorate of the Red Army Air Force to divert personnel away from their training so they could participate in the parade.

There is almost no doubt that if their units had retained their previous line-up, the Air Forces of the Baltic Special Military District would have been able to come close to achieving the tasks set out in decree No. 0020 issued by the People's Commissariat for Defence for 1941.

Events however began to unfold in line with the organisational and mobilisation measures described above, which were set out by the leadership of the country and the Army for 1941. In essence May was the last month in which the Red Army Air Force undertook full-scale combat training, and by the end of the month the mass transfer of personnel to the newly formed units had commenced.

It was in this same month that the process of formation began to gather speed and the new regiments began to acquire a specific outline, after having been formed first and foremost by transferring commanders and pilots.

Back on 27 March the process of appointing the commanders and their deputies for the regiments that were in the process of being formed was underway. Furthermore, despite the initial text of the directive, they were all drawn from the cadres of the Air Forces of the Baltic Special Military District.

Thus the Commander of the 236th Fighter Air Regiment Major P.A. Antonets was made Commander of the 1st Squadron of the 148th Fighter Air Regiment. The Commander of the 237th Fighter Air Regiment was to be the former pilot's competency inspector of the 6th Mixed Air Division, Captain I.P. Suvorov. The Commander of the 238th Fighter Air Regiment was to be the Assistant Commander of the 31st Fighter Air Regiment Major A.I. Syrov. The 239th Fighter Air Regiment Commander was to be the former Squadron Commander of the 42nd Fighter Air Regiment Captain A.I. Kurochkin. The Commander of the 240th Fighter Air Regiment was to be the Deputy Commander of the 42nd Fighter Air Regiment Major A.F. Obukhov.

At around the same time the strata of commanders in the district's formations was significantly 'purged' and out of the four deputy divisional commanders two of them were withdrawn and promoted to higher-ranking positions. The Deputy Commander of the 4th Mixed Air Division Brigade Commander A.N. Sokolov was made Divisional Commander in place of the outgoing General I.G. Pyatykhin. The Deputy Commander of the 6th Mixed Air Division Colonel V.A. Kitayev departed for the Transcaucasian Military District for the post of Commander of the 72nd Mixed Air Division. Only the Deputy Commander of the 8th Mixed Air Division Lieutenant-Colonel I.V. Yakubovich remained at his post.

It has to be said that it was the best pilots and commanders that were promoted, many of whom subsequently honoured by the Red Army Air Force. Thus out of the six who were made regimental commanders, three of them—Suvorov, Kurochkin, and Obukhov went on to become generals, and of the three who had just been appointed divisional commanders, they all went on to become generals.

Some time later on 15 April decrees were signed for those who had been appointed to the rank of squadron commanders, and naturally they were drawn exclusively from the ranks of the pilots of the Air Forces of the Baltic Special Military District.

This process reached an apogee at the end of May, and on 16 May the largest group of pilots in the regular units received their new postings to the ranks of deputy squadron commanders and flight commanders in the newly formed units.

After these reshuffles by 1 June only 35–40 experienced pilots remained in each of the regular regiments. It was entirely predictable that in accordance with standard document No. 15/21, to which the fighter aviation regiments were transferred, it was proposed that there should be 35 pilots in a Fighter Air Regiment that held command positions, from regimental commander to flight commander:

> Three of these were to be in the regimental directorate;
> Three each in the directorates of each of the four squadrons, so 12 men in total;
> There were to be a further five flight commanders in each in every squadron, so 20 men in total.

Naturally internal changes in personnel commenced in the units themselves: the flight commanders moved into the deputy squadron commander's positions, and the rank and file pilots took their places in turn. Thus many of the leaders mentioned above had themselves only graduated from flying school one year earlier, so in order to enhance their level of training the leadership of these divisions again arranged training courses for flight commanders that were drawn up under the formation headquarters. Correspondingly the sergeant pilots who had graduated from flying schools filled the positions left vacant by the rank and file pilots.

Thus in May in the 49th Fighter Air Regiment some 13 sergeant pilots, who had graduated in 1941, joined the 49th Fighter Air Regiment while 10 each joined the 21st and 38th Fighter Air Regiments. Unfortunately no accurate information exists regarding the other regiments but the assertion can be made with complete confidence that in the spring almost all the units in the district welcomed sergeant pilots, who had graduated in 1941, by way of augmentation.

At the beginning of June the majority of the newly appointed pilots left their units for their new postings, and their places were taken steadily by young pilots. The combat line-up in these units looked almost exactly the same as it had done in the winter, however if the quantitative indicators had not moved anywhere in comparison with January, then the qualitative indicator had certainly changed and not for the better.

As a result of the organisational and mobilisation measures that had been implemented experienced fighter pilots in regular units ended up being 'spread' around the 13 regiments and in fact should have formed a pool of instructors. Correspondingly in the course of the spring a significant number of regular personnel left the bomber regiments for new formations in other districts, while their places were taken by sergeants, pilots, and pilot observers. In the majority of units it was a struggle to fill two to three squadrons with trained personnel. For example regular pilots were moved from the 46th High-Speed Bomber Air Regiment into the 2nd, 3rd, and 5th Squadrons, and in the 54th High-Speed Bomber Air Regiment they were moved into the 3rd, 4th, and 5th Air Squadrons. The rest of the units welcomed young pilots drawn from the spring augmentation.

Apart from that gunner-radio operators began to join bomber regiments, who had graduated from the School of Junior Aviation Specialists in May 1941, the level of training of these gunner-radio operators left something to be desired. The Headquarters Director of the Air Forces of the Baltic Special Military District Brigade Commander Krupin reported the following:

On 20 May of this year the School of Junior Aviation Specialists released their graduates and they were sent to their units as gunners-radio-operators. They had undergone an accelerated training programme, where they received the minimum theoretical and practical knowledge of the art of warfare.

They can only become fully-fledged specialists when, in line with their practical work lectures in theory are organised for them in their specialist field.

The Commander of the Air Forces of the Baltic Special Military District has decreed the following:

That groups be formed of 10–15 individuals in the regiments and individual squadrons for the gunner/radio-operators who graduated in 1941, and that the responsibility for their training be placed on the shoulders of the regimental commanders as well as on the individual squadrons. Lectures should be arranged in the following disciplines:

1. Improving knowledge of the armament and of the radio equipment
2. To learn how to prepare the armament for firing in flight taking into account different meteorological conditions
3. Practice in bomb loading
4. How to acquire an expert knowledge of the calculations required for firing on air and ground targets as well as completing all the ground based firing exercises (on a firing range)
5. Improving practical work on the radio sets, by conducting interactive lectures in radio communication and in how to establish communication independently.
6. Improve aural reception and knowledge of transmitting using a key

The most adverse situation occurred in the 15th and 31st Fighter Air Regiments, where as a result of the transfer of regular personnel, the pilots who had with such difficulty graduated onto the MiG-1 and MiG-3 were transferred on equal terms to the newly formed units. As a result, by 1 June only 30 of the pilots who had been trained before the end of March remained in the 31st Fighter Air Regiment, and furthermore only 14 had completed the conversion programme. In connection with this the 4th Squadron was comprised entirely of trained personnel, whereas the 1st and 2nd received an approximately equal number of the remainder, the 3rd squadron did not operate the new aircraft at all, and their young pilots were trained on the UTI-4 and the I-16.

Still fewer pilots who had assimilated the new aircraft remained in the 15th Fighter Air Regiment. Of the 26 pilots who had completed their solo in the MiG-1 in the March there were only 14 left by 1 June, and in fact the only sub-division in the regiment in which all the MiG-3 pilots were concentrated remained the first squadron. The second squadron in the regiment continued their training on the I-153, while the 3rd and 4th led by several commanders began to train the young pilots on the UTI-4 and the I-16.

Specifically by 1 June 1941 both the 'old' and 'new' regiments had received their young pilots in place of their regular personnel and were in fact in the process of formation since they were forced to break the units in and introduce the young pilots to operations. Thus as a result of these measures not only were the newly formed but also the regular units, which had attained a more or less acceptable level of combat training by the end of May, forced to start the whole training process again from scratch. The commanders of the 15th and 31st Fighter Air Regiment also needed to start the whole process of conversion onto the MiG-3 all over again.

To the commanders of the Air Forces of the Baltic Special Military District's credit it should be noted that in the situation that had developed the commanders at all levels did attempt to complete the tasks that were put before them, and took very sensible and decisive measures.

Aside from the combat training the main tasks remained introducing the young pilots to operations, and conversion of the units on to new aircraft. In order to meet the first requirement a methodology had already been developed by the district Air Forces, which had been used successfully at the beginning of the year. In order to optimise and accelerate the tempo of the conversion onto the newest aircraft, however, a decision was taken to create two study centres, that the personnel in these units could pass through.

A fighter aviation aircrew conversion centre was set up in Siauliai on the 10th Fighter Air Regiment's base, and the pilot competency inspector of the Air Forces of the Baltic Special Military District Lieutenant-Colonel V.V. Sukhoryabov was appointed leader. The leadership of the 148th Fighter Air Regiment, totalling eight people in all, had converted onto the MiG-3 by the beginning of June. In the middle of the month however some 18 pilots arrived in Siauliai to undergo conversion, and for the most part they were squadron commanders and their deputies from the 42nd Fighter Air Regiment led by the Deputy Commander of the regiment, the future twice Hero of the Soviet Union V.A. Zaytsev.

On the airfield at Jelgava, however, a bomber and reconnaissance crew conversion centre had been in the process of being set up since the beginning of June. By 1 July 1941 the 46th High-Speed Bomber Air Regiment and the 312th Reconnaissance Air Regiment were due to commence flying at this centre on the Pe-2, and the conversion of air observation squadron personnel onto the SB was due to commence on that same day.

Apart from that, in accordance with the 'conversion programme' the personnel of the 9th and 54th High-Speed Bomber Air Regiments commenced their conversion at the Air Force Scientific Research Institute. Some five pilots from the 9th High-Speed Bomber Air Regiment underwent conversion, while another three from the 54th High-Speed Bomber Air Regiment also completed conversion. Apart from that, between the end of May–beginning of June four squadron commanders from the 40th High-Speed Bomber Air Regiment were sent to Moscow to undergo conversion training, along with the Regimental Commander Major Mogilevskiy. The commanders of the 61st Ground Attack Air Regiment Major Mamushkin and four squadron commanders, who succeeded in converting onto the Il-2 at the 1st Airbase District and accept five Il-2s from Factory No. 18. They saw in the first morning of the war in Vilnius, where they had spent the night on their long flight from Voronezh to Kedainiai.

On a regimental level the commanders were also trying to find the optimum structure for these units. For example in the 15th and 31st Fighter Air Regiments the remainder of the personnel who had already undergone conversion were not scattered thinly across all the squadrons, but were concentrated in the 1st Squadron of the 15th Fighter Air Regiment and the 4th Squadron of the 31st Fighter Air Regiment. This was in order that these sub-divisions at least could complete the full course of combat training planned for 1941.

The commanders of these formations gave their subordinate units specific tasks. Thus by way of a decree on the combat training tasks for the summer period the headquarters of the 8th Mixed Air Division were allocated the following—each crew should in the space of a month have achieved the following:

12 aerial firings;
six mock dogfights;
four bombing runs;
four cross-country flights.

On each of these flights the pilots were instructed to maintain radio contact with their unit's headquarters.

Furthermore the command of these formations were very realistic in assessing the capabilities of these young pilots. Only the regular squadrons in the 15th and 31st Fighter Air Regiments were instructed to undergo the maximum combat training course in the same year. The rest of the formations only needed to complete combat training in accordance with the second task of the combat training course No. 41, that is to say to train the squadron for combat in favourable weather conditions at all altitudes and to develop formation flying as a nine ship.

The Commander of the 8th Mixed Air Division Colonel Gushchin set the following tasks for the month of June: the regular pilots were to commence combat training in the MiG-3, and the entire cohort of young pilots were to complete their solo on the MiGs.

It has to be said, however, that in any case the capabilities of these units were nowhere near what they had been at the beginning of the year, and the small number of the experienced commanders who remained in these regular units began to be overloaded as a result of the pressure. Judging by the number of incidents and their nature the personnel suffered a decisive breakdown at the beginning of June.

Thus on 2 June in Kaunas the newly trained Flight Commander of the 4th Squadron of the 31st Fighter Air Regiment Lieutenant G.I. Gagushin taxied into an unserviceable MiG-3 on the runway. The pilot's hours up until that point on the MiG-3 amounted to four hrs 34 mins (just 33 landings).

On 6 June several accidents happened at once involving experienced deputy squadron commanders in the 15th Fighter Air Regiment:

The Deputy Squadron Commander Senior Lieutenant T.D. Kuzmin, an experienced pilot who had amassed 350 hrs, lost speed on a gliding descent into land and his MiG-3 fell from an altitude of one to one and a half metres onto the runway, and one of the wings broke off.

The Deputy Commander of the 4th Squadron Senior Lieutenant V.A. Voronov, who by this time had amassed seven hrs 23 mins (across 37 flights, with 640 flying hours in total) forgot to switch the fuel from the main to the centre-fuselage tank, and as a result as he came into land the engine failed and the aircraft, after losing speed, fell onto the runway from an altitude of three metres. The two sides of the MiG-3 were damaged, and in addition the undercarriage and propeller needed to be replaced, but nevertheless the aircraft was repairable.

The Deputy Commander of the 1st Squadron, Senior Lieutenant V.S. Martynenko, during a training flight with one of the young pilots in the UTI-4 ,'stayed up too long', and after using all the fuel landed back at the airfield with the engine having stopped, although in this case the aircraft was not damaged.

Interestingly Senior Lieutenant Voronov was also training young pilots in the UTI-4 prior to his sortie in the MiG, and even after that when he was making his second flight in the MiG-3 he forgot to switch the fuel feed from the main tank to the centre-fuselage tank. In any case the double pressure over the course of the first six months of the year on regular pilots, who took young pilots up for training flights, and in the second half of the day flew independently, made itself known—people were overwhelmed.

On 7 June it was the turn of the 31st Fighter Air Regiment and the Commander of the 4th Squadron Senior Lieutenant Kovshikov, just like Voronov, forgot to switch the fuel feed from the main tank to the centre-fuselage tank. As a result of which the engine failed and the pilot made an emergency landing back at the airfield, the aircraft was not damaged.

On 9 June a catastrophe occurred in the 35th High-Speed Bomber Air Regiment, as a result of a miscalculation on landing the aircraft flown by the Flight Commander of the 5th Squadron Senior Lieutenant P.N. Rabinovich, an experienced pilot who had amassed over 600 hrs, crashed. The Gunner/Radio-Operator Sergeant Venikov was not hurt, but the Navigator Lieutenant A.A. Popov was killed. According to the report on the accident the SB was in need of an overhaul, but German photographs of Tartu airfield testify that the aircraft was written off and broken up for spares.

On that same day, and in that very unit, as a result of a loss of orientation in cloud, Lieutenant Poddubniy's aircraft narrowly avoided a catastrophe. As he was trying to break through the cloud the Lieutenant miscalculated the angle and speed of his dive and whilst attempting to pull the aircraft out of a dive the outer skin on the sides was deformed.

These extraordinary events continued right up until the beginning of the war. Thus on 17 June during his second solo in the MiG-3 the Commander of the 2nd Squadron of the 42nd Fighter Air Regiment Captain G.A. Panteleyev was killed on Siauliai airfield.

Nevertheless, despite these difficulties the 'mechanism' of the Air Forces of the Baltic Special Military District continued to operate, although it was creaking. Although the young pilots would remind the air forces periodically of the shortcomings in their training, a positive outlook was on the horizon.

It is gratifying to note that not only did the young pilots fly relatively often but by June they had even begun to undertake air combat training flights. Thanks to a fortunate set of circumstances even the young personnel were able to complete the requirements of decree No. 0020 issued by the People's Commissariat for Defence, at least on the 'old' aircraft types, which is not difficult to ascertain looking at the results of combat training.

In accordance with the chronicle of events that took place in the Air Forces of the Baltic Special Military District in the first five months of 1941 it is easy to note that the units, which were due to convert onto the new aircraft in the first quarter of 1941 were able to achieve well deserved results in their combat training by 1 June, and were realistic candidates for fulfilling the tasks put before them in terms of combat training and the training of their young personnel in the course of 1941. Specifically those units that were not involved in the conversion process achieved an excellent level of combat training: the 40th High-Speed Bomber Air Regiment and the 38th Fighter Air Regiment. On the other hand one of the leaders in combat training in 1940 the 31st Fighter Air Regiment, which was the first to commence conversion onto the new aircraft in 1941 amassed only 700 hrs, which was a record low, and by the beginning of the summer the regiment was not combat capable.

The plans put forward by the Soviet command for the fulfilment of the organisational and mobilisation measures, and for the conversion onto the 'new' materiel in 1941, were already falling apart at the seams by the end of May.

The first blow was the fact that the factories were not able to establish a rhythmic production pattern for the 'newest' aircraft. In the end not only did reconnaissance and army aviation in this district not receive their 'newest' Yak-4 aircraft right up until the summer, but they did not receive the specified number of serviceable combat aircraft either that were stipulated in the standards, and they actually dropped out of combat training.

Apart from that even those aircraft that were, it seemed, established in production, suffered from such a number of design shortcomings that a significant amount of time was required for their eradication, and some of them could not be eradicated at all without a factory repair. For example owing to poor workmanship and the multitude of design shortcomings in the MiG-1 and MiG-3 fighters two of the best fighter regiments in the district were practically withdrawn from the combat training process for almost two months from April–the end of May 1941. As subsequent results were to demonstrate the issue of the technical reliability of the new aircraft and engines was not solved in 1941, and even if the German invasion had not happened, legitimate doubts arose concerning the successful continuation of combat training in those regiments that received their new aircraft between June–July 1941. Particularly considering the fact that almost all the units were to receive these new aircraft, and that the level of training for their personnel fell sharply owing to the arrival of newly qualified graduates from flying schools.

The second blow was the plan for the roll-out of the new units and formations, which was realised in May and led to the regular units being reformed. The main victims of this were again the units that were training their personnel on the new aircraft. Specifically this relates to the 15th and 31st Fighter Air Regiments In the Baltic Special Military District, where the sergeant-pilots together with very recent graduates from the aviation technical colleges were to arrive, following the departure of trained pilots. That is to say the conversion process had to be conducted all over again and only then could the regiments set about the planned combat training, which these units had not undertaken for almost the entire first half of the year, owing to the conversion programme.

The state of play with respect to the augmentation of the rest of the units with sufficient numbers of personnel was also at a critical level. For example if at the start of the year there was a basic skeleton, then only 30–40 men were left in each of them by 22 June. Approximately 20–40 percent of the regular personnel were withdrawn from the 'old' units as a result of the organisational and mobilisation measures and in their place the regiment was populated by graduate pilots from the flying schools. After the reduction of the regular pilots in the old regiments and their replacement with young pilots and the formation of new units formed of 'semi-trained' pilots who had just graduated from the flying schools it would have been much harder to organise the conversion process and the combat training than it would have been it the beginning of 1941, when there were 50–60 regular pilots in each of the regiments. Now the regiments were in the main comprised of young pilots, who still needed to be introduced to operations and, to put it simply, to be taught how to fly as well as converting onto the MiG-3 and Pe-2 almost without a break, and these were aircraft that even regular pilots found it hard to assimilate. How much time was spent on this could be judged by the similar springtime training provided to pilots who had graduated in 1940, which required between five to six months of training in the units themselves in order to commence combat training drills on the I-153, and I-16. To hope that the pilots who had graduated in 1941 and who had received inferior training would be able to set about combat training more quickly, and furthermore on the MiG-3 and the Pe-2, would have been simply naïve.

In actual fact by 1 June 1941 it became obvious that the timescales for re-equipping these units with new aircraft and for the roll-out of the new units had been disrupted. Saddest of all was the fact that the failure of these measures coupled with the ongoing problems with the technical condition of the materiel, put the process of combat training for the Red Army Air Force in 1941 under threat of disruption.

2.2 Air Force Logistics, Airfield Construction and the Air Defence System of the Baltic Special Military District in 1941

In the spring of 1941 the Red Army Air Force's aviation logistics system was augmented with new units, and in the Baltics this occurred within the confines of the roll-out of new units and formations in accordance with the directive issued by the People's Commissariat for Defence dated 24 January 1941. Airbases were required for the five newly formed fighter and one ground attack air regiment, which began to develop along with the regiments that were within their field of responsibility. By 1 June the 86th (responsible for the 236th Fighter Air Regiment), the 87th (the 237th Fighter Air Regiment), the 88th (the 238th Fighter Air Regiment), the 89th (the 239th Fighter Air Regiment), the 92nd (the 240th Fighter Air Regiment), and the 93rd (the 241st Ground Attack Air Regiment) airbases were in the initial stages of development and were only just beginning to be equipped with technology and with men.

Meanwhile the reforms had only just begun—at a meeting of the Commanders of the Air Force in January 1941 on the basis of the experience gained in the Soviet-Finnish War requirements were drawn up for the formation of an aviation logistics system, the requirements for which were attached to the decree issued by the People's Commissariat for Defence on 10 April 1941:

1. To acknowledge that the existing aviation logistics system does not facilitate manoeuvres, or the supply of aviation units both in peacetime, and especially in wartime. This system is completely unprepared for the transition from a peacetime to a wartime footing and in connection with this, for the redeployment of forces where necessary from one direction to another, or even a simple dispersal to forward airfields requires a great deal of time for the aviation logistics to attain combat readiness in anticipation of access to its bases.

2. Obligate the People's Commissariat for Defence to:
   a) Reconstruct the aviation logistics system to ensure its is able to remain at a permanent combat readiness to support the Air Force's combat operations from operational airfields;
   b) To make the aviation logistics system territorial on the basis of the following:
      i. Set up regional airbases in the border regions;
      ii. These regions should be structured as follows:
         A regional directorate with a view to this office serving three to four aviation divisions,
         Airbases with a view to them supporting one aviation division each,
   c) Put the proposal for the regional airbases, the administrative structure of an airbase itself, and the transfer to a new logistics system to the Committee for Defence under the Council of People's Commissars for approval by 15 March 1941.
   d) Complete the transfer onto a new logistics system by 1 July 1941.

In accordance with the decree issued by the Council of People's Commissars and the directive, the Red Army Air Force logistics were to consist of four regional airbases—the 8th, 9th, 10th, and 11th.

The 8th Regional airbase with its regional department in Tartu was to consist of the following:

The directorate and the 8th Signals Company, the 23rd, 24th, and 25th Anti-Aircraft Artillery Batteries and the 19th, 20th, 21st, and 22nd Airbases.

In turn the 19th Airbase would consist of a directorate, and the 199th Communications Company, and the 84th, 85th, 86th, and 87th Airfield Logistics Battalions.

The 20th Airbase consisted of a regional office, as well as the 120th Signals Company, and the 88th, 89th, 90th, and 91st Airfield Logistics Battalions.

The 21st Airbase consisted of a directorate, as well as the 121st Signals Company, and the 92nd, 93rd, 94th, and 95th Airfield Logistics Battalions.

The 22nd Airbase consisted of a directorate, as well as the 122nd Signals Company, and the 96th, 97th, 98th, and the 99th Airfield Logistics Battalions.

Out of the 12 newly formed airfield logistics battalions only four of them were reformed from the old airbases, the rest of the units needed to be formed from scratch using the personnel in the units and formations within the district.

The 88th Airfield Logistics Battalion was formed on the basis of the former 123rd old formation airbase and the 63rd High-Speed Bomber Air Regiment.

The 89th Airfield Logistics Battalion was formed on the basis of the former 38th old formation airbase and the 38th Fighter Air Regiment.

The 90th Airfield Logistics Battalion was formed on the basis of the former 20th old formation airbase and the 50th High-Speed Bomber Air Regiment

The 96th Airfield Logistics Battalion was formed on the basis of the former 44th old formation airbase and the 35th High-Speed Bomber Air Regiment.

The 9th Regional Airbase with its directorate located in Riga was structured as follows: A directorate with the 9th Signals Company, as well as the 26th and 27th Anti-Aircraft Batteries, the 5th and 15th Air Engineering Battalions, and the 23rd and 24th Airbases.

The 23rd Airbase consisted of a directorate, as well as the 123rd Communications Company, and the 100th, 101st, 102nd, 103rd, 104th, 105th, and 106th Airfield Logistics Battalions.

The 24th Airbase consisted of a directorate and the 124th Communications Company and the 107th Airfield Logistics Battalion.

All the airfield logistics battalions in this district were formed from the old airbases, of which only two (the 89th, and the 93rd) were new formations, while the rest were regular units. The 208th (the 21st Fighter Air Regiment), the 119th (the 148th Fighter Air Regiment), the 89th (the 239th Fighter Air Regiment), the 138th (the 40th High-Speed Bomber Air Regiment), the 116th (the 31st High-Speed Bomber Air Regiment), the 122nd (the 7th Long-Range Air Regiment), the 93rd (the 241st Ground Attack Air Regiment), and the 201st (the 49th Fighter Air Regiment) old formation airbases were reformed into the 100th, 101st, 102nd, 103rd, 104th, 105th, 106th, and 107th Airfield Logistics Battalions respectively.

The 10th Regional Air Base in Siauliai consisted of the following: a directorate and the 10th Signals Company as well as the 28th, 29th, 30th, and 31st Anti-Aircraft Artillery Batteries, the 3rd Air Engineering Battalion, as well as the 25th, 26th, and 27th Airbases.

The 25th Airbase consisted of a directorate, as well as the 125th Signals Company and the 109th, 110th, 111th, and the 122nd Airfield Logistics Battalions.

The 26th Airbase consisted of a directorate, as well as the 126th Communications Company and the 113th, 114th, 115th, and 116th Airfield Logistics Battalions.

The 27th Airbase consisted of a directorate, as well as the 127th Communications Company, and the 117th, 118th, 119th, and 120th Airfield Logistics Battalions.

Of the 12 newly formed airfield logistics battalions half of them had been reformed from the airbases, as well as four old and two newly formed battalions, and a further six battalions had to be formed from scratch.

The 109th Airfield Logistics Battalion was formed on the basis of the former 88th, an old formation airbase, and the 238th Fighter Air Regiment.

The 110th Airfield Logistics Battalion was formed on the basis of the former 13th old formation airbase and the 9th High-Speed Bomber Air Regiment.

The 111th Airfield Logistics Battalion was formed on the basis of the former 127th old formation airbase and the 46th High-Speed Bomber Air Regiment.

The 112th Airfield Logistics Battalion was formed on the basis of the former 206th old formation airbase, and the 10th Fighter Air Regiment.

The 117th Airfield Logistics Battalion was formed on the basis of the former 92nd old formation airbase and the 240th Fighter Air Regiment.

The 118th Airfield Logistics Battalion was formed on the basis of the former 140th old formation airbase and the 61st Fighter Air Regiment.

The 11th Regional Airbase in Kaunas was structured as follows: A directorate and the 11th Signals Company as well as the 32nd, 33rd, 34th, and 35th Anti-Aircraft Artillery Battalions, the 12th and 14th Air Engineering Battalions, and the 28th, 29th, and 30th Airbases.

The 28th Airbase consisted of a directorate, as well as the 128th Signals Company as well as the 121st, 122nd, 123rd, and 124th Airfield Logistics Battalions.

The 29th Airbase consisted of a directorate, and the 130th Communications Company as well as the 126th, 127th, 128th, and 129th Airfield Logistics Battalions.

The 30th Airbase consisted of a directorate, and the 130th Signals Company, and the 129th, 130th, 131st, 132nd Airfield Servicing Battalions.

Some of the airfield logistics battalions were reformed from airbases, four old and two newly formed bases, while the rest of the battalions were formed anew.

The 125th Airfield Logistics Battalion was formed on the basis of the former 110th airbase and the 54th High-Speed Bomber Air Regiment.

The 126th Airfield Logistics Battalion was formed on the basis of the former 204th airbase and the 42nd Fighter Air Regiment.

The 127th Airfield Logistics Battalion was formed on the basis of the former 87th airbase and the 237th Fighter Air Regiment.

The 128th Airfield Logistics Battalion was formed on the basis of the former 86th airbase and the 236th Fighter Air Regiment.

The 129th Airfield Logistics Battalion was formed on the basis of the former 213th airbase and the 31st Fighter Air Regiment.

The 130th Airfield Logistics Battalion was formed on the basis of the former 25th airbase and the 15th Fighter Air Regiment.

Apart from that 34 (Nos. 112–145) Airfield Servicing Companies were formed to clean the snow off the airfields.

An enormous amount of equipment as well as trained specialists was required to form this number of new units, which could not all be found at once. Even for the 19 battalions that had been formed from the airbases there was only enough equipment and men to man the units on a peacetime footing. In some locations however it was only possible to populate the newly formed units, in the best-case scenario, by the end of 1941.

Another problem, which was not solved even after the introduction of the changes to the logistical system, was the lack of technical specialists on the payroll of the air regiments. The point being that, for example, in accordance with the standard documentation for fighter air regiments (15/21), which had been introduced in April of that year in a regiment consisting of 63 fighters only 40 armourers were envisaged, even though this figure was completely inadequate. Crucially, the leadership of the Red Army Air Force were well aware of this.

The problems with the lack of armourers in a regiment's line-up were documented as a result of the fighting for Khalkhin-Gol and the Soviet-Finnish War, when on occasion some of the personnel had to step in to prepare the armament for an aircraft. During the course of the Soviet-Finnish War even the wives of the personnel in the 54th Air Brigade were drafted in to load the belts with shells. For reasons that remain unclear, despite the fact that the standards were changed in the period between 1940–1941 these shortcomings were not eradicated and the number of armourers was never increased.

Red Army Air Force units remained on a peacetime footing and were brought as close as possible to a wartime footing, to say nothing of the Air Force logistics. The peacetime footing contrasts sharply with that of a wartime footing and this circumstance, particularly in the case of a sudden enemy attack, put an aviation regiment in a vulnerable position. The reason for this is that meeting the demands during the course of combat operations with an airfield logistics battalion on a peacetime footing, and especially one that is not at full strength, would have been difficult to fulfil.

As already noted above in the previous section, the airfield construction plan for 1940 was not fulfilled and the work was due to be completed in 1941. Moreover the work was to have been completed within the confines of Directive No. 103151/op dated 28 September 1940 on the operational airfield construction plan for 1941.

> The Red Army Air Force airfield network, as a result of the border of the Soviet Union moving westwards, proved insufficient in terms of ensuring that the Air Force was based in the most important directions.
>
> The operational airfield construction plan for 1940, were it implemented in full, would in any case still not meet the needs of the Air Force in terms of operational airfields, particularly in the Soviet Union's newest republics and districts. Therefore the main task for the construction of airfields in 1941 would be to ensure that the decisive directions are provided with an adequate number of airfields on which the Air Force units would be based taking into account their possible augmentation.
>
> The construction of operational airfields in 1941 is to be conducted in accordance with the attached list. First and foremost the airfields that are to be built for fighter aviation should be constructed within a radius of up to 80 km from the border. All measures are to be taken to ensure that the plan for 1940 for the construction of new airfields be completed in full and that the only construction that is to be rolled-over into 1941 should be the retrofitting of these airfields in accordance with the tactical-technical requirements.

In accordance with this document the construction or redevelopment of 357 operational airfields was proposed across the entire USSR, including 47 in the Baltic Special Military District:

12 in Estonia
Eight in Latvia
27 in Lithuania

Interestingly in the Baltics the special prison squads from the People's Commissariat for Internal Affairs were not drafted in for the construction of the airfields. The 29 airfields would, it was proposed, be constructed by the five air engineering battalions already in the district and the rest were to be constructed with the help of civilian organisations.

This however was just the start of the process and by December 1940 a highly ambitious plan had been developed for the construction and redevelopment of the concrete runways formulated in directive No. 103640/op drawn up by the Headquarters Director and dated 17 December 1940.

> TO THE DIRECTOR OF THE PRINCIPAL DIRECTORATE OF THE AIR FORCE LIEUTENANT-GENERAL OF AVIATION COMRADE RYCHAGOV.
>
> THE PEOPLE'S COMMISSAR FOR DEFENCE HAS DECREED THAT:
> Your proposals to ensure the availability of flying operations all year round, including the winter and spring muddy periods be developed and presented within a 20-day timescale. The following should be used as a basis for the development of these proposals:
>
> 1. All available means must be employed to reduce the periods in which the airfields are out of action in the winter and spring by means of organising the necessary work to clear the airfields of snow in the winter. It is incumbent upon you to examine the question of bringing the airfields up to an acceptable operational standard as soon as possible in the spring, and to link this issue to cleaning the airfields of snow in winter.

Table 7 The provision of special equipment by the airfield logistics battalions in accordance with the standards and the actual situation

	Acc. to standard	Availability as of 1 April 1940	Shortage	To be delivered in 1941		Expected availability as of 1 April 1942	% of provision
				In the 3rd quarter	In the 4th quarter		
Refuelling vehicles	266	160	106	25	61	246	92
Oil and water servicing trucks	177	132	45	15	15	162	92
Automatic starters	167	126	41	10	31	167	100
Water spillage trucks	52	27	25	5	2	34	65
Fuel trucks	81	39	42	3	39	81	100
Tractor hauled fuel trucks	266	94	172	–	–	94	35
Mobile aircraft repair workshop	62	31	31	11	14	56	90
Compressor units	42	22	20	12	10	44	105
Photo processing truck (field)	90	48	42	18	10	76	84
Searchlight truck (for airfield brigades)	25	14	11	–	–	14	56
Searchlight trucks (for landing)	71	1	70	6	19	26	36
Searchlight trucks (for the airfield lighting service	48	2	46	12	23	37	80
Mobile weather trucks	48	14	34	3	–	17	35
AZS-1 Mobile charging stations	52	–	52	–	20	20	40
Al-6 Charging assemblies	9	15	None	–	–	15	167

Table 8 The provision of vehicular transport by the airfield logistics battalion according to the standards and the actual situation

	Acc. to the standard	Availability as of 1 April 1941	To be delivered in the 2nd quarter	To be delivered in the 3rd quarter	To be delivered in the 4th quarter
Light vehicles and pickups	344	91	15	194	41
Trucks weighing 1.5 tonnes	633	399	57	133	44
Trucks weighing between 3–5 tonnes	867	336	42	305	184
Buses	176	34	62	61	19
Mobile workshops	44	8	11	16	9
Refrigerated trucks	53	15	11	18	9
Vehicular transport as a whole	2,117	883			
Heavy tracked tractor vehicles	643	501	49	295	147
Light tracked tractor vehicles	349				
Tractors as a whole	992	501			

2. In order to ensure normal fighter and long-range bomber operations all year round, and also to ensure that these aircraft are able to operate at their maximum range, the construction of concrete runways needs to be examined as well as the issue of lengthening the runways in the existing airfields.

3. Two runways that are one kilometre in length and 150 m wide should be constructed on each of the airfields. The dimensions of the airfields should be up to 1.5 * 1.5 km. The construction of the runways and the expansion of the existing runways and airfields should be completed in 1941.

4. Aside from the completion of the work listed above the execution of the simplest measures should also be examined within your proposals that ensure year round flying operations at other permanent and operational airfields, such as: grass seeding, drainage, and asphalting of the runways, and so on.

5. When drawing up the calculations for the Western theatre of operations the number of permanent and operational airfields that in terms of the condition of their surfaces ensure year round flying operations without any interruptions needs to be taken into account.

   The plan for the construction and the calculations for the required funding and materials must be presented to me by 25 January 1941.

   The work must be prioritised as follows: the first priority should be the western border, the second priority should be the near eastern front, while the far eastern front should be the third priority.

In accordance with this plan the construction of 66 and the redevelopment of 20 concrete runways, as well as the construction of 81 macadam runways was envisaged across the entire territory of the USSR. Of these seven concrete, and six macadam runways were to be constructed in the Baltic region.

However since the measures specified in the decrees issued by the Council of People's Deputies and the Central Committee of the All-Union Communist Party (of Bolsheviks) No. P28/5 dated 25 February 1941 were yet to be started, the plans were reworked in favour of expanding the existing number of airfields and runways and were finally specified on 27 February 1941 in the 'Proposals for Ordering the Construction of Concrete Runways on the Airfields of the Red Army Air Force in 1941', which was signed by the Chief of the General Staff Zhukov and the Director of the Principal Directorate of the Red Army Air Force Rychagov.

On 1 March 1941 the new list of 240 airfields, on which it was proposed concrete runways would be constructed, was affirmed by the People's Commissar for Defence Marshal Timoshenko and furthermore all this work needed to be completed in 1941. Within the Baltic Special Military District itself 23 new concrete runways were to be constructed at the following locations: Vilnius (Parubanek), Riga (Greater Riga), Keidany (Kedainiai) Panevezys, Vaijnode, Raseiniai, Sirava, Telsiai, Ezere, Tarelki, Gluda (near Mitava), Slapaberze, Vindava (Pautskule), Bauska, Rumbula, Krustpils, Daugavpils (Zastenki), Kaupernieki, Vohma, Kuusiku, Ungru, Tapa, Tartu. Some of these runways, it was proposed, would be constructed on nine permanent airfields, while the rest were either designed for operational sites, or on completely new airfields. The final plan for the construction of concrete runways was appended to a directive issued by the Council of People's Deputies dated 24 March 1941.

On 3 March however changes to the directive dated 28 September 1940 were affirmed in accordance with which the construction of 164 new operational airfields was envisaged (of which

19 were constructed by the People's Commissariat for Internal Affairs) as well as 258 for which construction was brought forward, of which 46 were to be in the Baltic Region, and the construction of all of these was brought forward.

This however was still not the end—by 10 April in accordance with a new decree issued by the Council of People's Deputies a decision was taken in 1941 to construct an additional 365 operational airfields, and a further 11 were to be redeveloped. Thus in the whole of 1941 some 798 operational airfields were to be constructed or redeveloped, of these 539 were new and 258 were in the process of construction. Apart from fuel storage tanks, warehouses, and wells were to be constructed on 137 of the existing airfields. In total by the end of 1941 there were to be 1,818 Red Army airfields across the entire territory of the USSR, of which 275 were to be permanent and 1,543 were to be operational. These large-scale measures were conducted in accordance with the transfer of the Red Army Air Force to a new organisational basis, which proposed a transfer to a territorial basing system.

In the Baltic Special Military District an additional 20 operational airfields were to be constructed, of which four were to be in the area around Tallinn, seven in the Siauliai area, and nine in the Kaunas area. In total by the end of the year there were to be 91 functional airfields in this district.

Despite the fact that at many sites construction had begun back in 1940 even the preparatory work (establishing legal rights over the land, the topographical survey and design work) had still not been completed. By way of an example in the Baltic region the personnel of five air engineering battalions had started work at just 21 operational airfields by 20 May. The personnel of the 3rd Air Engineering Brigade built the airfields at Skvarbay, Kroky, Risgonis (Vepriai), and Markshtava. The 5th Air Engineering Battalion constructed the airfields at Poltsaama, Platone, Birzai, and Liksna. The 12th Air Engineering Battalion constructed the airfields at Preliai, Potsunai, Karmelava, Kivishki, and Kryzhaki. The 14th Air Engineering Brigade constructed the airfields at Gruzdziai, Nemaksciai, Girenai, and Rietavas. The 15th Air Engineering Brigade the airfields at Pautkulie, Dijdame, Peleki, and Guaduchie.

Apart from that, in March permission was given to employ airfield brigades to construct the airfields, which were formed of 7,000 men, with 220 tractors, 560 vehicles, 920 rollers, and to redeploy 25,000 workers from road building projects and to send students in their final years of study at the institutes of higher education specialising in road transport as well as students from the technical colleges in Moscow, Saratov, Omsk, and Kharkov. Even the local population were hired in the Baltic region, and 1,900 unskilled labourers were drafted in.

It would however not be possible to construct the rest of the airfields by hiring in civilian personnel as well as those serving in the various units, and therefore 100 construction battalions were formed between March–April, each of which consisted of approximately 1,000 personnel from the Airfield Construction Directorate of the People's Commissariat for Internal Affairs, of which 46 worked in the Baltic region. Thus in Lithuania there were 22 construction battalions (Nos. 464–485), while in Latvia there were 14 (Nos. 486–499), and in Estonia there were 10 (Nos. 454–463).

Despite the efforts that had been made and the concentration of construction units and other organisations the work progressed very slowly. According to a report by the Director of the 8th Directorate of the Principal Directorate of the Red Army Air Force Colonel Kuznetsov to the Chief of the General Staff in the Baltic Region as of 1 July work was underway on 46 operational airfields, all of which were undergoing construction. The status of the work was assessed as follows: preparation of the airfield was between 25–50 percent complete at 15 airfields, up to 25 percent at 10 airfields, but at 19 sites work on the construction of the airfield had yet to begin. Of the 30 new operational airfields earmarked for construction in 1941 a survey had only been completed on 22 of them while a topographical survey had only been completed at 17 of them.

Work on 23 airfields, where construction of the runway was set for 1 June, was also at the initial stages: topsoil had begun to be laid on 23 airfields, and concreting had commenced on five airfields.

The five airfields at which the concreting had commenced by 1 June were: Ezere, Vaijnode, Bauska, Kedainiai, and Slapaberze.

Considering practically half of the year had already gone by it was becoming clear that it would not be easy to complete the work within the given timescales. In a report the Director of the Principal Directorate of the Red Army Air Force Zhigaryev noted the following shortcomings:

> This report concerns the status of the work to construct runways on Air Force airfields, that has been carried out by the Principal Directorate of Airfield Construction, of the People's Commissariat for Internal Affairs, in accordance with a decree issued by the Council of People's Commissars of the USSR and dated 24 March of this year.
>
> The construction of the runways as of 1 June 1941 is at a preparatory stage.
>
> At the majority of the airfields under construction the work is progressing slowly, which threatens to disrupt the completion of the construction of the runways within the timescales set by the Government.
>
> The principal reasons for the unsatisfactory progress of the work are as follows:
>
> 1. The organisation of the work at the construction sites not having been thought through accurately enough together with delays in the start of the preparatory work;
> 2. The shortage of machinery for the construction work as well as shortages of the required tools;
> 3. Construction materials (stone, macadam, and cement) being slow to arrive at the construction sites, the material is arriving intermittently;
> 4. The technical documentation has still not been drawn up in full: the overall plans, as well as those for the ground levelling of the runways, and plans for the drainage and ground levelling of the airfields, and so on.

Judging by the reports and the descriptions of the issues with the construction, starting from the Principal Directorate of the Air Force level right up to the workforce, an entirely predictable picture was emerging. Having taken the decision to launch such a large-scale construction project across the entire territory of the USSR at once, none of the issues surrounding the design and the estimates for this project were ever considered at all nor was any preparatory work undertaken, which could not fail to influence the failure to meet the deadlines for the completion of the core work. Apart from that the constant expansion of the number of sites earmarked for construction meant that the plans were constantly being updated for support, as well as for the formation of new construction units, and for forwarding additional technology, and so on. That is to say the plan for the construction of new airfields and concrete runways was, along with the expansion of aviation units in 1941, an 'ideal' project so to speak, and the funds, the technology, and the workforce for this project were due to arrive as the construction work actually progressed. Naturally the leadership of the USSR had a great deal of experience in the construction of large-scale projects with limited technology, vehicles, and machinery, by maximising manual labour. To complete the allotted tasks within the course of one year was fanciful right from the start, and was a task, which was in fact only set at the end of the first quarter. True to form, in accordance with the initial plan for construction and the redevelopment of 66 concrete and 81 macadam runways this work was to have been completed within three years!

In the end this work only commenced in May 1941 and moreover as a result of all this work starting at the same time the conditions for the basing of the aviation units deteriorated even further. This was particularly acute at three airfields where concrete runways were under construction. Operating from these airfields after the formwork had been laid was made all the more complicated. Aircraft operating from the permanent airfields—Vilnius (Parubanek), Kedainiai, Riga (Greater Riga), Panevezys, Vaijnode, Vindava, Kuusiku, Ungru, Tartu—were only able to land and take off from very short runways, which remained free of construction work. This can clearly be seen on German reconnaissance photographs of the airfields at Vilnius, Kedainiai, and Riga. Nine regiments were based on these airfields, which represented half of the regular aviation units in this district, and naturally for them to function normally they needed to be redeployed to operational airfields. The reader however will recall that the degree of readiness for operational airfields was between zero to five percent, and as such basing these aircraft on these airfields did not provide a solution to the problem either.

The transfer to a territorial logistics system led to a dispersal of the technology that was already in short supply: the fuel tankers, oil and water servicing trucks, mobile aircraft repair workshops, and automatic starters, and so on, which were in chronically short supply, as well as the trained personnel for the newly formed regional airfields, airbases, and airfield logistics battalions. Moreover some of the newly formed structures had in fact initially been planned as reserves and were to spend the majority of their time standing idle in anticipation of the redeployment of regiments from other directions. Only a very rich country would be able to engage in such an irrational and highly wasteful use of resources, and the USSR did not belong among such countries. The newly formed units were due to be fully manned by 1942, but how the Air Force command were planning to ensure combat readiness of the logistics units in the course of 1941 is not clear.

The ill-considered and hastily organised construction of airfields led to the Air Force units being based even more closely together and this threatened the completion of the plans for combat training and conversion onto new aircraft.

Most importantly these measures over an extended period of time meant that the conditions for the servicing of the materiel deteriorated, the time taken for this work grew longer, and the congested deployment of the aviation units put them in a very vulnerable position in the event of any enemy attack.

2.3 The Condition of the Materiel and the Combat Strength in the Air Forces of the Baltic Special Military District by 22 June 1941

Another event, which has gone practically unrecorded in historical literature was the process of transferring the materiel of the regiments that had been re-equipped with the newest aircraft to the newly formed units and aviation technical colleges, which began at the end of May. Thus the 15th Fighter Air Regiment had transferred 30 I-153 aircraft to the 238th Fighter Air Regiment by 2 June. A further 39 'Chaikas' were transferred from the beginning of the month to the 236th Fighter Air Regiment and in total up until the outbreak of war 24 I-153s had been transferred to Alytus. The 10th and 31st Fighter Air Regiments finally surrendered their I-15bis aircraft to the 241st Ground Attack Air Regiment and in all the regiment received 27 'Bis' aircraft. The 237th Fighter Air Regiment received 13 I-153s from the 42nd Fighter Air Regiment. Then 13 I-153bis aircraft from the 61st Ground Attack Air Regiment were transferred to the 240th Fighter Air Regiment.

The bomber regiments also began to transfer their SB aircraft. In May three regiments transferred between 12–15 SB aircraft each to flying schools and the 312th Reconnaissance Air Regiment. On 24 May the 46th High-Speed Bomber Air Regiment transferred 10 SB aircraft to the Aviation Technical College in Krasno-Kutskoe and five were transferred to the 312th Reconnaissance Air Regiment. On 28 May the 50th High-Speed Bomber Air Regiment transferred a dozen of their oldest aircraft to the Balashov Flying School, and the 35th High-Speed Bomber Air Regiment transferred six SBs to the Taganrog Aviation Technical School and five SBs to the 312th Reconnaissance Air Regiment. The 54th High-Speed Bomber Air Regiment began the transfer of its aircraft at the beginning of June, and on 3 June six SBs were sent to the Totskaya Military Aviation Technical College. A further three were sent to the Voroshilov Military Aviation Technical College, while around 20–21 June five SBs were ferried to the 312th Reconnaissance Air Regiment.

These events were not recorded in many of the documents held in the higher level headquarters because the pre-war leadership of the Air Forces of the North-Western Front were already working in other positions and the personnel that replaced them were not in possession of the facts. Thus, information concerning 'super' regiments with hundreds of aircraft in the inventory continues to find its way into a number of publications to this day. Furthermore the newly appointed Soviet commanders began to make reference to this in the very first reports on combat activity. In an annual report dated 21 June 1942 the Commander of the 6th Air Army Major-General Kondratyuk noted:

> In the fighter air regiments the forward airfields received two sets of aircraft (the I-153s and MiG-3s, I-16s and MiG-3s), and moreover all the non-standard aircraft were destroyed in enemy air raids and also by brigades as they were evacuated since they could not be withdrawn to a location behind the lines in view of the rapidly changing situation.

Indeed the units of the Air Forces of the Baltic Special Military District were far from fully equipped with combat aircraft, and by the beginning of June the situation with respect to the equipping of the fighter air regiments and the high-speed bomber air regiments was even more tense than it had been during the winter of 1940–1941. The only situation that improved slightly concerned the 312th Reconnaissance Air Regiment's materiel, although this had little impact on the overall picture.

The MiG-1 and MiG-3 aircraft that the 31st, 15th, and 10th Fighter Air Regiments had received, as well as the Ar-2 bombers that the 46th and 54th High-Speed Bomber Air Regiments received in actual fact had limited combat capability owing to the manufacturing defects and technical unreliability of the aircraft themselves, and these regiments had in part transferred their old aircraft to the newly formed aviation units and flying schools. Interestingly the information concerning the difficult situation with respect to the new aircraft did nevertheless find its way into reports, and General Kondratyuk again noted: 'The pilots had not fully assimilated the new materiel (the MiG-3) aircraft and some of them stood unserviceable on the airfield (as the technical problems with the aircraft had not been eradicated at the manufacturing plants).'

Formally on paper as of 22 June 1941 the situation with respect to combat strength did not appear to be too bad. For example the combat strength of the regular regiments in the Air Forces of the Baltic Special Military District, which had yet to commence the process of re-equipping with the new materiel more or less corresponded to the standard of between 61–63 combat aircraft per regiment. The situation in the regiments that were undergoing conversion as well as the newly formed units was nowhere near as rosy.

Practically all these units, with the exception of the 15th and 31st Fighter Air Regiments, were in the course of re-equipping and had only just begun to receive their new materiel. The bomber regiments had already begun to transfer their old materiel to the higher education Institutions and the 312th Reconnaissance Air Regiments and in total by 22 June five bomber air regiments in the district had only been two thirds re-equipped. The newly formed units received older aircraft from the regular regiments, which represented between a quarter and a half of the standard number, while the 239th Fighter Air Regiment did not receive any aircraft at all.

Table 9 The combat strength of the Air Forces of the Baltic Special Military District – North-Western Front as of 22 June 1941

	Airfield	Type	Serviceable	Total	Crews
		Air Forces Baltic Special Military District—North-Western Front			
Air Force Directorate	Tallinn	SB	2	2	4[1]
		DS-2	1	1	8/13/2
		UT-2	1	1	
		Bucher-Brahms	1	1	
		The 4th Mixed Air Division			
4th Mixed Air Division Directorate	Tallinn	SB	2	2	2[2]
					6/9/2
38th Fighter Air Regiment	Tallinn	I-153	50	52	52
		I-15bis	3	5	64/-/-
		I-16	8	8	
35th High-Speed Bomber Air Regiment	Haapsalu	SB	34	39	46
		USB	2	3	59/65/86
50th High-Speed Bomber Air Regiment	Ungru	SB	30	34	46
		USB	4	4	69/64/74
63rd High-Speed Bomber Air Regiment	Kuusiku	SB	41	42	48
		USB	1	2	76/76/80
The Flight Commander's Courses	Tallinn	SB	7	8	?
		USB	2	2	
		SB	114	125	
		USB	9	11	
		I-153	50	54	
		I-15bis	3	5	
		I-16	8	8	

Notes

1 The numerator gives the figures for combat ready crews, while the denominator gives the figures for pilots, navigators, gunner/radio-operators.

2 Again the numerator gives the figures for combat ready crews, while the denominator gives the figures for pilots, navigators, gunner/radio-operators.

The 38th Fighter Air Regiment:

64 pilots in total, of whom 42 were in their second year or more of service and 22 of whom were in their first year of service, of these 12 who graduated in 1941 had not been introduced to operations.

Three type 5 I-16s were received in May from the 31st Fighter Air Regiment and five type 24/28 I-16s were received in June from the 21st Fighter Air Regiment.

The I-16 aircraft were transferred in order to arrange conversion onto the Yak-1.

Four squadrons at combat readiness.

The 35th High-Speed Bomber Air Regiment:

23 SB aircraft of the 201st series and 16 SBs up to the 201st series.

59 pilots, of whom 17 were in their first year of service, and of these nine had not been introduced to operations.

Five combat capable squadrons.

The 50th High-Speed Bomber Air Regiment:
14 SB aircraft of the 201st series and 20 SB up to the 201st series.

69 pilots, of whom 17 were in their first year of service and had not yet been introduced to operations.

Five combat capable squadrons.

The 63rd High-Speed Bomber Air Regiment:
41 SB aircraft of the 201st series, and one SB up to the 201st series.

76 pilots in total, of whom 40 pilots were in their first year of service, and of these 20 sergeant graduates of 1941 had not been introduced to operations.

Five combat capable squadrons.

The flight commander's courses:

Four SBs of the 201st series from the 63rd High-Speed Bomber Air Regiment and two SB aircraft up to the 201st series, and 2 SB aircraft up to the 201st series from the 35th High-Speed Bomber Air Regiment.

One USB each from the 35th and 50th High-Speed Bomber Air Regiments.

The 6th Mixed Air Division	Airfield	Type	Serviceable	Total	Crews
6th Mixed Air Division Directorate	Riga	SB	1	1	3
		I-153	1	1	3/10/-
21st Fighter Air Regiment	Riga	I-16	55	64	53
		I-153	1	1	69/-/-
		MiG-1	1	1	
		MiG-3	1	1	
148th Fighter Air Regiment	Liepaja	I-153	59	68	42
					57/-/-
239th Fighter Air Regiment	Ezere	–	–	–	10
31st High-Speed Bomber Air Regiment	Vaijnode	SB	48	60	43
		USB	2	3	59/82/74
40th High-Speed Bomber Air Regiment	Vindava	SB	43	54	58
	Piltene	USB	3	3	69/85/73
The Flight Commander's Courses	Riga	SB	10	10	?
		SB	92	125	
		USB	5	6	
		I-16	55	64	
		I-153	61	70	
		MiG-1	1	1	
		MiG-3	1	1	

The 21st Fighter Air Regiment:
There were 69 pilots and in total in the regiment, of whom 44 were in their second year of service or more while 25 are in their first year of service, of which 15 are 1941 graduates and have not been introduced to combat operations.

There were four squadrons at combat readiness.

In total the regiment had 33 type 5 I-16s, (of which four were unserviceable), nine type 17 I-16s, a single type 10 I-16, and 21 type 24/28 I-16s (of which five were unserviceable).

In accordance with the plan for the provision of air cover the regiment was to have been redeployed to Maliy Ryzhskiy and Rumbula airfields, whilst remaining a part of the forces at Bolshoy Ryzhskiy.

The 148th Fighter Air Regiment:
There were 57 pilots in total in the regiment, of whom 42 were in their second year of service or more, and 15 who were in their first year of service had not been introduced to operations, while eight had been trained on the MiG-3.

There were four combat squadrons comprising 42 crews.

In accordance with the plan to provide air cover the regiment was to have moved from Leipaja airfield to Ezere and Vaijnode.

The 239th Fighter Air Regiment:
There were 10 crews in this regiment.

In accordance with the plan for the provision of air cover the regiment was to have been redeployed to Bauska airfield.

The 31st High-Speed Bomber Air Regiment:
There were five squadrons at combat readiness.

In total there were 59 pilots in the regiment, of whom 12 were in their first year of service and had not been introduced to combat operations.

In accordance with the plan for the provision of air cover the regiment was to have been redeployed from Vaijnode airfield to Mitava and Platone airfields.

The 40th High-Speed Bomber Air Regiment:
There were five squadrons at combat readiness in this regiment.

In total there were 69 pilots in this regiment, of whom 11 were in their first year of service. Eleven regular pilots were away from the regiment and were undergoing conversion training in Moscow or attending training courses.

In accordance with the plan for the provision of air cover the regiment was to have been redeployed from Vindava airfield to Birzai, Krustpils, and Kaupernieki airfields.

There were four SBs from the 40th High-Speed Bomber Air Regiment and six from the 31st High-Speed Bomber Air Regiment that formed part of the Flight Commander's Courses.

The 10th Fighter Air Regiment:
In total there were 72 pilots in this regiment, of whom 40 were combat trained in the I-16.

There were four squadrons at combat readiness.

In connection with the roll-out of a study centre, which would use the regiment as its base, in June 1941 twenty MiG-3s were shipped to Siauliai at the end of May. Formally these aircraft were allocated to the 42nd Fighter Air Regiment, however owing to the familiar circumstances of 22 June 1941 these aircraft remained with the 10th Fighter Air Regiment. From 1 June onwards eight pilots from the 148th Fighter Air Regiment were trained on these same aircraft, and from mid June 19 pilots were trained on them from the 42nd Fighter Air Regiment. The pilots of the 10th Fighter Air Regiment who flew three dozen sorties in the MiG-3s in the March of that year did not succeed in resurrecting the conversion process right up until the beginning of hostilities. In fact 19 MiG-3 and MiG-1 aircraft were too much of a burden, considering that 10 of them were unserviceable. They could only be used if the regiment's pilots had received the required training.

In accordance with the plan for the provisions of air cover the regiment was to have been redeployed to Raseiniai and Nemaksciai airfields, whilst remaining, part of the forces based at Siauliai.

The 238th Fighter Air Regiment:
There were 12 crews in this regiment, and all the pilots were in their second year of service or more.

The 7th Mixed Air Division	Airfield	Type	Serviceable	Total	Crews
The 7th Mixed Air Division Directorate	Siauliai	SB	2	2	4 5/11/1
The 10th Fighter Air Regiment	Siauliai	I-16	27	35	40
		MiG-1	0	1	72/-/-
		MiG-3	10	19	
The 238th Fighter Air Regiment	Panevezys	I-153	27	30	12
The 9th High-Speed Bomber Air Regiment	Panevezys	SB	52	52	52 61/78/76
		USB	3	3	
The 46th High-Speed Bomber Air Regiment	Siauliai	SB	41	45	42 63/63/69
	Gruzdziai	Ar-2	9	11	
		USB	2	2	
The 241st Ground Attack Air Regiment	Mitava	I-15bis	25	27	15
		SB	95	99	
		Ar-2	9	11	
		USB	7	7	
		I-16	24	35	159
		MiG-1	0	1	
		MiG-3	10	19	
		I-153	27	30	
		I-15bis	25	27	

In accordance with the plan for the provision of cover the regiment was to have been redeployed to Linkuva, and Ioganishkeli airfields.

The 9th High-Speed Bomber Air Regiment:
There were 61 pilots in this regiment, of whom 12 pilots were in their first year of service and had not even introduced to combat operations.

There were five squadrons in this regiment at combat readiness.

All of the aircraft were 201 series SBs.

In accordance with the plan for the provision of cover the regiment was to have been redeployed to Svarbai airfield, whilst remaining a part of the forces based at Panevezys.

The 46th High-Speed Bomber Air Regiment:
The regiment had 31 SB aircraft that were 201st series machines, and 14 SBs aircraft that were up to the 201st series.

There were 63 pilots in the regiment, of whom 16 were in their first year of service and had not yet been introduced to combat operations.

There were three squadrons at combat readiness (the 2nd, 3rd, and 5th Air Squadrons).

In accordance with the plan to provide air cover the regiment was to have been redeployed to Gruzdziai and Dovschishki airfields.

The 241st Ground Attack Regiment:
There were 15 crews in this regiment, and all the pilots were in their second year of service.

In accordance with the plan to provide air cover the regiment was to have been redeployed to Ionishkis.

The 8th Mixed Air Division	Airfield	Type	Serviceable	Total	Crews
The 8th Mixed Air Division	Kaunas	SB	1	1	5
		I-16	2	2	5/1/3/-
The 15th Fighter Air Regiment	Kaunas	MiG-1	1	4	72
	Potsunai	MiG-3	55	57	
	Vincai	I-53	10	15	
		I-16	8	8	
		I-15bis	4	4	
The 31st Fighter Air Regiment	Kaunas	MiG-1	21	24	82
	Karmelava	MiG-3	23	28	
		I-16	8	13	
The 236th Fighter Air Regiment	Alytus	I-153	24	24	20
The 240th Fighter Air Regiment	Raseiniai	I-15bis	13	13	8
The 61st Ground Attack Air Regiment	Kedainiai	I-153	59	61	68
	Risgonis	I-15bis	3	5	
	Markshtava	Il-2	5	5	
		MiG-1	22	28	255
		MiG-3	78	85	
		I-153	93	100	
		I-16	18	23	
		I-15bis	20	22	
		SB	1	1	

The 15th Fighter Air Regiment:
In total there were 73 pilots in this regiment, of whom 30 were trained on the MiG-3. There is no data concerning the breakdown of pilots in terms of those in their first or second year of service (but there were no more than 40 pilots in their second year of service).

There was a single squadron that was at combat readiness: the 2nd Squadron consisting of 10 crews and 11 I-153s (one of which was unserviceable) based at Vincai.

In fact on the morning of 22 June there were two dozen pilots on Vincai airfield, 10 of whom were from the 15th Fighter Air Regiment and the same number from the 236th Fighter Air Regiment, who had arrived to ferry aircraft to Alytus.

There were three squadrons in the regiment that were partly combat capable—the 1st and 3rd Squadrons as well as the regimental directorate, and 31 MiG-1/3s (two of which were unserviceable) on Potsunai airfield; the 4th Squadron was based on Kaunas airfield with 10 crews, and 30 MiG-1/3s (three of which were unserviceable), eight I-16s, four I-153s (which were unserviceable as they were missing propellers and engines), and four I-15bis aircraft (which were awaiting transfer to other units).

Only the 1st Air Squadron had fully converted onto the MiG-3 (which consisted of 14 pilots), but even this formation did not manage to commence combat training flights and by 22 June a further 16 pilots in this regiment from the 3rd and 4th Squadrons had undergone conversion to fly solo in the MiG-3 and ahead of their training on the MiG they continued to train in the UTI-4 and I-16 in Kaunas and Potsunai.

In accordance with the plan for the provision of air cover the regiment covered Potsunai, Vincai, and Kaunas airfields.

The 31st Fighter Air Regiment:
In total there were 82 pilots in this regiment, and there is no data concerning the breakdown of pilots in terms of whether they were in their first or second year of service (in any case however there were no more than 35–40 remaining by 22 June 1941).

There were four squadrons in the regiment that were at partial combat readiness: these were the 1st, 2nd, and 4th Squadrons and the regimental directorate, consisting of 41 crews; there were 39 serviceable MiG-1/3s and two type 5 I-16s on Karmelava airfield; the 3rd Squadron consisting of 40 crews, 13 MiG-1/3s (eight of which were unserviceable), and 11 I-16s (five of which were unserviceable), on Kaunas airfield.

Only the 4th Air Squadron was fully trained on the MiG-1/3 but even this formation was not able to commence combat training flights, the pilots of the 1st and 2nd Air Squadrons were trained to fly solo in the MiG-3. A further 40 young pilots were concentrated in the 3rd Air Squadron and before they were trained on the MiG-3 they were transferred to Kaunas airfield and were trained on the UTI-4 and the I-16 at Kaunas airfield.

In accordance with the plan for the provision of air cover the 31st Fighter Air Regiment was to have redeployed to Kedainiai, Kroky, and Slapaberze airfields (all these airfields are in the vicinity of Kedainiai).

The personnel in these regiments had yet to commence aerial gunnery exercises. Apart from that the new aircraft remained substantially unarmed since one of the main design shortcomings of the first series remained the problem with the reliability of the armament, which had still not been overcome.

In fact the 15th and 321st Fighter Air Regiments were not capable of eradicating all the design shortcomings of the MiG-1/3s right up to the start of normal combat training.

The 236th Fighter Air Regiment:
There were three crews in this regiment, a further 12 pilots in the regiment departed for Vincai and Kaunas to ferry aircraft.

In accordance with the plan to provide air cover the regiment was to have been redeployed to Ukmerge airfield.

The 240th Fighter Air Regiment:
There were eight crews in this regiment, and of those only two flew the MiG-3, four that flew the I-16, and two the I-153.

In accordance with the plan to provide air cover the regiment was to have been redeployed to Daugavpils.

The 61st Fighter Air Regiment:
In total there were 68 pilots in this regiment, of whom 57 were actually serving in their unit, a further five were posted elsewhere, one was injured, and five were on leave.

There were five squadrons at partial combat readiness and the crews had only just begun to undertake combat training flights: the directorate, the 4th and 5th Air Squadrons at Kedainiai the 1st and 2nd Air Squadrons at Risgonis, and the 3rd Air Squadron at Markshtava airfield.

The regimental commander Major Mamushkin and four squadron commanders Captains Romanov, Andreyev, Filatov, and Senior Lieutenant Yemelyanov converted onto the Il-2, and ferried Il-2 aircraft to the regiment. On the morning of 22 June 1941 found them on Parubanek airfield in the area around Vilnius.

In accordance with the plan to provide air cover the regiment was to have been redeployed to Markshtava and Vepriai (Risgonis), both of which are in the area around Jonava.

The 57th Mixed Air Division	Airfield	Type	Serviceable	Total	Crews
The Directorate of the 57th Mixed Air Division	Vilnius	–	–	–	- 3/9/-
The 42nd Fighter Air Regiment	Vilnius	I-153	48	55	57 48/10/15
	Orany	I-15bis	20	21	
	Perloja	I-16	1	2	
The 49th Fighter Air Regiment	Daugavpils	I-153	35	38	57 75/80/15
	Liskna	I-16	20	23	
		I-15bis	2	2	
The 237th Fighter Air Regiment	Orany	I-153	13	13	13
The 54th High-Speed Bomber Air Regiment	Parubanek	SB	35	40	28 75/80/72
	Kivishki	Ar-2	7	12	
	Kryzhaki	USB	3	3	
		I-153	96	106	128
		I-15bis	22	23	
		I-16	21	25	
		SB	35	40	
		Ar-2	7	12	
		USB	3	3	

The 42nd Fighter Air Regiment:

Out of the 61 pilots in the regiment (all of which were in their second year of service or more) 17 were attending conversion courses in Siauliai and 12 were on courses outside the district. Apart from that it is possible that the pilots who graduated in 1941 have not been included in this number.

There were four squadrons that were at combat readiness: 30 crews, 30 serviceable I-153s, and type 5 I-16s, and the Fighter Air Regiment Directorate, based on Orany airfield, and two combat crews; the 1st Air Squadron at Orany with six combat crews; the 2nd Air Squadron at Perloja with seven combat crews, the 3rd Air Squadron at Perloja, with nine combat crews; the 4th Air Squadron at Orany airfield with six combat crews.

On the airfield at Vilnius there were 26 I-153s (nine of which were unserviceable), 21 I-15bis aircraft (of which three were unserviceable), and one unserviceable type 5 I-16, and the regiment did not have any crews at combat readiness.

In accordance with the plan for the provision of air cover the 42nd Fighter Air Regiment was to have been redeployed to Orany, Peloja, and Alytus airfields to enable them to participate in air combat.

The 49th Fighter Air Regiment:

In total there were four type 10 I-16s, some 14 type 18 I-16s, and five type 24/28 I-16s in this regiment.

In total the regiment had 73 pilots, of whom 48 were in their second year of service or more (four of them were away from their unit), while 25 were in their first year of service, of those 15 were 1941 graduates and had not been introduced to combat operations.

There were four squadrons at combat readiness: the 1st, and 3rd Air Squadrons that flew the I-153, and the 2nd and 4th Air Squadrons that flew the I-16.

In accordance with the plan for the provision of air cover the regiment remained at Dvinsk airfield.

The 54th High-Speed Bomber Air Regiment:

On Vilnius airfield there were 12 Ar-2s (five of which were unserviceable), 12 SB aircraft (of which five were unserviceable) and three USB aircraft, and the regiment did not have any crews at combat readiness.

There were 75 pilots in this regiment, of whom 12 were attending conversion courses away from their unit, 16 crews were posted elsewhere, and 12 pilots were in their first year of service and had not been introduced to combat operations.

There were three squadrons at combat readiness: the 3rd, 4th, and 5th, Air Squadrons, and 28 crews based on Kryzhaki and Kivishki airfields.

The 237th Fighter Air Regiment:

There were 13 crews on Perloja airfield.

In accordance with the plan for the provision of air cover the regiment was to have been redeployed to Pokulyanka airfield.

Individual units	Airfield	Type	Serviceable	Total	Crews
The 312th Reconnaissance Air	Rumbula	SB	6[1]	6	12
Regiment	Platone	USB	2	2	43/87/55
		U-2	7	11	
The 2nd Aerial Photographic	Kaunas	R-5	7	7	9
Detachment		U-2	1	1	9/15/-
The 112th Air Observation	Daugavpils	R-5SSS	1	7	12
Squadron		U-2	6	8	12/17/-
The 103rd Air Observation	Vilnius	R-5SSS	6[2]	7	14
Squadron		U-2	5	6	14/26/-
The 10th Air Observation	Ezere	R-5SSS	–	7	16
Squadron		U-2	3	5	16/24/-
The 11th Air Observation	Siauliai	R-5SSS	2	7	13
Squadron		U-2	4	5	21/18/-
The 16th Air Observation	Kaunas	R-5SSS	8[2]	8	15
Squadron		U-2	5	5	17/15/-
The 22nd Air Observation	Yagoda	Hawker Hart	7	7	18
Squadron		Henschel 126	5	5	18/18/-
		PTO-4	3	3	
		PON	3	3	
		Avro Anson	–	1	
		Miles	–	1	
The 24th Air Observation	Gulbene	SV-5	8	10	10
Squadron		Kod-1	1	3	18/10/-
		Kod-2	–	3	
The 29th Air Observation	Ukmerge	Anbo-41	12	12	18
Squadron		Anbo-51	9	9	18/20/-
		Gloster Gladiator	1	1	
The 65th Air Observation	Tartu	R-5SSS	4	4	16
Squadron		U-2	5	5	21/20/-

Notes

1 The 312th Reconnaissance Air Regiment: the data concerns combat strength as of 1 June 1941, apart from that at the beginning of June 15 SB were redeployed to the regiment, which comprised five aircraft each from the 35th, 46th, and 54th High-Speed Bomber Air Regiments. The regiment had 42 pilots, of whom 12 were in the liaison squadron and 31 served in the reconnaissance squadrons. The regiment had 12 trained crews in the 5th Air Squadron (liaison) flying the U-2. There were no combat crews in the reconnaissance squadrons, since the gunner/radio-operators were not trained.

2 According to other available data all the R-5SSS aircraft were listed as unserviceable.

Aside from the aircraft indicated in the tables there were small numbers of UTI-4, UT-1, UT-2, and U-2 training and liaison aircraft in these regiments. Apart from that the study centre at Mitava had seven Pe-2s, which were intended for the 54th High-Speed Bomber Air Regiment, but which were used to convert personnel onto the new materiel.

In total in these units there were 1,274 combat aircraft (of which 1,106 were serviceable), and 235 auxiliary aircraft (according to other data there were 1,125 serviceable aircraft). These aircraft were of the following types:

632 fighters (551 of which were serviceable): 297 I-153s (268 were serviceable), 155 I-16s (94 type 5s, nine type 17s, seven type 10s, 14 type 18s, and 16 type 24s, and 15 type 28s) (129 serviceable I-16s across all types), 105 MiG-3s (89 of which were serviceable), 30 MiG-1s (23 of which were serviceable) and 45 I-15bis aircraft (42 of which were serviceable). The remaining I-15bis aircraft in these regiments were not considered fully-fledged fighter aircraft. In the long run, to count these aircraft in the same vein as other fighters does not make any sense, since it was not considered a combat aircraft and the training of young personnel across all the regiments remained the preserve of the 'Bis' aircraft, except in the 240th Fighter Air Regiment where there were simply no other aircraft available. Characteristically the regular pilots of the Air Forces of the Baltic Special Military District did not utilise the I-15bis aircraft in combat operations at all.

There were 449 bombers (394 of which were serviceable): 392 SBs (of which 349 were serviceable), 27 USBs (of which 22 were serviceable), 23 Ar-2s (of which 16 were serviceable), and seven Pe-2s (according to other data 370 SBs and 24 USBs were serviceable).

There were 98 ground attack aircraft (87 of which were serviceable): 61 I-153s (of which 59 were serviceable). Apart from that five Il-2s were transferred to the 61st Ground Attack Air Regiment from Voronezh.

There were 21 long-range reconnaissance aircraft (in the 312th Reconnaissance Air Regiment): six SBs were listed on 1 June 1941, and apart from that a further 15 SBs were transferred to the regiment at the beginning of June.

There were 74 short-range reconnaissance aircraft (of which 53 were serviceable): 40 R-5SSS aircraft (of which 21 were serviceable), five Henschel 126s, seven Hawker Harts, 10 SV-5s (of which eight were serviceable), and 12 ANBO-41s.

There were 256 auxiliary, transport and training aircraft: seven R-5s, one R-5SSS, one R-6, 127 U-2s (of which 104 were serviceable), 31 UTI-4s (of which 26 were serviceable), 23 UT-1s (of which 21 were serviceable), eight UT-2s, seven S-2s (of which four were serviceable), nine ANBO-51s, five PTO-4s, 3 KOD-2s (all of which were unserviceable), three KOD-1s (of which one was serviceable), three PONs, one Dragon Rapide, one DS-2, one Bücker Jungmeister, one Bücker Brans, one Miles, one Avro (unserviceable), and one Gloster Gladiator.

In accordance with the delivery schedule for the materiel the units in the Air Forces of this district were due to receive around 200 new aircraft—122 MiG-3s, and 68 Pe-2s.

In accordance with this plan the new materiel was to be distributed as follows:

The 10th Fighter Air Regiment—60 MiG-3s;
The 31st Fighter Air Regiment—nine MiG-3s;
The 42nd Fighter Air Regiment—40 MiG-3s;
The 148th Fighter Air Regiment—15 MiG-3s;
The 9th High-Speed Bomber Air Regiment—25 Pe-2s;
The 50th High-Speed Bomber Air Regiment—14 Pe-2s;
The 54th High-Speed Bomber Air Regiment—29 Pe-2s.

Out of those deliveries stipulated in the plan only seven Pe-2s that had been allocated to the 54th High-Speed Bomber Air Regiment, but which were used by the study centre, had arrived in the district by the outbreak of war. These were delivered along with six Pe-2s that were delivered to the 50th High-Speed Bomber Air Regiment (these were still not listed in the regiment's inventory). The rest of the aircraft were received but only in part, during the course of combat operations. The 15th, 31st, and 148th Fighter Air Regiments, while the 9th, 35th, 40th, 50th High-Speed Bomber Air Regiments received only two dozen Pe-2s.

In summing up the calculations concerning the numbers of aircraft we note that in the Air Forces of the Baltic Special Military District these had increased in comparison with the winter of 1940–1941 by approximately 100 aircraft in all, while the number of fighter aviation units in the district had again grown by almost double from eight to 13 regiments. In total, instead of the re-equipping with new aircraft in place of the old that was required at the beginning of the year, the units of the Baltic Special Military District were only partly augmented, and moreover with MiG-1 or MiG-3 aircraft that were very unreliable from a technical perspective. As a result of this the old materiel that served in the 15th and 31st Fighter Air Regiments was scattered around the regiments that were in the process of being formed and both these regiments, along with the 10th Fighter Air Regiment were in fact left with barely any reliable combat aircraft at all. The situation in the 21st and the 49th Fighter Air Regiments, which had divided all the later type I-16s amongst themselves, was only slightly better. In total the 21st Fighter Air Regiment, which included 21 type 24/28 I-16s in its inventory, continued to operate type 5, 10, and 17 I-16s, while the 1st and 3rd Squadrons of the 49th Fighter Air Regiments operated the I-153.

Only in the 38th, 42nd, and 148th Fighter Air Regiments did the situation with respect to materiel remain more or less normal, since these regiments had yet to hand over their I-153s to the new formations, although they had still not succeeded in eradicating all the mass of design shortcomings in the 'Chaikas'. Brigade No. 1 continued to work at Baltic Special Military District units right up until the outbreak of war.

The number of ground attack units had almost doubled, but the number of aircraft remained at the same level as it had been at the beginning of the year. Moreover the 61st Ground Attack Air Regiment handed over almost all its I-15bis aircraft to the 240th Fighter Air Regiment. On the formation of the 241st Ground Attack Air Regiment 27 aircraft of the same type arrived from the 10th and 31st Fighter Air Regiments, while the regiment required a further 36 aircraft to be fully equipped in accordance with the standard.

The 61st Ground Attack Air Regiment was among the first regiments to receive the newest Il-2 ground attack aircraft. The five Ilyushins were ferried under their own power by Regimental Commander Major Mamushkin and four squadron commanders from Voronezh. They did not however reach the unit until the outbreak of war, and 22 June found them on Vilnius airfield.

The number of bombers in the Air Forces in this district even reduced slightly, while the arrival of new aircraft had only just begun. In total in the bomber regiments the process of re-equipping onto the new materiel was only just getting underway, and after receiving three dozen new aircraft the units handed over 50 SB aircraft to the 312th Reconnaissance Air Regiment and flying schools, which significantly reduced their combat effectiveness.

The tense situation concerning the reconnaissance aviation materiel did not improve significantly. The only regiment to receive any augmentation was the 312th Reconnaissance Air Regiment, but up until June only six SBs and two USBs had been delivered, which did nothing to enable a significant increase in the intensity of combat training. At the beginning of June there were no fully trained reconnaissance crews in the regiment. The air observation squadrons remained on their own with their ancient R-5SSS, the majority of which ended up being 'laid up' unused, and the personnel prepared to re-equip with the SB.

The quality of the 'old' aircraft in comparison with the preceding year did not diminish, while the defects that came to light based on the results of the operation of the new materiel in June 1941 did not provide any basis for optimism either.

The situation in terms of bringing the MiG-3 up to standard was very accurately described in an ancient proverb known as 'robbing Peter to pay Paul'. In May 1941 in connection with the weakness in the aircraft's standard armament, which consisted of just three machine guns—one BS and two ShKAS guns—work was undertaken on additional armament on all the aircraft that had already been manufactured to fit underwing pylons with BK machine guns. It would appear that the issue with the armament had been solved, but doing this overloaded the aircraft and the weight of the aircraft grew from series to series. When fitted with the underwing machine guns the MiG lost speed and manoeuvrability. The main issue, however, was that the handling and stability had deteriorated. In the end, following comparative testing of aircraft fitted with the BK and those fitted with the standard armament (the difference in speed was between 35 km/h at low level to 20 km/hr at an altitude of 8,000 m), a decision was taken to remove the underwing BK guns. At the same time the ventral fuel tanks on all the aircraft that had already been manufactured were replaced with smaller examples. The decree for this was received by the Baltic Special Military District on 10 June 1941 and was carried out over the course of a week. The BK guns were removed from all aircraft and as a result by 22 June the MiGs were left without reliable armament.

By 22 June 1941 the situation with respect to the materiel in the Air Forces of the Baltic Special Military District grew worse. This occurred firstly because of the disruption in the deliveries from the factories of the newest aircraft, and secondly because of the formation of the new units for which the old aircraft in the regular regiments were transferred by way of augmentation.

In total by 22 June 1941 formally there were 13 fighter air regiments, eight bomber air regiments, two ground attack air regiments, and one reconnaissance air regiment in the Air Forces of the Baltic Special Military District. The 'old materiel' however in the regular regiments had by that time been scattered around the new formations and the flying schools, and the new materiel was arriving relatively slowly. Therefore the majority of the regular regiments in June 1941 were left without a standard set of the 'older types' of aircraft. Apart from that as a result of the re-equipment onto new aircraft that had not happened back in 1940, many of the units retained their rare type 5 I-16s, I-15bis, R-5SSS, and SB aircraft up until the 201st series in significant numbers. These aircraft were morally and physically obsolete and were in need to immediate replacement. The new regiments however had only just begun to receive their new aircraft and the personnel were only at the early stages of their training. In reconnaissance aviation no significant changes had taken place up until June 1941, and almost none of the reconnaissance units in the district were combat capable.

The newest aircraft with their clusters of design shortcomings and defects did not instil optimism either, especially in the context of the unresolved problems with the failures in the armament of the MiG-3s and the cracks in the engine mountings on the Ar-2s. Thus the 15th and 31st Fighter Air Regiments, which had been 100 percent equipped with new aircraft, and which had handed over three quarters of their old aircraft, were only at partial combat readiness. The 10th Fighter Air Regiment and the 35th, 46th, 50th, and 54th High-Speed Bomber Air Regiments were only partially combat capable owing to the fact that approximately one third of the old aircraft had been withdrawn from these regiments.

In fact in June 1941 the regular units remained the most combat capable since they had not started to transfer their aircraft, nor had they begun to send a significant proportion of their personnel, to the newly formed regiments and colleges.

Conclusions

As a conclusion to this part it should be noted that the organisational and mobilisation measures taken in 1941 were arranged in such a way that the USSR would, so to speak, end up in a vacuum and would be separated from its western neighbour by an impenetrable barrier, that is to say in actual fact without protection of some kind from an external influence.

The Red Army Air Force was at the initial stage in terms of implementing the processes below:

- Reforming and breaking in the units and sub-divisions in their new format;
- Training the new personnel and introducing them to combat, and moreover thousands of the new pilots and, navigators, and gunner/radio-operators who had arrived at their units only had to start their training and some time later would become combat crews;
- Conversion onto new aircraft that were subject to a great number of design, and manufacturing defects;*
- The formation and reformation of logistics units;†
- The construction of airfields, which had begun immediately on all the airfield sites including the construction of concrete runways at 240 airfields. This did not lead to an improvement in the basing of these aircraft overnight since the date on which these new structures would come on stream remained some time away, and the fact that instead of the expansion of the network of airfields in the summer of 1941 the reverse of this process was actually happening.‡

The results of these processes that occurred in the Red Army Air Force in the first half of 1941 was the reduction in the combat capability of the majority of regular units in the Red Army Air Force, and the almost complete lack of combat capability in the regiments and squadrons that had only just been formed in 1940 and 1941.

---

* Furthermore the problems with the manufacture of modernised aircraft and powerful engines and the inability of the Soviet aviation industry to correct the situation over the course of a significant period of time in the end gave rise to the basic premise for the disruption in the re-equipping of the Red Army Air Force between 1938–1940 and the disruption in the roll-out of the new aviation units in 1941. The hysteria that followed that was based on the chronic failures in testing of the 'new' I-28, I-180, SPB, VIT and other aircraft ended in the launch of the MiG-3, Yak-1, LaGG-3, Pe-2, and Il-2 into production without even eradicating their obvious design shortcomings and without conducting repeat state and combat testing. In fact there was no prospect of these decisions being realised successfully, and the launch of the 'new aircraft types' into production, between 1940–1941, was initially under threat of disruption. The following aircraft were in service with the front line units of the Red Army Air Force by 22 June 1941 in significant numbers; I-16s and I-15bis aircraft fitted with M-25/25V engines, SB aircraft (up to 221st series), DB-3s fitted with M-86/87 engines, R-5s, and R-5SSS aircraft, R-Zets, R-10s, and TB-3s. Meanwhile back in the spring of 1941 German fighter aviation units had begun to receive new aircraft en masse that were of the next generation so to speak: these were the Bf 109F-4 fitted with the DB 601E engine rated at 1,350 h.p., the Ju-88A-4 (fitted with Jumo-211J engines rated at 1,340 h.p.) and the Do 217 (fitted with the BMW-801 engines rated at 1,540 h.p.). The long-range reconnaissance squadrons in the *Luftwaffe* were almost 100 percent equipped with Ju-88D-1 and Bf 110s, and the short-range squadrons received the distinctive 'Frame'—the FW 189A-1. The Red Army Air Force did not have a chance to rectify this situation with respect to armament at all, since they were on the threshold of war.

† The transfer to the new logistics system began literally in June and the augmentation of the newly formed logistics units, first and foremost the airfield logistics battalions with materiel and personnel in accordance with the new standards had yet to begin. These units remained like this up until the outbreak of war, that is to say with equipment that they had inherited from the airbases, and they did not receive technology or personnel by way of augmentation.

‡ Unfortunately the construction of the new airfields and runways in the end turned into a senseless waste of enormous materiel resources and human effort. It was true that in the summer this did not play a particularly significant role since almost any site with a level surface could be used to base these aircraft on, which were located near approach roads. Apart from that, by way of an example, for the units equipped with I-15bis, I-153, and I-16 aircraft, which were not fitted with lift devices and which had inefficient braking systems, concrete runways were irrelevant. Considering that almost none of the young pilots who had recently joined the units had mastered take-off and landing, expecting them to take-off and land on concrete runways would amount to a suicide mission.

Today it is difficult to assert whether these events were brought about by attitudes among the highest political leadership of the USSR, who were looking to reach agreements with Germany, or whether this was simply a strategic blunder by the leaders of the People's Commissariat for Defence, and the Red Army Air Force, who for the third time in four years ignored common sense in their organisation of similar reforms. Nevertheless the way these events unfolded was the worst possible scenario, and there was neither the time nor the resources to implement the full set of measures envisaged by Red Army command.

It should be underlined that to reproach the commanders of the Air Forces of the Baltic Special Military District, the units and formations and also the pilots to a large extent makes no sense. In fact the opposite is true, in that the commanders at all levels as well as the experienced pilots made a truly titanic effort to introduce the young flight crews to operations and to convert the regular pilots onto the newest aircraft. Following the disbandment of the regular units however there was simply neither the effort available, nor first and foremost the time, to repeat the training process.

There is every likelihood that the commanders of the Air Forces of the Baltic Special Military District understood entirely how serious the developing situation was, and as much as they were able, tried to force the pace of combat training and of the conversion onto new aircraft. There was however no time left, and Soviet pilots were to undergo a test in the coming days, since the *Wehrmacht* had completed their concentration of forces on the Soviet-German border.

Photographs taken of an accident that occurred on 4 January 1961. The pilot from the 4th Squadron, 15th Fighter Air Regiment Junior Lieutenant V.I. Yermolayev crashed his I-15bis on landing (the aircraft bore the factory No. 5553, and was fitted with an M-25V engine No. 1912605).

An accident involving an I-153 aircraft (No. 6792 fitted with an M-62 engine No. 1177), on Daugavpils airfield on 21 January 1941. The pilot was Adjutant of the 2nd Squadron, 38th Fighter Air Regiment Senior Lieutenant F.F. Turkin.

An emergency landing by an I-153 aircraft (No. 6791 fitted with an M-62 engine No. 1177), on Daugavpils on 21 January 1941. The pilot Lieutenant V.V. Rozhnov of the 3rd Squadron, 49th Fighter Air Regiment.

The leader of the Air Force Scientific Research Institute aircrew conversion Brigade for the aircrew of the 31st Fighter Air Regiment onto MiG-1 aircraft Colonel Mikhail Ivanovich Martselyuk.

Air Force Scientific Research Institute test-pilot Senior Lieutenant Leonid Mikhaylovich Kuvshinov, he later was awarded the title of Hero of the Soviet Union.

A crash involving an I-153 (bearing the factory No. 6494 and fitted with an M-62 engine No. 1566) on Tallinn airfield, on 24 February 1941. The pilot from the 2nd Squadron Lieutenant D.M. Bykovets was killed.

A catastrophe with an I1-5bis (No. 4999 and fitted with an M-25V engine No. 199880) on Siauliai airfield on 1 February 1941. The Head of the Transport and Airborne Assault Service of the 4th Squadron, 10th Fighter Air Regiment Lieutenant Ya.P. Kolbasuk was killed.

An accident involving an SB aircraft (No. 12/111 fitted with two M-103 engines Nos. 843–491; 843–406) that occurred on Tartu airfield on 14 February 1941. The crews were as follows: the pilot was Assistant Commander of the 2nd Squadron Senior Lieutenants A.K. Razumeychik, the navigator was Captain L.M. Yumin, and the gunner/radio-operator Junior Sergeant P.V. Salinkov were unhurt.

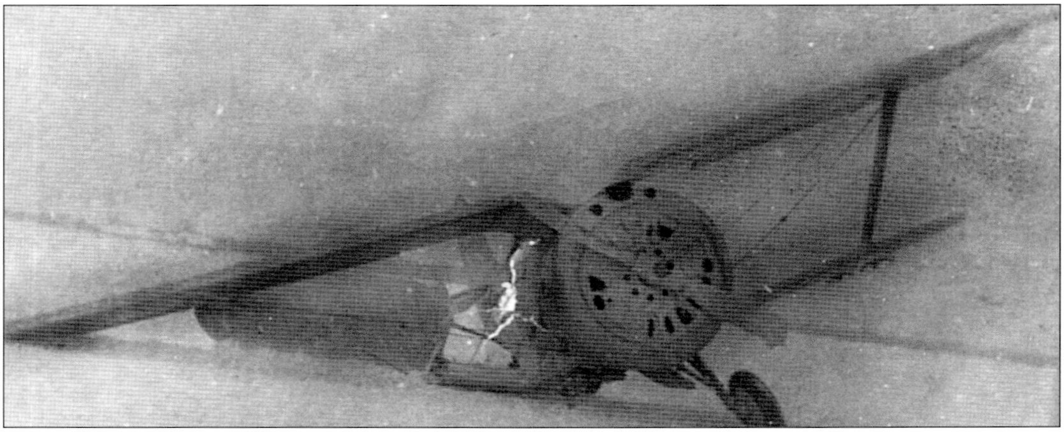

An accident with an I-153 aircraft (No. 7388 and fitted with an M-62 engine No. 1839) on Liepaja airfield on 25 February 1941. The pilot was from the 4th Squadron, 148th Fighter Air Regiment V.M. Bondarenko.

An accident on the runway of Potsunai airfield on 17 March 1941, the Commander of the 2nd Squadron, 15th Fighter Air Regiment Captain A.P. Sorgin in a MiG-1 aircraft (No. 2065 fitted with an AM-35A engine No. 0024) collided with a U-2 aircraft (No. 15560 fitted with an M-11 engine No. 1617417).

An accident with an SB aircraft (No. 1/331 fitted with M-103A engine Nos. 043-134 and 043-135) on Ungru airfield on 17 March 1941. The pilot was the Commander of the 50th High-Speed Bomber Air Regiment Colonel F.A. Agaltsov.

The Head of the Directorate of the Air Forces of the 8th Army Major-General of Aviation Aleksandr Petrovich Andreyev

He was born on 27 August 1901 in Novaya Bukhara, Bukharsk khanate.

He joined the Red Army from September 1919 and was a Red Army soldier serving in the military commissariat in Kushka castle. In March 1920 he was sent to study in Tashkent at the Turkestan Cavalry and Artillery Battalion. From May 1922 he was an Adjutant at the Directorate of Artillery on the Turkestan Front, from November he was a Platoon Commander in the 1st Separate Mountain Battery. He fought on both the Bukharsk, and Fergansk Fronts.

From August 1923 to November 1925 he studied in the Military School for Pilots and Observers in Leningrad (in 1925), and the School of Aerial Gunnery and Bombing in Serpukhov. On completion of his studies in November he was made a pilot-observer in the 2nd Light Bomber Air Squadron in Vitebsk. From March 1928 until March 1929 he was on a government tour of duty in Afghanistan, and on return he was made Assistant Commander of the 26th Separate Artillery Correction Air Detachment in Yegorevsk. From March 1930 he was an acting Chief of Staff of the 28th Separate Artillery Correction Air Detachment in Voronezh. From October 1930 until May 1932 he studied at the Zhukovskiy Military Aviation Academy of the Worker's and Peasant's Red Army Air Force, and on completion of his studies there he was made a Chief of Staff of the 83rd Fighter Air Brigade. From November 1936 he was the Commander of the 13th High-Speed Bomber Air Squadron of the Air Forces of the Belorussian Front, and in May 1937 he was made Commander of the 51st High-Speed Bomber Air Brigade of the Air Forces of the Special Red Banner Far East Army, and he was made a Brigade Commander on 19 February 1938.

From May until March 1939 he participated in the fighting in Spain. From 19 April 1939 he was made acting Commander of the Air Force Directorate of the Special Red Banner Far East Army, and from 21 January 1940 he was confirmed in this post and was made Major-General of Aviation on 4 June 1940. From 8 August 1940 he was made Commander of the 50th Air Division and continued to fulfil the duties of Commander of the Air Force Directorate of the Special Red Banner Far East Army. On 27 March 1941 he was made Commander of the Directorate of the Air Forces of the 8th Army in the Baltic Special Military District.

He participated in the Great Patriotic War and on 20 October 1942 he was made Commander of the 276th Bomber Air Division. From September 1944 he carried out the duties of the Head of the Aviation Department of the Union supervisory committee in Finland.

In October 1947 he was made Commander of the 13th Air Army of the Leningrad Military District. From 1 June 1948 he was acting Commander of the 275th Fighter Air Division. He served as a Military Attache in Finland. From 15 December 1951 he studied at the Higher Aviation School under the K.E. Voroshilov Higher Military Aviation Academy. On 8 October 1952 he was made Commander of the Air Forces of the Southern Ural Military District, and was made Lieutenant-General of Aviation on 18 February 1958. From 4 April 1958 he was a Commander of the Air Forces of the Baltic Special Military District. From 3 October 1960 he was at the disposal of the Chief Directorate of Air Force Personnel. From 25 February 1961 he was retired to the reserves. He died in 1987.

He was awarded the order of Lenin, and the Order of the Red Banner, and the Orders of Suvorov 2nd class, and Kutuzov 2nd class, as well as the Order of the Patriotic War, as well as the Red Star, and other medals.

The Head of the Air Force Directorate of the 11th Army Major-General Viktor Alekseyevich Chumakov

He was born on 16 August 1899 in the village of Solodovka, in the Leninsk district, Stalingrad Region.

He joined the Red Army in November 1918 and was a Red Army Soldier. He graduated from the Commander's Courses in the 1st Cavalry Army and on 20 November 1920 he was made Commander of a Squadron in the 112th Cavalry Regiment. From March 1921 he held this same position in the 62nd Cavalry Regiment, 11th Cavalry Division. He fought on the Tsaritsyn, Southern, and Western Fronts.

He graduated from the Higher Cavalry School of the Workers' and Peasants' Red Army (between 10 January 1921 to August 1923). From August 1923 he was the Commander of a Cavalry Squadron in the 22nd Cavalry Regiment, 4th Cavalry Division. From 19 November 1924 he was the Chief of Staff and subsequently Assistant Commander of the 24th Cavalry Regiment, 4th Cavalry Division. From 8 November 1926 he was the Chief of Staff of the 21st Cavalry Regiment, 4th Cavalry Division, He attended Development Courses for the Supreme Commanders at 'Vystrel' from 17 December 1928. In December 1930 he was made Assistant Commander of the Moscow Military District Headquarters sector of the Higher Education Institution. In 1932 he attended one course at the Fruntze Academy. From February 1933 he was the Commander of the 35th Cavalry Regiment, and the 22nd Cavalry Division and was made a Colonel on 13 March 1938. On 20 October 1937 he was acting Commander of a Separate Cavalry Brigade of a Separate Rifle Corps in Mongolia. On 15 September 1938 he became a Lecturer in Tactics at the Development Courses for the Supreme Commanders organised by the Workers' and Peasants' Red Army. He participated in the Soviet-Finnish War and on 18 January 1940 he was made Chief of Staff of the 113th Rifle Division. He became a Major-General on 04 June 1940. On 25 October 1940 he attended a focus group at the Operations Faculty of the Zhukovskiy Military Aviation Academy. On 27 May 1941 he was made Commander of the Air Force Directorate of the 11th Army in the Baltic Special Military District. He participated in the Great Patriotic War. On 20 September 1941 he was made Chief of Staff of the Air Forces of the North-Western Front. From May 1942 he was made Deputy Commander of the 6th Air Army, and from October 1942 of the 4th Air Army. On 25 May 1943 he became Senior Lecturer and Head of the Course at the Frunze Academy. On 14 December 1956 he was retired to the reserves.

He was awarded the Order of Lenin, and the Order of the Red Banner three times, as well as the Orders of Kutuzov 2nd class, B. Khmelnitskiy 2nd class, and the Red Star, as well as other medals.

The Commander of the 8th Mixed Air Division
Nikolai Stepanovich Toropchin

He was born on 19 October 1904 in the village of Vozdvizhenskoe, in the Vozdvizhenskoe district, Orenburg region. He joined the Red Army on 15 April 1923 and was a Red Army soldier in the 52nd Rifle Regiment, 18th Rifle Division. From August 1923 he was a student at the Yegorovsk school of Military Theory (this later became the Leningrad School of Military Theory of the Air Forces of the Worker's and Peasant's Red Army). From August 1925 he was a student of the A.F. Myasnikov 1st Military Pilots' School. From November 1926 he was a student of the Serpukhov Higher School of Aerial Combat and Bombing (known as STRELBOM). In August 1927 he became a Junior Pilot in the 70th OIAO, and subsequently became a Senior Pilot and a Flight Commander In December 1931 he was made Commander of a Detachment in the 2nd Separate Fighter Air Squadron. From October 1932 he attended the Development Courses for Supreme Commanders under the Zhukovskiy Military Aviation Academy of the Air Forces of the Workers' and Peasants' Red Army. In May 1933 he was made Commander of a Detachment in the 119th Fighter Air Squadron, and from September he was made the Squadron's Chief of Staff. In March 1934 he was made Commander of the 54th Separate Reconnaissance Aviation Department. From November 1934 he attended the Lipetsk Higher School of Tactical Flying under the Air Forces of the Workers' and Peasants' Red Army. In December 1935 he was made Commander of the 120th Fighter Air Squadron of the Air Forces of the Transbaikal Military District. In March 1938 he was made Commander of the 36th Fighter Air Regiment. In November 1938 he was made Commander of the 25th Fighter Air Regiment, 59th Fighter Air Brigade, of the Air Forces of the Leningrad Military District. In September 1939 as part of a brigade he participated in the Red Army's entry into Western Ukraine.

He participated in the Soviet-Finnish War. He carried out 48 combat sorties and fought in 10 air battles. By way of a decree issued by the Presidium of the Supreme Soviet of the USSR issued on 21 March 1940 Major N.S. Toropchin was awarded the title of Hero of the Soviet Union.

From September 1940 he was made Deputy Commander of the 25th Mixed Air Division of the Air Forces of the Transbaikal Military District. On 26 May 1941 he was made Commander of the 8th Mixed Air Division of the Air Forces of the Baltic Special Military District.

He participated in the Great Patriotic War. From July 1941 he took up command of the 8th Mixed Air Division. In March 1942 he was made Commander of the 125th Fighter Air Division of the Air Defence System, becoming a Major-General of Aviation on 10 October 1943. In May 1943 he was made Commander of the 36th Fighter Air Division of the Air Defence System. In April 1945 he was made Commander of the 106th Fighter Air Division of the Air Defence System. In April 1947 he was made Commander of the 2nd Guard's Fighter Air Division. From March 1949 he was at the disposal of the Commander of the country's Air Defence forces and then in July he was made Head of the Air Defence Commander's Auxiliary Control Point (ACP) for the Air Defence of the Moscow Region. From December 1951 he attended the Higher Aviation Courses under the K.E. Voroshilov Higher Aviation Academy. He was made Head of the Directorate of Combat Training for the Air Defence Forces of the Stalingrad region. From July 1953 he was made Head of the 5th Directorate of the country's Air Forces. From August 1954 he was the Commander of the Tavrichesk region's Air Defence Corps. From October 1955 he was made Deputy Head of the country's air defence forces for battle management and the Duty General of the Directorate of the Commander in Chief of the country's air defence forces. In October 1958 he was retired to the reserves, he died on 7 May 1987.

He was awarded the Order of Lenin twice, and the Order of the Red Banner three times, as well as the Orders of the Patriotic War 1st class, and other medals.

The navigator Senior Lieutenant Ivan Antonovich Aksyutin from the 4th Squadron, 31st Fighter Air Regiment. In this post-war photo he holds the rank of Major.

The Flight Commander of the 4th Squadron, 31st Fighter Air Regiment Junior Lieutenant Sergey Nikolayevich Akimov.

The remains of a MiG-3 aircraft (No. 2172 fitted with an AM-35A engine No. 9EA0344), which was destroyed in an accident on 10 April 1941. The pilot Junior Lieutenant Sidor Aleksandrovich Yevtushenko was killed.

The remains of a MiG-3 aircraft (No. 2172 fitted with an AM-35A engine No. 9EA0344), which was destroyed in an accident on 10 April 1941. The pilot Senior Lieutenant Ivan Antonovich Aksyutin bailed out of this aircraft by parachute.

An aerial photograph of Kaunas airfield taken on 10 April 1941 from on board a reconnaissance aircraft from Aufkl.Gr.Ob.d.L.

The Deputy Commander of the 10th Fighter Air Regiment Aleksandr Ivanovich Serenko.

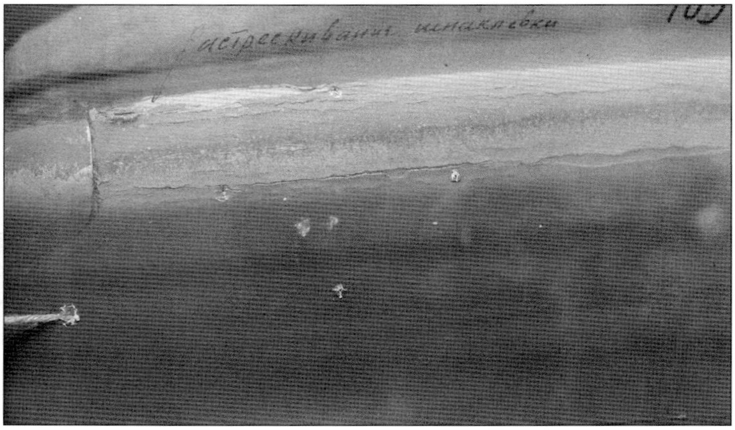

Cracks in the tail fin of a MiG-3 aircraft.

An accident that happened with an SB aircraft (No. 8/80 fitted with two M-100A engines Nos. 3-142 and 2-451) on Kuusiku airfield on 4 April 1941. The crew consisted of pilot Junior Lieutenant I.V. Melnikov, and the observer Lieutenant Aladyev. The gunner/radio-operator was Junior Sergeant Kosenko, they were unhurt.

An accident that happened with a MiG-1 aircraft (No. 2064 fitted with an AM-35A engine No.0150) on Kaunas airfield on 30 May 1941. The pilot was Deputy Commander of the 1st Squadron, 15th Fighter Air Regiment Senior Lieutenant P.M. Chepikov was unhurt, but the aircraft was beyond repair.

An accident with an I-153 aircraft (No. 7332 fitted with an M-623 engine No. 1749) on Liepaja airfield on 8 May 1941. The pilot was Junior Lieutenant K.I. Yakovlev from the 148th Fighter Air Regiment, who was unhurt ,but the aircraft was was beyond repair.

An accident that happened with a USB aircraft (No. 8/216 fitted with M-103 engines Nos. 933-194 and 023-1755) on Vaijnode airfield on 18 May 1941. The pilot was Sergeant M.S. Nebolsin from the 4th Squadron, 31st High-Speed Bomber Air Regiment. The instructor Captain N.A. Petrov was unhurt, but the aircraft was beyond repair.

An accident with an I-153 (No. 7344 fitted with an M-62 engine No. 3614) on Liepaja airfield on 21 May 1941. The pilot was Deputy Commander of the 2nd Squadron, 148th Fighter Air Regiment Senior Lieutenant L.D. Smirnov.

An emergency landing by a type 5 I-16 (No. 521084 fitted with M-25A engine No. 250887) in the area around Siauliai on 21 May 1941. The pilot from the 2nd Squadron, 10th Fighter Air Regiment Junior Lieutenant N.S. Semashev was unhurt but the aircraft was beyond repair.

A landing accident that occurred with an SB (No.18/117 fitted with two M-103 engines Nos. 923-233 and No 923-235) on 28 March 1941. On Vekhma airfield. The crew were from the 35th High-Speed Bomber Air Regiment and consisted of pilot Sergeant I.N. Myslivets, navigator Lieutenant Metelskiy, and gunner/radio-operator Junior Sergeant Lopatin. They were unhurt but the aircraft required a factory repair.

A landing accident that occurred with an SB (No.18/117 fitted with two M-103 engines Nos. 923-233 and No 923-235) on 28 March 1941. On Vekhma airfield. The crew were from the 35th High-Speed Bomber Air Regiment and consisted of pilot Sergeant I.N. Myslivets, navigator Lieutenant Metelskiy, and gunner/radio-operator Junior Sergeant Lopatin. They were unhurt but the aircraft required a factory repair.

An accident with a type 5 I-16 (No. 5210312 fitted with an M-25V engine No. 1913381) on 27 May 1941 in the area around Kaunas. The pilot was the Commander of the 4th Squadron, 31st Fighter Air Regiment Senior Lieutenant B.I. Kovshikov. He was unhurt but the aircraft was beyond repair.

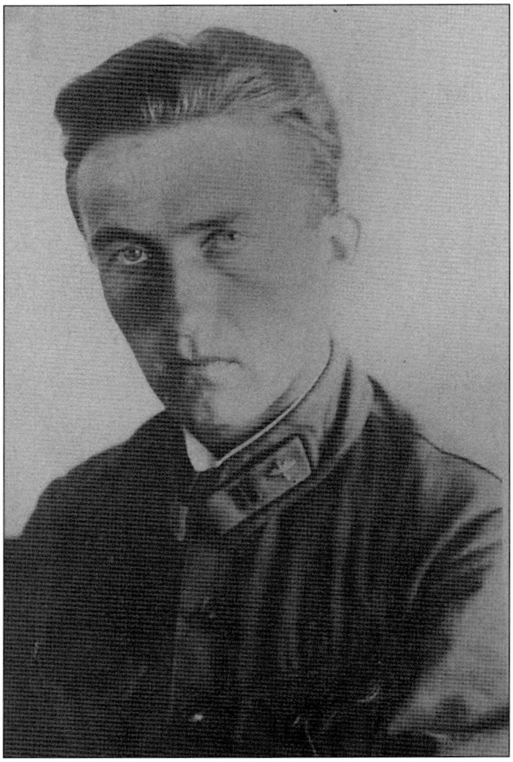

Commander of the 57th Mixed Air Division Kuzma Aleksandrovich Katichev

He was born on 25 October 1905 in the village of Danilovch, Roslavlsk district, Smolensk region.

He joined the Red Army from June 1926 and was a student at the School of Military Theory of the Air Forces of the Workers' and Peasants' Red Army in Leningrad. From May 1927 he was a student of the 2nd Military Aviation School for Pilots named after the *Osoaviakhim* of the USSR, after he had completed his studies at the 2nd Higher Aviation School in December 1928 he was retained as a Junior Pilot. From May 1929 he was a Junior Pilot and a Flight Commander in the 17th Air Observation Squadron. From May 1932 he was Flight Commander of the 71st Separate Fighter Air Detachment. From December 1933 he was the Commander of a Detachment in the Special Purpose Squadron. By way of a decree issued by the Central Executive Committee of the USSR dated 25 May 1936 for testing the prototype weaponry on these aircraft Captain K.A. Katichev was awarded the Order of the Red Star. From November 1937 he was acting Commander of the Special Purpose Squadron. In June 1938 he was made Assistant Commander of the 57th Air Brigade, becoming a Colonel on 17 February 1932. From September 1939 he was acting Commander of the 2nd Fighter Air Brigade.

He participated in the Soviet-Finnish War, and from February 1940 he was Commander of the 153rd Fighter Air Regiment. He personally completed 18 combat sorties and by way of a decree issued by the Presidium of the Supreme Soviet of the USSR dated 20 May 1940 he was awarded the Order of the Red Star. On 26 April 1940 he was made Commander of the 2nd Fighter Air Brigade. On 8 August 1940 he was made Deputy

Commander of the 7th Mixed Air Division of the Air Forces of the Special Military District. On 27 March 1941 he was made Commander of the 57th Mixed Air Division.

He participated in the Great Patriotic War and on 22 November 1942 he was made Commander of the Air Forces of the Moscow Military District and Major-General of Aviation on 1 July 1944.

In January 1948 he enrolled as a student attending higher aviation courses at the K.E. Voroshilov Higher Military Aviation Academy. In October 1949 he was made Head of the Directorate of Accident Investigation and Flight Safety at the Principal Headquarters of the Air Force. In September 1954 he was engaged in lecturing at the K.E. Voroshilov Higher Military Aviation Academy. On 27 September 1960 he was retired to the reserves. He died on 2 December 1977.

He was awarded the Order of Lenin, as well as the Order of the Red Banner four times, the Order of the Patriotic War 1st class, and the Order of the Red Star, as well as other medals.

The Commander of the 236th Fighter Air Regiment
Major Pavel Andreyevich

He was born on 3 June 1910 in the Dniepropetrovsk Region, Novomoskovskoe district, in the village of Nikolayevka.

He joined the Red Army from 1932 and in 1933 he graduated from the 9th Higher Aviation School (in Kharkov). From 15 December 1933 he was a pilot of the 52nd Artillery Correction Detachment. On 15 July 1934 he became a Junior Pilot of the 118th Fighter Air Squadron. For his successes in assimilating aviation technology and for his capable leadership in military, and political training he was awarded the Order of the Badge of Honour (on 25 May 1936).

He participated in the fighting in Spain from October 1936 until 30 January 1937. He was awarded the Order of the Red Banner on 2 January 1937.

On 8 March 1937 he was made Commander of a Flight in the 118th Fighter Air Squadron and became a Senior Lieutenant on 8 March 1937. From 2 December 1937 he was made Commander of a Detachment in the 68th Fighter Air Squadron, and a Captain on 26 February 1938. On 9 May 1938 he was made Commander of a squadron in the 16th Fighter Air Regiment, becoming a Major on 17 February 1939. From September 1939 he attended the Lipetsk Higher School of Tactical Flying.

He participated in the Soviet-Finnish War.

He was a Squadron Commander in the148th Fighter Air Regiment from December 1939. On 27 March 1941 he was made Commander of the 236th Fighter Air Regiment.

He participated in the Great Patriotic War.

He was made a Colonel on 22 May 1941. From 17 December 1942 he was at the disposal of the Commander of the 2nd Mixed Air Corps. From 10 April 1943 he was a pilot and an inspector of piloting techniques in the Directorate of the 10th Fighter Air Corps. On 9 August 1945 he was made Deputy Commander of the 279th Fighter Air Division and a Colonel from 5 August 1948. From 8 February 1949 he was a Deputy Commander of the 129th Fighter Air Division. On 21 August 1950 he was made Deputy Commander of the 107th Fighter Air Division. From 14 October 1952 he attended development courses for commanders, and chiefs of staff of the division under the Air Army. On 29 April 1953 he was working overseas. On 13 February 1956 he was retired to the reserves.

He was awarded Orders of the Red Banner, the Patriotic War, 1st, and 2nd class, and other medals.

The Commander of the 237th Fighter Air Regiment
Ivan Pavlovich Suvorov

He was born on 5 September 1909 in the village of Yermakovo, Galichsk district, Kostroma region.

He joined the Red Army on 21 December 1929 voluntarily. He was a student of the School of Military Theory of the Air Forces of the Red Army in Leningrad. From 1 June 1931 he was a student of the 2nd Higher Aviation School. On 8 July 1932 he was made an inspector of piloting techniques at the 14th Higher Aviation School. From 22 October 1938 he was made inspector of piloting techniques of the 20th Fighter Air Regiment. On 28 March 1939 he was made an inspector of piloting techniques of the 18th Air Brigade, becoming a Captain on 31 December 1939.

He participated in the Red Army's march into Western Belorussia.

He participated in the Soviet-Finnish War and from 1 October 1940 he was Deputy Commander, and then Squadron Commander of the 25th Fighter Air Regiment.

On September 9 1940 he was made an inspector of piloting techniques in the 6th Mixed Air Division. From 27 March 1941 he was made Commander of the 237th Fighter Air Regiment.

He participated in the Great Patriotic War. From November 1942 he was acting navigator in the 211th Fighter Air Regiment. From 14 April 1942 he was made acting Commander of the 745th Fighter Air Regiment. From 31 July 1942 he was acting Commander of the 147th Fighter Air Division of the Air Defence System. On 6 September 1944 he was made Deputy Commander of the 106th Fighter Air Division of the Air Defence System, becoming a Lieutenant-Colonel on 19 December 1944. In December 1944 he was made Commander of the 147th Fighter Air Division of the Air Defence System.

He participated in the fighting against Japanese forces in 1945, becoming a Colonel on 8 March 1946.

On 5 April 1948 he was made Deputy Commander of the 123rd Fighter Air Division of the Air Defence System. From 11 October 1948 he attended development courses for commanders and chiefs of staff of the division under the Air Army. He became a Major-General of Aviation on 3 August 1950. On 14 February 1951 he was made Commander of the 123rd Fighter Air Division of the Air Defence System. From 14 June 1952 he was Commander of the 50th Fighter Air Corps. On 4 September 1953 he was made Deputy Commander of the Air Defence System of the 30th Air Army. From 11 November 1954 he attended higher aviation courses at the K.E. Voroshilov Higher Aviation Academy. On 15 November 1955 he was made an Inspector-General of the Fighter Aviation Inspectorate of the Air Defence System under the Principal Inspectorate of the Ministry of Defence of the USSR. On 27 March 1957 he was at the disposal of the Principal Reconnaissance Directorate at General Headquarters. From 3 June 1957 he was acting Head of Soviet Military Liaison Mission under the Commander in Chief of American Forces in Germany. From 24 October 1958 he was the Head of Combat Training Department and of the higher education institutions in the Directorate of the Air Forces of the Southern Forces Group. From 17 December 1959 he was made duty officer at the Control Point that controls flights at Air Force General Headquarters. On 15 March 1961 he was retired to the reserves. He died on 12 June 1982 in Moscow. He was awarded the Order of the Red Banner twice, as well as the Orders of the Patriotic War 1st class, and of the Red Star, and other medals.

The Commander of the 238th Fighter Air Regiment
Major Anisim Ivanovich Syrov

He was born on 28 February 1904 in Mozdok.

He joined the Red Army from October 1926 he was a student of the School of Military Theory of the Air Forces of the Red Army in Leningrad. From January 1928 he was a student at the 3rd Higher Aviation School. From July 1929 he was a Junior Pilot in he 17th Fighter Air Squadron and subsequently became a Flight Commander from November 1930. On 13 June 1934 he was made a Detachment Commander of the 117th Fighter Air Squadron. From 20 November 1934 he was made Detachment Commander of the 116th Fighter Air Squadron. From May 1935 he was a Deputy Commander of Military Unit 1019 becoming a Captain on 14 March 1936. On 19 March 1937 he was made Detachment Commander of the 2nd Higher Aviation School. From 9 October 1938 he was made Squadron Commander of the 42nd Fighter Air Regiment, becoming a Major on 25 July 1940. On 19 November 1940 he was made Deputy Commander of the 31st Fighter Air Regiment. On 27 March 1941 he was made Commander of the 238th Fighter Air Regiment.

He participated in the Great Patriotic War.

From 16 August 1941 he was a Commander of the 293rd Fighter Air Regiment and failed to return from a sortie on 27 March 1942.

The Commander of the 239th Fighter Air Regiment
Aleksey Innokentyevich Kurochkin

He was born on 25 May 1911 in the Orekhovo-Zuyevo, Moscow region.

He joined the Red Army on 26 May 1931 as a student of the A.F. Myasnikov 1st Higher Aviation School. From 20 August 1932 he enrolled at the Higher Military Pilot's School, becoming a Flying Instructor, Flight Commander, and a Assistant Head of the Flying School, and a Captain on 12 February 1938. From 12 February 1939 he attended higher courses in tactical flying in Lipetsk. From 20 October 1939 he was a Squadron Commander of the 42nd Fighter Air Regiment. On 27 March 1941 he was made Commander of the 239th Fighter Air Regiment.

He participated in the Great Patriotic War. From 12 December 1943 he was made a Deputy Commander of the 235th Fighter Air Division. From 13 February up to 9 March 1943 he was an acting Commander of the 235th Fighter Air Division. From 17 November 1943 he was made Deputy Head of the Flying Section of the Higher Officers' School of Air Combat of the Air Forces of the Red Army. From 1 March 1947 he was Deputy Commander of the flying section of the higher officer's courses in Tactical Flying.

From 11 October 1948 he attended development courses for the supreme commanders and chiefs of staff of the divisions under the Military Aviation Academy. On 8 June 1949 he was made Head of the Kachinsk Higher Aviation College. From 4 October 1952 he attended higher aviation courses at the Military Academy of the K.E. Voroshilov Military Aviation Academy. On 14 January 1955 he was made Head of the Borisogleb Higher Aviation College. He became a Major-General of Aviation on 18 December 1958. From 10 November 1960 he was made Head of logistics in the Air Forces of the Moscow Military District. On 16 March 1970 he was retired to the reserves, he died on 26 March 1978.

He was awarded the Order of Lenin, and the Order of the Red Banner 4 times, and the Orders of the Patriotic War 1st class, and 2nd class, and the Orders of the Red Star and other medals.

The Commander of the 240th Fighter Air Regiment, Veniamin Vsevolodovich Andreyev

He was born on 13 June 1908, in the Sverdlovsk region, in the town of Lysva.

He joined the Red Army on 15 October 1930 and was a student of the Regimental School of the 169th Rifle Regiment, 57th Rifle Division. In December 1930 he was enrolled as a student in the 7th Higher Aviation School. From 18 December 1932 he attended development flight commander's courses in the Kharkov Military District

On 3 October 1934 he was made Flight Commander in the 106th Fighter Air Squadron, and became a Lieutenant on 14 March 1936. He subsequently from June 1936 he became the Commander of a Detachment and on 3 October 1936 he became a navigator in the 106th Fighter Air Squadron, and a Senior Lieutenant on 22 April 1937. From June 1938 he became an inspector of piloting techniques in the 15th Fighter Air Regiment. On 29 August 1938 he was made Squadron Commander of the 15th Fighter Air Regiment, becoming a Captain on 31 October 1938.

He took part in the Soviet-Finnish War.

From October 10 1940 he was made Deputy Commander of the 15th Fighter Air Regiment. On 27 March 1941 he was made Commander of the 240th Fighter Air Regiment.

He participated in the Great Patriotic War.

He became a Major 15 June 1940 and from 16 November 1942 he was made Commander of the 822nd Fighter Air Regiment of the Air Defence System, and a Lieutenant-Colonel on 12 October 1944. On 7 December 1944 he was made Deputy Commander of the 141st Fighter Air Division of the Air Defence System. From 6 January 1947 he was made Commander of the 933rd Fighter Air Regiment of the Air Defence System, becoming a Colonel on 16 May 1949. On 23 January 1950 he was made Deputy Commander of the 155th Fighter Aviation Division of the Air Defence System. From 7 March 1951 he was acting Commander of the 64th Fighter Air Corps. On 29 May 1952 he was made Deputy Commander of the Air Defence of the Caucasian Border Region. From 24 July 1953 he was the Deputy Head of the 7th Air Defence System directorate. From 11 September 1954 he was Deputy Commander of Fighter Aviation in the Air Defence System of the Transcaucasian Military District.

He was awarded the Order of the Patriotic War 1st class twice, and the Order of the Red Star, and other medals.

The Commander of the 241st Ground Attack Air Regiment Aleksey Filippovich Obukhov

He was born on 14 August 1904 in the town of Kirillov, Volochayev Region.

He joined the Red Army in November 1926, and was a cadet of the 22nd Separate Mortar Battery, from October 1927 he was a student of the 2nd Leningrad Artillery School. In April 1931 he became a Platoon Commander of the 4th Corps Artillery Regiment. From May 1932 he attended lectures at the Military School of the All-Russian Central Executive Committee for commanders and combined military and political leaders. From October 1932 he was made Commander of the Artillery Fleet of the 4th Corps Artillery Regiment.

From 27 February 1933 he attended the 2nd Higher Aviation School (in Borisoglebsk). In November 1934 he was made Section Commander of the 26th Separate Fighter Air Detachment, becoming a Senior Lieutenant on 19 March 1936. From May 1936 he was an instructor of the 92nd Fighter Air Brigade. From July 1937 he was a Commander of a Detachment in the 92nd Fighter Air Brigade.

He participated in fighting in China from 28 June 1938 to 5 August 1939 he was a Section Commander, and an Assistant Group Commander, he completed 42 combat sorties. From the report on his government tour of duty: 'He participated in five air battles. He was disciplined, consistent, brave, and decisive in battle. He is recommended for the Order of the Red Banner, and the Red Star. This attests to the position of Commander of a Fighter Regiment with an award of the rank of Colonel.'

On 9 October 1939 he was made Deputy Commander of the 42nd Fighter Air Regiment, becoming a Major (on 5 November 1939), and from 27 March 1941 he was made Commander of the 241st Ground Attack Air Regiment.

He participated in the Great Patriotic War.

He became a Lieutenant-Colonel on 9 January 1942. On 18 May 1942 he was made a Commander of the 225th Ground Attack Air Division, becoming a Colonel on 22 November 1942. From 29 July 1944 he was acting Commander of the 214 Ground Attack Air Division. On 12 February 1945 he was made Commander of the 227th Ground Attack Air Regiment. From 30 September 1946 he was Commander of the 206th Ground Attack Air Regiment. From April to June 1948 he was an attendee at development courses for the commanders, and chiefs of staff in this regiment under the Military Aviation Academy. He was subsequently to command the 206th Ground Attack Air Regiment again, becoming a Major-General on 11 May 1949. From 20 January 1952 he was an attendee at Higher Aviation Courses under the Voroshilov Military Aviation Academy. On 14 November 1953 he was made Commander of the 8th Guard's Bomber Air Division. On 30 August 1956 he was retired to the reserves.

He was awarded the Orders of the Red Banner 2nd class, and of Suvorov 3rd class, as well as the Red Star and other medals.

The Commander of the 4th Mixed Air Division Brigade Commander Andrey Nikolayevich Sokolov

He was born on 6 February 1896 in the village of Rozhdestveno in the Novo-Petrovsk district, Moscow region.

He participated in the First World War from June 1917 onwards, he was a Platoon Commander in the 21st Light Mortar Battalion of the 9th Army, and he held the rank of Senior Warrant Officer.

He joined the Red Army in March 1918, as a volunteer. He was a Platoon Commander and a Battery Commander in the Artillery Battalion of the Western Rifle Division. From May 1920 he was the Head of an operational department of the 6th Cavalry Division, 1st Cavalry Army. From September 1920 he was the Chief of Staff of the 6th Cavalry Division, 1st Cavalry Army. From December 1920 he attended the Red Army Military Academy. From February 1921 he was the Chief of Staff of the Artillery Group of the 7th Army. From April 1921 he attended the Red Army Military Academy. From July 1921 he was the Chief of Staff of the 3rd Cavalry Corps on the Western Front. From May 1922 he was in the Red Army headquarters reserve. From September 1922 he was the Head of Department at the Moscow City Courier Corps of the Unified State Political Department. From September 1923 he attended the Leningrad Military Aviation School for Pilot-observers. From June 1924 he was a trainee pilot-observer in the 3rd Separate Reconnaissance Air Squadron of the Air Forces of the Kiev Military District. From July 1924 he was a Senior Instructor in the Leningrad School of Military Theory of the Air Forces of the Red Army. From April 1925 he was a trainee pilot at the 2nd Military Aviation School for Pilots named after the *Osoaviakhim* of the USSR. From July 1925 he was a trainee pilot at the 3rd Military Aviation School for pilots and observers. From September 1925 he was the Commander of a Detachment in the 7th Separate Reconnaissance Air Squadron of the Air Forces of the Leningrad Military District. From June 1926 he was Commander of the 1st Separate Reconnaissance Air Detachment of the Air Forces of the Leningrad Military District From January 1927 he was Commander of the 34th Air Squadron of the of the Air Forces of the Leningrad Military District, and from December 1927 he was Commander of the 56th Air Squadron of the Air Forces of the Leningrad Military District. From January 1929 he was Squadron Commander of the 3rd Military Aviation School for Pilots and Observers. From January 1930 he was the Commander of the 46th Air Squadron of the Air Forces of the North-Caucasian Military District. In 1930 he attended development courses for supreme commanders under the Zhukovskiy Military Aviation Academy of the Worker's and Peasant's Red Army From August 1933 he was Commander of the 11th Air Brigade of the Air Forces of the Moscow Military District, becoming a Brigade Commander on 28 November 1935. On 30 May 1936 for his outstanding successes in assimilating new combat materiel, and in combat, and political training he was awarded the Order of Lenin. From January 1937 he was Commander of the 93rd Air Brigade, Special Purpose Aviation. From February 1938 he was at the disposal of the Red Army Supreme Commanders Directorate. In August 1938 he was retired to the reserves. In June 1939 he was reinstated to the ranks of the Red Army as Head of a Flight-Test station at

Factory No. 22 of the People's Commissariat for the Aviation Industry working on the '1000'. On 19 July 1940 he was made Deputy Commander of the 2nd Mixed Air Division, and from 8 August 1940 Deputy Commander of the 4th Mixed Air Division. On 27 March 1941 he was made Commander of the 4th Mixed Air Division.

He participated in the Great Patriotic War. From October 1941 he was the Head of the Stalingrad Higher Aviation College, becoming a Major-General on 28 May 1943. On October 1944 he was made the Deputy Commander of the Air Forces of the North-Caucasian Military District, responsible for the Higher Education Institution. In November 1945 he was made Commander of the Chernigov Higher Aviation College. From October 1946 he was made the Head of the 2nd Balashevsk Higher Aviation College. From December 1949 he was made Deputy Head of the Principal Directorate of the Civilian Air Fleet. He was Senior Lecturer at the Faculty of the Art of Operations in the Aviation Faculty of the K.E. Voroshilov Higher Military Aviation Academy. He died on 11 November 1952.

He was awarded the Order of Lenin twice, as well as the Orders of the Red Banner, Red Star, and the Patriotic War 2nd class, as well as other medals.

The Deputy Commander of the 6th Mixed Air Division Colonel Vladimir Alekseyevich Kitayev

29 May 1908 in Verkhneudinsk–4 December 1986, Zhda-Russkiy). He joined the Red Army from July 1926 he graduated from the School of Military Theory of the Workers' and Peasants' Red Army in Leningrad in 1927, and the A.F. Myasnikov 1st Military Pilots' School in 1929, as well as graduating from courses in operations under the Military Aviation Academy named after professor N.E. Zhukovskiy in 1939.

V.A. Kitayev in July 1926 was called up to join the Worker's and Peasant's Red Army and was sent to the Lenin School of Military Theory of the Workers' and Peasants' Red Army. After graduating from here in 1927 he continued his studies in the A.F. Myansikov 1st Military Pilots' School. In June 1929 he was made Junior Pilot in the 52nd Ground Attack Air Regiment of the Air Forces of the of Belorussian Military District in Gomel. From September 1930 he continued his service in the 19th Air Squadron, which had been re-deployed initially to Bryansk, and hence to Moscow, and to Khabarovsk, performing the duties of a Flight Commander, as well as that of a Detachment Commander, a Chief of Staff, and a Squadron Commander. From April 1938 he was an Assistant Commander of the 58th Air Brigade from the Air Forces of the Belorussian Military District in Mogilev, from April to October 1938 he was in temporary command of this brigade. He took part in the Red Army's march into Western Belorussia. In 1939 V.A. Kitayev was sent to attend courses in operations under the Military Aviation Academy of the N.E. Zhukovskiy Worker's and Peasant's Red Army, on completion of which he was made Commander of the 49th Fighter Air Regiment of the Air Force in the November, the unit was based in Lida. In this position he took part in the Soviet-Finnish War between 1939–1940. For successful completion of his orders in commanding this regiment he was awarded the Order of the Red Banner. Colonel V.A. Kitayev personally completed 59 combat sorties. From May 1940 he performed the duties of Deputy Commander of the 6th Mixed Air Division of the Air Forces of the 8th Army of the Baltic Special Military District in Riga. In April 1941 he was made Commander of the 72nd Mixed Air Division of the Air Forces of the Western Caucasian Military District. With the outbreak of the Great Patriotic War Colonel V.A. Kitayev continued to command this division. From August 1941 he was carrying out the duties of the Commander in Chief of the Air Forces of the 44th, and of the Primorskoye Armies. From July 1942 he took up command of the 283rd Fighter Air Division. It was whilst he held these positions that he participated in the fighting on the Crimean, South-Western, Stalingrad, and Don fronts. After the conclusion of the battle of Stalingrad in February 1943 Colonel V.A. Kitayev, as one of the best Commanders in the division, was assigned to the 274th Fighter Air Division, 1st Fighter Corps, 3rd Air Army on the Kalinin Front. Major-General of Aviation of V.A. Kitayev in this period flew 174 combat sorties, and fighting in 31 air battles, In which he personally shot down nine enemy aircraft. After the war V.A. Kitayev up until October 1945 continued to command this same division. From February 1946 he was the Commander of the 16th Guard's Fighter Air Division in the Belomorsk Military District. In March 1947 he was made Deputy Commander of the 336th Fighter Air Division of the Baltic Military District. In November he was made Deputy Commander of the 275th Fighter Aviation Division, 13th Air Army. In September 1948 he was retired to the reserves.:

He was awarded the Order of the Red Banner three times, as well as the Orders of Kutuzov 2nd class, and the Order of the Patriotic War 1st class, and the Order of the Red Star, as well as other medals.

Deputy Commander of the 8th Mixed Air Division Lieutenant-Colonel Ivan Vasilyevich Yakubvich, he was the only one of the Deputy Commanders of the Divisions in the Air Forces of the Baltic Special Military District to remain in his post after the roll out of the new units, and formations in Spring 1941.

An accident with a MiG-3 from the 31st Fighter Air Regiment (No. 2166 fitted with an AM-35A engine No. 9EA0354) in Kaunas on 2 June 1941. Another MiG-3 collided with this aircraft, which was being flown by Flight Commander of the 4th Squadron Lieutenant G.I. Gagushin.

An accident that happened with a MiG-3 (No. 2373 fitted with an AM-35A engine No. 03247) on Kaunas airfield on 6 June 1941. The pilot was Deputy Commander of the 4th Squadron, 15th Fighter Air Regiment Senior Lieutenant V.A. Voronov.

This same aircraft is inspected by German soldiers following the capture of Kaunas.

An accident that happened with an SB aircraft (No. 19/203, fitted with two M-103A engines No. 923-485), on Tartu airfield on 9 June 1941. Of the entire crew from the 5th Squadron, 53rd High-Speed Bomber Air Regiment Flight Commander Senior Lieutenant P.N. Rabinovich, and gunner/radio-operator Sergeant Venikov were unhurt, but navigator Lieutenant A.A. Popov was killed. According to the accident report the aircraft required a major repair.

This same aircraft in a German photograph, evidently the aircraft was not repaired and iwas written off, and broken up for spares.

An accident with a I-153 (No. 6518 fitted with an M-62 No. 960) in the area of Tallinn airfield. On 10 June pilot of the 3rd Squadron, 38th Fighter Air Regiment Junior Lieutenant I.M. Ilyin bailed out by parachute, and the aircraft crashed in a flat spin.

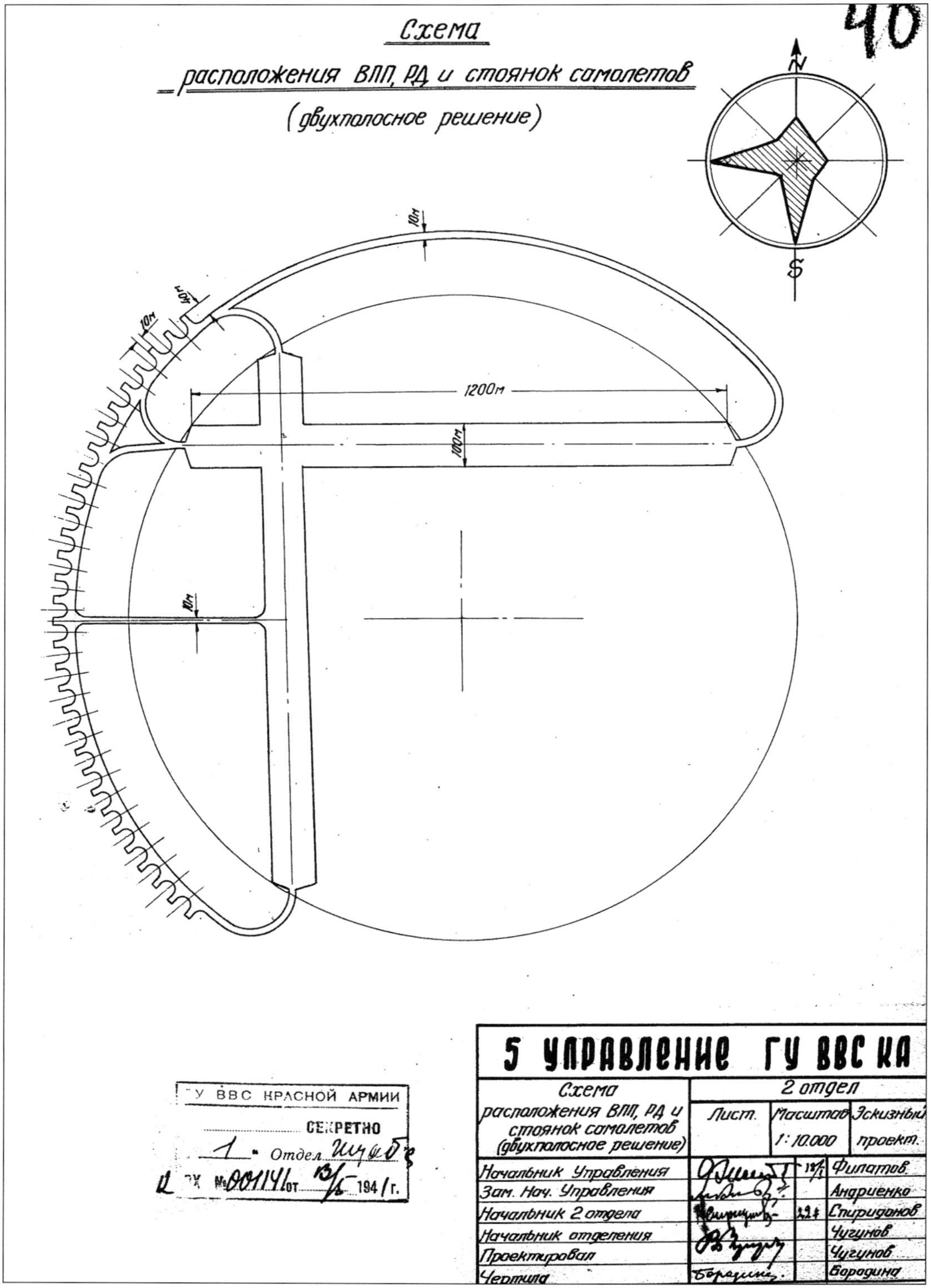

A plan of the distribution of the runways, taxiways, and aircraft hard standings from a standard design for an airfield for 1941.

The personnel are laying down the metal framework ahead of concreting the runway, spring 1941.

3

War on the Doorstep

The *Luftwaffe* Alignment that Opposed the Baltic Special Military District. A Comparison of Both the Soviet and German Aviation Alignments, the Plans of Both Sides, and the Reconnaissance Measures.

3.1 The *Luftwaffe* Alignment that Opposed the Baltic Special Military District. A Comparison of the Soviet and German Aviation Alignments.

What did the *Luftwaffe* aviation alignment that was lined up against the Air Force units of the Baltic Special Military District comprise of?

Firstly, these were units and formations that were deployed to support the forces of Army Group 'North', that included *Luftflotte* 1 and I. *Fliegerkorps* in its line-up, and which had advanced via the Baltic to Leningrad.

Secondly the units and formations that comprised the *Luftflotte* 2 and VIII. *Fliegerkorps* that had been deployed in the area around Suvalok, and was prepared to attack both the forces of the Soviet Western District, and against the left flank of the Baltic District.

I. *Fliegerkorps* comprised the entire 1st, 76th, and the 77th Bomber Wings (KG 1, KG 76, KG 77), the 54th Fighter Wing (JG 54) as well as the headquarters of the second group of the 53rd Fighter Wing (JG 53) and the 5th Squadron of the 122nd Long-Range Reconnaissance Group (5.(F)/122).

Aside from the I. *Fliegerkorps*, the so-called *Fliegerführer Ostsee* also came under the wing of the *Luftflotte* 1, which was to have seen action over the Gulf of Finland in conjunction with the fleet, as part of a separate bomber group (KGr. 806) and three squadrons of the 125th Group of Maritime Reconnaissance Crews (1.2.3./(F)125).

The reserve training groups of the 54th, and 52nd Fighter Wings (Erg./JG 52 and the Erg./JG 54) were based on airfields behind the lines as part of *Luftflotte* 1.

The reconnaissance units were represented by the 2nd Squadron of the High Command Reconnaissance Group (2.(F)/Ob.d.L) and the 1st Weather Reconnaissance Squadron (*Wekusta* 1).

VIII. *Fliegerkorps* was a formation which comprised units equipped with strike aircraft. The principal aim of these units was to strike ground and naval surface targets in conjunction with the tank groups of the *Wehrmacht*:

The Headquarters, and the II and III Groups of the 1st Dive Bomber Wing (StG 1), Headquarters, I and II groups of the 2nd Dive Bomber Wing (StG 2);

The second group (ground attack) and the 10th Squadron of the 2nd Training Wing (II.(S)/LG 2 and 10.(S)/LG 2).

The Headquarters, and the I and II Groups of the 26th Heavy Fighter Wing (ZG 26).

The Headquarters, and the II and III Groups of the 2nd Bomber Squadron (KG 2), and apart from that the Second Group of the 52nd Fighter Wing (II./JG 52) and the third group of the 53rd Fighter Wing (III./JG 53), was subordinate to the headquarters of this same squadron.

The 2nd Squadron of the 11th Long-Range Reconnaissance Group (2.(F)/11).

The reconnaissance units were directly subordinate to Army Group Command, as well as that of the tank groups, and the field armies. The so-called 'Air Command' (*Kommander der Luftwaffe—Koluft*) was part of the army groups, field armies, and tank groups, and apart from the reconnaissance squadrons the liaison squadrons, and the anti-aircraft artillery units these were also part of the *Koluft*.

One separate 'highlight' was that the short-range reconnaissance units were not only subordinated to the army and motorised corps, but also to the tank divisions, which undoubtedly gave the German mobile formations significant advantages over the enemy.

All the German units were at a strength that was close to the standard numbers, and had excellent tactical training, as well as combat experience.

Table 10 The constituents of the German alignment

***Luftwaffe* 1, Norkitten, General *Oberstern* Keller**

Unit	Airfield	Aircraft type	Quantity	Commander
2.(F)/Ob.d.L[1]	Norkitten Seerappen	Do 215 Ju-88D	22/14	*Hauptmann* Dietrich
Wekūsta 1	Jürgenfelde	He 111H Ju-88A Do 17Z Ju-52/3m	2/1 2/2 2/2 1/1	*Oberleutnant* Kater

Note

1 This unit regrouped from the Do 215 onto the Ju-88D, and by all accounts, owing to this they had a double quota of aircraft. Evidently up until 22 June 1941 the crews were still being converted onto the Junkers, since the Do 215s were not used in combat.

I. *Fliegerkorps*, Gumbinnen, General der Flieger Forster

Unit	Airfield	Aircraft type	Quantity	Commander
Stab/KG 1	Powunden	He 111H	1/1	*Oberstleutnant* Angerstein
II./KG 1	Powunden	Ju-88A	29/27	*Hauptmann* Stams
III./KG 1	Eichwalde bei Labiau	Ju-88A	30/29	*Major* Lehwess-Litzmann
Stab/KG 76	Gerdauen	Ju-88A	1/ -	*Oberstleutnant* Bormann
I./KG 76	Gerdauen	Ju-88A	30/22	*Hauptmann* v. Sichart
II./KG 76	Jürgenfelde	Ju-88A	30/25	*Hauptmann* Riedesel zu Eisenbach

Unit	Airfield	Aircraft type	Quantity	Commander
III./KG 76	Schippenbeil	Ju-88A	29/22	*Major* v. Benda
Stab/ KG 77	Heiligenbeil	Ju-88A	1/1	*Oberstleutnant* Raithel
I./KG 77	Jesau	Ju-88A	30/23	*Hauptmann* Pötter
II./KG 77	Wormditt	Ju-88A	31/23	*Hauptmann* Peltz
III./KG 77	Heiligenbeil	Ju-88A	29/20	*Major* v. Frankenberg
Stab/JG 54	Lindental	Bf 109F	4/3	*Major* Trautloft
I./JG 54	Rautenberg	Bf 109F	40/34	*Hauptmann* v. Bonin
II./JG 54	Trakehnen	Bf 109F	40/33	*Hauptmann* Hraback
III./JG 54	Blumenfeld	Bf 109F	40/35	*Hauptmann* Lignitz
II./JG 53	Neusiedel	Bf 109F	25/24[1]	*Hauptmann* Bretnütz
5.(F)/122	Jürgenfelde	Ju-88D Bf 110	9/8 3/2	*Major* Banke

Note

1 Only the Headquarters of the 4th, and 5th Air Squadron Groups remained in the East, but only the total number of aircraft along with those of the 6th Air Squadron in terms of 35/33 aircraft is known. Strength is put at 25/24 aircraft.

***Fliegerführer Ostsee*, Königsberg, *Oberstleutnant* von Wild**

Unit	Airfield	Aircraft type	Quantity	Commander
K.Gr. 806	Prowehren	Ju-88A	30/18	*Major* Emig
1.(F)/125	Fischhausen	He 60	9/5	
2.(F)/125		He 114	9/9	
3.(F)/125		Ar 95	9/8	

Air Command Army Group North (*Koluft Heeresgruppe Nord*), Insterburg

Unit	Airfield	Aircraft type	Quantity	Notes
1.(F)/22	Insterburg	Ju-88D	7/5	
3.(F)/Nacht	Insterburg	Do 17P	10/3	
KGr.z.b.V. 106	Insterburg	Ju-52/3m	44/8	
Kurierstaffel 9				

Air Command of the 18th Army (*Koluft Armee-Oberkommando* 18), Eichwalde bei Labiau, *Osberstleutnant* Dr Stein

Unit	Airfield	Aircraft type	Quantity	Notes
3.(F)/22	Eichwalde bei Labiau	Ju-88D	9/6	
2.(H)/21	Margen	Hs 126B-1	7/7	Operated in conjunction with the 38 Air Corps
4.(H)/21	Memel	Hs 126B-1	6/5	Operated in conjunction with the 26th Air Corps
7.(H)/21	Wolfsberg	Hs 126B-1	7/5	Operated in conjunction with the 1st Air Corps
Kurierstaffel 12				

The Air Command of the 4th Panzer Group (*Koluft Panzer-Armee-Oberkommando* 4), Ragnit, *Oberstleutnant* Günther Lohmann.

Unit	Airfield	Aircraft type	Quantity	Notes
4.(F)/33	Ragnit	Bf 110	9/9	
Headquarters of the 23rd Reconnaissance Group (*Gruppenfliegerstab* 23).				
4.(H)/31	Tilsit	Fw 189A-1	9/9	Operated in conjunction with the 41st Mechanised Corps
2.(H)/23	Tilsit	Hs 126B-1	7/7	Operated in conjunction with the 1st Panzer Division
3.(H)/23	Ragnit	Hs 126B-1	7/7	Operated in conjunction with the 6th Tank Division
Headquarters of the 13th Reconnaissance Group (*Gruppenfliegerstab* 13).				
8.(H)/32	Lindengarten	Hs 126B-1	7/6	Operated in conjunction with the 56th Mechanised Corps
3.(H)/41	Lindengarten	Hs 126B-1	7/5	Operated in conjunction with the 8th Tank Division
Kurierstaffel Panzer-AOK 4				

Air Command of the 16th Army (*Koluft Armee-Oberkommando* 16), Ebenrode, *Oberstleutnant* von Wurmb.

Unit	Airfield	Aircraft type	Quantity	Notes
1.(H)/12	Ebenrode	Fw 189A-1	9/9	Operated in conjunction with the 28th Air Corps
2.(H)/13	Ebenrode	Hs 126B-1	7/6	Operated in conjunction with the 2nd Air Corps
4.(H)/23	Neuweide	Hs 126B-1	5/4	Operated in conjunction with the 10th Air Corps
Kurierstaffel 2				

VIII. *Fliegerkorps*, Suwalki, General der Flieger von Richthofen

Unit	Airfield	Aircraft type	Quantity	Commander
Stab/KG 2	Arys-Rostken	Do 17Z	11/5	*Oberstleutnant* Rieckhoff
I./KG 2	Arys-Rostken	Do 17Z	35/19	*Major* Lerche
III./KG 2	Lyck	Do 17Z	41/23	*Oberstleutnant* Conrady
III./KG 3	Suwalki	Do 17Z	44/18	*Major* Rathmann
Stab/StG 1	Radczki	Ju-87B Bf 110	3/2 6/3	*Major* Hagen
II./StG 1	Radczki	Ju-87B	39/28	*Hauptmann* Keil
III./StG 1	Radczki	Ju-87B	39/24	*Hauptmann* Mahlke
Stab/StG 2	Praschnitz	Ju-87B Bf 110	3/3 6/4	*Major* Dinort
I./StG 2	Praschnitz	Ju-87B	35/19	*Hauptmann* Hitschhold
III./StG 2	Praschnitz	Ju-87B/R	39/20	*Hauptmann* Steen
Stab/ZG 26	Suwalki	Bf 110C/E	4/4	*Oberstleutnant* Schalk
I./ZG 26	Suwalki	Bf 110C/E	38/17	*Hauptmann* Kaminski
II./ZG 26	Suwalki	Bf 110C/E	36/30	*Hauptmann* v. Rettberg

Unit	Airfield	Aircraft type	Quantity	Commander
Stab/JG 27	Subolewo	Bf 109E	4/4	*Major* Schellmann
II./JG 27	Berzniki	Bf 109E	40/31	*Hauptmann* Lippert
III./JG 27	Subolewo	Bf 109E	40/14	*Hauptmann* Dobislav
II./JG 52	Subolewo	Bf 109F	39/37	*Hauptmann* Woitke
III./JG 53	Subolewo	Bf 109F	38/36	*Hauptmann* Wilcke
II.(S)/LG 2	Praschnitz	Bf 109E	38/37	*Major* Weiss
10.(S)/LG2	Praschnitz	Hs 123	22/17	
2.(F)/11	Suwalki	Do 17P	12/10	*Hauptmann* Randel-Semper

Air Command of the 3rd Panzer Group (*Koluft Panzer-Armee-Oberkommando* 3), Suwalki, *Oberstleutnant* Hans Berger

Unit	Airfield	Aircraft type	Quantity	Commander
2.(F)/33	Dubowo	Bf 110	9/8	
Headquarters of the 11th Reconnaissance Group (*Gruppenfliegerstab* 11)				
4.(H)/12	Dubowo	Hs 126B-1	10/10	Operated in conjunction with the 39th Mechanised Corps
1.(H)/11	Dubowo	Fw 189A-1	6/6	Operated in conjunction with the 7th Panzer Division
1.(H)/13	Dubowo	Hs 126B-1	7/6	Operated in conjunction with the 20th Tank Division
Headquarters of the 21st Reconnaissance Group (*Gruppenfliegerstab* 21)				
7.(H)/13	Krusznik	Hs 126B-1	7/7	Operated in conjunction with the 57 Mechanised Corps
3.(H)/12	Krusznik	Hs 126B-1	7/7	Operated in conjunction with the 12 Tank Division
2.(H)/32	Krusznik	Hs 126B-1	6/5	Operated in conjunction with the 19th Tank Division
Kurierstaffel Panzer-AOK 3				

Air Command of the 9th Army* (*Koluft Armee-Oberkommando* 9). General Major Albert Müller-Kahle

Unit	Airfield	Aircraft type	Quantity	Commander
4.(H)/10		Fw 189A-1	8/7	Operated in conjunction with the 5th Air Corps
2.(H)/12		Hs 126B-1	7/6	Operated in conjunction with the 6th Air Corps

* The remainder of the units from those that comprised this command operated in the Grodno direction against the forces of the Western Front.

In total this amounted to 1,242 combat aircraft, of which 916 were serviceable:

402 bombers (of which 276 were serviceable), of which 270 were Ju-88s (210 of these were serviceable), 131 Do 17Zs (of which 65 were serviceable) and one He 111 (of which one was serviceable).
158 Ju-87B/R dive-bombers (of which 96 were serviceable).
272 single-engine fighters (of which 215 were serviceable), of those 188 Bf 109F-1/2s (of which 166 were serviceable), 84 Bf 109E-1/4/7s (of which 49 were serviceable).
78 Bf 110C/E heavy fighters (of which 51 were serviceable).
12 Bf 110s under the headquarters of the dive bomber squadrons (of which seven were serviceable).
60 ground attack aircraft (of which 54 were serviceable), of which 38 were Bf 109Es (and 37 of these were serviceable), and 22 Hs 123 aircraft (of which 17 were serviceable).
124 long-range reconnaissance aircraft (of which 93 were serviceable) of which 27 were Ju-88Ds (of which 21 were serviceable), 21 Bf 110s (of which 19 were serviceable), 22 Do 215s (of which 14 were serviceable), 24 Do 17P/Zs (of which 15 were serviceable), two He 11Hs (of which one was serviceable), one Ju-52 (of which one was serviceable), and also 28 Ar 95/He 60/He 114/Ju-52s (of which 23 were serviceable).
136 short-range reconnaissance aircraft (of which 124 were serviceable), of which 32 were Fw 189A-1s (some 31 of these were serviceable) and 104 were Hs 126B-1s (of which 93 were serviceable).

The relatively high number of unserviceable aircraft can be explained for the most part by the fact that the units of the VIII. *Fliegerkorps* had only just left the battles in the Balkans just a few weeks previously.

In total the Germans concentrated the headquarters of nine wings against the Air Forces of the Baltic Special Military District consisting of two air corps, of these six were bomber wings (including two dive bomber wings) and three were fighter wings (including one heavy fighter wing):

11 bomber groups, which amounted to 34 squadrons in total (including the KG 2 headquarters squadron);
Four groups of dive bombers, 12 squadrons in total;
Eight fighter groups, 23 squadrons, and 10 headquarters flights;
Two heavy fighter groups, six squadrons and three headquarters flights (together with one projected squadron);
One augmented ground attack group, four squadrons;
12 long-range reconnaissance squadrons;
19 short-range reconnaissance squadrons.

In certain circumstances, training squadrons in the training reserve groups in the 52nd and 54th Wings that were deployed in airfields behind the lines in East Prussia may well have taken part in combat activity.

1. Aviation District (*Luftgau-Kommando* I) Königsberg, *General Leutnant* Putzier.

Unit	Airfield	Aircraft type	Quantity	Commander
Erg.JGr. 52[1]	Neuhausen	Bf 109 E	30/19	
Erg.JGr. 54[2]	Neukuhren	Bf 109 E	24/19	

Notes
1 This included a training squadron of 12 Bf 109E aircraft (of which two were unserviceable), and 11 pilots.
2 This included a training squadron of 11 Bf 109Es (of which four were unserviceable), four Bf 109Fs (of which one was unserviceable), and 13 pilots.

Luftwaffe formations and units were situated in a single echelon and were ready to go into battle at full strength.

In the immediate first echelon of the Air Forces of the Baltic Special Military District there were four aviation divisions, 10 fighter, five bomber, and two ground attack regiments.

There were 21 combat capable squadrons of SBs (of which four were at limited combat readiness):

Five squadrons from the 9th High-Speed Bomber Air Regiment;
Five squadrons from the 31st High-Speed Bomber Air Regiment;
Five squadrons from the 40th High-Speed Bomber Air Regiment;
Three squadrons from the 46th High-Speed Bomber Air Regiment (and two squadrons with limited combat readiness);
Three squadrons from the 54th High-Speed Bomber Air Regiment (and two with limited combat readiness);
Three combat capable fighter squadrons, of which nine operated I-153s and four operated I-16s.
Four squadrons from the 148th Fighter Air Regiment;
Four squadrons from the 10th Fighter Air Regiment;
One (the 2nd) squadron from the 15th Fighter Air Regiment;
Four squadrons from the 42nd Fighter Air Regiment;
Seven fighter squadrons with limited combat capability that operated MiG-1/3s and I-16s;
Three squadrons from the 15th Fighter Air Regiment;
Four squadrons from the 31st Fighter Air Regiment;
Four projected squadrons from the line-up of the 236th, 237th, and 240th Fighter Air Regiments, which had limited combat capability, operating the I-153, and the I-15bis.
Five ground attack squadrons, with a limited combat capability, that operated I-153s from the 61st Ground Attack Air Regiment.
One estimated squadron with limited combat capability from the 241st Ground Attack Air Regiment
Four corps reconnaissance squadrons (the 10th, 11th, 16th, and 103rd Air Observation Squadrons) and a separate aerial photographic detachment (the 2nd Aerial Photographic Detachment), which did not have any combat capable materiel.

There was an aviation division in the second echelon of the Air Forces of the Baltic Special Military District, three fighter, three bomber regiments, and one reconnaissance regiment.

There were 15 combat capable bomber squadrons equipped with SBs:

Five squadrons from the 35th High-Speed Bomber Air Regiment;
Five squadrons from the 50th High-Speed Bomber Air Regiment;

Five squadrons from the 63rd High-Speed Bomber Air Regiment;

12 combat-capable fighter squadrons, six operating the I-153, and six operating the I-16:
Four squadrons from the 21st Fighter Air Regiment;
Four squadrons from the 49th Fighter Air Regiment;
Four squadrons from the 38th Fighter Air Regiment;

Five corps reconnaissance squadrons (the 22nd, 24th, 29th, and 65th Air Observation Squadrons).
Four long-range reconnaissance squadrons from the 312th Reconnaissance Air Regiment, which were not combat capable.

Table 11 A comparison of the *Luftwaffe* and the Air Forces of the Baltic Special Military District alignments (displaying data for combat capable aircraft only)

Luftwaffe alignment		The Air Forces of the Baltic Special Military District	
I. *Fliegerkorps*	*VIII. Fliegerkorps*	1 Provisional echelon	2 Provisional echelon
	Fighter squadrons		
11 squadrons and 5 headquarters flights 129 Bf 109F	**12 squadrons and 5 headquarters flights** 73 Bf 109F 49 Bf 109E In total 122 Bf 109	**13 squadrons** 80 I-153 27 Type 5 I-16s **11 squadrons with limited combat readiness** 75 MiG-1/3 Seven I-15bis 35 I-153 In total 224 fighters	**12 squadrons** 86 I-153 75 I-16 In total 161 fighters
	Bomber squadrons		
24 squadrons 210 Ju-88A	**10 squadrons** 65 Do 17Z	**21 squadrons (and 4 with limited combat readiness)** 207 SBs	**15 squadrons** 114 SBs
	Dive bomber, heavy fighter, and ground attack squadrons		
–	**22 squadrons and 3 headquarters squadrons** 96 Ju-87 B/R 58 Bf 110C/E 37 Bf 109E 17 Hs 123 In total 208 strike aircraft	**5 squadrons** 59 I-153 **1 squadron with limited combat capability** 15 I-15bis In total 74 strike aircraft	–
	Long-range reconnaissance squadrons		
10 squadrons	**2 squadrons**	–	–
	Short-range reconnaissance squadrons		
11 squadrons	**8 squadrons**	**4 squadrons**	**7 squadrons**

In a quantitative analysis of the warring alignments it is possible, it would appear, to state that the forces were almost 100 percent equal. There were 1,274 combat aircraft in the line-up of the Air Forces of the Baltic Special Military District, against the *Luftwaffe's* 1,242 aircraft.

In a comparison of the numbers of combat capable squadrons and crews however this parity immediately disappears.

As far as fighter aviation was concerned there were 24 fighter squadrons that could go into battle at any given time from the Air Forces of the Baltic Special Military District. Of these 13 were combat capable, which included nine that operated I-153s (a total of 80 crews) and four that operated the I-16 (a total of 27 crews). A further four estimated squadrons, and seven squadrons with limited combat capability and which flew the MiG-1/3 and the I-16 were also included in that number.

Against them were 23 fighter squadrons and 10 headquarters flights (approximately a further three estimated squadrons), consisting of 202 Bf 109Fs, and 49 Bf 109Es.

The *Luftwaffe*'s fighter aviation alignment only exceeded the first echelon of the Air Forces of the Baltic Special Military District by a small margin, but the *Luftwaffe* held the qualitative advantage. The Soviet pilots just did not have any aircraft that were capable of countering the Bf 109F. Almost half of the fleet consisted of what were clearly obsolete Type 5 I-16s, and I-15bis aircraft that were only good for use as training machines, as well as the technically unreliable MiG-1s / MiG-3s with their armament that had not been finely tuned. The principal aircraft serving in fighter aviation in the Baltic Special Military District however was the I-153. For all its advantages, however, this aircraft was not always capable of catching a Ju-88, let alone German fighters. 'Chaika' pilots could only engage the fighter aircraft in combat in favourable conditions or if the enemy themselves actually attacked the Soviet biplane.

In the line-up of the I. *Fliegerkorps* there were in total 153 fighter pilots. Of those in the headquarters of JG 54 there were three pilots, in I./JG 54 there were 40 pilots, in II./JG 54 there were 46 pilots, and in III./JG 54 there were 39 pilots, while in the II./JG 53 (the headquarters of the 4th and 5th Air Squadrons) there were approximately 25 pilots.

In the line-up of the VIII. *Fliegerkorps* there were in total 135 combat-capable fighter pilots. Of those in the Stab/JG 27 there were 4 pilots, in II./JG 27 there were 36 pilots, and in III./JG 27 there were 24 pilots, in II./JG 52 there were around 35 pilots, and in III./JG 53 there were 36 pilots.

In total there were only 331 pilots in the units (which included those not combat capable), given a standard strength of 316. Of those there were 114 experienced pilots (those who already had combat experience), and of those there were 43 aces (pilots who had recorded five or more kills). In terms of combat experience an approximate distribution would be as follows: there were 94 pilots who had been engaged in combat for more than a year (in the campaigns in Norway, Denmark, and France as well as earlier campaigns), and 32 who had been engaged in combat activity for between six months to a year (in the Battle of Britain and later), as well as 56 who had been engaged in combat for less than six months (since the beginning of 1941). There were in addition the 149 newest pilots who had joined the units in the Spring–Summer of 1941. Thus, as a minimum 126 pilots had acquired significant combat experience (or 40 percent of the standard strength), and a further 56 had insignificant combat experience (this amounted to 18 percent of the standard strength).

In terms of ground attack aviation the situation was even worse. The *Luftwaffe's* advantage in terms of the number of units was four times larger, and in terms of aircraft it was three times larger. Considering the combat capabilities of the German strike aircraft and the training of their crews, the advantage seems even more imposing.

There is little point in discussing the situation with respect to reconnaissance aviation, as there was a complete lack of combat capable long-range reconnaissance units in the Air Forces of the Baltic Special Military District. In terms of short-range reconnaissance aviation, however, the advantage for the *Luftwaffe* was in the order of five, and taking into consideration the qualitative edge, this position was one of an absolute advantage. All the German aircraft were specially designed machines, and the Fw 189, or as that aircraft was still known by its nickname the 'Frame', set the standard for a reconnaissance aircraft right up until the end of the Second World War.

An approximate comparison only remained in bomber aviation due to the fact that the units of the 4th Mixed Air Division were very capable of operating within the territory of East Prussia from their own airfields in Estonia. However all the 24 squadrons of the I. *Fliegerkorps* were equipped with the newest Ju-88s, and as such there is no point in discussing any parity of forces in terms of this category.

Even when the fact that part of the forces of the VIII. *Fliegerkorps* were mobilised against the Air Forces of the Baltic Special Military District in the Grodno direction is taken into consideration, the *Luftwaffe* alignment still held a measurable quantitative advantage over the first echelon of the Air Forces of the Baltic Special Military District. Taking into consideration the absolute advantage the Germans had in fighter aviation however the battle for air superiority for the Air Forces of the Baltic Special Military District was a hopeless one from the very outset.

In principal the commanders of the Air Forces of the Baltic Special Military District did have the potential to augment their forces. The 21st, 49th, and 38th Fighter Air Regiments under the 4th Mixed Air Division were based in the second echelon of the Air Forces of the Baltic Special Military District. All three regiments were fully equipped units—12 squadrons of 'Ishak' and 'Chaika,' as well as 86 I-16s, of which 45 were later series aircraft, and 90 I-153s comprised half of the combat-capable sub-divisions in the Air Forces of the Baltic Special Military District's fighter aviation. Their participation in the first air battles would have, if not changed the situation, then at least enabled a prevention of a complete routing of the forward units.

Naturally driving the enemy out of Riga, or Daugavpils, and even out of Tallinn for that matter was unrealistic, but for the most part deploying these units closer to the theatre of operations would not have posed any particular difficulties. Apart from that the staging airfields could be used for operations conducted by the 21st, and the 49th Fighter Air Regiment.

Subsequent events however were to illustrate that although an augmentation of forces was envisaged in the plans for the provision of cover, it was not realised even in the critically unfolding situation that held sway at the beginning of the war.

3.2 The Plans of the Different Sides – Reconnaissance

The *Luftwaffe* command ordered their units and formations to neutralise the air forces of the Red Army as a first priority, and moreover neither support for the *Wehrmacht's* troops on the ground, nor the task of destroying the corresponding reserves, and the infrastructure behind the Soviet lines was taken into consideration. Even the 8th Air Corps (VIII. *Fliegerkorps*), which had gained a reputation for close support of ground troops on the battlefield, was nevertheless also given the following order:

> Suppression of enemy Air Forces and gaining air superiority is critical right at the outset by means of attacks on the airfields and by engaging enemy fighters in combat.
>
> The first planned missions should be as follows: attacks on the airfields with the aim of suppressing enemy Air Forces during the initial attack. Destruction of the channels of communication, and of the dissemination of information.
>
> Destruction of the command headquarters housing the enemy's operational leadership. Bombing of the main areas where the enemy's troops are concentrated, as well as military technology, and munitions. Close air support of armoured tank forces.

Undoubtedly the principal component of the German plan was that *Luftwaffe* command was planning to mobilise practically all its subdivisions not only of bomber, but also of fighter aviation in the initial attacks on the airfields, the only exception being the groups of dive bombers.

Special weaponry and ammunition was developed for the *Luftwaffe* aircraft and was tested in the course of armed combat to enable them to be effective against the airfields.

The principal weapon for effective action against enemy aviation on the airfields themselves became the SD-2, and SD-10 high-explosive bombs with which the Bf 109E and Bf 110 were armed, with 96 SD-2 bombs each, as well as the Do 17Z and Ju-88As with 360 SD-2s each. Apart from that, in the bomber groups some of the Ju-88A, and Do 17Z aircraft were armed with the so-called 'A' variant, that is to say they each carried some twenty 50 kg SD 50 high explosive fragmentation bombs in their bomb bays. In fighter aviation units pilots serving in a series of subdivisions, as a rule one squadron in each group, would be trained as fighter-bomber crews and would carry one 250 kg, or four 50 kg bombs on a ventral pylon.* Thus even small groups of German aircraft operating at low level could literally cover an airfield with an avalanche of bombs. In addition all the German fighters and some of the bombers had gun armament, which enabled them to strafe an airfield effectively after it had been bombed.

Another idiosyncrasy of the German plan was that the first attacks would be made by individual crews, and flights, specially trained in night flying. Their orders were to destroy the runways and carry out reconnaissance on the airfields they were attacking. These attacks were to be carried out simultaneously with the start of the artillery preparations.

A very well organised aerial reconnaissance revealed the number of aircraft on practically all the Soviet bases and enabled the Germans to prepare detailed plans for the participants in the subsequent raids. Apart from that, active reconnaissance flights from the opening minutes of the invasion, and thereafter flown constantly, enabled the Germans to quickly define the airfields to which Soviet units had been redeployed, having escaped the first few attacks, and to attack them almost immediately without allowing those units an opportunity to get themselves organised.

Training for this invasion began with flights by high altitude reconnaissance aircraft from the so-called Rohwel Group (*Gruppe-Rohwel-Aufkl.Gr.Ob.d.L.*) over Soviet territory from January 1941 onwards. The first flight over the aerial reconnaissance stations was recorded as having taken place on 6 January.†

Specially developed He 111s and Do 215s fitted with high altitude engines were used in these activities, and two to three aircraft each were drawn from the 1st, 2nd, and 3rd Squadrons. The 1st Squadron operated from Tana airfield in Norway, and the 2nd Squadron operated from Seerappen airfield in East Prussia (directly opposite the Air Forces of the Baltic Special Military District), while the 3rd Squadron operated from the Krakow airfield. The 4th Squadron flew five Ju-86P aircraft (that were fitted with pressurised cabins, and diesel engines with turbo-compressors), and two or three prototype Ju-88Bs from Bucharest as well as from Plovdiv and Krakow airfields. All

* Aircraft of the Air Forces of the Baltic Special Military District did not have any weaponry and ammunition that was analogous. As a rule the SB bombers carried a bomb load of between six to eight FAB-100 or FAB-50 bombs, while I-153 fighters carried two FAB-50s, and two small calibre fragmentation bombs (25, 12, 10, or eight kg). In terms of gun fighters there were 15 type 28 I-16s, and nine type 17 I-16s in the district, the majority of which were in the 21st Fighter Air Regiment, which accordance with pre-war plans were to be used as a regiment that formed part of the Air Defence System of Riga. Therefore it would be futile to rely on the effectiveness of attacks using this weaponry, considering German airfields were so saturated with air defence systems.

† Aircraft in Rohwel's group began reconnaissance flights over the territory of the USSR back in 1934 and continued their activities right up until August 1939. After the conclusion of the non-aggression pact between the USSR and Germany flights ceased temporarily, but reconnaissance resumed in December 1939 and was conducted during the course of 1940–1941.

these aircrafts had civilian identification markings and were unarmed (by way of an example the only aircraft to be lost during the course of these flights was a Ju-86P, which bore the civilian registration D-APEW, and was unarmed).

The main targets on Soviet territory were the roads and railways, sea and river ports, industrial enterprises, and of course the airfields.

The Germans tried to camouflage their extensive activities, and to cross the border secretly German crews would as a rule gain as much altitude as possible and use cloud cover. As far as the 2nd Squadron was concerned the crews would usually commence their flight from Seerappen airfield near Königsberg, and the aircraft would then gain altitude over the Gulf of Finland and whilst conducting aerial reconnaissance in the Baltic Region and in Belarussia they would have crossed the border somewhere around the Brest area, after which they would head back to their home base over German territory. However it was difficult to remain unseen given such a wide tract of operation. Despite the fact that the Red Army did not have a radar system, the aerial reconnaissance posts recorded a relatively high number of aircraft overflying the border:

> On 24 January 1941, an unidentified twin-engine aircraft. At 1745 hrs in the area around Kunigishki (34 km to the south of Liepaja) a German aircraft flew across the border, which, after flying a circuit over Shaki (47 km south of Raseiniai), departed back towards the west on a heading of 240°.
>
> On 2 February 1941, an unidentified twin-engine aircraft. At 1615 hrs in the area around Vainutas (44 km to the west of Marijampole) a German aircraft crossed the border, which after flying a circuit over Vistytis, departed back towards the west.
>
> On 4 February 1941, A single, unidentified twin-engine aircraft. At 1634 hrs in the area around Vainutas (72 km south-west of Telsiai) a German aircraft crossed the border, which having set course for Naumiestis (10 km west of Vainutas) turned back towards German territory.
>
> On 5 February 1941, a single Heinkel 111 aircraft. At 0957 hrs in the area around Palanga (63 km south of Liepaja) a German aircraft crossed the border, and proceeded to fly 11 km inside our own territory and as one of our fighter aircraft drew near, departed on a heading of 270°.
>
> On 7 February 1941, a single, unidentified twin-engine aircraft. At 0940 hrs in the direction of Palanga (63 km south of Liepaja) a German aircraft crossed the border, which flew out to sea on a heading of 240°. Two fighters that had been scrambled were not able to locate the German aircraft due to low cloud and poor visibility.
>
> 12 February 1941. A single 'Heinkel 111' aircraft. At 0950 hrs in the area around Liepaja a German aircraft crossed the state border. A flight of fighters that had been scrambled could not find the German aircraft as it had vanished into cloud.
>
> 14 February 1941. A single 'Heinkel 111' aircraft. At 0955 hrs in the area around Kalnishtis (33 km south of Liepaja) a German aircraft crossed the state border, and flew on a heading of 360° to Akmendziras (11 km south-west of Vindava). A flight of fighter aircraft were not able to find this aircraft due to low cloud, and poor visibility.
>
> 3 March 1941. A single, unidentified twin-engine aircraft. At 0835 hrs a German aircraft crossed Palanga at a heading of 180° and flew away towards German territory. The fighters were not scrambled as the airfields were unsuitable.
>
> 5 March 1941. A single 'Dornier 17'. At 1627 hrs in the area around Palanga a German aircraft crossed the state border. In the area around Liepaja this aircraft was fired upon by anti-aircraft artillery, after which it departed towards the sea losing altitude. The fighters were not scrambled because the airfields were unsuitable.

The Commander of the Red Army Air Force Lieutenant-General Rychagov, in a report to the People's Commissar for Defence Marshall Timoshenko, dated 4 April 1941 noted that from 1 January 1941 to 25 March 1941 some 25 German aircraft had crossed the border (in the Baltic region the principal direction of these flights was noted as Liepaja–Palanga), and for the majority of flights the reason was clearly not a loss of orientation, and it was proposed that this situation could be utilised to prepare retaliatory action:

> Fighters scrambled to intercept do not have the right to fire at German aircraft that have crossed the border.
>
> There were no incidents of German aircraft firing at our aircraft as they crossed the border in 1940 either.
>
> I consider it necessary, using the fact of the lack of any instances of German aircraft firing on our aircraft crossing the German border, to carry out photographic reconnaissance on what for us are the most important border areas, and fortifications. I await your instructions.

While the Soviet leaders held meetings the activity among German reconnaissance aircraft increased sharply. The first 10 days of April set a new record for the level of border incursions in the Baltic direction. Soviet fighters were regularly scrambled to intercept German reconnaissance aircraft in response to signals from the aerial reconnaissance system, but the high altitude at which the German crews operated as a rule did not enable the pilots of the I-15, and I-153s to draw near. An attempt by several pilots who remained at Kaunas, and whom had been trained in the MiG-3, to intercept a high altitude reconnaissance aircraft, led to the loss of two aircraft on 10 April, as well as one pilot.

> On 3 April 1941. A single twin-engine, unidentified aircraft, H=9,000. At 1225 hrs a German aircraft crossed the state border in the area around Kunigishi (85 km south-west of KAUNAS) and flew over Naumiestis, Shaki, Kaunas, Raseiniai, and Shavli. Without flying a further 15 k to Jelgava it changed course, and flew along the railway line to Tilsit. A flight of fighters from Shavli airfield took-off, and followed the German aircraft to the border. Two MiG-3 fighters from Kaunas airfield, that followed the intruder to Raseiniai, returned to Kaunas due to a technical failure.
>
> On 5 April 1941. A single 'Heinkel 111' aircraft, H=4,000. At 0810 hrs a German aircraft was discovered in the area around Lake Pape (35 km south of Liepaja) on a northerly heading. In the area around Lake Liepaja this intruder was intercepted by our own fighters and after changing course, flew out to sea. As they followed the intruder our fighters fired 20 warning bursts of machine gun fire and followed the aircraft out to sea to a distance of 30 km.
>
> On 8 April 1941, a single, twin-engine, unidentified aircraft, H=6,000. At 1135 hrs this aircraft flew north along the coast in the area around Palanga, and flew over Shavli, and Jelgava at 1308 hrs, flying on towards German territory in the area around Palanga. On encountering two I-153 aircraft that had taken off from Palanga airfield and a flight of I-153s that took off from Liepaja airfield the intruder flew out to sea. A flight of I-16s that took off from Shavli airfield was not able to reach the intruder. Captain Serenko chased after the intruder, broke away from the flight, lost orientation and made an emergency, wheels-up landing in the area around Ostrov.
>
> Two I-16s that took off from Riga airfield did not locate the intruder.
>
> On 8 April 1941. A single Do 17 aircraft. At 1350 hrs a German aircraft flew north along the coast in the area around Palanga. After flying as far as Liepaja and after encountering a flight of I-153s that had taken off from Liepaja airfield the German aircraft flew out to sea.

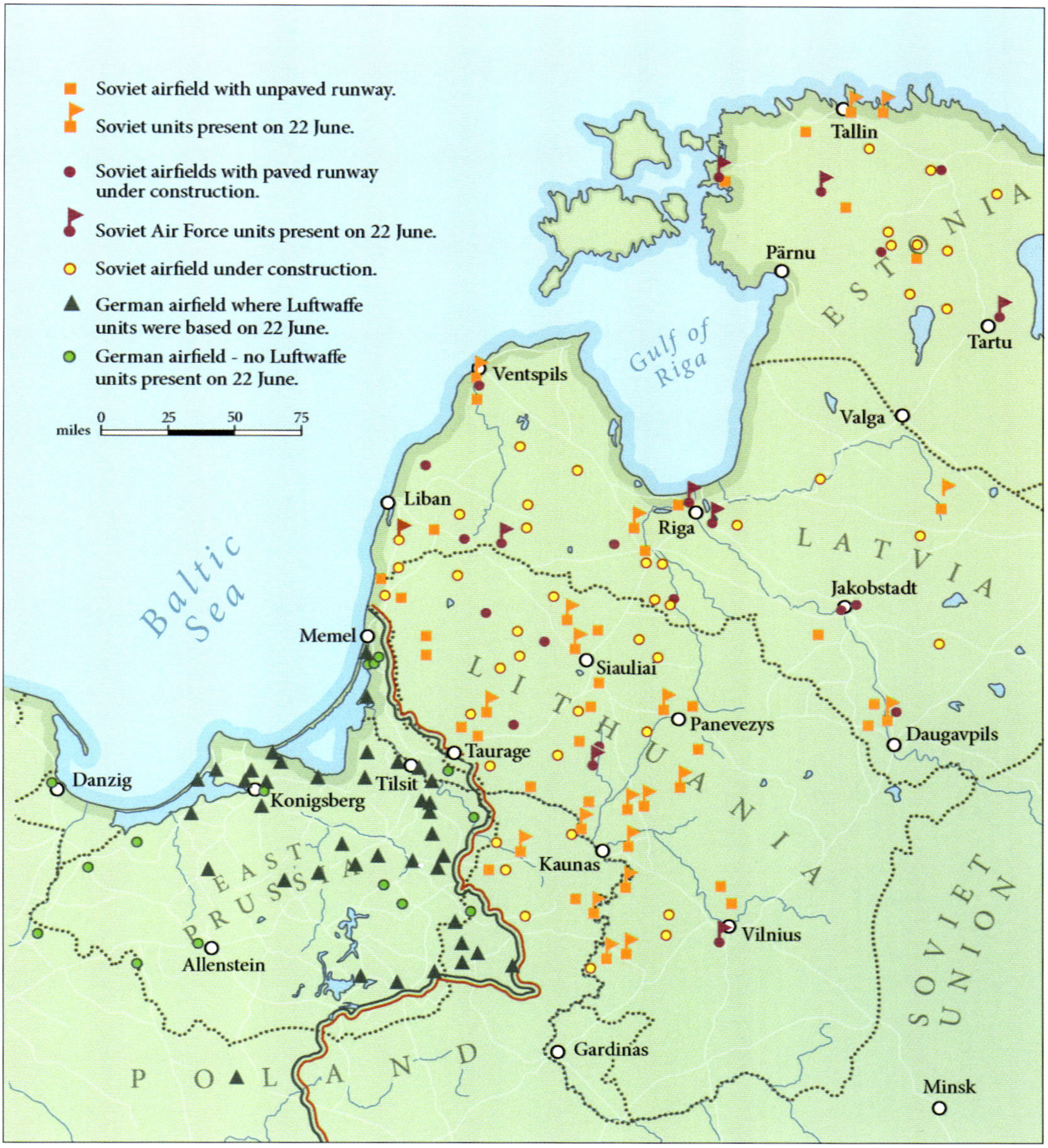

Map 1 The situation at 4 a.m. on 22 June 1941.

Map 2 Sites for the construction of new operational airfields in the Baltic region, in 1941.

Map 3 Directions of operations over Soviet territory for reconnaissance aircraft from the Long-Range Air Reconnaissance Air Group (Aufkl.Gr.Ob.d.L) or as it was often dubbed 'Rowehl's Group'.

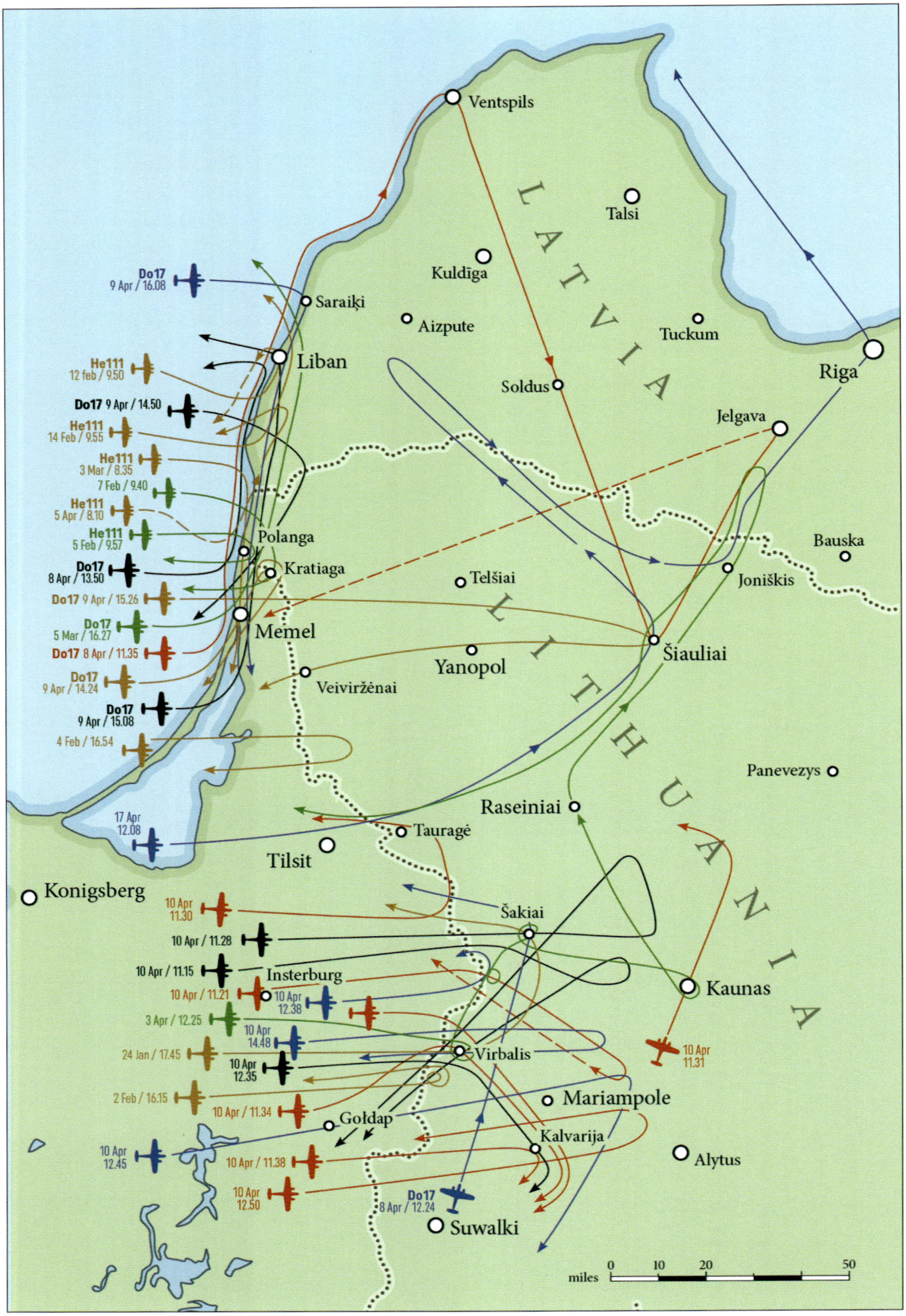

Map 4 Violations of the state border of the USSR from 1 January to 10 April 1941.

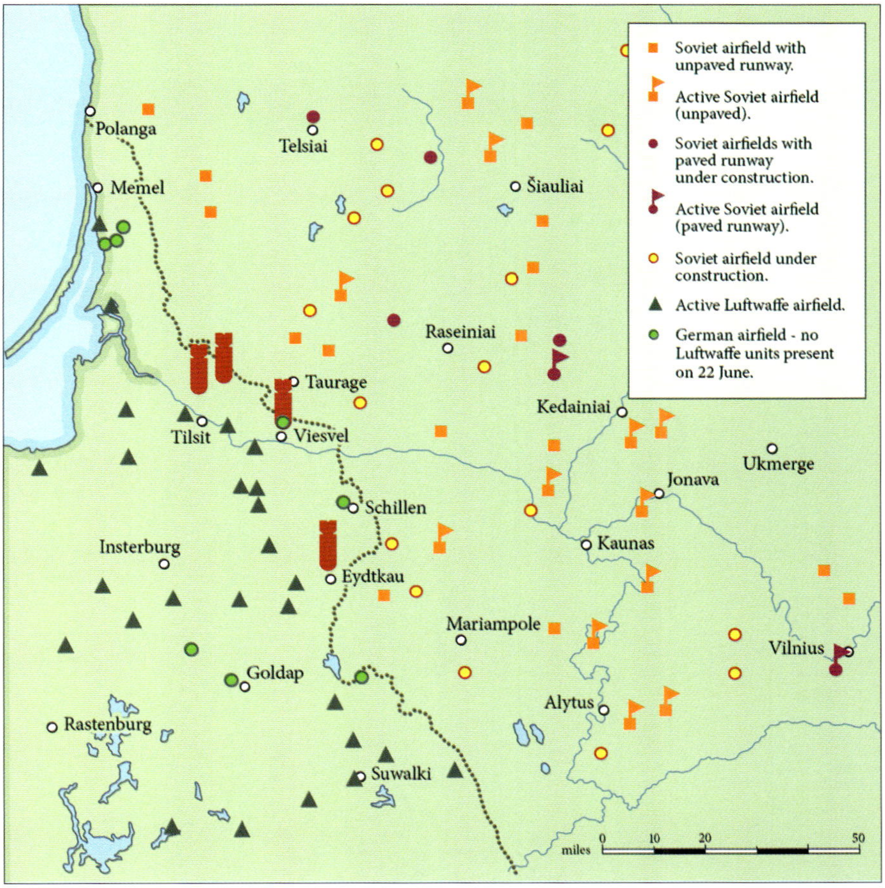

Map 5 Bombing attacks carried out by the 9th, and 46th High-Speed Bomber Air Regiments on the morning of 22 June 1941.

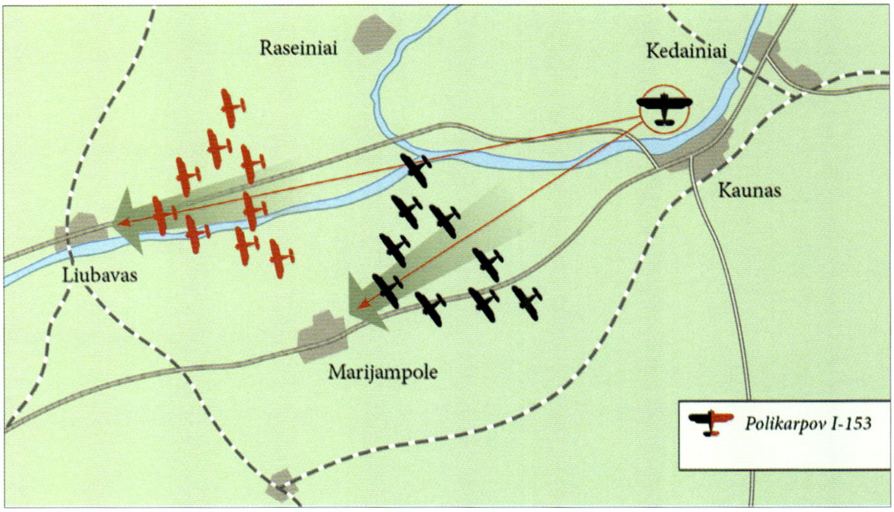

Map 6 The first combat sortie for aircraft of the 61st Ground Attack Air Regiment to attack advancing German forces in the area around Kalvarija and Lyubavas. From the history of the 61st Ground Attack Air Regment.

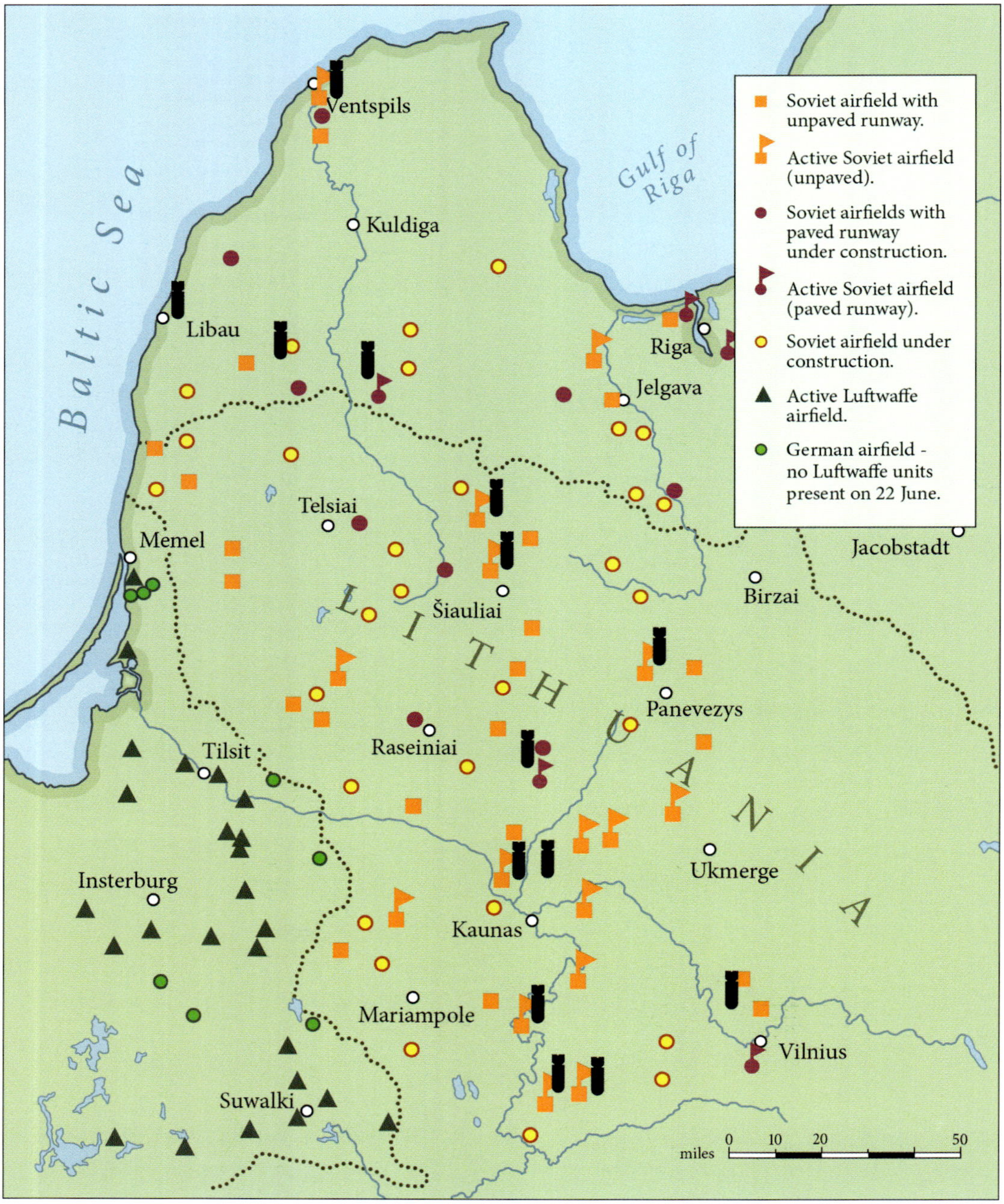

Map 7 Raids by *Luftwaffe* aircraft on the airfields of the Air Forces of the North-Western Front on 22 June 1941.

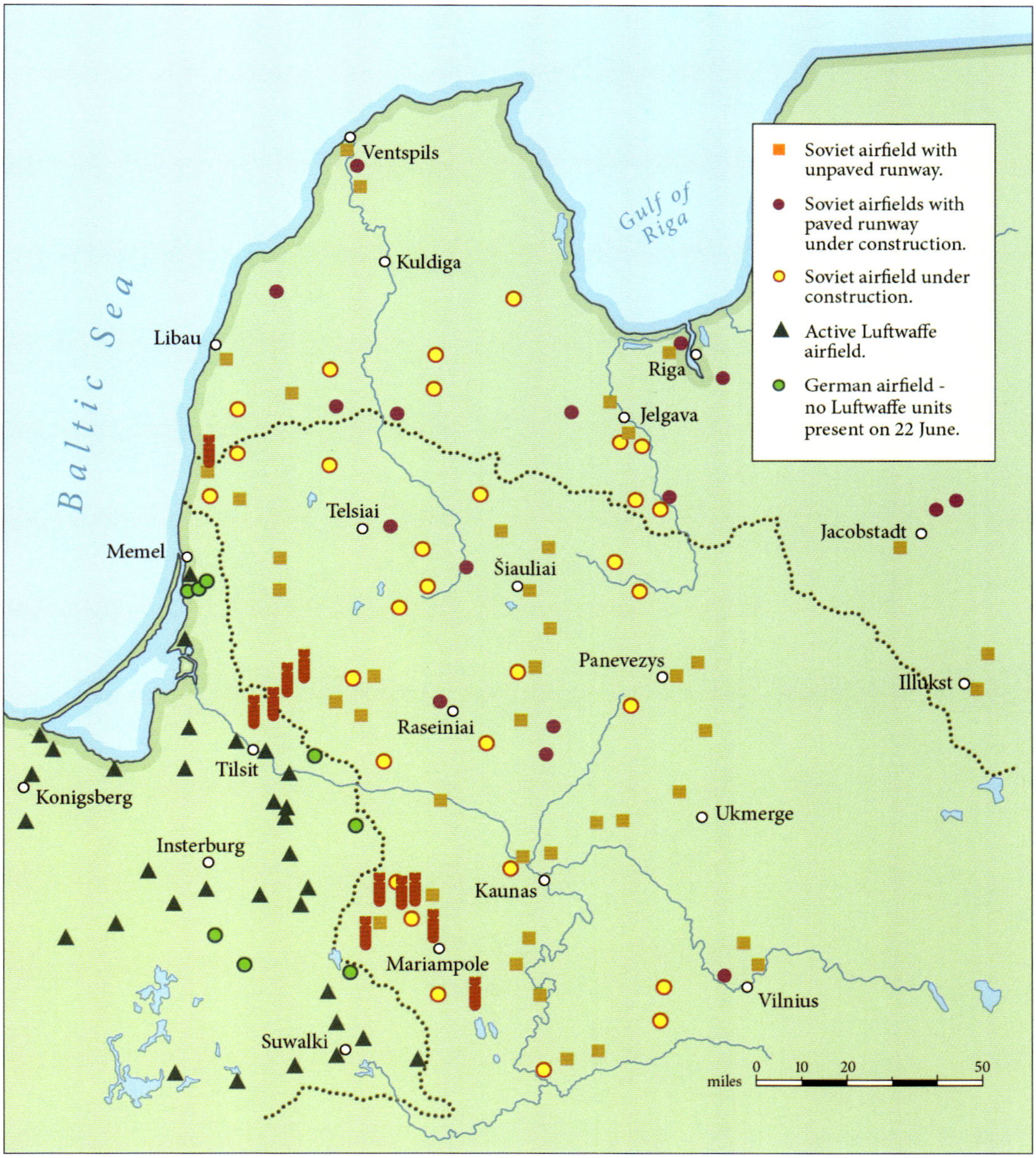

Map 8 Bombing raids carried out by North-Western Front aircraft on advancing *Wehrmacht* forces on 22 June 1941.

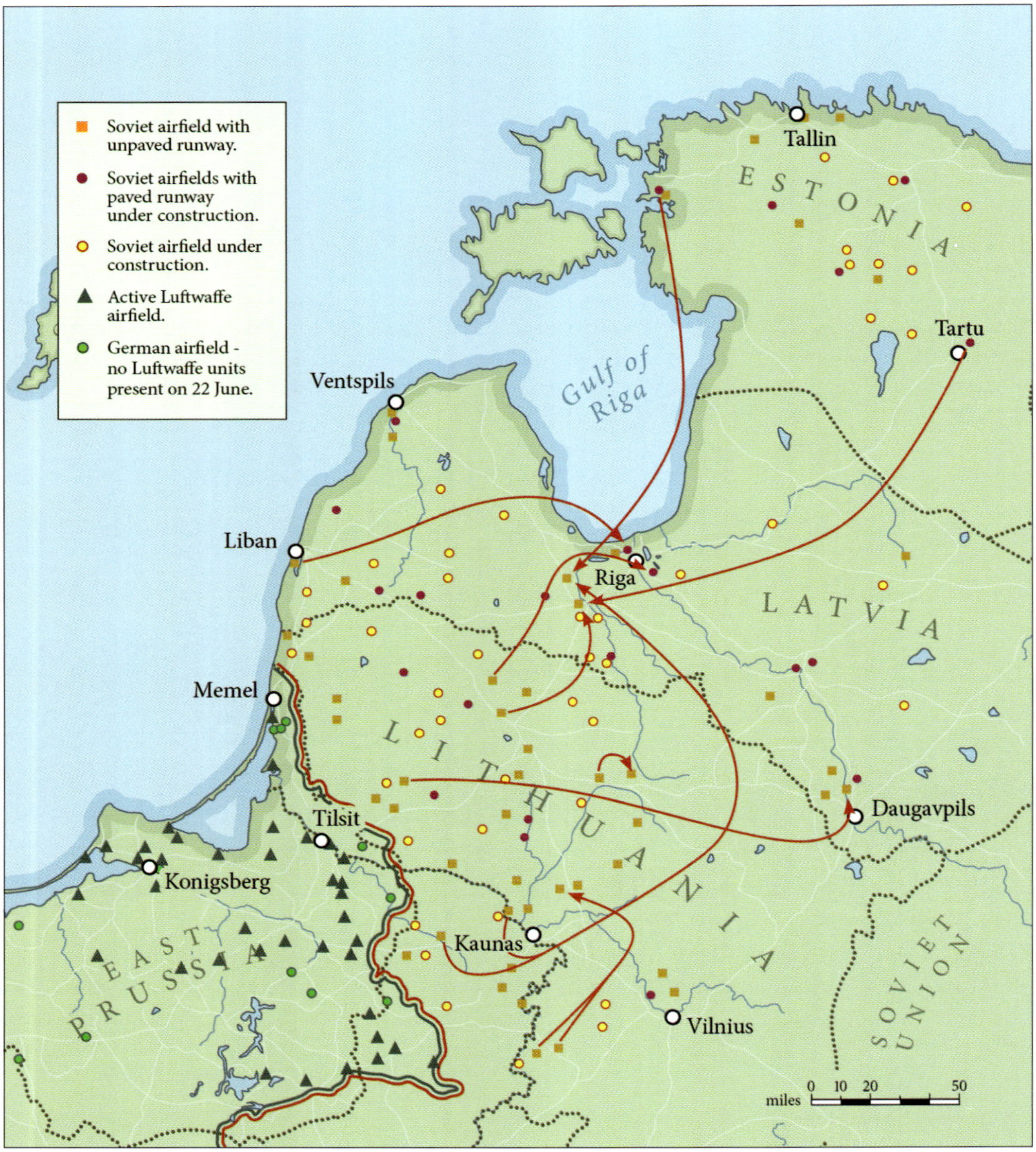

Map 9 The redeployment of the aircraft of the Air Forces of the North-Western Front in the second half of the day on 22 June 1941.

Colour profiles

The Air Forces of the North-Western Front:

There was no overall system of markings for aircraft of the air forces of the Red Army by the outbreak of the Great Patriotic War. I did not find any decrees governing the application of numerical designations for that time in the funds of the Central Archive of the Ministry of Defence. There is, however ,partial information available from different documents, such as the orders of battle for the units, information concerning the condition of the aircraft engine fleet, information concerning the losses in terms of materiel, emergency orders, and other information. In the course of processing similar documentation, as well as analysing photo-documents that are available in large quantities I succeeded in revealing two principal numbering systems on aircraft serving in the aviation units. The first, and the most widespread, was the so-called 'colour' system, naturally the name of this system is provisional. Under this numbering system aircraft serving in a regiment were organised as follows. Each squadron had coloured numbers ranging from 1–15 written in Arabic numerals. Furthermore the vast majority of units used the following colours for their numerals across the squadrons:

1st Squadron—red
2nd Squadron—light blue/dark blue
3rd Squadron—yellow
4th Squadron—white
5th Squadron—black/green

Naturally in certain units there were idiosyncrasies, for example, the numbering of aircraft in the first squadron could be applied in light blue, and those in the fifth in red. A number, as a rule, was painted onto the aircraft's rudder, the size of the numbers was not regulated.

Aircraft flown by the commanders of these squadrons, according to this system, were as a rule designated by the letter E. Aircraft flown by the regimental commanders and their deputies in the political units were designated using the letter K. As has been noted previously, however, there was no overarching regulation, and therefore the regimental and squadron commander's aircraft were often simply adorned with the number 1 or some other number. The number for training aircraft was very often a 0. An aircraft designated in this way, from the 40th High-Speed Bomber Air Regiment, was photographed by German soldiers on Ventspils airfield, for example.

Most of the units in the Air Forces of the North-Western Front specifically had a 'numeric' numbering system, however there were exceptions. This applied to I-153 aircraft from the 15th and 148th Fighter Air Regiments, which had a sequential numbering system in each squadron.

This system, let us call it provisionally a 'numerical' system, was also relatively widely used in the air forces of the Red Army. Numbers—and as a rule, these were two-digit numbers—were also painted on the rudder, and furthermore each squadron was given their range, as follows:

1st Squadron: 1–20;
2nd Squadron: 21–40;
3rd Squadron: 41–60;
4th Squadron: 61–80;
5th Squadron: 81–100.

Apart from that, aircraft from the 148th High-Speed Bomber Air Regiment had different coloured numbers, and therefore the 148th Fighter Air Regiment had some sort of a mixed 'colour-numerical' numbering system, which was very rarely applied in practice.

Interestingly during the course of the conversion onto the MiG-3 the 15th Fighter Air Regiment transferred from a 'colour' numbering system.

1) An SB, bearing the tactical No. 4 from the 9th High-Speed Bomber Air Regiment, which had been abandoned due to a failure on Panevezys airfield. On the rudder the designation symbol for an aircraft serving in this regiment, the figure 9 painted into the emblem of the Air Forces of the Red Army. The Artist is Vladimir Kamskiy.

2) An SB, bearing the tactical No. 5 from the 9th High-Speed Bomber Air Regiment that had been damaged by German aircraft and abandoned on Panevezys airfield, since it had not been possible to evacuate it. The artist is Vladimir Kamskiy

3) A USB, bearing the tactical No. 6, and the factory No. 8/216 (M-103 Nos. 93 3-194 and 023-1755) from the 31st High-Speed Bomber Air Regiment. The pilot of this aircraft was Sergeant M.S. Nebolsin, and the flying instructor was Captain N.A. Petrov. This aircraft was destroyed in an accident due to engine failure on Vaijnode airfield on 18 May 1941. The artist is Vladimir Kamskiy.

4) An SB bearing the tactical No. 10 of the 31st High-Speed Bomber Air Regiment, damaged by German aircraft and abandoned on Daugavpils airfield since it was not possible to evacuate it. Aircraft from the 31st High-Speed Bomber Air Regiment typically carried a small star above their tactical number. The artist is Vladimir Kamskiy.

5) A USB bearing the tactical No. 4 black from the 35th High-Speed Bomber Air Regiment, which had been damaged by German aircraft and abandoned on Riga airfield, since it had not proved possible to evacuate it. The artist is Vladimir Kamskiy.

6) An SB bearing the tactical No. 6 light-blue, and the factory No. 18/117 (M-103 Nos. 923-233 and 923-235) from the 2nd Squadron, 35th High-Speed Bomber Air Regiment. The pilot of this aircraft was Sergeant I.N. Myslivets, the navigator was Junior Lieutenant M.N. Metelskiy, while the gunner/radio-operator was Sergeant P.A. Lopatin. This aircraft carried out an emergency landing on Vohma airfield on 23 May 1941. Aircraft from this regiment typically carried a 'split' pilot's cap, which was preliminarily applied to these aircraft during the period of the formation of the 35th and 50th High-Speed Bomber Air Regiments that came under the 71st High-Speed Bomber Brigade in 1939. The artist is Vladimir Kamskiy.

7) An SB, bearing the tactical No. 7 black, and the factory No. 19/203 (M-103 Nos. 923-685 and 923-485) from the 4th Squadron, 35th High-Speed Bomber Air Regiment. The pilot was Senior Lieutenant P.N. Rabinovich, the navigator was Lieutenant A.A. Popov, and the gunner/radio-operator was Sergeant Vanenkov. This aircraft was destroyed in an accident on Tartu airfield on 9 June 1941. The pilot and the gunner were unhurt, but the navigator Anatoliy Aleksandrovich Popov was killed. The artist is Vladimir Kamskiy.

8) An SB bearing the tactical No. 8 yellow from the 3rd Squadron, 35th High-Speed Bomber Regiment that had been damaged by German aircraft and abandoned on Platone airfield, since it had proved impossible to evacuate it. The artist is Vladimir Kamskiy.

9) A USB bearing the tactical No. 0 red from the 40th High-Speed Bomber Air Regiment, which had been damaged by German aircraft and abandoned on Ventspils airfield, since it had not proved possible to evacuate it. The artist is Vladimir Kamskiy.

10) A USB bearing the tactical No. 4 red from the 40th High-Speed Bomber Air Regiment, which had been damaged by German aircraft and abandoned on Riga airfield, since it had not proved possible to evacuate it. Almost all the aircraft of the 40th High-Speed Bomber Air Regiment carried on their rudders a small, stylised illustration of a bolt of lightning. The artist is Vladimir Kamskiy.

11) An SB bearing the tactical No. 12 yellow from the 40th High-Speed Bomber Air Regiment, which had been damaged by German aircraft and abandoned on Ventspils airfield since it had not proved possible to evacuate it. The artist is Vladimir Kamskiy.

12) An SB bearing the tactical No. 9 red from the 40th High-Speed Bomber Air Regiment, which had been damaged by German aircraft and made an emergency landing. The artist is Vladimir Kamskiy.

13) An SB bearing the tactical No. 8 black from the 4th Squadron, 40th High-Speed Bomber Air Regiment, the pilot of this aircraft was Junior Lieutenant A.V. Antiforov, the navigator was Junior Lieutenant Ryzhkov, the gunner/radio-operator was Junior Sergeant Rykov. This aircraft was damaged as a result of an anti-aircraft shell hitting the starboard engine on 22 June 1941, and it made an emergency landing on Siauliai airfield. The artist is Vladimir Kamskiy.

14) An SB bearing the tactical No. 7 blue of the 2nd Squadron, 46th High-Speed Bomber Air Regiment. This aircraft made an emergency landing after a battle with a Bf 109F from II./JG 53 on Siauliai airfield. The artist is Vladimir Kamskiy.

15) An SB bearing the tactical No. 2 of the early production series from the 46th High-Speed Bomber Air Regiment, which had been abandoned owing to a failure on Siauliai airfield. The artist is Vladimir Kamskiy.

16) An Ar-2 bearing the tactical No. 3 white of the 46th High-Speed Bomber Air Regiment, which had been abandoned on Siauliai airfield. The artist is Vladmir Kamskiy.

17) An Ar-2 bearing the tactical No. 2 red from the 46th High-Speed Bomber Air Regiment, which had been abandoned owing to a failure on Siauliai airfield. The artist is Vladimir Kamskiy.

18) An SB bearing the tactical No.10 black, and the factory No. 8/80 (M-100A Nos. 3-142 and 2-451) of the 5th Squadron, 50th High-Speed Bomber Air Regiment. The pilot of this aircraft was Junior Lieutenant I.V. Melnikov, navigator Lieutenant Aladyev, gunner/radio-operator Junior Sergeant Kosenko. This aircraft was destroyed in an accident on Kuusiku airfield on 4 April 1941. Aircraft in this regiment displayed a split pilot cap, analogous to that displayed by aircraft from the 35th High-Speed Bomber Air Regiment. The artist is Vladimir Kamskiy.

19) An SB bearing the tactical No. 3 of the 54th High-Speed Bomber Air Regiment that had been abandoned on Vilnius airfield owing to a failure. This aircraft is interesting by virtue of it being fitted with RS rocket mountings, with five launchers under each wing. The artist is Vladimir Kamskiy.

20) An SB bearing the tactical No. 9 of the 54th High-Speed Bomber Air Regiment, which had been abandoned due to a failure on Vilnius airfield. The artist is Vladimir Kamskiy.

21) An I-153 bearing the tactical No. 2 red, flown by the Deputy Commander of the 1st Squadron, 61st Ground Attack Air Regiment, Senior Political Instructor A.M. Lagutn, which made an emergency landing owing to battle damage on Kaunas airfield. This is a later series aircraft, and has been fitted with a radio, and has been armed with three machine guns: a 12.7-mm BS machine gun, and a 7.62-mm ShKAS. The artist is Vladimir Kamskiy.

22) I-153s Nos. 1, 2, 3, 4, 7, and 12 of the 4th Squadron, 61st Ground Attack Air Regiment that had been abandoned due to battle damage on Kedainiai airfield. The artist is Igor Zlobin.

23) An Il-2 bearing the tactical No. 1, 2, 3, 4, 5 from the 61st Ground Attack Air Regiment, which had been abandoned on Vilnius airfield since it had not proved possible to evacuate it. The artist is Igor Zlobin.

24) An I-15bis bearing the tactical No. 2 white, from the 241st Ground Attack Air Regiment, June 1941. This aircraft had been transferred from the 10th Fighter Air Regiment and bears identification markings from the 4th Squadron, 10th Fighter Air Regiment. The artist is Igor Zlobin.

25-26) An R-5SSS bearing the tactical Nos. 2 and 5 from the 11th Air Observation Squadron, these aircraft were unserviceable and as a result were abandoned on Siauliai airfield since it had not proved possible to evacuate them. The artist is Aleksey Valyayev-Zaytsev.

27) An R-5SSS bearing the tactical No. 6 from the 103rd Air Observation Squadron, this aircraft was unserviceable and consequently was abandoned on Vilnius airfield since it had not proved possible to evacuate this machine. The artist is Aleksey Valyayev-Zaytsev.
The majority of the corps reconnaissance squadrons in the Air Forces of the North-Western Front were armed with R-5SSS light ground attack aircraft that had been transferred from the 61st Ground Attack Air Regiment, these aircraft carry tactical numbers from the various squadrons in the 61st Ground Attack Air Regiment.

28-29) R-5 photo-reconnaissance aircraft bearing the tactical Nos. 3 and 5 from the 2nd Aerial Photoreconnaissance Detachment, these aircraft were unarmed and were used to carry out aerial photoreconnaissance of the territory of the Baltic republics that became part of the USSR. On 22 June 1941 these aircraft were damaged and were abandoned on Kaunas airfield since it had not proved possible to evacuate them. The artist is Aleksey Valyayev-Zaytsev.

30) This Hs 126 from the line-up of the 22nd Air Observation Squadron was damaged and abandoned on Yagola airfield. This aircraft previously belonged to the Air Forces of Estonia and has the standard aircraft camouflage used by the *Luftwaffe*, the Estonian insignia have been painted out and the red stars and the tactical No.1 has been applied over them. The artist is Aleksey Valyayev-Zaytsev.

31) An ANBO 41 from the line-up of the 29th Air Observation Squadron, this aircraft was damaged and abandoned on Ukmerge airfield since it had proved impossible to evacuate it. This aircraft previously belonged to the Lithuanian Air Force and wears the registration number 898. The Estonian insignia have been painted out and the red stars have been painted over them. The artist is Aleksey Valyayev-Zaytsev.

32) A type 5 I-16 bearing the tactical No. 7 white, and the factory No. 521804, and fitted with an M-25a engine No. 250887 from the 2nd Squadron, 10th Fighter Air Regiment. The pilot, Junior Lieutenant N.S. Semashev, made an emergency landing in the area around Siauliai on 21 May 1941. The artist is Igor Zlobin.

33) An I-15bis bearing the tactical No. 1 white, and the factory No. 4999 and fitted with an M-25V engine No. 199880 from the 4th Squadron, 10th Fighter Air Regiment. This aircraft was destroyed in an accident on Siauliai airfield on 1 February 1941. The Head of the Transport and Airborne Assault Service Ya.P. Kolbasyuk was killed. The artist is Igor Zlobin.

34) A UT-4 aircraft from the 10th Fighter Air Regiment that was abandoned on Riga airfield since it had proved impossible to evacuate it. The artist is Igor Zlobin.

35) Type 5 I-16s from the 10th Fighter Air Regiment, which were abandoned on Siauliai and Riga airfields due to damage and since it was impossible to evacuate them. The artist is Igor Zlobin.

36) MiG-3s bearing the tactical Nos. 1 and 2, which had been transferred on 22 June 1941 from the line-up of the 42nd Fighter Air Regiment to the 10th Fighter Air Regiment. These aircraft were damaged and were abandoned on Siauliai airfield since it had not proved possible to evacuate them. The artist is Igor Zlobin.

37) A UTI-4 aircraft bearing the tactical No. 4, this aircraft was damaged as a result of bombing on the part of the *Luftwaffe* and was abandoned on Kaunas airfield since it had proved impossible to evacuate it. The artist is Igor Zlobin.

38) An I-153s bearing the No. 28, this aircraft was damaged as a result of bombing on the part of the *Luftwaffe* and was abandoned on Kaunas airfield since it had proved impossible to evacuate it. The artist is Igor Zlobin.

39) An I-15bis bearing tactical No. 8 white, and factory No. 5553, the aircraft is fitted with an M-25V engine No. 1912605, from the 4th Squadron, 15th Fighter Air Regiment. The pilot was Junior Lieutenant V.I. Yermolayev. This aircraft was destroyed in an accident on 4 January 1941. This aircraft previously belonged to the 42nd Fighter Air Regiment and wears its previous tactical number. The artist is Igor Zlobin.

40) A MiG-3 bearing the tactical No. 5 white, and the factory No. 2373, and fitted with an AM-35A engine No. 03247 from the 4th Squadron, 15th Fighter Air Regiment. This aircraft was destroyed in an accident on Kaunas airfield on 6 June 1941. The pilot was Deputy Commander Senior Lieutenant V.A. Voronov. This represents the 'colour' numbering system used in the Red Army Air Force on MiG-3s of the 15th Fighter Air Regiment, as an example. The artist is Aleksandr Kazakov.

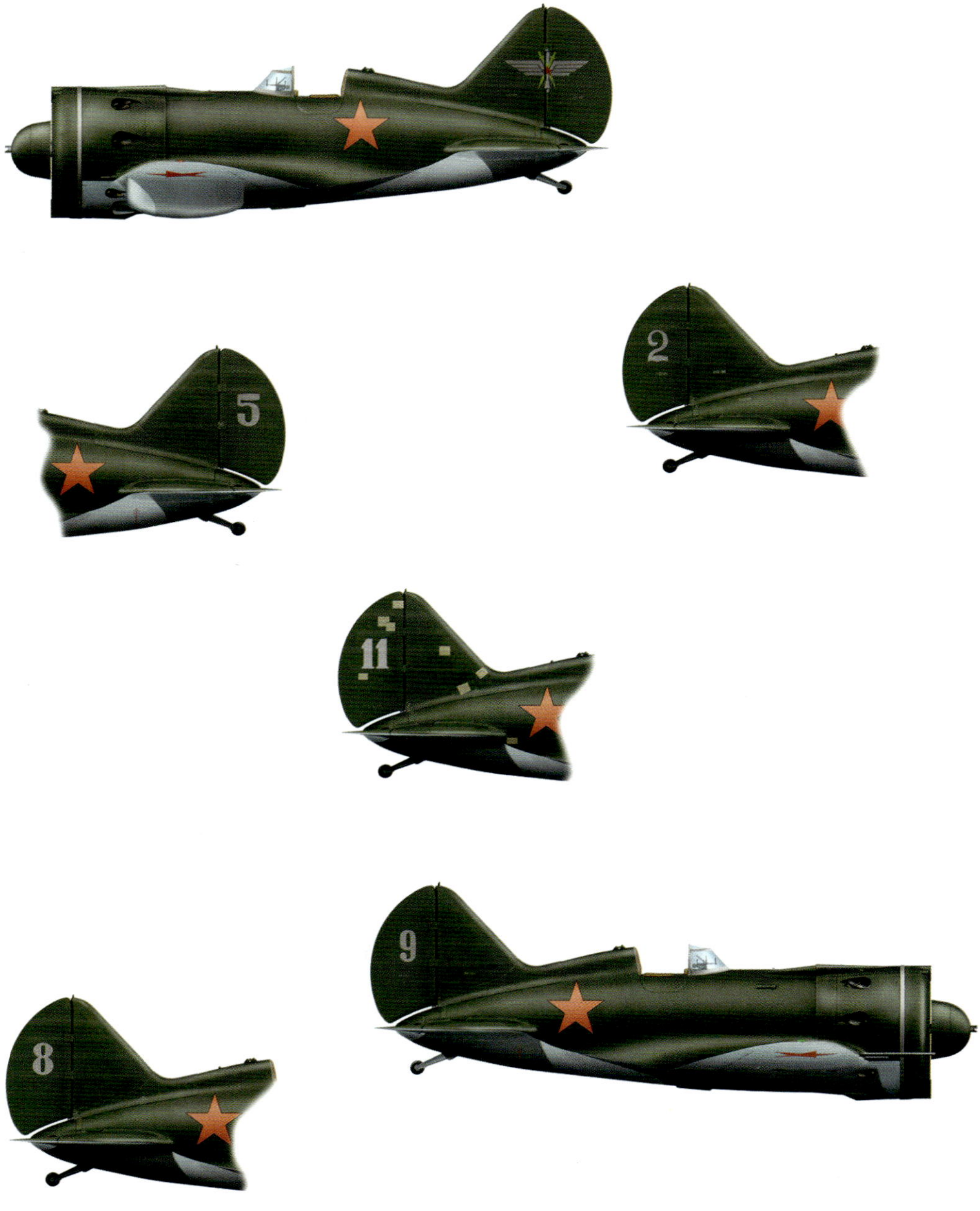

41) Type 24 and 28 I-16s from the 21st Fighter Air Regiment, these aircraft were abandoned as they had been damaged on Riga airfield in June 1941. The artist is Igor Zlobin.

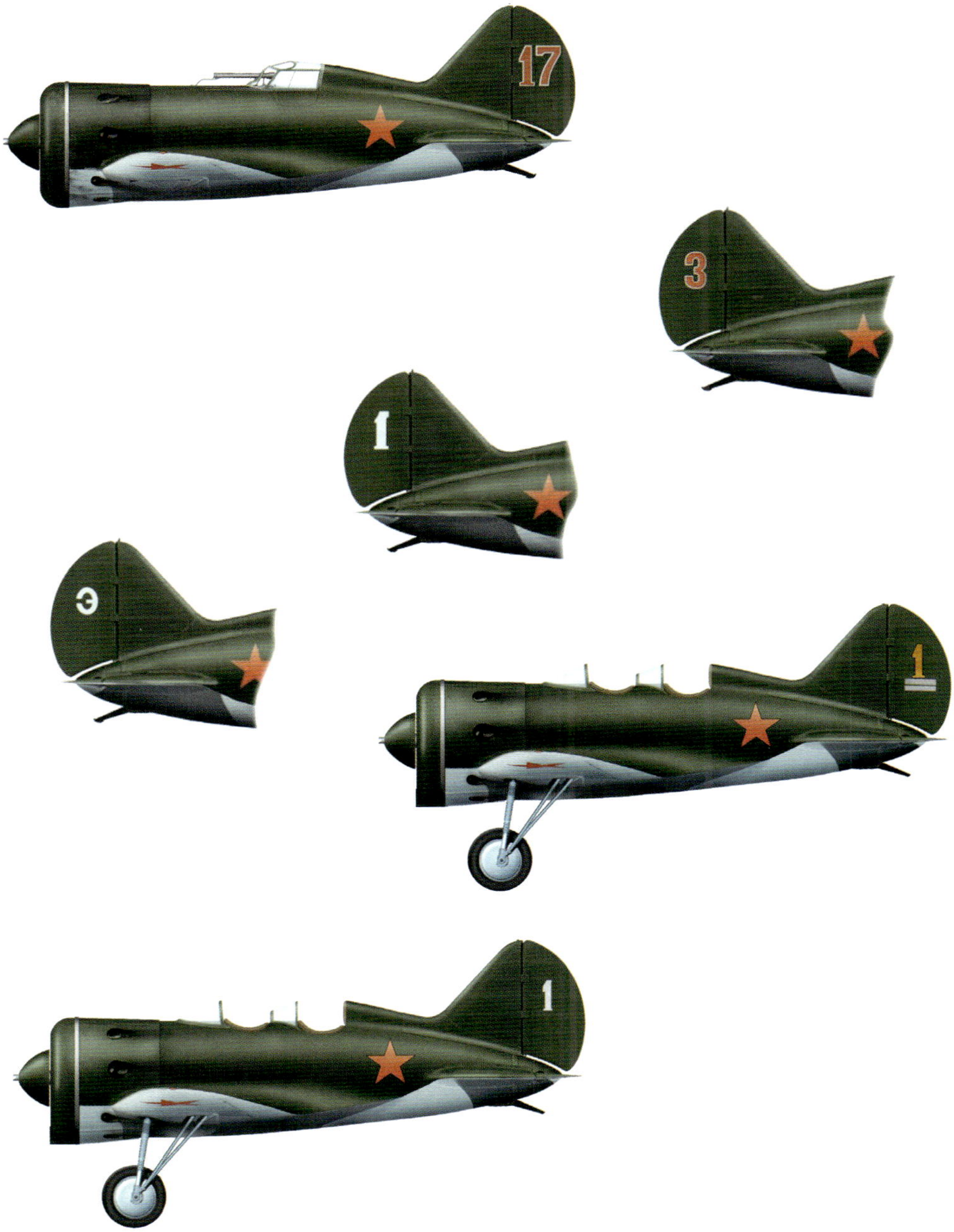

42) A type 5 I-16 and a UTI-4 from the 31st Fighter Air Regiment, these aircraft were abandoned on Kaunas airfield as a result of battle damage and technical failure on June 22 1941. The artist is Igor Zlobin.

43) A type 5 I-16 bearing the factory No. 5210312 and fitted with an M-25V engine No. 1913381, from the 4th Squadron, 31st Fighter Air Regiment. This aircraft was destroyed in an accident on 27 May 1941 in the area around Kaunas. The pilot of this aircraft Senior Lieutenant B.I. Kovshikov was unhurt. In place of a tactical number the aircraft carries the emblem of the Air Force on the rudder. The artist is Igor Zlobin.

44) A MiG-1 bearing the tactical No. 11 blue from the 2nd Squadron, 31st Fighter Air Regiment. This aircraft was abandoned due to a technical failure on Kaunas airfield on 22 June 1941. The artist is Vladimir Kamskiy.

45) A MiG-3 bearing the tactical No. 4 yellow, from the 3rd Squadron, 31st Fighter Air Regiment. This aircraft was damaged and was abandoned on Kaunas airfield on 22 June 1941. The artist is Vladimir Kamskiy.

46) A MiG-1 bearing the tactical No. 6 red from the 1st Squadron, 31st Fighter Air Regiment. This aircraft was abandoned during the withdrawal due to a technical failure on Riga airfield in June 1941. The artist is Vladimir Kamskiy.

47) A MiG-1 bearing the tactical No.7 white, from the 4th Squadron, 31st Fighter Air Regiment. This aircraft was abandoned during the withdrawal from Riga airfield due to a technical failure, in June 1941. The artist is Vladimir Kamskiy.

48) A MiG-3 bearing the tactical No. 11 white, the factory No. 2166, and fitted with an AM-35A engine No. 9EA0354 from the 4th Squadron, 31st Fighter Air Regiment. This aircraft was damaged as a result of a collision with another MiG-3 on Kaunas airfield on 2 June 1941. The artist is Vladimir Kamskiy.

49) An I-153 bearing the tactical No. 18 blue, and the factory No. 6494, and fitted with an M-62 engine No. 1048 from the 2nd Squadron, 38th Fighter Air Regiment The pilot was Adjutant Senior Lieutenant F.F. Turkin. This aircraft was destroyed on Tallinn airfield on 13 January 1941. The artist is Igor Zlobin.

50) An I-153 bearing the tactical No. 8 blue, and factory No. 6518, and fitted with an M-62 engine No. 1566 from the 2nd Squadron, 38th Fighter Air Regiment. This aircraft was destroyed in an accident on Tallinn airfield on 24 February 1941. The pilot Lieutenant D.M. Bykovets was killed. The artist is Igor Zlobin.

51) An I-153 bearing the tactical No. 1 red, and the factory No. 6518, and fitted with an M-62 engine No. 960 from the 3rd Squadron, 38th Fighter Air Regiment. The pilot of this aircraft was Junior Lieutenant I.M. Ilyin, who baled out by parachute. The aircraft crashed in a flat spin in the area around Tallinn on 10 June 1941. The artist is Igor Zlobin.

52) An I-15bis bearing the tactical No. 3 white from the 42nd Fighter Air Regiment that was abandoned due to a technical failure on Vilnius airfield. The artist is Aleksandr Kazakov.

53) An I-15bis bearing the tactical No. 3 white from the 42nd Fighter Air Regiment that was abandoned due to a technical failure on Vilnius airfield. I-15bis aircraft with large painted numbers were transferred from the 67th Fighter Air Regiment in 1940 and wear the old tactical numbers. The artist is Aleksandr Kazakov.

54) UTI-42s from the 42nd Fighter Air Regiment that were abandoned either due to accident damage or a technical failure on Orany airfield on 22 June 1941. The artist is Aleksandr Kazakov.

55) An I-153 bearing the tactical No. 12 red, from the 1st Squadron, 42nd Fighter Air Regiment that was abandoned on Orany airfield due to battle damage on 22 June 1941. The artist is Aleksandr Kazakov.

56) An I-153 bearing the tactical No. 1 blue, from the 2nd Squadron, 42nd Fighter Air Regiment, which was abandoned due to battle damage on Orany airfield on 22 June 1941. The artist is Aleksandr Kazakov.

57) An I-153 bearing the factory No. 7997, and the tactical No. 10 yellow from the 3rd Squadron 42nd Fighter Air Regiment, which was abandoned due to battle damage on Vilnius airfield on 22 June 1941. The artist is Aleksandr Kazakov.

58) An I-153 bearing the tactical No. 8 white, from the 4th Squadron, 42nd Fighter Air Regiment, which made an emergency landing and was abandoned on Orany airfield on 22 June 1941. The artist is Aleksandr Kazakov.

59) A collage showing the rudder markings on I-153s serving in the 42nd Fighter Air Regiment, which have been researched using photographs. Small tactical numbers are typical for aircraft from this regiment. The artist is Aleksandr Kazakov.

60) A collage showing the rudder markings on I-15bis aircraft from the 42nd Fighter Air Regiment that have been researched using photographs. I-15bis aircraft with small tactical numbers were transferred from the 67th Fighter Air Regiment in 1940. The artist is Aleksandr Kazakov.

61) A type 18 I-16 and an I-153 from the 49th Fighter Air Regiment, which were abandoned due to battle damage and technical failures on airfields in the area around Daugavpils in June 1941. The artist is Igor Zlobin.

62) An I1-53 bearing the tactical No. 5 black, and the factory No. 6791, and fitted with an M-62 engine No. 1177 from the 3rd Squadron of the 49th Fighter Air Regiment. The pilot of this aircraft Lieutenant V.V. Rozhnov made an emergency landing on Daugavpils airfield on 21 January 1941. The artist is Igor Zlobin.

63) I-153s from the 148th Fighter Air Regiment that were abandoned due to battle damage or technical failures on Liepaja and Riga airfields in June 1941. The artist is Igor Zlobin.

64) An I-153 bearing the tactical No. 44 yellow and the factory No. 7344 and fitted with an M-62 engine No. 3614 from the 3rd Squadron, 148th Fighter Air Regiment. The pilot of this aircraft was Deputy Squadron Commander Senior Lieutenant L.D. Smirnov. This aircraft was damaged in an accident on Liepaja airfield on 21 May 1941. The artist is Igor Zlobin.

65) I-153s from the 236th Fighter Air Regiment that were abandoned due to battle damage on Alytus airfield on 22 June 1941.

66) I-153s from the 238th Fighter Air Regiment that were abandoned due to battle damage on Panevezys and Skverbai airfields in June 1941. All the I-153s from the 236th, and 238th Fighter Air Regiments were transferred to these units at the beginning of June 1941 from the 15th Fighter Air Regiment, and wear tactical markings of aircraft from the 15th Fighter Air Regiment. The artist is Igor Zlobin.

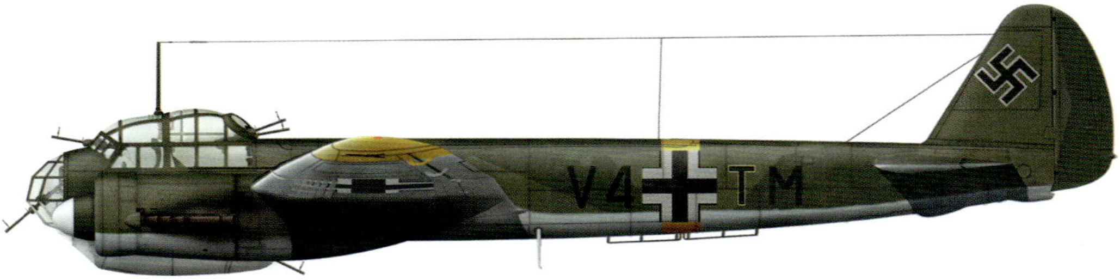

67) A Ju 88A-5 from 4./KG 1 bearing the code V4+TM, June 1941. The artist is Igor Zlobin.

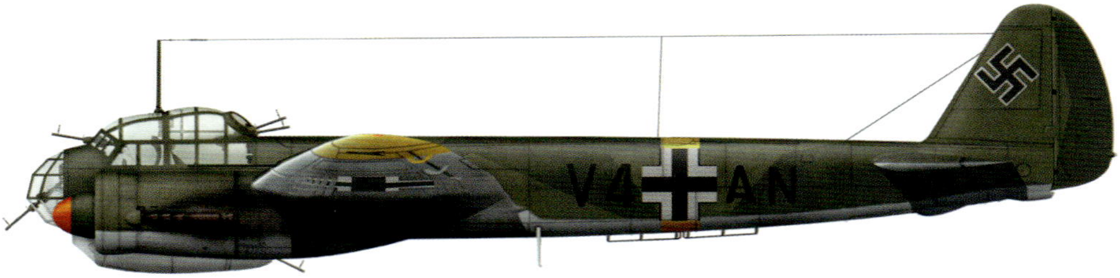

68) A Ju-88A-5 from 5./KG 1 bearing the code V4+AN this aircraft was shot down in the area around Narva on 5 July 1941. The artist is Igor Zlobin.

69) A Ju-88A-5 from 8./KG 1 bearing the code V4+HS, June 1941. The artist is Igor Zlobin.

70) A Ju-88A from 3./KG 76 bearing the code F1+CL, June 1941. The artist is Igor Zlobin.

71) A Ju-88A-5 from 4./KG 76 bearing the code F1+MM, this aircraft was damaged in June 1941. The emblem of aircraft from the II./KG 76 is an English goose in the crosshairs of a sight. The artist is Igor Zlobin.

72) A Ju-88A-5 from 7./KG 76 bearing the code F1+JR, June 1941. A distinguishing feature of aircraft from III./KG 76 was the thin white line around the fuselage, the emblem of the 7th Squadron is a crocodile standing on its hind legs. The artist is Igor Zlobin.

73) A Ju-88A-5 from 5./KG 77 bearing the code 3Z+BN, June 1941. The artist is Igor Zlobin.

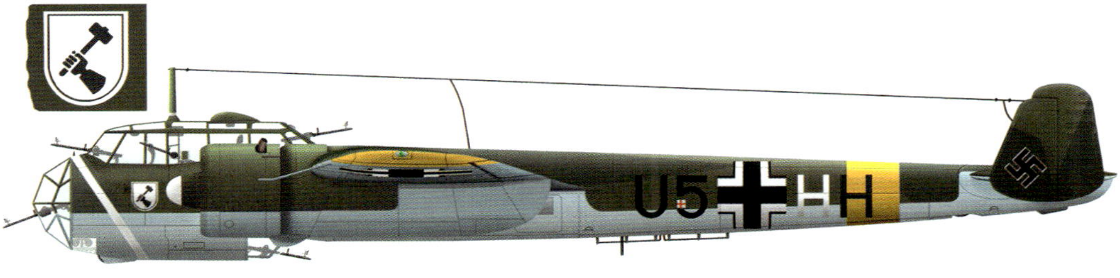

74) A Do 17Z from 1./KG 2 bearing the code U5+HH, summer 1941. This aircraft bears the stylised emblem of the 2nd Bomber Wing a 'wooden mallet'. A thin line around the nose section of the fuselage was also a distinguishing feature of aircraft from KG 2, and was painted in the wing's colours. The artist is Aleksey Valyayev-Zaytsev.

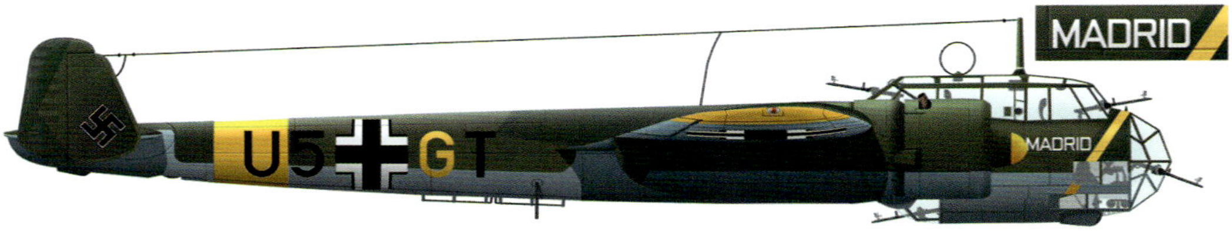

75) A Do 17Z from 9./KG 2 bearing the code U5+GT, summer 1941. This aircraft has been named 'MADRID' and was destroyed in an emergency landing in the area around Demidov, on 24 July 1941. The artist is Aleksey Valyayev-Zaytsev.

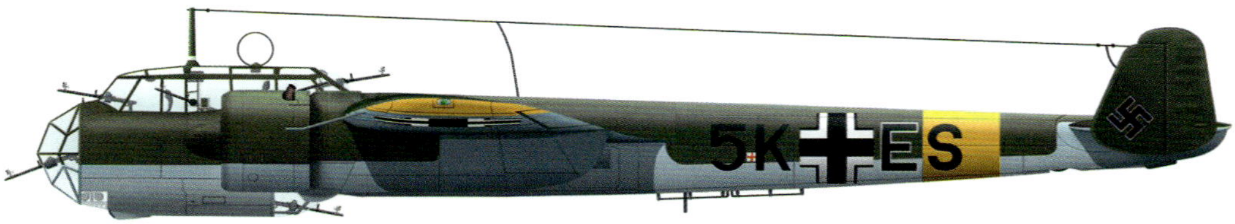

76) A Do 17Z from 8./KG 3 bearing the code 5K+ES, summer 1941. A distinguishing feature of the aircraft of the 8th Air Corps were the broad, yellow lines around the fuselage. The artist is Aleksey Valyayev-Zaytsev.

77) A Do 215 from Aufklärungsgruppe O.b.d.L, bearing the code T5+BC, Summer 1941. The 2nd Squadron O.b.d.L carried out reconnaissance in the interests of the Headquarters of the 1st Air Fleet. The artist is Aleksey Valyayev-Zaytsev.

78) A Do 17Z from *Wekūsta* 1, bearing the code D7+EA, June 1941. This weather reconnaissance squadron was subordinated to the headquarters of the 1st Air Fleet and operated in the interests of all the aviation units that operated within the confines of the responsibility of Army Group 'North'. The artist is Aleskey Valyayev-Zaytsev.

79) A Ju-88D-1 from 1.(F)/22, bearing the code 4N+Lh, summer 1941. This squadron carried out reconnaissance in the interests of the headquarters of Army Group North's Air Command. The artist is Igor Zlobin.

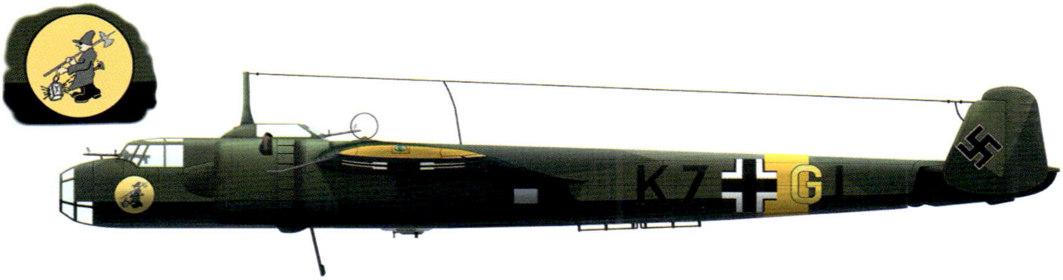

80) A Do 17Z from *Wekūsta* 1 from 3.(F)/Nacht, bearing the code K7+GL, June 1941. This squadron carried out reconnaissance in the interests of the headquarters of Army Group North's Air Command. The artist is Aleksey Valyayev-Zaytsev.

81) A Ju-88D from 5.(F)/11, bearing the code F6+MN, summer 1941. This squadron carried out reconnaissance in the interests of headquarters of the 1st Air Corps. The artist is Igor Zlobin.

82) A Do 17P from 2.(F)/11 bearing the code 6M+DK, June 1941. This squadron carried out reconnaissance in the interests of the headquarters of the 8th Air Corps. The artist is Aleksey Valyayev-Zaytsev.

83) A Ju-88D-1 from 3.(F)/22, bearing the code 4N+GL, summer 1941. This squadron carried out reconnaissance in the interests of the headquarters of the 18th Army's Air Command. The artist is Igor Zlobin.

84) A Bf 110E from 4.(F)/33, bearing the code H8+CM, June 1941. This squadron carried out reconnaissance in the interests of the headquarters of the 4th Panzer Group's Air Command. The artist is Igor Zlobin.

85) A BF 110E from the headquarters of StG1, bearing the code A5+ED, June 1941. The Bf 110A aircraft under the headquarters of the dive bomber wings were used as reconnaissance aircraft. In particular the reconnaissance crews flying the Bf 110E aircraft from the headquarters of the StG1 from 22–24 June conducted aerial photoreconnaissance of the Kaunas, Vilnius, Daugavpils, and other airfields. The artist is Igor Zlobin.

86) An Hs 126B-1 from 3.(H)/23, bearing the code 6K+DL, summer 1941. This squadron carried out reconnaissance in the interests of the headquarters of the 6th Panzer Division. The artist is Aleksey Valyayev-Zaytsev.

87) An Hs 126B-1 from 3.(H)/23 bearing the code 6K+D, summer 1941. This squadron carried out reconnaissance in the interests of the headquarters of the 6th Panzer Division. The artist is Aleksey Valyayev-Zaytsev.

88) An HS 126B-1 from 4.(H)/23, bearing the code 6K+DM, summer 1941. This squadron carried out reconnaissance and artillery correction for the X Army Corps, 16th Army. The artist is Aleksey Valyayev-Zaytsev.

89) An HS 126B-1 from 3.(H)/41, bearing the code C2+FL, summer 1941. This squadron conducted reconnaissance in the interests of the 8th Panzer Division. The artist is Aleksey Valyayev-Zaytsev.

90) An Hs 126B-1 from 8.(H)/32, bearing the code M4+GS, summer 1941. This squadron carried out reconnaissance in the interests of the headquarters of the LVI Motorised Corps. The artist is Aleksey Valyayev-Zaytsev.

91) An HS-126B-1 from 2.(H)/12 bearing the code P2+HK, summer 1941. This squadron carried out reconnaissance and artillery correction for the XXVIII Army Corps, 16th Army. The artist is Igor Zlobin.

92) A FW-189A-1 from 1.(H)/12, bearing the code H1+EH, June 1941. This squadron carried out reconnaissance and artillery correction for the XXVIII Army Corps, 16th Army.

93) A Fw 189A-1 from 1.(H)/11 bearing the code 6M+DH, June 1941. This squadron carried out reconnaissance in the interests of the headquarters of the 7th Panzer Division. In spite of conventional wisdom, the famous Fw 189 reconnaissance aircraft, or 'frames' as they were known in the Red Army, had appeared on the front line from 22 June 1941 onwards, and in large numbers at that, and by the outbreak of the campaign against the USSR the Germans had succeeded in equipping more than a dozen squadrons with these new aircraft. The artist is Igor Zlobin.

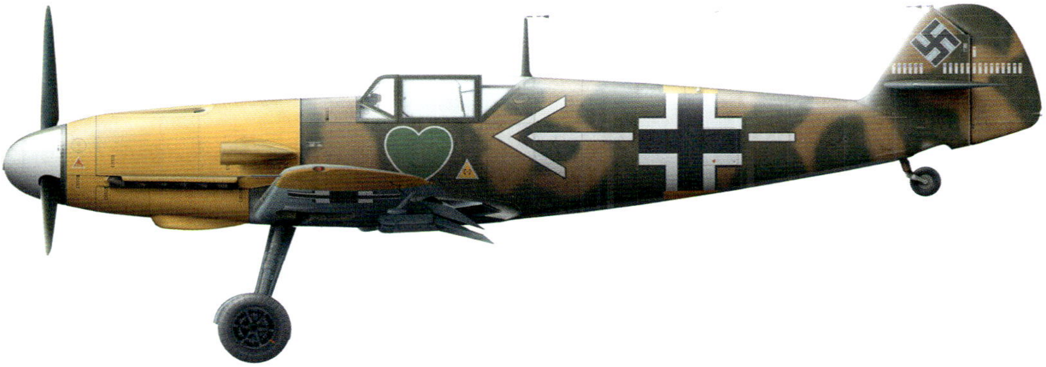

94) A Bf 109F-2, W.Nr. 5761, flown by the Commander of JG 54 Major Hannes Trautloft. This aircraft has a non-standard livery, the badges denoting aerial victories have been applied in a line, horizontally, and on the side is Trautloft's personal emblem, a 'green heart,' which in time would become the emblem of the entire wing. On the evening of 22 June this aircraft was shot down by fire from gunners in an SB from the 40th High-Speed Bomber Air Regiment. The artist is Vladimir Kamskiy.

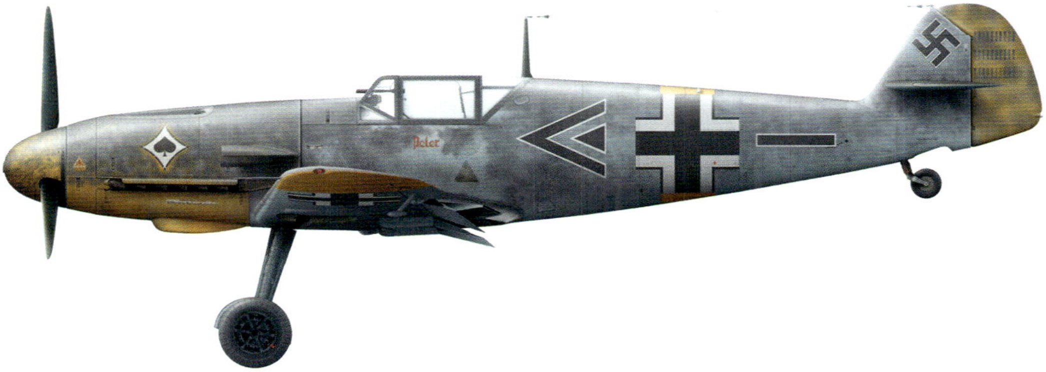

95) A Bf 109F-2, W.Nr. 6674 flown by the Commander of II./JG 53 Hauptmann Heinz Bretnütz. On the aircraft's cowling is the emblem of JG 53 the 'ace of spades'. On the rudder are the markings denoting 31 victories, the badge showing the octane number of the fuel has been painted out, and alongside it on the aircraft's flank is the inscription 'Peter'. The artist is Vladimir Kamskiy.

96) A Bf 109F-2 bearing the tactical No. 1 white, flown by Captain Richard Seiler, Summer 1941. On the side is a drawing—a cylinder—the pilot's symbol from the time of the Spanish Civil War, on the rudder are the insignia denoting 21 victories, which Seiler attained on 21 August 1941. The artist is Vladimir Kamskiy.

97) A Bf 109F-2 bearing the tactical No. 9 white, flown by the Commander of the 4./JG 54 *Oberleutnant* Hans Philipp, August 1941. Behind the cowling is the emblem of the II Group JG 54, underneath the canopy is the pilot's personal emblem while on the rudder are insignia denoting 58 victories. On 22 June this pilot claimed a victory over an SB from the 40th High-Speed Bomber Air Regiment, and this victory is confirmed by Soviet documents. The artist is Vladimir Kamskiy.

98) Bf 109F-2 bearing the tactical No/ 10 white from the line-up of 7./JG 54 in summer 1941. The JG 54 aircraft is distinguished by its unusual camouflage. The artist is Vladimir Kamskiy.

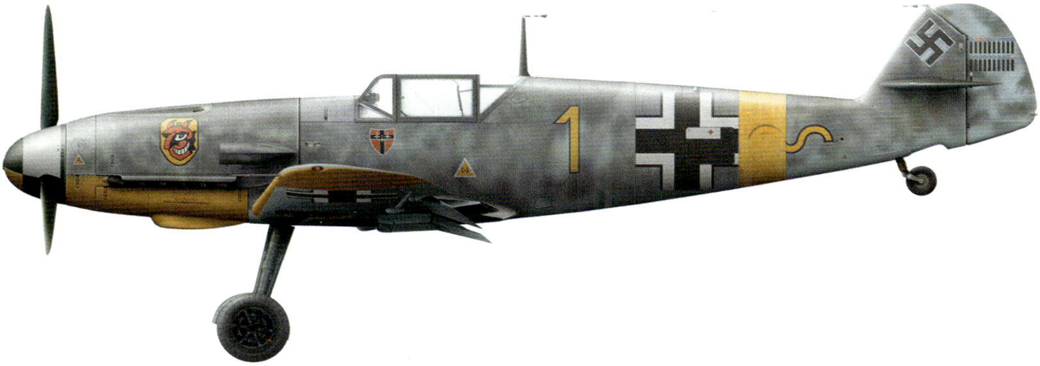

99) A Bf 109F-2 W.Nr. 9207, flown by the Commander of the 9./JG 54 *Oberleutnant* Hans Ekkerhard-Bob, this aircraft was lost on 23 June 1941 following a battle with a group of SB aircraft from the line-up of the 3rd Squadron, 9th High-Speed Bomber Air Regiment. On the cowling is the emblem of the 9th Squadron, while under the canopy is that of the III Group JG 54, and on the rudder are the insignia denoting the 21 victories attained on the Western Front. The artist is Vladimir Kamskiy.

100) Bf 109F-2 bearing the tactical No. 3 black W.Nr. 5434, flown by 5./JG 53 pilot Josef Wurmheller, July 1941. On the rudder are the insignia denoting the 18 victories he had attained. On the evening of 22 June the pilot claimed a victory over an SB-50 of the High-Speed Bomber Air Regiment, this victory however is not confirmed by Soviet data. The artist is Vladimir Kamskiy.

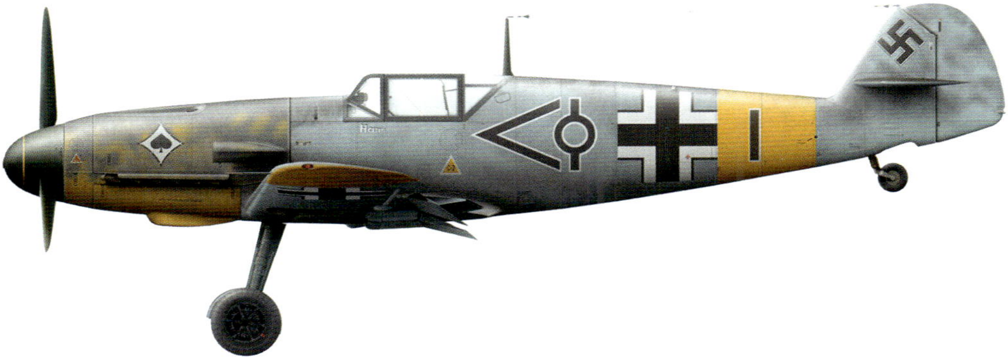

101) A Bf 109F-2 W.Nr. 8085, flown by the technical officer of the headquarters of III./JG 53 Leutnant Jürgen Harder, June 1941. Under the canopy is the inscription 'Naggo', while on the rudder is a badge denoting a victory in aerial combat attained on 22 June over a MiG-3 from the 15th Fighter Air Regiment in the area around Potsunai airfield. The artist is Vladimir Kamskiy.

102) A Bf 109F-2 bearing the tactical No. 2 white W.Nr. 6702,flown by a pilot from the 7./JG 53 *Feldwebel* Hermann Neuhoff. On the rudder are insignia denoting 16 victories he attained. On 22 June this pilot claimed two Soviet aircraft shot down. The artist is Vladimir Kamskiy.

103) A Bf 109F-2 bearing the tactical No. 3 black, flown by *Leutnant* Herbert Schramm, a pilot from 8./JG 53, September 1941. On the rudder are the insignia denoting the 33 victories he attained. In combat on 22 June this pilot claimed two Soviet aircraft shot down. The artist is Vladimir Kamskiy.

104) A Bf 109F-2 bearing the tactical No. 11 yellow, flown by *Leutnant* Erich Schmidt, August 1941. On the rudder are the insignia denoting the victories he attained. In combat on 22 June this pilot claimed four Soviet aircraft shot down. The artist is Vladimir Kamskiy.

105) A Bf 109F-2 bearing the tactical No. 3 white, from the 4./JG 52, summer 1941. Underneath the canopy the emblems of JG 52 and the 4th Squadron can be seen, while on the rudder are the insignia denoting his four victories attained in aerial combat. The artist is Vladimir Kamskiy.

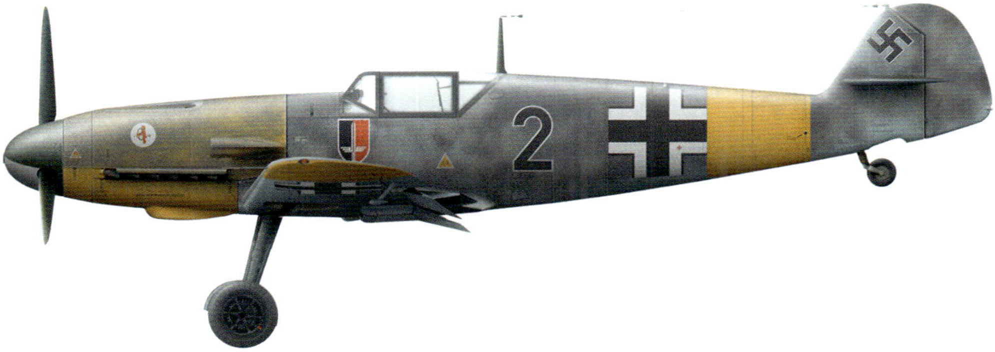

106) A Bf 109F-2 bearing the tactical No. 2 black, from 5./JG 52, summer 1941. On the aircraft's cowling the emblems of the 5th Squadron have been applied, while under the canopy is the emblem of JG 52. The artist is Vladimir Kamskiy.

107) Bf 109F-2 bearing the tactical No. 4 yellow, from 6. /JG 52. And flown by *Unteroffizier* Bernhard Wilskiy, autumn 1941. Underneath the aircraft's canopy the emblem of the 6th Squadron has been applied, while on the rudder are the insignia denoting the 11 aerial victories attained. On the morning of 22 June as part of a headquarter's section from II./JG 52 this pilot claimed a victory over an I-153 from the 42nd Fighter Air Regiment over Orany airfield. The artist is Vladimir Kamskiy.

108) A Bf 109E from the headquarter's section of II./JG 27, June 1941, aircraft of the JG 27 on 22 June attacked Alytus, Orany, and Vilnius airfields using SD-2 bombs and machine gun fire on more than one occasion. The artist is Vladimir Kamskiy.

109) A BF 109E bearing the tactical No. 10 black from the line-up of the 5./JG 27, June 1941. The artist is Vladimir Kamskiy.

110) A Bf 109E bearing the tactical No. 12 white, from the line-up of the 7./JG 27, June 1941. This aircraft has a pylon for carrying a 2.5 kg bomb, as well as SD-2 fragmentation bombs. Aircraft from III./JG 27 were marked up in a distinctive style when it came to painting the numbers on the aircraft's cowling, and to the group's emblem under the canopy. The artist is Vladimir Kamskiy.

111) A Bf 110E from 5./ZG26, and bearing the code 3U+CM, June 1941. On the aircraft's nose is the emblem of the squadron, while on the engine cowling is the emblem of the II group. Aircraft from ZG 26 on 22 June attacked Alytus airfield at around 0400 hrs using SD-2 bombs, and machine-gun fire. The artist is Igor Zlobin.

On 8 April 1941. A single Do 17 aircraft, and a single, unidentified aircraft, H=6,000–8,000. At 1224 hrs two German aircraft crossed the state border from the area around Suwalki. After flying up to Shaki (60 km north-north-west of Kaunas) and after encountering two MiG-3 aircraft, and five I-153s that had taken off from Kaunas the German aircraft flew on towards German territory in the direction of Tilsit.

On 9 April 1941 a single Do 17 aircraft, H=7,000. Between 1426–1545 hrs a German aircraft crossed the state border in the area around Mikoliskiai (15 km east of Klaipeda). After flying via Shavli the intruder flew on towards German territory in the area around Veivirzenai. After taking off from Shavli airfield four I-16s were not able to intercept the intruder as it had flown on towards German territory at high speed.

On 9 April 1941. A single Do 17 aircraft, H=6,000. Between 1450–1510 hrs the German aircraft appeared in the area around Rucava (30 km south of Liepaja). After penetrating deeper into our territory 25 km to the east, the intruder turned away in the direction of Klaipeda.

9 April 1941, a single Do 17 aircraft. H=6,000–8,000. Between 1410–1508 hrs a German aircraft flew from the direction of Klaipeda on a northerly course, and after encountering our fighters in the area around LIEPAJA flew out to sea.

9 April 1941, a single Do 17 aircraft, H=4,000. Between 1608–1627 hrs a German aircraft appeared in the area around Ziemupe (20 km to the north of Liepaja), and flew up to the border on a northerly heading, and turned back towards German territory. On encountering our own fighters that had taken off from Palanga, Liepaja, and Riga airfields (these comprised of six I-16s, and 11 I-153s), the intruder flew out to sea losing altitude.

10 April 1941, a single Do 17 aircraft, H=8,000. Between 1115–1225 hrs a German aircraft crossed the state border in the area around Syntovty (15 km north-east of Naumiestis), and flew via Vysoka-Ruda (30 km to the south-west of Kaunas), Shula (Brazuki, 25 km west of Kaunas), and at 1228 hrs in the area around Kunigishki the aircraft turned back towards German territory.

10 April 1941, a single, unidentified aircraft, H-4,000. Between 1121–1128 hrs a German aircraft crossed the state border over the area around Naumiestis, and after flying over Novaja Huta (35 km south of Kaunas) departed back to German territory.

10 April 1941, a single unidentified aircraft, H=11,000. At 1128 hrs a German aircraft crossed the state border to the west of Shaki, and after having passed over Ligaine (25 km north-west of Kaunas), Ariogala, (50 km north-west of Kaunas) the aircraft flew back to German territory over Virbalis.

10 April 1941, a single unidentified aircraft. At 1131 hrs a German aircraft appeared over Kaunas, and subsequently flew over the area around Kedainiai.

10 April 1941, a single, unidentified aircraft, H=4,000. At 1130 hrs a German aircraft flew 15 km into Soviet territory, in the area over Sokoline (35 km north-east of Tilsit) and after turning round, flew back towards German territory.

10 April 1941 a single, unidentified aircraft, H=8,000. At 1134 hrs a German aircraft crossed the state border in the area around Kunigishki, and after flying over Meskine (75 km south-west of Kaunas), flew back to German territory.

10 April 1941, a single, unidentified aircraft, H=5,000. At 1138 hrs a German aircraft crossed the state border in the area around Maltsov (30 km north-east of Suwalki), and after flying 15 km into our territory, flew back to German territory.

10 April 1941, a single unidentified aircraft, H=7,000. At 1235 hrs a German aircraft crossed the state border in the area around Virbalis, and after flying via Meskine returned to German territory.

> 10 April 1941, a single unidentified aircraft. At 1238 hrs a German aircraft crossed the state border in the area around Shukele (10 km south of Naumiestis), and after flying over Naumiestis, flew back to German territory.
>
> 10 April 1941, a single, unidentified aircraft, H=7.000. Between 1235–1245 hrs a German aircraft crossed the state border in the area around Grozishke, and after flying over Novaja Huta on a southerly heading flew back to German territory.
>
> 10 April 1941 a single unidentified German aircraft. At 1250 hrs a German aircraft crossed the state border in the area around Maltsov, and after flying over Raudonikiai (45 km south-west of KAUNAS, flew back to German territory via Kamin (30 km north of Suvalki).
>
> 10 April 1941 a single, unidentified aircraft at an altitude of 4,000 m. At 1448 hrs a German aircraft crossed the state border in the area around Virbolis, and after flying over Dembova-Buda (30 km south-west of Kaunas) flew back to German territory.
>
> 10 April 1941, a single, unidentified twin-engine aircraft. Between 1600–1621 hrs over the sea 10 km south of Liepaja, and over the sea 35 km north of Liepaja.

Evidently there were a maximum of one or two aircraft operating over Soviet territory on 10 April, which after gaining altitude, passed over the area from Kaunas–Kedainiai, taking some photographs and then departing towards their home territory. This evidently involved several aircraft. In view of their intelligent actions the German reconnaissance crews were able to complete their mission, and brought some very clear images of the Kaunas airfield cluster back to their home bases.

The Soviet fighters however did not cope well with their sorties, they were not able to intercept the intruders and lost Junior Lieutenant Evtushenko who was killed, two MiG-3s were completely destroyed, and two were damaged.

In the final few days of April and the beginning of May the German reconnaissance activity over the Baltic region dropped sharply. In total over the course of one or two days flights were only recorded on 11, 12, 17, and 18 April, and on 8 May.

It is possible that this was linked to combat activity in the Balkans, and to the transfer of German reconnaissance activity to a zone comprising the Western Special Military District, and the Kiev Special Military District.

Active operations over the Baltic region resumed from the end of May and did not cease right up until the start of the war.

On 28 May 1941 unidentified aircraft, flying at an altitude of between 6,000–9,000 m appeared over Kretinga, and Marijampole.

On 29, 30, and 31 May aircraft were noted over Kretinga.

On 1 June 1941 an unidentified aircraft was operating over the area around Alytus.

On 2 June 1941 an unidentified aircraft was noted in the area over Shaki.

On 3 June 1941 unidentified aircraft were noted in the area over Kretinga at an altitude of 9,000 m.

On 4 June 1941 unidentified aircraft were noted in the area over Alytus.

On 5 June a Heinkel He 111 aircraft at an altitude of 6,000 m was noted in the area around Alytus, and a Do 17 was noted in the area around Yurbarkas, and Erzhvilskiy, H=7,000.

On 6 June a Do 17 aircraft at an altitude of 8,000 m crossed the border three times in the area around Kunigishki, and Shkuli.

On 8 June two aircraft crossed the border.

On 9 June two aircraft crossed the border.

On 16 June between 2235–2250 hrs a single He 111 was noted in the area around Zhigaitsy (20 km south-west of Taurage), which flew back to their home territory via Vistytis.

On 19 June German aircraft crossed the border no less than four times in the areas around Taurage, Mariampol, and Alytus.

On 20 June two aircraft crossed the border.

Moreover far from all these flights by German aircraft were detected by the aerial reconnaissance posts.

On 17 June 1941 in his next report to Marshall Timoshenko the Commander of the Air Forces of the Red Army Lieutenant-General Zhigaryev again noted the fervent reconnaissance activity being conducted by the Germans and again requested retaliatory strikes, as well as the resumption of reconnaissance over German territory:

> In the period from 1 January 1941 to 10 June 1941 there were 122 incidents of foreign aircraft crossing the state border of the USSR...
>
> A study of these incidents has revealed that violations of the state border, which up until April 1941 were sporadic in nature, have since April become a mass phenomenon, which on certain days has resembled an entire reconnaissance operation.
>
> 9 April 1941. In the period from 1424–1608 hrs five German aircraft crossed the border of the Lithuanian SSR.
>
> 10 April 1941. In the period from 1121–1428 hrs some 14 German aircraft crossed the state border of the Lithuanian SSR...
>
> The most intensive flights in which aircraft crossed the state border occurred in the following areas: RIGA, LIEPAJA, SHAVLI, and KAUNAS.
>
> The reconnaissance nature of these flights was evidenced by the presence of photographic film on a Ju-86 that was forced to make an emergency landing in the area around Rivne on 15 April 1941, which had been used to capture images of the railway line from MALIN to STREMIGOROD (on the stretch of line from KIEV–KOROSTEN).
>
> All this is testimony to the fact that the western border regions of the USSR are being systematically subjected to reconnaissance, and are being photographed by German aviation.
>
> Our fighters, which have taken off to intercept these aircraft, do not have the right to fire at German aircraft that have crossed the German border.
>
> In turn however there have not been any instances of aircraft crossing our state border from Germany.
>
> In my report, which was sent to you under No. 159172 dated 4 April 1941 all the instances of violations of the state border by German aircraft between 1 January 1941 to 25 March 1941 are analysed, and the question was raised concerning the organisation of photoreconnaissance of German territory.
>
> I consider it necessary once again to raise this question of taking advantage of the fact that our aircraft are not being fired upon from the German side when they have crossed the German border, to conduct photoreconnaissance of the principal directions and assets on the German border territory.
>
> I have presented an analogous report to Comrade I.V. STALIN.

However there was neither the means, nor the time to organise adequate measures. Nevertheless, in accordance with the so-called 'Plans to provide cover', the Soviet Command also envisaged widespread combat activity to gain air superiority, which was fully concordant with the enemy's plans.

> The following orders are put before the units of the Air Forces of the Baltic Special Military District by the People's Commissar of the USSR for the period of the provision of cover:

1. To destroy enemy aviation from the first few days of the war and gain air superiority by conducting successive attacks using combat aircraft on the established bases, and airfields as well as by means of aerial combat.
2. To provide stubborn support to the district's troops during the mobilisation, and their concentration of forces, and also protect normal operation of the railways and prevent the enemy aircraft from getting through to the district itself, or into the country's interior, by using fighter aviation in close cooperation with the district's entire Air Defence System.
3. Destroy the enemy's navy, and transport jointly with naval aviation and the Red Banner Baltic Fleet in the Baltic Sea, and do not allow the marines to land on the islands of Saaremaa, and Hiiumaa, or on the coast on the district's outer borders.
4. Destroy the advancing enemy in cooperation with ground forces, and do not allow the enemy's large, motorised or mechanised forces to break through the district's defensive front line.
5. Destroy and delay the build up of enemy forces by attacking the railway junctions of Königsberg, Marienburg, Marienwerder, Preussisch-Elau, Allenstein, Insterburg, and on the railway bridges across the Visla river on the Danzig, Bydgoszcz section, as well as the alignments of forces.
6. Destroy the port of Klaipeda.

In order to realise this scenario the participation of seven bomber, two ground attack, and eight fighter regiments was envisaged in the course of the first 15 days of the operation:

> The 6th Mixed Air Division, with the 148th Fighter Air Regiment and the 40th High-Speed Bomber Air Regiment, were given the following orders: the 148th Fighter Air Regiment was to carry out three sorties as a regiment to destroy enemy aviation on the airfields at Königsberg, Elbing, Marienburg, and Marienwerder, and five sorties as a regiment to provide cover for the activities of the bombers of the 40th High-Speed Bomber Air Regiment in their attacks on these same airfields.
>
> The 57th Mixed Air Division, with the 42nd and 49th Fighter Air Regiments, and the 54th High-Speed Bomber Air Regiment, was ordered to carry out three sorties as a regiment to attack the enemy airfields at Allenstein, Lyubavas, Nowe-Myasto, and Merunchey, while the 42nd Fighter Air Regiment was to conduct a further three sorties as a regiment to escort the bombers of the 54th High-Speed Bomber Air Regiment during their attacks on these same airfields.
>
> The 8th Mixed Air Division, with the 15th, 31st, 236th, and 240th Fighter Air Regiments, and the 61st Ground Attack Air Regiments was to carry out three sorties as a regiment to attack enemy aviation on the airfields at Vishvill, Insterburg, Darkehmen, and Goldap.
>
> The 7th Mixed Air Division with the 10th and 238th Fighter Air Divisions and the 9th and 46th High-Speed Bomber Air Regiments, as well as the 241st Ground Attack Air Regiment, envisaged that the airfields at Klaipeda, Polessk, Insterburg, and Vishvill would be attacked no less than three times.
>
> For the 4th Mixed Air Division, the targets for the 35th, 50th, and 63rd High-Speed Bomber Air Regiments were to be the airfields, and the port of Klaipeda.

The achievements of Soviet reconnaissance have been glorified across the media in recent years, in books, on television, and in the cinema. However if the level of intelligence gained from agents was at the level it should have been, then undoubtedly the situation with respect to aerial reconnaissance, and signals intelligence would have been much worse. As already mentioned above special reconnaissance units, such as Rohwel's group, designed to ensure that the People's Commissariat for Defence, General Staff, and the Principal Directorate of the Air Forces of the Red Army were kept up to date with intelligence just did not exist in the air forces of the Red Army. At the level of the air forces of the military districts the situation was also a very complicated one, and this is despite the availability of one or two reconnaissance regiments in the line-up of any one of the border districts. All the reconnaissance regiments began to be formed in the second half of 1940 and were only equipped by June of 1941 partly with Yak-2 and Yak-4 aircraft and partly with SBs, albeit with great difficulty. In the end the units only commenced combat training from spring 1941 onwards, and there were only a few combat capable crews among their number.

It is possible that it was this same lack of combat capable crews for reconnaissance aircraft as well as specially equipped aircraft that to a great extent influenced the decision made by the leadership of the Red Army, and also of the USSR, not to issue an order to conduct aerial reconnaissance over the territory of Eastern Prussia, Poland, Finland, and Romania, in the spring of 1941.

It was for this reason that information on the targets in the adjacent territories had to be compiled by headquarters at all levels based on the so-called 'target information lists', which were drawn up back in the 1930s. At that time these were very detailed, right up to panoramic aerial photography detailing airfields, bridges, stations, factories, plants, military barracks, government buildings, and so on.

Apart from that the target designations were compiled on the basis of the information gathered from agents in the winter of 1940–1941 concerning the airfields in East Prussia. Overall it has to be said that the majority of the stationary airbases such as Königsberg Devau, Danzig, Elbing, Marienburg, Marienwerder, and Allenstein, were known to Soviet reconnaissance crews, correspondingly:

Gumbinnen was the headquarters of the 1st Air Corps;
Seerappen—2.(F)/Ob.d.L.;
Eichwalde bei Labiau— III./KG 1 and 3.(F)/22;
Gerdauen—was the headquarters of the 1./KG 76;
Heiligenbeil—was the headquarters of the III./KG 77;
Jesau—I./KG 77;
Memel (Klaipeda)—4.(H)/21.
Neukuhren—Erg.JG 54;
Neuhausen—Erg.JG 52;
Pillau—1.,2.,3.(F)/125.

Even the many operational airfields and landing sites of the 1st Air Fleet in East Prussia, and of the 8th Air Corps, 2nd Air Group in Poland, which were not hidden either from the observant eyes of the Soviet field station, were well-known and the information on them held by the headquarters of the Soviet air regiments, and divisions was as follows:

Insterburg—1.(F)/22, 3.(F)/Nacht, KGr.z.b.V.106;
Ragnit—4.(F)/33 and 3.(H)/23;
Tilsit—4.(H)/31 and 2.(H)/23;
Ebenrode—1.(H)/12 and 2.(H)/13;
Arys-Rostken—Headquarters. and I./KG 2;
Lyck—III./KG 2;
Suwalki—Headquarters., I., II./ZG 26, III./KG 3, 2.(F)/11.

Evidently from the above intelligence some of the airfields known to Soviet intelligence were even in the hands of German aviation units, but the Soviet commanders, owing to a lack of up-to-date information, were not aware of the number or the location of the *Luftwaffe* aircraft based there. They did not even have any idea if there were any enemy combat aircraft located on these airfields or not. That is to say that even in the event of the first preemptive strike on German airfields the effect of similar actions would first and foremost be minimal, but losses on the contrary would be very heavy since many of the German airfields that were earmarked for attacks under the plan for the provision of cover, were located deep inside German territory and the *Luftwaffe's* combat units were absent from these airfields. Furthermore the routes of the flights made by Soviet aircraft took them over German fighter bases, which were rich in air defence systems.

Soviet headquarters were only able to rely on agent intelligence in order to plan the attacks on the German airfields, although they were not able to provide up-to-date information, and often on the contrary, they would feed the command disinformation.

This, for example was how the *Luftwaffe* alignment were assessed in Intelligence report No. 2 written by the headquarters of the Baltic Special Military District dated 2000 hrs on 21 June 1941:

> First. The Siauliai direction.
> Tilsit: An air group of up to 63 aircraft.
> Königsberg: Headquarters of the 1st Air District, up to 300 unidentified aircraft are located on Königsberg airfield.
> Pillau: an aviation unit of up to 100 hydroplanes, and up to 50 Ju-87s.
>
> Second. Kaunas–Vilensk direction.
> Insterburg: the 16th Air Group,* with up to 170 aircraft.

As a result of what was, to put it mildly, 'modest' intelligence on the German airfields that were earmarked for attacks according to the Air Forces of the Baltic Special Military District's 'Plan for the Provision of Cover', in reality only the airfields at Insterburg, Tilsit, Ragnit, Labiau, Königsberg, and Memel (Klaipeda) were actually occupied by *Luftwaffe* combat units. The other German bases that had been designated for attacks were not occupied by *Luftwaffe* combat units, but the actions of the Air Forces of the Baltic Special Military District on the airfields at Danzig, Elbing, Marienburg, Marienwerder, Allenstein, and Goldap, from an operational perspective had been ineffective, and in fact, would have been represented attacks on empty locations.

The schematic diagrams that the Soviet headquarters had in their possession could not in any way be compared with the detailed photomaps taken by the German reconnaissance aircraft. Aside from the locations of the airfields the German commanders and pilots had at their disposal up-to-date 'panoramas' of the airfield they were attacking or any other target, which were detailed right down to the individual locations of each Soviet aircraft. This enabled them to effect well-planned, precise attacks right onto the runways, aircraft, hangars, and so on, as opposed to on the airfield as a whole. Moreover with the help of photographic monitoring German reconnaissance personnel were able to adjust these attacks almost in real time.

Considering that the units of the Air Forces of the Baltic Special Military District:

> Did not have up to date reconnaissance information on the composition, or the location of the enemy alignment;

* It is completely obvious that this relates to 'the 16th Army's Aviation Command' (*KoLuft Armee-Oberkommando* 16), which consisted of just three short-range reconnaissance squadrons (21 combat aircraft). Even taking into account the 1.(F)/22, 3.(F)/Nacht, KGr.z.b.V. 106 that were based there the number of aircraft would only increase to 82.

Were concentrated in two distant echelons, and that their strength had diminished, and the fact that it was envisaged that not all of the units would participate in the raids on the German airfields;

Had not engaged in specialised combat training for combat activity against enemy airfields, in the same way that the *Luftwaffe* pilots had;

Did not have any specialised ammunition, or gun armament;

It has to be said that the Soviet Air Forces were completely unprepared to carry out the order that had been put before them to destroy German aviation on their airfields.

It has to be said that in contrast to the Soviet airfields, which as a rule were defended by between one to three 'Maxim' quadruple machine guns, which became part of the airfield servicing battalions as standard (since the anti-aircraft airfield servicing area batteries had not yet been formed) the German airbases were defended by powerful anti-aircraft artillery, including large-calibre guns. Thus the Command of the Air Forces of the 18th Army (*KoLuft Armee-Oberkommando* 18) had in its line-up I./51, II./36, I./111 motorised anti-aircraft batteries. The Command of the Air Forces of the 4th Panzer Group (*KoLuft Panzer-Armee-Oberkommando* 4) had I/3, II/23, II/411 motorised anti-aircraft, and 83 and 92 light motorised anti-aircraft batteries in their line-up. The Command of the Air Forces of the 16th Army (*KoLuft Armee-Oberkommando* 16) had I./13, I./291, I./411 motorised anti-aircraft batteries at their disposal. The Command of the Air Forces of the 3rd Panzer Group (*KoLuft Panzer-Armee-Oberkommando* 3) had I./29, and I./36 motorised anti-aircraft, and 73, 74, 75, and 84 light motorised anti-aircraft batteries. In the event of an air attack they undoubtedly would have inflicted heavy losses.

Conclusions

The *Luftwaffe* Command concentrated all the forces of their alignment in the first echelon. In fact there were only two training reserve groups that were left in the reserve in East Prussia. Apart from that the German units were not spread out along the entire backbone of the border, but were concentrated in two areas, which enabled German command to manoeuvre their forces over a wide area, and to create an overwhelming advantage in terms of strength in the appropriate direction.

Soviet Command, on the other hand, had spread their forces over several hundreds of kilometres both on the front line, and to some depth. Moreover this was not a situation that was forced upon them, but this configuration was planned in accordance with the plans for the provision of cover. Considering the Red Army's 'traditional' problems in terms of communication equipment and in the organisation of cooperation between units, this distribution could certainly not be termed an optimal one.

Owing to the absence of aerial photoreconnaissance Soviet commanders did not have any accurate information on the basing of German aviation units on one airfield or another, neither were they aware of the deployment of the *Luftwaffe's* principal forces, which created the prerequisites that meant the forthcoming attacks were misplaced and led to a useless distribution of forces and hardware in the battle for air superiority, and to senseless losses.

In fact the division of forces over several echelons automatically condemned Soviet pilots to conduct combat operations in conditions in which the enemy had the upper hand numerically. Therefore even taking into consideration that the Germans only used part of their forces against the Air Forces of the Baltic Special Military District, it nevertheless has to be said that Soviet pilots had almost no chance of emerging from this stand-off as the victors. *Luftwaffe* Command could at any moment create a localised advantage in terms of their strength of forces in the required direction, and hit the Soviet units located there, after which they would be able to continue to destroy the aircraft in other directions, all the time having the upper hand in terms of their strength of forces.

Thus a grave conclusion has to be made, that the actions of the Air Force were, according to the plan for the provision of cover, set to fail from the outset.

Luftwaffe Command, aside from their other advantages, held the initiative of the first pre-emptive strike, which German commanders used to the full, employing it brilliantly during the course of the battle for air superiority.

3.3 The Strange War of the Air Forces of the Red Army

Luftwaffe command conducted out the redeployment of its principal forces right on the eve of Operation Barbarossa in small groups. Since the atmosphere however had already become strained by the flights carried out by reconnaissance aircraft that began back in the spring, the tension grew and the Soviet side were quite sensible in their response.

The military leadership of the USSR took very definitive steps aimed at countering the aggressive policy of their western neighbour. Thanks to the Air Forces of the Baltic Special Military District's surviving documents the training of the district's air forces for the forthcoming combat activities can be assessed in some detail. The onset of war was completely obvious to district command, and the armed forces were trained for this. Judging by the surviving documents these activities commenced no later than 14 June 1941, when the formations were ordered to advance towards the border. The air forces, and the air defence system, however, had begun to be brought up to combat readiness on 18 June:

> ORDER No. 00229 TO THE DIRECTORATE OF THE BALTIC SPECIAL MILITARY DISTRICT 18 June 1941, Riga.
>
> With the aim of bringing the Baltic theatre of military operations up to combat readiness as soon as possible I ORDER:
>
> 1. That the Head of the air defence zone bring the district's entire air defence system up to combat readiness by the end of the day on 19 June 1941, for which it is necessary to:
>   a) Organise a round the clock watch on all the air observation posts, and provide them with continuous communications;
>   b) Prepare all anti-aircraft artillery and searchlight batteries, after ensuring a round the clock watch on the batteries, and organising uninterrupted communications between them, and after having prepared them carefully from an engineering perspective, and having supplied them with ammunition;
>   c) Arrange cooperation between fighter aviation with anti-aircraft units;
>   d) Arrange uninterrupted communications for the air observation posts, with fighter stations;
>
>   Construction of the command posts should be completed by 1 July 1941, starting with the battery commander up to the district brigade commander.
>
>   19 June 1941 Report on the level of cover on the part of the dive bombers for the large railway, and road bridges, ammunition stores, and critical assets.
>
>   Ensure by 21 June 1941 that in conjunction with local air defence, blackouts are in place for the cities of Riga, Kaunas, Vilnius, Dvinsk, Jelgava, Liepaja, and Siauliai, and ensure that they have fire protection as well as medical assistance for the injured, and identify the facilities that could be used as bomb shelters;

e) Expedite as much as possible all the organisational measures, completing them no later than 1 July 1941. Check that these measures mentioned above are being implemented both personally, and via the district's employees.

2. The head of communications in the district is ordered to bring all communications within the territory of the district up to combat readiness, for which it is necessary to:
   a) Deploy the commanders along with the required equipment to the front line, and army command posts no later than the morning of 20 June 1941 to enable them to organise communication centres in these command posts. Use inputs that can be activated at a moment's notice. Systematically check the communications with the command posts, and post the appropriate commanders to them;
   b) Arrange, and systematically check the operation of the radio stations in accordance with the my agreed timescale:

      Pay particular attention to the radio communications with border corps, and divisions, as well as with border troops, aviation, and aerial reconnaissance services.

      Appoint one of your deputies as the head of radio communications in order to ensure that the entire radio network is managed properly.

      Report the results of the checks on the operation of the radio network to the Chief of Staff daily at 0900 hrs, 1300 hrs, and 2100 hrs;
   c) Expedite the installation of SIG-2 systems across the entire aerial reconnaissance network, this should be completed no later than 23 June 1941;
   d) Inform and prepare the communications commanders, who should be ready by the morning of 20 June 1941, of the order from the commanders of the formations to take the communications centres I have appointed under their control...
   e) The head of the Engineering Directorate, along with the Commander of Air Forces is to prepare and submit to me no later than 21 June 1941 a plan for the protection of the airfields from airborne troop landings, after identifying the hardware, and the forces required to achieve this goal.
   f) Commander Lieutenant-General Safronov's Deputy, along with the commanders of the Air Forces, and the head of the Operations Department is to prepare a plan, and submit this to me no later than 24 June 1941, for the defence against airborne troop landings in those areas that are most likely to be affected. Make provision for the deployment of armoured trains to combat airborne troops, with infantry assault troops on board, as well as battalions of T-27 tanks, and the Riga, and Vilensk Infantry Colleges, which would be deployed by road transport.

In accordance with this order by 19 June the aviation regiments and divisions in the Air Forces of the Baltic Special Military District were brought up to combat readiness, and the dispersal of the materiel around the operational airfields began.

In accordance with a report on the combat activities of the 42nd Fighter Air Regiment, which was written by the Deputy Squadron Commander of the 4th Squadron's Political Unit Senior Political Instructor Smirnov, the alarm was raised among the regiments on 19 June 1941:

> On 19 June 1941 at 1300 hrs the combat alert was sounded. At this time two squadrons as well as the leadership of the regiment were in Vilnius attending the funeral of Captain Georgiy Alekseyevich Panteleyev (the Commander of the 2nd Squadron), who was killed in an accident with a MiG-1 on his fifth solo flight on Siauliai airfield. After the alert had been sounded all the personnel that had travelled to the funeral left immediately for Varena. Over

> the course of the 19–20–21 June and into the night of 22 June the personnel were at the airfield and spent the night underneath their aircraft.

On 20 June the headquarters of the 7th Mixed Air Division, in accordance with order No. 1/OP withdrew from Jelgava to a reserve command post in the forest 5 km to the south-west of Siauliai.

The 46th High-Speed Bomber Air Regiment, 7th Mixed Air Division also received an order to redeploy on 20 June:

> Order No. 019 to the 46th High-Speed Bomber Air Regiment dated 20 June 1941.
>
> 1. Redeploy the regiment, and the airbase to the operational Gruzdziai airfield today...
>
> ...
>
> 7. The flight echelon is to be redeployed on 21 June 1941. The time of departure is to be advised.
>
> 8. By 1800 hrs on 21 June 1941 the Commander of the airbase is to draw up a plan for the defence of Gruzdziai airfield from air and ground attacks, as well as for the airfield's security, and is to present this report to me for approval.

These measures are also confirmed in the memoirs of the men themselves. The Deputy Commander of the 6th Mixed Air Division's Political Unit Regimental Commissar Rytov noted in his memoirs: 'On the eve of the 22 June we finally received the order to disperse the aircraft around the field airfields and to ensure they were carefully camouflaged.'

A pilot of the 148th Fighter Air Regiment Junior Lieutenant A.P. Degtyarev recalled:

> Command knew in advance about the attack by Hitler's forces on the Soviet Union. How did I come to this conclusion? Back on 19 June our regiment was scrambled at 0400 hrs in the morning, but we sat there on the airfield for days without the all clear being sounded. Recently the aircraft have been deployed around the airfield on its outer edges, the aircraft were camouflaged, trenches were dug, and combat bombs weighing 25 kg each were recently delivered. On 21 June our Regimental Commander was summoned by the Commander of the Baltic Special Military District to a meeting in Riga [this relates to a meeting at which, by all accounts, the order dated 18 June was disseminated to the commanders of the units, and formations]. He returned that same day, and we knew nothing. All this makes me think that the district headquarters knew about the onset of war.

The head of the 148th Fighter Air Regiment Cholok noted that the order to execute these measures had been issued with perfect timing between 18–20 June at a meeting at the headquarters of the Air Forces of the Baltic Special Military District:

> At around 20 June at a meeting in the Commander of the 6th Mixed Air Division and the Commander of the District Air Force's office in Riga the Regimental Commander received an instruction to carry out a series of measures aimed at raising the level of the unit's combat readiness: Although this was normal since at every meeting someone among us was given the very strictest of instructions, this time they seemed more significant to us.

Assuming that this was the case that these measures began to be put in place on 19 June, it is more than likely that this refers either to the evening of 18 June, or to the morning of 19 June 1941:

18–20 June the aircraft of the 15th, and the 31st Fighter Air Divisions, and the 61st Ground Attack Air Regiment, and the 8th Mixed Air Division were also redeployed among the field airfields:

> The 31st Fighter Air Regiment; three squadrons were redeployed to Karmelava on 18 June, and on 20 June the unit was brought up to combat readiness.
> The 15th Fighter Air Regiment; by 20 June the directorate, as well as the 1st, and 3rd Squadrons had been redeployed to the airfield in Potsunai, while the 2nd went to Vincai.
> The 61st Ground Attack Air Regiment; the 1st and 2nd Squadrons were redeployed to the airfield at Markshtava, and the 3rd Squadron went to Risgonis.
> The 40th High-Speed Bomber Air Regiment was redeployed to the airfield at Piltene.
> The 31st High-Speed Bomber Air Regiment was redeployed to the airfields at Jelgava, and Platone.
> The 54th High-Speed Bomber Air Regiment; three squadrons were redeployed to the airfields at Kryzhaki, and Kivishki.
> The 42nd Fighter Air Regiment; all the combat crews were redeployed to the airfields on Orany, and Perloja.

Subsequently, at least from the morning of 20 June onwards (more than likely this rebasing of the headquarters' structures from Riga to Panevezys took place on the night of 19–20 June) the directorate of the North-Western Front was deployed at a command post in the area around Panevezys. This was where the headquarters of the air forces of the South-Western Front was located, and this is confirmed by operations reports written by the district headquarters, and by the headquarters of the district's air forces dated 20 June 1941.

Operations report No. 2 dated 0500 hrs on 21 June 1941, written by the headquarters of the Air Forces of the Baltic Special Military District, Panevezys: 'The Air Forces units in the course of the night of 21 June 1941 did not engage in combat, one squadron in each regiment was at readiness condition No. 2 for the entire night. The rest were engaged in combat training.'

Operations report No. 3 dated 1700 hrs on 21 June 1941, written by the headquarters of the Air Forces of the Baltic Special Military District, Panevezys: 'The Air Force units in the course of the day on 21 June 1941 were engaged in combat training and camouflaging materiel on the airfields. In each regiment one squadron was on watch at readiness condition No. 2.'

Interestingly all the measures that were taken by district command and which were aimed at not antagonising the situation were hidden, first and foremost from their own personnel, and resembled preparations for an exercise. The Chief of Staff of the 148th Fighter Air Regiment Cholok writes about this directly:

> On 21 June the aircraft were dispersed and ammunition was prepared. Although it was clear to everybody that this was no ordinary training all these measures were carried out, and were explained as large scale exercises which were to be conducted by the People's Commissariat for Defence, and that the regiment was being called upon to ensure that these exercises were being supported by their own combat readiness.

A pilot in the 31st Fighter Air Regiment N.I. Petrov also confirms this, he was among a group of pilots for whom the story about the exercises was also fabricated:

> During a flight from Kaunas to the airfield at Karmelava after a scramble, this was three days prior to 22 June 1941, we were informed that district wide exercises would be conducted by

> the Air Forces of the Baltic Military District. On arrival at Karmelava airfield everything that could have been had already been brought up to combat readiness, for the (notional) combat activity from 20–21 for the purposes of exercises.

Overall the aviation of the Air Forces of the Baltic Special Military District saw in the morning of 21 June 1941 in a completely combat capable state, with one squadron each maintaining readiness level No. 2 in every regiment. At this very same time the troops in the Baltic Special Military District's second echelon (specifically the Western Special Military District, the Kiev Special Military District, and the Odessa Military District) had begun to move up to the border from 14–18 June. The engineering units in the district were ordered to stop building the pillboxes and to withdraw the construction units from the border, while the sapper units began to reconnoitre the border objectives with the aim of installing fences and laying mines in the critical tank approach routes, as well as destroying the bridges. The training of the troops in the Baltic Special Military District in countering aggression on the western border at the end of June 1941 was completely obvious.

For reasons that are unclear the pragmatic development of events was interrupted on the evening of 21 June 1941 (and actually on the night of 21–22 June) and from that moment on the logic in the actions of the leadership of the country and the army collapsed decisively. The tragically notorious Directive No. 1 set all the chaos in motion, and a time bomb in terms of point 2 had been planted in what was overall a relatively sensible narrative.

> The military councils of the Leningrad Military District, the Baltic Special Military District, the Kiev Special Military District, and the Odessa Military District.
>
> 1. Over the course of the 22–23 June 1941 a sudden attack by the Germans is possible on the front lines of the Leningrad Military District, the Baltic Special Military District, the Kiev Special Military District, and the Odessa Military District. The combat activity may begin with acts of provocation.
>
> 2. **The mission for our forces is not to give into any provocation, which could give rise to widespread implications.**
>   At the same time the forces of the Leningrad, Baltic, Western, Kiev, and Odessa districts should be at full readiness to counter a sudden attack from the Germans or their allies.
>   I order:
>   a) The firing points in the fortified sectors on the state border to be quietly occupied on the night of 22 June 1941;
>   b) Disperse all aviation, including front line aircraft around the field airfields, and camouflage them carefully before dawn on 22 June 1941;
>   c) Bring all units up to combat readiness. The troops are to remain dispersed, and camouflaged;
>   d) Bring air defences up to full combat readiness without the additional mobilisation of designated personnel. Prepare measures for the blackout of cities, and other assets;
>   e) Do not carry out any further measures without any special orders.
>   Timoshenko, Zhukov.
>   21 June 1941.

This directive was received at the headquarters of the Baltic Special Military District at approximately 0130 hrs. The commander, Lieutenant-General F.I. Kuznetsov, who had finalised this document, sent it to the headquarters of the 8th, 11th, and 27th Armies, in accordance with which the following orders were issued:

A DIRECTIVE ISSUED BY THE COMMANDER OF THE BALTIC SPECIAL MILITARY DISTRICT DATED 22 JUNE 1941 TO THE MILITARY COUNCILS OF THE 8th and 11th ARMIES CONCERNING THE MEASURES IN CONNECTION WITH THE POTENTIAL INVASION BY THE GERMANS IN THE PERIOD FROM 22–23 JUNE 1941.

TOP SECRET
22 June 1941, 0225 hrs.

1. It is possible during the course of 22–23 June 1941 that a sudden invasion may take place on the part of the Germans on our positions. This invasion may begin suddenly with acts of provocation.
2. The mission for our forces is not to give in to these acts of provocation by the Germans, which could give rise to widespread implications.
   At the same time our forces should be at full combat readiness to counter any sudden attack from the Germans, and to defeat any attack.

I ORDER:
1. That the defences in the principal zone be quietly manned in the course of the night of 22–23 June 1941. Draw the sentry posts out to the forefield to guard the pillboxes, while the subdivisions which are intended for the defence of the forefield, are to be kept in reserve. Cartridges, and shells are to be distributed.
   In the event of any acts of provocation on the part of the Germans do not open fire. Until German aircraft start to fly over our territory, and until they begin to engage in combat activity, do not open fire.
2. In the event of large scale enemy forces going on the offensive they are to be defeated.
3. The directorate of forces is to be left firmly in the hands of the commanders.
4. The leadership, as well as Red Army soldiers are to be kept informed of the situation.

…

8. The Air Defence materiel and the troops are to be brought up to combat readiness level No. 1, after preparing the cities and other assets for blackouts.
9. Anti-tank mines, and low visibility obstructions are to be put in place immediately.
10. Report the completion of these orders, as well as any violation of the border immediately.

This directive succeeded in reaching all the formations, and units of the district's air forces (which practically made up the front line) prior to the start of combat activity by the Germans.

The documents, as well as the memoirs of the participants record the time the units were put on alert—this occurred somewhere between 0300–0330 hrs in the morning of 22 June.

According to 'Operational report No.1' written by the headquarters of the 57th Mixed Air Division the alert was sounded in the units comprising the formation at 0325 hrs in the morning of 22 June.

A report on the combat activities of the 42nd Fighter Air Regiment by Senior Political instructor Smirnov gives an even earlier time of approximately 0315 hrs:

> At 0315 hrs on 22 June the combat alert was sounded by the Chief of Staff Captain Redkin. The personnel, who were located in tents, had manned their aircraft five minutes later.
>
> We were ordered to make all the preparations for a sortie. The machine guns were armed, but the bombs were not fitted underneath the aircraft.

In a political report the Deputy Commander of the 148th Fighter Air Regiment's Political Unit, Battalion Commissar Golovachev notes that the alarm was sounded in the regiment at 0305 hrs on 22 June 1941.

A pilot who was on duty that night on Liepaja airfield from the 148th Fighter Air Regiment, A.D. Ocherednikov, recorded precisely the time at which the directive was received: 'From 21–22 June 1941 I took the place of the duty officer in the Batpuri [Liepaja airfield] locality. At 0315 hrs the alarm was raised.'

His words are confirmed by another pilot in the 148th Fighter Air Regiment Junior Lieutenant A.P. Degtyarev, according to his memoirs the alarm was raised at 0330 hrs: 'On 22 June at 0330 hrs we were scrambled again, and when we got to our aircraft we started them up, warmed up the engines, and awaited further instructions.'

S.A. Ovchinnikov, a former technician in the 3rd Squadron, 148th Fighter Air Regiment wrote:

> This happened at 0200 hrs [it seems he is confused and that this should be read as 0300 hrs] on the Sunday, we were scrambled. We lived some 600–800 m from the airfield. After running quickly to our aircraft we began to ready them for a sortie, that is to say we tried to start the engines and we fed the cartridge belts into the machine gun feed block. I say 'we', but I am speaking for myself, for the engine specialists, and for the crew commander—the pilot. We were a crew—a pilot, technician, and engine specialist. It was still dark when crew commander Comrade Levin reported on command that the aircraft was combat ready. After which we all stepped away from the aircraft, sat on the grass, and had a smoke. Approximately an hour went by from the time the alarm was raised to the time the aircraft was ready, maybe a little more.

Almost the same thing happened in other divisions and regiments in the district's air forces, an example of this is this excerpt from the memoirs of a pilot of the 4th Squadron, 31st Fighter Air Regiment, Petrov:

> On 21 June on the Saturday I took the place of the unit's duty officer. At 0300 hrs in the morning of 22 June the Chief of Staff of the Mixed Air Division that we were a part of called, and ordered me to sound the alarm, and for the regiment's Chief of Staff to call the Divisional Headquarters on reaching the command post. He went on to ask 'Are you a pilot? Then we will get someone to replace you.' I immediately remembered that in the combat Statute for the air forces it states that if the alarm is sounded a member of ground crew, a technician, that is also a member of an operational crew is relieved of carrying out his internal duties and is to begin to carry out his principal duties. I thought this was it and the war had begun. I immediately handed over to the regimental Chief of Staff Captain Sergeyev and sounded the alarm for the regiment, I was relieved of my duties. As the ground crew arrived at the aircraft a short time later after just a few minutes green flares shot up from the regimental command post.

Thus with some accuracy it can be established that by 0400 hrs on 22 June the regiments of the 6th, 7th, 8th, and 57th Divisions of the Air Forces of the South-Western Front (the Baltic Special Military District) had succeeded in responding to the alarm and even in preparing their materiel for combat activity right up to starting the engines and elevating their machine guns. To quote the words of the Commander of the 148th Fighter Air Regiment G.N. Zaytsev: 'All the aircraft were dispersed, the guns had been tested.'

The subsequent course of events was inextricably linked to the 'sword of Damocles' that was hanging over the heads of the majority of the commanders of the divisions and regiments in terms of the orders issued by the above mentioned command. 'Do not give into acts of provocation' and 'In the event of any acts of provocation on the part of the Germans do not open fire. Until German aircraft start to fly over our territory, and until they begin to engage in combat activity, do not open fire.'

From the texts of the directives, and of the memoirs of the personnel it is very obvious that in setting the goals for their subordinates each successive commander in the hierarchy used ever more 'dangerous' phraseology, and objectives, and in the end the directive would reach the regimental commanders in a very 'interesting' format. G.N. Zaytsev in his memoirs cites an instruction given by the Commander of the 7th Mixed Air Division:

> We have been given an order to be at combat readiness, but not to shoot down a single enemy aircraft, but just to force them to land! This was communicated to everyone. In response to some confused questioning it was confirmed that we were to 'force the aircraft to land and that was all!' This was how it was written in the original, evidently it should read 'force them to land and that's it!')

That is to say in place of a concise command to take specific action to destroy the enemy that had crossed the border, the personnel were fed contradicting phraseology and instructions to interpret the situation at hand, and for them to decide for themselves if a given situation represented an act of war or provocation. One of the first to describe this absurdity was Hero of the Soviet Union Colonel-General of Artillery N.M. Khlebnikov back at the beginning of the 1970s. He saw in the war as a colonel, and as the head of artillery in the 27th Army. Colonel Khlebnikov on the night of 21–22 June was at district headquarters along with the Deputy Commander of the Baltic Special Military District Lieutenant-General E.P. Safronov, who took the rap for Lieutenant-General Kuznetsov, who had left for the 11th Army. He recalled in some detail that immediately after the text of the directive had been received the commanders of the different levels literally showered district headquarters with questions, but they did not get the explanation they deserved:

> At approximately 0230 hrs constant phone calls began to come in from individual units. The Commanders asked: what are we supposed to make of the directive from district command? How are we supposed to discern provocation from a real attack, if the enemy undertakes combat activities?
>
> Egor Pavlovich's (Safronov's) position was a difficult one: what were we to tell them if we had not seen this directive with our own eyes? The District Commander issued this order to the troops in the first echelon, without informing his deputy.

In fact after the receipt of Directive No. 1 commanders at all levels were forced to take extraordinarily responsible decisions independently as to whether combat activities had actually commenced or not, and Soviet pilots were put in what was a very strange position: directives issued by their own command actually ordered them, so to speak, to force an enemy that was armed to the teeth to land simply by manoeuvring! To a large extent if this directive had not reached the units in the district at all the atmosphere would have been much more healthy, and the commanders would not have had the 'food' for the doubts, and the discussions that took place around that time, and which were completely unnecessary.

Apart from the factors that have been stated above there was another reason why, despite the combat readiness of the Soviet units, the first attack by the *Luftwaffe* was successful. The point being that the flight time from the border to the principal, first line Soviet airfields, was in the region of 10–15 minutes and this was nowhere near enough time for the aerial reconnaissance posts to successfully send the radiograms, and for the formations, and unit headquarters to decipher them and scramble their fighters. For example, during joint exercises held in May the 8th Mixed Air Division and the 41st Aerial Reconnaissance Battalion revealed the following shortcomings:

> The exercises that were held along with the 41st Aerial Reconnaissance Battalion on 9 May highlighted the following shortcomings in the work of the radio operators (and of the duty officers) in the aviation garrisons:
>
> In the 15th and 31st Fighter Air Regiments preparation of the radio stations was poorly carried out (the feed to the receivers was absent), which had a detrimental effect on the quality of the radiograms as they were received.
>
> The preparation of the radio stations in the 42nd and the 61st Fighter Air Regiments, and the signal companies in the 8th Air Division was carried out perfectly satisfactorily.
>
> 2. Of the 18 radiograms sent by the aerial reconnaissance posts (Alytus seven, and Mariumpole 11):
>
>   The signals company of the 8th Air Division received eight of them, while six of them were distorted;
>
>   The signals companies in the 61st Ground Attack Air Regiment received 15, while seven were distorted;
>
>   The signals companies in the 42nd Fighter Air Regiment received 15, while 12 of them were distorted;
>
>   The signals companies in the 15th Fighter Air Regiment received five, while five them were distorted.
>
>   These distortions happened, in the main, due to insufficient training on the part of the radio operators, and the radiograms not having been sent accurately from the aerial reconnaissance posts.
>
> 3. The time taken for the radiograms to travel from the reconnaissance points to the duty officer was at least one and a half to two minutes, with the maximum being 10–13 minutes, while from the duty officer to the duty squadron took two to three minutes, which does not ensure that the duty squadron would be able to get off the ground quickly.
>
> 4. The duty officers in the aviation garrisons did not maintain a flight plan for the aircraft, since they were guided solely by a map showing the aerial reconnaissance posts.
>
>   The way the duty officer handled the radiograms he received was sluggish, he did not respond with any urgency, which suggests that the briefing the duty officer received from the heads of the operations departments within the regiments was insufficient. Despite the fact that the instructions that I affirmed required the duty officer to receive a daily briefing from the heads of the operations departments within the regiments, the duty officer in the 15th Fighter Air Regiment had not been briefed, as a result of which his knowledge of his duties was poor.

Considering the first attacks were made by German aircraft to coincide with the first artillery salvos, and in many cases before this, Soviet fighters had practically no way of meeting these aircraft in the air.

Theoretically the first attack was meant to be repelled by the anti-aircraft machine gun platoons, which were incorporated as standard in the line-up of each of the three companies of the airfield servicing battalions, and the anti-aircraft batteries of the reserve artillery battalions. The Red Army however saw in the war without having been mobilised fully, and apart from that many of the units and formations had only just been formed, and were at the stage of being deployed, and equipped. Therefore the anti-aircraft batteries in the reserve artillery battalions were not fully equipped and out of what were the standard three M-4 anti-aircraft machine gun installations in wartime, there was practically just the one quadruple 'Maksim' machine gun each in the anti-aircraft artillery machine gun platoons of the airfield servicing battalions by 22 June. Considering that some of the regiments had been successfully dispersed around two to three airfields, it turned out that each of the airfields, even theoretically, could only be covered by one or two machine guns. A further negative factor was that the anti-aircraft platoons were subordinated to the commanders of the airfield servicing battalions, and the level of their training for combat operations was relatively low. During the course of exercises that were held in the spring, as a rule, out of the two or three machine gun crews that were trained to counter an attack from a likely enemy, in practically all cases, only one or two crews were able to fire for a number of reasons. On some occasions the crews were not able to bring their machine guns up to a condition in which they would be combat capable.

In transferring directly to a description of the combat activity itself, we note again that reproaching the commanders, and the personnel of the Air Forces of the Baltic Special Military District for the situation that had unfolded would be completely prejudicial. On the contrary, across all levels the commanders of the district were working very hard trying to correct the situation that had been brought about by the upper leadership, and were trying to meet the oncoming war fully armed. The 'crunch time' was upon them, however, and in the pre-dawn twilight German aircraft taxied out for take-off. The Commander of JG 54 *Major* Hannes Trautloft described in his diary the preparations, as well as the first sortie on 22 June 1941:

> At 0330 hrs when I arrived at the airfield the stars were still shining brightly in the night sky. The grass was heavy with dew and my boots quickly became damp.
>
> The airfield had already been awake for some time. Around 45 aero-engines were in operation simultaneously, gradually warming up. Their monotonal drone was interspersed with booms emanating from the engines that had just been started, in the darkness orange and yellow flames could be seen shooting out of their exhaust manifolds. The air was filled with a strange smell, which was made up of the smell of the earth, the grass, the flowers, and of the oil, and petrol. The first birds had begun to chirp. The sky was lightening in the east, and the darkness, and shadows were steadily dissipating.
>
> This was a pivotal day in terms of our fate, and everyone on the airfield knew this. I took my place in a cold cockpit, the straps were wet, and clammy. A technician helped me to strap in. As I closed the canopy I heard the valedictory cries of 'Hals und Beinbruch!' [this was a traditional greeting to bring good luck to pilots in the *Luftwaffe*, and literally translated it means 'Go break your leg, go break your neck!'] My throat was dry and my heart was pounding faster than usual.
>
> At 0350 hrs we took off. All the squadrons in the 1st Air Corps were ordered to cross the Soviet border at 0400 hrs. As we crossed it the border would literally come alive. At 0405 hrs artillery fire would break out along its entire length. We could clearly see the flashes from the exploding shells. At this very moment a huge drama was unfolding, which could change not only our fate, but the entire course of history!
>
> My pilots were on the alert, I knew this from the first combat sorties in other campaigns. There was so much of the unknown ahead of us, What will the Russians do? Will our attack

> come as a surprise to them? Will we encounter their fighters? Were their aircraft better than ours?

The thorough *Luftwaffe* preparations for this operation, along with the processes described above in the Red Army bore fruit and in the course of the first sortie German pilots encountered almost no resistance from their Soviet counterparts: 'The first sortie answered our questions quickly, the majority of Soviet airfields turned out to be bereft of any kind of defence.

The Commander of the 1st Air Fleet General A. Keller.

Commander of the 8th Air Corps General F. von Richthofen.

A Bf 10F from the headquarter's flight of the 54th Fighter Wing (I./JG 54).

Bf 109F fighters from the 2nd Squadron, 1st Group, 54th Fighter Wing (JG 54) on a forward airfield in the Baltic region.

A Bf 109F from the 4th Squadron, II Group 54th Fighter Wing (II./JG 54) on a forward airfield in the Baltic Region.

A Bf 109f of the 7th Squadron, III Group, 54th Fighter Wing (III./JG 54) stand out with their non-standard camouflage.

A Bf 109f flown by the Commander of the III Group 53rd Fighter Wing (II./JG 53) *Hauptmann* Heinz Bretnütz.

A Bf 109F flown by the Commander of the 7th Squadron III Group, 53rd Fighter Wing (III./JG 53) *Oberluetnant* Heinz Altendorf).

A Bf 109F from the II Group, 52nd Fighter Wing (II./JG 52) on a forward airfield in June 1941.

Bf 109E from the 8th Squadron, III Group, 27th Fighter Wing (III./JG 27) on an airfield in the area around Suwalki.

A Bf 109E from the II Group, 27th Fighter Wing (II./JG 27) camouflaged on the edge of the airfield in the area around Suwalki.

Ju-88A-5 bombers from the II Group, 1st Bomber Wing (II./KG I) on a forward airfield, summer 1941.

A Ju-88A from the 9th Wing, III Group, 1st Bomber Wing (III./KG 1) the emblem of the squadron can clearly be seen on the nose—a monogram with the inscription 'Hindenburg'.

Fuelling a Ju-88A-5 from the 4th Squadron, 76th Bomber Wing (II./KG 76) the aircraft's code can be seen on the tail section, F1+GM.

Fuelling a Ju-88A-5 from the 4th Squadron, 76th Bomber Wing (II./KG 76) the aircraft's code can be seen on the tail section, F1+GM.

Ju-88A-5 bombers from III Group, 76th Bomber Wing (III./KG 76) the distinguishing marking of this group's aircraft is the thin white line across the fuselage.

A Ju-88A-5 from the 1st Squadron, 1st Group, 77th Bomber Wing (I./KG 77), alongside these aircraft, a dummy horse has been tethered to a trailer.

Technical servicing of a Ju-88A-5 from the 4th Squadron, II Group 77th Bomber Wing (III./KG 77).

A Do 17Z from the 2nd Squadron, I Group, 2nd Bomber Wing (I./KG 2), June 1941.

A Do 17Z of the 8th Squadron, II Group, 3rd Bomber Wing (III./KG 3), June 1941. Aircraft of the 8th Air Corps were distinguishable by broad yellow lines that were painted around the fuselage in the area around the tail fin.

Technical personnel from the 1st Group, 26th Heavy Fighter Wing, against a backdrop of Bf 110 aircraft from the 3rd Squadron, June 1941.

Technical personnel prepare Ju-87B-2 from the 4th Squadron, II Group, 1st Dive-Bomber Wing (II./StG1), June 1941.

Technical personnel prepare Ju-87B-2 from the 4th Squadron, II Group, 1st Dive-Bomber Wing (II./StG1), June 1941.

Starting the engine on a Ju-87B-2 from the 3rd Squadron, 1st Dive Bomber Wing, June 1941.

A Ju-87B-2 from the 2nd Squadron, I Group, 2nd Dive Bomber Wing takes off.

A Bf 109E from the 5th Squadron, II Group, *Lehrgeschwader 2* (II./LG2) prepared for a bombing raid on June 1941. 96 SD-2 bombs have been fitted on ventral pylons.

The *Luftwaffe* had a powerful reconnaissance aviation branch with modern aircraft in service. In this photo is a Bf 110 from the 4th Squadron, 33rd Long-Range Reconnaissance Group. In summer 1941 this unit carried out reconnaissance in the interests of the 4th Panzer Group.

Ju-88D-1 reconnaissance aircraft from the 1st Squadron, 22nd Reconnaissance Group, in June 1941 were in the reserve in the zone of the Army Group North.

Technical staff repair an engine on an Hs 126 from the 3rd Squadron, 41st Reconnaissance Group, carried out reconnaissance in the interests of the headquarters of the 8th Panzer Group.

An Hs 126 from the 2nd Squadron, 23rd Reconnaissance Group, were operated by the Headquarters of the 1st Panzer Group.

Apart from the Hs 126 there were three squadrons that were equipped with the newest reconnaissance aircraft in the shape of the FW 189As-1s in the *Luftwaffe's* reconnaissance alignment, that were deployed against the forces of the North-Western Front. In this photo the crew pose against a 'Frame' from the 4th Squadron, 31st Reconnaissance Group, which was operated by the Headquarters of the XXXXI Motorised Corps.

German anti-aircraft artillery posed a huge threat to aircraft, since it was equipped with modern guns, and crewed by very well trained personnel. In this photo the crew of a legendary 88 mm anti-aircraft gun prepare it for battle.

A 37 mm gun opens fire.

Personnel pose next to a 20 mm gun.

A fearsome weapon was the quadruple mounted anti-aircraft gun and in the summer of 1941 the Red Army did not have anything to match it.

Thanks to the availability of high speed, halftrack tractors, heavy anti-aircraft artillery could keep up with panzer columns.

20 and 37 mm weapons, thanks to their compact gun carriages, could easily be accommodated in the superstructures of high-speed, semi-half track tractors, as well as cross-country vehicles. They were therefore used ubiquitously in orders of battle, and as light armoured personnel carriers, and moreover not only against an aerial enemy, but against any other targets as well.

German infantry divisions did not have anti-aircraft guns, and as standard they were equipped with MG-34 dual mounted anti-aircraft guns, and special single axle carts were used to transport them.

The principal anti-aircraft gun for the Red Army in the 1930s was the 76.2 mm K-3 guns, which were the standard design for 1931. In the summer of 1941 this gun along with a modernised version that was standard for 1938, remained the most widespread anti-aircraft gun in service with the Air Defence System.

Another standard weapon in the arsenal of the Air Defence System were the dual mounted, triplicated, and quadruple mounted 'Maksim' machine guns. This photo shows the most widespread variant the ZPU-4 quadruple variant, which was manufactured by N.T. Tokaryov in 1931.

The ZPU-4 gun carriage was also designed for installation in the superstructures on a GAZ-AAA vehicle. Up until the advent of the 25 and 37-mm and the large-calibre DShK machine guns, the ZPU-4 in a GAZ-AAA was the only mobile means of providing cover for motorised units on the march.

The new generation of anti-aircraft artillery entered service in 1939, this was the powerful 85 mm 52-K semi-automatic anti-aircraft gun, which subsequently became the principal anti-aircraft gun in service with the air defence dystem units.

The first automatic automatic anti-aircraft gun that entered service with the Red Army was the 37 mm 61-K gun. This gun was produced en masse and subsequently became the main weapon of war against enemy aircraft at low level.

A 12.7 mm large-calibre DShK machine gun, which is a wonderful example of a light weapon. It is in service with several dozen countries and up until now has been used successfully in the course of local conflicts.

A SD-2 fragmentation bomb.

A suspension point for SD-2 bombs underneath an Bf 109E fighter.

A suspension point with SD-2 bombs underneath an Bf 109E in field conditions, July 1941.

A Bf 109E from II./G 27 fully loaded with SD-2 bombs, this photograph was taken in June1941.

SD-2 bombs suspended underneath the wing of a Bf 110 fighter-bomber.

A suspension point for SD-2 bombs in the bomb bay of a Ju-88A.

SD-50 fragmentation bombs were the principal armament for the aircraft of the *Luftwaffe's* I Air Corps in combat with Soviet aircraft on their own airfields.

Four SD-50 bombs suspended underneath a Bf 109F fighter.

A 250 kg bomb suspension point underneath a Bf 109F fighter.

A high-altitude reconnaissance Ju-86P aircraft from the 4.(F) Gr.Ob.d.L, bearing the code D-APEW, which made an emergency landing due to engine failure on 15 April 1941 in the area around Rivne. This was the only aircraft lost during the course of reconnaissance over the territory of the USSR in the spring of 1941. It is very likely that this aircraft also carried out flights over the Baltic region.

An aerial photograph of Siauliai airfield taken on 8 June 1941, from on board a German reconnaissance aircraft. The aircraft standing in groups or on their own around the airfield can clearly be seen.

An aerial photograph of Kaunas airfield taken on 8 June 1941 from on board a German reconnaissance aircraft. The hard standings housing Soviet aircraft are clearly visible.

An aerial photograph of Riga airfield taken on 20 June 1941 from on board German reconnaissance aircraft, The concrete runway that is being constructed in accordance with a standard design is clearly visible.

Information, and maps that the units of the Air Forces of the Baltic Special Military District of the targets in the shape of the German airfields that were designated for attack in accordance with the 'plan for the provision of cover', and which were not occupied by German forces: These were: Königsberg-Devau, Danzig, Elbing, Marienburg, Allenstein, Darkehmen, and Goldap.

Экз. № 15

СВОДНАЯ ТАБЛИЦА

АЭРОДРОМОВ, ПОСАДОЧНЫХ ПЛОЩАДОК И ГИДРОАЭРОДРОМОВ ГЕРМАНИИ.

1. ВОСТОЧНАЯ ПРУССИЯ.

Наименование.	Классификация.	Местонахождение по ориентирам.	Координаты.	Размер.	Выс. над уров. моря (вм)	Описание объекта	[illegible]	СХЕМА.
ДЕВАУ	аэродром	4,5 км сев.восточнее центра города КЕНИГСБЕРГ, 500 мт юго-восточн. пункта ДЕВАУ и южнее ж.д. и шоссе КЕНИГСБЕРГ-НОЙХАУЗЕН.	20°34'25" Вост.долг. 54°43'35" северной широты.	880х575	20мт	Аэродром имеет форму неправильного квадрата, наибольшее протяжение его по диагонали 1250х1100. Летное поле засеяно травой. Аэродромные строения расположены в восточной части. К аэродрому с зап. части ДЕВАУ подходит шоссейная дорога. Подходы затруднены с северной и западной стороны. На аэродроме имеется: 1) Казармы, 2) Аэропорт, 3) Ангары (всего 4), 4) Стационарный прожектор, 5) Флюгер. Аэродром оборудован для ночных полетов. В Ю.З. части в 500 мт от аэродрома стрельбище...........	.	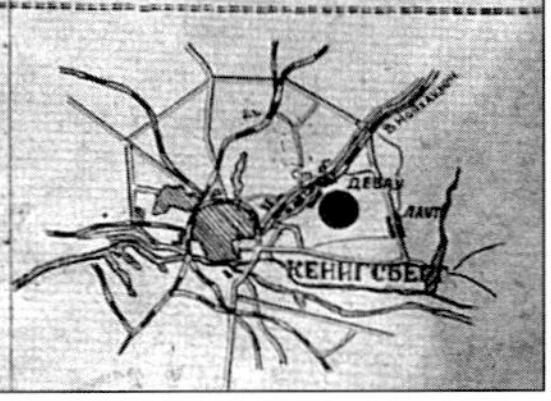
ДАНЦИГ	аэродром	Сев.зап.окраина г. ДАНЦИГ (сев. ж.д. ДАНЦИГ-ГДЫНЯ в 100 мт. и зап. шоссе - ДАНЦИГ-БРЕЗЕН.).	18°36'25" Восточн. долготы. 54°23'25' северной широты.	900х900	19мт	Аэродром имеет форму многоугольника наибольшее протяжение площади с Юго-зап. на Сев. Восток 950 мт. и с Востока на Запад 1200мт. Аэродромные строения размещаются в юго-западной и юго-восточной части аэродрома с этих направлений подходы затруднены, с других направлений открыты. Граница аэродрома обнесена стационарными знаками. На аэродроме имеется: 1) Один ангар с указателем ветров, 2) Радиостанция. 3) Бензохранилище. 4) Помещение авиашколы.	.	
ЭЛЬБИНГ	аэродром	50 км Ю.В. ДАНЦИГ На южной окраине ЭЛЬБИНГ и Ю.Ю.З. в 500 мт. ж.д. ст. У жел. дороги ЭЛЬБИНГ - ОСТЕРОДЕ	19°26'00" восточной долготы. 54°10'30" северной широты.	100х800 (900х600).	2мт	Форма летного поля - неправильный многоугольник, покрыто травянистым покровом на песчаном грунте. Подходы стеснены с Сев. и Вост. прилегающими строениями. Отдельные препятствия высотой до 45м. расположены на С-З (1,5-2км от аэродрома), фабричные трубы. В юго-восточной части имеется: 1) Ангар, 2) Бензохранилище на 500л., 3) Ремонтные мастерские, У ангара имеется конусный ветроуказатель. Ночное электрооборудование имеется.	.	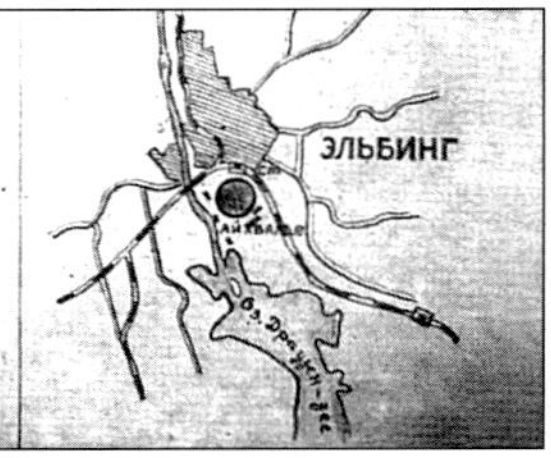
МАРИЕНБУРГ	Аэродром.	4,5км. Восточнее г. МАРИЕНБУРГ в 1,4 км южнее жел. дор. МАРИЕНБУРГ-ЭЛЬБИНГ на южном берегу старого русла р. НОГАТ.	19°07'25' восточной долготы. 54°01'37" северной широты.	700х600 (общ. площадь 420-000 кв. мт.)	5мт.	Имеет форму многоугольника, площадь засеяна травой. Подходы со всех направлений открыты. В северной части имеется 1 ангар. К аэродрому с севера подведено шоссе. Летный состав живет в городе и в поселке что в 1,5 км Ю.З аэродрома. Электрооборудование имеется:	Аэродром школьный.	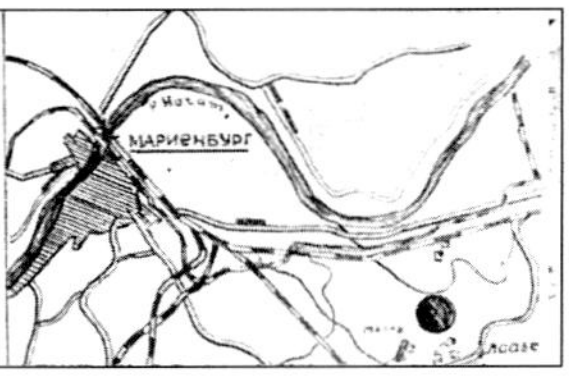
АЛЛЕНШТЕЙН. (ДЕЙТЕН)	Аэродром.	4,4км западнее АЛЛЕНШТЕЙН южнее в 700х800 мт. оз. Ойфль-Зее у шоссе АЛЛЕНШТЕЙН-ОСТЕРОДЕ С.З. окраина села ДУЙТЕН.	20°24'35" восточной долготы. 53°46'50' северной широты.	600х600 (общ. площадь 36000кв. мтр.)	135 мт.	Имеет форму квадрата, рабочая площадь имеет улучшенную часть в виде неправильного треугольника и засеяно травой. Подходы затруднены с юга и юго-востока прилегающими строениями и телефонным проводом высотою до 14мт. Наиболее удобны с запада и востока. Служебное здание и конусный указатель ветров расположен на Ю.В. окраине аэродрома у ДЕЙТИН.		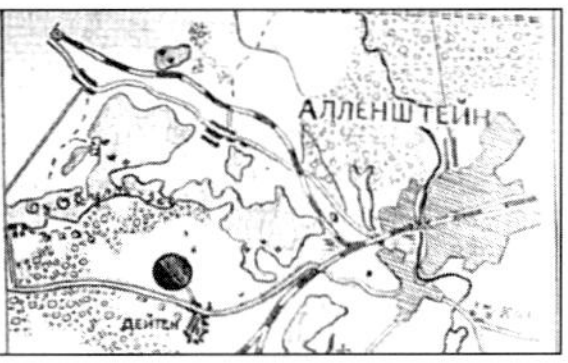
ДАРКЕМЕН	посадочная площадка	25км Ю.Ю.Зап. ГУМБИНЕН в 2 км Ю-Во ДАРКЕМЕН и в 2км Сев. вост. БАГДОНЕН На Ю.З окр. Пуйквален	предположительно 22°02'30' восточной долготы 54°23'20" северной широты.					
ГОЛЬДАП	посадочная площадка.	33 км. Ю.Ю. восточн. ГУМБИНЕН 2,5км Юго-Зап ГОЛЬДАП между шоссе и рекой. (предположительно) у д. Шенеберг	22°16'25" восточной долготы. 54°17'30" северной широты.					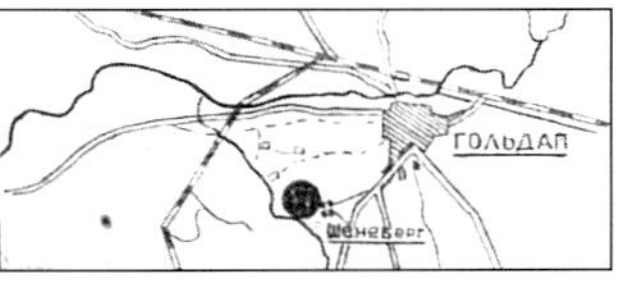

	ПИЛАУ	Гидроаэродром.	37,5 км.западнее гор. КЕНИГСБЕРГ в заливе ФИШХАУ ХЕНЕР-ВИК на сев. восточной окраине гор. ПИЛАУ.	19°56'30" восточной долготы. 54°39'35" северной широты	600х300	На аэродроме имеется: 3 наземных ангара 100х24 и высотой 10 шт. вместительностью каждый на 17 гидропланов. Спуск.

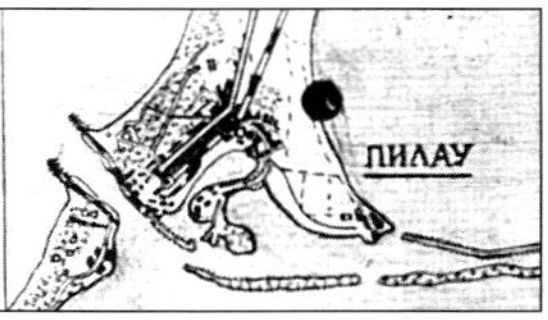

21	ГУМБИНЕН	Аэродром	3км зап. ГУМБИНЕН (что 55км D.D. Восточнее) ТИЛЬЗИТ. Расположен между ж.д. и шоссе ГУМБИНЕН.-ИНСТЕРБУРГ в 500мт зап. [illegible] и на [illegible] окраине Станнайтшен.	20°07'25" восточной долготы 54°36'00" северной широты.		55м.	

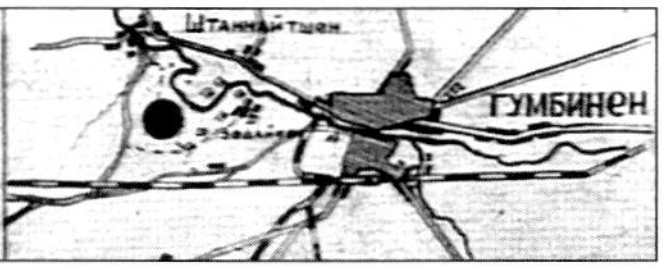

	ЗЕЕРАППЕН	Аэродром	14,7км.зап.центра г.КЕНИГСБЕРГ Между жел.дорогой и шоссейной дорог. КЕНИГСБЕРГ-ФИШХАУЗЕН.(сев.жел.дороги) и в 1000мт. Юго-зап. ЗЕЕРАППЕН, на зап.берегу Реки.	20°16'20" восточн. долготы 54°44'30" северной широты.	Около 1000х 1000	10-15 шт	Имеется 3 наземн. ангара разм. 100х50 мт; 18 складов и 4 казармы разм. 60х20 мт.

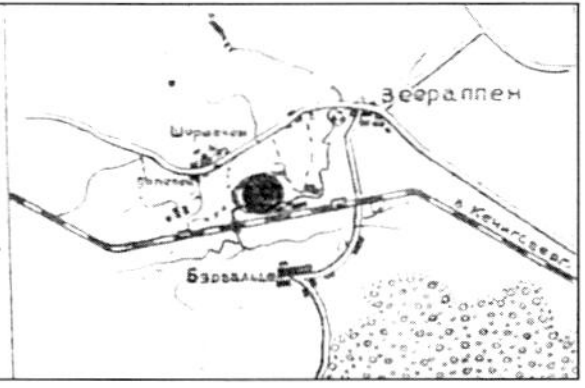

	ЛАБИАУ	посадочная площадка.	41км сев. Восточнее г. КЕНИГСБЕРГ. На южной окраине ЛАБИАУ (южнее жел. дороги в 1 км).	21°05'35" восточной долготы 54°50'50" северной широты.			

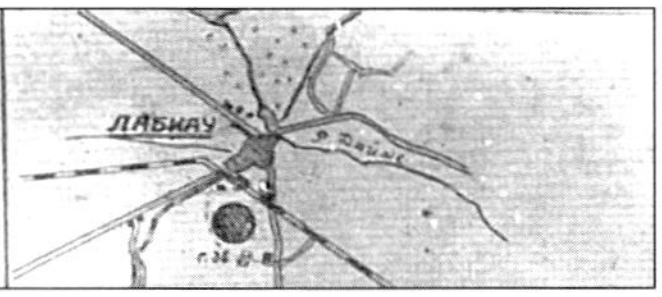

	ГЕРДАУЕН	Посадочн. Площадка	45 км Юго-Зап. ИНСТЕНБУРГ в 3,5 км. Ю.Зап.ГЕРДАУЕН в Районе АРНСДОРФ (южная окраина)				

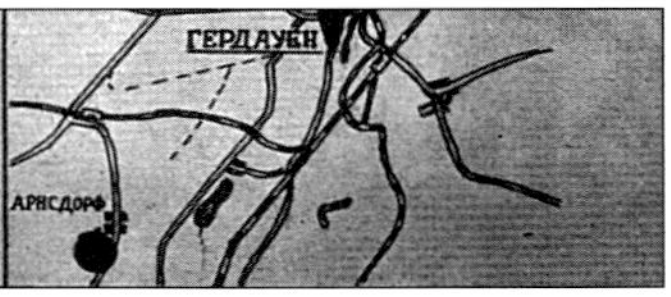

	ХАЙЛИГЕНБАЙЛЬ	Аэродром.	в 46 км Ю.З. г. КЕНИГСБЕРГ в 1 км. Ю.З. г. ХАЙЛИГЕНБАЙЛЬ		600х 400		На аэродроме имеется 5 ангаров 40х15 два здания мастерских. В р-не аэродрома 10 небольших зданий.

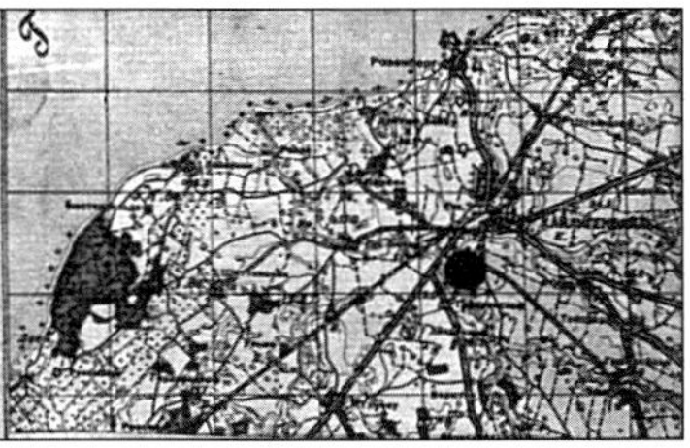

	ЕЗАУ (ЙЕЗАУ)	Аэродром	18,2км Ю.Ю. Восточн. г. КЕНИГСБЕРГ. Предположительно на Сев-восточной окраине ЕЗАУ.	20°38'20" восточной долготы. 54°32'00" северной широты.			

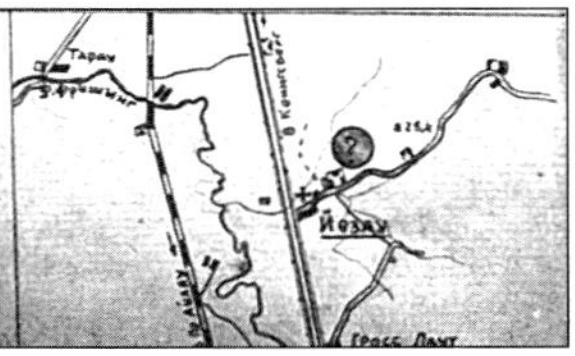

	НОЙКУРЕН	Аэродром	31 км. Сев.Сев.зап. г.КЕНИГСБЕРГ 500мт Сев.восточн.стыка жел.дорог КЕНИГСБЕРГ-НОЙКУРЕН и НОЙКУРЕН КРАНЦ в 1 км. Юго-восточнее села НОЙКУРЕН.	20°14'45" восточной долготы. 54°56'57" северной широты.	1000х 1000	20мт	Имеется 5 наземных ангаров

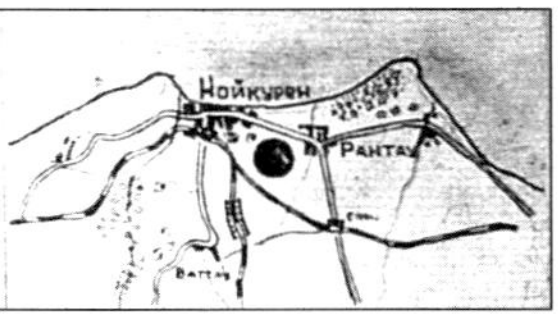

23	ЛЫК	Аэродром	3,5км восточнее ЛЫК (что 45 км Ю.З СУВАЛКИ). Южнее в 100-150мт шоссе ЛЫК-СЕНТКЕН на ЮЗ окраине [illegible]. Цилазек	22°25'00" восточной долготы 53°40'20" северной широты.		130мт	

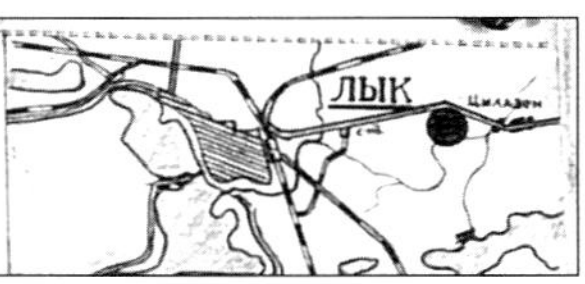

НОЙХАУЗЕН	Аэродром	12 км.Сев.восточн. центра г.КЕНИГСБЕРГ Между ж.дорогами КЕНИГСБЕРГ-ТИЛЬЗИТ и узкоколейной КЕНИГСБЕРГ-ТАПИАУ, на сев.зап.окраине НАЙХАУЗЕН.	20°37'35" восточной долготы. 54°45'02" северной широты.	800 x400	20 мт.	Имеется 3 назем. ангара разм.100x20 шт. [illegible]	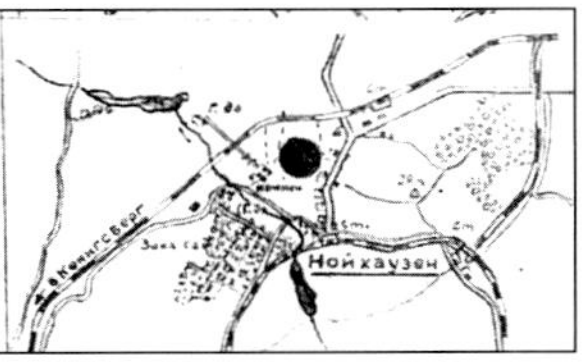
ИНСТЕНБУРГ	аэродром	2,5км южнее г. ИНСТЕНБУРГ в 500 мт восточ.ж.д. ИНСТЕНБУРГ-ДАР- КЕМЕН на восточн. окраине ст.ХЕРМАН- НСХОФ.	21°48'22" восточн. долготы. 54°36'00 северной широты.	600x500 (600x400) общ.про- щадь 240.000 кв.м.	35м	Форма летного поля почти пра- вильный прямоугольник имеющий растяжение с запада на восток Поле имеет травянистый покров В центре летного поля имеется белый круг.Подходы затрудне- ны с запада прилегающими строе ниями. С севера в 200-300мт. от границы аэродрома проходит линия высокого напряжения.На аэродроме имеется 1 ангар и несколько служебных зданий и складских помещений.в запад- ной части аэродрома.Имеется электрооборудование для ноч- ных полетов.	
РАГНИТ.	Аэродром	предположительно В 4 км сев.сев.за- паднее г.РАГНИТ (что в 10,5км D.В. ТИЛЬЗИТ) в кольце- вом изгибе р.НЕМЕНЬ около им.НАЙТЕН (ст. НОВОЗЕДЕН).	22°00'00" восточн. долготы 50°04'10" северн. широты	600x400 (100x400		Ангаров нет, аэродром в стадии строительства.	
ТИЛЬЗИТ	аэродром	7км.зап.ТИЛЬЗИТ между шоссе и ж. дорогой идущ. к западу от ТИЛЬ- ЗИТ в 1,1 км. Юго-восточнее АЛЬТ-ВЕЙНОНЕН и в 200м. вост.ШИЛЬ- ГЕЛЛЕР.	21°48'00' восточн. долготы 55°05'00' северной широты.	800x900 (600x400)	10м	Форма летного поля-неправиль- ный прямоугольник,вытянутый с С-З на Ю-В. Поле покрыто травянистым покровом на перва- ном грунте.Подходы стеснены с севера отдельными прилегаю щими строениями высотой до 10мт. Вцентре летного поля белый круг с надписью "ТИЛЬЗИТ" Аэродром имеет ное электрообо- рудование. На аэродроме в се- верной его части имеется: 1)Здание управления; 2)конус- ный ветроуказатель; 3)3 на- земных ангара размером 100x 25, и 4) 4 бензобака на 10000 литров.5)Жилые дома.Один дом 3-х этажный. Господствующие ветры Зап.и Юго-западные. Аэродром огражен железными штангами.	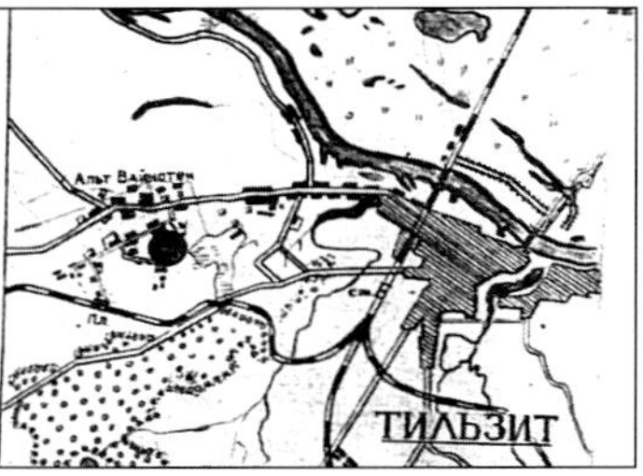
КЛАЙПЕДА (МЕМЕЛЬ)	аэродром	2,2км D.D-Восточн. КЛАЙПЕДА.Западнее ж.д. и шоссе на ТИЛЬЗИТ, на южной окраине дер.РУМШИШ- КИ.	21°10'00" Восточной долготы. 55°41'48" северной широты.	1000x500		Аэродром имеет форму непра- вильного четырехугольника рас- тянутого с юго-запада на сев. восток.По южной стороне аэрод рома проходит ж.дорога на ле- сопильный завод в.СМИЛЬТЕНЕ. летное поле засеяно травой. Через центр аэродрома проходит закрытое для проезда шоссе из РУМШИШКИ в лесопильный завод "ЭММЕРА".На аэродроме имеется: 1)Один наземный ангар на 20 с-тов; 2)Служебное здание.В настоящее время строятся 2 подземных ан- гара размеры и место не уста- новлено.	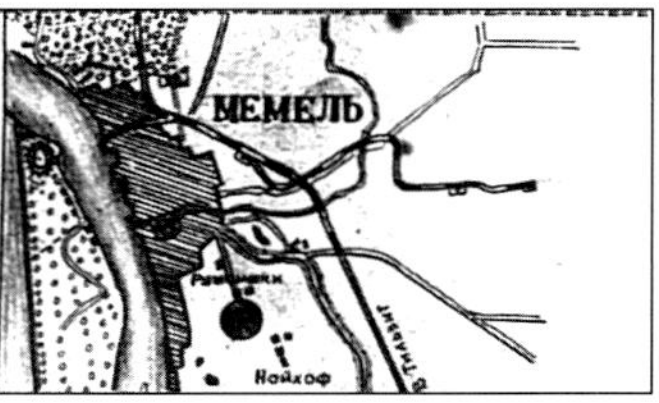
ШТАЛЛЮПЕНЕН	посадочная площадка.	24км Восточнее ГУМБИНЕН в 3 км. D.3 ШТАЛЛЮПЕНЕН юж- нее ж.д.дороги.На D.3 окраине гросс. ЖИБАЛЕН. (грос.ВАН- НАГУПХЕН)	22°33'20" восточной долготы. 54°37,00 северной широты.				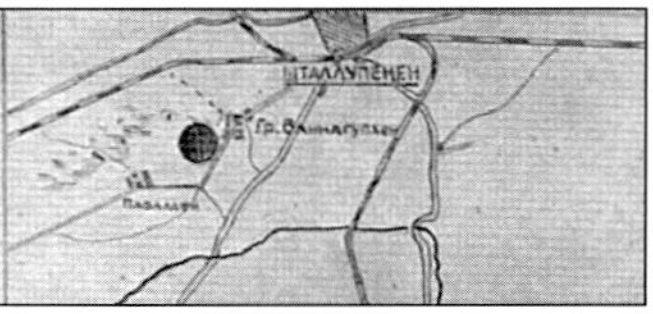
	Аэродром	Предположительно в 4км D.В АРИС (что в 72км D.3.СУВАЛКИ) на зап.окраине с.ВЕРСМИНЕН и восто чнее шоссе АРИС ИОГАННИСБУРГ.	21°58'50" восточной долготы. 54°47'30" северной широты.				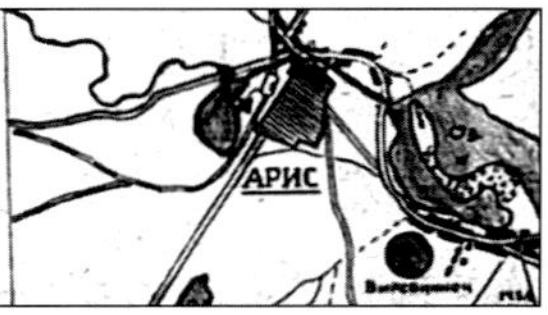
	Аэродром	2км. юж. Сувалки [illegible] [illegible]		2000 x2000			

General W. Richthofen issues an order to officers of the Headquarters of the 8th Air Corps.

Generals Keller (in the centre) and Ferster (on the right) inspect the 54th Fighter Wing, on the left is Major Trautloft, and his fourth Adjutant, *Oberleutnant* O. Katz.

Major Trautloft on take-off in the cockpit of his Messerschmitt, the engine is already running it is possible that this photograph was taken on the morning of June 22 1941. On the side of the aircraft is Trautloft's personal emblem the 'green heart', which in time became the emblem of the whole squadron.

4

The Battle in the Air over the Soviet Baltic Region

4.1 The First Attacks by Luftwaffe Aircraft on Soviet Airfields

The aircraft of the I. *Fliegerkorps* and the VIII. *Fliegerkorps*, as mentioned above, conducted their first raids against Soviet airfields just 10 mins before the start of the artillery bombardment, set for 0405 hrs Moscow time. For example, at 0355 hrs Bf 110 aircraft from the 5/ZG 26 attacked Alytus airfield, and a few minutes later at 0357 hrs a group of seven Ju-88s from the III./KG 1 dropped bombs on the runway of Liepaja airfield.

The details of the raid by the German *zerstörers* on Alytus airfield have unfortunately not survived, but the attack on Liepaja is well documented in the memoirs of veterans of the 148th Fighter Air Squadron. Former pilot A.P. Degtyarev recalled the circumstances of the raid in minute detail:

> At precisely 0400 hrs a Ju-88 aircraft appeared over our airfield, and on seeing their silhouettes we took them to be our own SBs as the airfield was covered in fog. They made several approaches and then began to bomb and strafe the airfield with their machine guns. We were not able to scramble due to the fog, nor had we received any orders to do so, we could only watch what was happening. Many of our own aircraft caught fire and we were forced to hide in ditches. Our parachute rigger Agoyan [actually this was Ya.F. Eloyan] was killed at this time by shrapnel from a bomb. Only then did we realise that the war had started.

Degtyarev's story is supported by the recollections of the regimental commander G.N. Zaytsev and those of another pilot A.D. Ocherednikov. They both mention that it was indeed the fog that prevented the regiment's pilots from taking off. Mention is also made of the political report concerning the actions of the 148th Fighter Air Regiment, which was compiled on 25 June by Battalion Commissar G.M. Golovachev, so there is no reason to doubt this information. It is strange though that the fog did not prevent the German crews from bombing the airfield accurately and not only damaging the airfield, but actually destroying four of the regiment's aircraft. This was recorded in the Combat Journal of the 27th Army: 'At 0400 hrs seven enemy aircraft bombed the airfield in Liepaja. Four aircraft were destroyed on the ground and three red army soldiers were injured. One enemy aircraft made an emergency landing in the forest nearby, while the other six turned for home.'

The Germans do not provide any confirmation of their bomber having made an emergency landing. Judging by the memoirs of the 7./KG 1 *Uberleutnant* M. von Cossart it was not the fog that was behind the lack of resistance from Soviet fighters but the suddenness of the attack. Von Cossart also notes that bombs hit the aircraft hard standings and that one anti-aircraft gun did open fire but did not inflict any damage on the enemy. Unfortunately, however, the enemy's losses were not restricted to just four aircraft that were destroyed during the bombing. When a flight from the 3rd Squadron returned a few minutes later following their spell on duty at Palanga operational airfield, two I-153s hit bomb craters on landing and ground looped. None of the pilots were injured but the aircraft were destroyed and were beyond economical repair.

The enemy attacked the rest of the Soviet airfields at approximately 0410–0425 hrs. The following is taken from intelligence report No. 3 dated 1200 hrs on 22 June 1941 complied by North-Western Front Headquarters:

> Following an artillery bombardment enemy air forces violated the state border and from 0415 hrs on 22 June 1941 they carried out raids on airfields, bombing a series of sites within our own territory...
>
> ...At 0415 hrs a group of aircraft were active over Vindava [at] 0418 hrs five aircraft strafed Vistytis and these same aircraft were then active over Kalvarija, [at] 0425 hrs bombs were dropped on Jurbarkas, and [at] 0420 hrs up to a regiment of aircraft bombed Kaunas, and Kalvarija.

According to the Combat Journal of the 40th High-Speed Bomber Air Regiment at 0407 hrs 12 enemy aircraft bombed Vindava airfield.

At 0410 hrs dozens of twin-engine aircraft dropped bombs on Kedainiai airfield. Despite the fact that back at 0350 hrs the alarm had been sounded by the headquarters of the 61st Ground Attack Air Regiment the pilots of the 4th and 5th Squadrons did not have sufficient time to prepare for a sortie. The raid was so sudden, and the aerial reconnaissance posts did not report enemy aircraft crossing the border, and as a result the enemy aircraft headed back towards the west without encountering resistance. Divisional headquarters did not provide any explanation of what was happening in response to requests from regimental headquarters. Neither was any explanation forthcoming from the leadership of the Air Force command commission ('this commission, which was led by General Sinyakov arrived on 21 June in order to inspect the units within the Kiev Special Military District'). Regimental headquarters reported that there had been a raid on the operational airfields at Risgonis and Markshtava and ordered that preparations be made for a combat sortie and bombs to be loaded onto the aircraft. After this communications with these airfields were lost, and any further communications were achieved by means of liaison aircraft.

The airfields in Kaunas and Panevezys were subject to the most powerful attacks. Thus Kaunas airfield at 0415 hrs was attacked in succession by several squadrons of Ju-88s from KG 77, which were escorted by Bf 109s from Stab II./JG 54 (this series of attacks continued over a period of 25 mins from 0415 hrs up to 0440 hrs.)

The first raid on Kaunas is described in the memoirs of both Soviet and German pilots. From the diary of the Commander of the 54th Fighter Wing H. Trautloft:

> Our target was the airfield in Kaunas. Ahead of us we could already see the dark contours of the city and the airfield, and at that same moment to the east the sun was rising on the horizon, illuminating us with its bright rays. Bombers dropped their bombs on the airfield and we could see how they were exploding amongst the aircraft parked there. Suddenly two Soviet fighters appeared in front of us but did not engage us in combat and vanished as quickly as they had appeared. We turned back. Many border locations were on fire and columns of black smoke climbed high into the sky.

Soviet pilots A.E. Shvarev and B.V. Veselovskiy, who found themselves in Kaunas completely by chance that morning, also recalled the details of this first raid. Shvarev arrived to ferry a U-2 aircraft to Alytus, which was intended for the 236th Fighter Air Regiment, and Veselovskiy had arrived in a group of four pilots the previous day in order to ferry two I-16s and two UTI-4s to Karmelava. Neither of these pilots were members of a crew, and as such they were caught unawares by the war, not on the hard standings but resting in hostels. Firstly let us open the floor to Shvarev since not only does he remember the time of the first raid very accurately but first and foremost he was in the cockpit of one of the fighters that Trautloft mentions in his memoirs:

> I spent the night of Saturday 21–Sunday 22 June 1941 staying with friends from the 31st Fighter Air Regiment [up until 25 May 1941 Shvarev had served in the 31st Fighter Air Regiment] At approximately 0400 hrs we heard the anti-aircraft guns open fire. Up until that point there had been a rumour going around that exercises were imminent. We decided there and then that the exercises had started. Kaunas airfield however was visible from the house we were staying in. There was a meat factory next to the airfield. Then suddenly I noticed a glow and I said: guys this is no exercise, look the hangar is on fire.

According to the memoirs of Shvarev several experienced pilots from the 3rd Squadron, 31st fighter Air Regiment, which Aleksandr Yefimovich had joined, had attempted to scramble and attack the enemy aircraft that had bombed Kaunas airfield during the course of this attack, but unfortunately the Soviet pilots were not able to achieve anything:

> We got dressed quickly and ran to the airfield. None of the bosses were there. A hangar was on fire. Since we had only just arrived on the scene we tried to pull the aircraft out of the hangar. We sat in the aircraft and the Flight Commander Volchok gave the order:* Take off after me! We began to take off in pairs. A group of He 111s were flying towards us—a formidable aircraft with powerful on-board weaponry [these were actually Ju-88s]. We flew towards them and opened fire, but as luck would have it the MiG-3s were fitted with 12.7mm BS machine guns, which would often jam—they would just chug and stop firing. The Germans however were firing at us using machine guns. After the first raid around 40 holes were discovered in my aircraft, and a further eight bullets had lodged in my parachute.

Boris Vasilyevich Veselovskiy unfortunately did not record the time of the start of the raid but details are also reflected in his memoirs that Shvarev did not mention:

> A powerful explosion woke me up from my sleep. I got up. The large window reflected the dawn of Sunday 22 June 1941. On the grass runway, which was silvery-grey from the dew, I noticed craters, like a dotted line covering the entire airfield. From these craters grey clouds of smoke rose up, similar to those that rise up from cement practice bombs.
>
> I decided that the exercises had started and shouted loudly:
>
> Get up scallywags! We are sleeping and the 7th Division is already gouging out the airfield [again we see that the notion of supposed exercises had really taken root in the minds of air force personnel].
>
> Our own Lithuanian division was the 8th, and the 7th was based in Latvia. On exercises we were supposed to act as the enemy.

* Stepan Andreyevich Volchek, Flight Commander and Junior Lieutenant. He was later to become a Lieutenant and Flight Commander of the 293rd Fighter Air Regiment. He failed to return from a combat sortie on 13 May 1942.

> The guys had hardly lifted their heads in response to my shout when a fresh rumble of explosions began and we noticed that on the far side of the airfield, on the 15th Regiment's dispersal, the crates with the MiGs had been smashed to splinters and that fires were breaking out in the hangars.
>
> After we realised that this was no exercise we started to get dressed at once, aiming to leave the house as soon as possible and run to the airfield.
>
> We got our breath back and noticed the buildings where we had spent the night. They had been completely destroyed. The headquarters buildings for the other squadrons were on fire. An enormous fire was raging in the 15th Regiment's area. Four groups of three *Heinkel* He 111 bombers [these were actually Ju-88s] appeared suddenly over the airfield at relatively low level accompanied by Messerschmitts.
>
> As soon as we could we took cover at the foot of a ditch. Explosions from the bombs covered the runway.
>
> We decided to try and get to the surviving aircraft individually and to try and take-off on the edge of the airfield. The main runway was covered in craters.

We note that Veselovskiy mentioned that the Germans thoroughly ploughed up the runway and that the principal blow delivered by the German aircraft was aimed at the southern part of the airfield, where the hard standings were located for the 15th Fighter Air Regiment and the 16th Air Observation Squadron. The Soviet pilot's words are confirmed by a number of photographs taken after the Germans had captured Kaunas, which show several dozen hulks of aircraft standing in three rows on the edge of the airfield. This was all that remained of the materiel belonging to the 15th Fighter Air Regiment and the 16th Artillery Correction Squadron following the raids of 22 June. Unfortunately it has not been possible to determine how many combat aircraft were destroyed in the first raid and how many were destroyed in subsequent raids, since the corresponding documents detailing the 8th Mixed Air Division's losses were not found.

The personnel of the 9th High-Speed Bomber Air Regiment on the night of 21–22 June were developing a training 'evasion' scenario, and after completion of these exercises, which finished at 0300 hrs they rested in a camp close to the airfield. At 0425 hrs in the morning the regiment were put on alert and at 0430 hrs a dozen twin-engine *Luftwaffe* bombers attacked Panevezys. The bombardment continued for approximately 15 mins and cost the regiment seven SBs destroyed and 14 damaged, five of which were subsequently repaired. Apart from that, the 238th Fighter Air Regiment that was also based on this same airfield suffered considerable losses and lost half of their materiel, three I-153s were burnt out and a further 11 were damaged in various ways.

The majority of Soviet airfields were attacked by small groups of German bombers and fighters. As a rule, in each of these groups the number of aircraft ranged from a flight to a squadron and far from all these attacks were as effective as the raids on Panevezys and Kaunas had been.

Thus, according to Intelligence report No. 1 written by the headquarters of the 31st Fighter Air Regiment and dated 0900 hrs on 22 June 1941 Karmelava airfield was bombed from an altitude of 1,000 m by three twin-engine bombers identified as He 111s (they were actually Ju-88s). According to N.I. Petrov's memoirs this attack did not inflict any damage on the materiel but the runway was damaged. Having seen the oncoming German aircraft the 4th Squadron in the regiment was scrambled. Unfortunately, however, the aircraft began to get airborne just as the bombs began to fall on the airfield and the Soviet pilots were not able to catch the German aircraft up; they themselves were lucky to escape without incurring losses.

The airfields of the 42nd Fighter Air Regiment at Varena and Perloja were subject to attacks at 0420 hrs. From a report on the combat activity of the 42nd Fighter Air Regiment written by Senior Political Instructor Smirnov:

> Nine Messerschmitt-109s [this is how it appears in the text] appeared over the airfield [this refers to Varena airfield] at 0420 hrs dropping onto a line of parked, camouflaged aircraft. The Me-109s strafed them as they came out of a shallow dive and as a result eight aircraft were damaged including a single UTI-4 aircraft, which had its oil tank ruptured. A single I-153 aircraft was set alight but the fire was rapidly put out by technicians using a fire extinguisher.

Interestingly, in operations report No. 1 the headquarters of the 57th Mixed Air Division makes no mention of this raid, but a raid by three Do 17 aircraft on this airfield is mentioned that was also timed at 0425 hrs. Evidently attacks by different German subdivisions are described in these documents: the operations report mentions the first attack by a flight of Do 17Z aircraft on Perloja airfield, while a report written by Senior Political Instructor Smirnov mentions the subsequent attack by fighter-bombers on Varena airfield.

Siauliai airfield was also attacked at 0425 hrs by eight or nine Bf 109F aircraft at low level. The Combat Journal of the 7th Mixed Air Division records that the enemy made three attacks. Operations report No. 1 written by the headquarters of the 10th Fighter Air Regiment dated 1300 hrs on 22 June adds more detail: 'At 0420 hrs nine Me-109 enemy fighter aircraft attacked Siauliai airfield, strafing the air traffic control buildings and the southern edge of the forest in the area around the camp.'

We note that the first attacks by *Luftwaffe* aircraft on Soviet airfields for the most part were not 'crushing blows' and represent battle reconnaissance of a kind. In accordance with the entries in the war diary written by Army Group North, some 76 Ju-88s and 90 Bf 109s took off in the first wave of aircraft in I. *Fliegerkorps*: '0300 hrs. In the Army Group North zone the 1st Air Fleet consisting of 76 bombers and 90 fighters are to cross the Soviet border with the aim of attacking seven airfields.'

The enemy did not put all its forces into action by any means, and the principal orders for the small groups of aircraft in these raids were to destroy the runways and to define the number and disposition of aircraft on the airfields, the location of the anti-aircraft guns and so on. Furthermore the use of almost all the available fighters and only a third of the bombers was undoubtedly linked to the fact that the commanders of the 1st Air Corps wanted to provide a reliable escort for their ground attack aircraft in the course of the first raid, and during subsequent raids. Since in a technical sense the fuelling and arming of the bombers was a long, and labour intensive process, using the bombers with a time interval of two to three echelons between them meant that each wave of attack aircraft could be escorted by fighters that were located on airfields close to the border and which were able to refuel and rearm rapidly, rather than Ju-88s. Moreover the destruction of the materiel, given a favourable set of circumstances, was not of course ruled out.

This thinking is supported by the Chief of Staff of the 148th Fighter Air Regiment Major Cholok:

> At around 0400 hrs in the morning a group of aircraft appeared over the airfield but a thick fog meant it was impossible to determine who they belonged to. Subsequently we would recognise them by the characteristic sound of their engines but at the time we did not have any experience of this.
>
> The sound of machine gun fire was heard in the air. Several officers mentioned that exercises had commenced featuring simulated air combat. Then however it emerged that in one of the squadrons the parachute rigger Ilovayskiy [Ya.F. Eloyan] had been killed. Meanwhile the aircraft broke into the circuit and started to bomb the airfield. Explosions from the bombs as well as fires broke out both on the airfield itself, and in the surrounding neighbourhood.
>
> The confusion however did not last long. Steps were immediately taken to repair the runways on the airfield. Evidently the enemy had set themselves a target of destroying the

> runways in the first bombing raid so that they could then take out the personnel, aircraft, fuel and ammunition stores in subsequent raids.

The Germans were evidently planning to attack large airbases that had been carefully reconnoitred up until the beginning of the war using several groups of aircraft at once, without waiting for the results of their reconnaissance. This relates to Kaunas, Alytus, Kedainiai, Siauliai, and Panevezys airfields.

Losses in the Air Forces of the North-Western Front from the first attacks by *Luftwaffe* aircraft on the airfields were not less than 70–80 aircraft destroyed or damaged from the 15th, 31st, 42nd, 148th, 236th, 237th, and 238th Fighter Air Regiments and the 9th and 40th High-Speed Bomber Air Regiments. Unfortunately owing to the loss of documentation from many of the units and formations there is a good chance that establishing the number of Soviet aircraft lost as a result of the first raid, down to individual examples, would not prove possible.

This damage was relatively palpable but as far as the overall number of aircraft in the units is concerned they were for the most part no more than five to 10 percent. Relatively significant losses were incurred by the 9th High-Speed Bomber Air Regiment and the 238th Fighter Air Regiment, which lost up to 40 percent of their materiel as well as the 15th Fighter Air Regiment, and the 16th Air Observation Squadron. It has to be said, however, that unserviceable R-5SSS aircraft stood in rows on the edge of Kaunas airfield that belonged to the 16th Air Observation Squadron as well as obsolete I-15bis aircraft that were not assigned to a combat unit, together with training and unserviceable UTI-4s and type 5 I-16s and I-153s belonging to the 15th Fighter Air Regiment. In the 238th Fighter Air Regiment however there were only 11 pilots so the number of combat capable crews did not reduce in proportion with the loss of 14 aircraft.

Thus the potential of the majority of the Soviet units was only slightly reduced by the first raids. The 'first half' so to speak had been won by the enemy as a result of the element of 'tactical surprise', but 'normal playing time' was still ahead and the Soviet units would not be taken by surprise any longer.

We note that the enemy, thanks to the intelligence information that they had gathered prior to the start of hostilities, attacked practically all the large airfields in the Air Forces of the North-Western Front's 'first' echelon'. The operational airfields of Vincai, Potsunai, and Raseiniai, the Germans did not discover right up until the end of the first day of the war, as well as Vilnius airfield, which the VIII. *Fliegerkorps* evidently did not have the available forces to attack.

The German successes would have been without doubt modest were it not for the interruption in the construction of the operational airfields. This meant that many of the units on 19–20 June and also in the period after the raids had nowhere to redeploy to, since on the majority of newly built airfields and sites ground work or concreting was underway, which restricted runway operations.

Nevertheless with the onset of combat operations the intensity of German aerial reconnaissance increased dramatically. By way of an example this is how Senior Political Instructor Smirnov described the situation:

> At 0405 hrs via the airfield [this relates to Varena airfield] an 'unidentified' bomber aircraft approached from the west flying in the direction of Vilnius at an altitude of 1,000–1,200 m. A few minutes later a further Me-110 bomber flew at this same altitude and in this same direction. After turning 180° over two to three kilometres outside of the airfield and descending to an altitude of 200–300 m the aircraft passed over the camp dropping several bombs and strafed the camp using machine gun fire from all its on board machine guns.
>
> Without any orders forthcoming from command to scramble, I as the Deputy Commander of the Political Section in the 4th Duty Squadron ordered the flight to scramble. After increasing speed the Me-110 aircraft departed to the west.

Over Karmelava, judging by this very same intelligence report No. 1 written by the headquarters of the 31st Fighter Air Regiment, a reconnaissance Bf 110 suddenly appeared at 0500 hrs and flew a circuit of the airfield at low level, and aside from their reconnaissance activities the Germans strafed aircraft on the ground. All the regiment's aircraft having completed their first combat sortie had landed just a few moments before this happened and so this German reconnaissance aircraft departed 'homeward' without incurring any damage and with updated reconnaissance data.

All the Soviet airfields that morning were visited on more than one occasion by the crews of German reconnaissance aircraft. For example between 0645–0745 hrs the crews of 4.(F)/33 and 8.(H)/32 established the following as a result of their reconnaissance sorties:

On Kedainiai (north) airfield there were eight fighters
On Kinelawia [this refers to Kedainiai] there were 26 fighters
On Siauliai there were 15 unidentified aircraft.

The *Luftwaffe* reconnaissance crews finalised the results of the first raids and attempted to discover the airfields belonging to the Air Forces of the Baltic Special Military District that had not been revealed until the start of combat operations, in order to inflict their main attacks. These raids were, in accordance with German thinking, to take a deadly turn.

An aerial photograph of Kaunas airfield taken on 23 June 1941 the traces of German aerial attacks on the first day of the war can be clearly seen. In the bottom left hand corner are the aircraft of the 15th Fighter Air Regiment, and the 16th Air Observation Squadron that were destroyed on the ground.

Photographs of Kaunas airfield enable an analysis to be made of the effectiveness of the German attacks made on the first day of the war. In the photo the remains of these same aircraft can be seen as from the previous page. What is clearly evident is that almost all the aircraft from the 15th Fighter Air Regiment and the 16th Air Observation Squadron standing in three rows were completely burnt out, or suffered significant damage.

In the foreground is an I-153 bearing the tactical No. 28 from the 15th Fighter Air Regiment, it was from this aircraft that the first photograph was taken.

A MiG-3 from the 15th Fighter Air Regiment, the aircraft is standing on the far right in the front row.

The MiG-3 and I-15bis, and I-153s that stood in the front row were all burnt out.

A MiG-3 bearing the tactical No. 2 white from 4th Squadron, 15th Fighter Air Regiment one of few that did not incur significant damage.

Unserviceable, and partially dismantled without engines or propellers these I-16 and MiG-1 aircraft from the 31st Fighter Air Regiment had been standing on the other side of the airfield, the former Deruluft airfield.

MiG-1s and I-16s from the 31st Fighter Air Regiment, which were damaged on their hard standings.

An R-5 from the line-up of the 2nd Aerial Photography Detachment, a UTI-4, and a MiG-2 from the 15th Fighter Air Regiment, these aircraft do not have any obvious damage and were evidently abandoned due to technical failures.

A photograph of Panevezys airfield that was taken by the Germans, in the foreground is a TB-3 that had been destroyed in an accident back in 1940, while in the background is a row of I-153s from the 238th Fighter Air Regiment.

Those same 'Chaikas' from the 238th Fighter Air Regiment in close up, the tactical numbers 3, 7, 9, 16, 21, 25, and 26.

SB, and USB from the 9th High-Speed Bomber Air Regiment, this photograph is taken from the other side of the airfield close to the former Lithuanian barracks.

On the SB in the other photograph the tactical No. 4, and the emblem of the 9th High-Speed Air Regiment were visible, here the No. 9 has been written into the Air Force emblem.

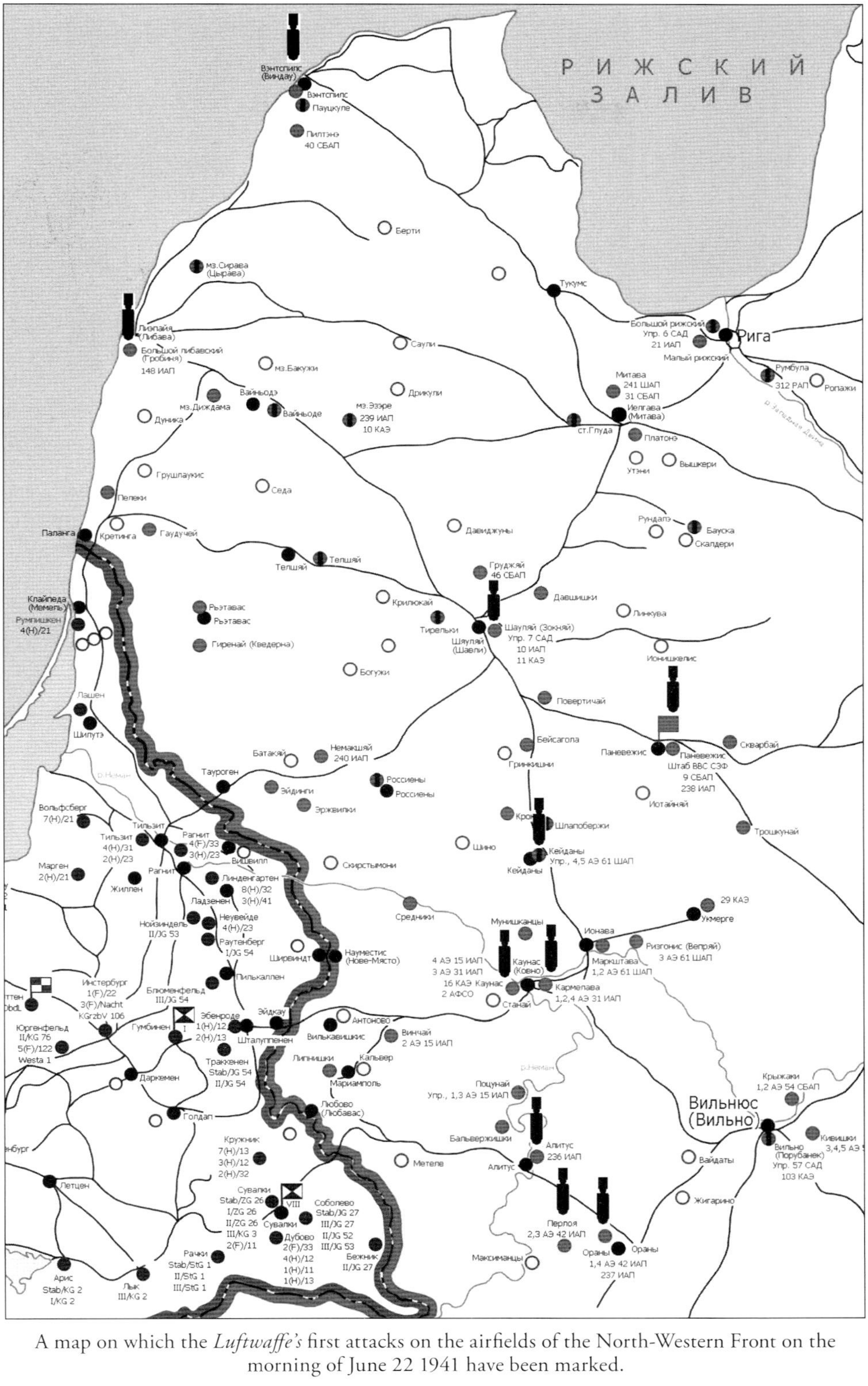

A map on which the *Luftwaffe's* first attacks on the airfields of the North-Western Front on the morning of June 22 1941 have been marked.

4.2 The First Air Battles

Across practically the entire zone of the North-Western Front the first attack by the *Luftwaffe* really was a sudden one, and in certain locations: such as Kaunas airfield, Panevezys, Liepaja, Alytus, and Varena they were also quite effective.

As indicated above, the serious influence of the terms of Directive No. 1 weighed on the minds of commanders at all levels. In accordance with these terms aside from implementing the plans for the provision of cover accurately and conducting retaliatory strikes on enemy airfields, which in this situation would have been completely logical, almost every commander from the front line commanders to junior lieutenants were called upon to make an independent decision in such an unbelievably complex situation. Naturally all the commanders acted in their own way, they were ordinary people with all their inherent strengths and weaknesses. The commander of the North-Western Front Colonel-General Kuznetsov, as was discussed above, accepted Directive No. 1 as an order not to give in to provocation and translated this to his troops with an even more ambiguous form of words: 'In the event of any provocation by the Germans do not open fire. During the course of their flights over our territory German aircraft have not yet opened fire, while enemy aircraft have yet to commence hostilities.' In the end, as it reached regimental level this instruction was interpreted as meaning no enemy aircraft should be shot down but should be forced to land and correspondingly the regimental commanders were forced to carry out these absurd instructions.

By way of an example the Commander of the 31st Fighter Air Regiment Major Putivko scrambled all three squadrons in the regiment based at Karmelava airfield immediately after he discovered the flight of twin-engine bombers flying towards the airfield. This is how a veteran of this regiment N.I. Petrov recalled the details of this first sortie:

> Green rockets shot up into the air from the regimental command post. The alarm had been raised many times recently (though these were training scenarios) and so everything had been worked out and played out, in terms of who did what and when concerning the crew's actions both in the air and on the ground. After receiving the signal to scramble we began to take off as a flight, taxying out and taking-off virtually straight from the hard-standings.

Unfortunately the pilots of the 31st Fighter Air Regiment were not able to catch the enemy aircraft and after forming up into a group of nine MiGs over the airfield the Lead Deputy Squadron Commander Senior Lieutenant V.Ya. Volkov continued to fly in the direction of Kaunas:*

> We formed up in a line of nine aircraft after take-off. The lead pilot was Senior Lieutenant Volkov. We set course for Kaunas in a turn to port and after climbing to an altitude of 1,550 m we could see Kaunas airfield. The hangars were on fire, as was the building in front of the hangars, and the regimental headquarters.
>
> As we flew closer we could see that the railway station to the west of Kaunas was on fire. Flying over Kaunas airfield itself we could see several craters from bombs in the runway. To the left, at an altitude higher than 700 m a flight of two pairs of Me-110s and four Me-109s were heading west at high-speed, trailing smoke. Below them on a reciprocal heading were six I-153 'Chaika' aircraft, these were our neighbours from the 15th Fighter Air Regiment. After flying west for 15 mins at an altitude of 3,000 m we turned back, the sky was calm. As we

* Deputy Squadron Commander Senior Lieutenant Yakov Georgevich Volkov, born in 1907, failed to return from a combat sortie on 5 May 1941.

> approached our own airfield in a descent down to 1,000 m and at high speed, we had already spent 35 mins in the air (the duration for a 1st series MiG-3 was 45 mins). The neighbouring squadrons approached and made their landings. Everyone landed safely despite the fact that there were no landing markers, aircraft approached the airfield to land from different directions, whichever was the most convenient for each squadron without them getting in each other's way.

It is worth noting from Petrov's account that there were a group of nine MiGs over Kaunas airfield aside from the group of six I-153s (which he had identified as aircraft from the 15th Fighter Air Regiment) that faced the German aircraft. For unknown reasons this large group of Soviet fighters did not even attempt to attack the enemy aircraft, which furthermore were actually outnumbered even though the Soviet pilots could clearly see that Kaunas airfield was on fire. Petrov makes no mention of this but it is evident that the lead group of were given orders that were accordant with the directive and they were not allowed to attack the enemy aircraft first.

The fact of the order 'not to open fire on the enemy' is also confirmed in the memoirs of a participant in the first combat sortie by aircraft from the 10th Fighter Air Regiment, V.I. Klimenko. Judging by his story the flight commander's courses did not raise the alarm and as such the morning of 22 June for Klimenko was not disturbed by the sounding of the alarm, but by the explosions of German bombs:

> I heard the drone of aircraft.
>
> I thought that it was a raid from Panevezys, and that it had probably been missed. I opened the door of the tent and looked out. There were 'crosses' above us and traces of machine gun fire around the tents. I shouted out: 'Guys, it's war!' 'Get out of here—what sort of a war?' 'See for yourself, it's a raid.' Everyone jumped out of the tents and there were dead and wounded already in neighbouring tents. I put on my flying suit, and my knee-pad and ran to the hangar. I said to the Technician 'Pull the aircraft out.' The duty aircraft however that had all been parked in a line were already on fire [for the most part these were the unserviceable aircraft in the 10th Fighter Air Regiment]. I started the engine, got into the aircraft, and took off. I flew around the airfield, I did not know where to go or what to do! Suddenly a fighter came towards me. I rocked my wings as if to say: 'Attention! Follow me' I recognised Sashka Bukach, a neighbouring Flight Commander and we crossed the border. After we crossed the border we noticed that villages were on fire and columns of military vehicles were on the move. Sashka went into a dive and I watched the tracer coming from his aircraft, he was attacking them. I followed him. We attacked the German forces. It was impossible to miss, so dense were the columns. For some reason they were silent, the anti-aircraft guns were not opening up. I was afraid of breaking away from the lead pilot, I would have got lost! We made two approaches. We arrived back at the airfield and taxied into an aircraft shelter. A car arrived from the command post: 'Did you take off?' 'We did take off' 'Get yourselves over to the command post.' We arrived at the command post. The regimental commander said: 'Arrest them and put them in the guard house. Ground them from flying. Who ordered you to attack? Did you know what you were firing at? I don't know either. This may just be provocation of some kind, and you opened fire. Did you even know who they were? Could they not have been our troops?'
>
> The losses were heavy, many aircraft were set on fire, and the hangars were also ablaze. [Evidently the veteran is referring to the losses on the first day]. We were the only ones from our regiment to give any kind of rebuke, without waiting for an order.

The Combat Journal of the 7th Mixed Air Division confirms Klimenko's story completely. At 0445 hrs the Commander of the 10th Fighter Air Regiment Major Derevin received an order: 'From the Commander of the 7th Mixed Air Division to the Commander of the 10th Fighter Air Regiment. Provide cover for the area around Siauliai.' At 0450 hrs all the serviceable aircraft in the regiment began to take to the skies. The patrol continued up to 0545 hrs at altitudes of between 2,000–4,000 m but there were no encounters with enemy aircraft.

Evidently the fact that three dozen fighters from the 10th Fighter Air Regiment were in the air meant that a powerful second bombing of Siauliai airfield was avoided. In intelligence report No. 3 written by the headquarters of the North-Western Front notes the operations carried out by a large group of German aircraft in this area: 'At 0442 hrs on 22 June 1941 up to 45 aircraft bombed Siauliai airfield. An air battle took place over Siauliai airfield.' The lack of bombing of this airfield makes it possible to propose that the *Luftwaffe* crews did not try to push their luck and did not decide to attack the airfield, which was protected by such a large group of fighters. Nevertheless judging by Klimenko's account and the Combat Journal of the 7th Mixed Air Division the Commander of the 10th Fighter Air Regiment Major Derevin, although he did scramble his regiment, did not allow any of his pilots to open fire on the enemy.

It is known that the aircraft of the 42nd Fighter Air Regiment also scrambled after the German aircraft appeared over Varena. It is likely that the Commander of the Regiment Major Belousov also gave his pilots the following order: Drive the enemy aircraft out of Soviet territory or force them to land. Even after an attack by Messerschmitts on the airfield the pilots in the regiment did not take the decision to attack first.

The Commander of the 148th Fighter Air Regiment Major Zaytsev decided not to scramble even a single aircraft at all before any firm orders were received from the headquarters of the 6th Mixed Air Division. Although the Commander of the Division Fyodorov was in no hurry to issue an order for a combat sortie either. The Deputy Political Instructor of the regiment Golovachev recorded this response: 'We received a response to our report from Divisional Headquarters, which stated that it was evidently "Fascist propaganda", which naturally commanded moderation and restraint.'

While the Soviet command dragged their heels, German pilots continued to attack, and if Siauliai succeeded in avoiding a second attack then in other locations German crews went all out.

At 0430 hrs a second group of nine Ju-88 aircraft approached Kedainiai airfield. This time several aircraft from the 61st Ground Attack Air Regiment did manage to get airborne, however they were not able to have any effect on the German bombers. The Bf 109s escorting the Junkers from JG 54 attacked the I-153s as they were getting airborne and shot down three aircraft, furthermore the Deputy Squadron Commander Senior Lieutenant V.G. Andreychenko was killed. A further two pilots, Deputy Squadron Commander Senior Lieutenant P.I. Kamyshnoy, and Flight Commander Lieutenant I.T. Abramchenko managed to bail out of their damaged aircraft by parachute. A further two I-153s were retired from the battlefield and their pilots Junior Lieutenant P.A. Selyakin and Lieutenant N.S. Geyko were in a state of shock at how serious the air battle had become. After they had flown to Risgonis where they performed a wheels-up landing, the aircraft were damaged and were beyond economical repair. The pilots of the Messerschmitts, however, 'took courage' so to speak and after making short work of the I-153s they attacked the airfield once again. Squadron Commander *Oberleutnant* Adolf-Waldemar Kinzinger took out two Soviet aircraft [two DJ-6s at 0330 hrs Berlin time] and *Unteroffizier* Fritz Tegtmeier claimed a single DJ-6 although for some reason his victory did not count. These were the first aircraft shot down in the air battles in the skies over the Baltic region.

Despite the fact that the materiel of the 61st Ground Attack Air Regiment had been dispersed, in the course of the first two raids the Germans succeeded in destroying three 'Chaikas' on the ground after which the airfield structures as well as the block belonging to the regimental command were bombed. The crews manning the machine gun quads in the 118th Airfield Servicing Battalion attempted to return fire and even reported that one German aircraft had been destroyed, which given the poor training these crews received is very doubtful.

For 5./JG 27 VIII. *Fliegerkorps* the first combat sortie was due to take place by 0410 hrs Berlin time. However according to the memoirs of a pilot in the squadron *Unteroffizier* Hans Niederhofer the aircraft only took off at 0435 hrs when 13 Bf 109Es led by Squadron Commander *Leutnant* Hans Witzel took off to attack the airfield that formed the base for the 236th Fighter Air Regiment in Alytus.

At almost the same time Stab 7./JG 53 was just getting airborne from Sobolevo airfield. This group was led by Commander *Hauptmann* Wolf-Dietrich Wilcke. The 'Ace of Spades' also set off in the direction of Alytus and their orders were to escort the attack aircraft from 5./JG 27.

At approximately 0440–0450 hrs Messerschmitts from 5/JG 27 dropped SG-2 bombs on the hard standings and began to attack the airfield with machine gun fire. At that time a flight of I-153s appeared in the skies over the airfield that had taken off—judging by the memoirs of the Deputy Commander of the Political Section of the 236th Fighter Air Regiment Senior Political Instructor I.G. Taldykin—to intercept a group of German bombers that had taken off in the direction of Kaunas. The flight consisted of the leader, Deputy Squadron Commander Senior Lieutenant B.M. Bugachev, his wingman Junior Lieutenant S.G. Koshkin, and Taldykin. The Soviet pilots did not succeed in catching the bombers but on their return to their airfield they were called upon to counter-attack by two squadrons of German fighters.

All three Soviet pilots were experienced soldiers, veterans of the Soviet Finnish War, but naturally given such a numerical advantage their chances of victory were almost nil. In the ensuing merry-go-round, however, Soviet pilots forced the Germans to sweat to some degree for a while and the pilots of the *Luftwaffe*, who had an absolute quantitative and qualitative advantage, were only able to emerge victorious after a tense 20 minute battle.

The enemy are very scant in their description of this battle. According to their information the German group fought not one but two flights of Soviet aircraft, which they identified as I-15s. This suggests that Burgachev's flight fought first the attack aircraft from 5./JG27 and then fighters from JG 53 in turn. The *Luftwaffe* pilots reported that they were able to shoot down five Soviet aircraft without incurring any losses. Correspondingly a single victory over one I-15 at 0454 hrs was allegedly recorded by *Leutnant* Hans Witzel, and another at 0505 hrs by a pilot from the 7./JG 53 *Feldwebel* Werner Stumpf and another three victories over I-15s at 0500 hrs, 0505 hrs, and 0510 hrs were recorded by *Hauptmann* Wolf-Dietrich Wilcke.

However in the air battle itself the Germans succeeded in shooting down only two Soviet fighters. First of all Junior Lieutenant Koshkin was shot down and killed, then the enemy shot down a 'Chaika' flown by Senior Political Instructor Taldykin. He was injured but managed to bail out by parachute. The Germans did not succeed in shooting down the leader of the Soviet flight, and future ace with 11 victories to his credit, Boris Maksimovich Burgachev. Only after he had run out of fuel when attempting to land did the Germans try to strafe his aircraft on the landing roll. It is practically 100 percent certain that Wilcke added this defenceless aircraft to his tally.* The I-153 ground looped and Boris Maksimovich was injured but in contrast to the majority, and possibly all the German pilots that took part in the battle, he returned to the formation following a four-month recovery period. He later survived the entire war and in 1945 he participated in the victory parade in Moscow.

* A surprising fact is that both of the surviving Soviet pilots from this battle, Taldykin and Burgachev, recorded their memoirs of this battle, and furthermore it is interesting that these pilots did not meet again after 22 June but their memoirs confirm the course of the battle, and corroborate one another.

These battles became the first air battles between Soviet and German aircraft in the skies over the Baltic region. Taking into account that in the course of the first sortie aircraft from the 15th Fighter Air Regiment most likely took part between 0400 hrs and 0500 hrs in the morning, more than a hundred Soviet fighters took to the skies. Not one of them, however, attempted to attack the *Luftwaffe* aircraft first since the Soviet pilots had received an absurd order not to open fire on German aircraft before the enemy went on the attack. As a result only two air battles took place, the result of which alas turned out to be logical. The quantitative and qualitative advantage of the *Luftwaffe* fighters played its part. Soviet losses consisted of eight 'Chaikas', of which the 61st Ground Attack Air Regiment lost three I-153s shot down and two damaged (which were later written off) and one pilot was killed. The 236th Fighter Air Regiment lost two I-153s shot down in air combat, and a single aircraft that was destroyed as a result of battle damage, one pilot was killed, and two were injured.

Passive action by Soviet fighters enabled the German crews to complete the orders they had been set for the neutralisation of Soviet airfields and the fact that Soviet pilots did not attack them played into their hands in what would have proved an inopportune moment for air battles to have taken place. Apart from that both sides evidently were, in a purely psychological sense, completely unprepared at that time and were not ready for a decisive battle. This is confirmed by the episode over Siauliai, and as such the main air battles were still to come.

The Commander of 1./JG 54 *Oberleutnant* Kinzinger in the cockpit of a Bf 109F. This officer became the first pilot who attained an aerial victory over an aircraft of the Air Forces of the North-Western Front on the morning of 22 June, and most likely was one of the first to attain a victory in the Great Patriotic War.

Ivan Terentyevich Abramchenko, Lieutenant, and Flight Commander of the 61st Ground Attack Air Regiment was shot down on the morning of 22 June by Messershcmitts from 1./JG 54.

Pavel Ivanovich Kamyshnoy, Senior Lieutenant Deputy Commander of the 4th Squadron, 61st Ground Attack Air Regiment, was shot down in the first air battle on 22 June over Kedainiai by Messerschmitts from 1./JG 54.

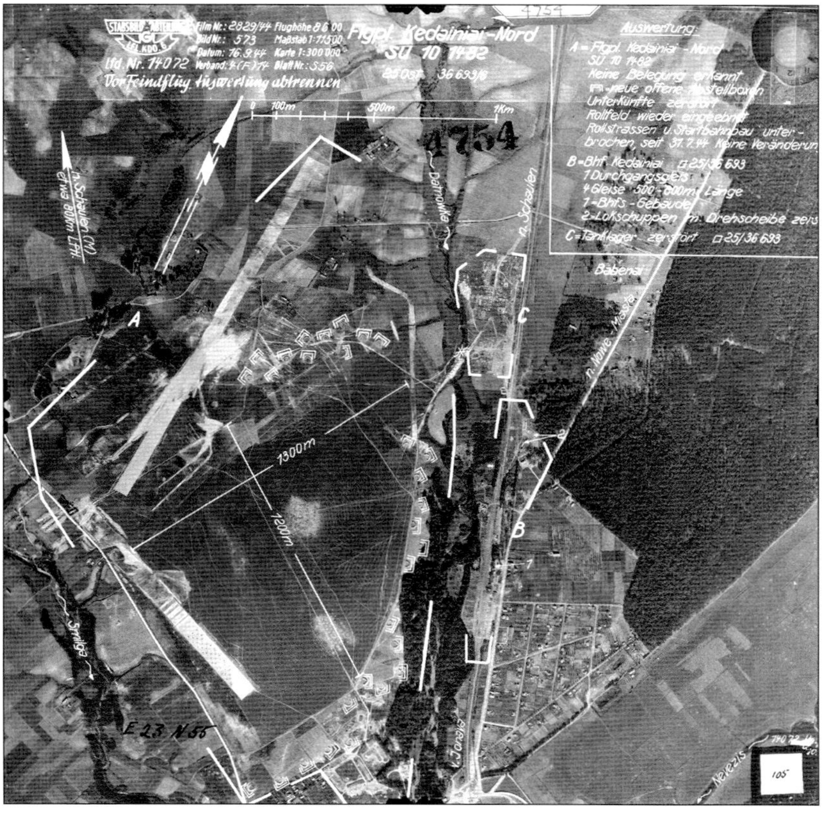

An aerial photograph of Kedainiai taken in 1944. The concrete runway, which had not been completed in 1941, and the runway's concrete section, which was blown up by the Germans during their withdrawal, is clearly visible in the bottom left hand corner.

German soldiers posing next to I-153, and I-15bis aircraft of the 61st Ground Attack Air Regiment on Kedainiai airfield, June 1941.

German soldiers posing next to I-153, and I-15bis aircraft of the 61st Ground Attack Air Regiment on Kedainiai airfield, June 1941.

German soldiers posing next to I-153, and I-15bis aircraft of the 61st Ground Attack Air Regiment on Kedainiai airfield, June 1941.

An I-153 bearing the tactical No. 1 white, from the 4th Squadron of the 61st Fighter Air Regiment, this aircraft made an emergency landing on Kedainiai airfield.

An aerial photograph of Alytus airfield taken in 1944. The part of the airfield destroyed in bombing raids, and strafing attacks, partly in 1941 can be clearly seen. In the lower part of the photograph the 'northern' bridge that was destroyed in 1944 can be clearly seen. It was across this bridge at around 0100 hrs on 22 June 1941 that tank crews from the 7th Panzer Division crossed to the eastern side.

Commander of the III./JG 53 *Hauptmann* Wolf-Dietrich Wilcke in the cockpit of a Bf 109F.

Boris Maksimovich Bugarchev, Senior Lieutenant Deputy Commander of the 236th Fighter Air Regiment, was injured in air combat with German fighters on the morning of 22 June 1941 over Alytus airfield.

Stepan Gavrilovich Koshkin, Lieutenant, Flight Commander of the 236th Fighter Air Regiment, was killed in an air battle with German fighters on 22 June 1941 over Alytus airfield.

Ivan Gordeyevich Taldykin, Lieutenant, and Flight Commander of the 263th Fighter Air Regiment's political unit, was injured in air combat with German fighters on the morning of 22 June 1941 over Alytus airfield.

An I-153 bearing the tactical Nos. 27 and 31, these aircraft were damaged by German aviation, and were abandoned on Alytus airfield on 2 June 1941.

MiG-3s abandoned on Alytus airfield on 22 June 1941. At present the allocation of these aircraft is not known.

4.3 The Strange War Continues. The Non-Existent Retaliatory Strike by the Air Forces of the South-Western Front, and the Second Raid by Luftwaffe Aircraft on Soviet Airfields

While the pilots returned after their first combat sorties to their airfields the Chiefs of Staff on both sides were feverishly holding meetings, analysing, and making decisions on which would depend the result of the confrontation that had only just begun. If everything went according to plan for *Luftwaffe* command then the commanders of the Red Army would be forced to improvise. The point being that despite the reports from the headquarters in the western military districts concerning mass raids by German aircraft on Soviet airfields, and the *Wehrmacht's* crossing of the state border of the USSR, Soviet military leadership were in no hurry to issue actual orders to counter the aggression and the main document that regulated the actions of the Soviet military, remained that same Directive No. 1.

In contrast to the leadership of the USSR and the Red Army the Commander of the Air Forces of the North-Western Front, General Ionov, reacted quickly and accurately to the German attack 'in a soldierly manner'. Unambiguous orders began to arrive at the headquarters of the various formations from the Commander of the Air Forces of the North-Western Front. Specifically the headquarters of the 7th Mixed Air Division received an order at 0440 hrs from the Commander of the Air Forces of the North-Western Front. The text of his order in the logbook in which all the orders the division received were recorded, literally sounds like this: 'The Commander of the Air Forces of the Baltic Special Military District to the Commander of the 7th Mixed Air Division. Destroy the enemy.' Just 13 minutes later at 0453 hrs the headquarters of the 9th and 46th High-Speed Bomber Air Regiments received a corresponding order from divisional headquarters, which literally read: 'Destroy the enemy alignment and the aircraft on the airfields around Tilsit, Ragnit, and Zhillen. Take-off immediately.'

Considering that the front line headquarters and the headquarters of the 7th Mixed Air Division, and the 9th and 46th High-Speed Bomber Air Regiments were located very close to one another in Panevezys, Siauliai, and Gruzdziai it is no surprise that it was these same units that were the first to receive these new orders and the headquarters of the 9th High-Speed Bomber Air Regiment located as it was in Panevezys alongside the Air Forces of the North-Western Front received them almost immediately. Naturally these units began to act just as quickly; the 9th High-Speed Bomber Air Regiment took off straight away while the 46th High-Speed Bomber Air Regiment took off at 0540 hrs.

The orders formulated by the Commander of Air Forces reached the headquarters of the other formations a little more slowly and correspondingly it took some time for the orders to reach the units under them. By way of an example the headquarters of the 4th Mixed Air Division only passed this order on to the 35th, 50th, and 63rd High-Speed Bomber Air Regiments at 0600 hrs. the following is an extract from combat order No. 01/OP written by divisional headquarters:

> The 50th High-Speed Bomber Air Regiment is to prepare for the destruction of the enemy aircraft on the airfield north of Klaipeda. The approach was to be over the sea and the departure is to be a turn to port towards Tukumus, Ruhnu Island. The route, ordnance, and altitude are to be decided by the Regimental Commander. Take-off is on my orders relayed over the command post telephone system via Brigade Commander Sokolov...
>
> The 35th High-Speed Bomber Air Regiment is to prepare for combat activity aimed at destroying aircraft on an airfield two and a half kilometres south-east of Klaipeda. The approach is to be over the sea and the departure is to be via a turn to port towards Busk, Valk. The route, ordnance, and altitude are to be decided by the Regimental Commander. Take-off

> is on my orders relayed over the command post telephone system via Brigade Commander Sokolov.
>
> The 63rd High-Speed Bomber Air Regiment is to be prepared for the destruction of the concentration of enemy forces in the area around Klaipeda. The approach is to be achieved over the sea with the departure being via a turn to port towards Ruhnu. The route, ordnance, and altitude are to be decided by the Regimental Commander. Take-off is on my orders relayed over the command post telephone system via Brigade Commander Sokolov.

The texts of the orders for the 4th, and 7th Mixed Air Division headquarters as a whole corresponded to the orders that had been spelled out in the relevant points in the 'plan for the provision of cover'. The information that General Ionov ordered was to be hidden in the bags containing the plans is missing and it is more than likely that these orders were drawn up individually for each of the headquarters of the various formations as the situation developed. However it is completely obvious that the Commander of Air Forces used the 'plan for the provision of cover' as the basis on which to produce the orders, with his concept of fighting for air superiority by attacking the enemy airfields.

The receipt of the order from the 7th Mixed Air Division almost coincided with the end of the German raid on the 9th High-Speed Bomber Air Regiment's base at Panevezys airfield, and furthermore owing to the losses that had been incurred in carrying out the order put before them only 26 combat aircraft were sent forward. The 5th Squadron became the leader of the regiment and they were led by Squadron Commander Captain M.A. Krivtsov. This squadron had evidently suffered the least from the German attack. The target for the attack was the railway station in the town of Tilsit. According to the testimony of one of the navigators, who took part in this raid the leader did not take the aircraft straight towards Tilsit, but first made a wide detour towards Suwalki and only then did he set off for the target and moreover the aircraft climbed to an altitude of 7,500 m. It would appear that the time lost in making this manoeuvre was more than compensated for by the fact that they succeeded in achieving an element of surprise. The anti-aircraft guns opened fire only after the Soviet aircraft had dropped their bombs at approximately 0620 hrs on their target and had set off on their departure heading in a shallow dive without incurring losses.

Other squadrons, one of which was led by Regimental Commander Major Skitev, took off as they attained readiness and attacked a range of targets around Tilsit at an altitude of 4,000 m. According to operational report No. 1 written by the headquarters of the 9th High-Speed Bomber Air Regiment, the enemy dealt a definitive blow: 'As a result of the bombing Tilsit railway station is ablaze.' However during the course of these sorties the first losses were also incurred and three crews from the 4th Squadron were shot down by anti-aircraft artillery over the target. From a report written by the Regimental Commander it is known that out of the four SB aircraft that came under concentrated fire from the German ant-aircraft artillery batteries, three aircraft were shot down and only the crew led by the Deputy Regimental Commander of the Political Unit, Battalion Commander Dorofeyev, returned from the mission.

The headquarters of the 164th Anti-Aircraft Artillery Regiment also mentions a raid by a group of four Soviet bombers on Tilsit between 0640–0645 hrs although the aircraft type is entered tentatively as TB-3s.

The actions by Soviet aircraft did not go unnoticed. In the documents belonging to the German 1st Panzer Division that had advanced from the area around Tilsit to Taurage there is an entry that was made at 0600 hrs (Berlin time): 'The first air attacks were conducted over the command post and the Arko 30 command post is being bombed.'

Following the return to Panevezys all the serviceable aircraft in the 9th High-Speed Bomber Air Regiment were almost immediately redeployed to Skverbai airfield, with the aim of forestalling retaliatory strikes by the enemy.

The second bomber air regiment in the 7th Mixed Air Division, namely the 46th High-Speed Bomber Air Regiment, did not conduct any night flights that weekend so the regimental command required only about an hour to prepare the regiment's aircraft for the next sortie. The first aircraft took off at 0559 hrs and further events are given only a meagre description in operational report No. 1:

> I report that between 0640–0645 hrs on 22 June 1941 the 2nd and 3rd Air Squadrons in the 46th High-Speed Bomber Air Regiment conducted a bombing raid with 18 aircraft. The 2nd Air Squadron destroyed the concentration of forces in the area around Tilzin, and Taurage at an altitude of 3,600 m. During the course of the bombardment by five SB aircraft from the 2nd Air Squadron five SB aircraft along with their crews failed to return. In total 36 FAB-100, and 18 FAB-50 bombs were dropped.
>
> The 3rd Squadron destroyed the railway station in Zhillen from an altitude of 3,500 m, and five crews failed to return from the mission. In total 36 FAB-100, and 18 FAB-50 bombs were dropped.

The Combat Journal of the 46th High-Speed Bomber Air Regiment and the German data enable a relatively detailed description of the first combat sorties by the squadrons in the regiment.

The 2nd Squadron under the command of Squadron Commander Gryzlov at 0645 hrs bombed a river crossing together with the concentration of German forces in the area around Vishvill. Why Soviet aircraft ended up over Vishvill when their targets were located in the area around Ragnit is not clear. Seemingly the squadron got lost and 'missed' Ragnit, which in actual fact was a suburb of Tilsit and after circling for some time over the area they attacked targets in areas that were slightly to the east of the town of Vishvill on the banks of the Neman. This is confirmed by the diagram in the regimental album where the target for the aircraft in the 2nd Squadron is shown as Vishvill, but is named incorrectly. German sources confirm this action and in accordance with their data at 0545 hrs (Berlin time) a group of eight Soviet bombers attacked the river crossing used by the forces of the 56th Motorised Corps in the area around Vishvill, but without success. A bridge near Vishvill was an important strategic point that was acting as the main crossing for the 56th Motorised Corps and was heavily defended. Almost immediately at 0648 hrs Soviet aircraft were fired upon by anti-aircraft artillery and at 0650 hrs they were attacked by a group of Bf 109s. The German patrol was led by the Commander of II./JG 53 *Hauptmann* Heinz Bretnütz who at that time was one of the best aces in the *Luftwaffe* with 31 victories to his credit. After he had started to attack the Soviet group in the area around the target the German fighters continued to pursue the SBs right up to Nemaksciai. As a result of the battle two SBs were shot down and a further two made emergency landings on Soviet territory, while another two made emergency landings on Siauliai airfield. The aircraft flown by the leader of the German group was shot down by return fire from the gunners, and he himself was seriously injured in the leg. Bretnütz had enough strength to make an emergency landing but on Soviet territory in the area around Erzvilkas. Despite the fact that he was taken in by a Lithuanian family and on 26 June was handed over to German units, on 27 June Bretnütz died in hospital owing to the onset of gangrene.

The victories that the German pilots in II./JG 53 claimed are as follows:

> *Hauptmann* Walter Spies, Stab II./JG 53: SB aircraft at 0652 and 0654 hrs
> *Oberfeldwebel* Walter Margstein, 4./JG 53: an SB at 0654 hrs
> *Oberfeldwebel* Stefan Litjens 4./JG 53: an SB at 0656 hrs
> *Unteroffizier* Herbert Rollwage 4./JG 53: SB aircraft at 0657 hrs and 0658 hrs
> *Leutnant* Gerhard Stengel: 4./JG 53: an SB at 0659 hrs
> *Hauptmann* Heinz Bretnütz, Stab II./JG 53 an SB at 0659 hrs.

In contrast to the Combat Journal, in their operational report the 46th High-Speed Bomber Air Regiment note five crews as having been lost. It is possible that one aircraft was destroyed during an emergency landing on Siauliai airfield.

It has to be said, however, that the enemy overstated their achievements by almost double. Thus eight Soviet bombers were recorded in the German pilots' tally whereas in reality they had only shot down four aircraft. Although a further two did make emergency landings due to battle damage on Siauliai airfield. In turn the Soviet crews claimed that they had succeeded in setting two German fighters on fire by using joint fire with the air gunners when all of the crews worked together. Bf 109F-2 W.Nr.6674 flown by Bretnütz became the first aircraft that the Germans lost in the course of the air battles over the Baltic region. ('This aircraft was initially listed as a 100 percent total loss, but was subsequently found and repatriated').

The 3rd Squadron led by Captain Gavrilov were to have attacked the station at Zhillen, however judging by the entries in the regiment's Combat Journal and German data these bombs were dropped on a completely different site.

According to the Combat Journal of the 46th High-Speed Bomber Air Regiment at 0635 hrs the squadron was fired upon by anti-aircraft artillery in the area around Tilsit, and at 0640 hrs was fired upon again by anti-aircraft artillery in the area around Taurotenen (which was a town 10 km south of Tilsit) and at 0645 hrs the crews dropped their bombs on Zhillen station. Subsequently at 0653 hrs in the area around Malomozhayskoye and Kraupishken (Malomozhayskoye is a town 10 km east of Zhillen) they were attacked by a group of Bf 109s.

However, according to German data at 0645 hrs the group of Soviet aircraft bombed a railway station in Eydtkau. Indeed judging by the chronometry it is obvious that it would have been possible to fly a distance of 30 km, of which 20 km would have been from Tilsit to Zhillen and a further 10 km from Zhillen to Malomozhayskoye in the course of 18 minutes three or four times at least. This kind of distance (of between 90–100 km) divides Tilsit from Eydtkau. There is every likelihood that the navigator of the 3rd Squadron made a miscalculation and instead of Tilsit he reached another town, but in East Prussia with its densely populated territory this is not surprising. Evidently this was one of the towns along the railway line from Tilsit–Stallupönen or from Lazdennen–Stallupönen. Judging by the map showing the sorties undertaken by the 46th High-Speed Bomber Air Regiment on 22 June 1941 it was actually Lazdennen, which was located 40 km east of Tilsit on a tributary of the River Neman known as the Sesupe. Evidently after mistaking it for Tilsit and after having flown for 50 km, which is actually 10 minutes' flying time, the Soviet pilots dropped their bombs on Eydtkau station, mistaking it for Zhillen.

The Soviet bomber pilots were unlucky, since all the fighter bases of the *Fliegerkorps* were located in the area in which they were flying. It is therefore no surprise that this squadron was also subject to attacks from German aces. There is every possibility that the group of SBs flew right over the airfield at Rautenberg (10–12 km west of Lazdennen) from which German fighter aircraft from I./JG 54 took off to chase them. Considering the relatively safe flying altitude of 3,500 m the Germans were able to catch up with the Soviet crews deep within Soviet territory even after they had successfully dropped their bombs on a town such as Eydtkau, which stands on the border, and had departed east towards Kaunas. The German pilots were led by an experienced pilot, and a veteran of the Spanish Civil War and also of the battles on the Western Front. *Hauptmann* Reinhard Seiler, although there were other aces within the group. According to Western information the tally was opened by *Oberleutnant* Kinzinger, who had excelled in combat over Kedainiai. He shot down an SB at 0651 hrs Moscow time. *Luftwaffe* pilots continued this persecution for another seven minutes at least, and the next six victories were recorded north-west of Kaunas. The leader *Hauptmann* Seiler became a hero of the battle, scoring a hatrick. These were his 4th, 5th, and 6th victories in the Second World War.

The victories claimed by the pilots of I./JG 54 were as follows:

Oberleutnant Adolf-Waldemar Kinzinger I./JG 54: at 0651 hrs
Unteroffizier Peter Siegler 2./JG 54: an SB at 0655 hrs
Hauptmann Reinhard Seiler, Stab I./JG 54: an SB to the north-east of Kaunas at 0655, 0657, and 0658 hrs.
Leutnant Günther Raub, 2./JG 54: two SB aircraft at 0657 hrs and 0658 hrs.

In accordance with the results of the battle the Soviet side acknowledged that five SBs had been lost. According to the Combat Journal they were lost without trace, apart from that a further aircraft made an emergency landing on Panevezys airfield due to battle damage and the gunner Petty Officer D.P. Petrov was injured. Only three aircraft retuned to Gruzdziai.

However paradoxical the heavy losses in the 2nd and 3rd Squadrons of the 46th High-Speed Bomber Air Regiment sound, they were to a great extent predetermined by the successful raids conducted by the 9th High-Speed Bomber Air Regiment. The bomber regiments in the 7th Mixed Air Division incidentally were allocated targets in this same region—the triangle formed of Tilsit–Ragnit–Zhillen—and the German Air Defence System was already at full strength. It has to be said that the Divisional Commander Colonel Petrov understood the danger of an interception and at 0530 hrs he ordered that the bombers of the 46th High-Speed Bomber Air Regiment be escorted by a group of nine I-16s from the 10th Fighter Air Regiment. Unfortunately, for the crews of the 46th High-Speed Bomber Air Regiment, however, in accordance with the preceding order all the aircraft in the 10th Fighter Air Regiment from 0450 hrs were in the air covering Siauliai and did not have any time to prepare to escort the SBs.

For the German pilots sitting in their Messerschmitts the SBs flying as they were without an escort were an easy target, in that both groups were led by the most experienced pilots, who were veterans of the Spanish Civil War and of the battles in Europe—namely *Hauptmann* Seiler, and Bretnütz. There was therefore nothing strange about the results of these battles, and the losses that were incurred by the 46th High-Speed Bomber Air Regiment. We note that even though the crews in both Soviet squadrons were without fighter cover and incurred heavy losses they nevertheless managed to maintain the formation, and to shoot down one of the attacking enemy aircraft. The German pilots, on the other hand, should be given their due as they went about their mission very professionally. Attention is drawn to the high percentage of victories claimed by the Germans against the Soviet aircraft that were actually shot down. The ratio is approximately 2:1 and 1.5:1.

It would appear that a description of this episode could end there, were it not for one important aspect. The point being that by that time when the Soviet aircraft were already in the air, at 0615 hrs precisely an order arrived at the headquarters of the 7th Mixed Air Division from the headquarters of the Air Forces of the North-Western Front to abort the combat sortie: 'Do not fly across the border to destroy enemy aircraft on their own territory. Order the aircraft that have already taken off to land back at their own airfields.' Naturally this order was a repeat of the order received by the headquarters of the North-Western Front from the People's Commissar for Defence for which there is documentary confirmation:

> The report written by the Commander of the North-Western Front dated 22 June 1941 to the People's Commissar for Defence of the USSR concerning the commencement of hostilities by the Germans at 0610 hrs on 22 June 1941.
>
> At 0400 hrs on 22 June 1941 the Germans commenced their combat activities. Enemy Air Forces bombed the airfields at Vindava, Panevezys, Siauliai, and Kaunas. Palanga, Taurage, and Kalvarija were fired upon using artillery.

> Enemy tanks are advancing in Taurage. The infantry are on the move in Shaki (up to a regiment of infantry) and in Vistytis and Kalvarija the numbers of enemy forces are being finalised. I have issued an order to push the enemy back using counter-attacks and to take prisoners. Our Air Force is in the air. Do not cross the border until I am in receipt of your order, I received your order via General Safronov not to cross the border voluntarily. I have taken steps to ensure that the enemy can be bombed without overflying the border.

Similar orders not only induced nervousness and confusion. In fact this abiding tragicomedy that played out in the way the leadership of the USSR and Red Army Command conducted themselves, made the situation for the air forces on the border airfields even worse. While Soviet military leaders, ignoring the war, indulged in exercises in writing politically correct orders, German aircraft were preparing for the next raid on Soviet airfields.

This order, however, was only partially fulfilled. Only one group of nine SB aircraft from the 5th Squadron of the 46th High-Speed Bomber Air Regiment led by Captain Bugay returned to their airfield having cut short the fulfilment of their combat order. Other groups from both regiments, let us remember, dropped their bombs on their allotted targets. Naturally the first thing to suggest is that these problems were linked to the unsatisfactory condition of the communication equipment or the poor training of the radio-operators, but in this case there was a totally different reason.

An unknown chronicler from the 5th Squadron, 9th High-Speed Bomber Air Regiment, writing about the history of the regiment, tells of how Squadron Commander Krivtsov received a radiogram on the curtailment of the combat sortie and ordering a return to base literally on his bombing run. The leader closed the bomb bay doors on his SB but a few seconds later he opened them again and began to drop bombs on his target. Thus Captain Krivtsov became the first pilot in the Red Army Air Force to drop bombs on Germany in the Great Patriotic War, not only by decree of providence, but also by dint of a personal decision.

Unfortunately, apart from the aircraft in the 9th and 46th High-Speed Bomber Air Regiments, 7th Mixed Air Division, not one of the other formations succeeded in sending their aircraft off to carry out raids on German airfields. This in essence became the same Rubicon that the Air Forces of the North-Western Front on the morning of 22 June 1941 had failed to cross. The majority of Soviet aircraft remained on their bases and the *Luftwaffe* units were given an opportunity to rearm and refuel their materiel in a trouble free environment, preparing for a repeat raid on Soviet airfields.

Undoubtedly if the aircraft in the majority of the units in the Air Forces of the North-Western Front were at that moment engaged in raids on German bases this would have had a serious effect on the realisation of German intentions. Firstly, the majority of the German fighters would have been busy countering the Soviet attacks, and correspondingly they would not have been able to participate in a repeat attack. Secondly, it is possible that some of the German aircraft would have been destroyed or damaged and they would have been unable to participate in subsequent raids. Thirdly, a second raid by German aircraft would have been delayed and given a specific set of circumstances it would have been directed against empty airfields. Overall ,however, this confrontation would have assumed the character of a classic exchange of attacks, that is to say a completely standard form of warfare.

Apart from that it is worth taking into consideration the moral factor of this 'stop-order'. Following the first bombing runs the personnel would have been dying to get their own back on the enemy, and any ban on firing at German aircraft and then to bomb targets beyond the River Neman would have confused the pilots to say the least. The Deputy Commander of the Political Unit of the 6th Mixed Air Division Regimental Commissar Rytov confirms receipt of an order stating this same thing, along with the headquarters of the 4th and 7th Mixed Air Divisions and noted the reaction among the leadership of the division to similar orders:

> An officer from the operations department came in holding the radiogram he had just received. We literally pored over it but there was nothing new in it at all: do not give in to provocation, and individual enemy aircraft were not to be shot down! We are being beaten into the ground and we are keeping shtum. 'I don't understand it' the officer exclaimed in frustration [this refers to the Commander of the 6th Mixed Air Division] and slammed the piece of paper down on the table.

Interestingly, from then on in documents written by the 3rd Directorate of Red Army General Headquarters (Counter-intelligence) the actions of the 6th Mixed Air Division were described relatively briefly and in actual fact they incriminated the Divisional Commander for obeying the orders from his own command to the letter.

> In the 6th Mixed Air Division by fault of its Commander who still feared provocation no resistance was offered to the fascists after the first raid. Therefore the Germans, in spite of the fact that the Soviet numerical superiority was almost twice that of theirs, gained air superiority almost immediately. Only after a certain period of time have the regimental commanders taken steps to counter these attacks on their own initiative.

Naturally it would have been easy to reason with counter-intelligence personnel, but it would be interesting to see what they would have done had they been in Colonel Fyodorov's shoes—would they themselves have not carried out the orders given to them by their front line commander, by the People's Commissar for Defence, and the Chief of Staff? It is completely obvious that the leadership of the country and the commanders of the army did have to react in some way to the actions of the enemy, such as declaring war, for example, for a start. Soviet leadership on the other hand as mentioned above were playing it safe at the time, ordering aircraft to be recalled and also that the border was not to be crossed.

Correspondingly the subsequent actions of the Air Forces of the North-Western Front were played out with a keen eye on orders from Moscow. Air Force Headquarters made an almost immediate U-turn, ordering formations and units to prepare for attacks on the enemy that had invaded Soviet territory. By 0620 hrs the formations had received new orders from the Commander of front line air forces that mirrored orders received from the People's Commissar for Defence almost word for word.

Thus the 7th Mixed Air Division made the following entry in the orders log: 'Have units on readiness to destroy the enemy's ground forces as well as any aircraft that have crossed, or flown into our territory. Do not cross the border but be prepared to carry out attacks in the area around Shaki, and Taurage on the enemy's troops, and aircraft.'

The headquarters of the 4th Mixed Air Division received a very similar text at 0632 hrs: '1. Be at readiness to destroy the enemy's ground forces in the Shaki, and Taurage sector 2. Be prepared for evasion manoeuvres 3. The order to take off will be issued in a separate order 4. An order for Klaipeda remains a secondary priority.'

At that moment, however, almost supernatural forces interfered in the course of the battle. It is well known that fortune favours the brave and the decisive, and despite the cessation of raids in accordance with the plan for the provision of cover the military powers were 'smiling' on the Air Forces of the North-Western Front and its command. This happened because of that same first attack by several groups of bombers from the 9th and 46th High-Speed Bomber Air Regiments, which forced the enemy to concern themselves with the defence of their own airfields.

The Commander of the *Luftflotte* 1, by all accounts, was concerned about a retaliatory strike and this was completely logical. Firstly the Germans had started the war, and evidently they took their enemy seriously although naturally they had no idea that the Soviet pilots had been ordered not to cross the border and not to be the first to fire on German aircraft! Secondly, and this is without a doubt, the stimulus for this was the bombing of Tilsit, Vishvill, and Eydtkau, which was actually carried out at the time the German aircraft were being refuelled and rearmed after they had returned to their airfield, as a result of which the first groups of Soviet bombers did not encounter a single German fighter in the air.

Therefore in response not even to the attack but to the thrust by the Air Forces of the North-Western Front, the Germans actually cancelled the second sortie by their fighters aimed at carrying out a second attack on the airfields and began to counter the attacks by aircraft of the 46th High-Speed Bomber Air Regiment. The Commander of JG 54, H. Trautloft,noted in his diary that the start of the second raid on Soviet airfields was recorded at 0615 hrs, however instead of this the fighters carried out an airfield manoeuvre to avoid Soviet attacks, changing the airfield on which they were based.

It has to be said that the Germans began to suspect that something strange was to be anticipated from the Air Forces of the North-Western Front in the course of the first raid. Thus at 0705 hrs Junkers aircraft from III./KG.1 again attacked Liepaja airfield unopposed, destroying 11 I-153 aircraft. The Regimental Commander Zaitsev mentions the losses but for some reason he does not mention the sortie that was undertaken to intercept the attack: 'Our airfield was not damaged either after the 2nd raid although around 10 aircraft were damaged that stood in a line minus their engines and which had not been dispersed as they were unserviceable aircraft. Bomb craters had appeared on the runway.'

The Commander of the 7 *Staffel* that carried out the attack on Liepaja recalled that Soviet aircraft were airborne but were acting very strangely:

> Although a large number of fighters were standing on the airfield, neither the first nor the third raids encountered any resistance. If the first raid did evidently come as a surprise...
>
> During the course of the second attack the Rata aircraft were brought up to combat readiness just as the German bombers approached. The Russians did take off and engage us in combat but no formation of any kind was discernible in the way they carried out their attack, they were not even arranged in pairs or in sections. Each of the aircraft attacked individually firing from a distance of around 500 m and after they had finished their attack, they would enter a dive.

The *Luftwaffe* pilots got the wrong end of the stick with these manoeuvres, interpreting them as the overall weakness in the training of red Army aviation crews. The reader however will already be aware that the real reason the pilots of the 148th Fighter Air Regiment fired past their targets was an order not to shoot down the enemy aircraft, but to force them to land. Deputy Political Instructor of the 6th Mixed Air Division A.G. Rytov confirms the fact that divisional command continued to fulfil Directive No. 1 even after the first raid on Liepaja as well as the subsequent orders from the People's Commissar for Defence, which did not permit pilots in the 148th Fighter Air Regiment to shoot down the German aircraft. Judging by his memoirs after the first raid he flew to Liepaja himself and attempted to bolster regimental command:

> 'What about the German parachutists?' I asked Zaitsev, watching the aircraft take off not to intercept the bombers but to fly alongside them. An order was an order and they were not to be shot down.
>
> 'How long are we going to play cat and mouse?' Zaitsev asked as we climbed out of the ditch. 'Look what these low-lifes have done—he gestured towards the smoke-covered airfield with his hand—we are being bombed, we are bathing in blood, and yet we cannot touch them.'

> I reasoned with the Regimental Commander although he was simmering with indignation on the inside—'Just hold on Zaitsev, we haven't received an order.'
> The Junkers aircraft began to drop high explosive and incendiary bombs. No, this was no provocation, but the start of a real war!

It is not hard to imagine how combat pilots—veterans of the war with Finland—would have felt, and how they would have reacted to this 'theatre of the absurd'. Their restraint can only be admired, but by all accounts, after the second raid and the warning shots fired past the Junkers aircraft their nerves began to get the better of them, especially since the regiment's losses began to increase. A.G. Rytov conveys this tense atmosphere and according to his memoirs it turned out that the personnel actually rebelled and refused to carry out the orders they received from command:

> Commissar Golovachev approached us. His eyes were bloodshot.
> 'How long are we going to have our hands tied?' He kicked a stone out from under his foot in indignation. To sum up, I report as follows: the pilots have decided to attack, without waiting for an order from on high. I will stand with them in answering for the consequences.

Rytov evidently could only complain higher up the chain:

> I spoke to a member of the district's Military Council and reported the situation at Liepaja in the hope of receiving advice or an order. He however did not say anything of substance. He just reminded us of one thing: If anything happens, let me know.
> It became clear that in this most difficult, and complicated situation one had to rely solely on one's own military experience, and act as one's party conscience would dictate.

Owing to the limited number of documents and memoirs that survive it is very difficult to establish what was happening at this time on the majority of airfields. By all accounts however a similar situation to the one that held sway on the morning of 22 June was prevalent in almost every regiment, whose pilots continued to rock their wings and fire into the air, and naturally were not able to impede the German bombers.

It was true that common sense did gradually come to the surface and several commanders did nevertheless respond to the repeated German raids not by rocking their wings but by firing. For example Senior Political Instructor Smirnov testifies to the fact that the Commander of the 42nd Fighter Air Regiment came to the necessary conclusion after the enemy's first appearance in the area around Varena airfield and the second raid by *Luftwaffe* aircraft gave rise to a highly appropriate response.

At 0625 hrs a Bf 109 attacked Varena airfield. According to the Combat Journal of the 57th Mixed Air Division 12 I-153s took off to counter them and at an altitude of 800 m they engaged them in combat. As a result the enemy broke off the attack and departed back to their own territory. No losses were incurred on either side.

The attacks on Varena, Alytus, Liepaja, Ventspils, and Kedainiai represented the second wave of attacks on Soviet airfields, which began between 0630–0700 hrs in the morning. However as mentioned above almost none of the fighters from I. *Fliegerkorps* participated in these raids while aircraft from the VIII. *Fliegerkorps* were at that time active in the air forces zone on the Western Front and as such the activity involving German aircraft in the zone of the Western Front was relatively insignificant and did not inflict any serious damage on Soviet units. Arguably the most serious losses were in Liepaja, but the total number of aircraft destroyed could be estimated at between 20–25 aircraft, which had almost no effect on the combat capability of the Air Forces of the North-Western Front.

Again we note that as a result of the retaliatory attack by aircraft from the 9th and 46th High-Speed Bomber Air Regiments (the actions of just four dozen Soviet bombers) that had in essence just designated their targets for the attack, was enough to interrupt a second sortie by the aircraft of *Luftflotte* 1. This undoubtedly was the reason behind the low level of effectiveness in the activity of the second wave of German bombers, which were left without support and without a fighter escort.

Nevertheless, the enemy hardly incurred any losses in the air or on the ground. Despite the favourable conditions neither the Soviet fighters nor the bombers were able to inflict any kind of damage on the enemy. This took place because the Soviet fighters were banned from attacking the enemy aircraft first, as a result of which the German bombers, having dropped their bombs, turned back towards home without having encountered any resistance. The bombers of the 9th and 46th High-Speed Bomber Air Regiments did not have any up to date reconnaissance information on the disposition of German aircraft on the airfields, as a result of which the crews bombed secondary targets. The cessation of the second sortie by other bomber regiments in the Air Forces of the North-Western Front however enabled the *Luftflotte* 1 units to prepare for the next attacks in favourable conditions.

The sensible, and timely decisions taken by General Ionov were cancelled by commanders higher up the chain and this meant that the Germans only received a warning signal instead of a powerful retaliatory strike 'in pursuit'. Despite the fact that as a result of this the enemy reduced its activities dramatically in the skies over the Baltic region the initiative remained in hands of the *Luftwaffe*, and considering the fact that the Germans had hardly incurred any losses and had carried out supplementary reconnaissance on the disposition of Soviet airfields they had a real chance of inflicting a decisive blow on the Air Forces of the North-Western Front.

The last photograph of A.P. Ionov.

The Commander of the 5th Squadron, 9th High-Speed Bomber Air Regiment Captain Mikhail Antonovich Krivtsov, was the first Soviet pilot to drop bombs on German territory at approximately 0615 hrs on the morning of 22 June 1941.

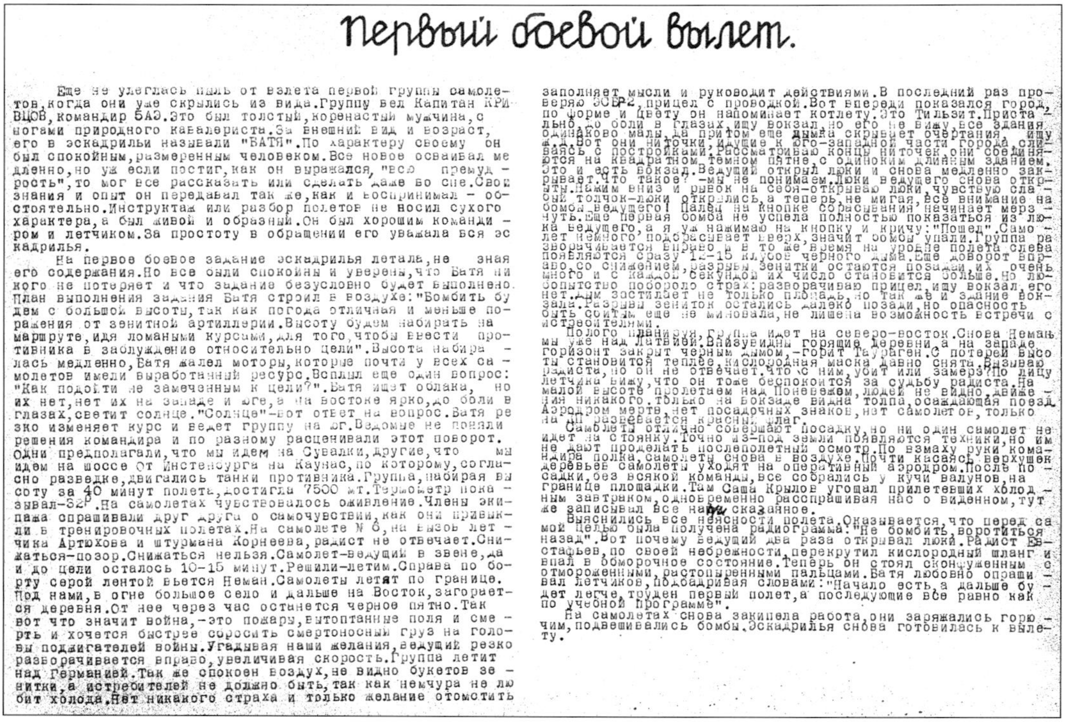

Первый боевой вылет.

Еще не улеглась пыль от взлета первой группы самолетов, когда они уже скрылись из вида. Группу вел Капитан КРИВЦОВ, командир БАЭ. Это был толстый, коренастый мужчина, с ногами природного кавалериста. За внешний вид и возраст, его в эскадрильи называли "БАТЯ". По характеру своему он был спокойным, размеренным человеком. Все новое осваивал медленно, но уж если постиг, как он выражался, "всю премудрость", то мог все рассказать или сделать даже во сне. Свои знания и опыт он передавал так же, как и воспринимал – обстоятельно. Инструктаж или разбор полетов не носил сухого характера, а был живой и образный. Он был хорошим командиром и летчиком. За простоту в обращении его уважала вся эскадрилья.

На первое боевое задание эскадрилья летала, не зная его содержания. Но все были спокойны и уверены, что Батя никого не потеряет и что задание безусловно будет выполнено. План выполнения задания Батя строил в воздухе: "Бомбить будем с большой высоты, так как погода отличная и меньше поражения от зенитной артиллерии. Высоту будем набирать на маршруте, идя ломаными курсами, для того, чтобы ввести противника в заблуждение относительно цели". Высота набиралась медленно, Батя жалел моторы, которые почти у всех самолетов имели выработанный ресурс. Всплыл еще один вопрос: "Как подойти не замеченным к цели?". Батя ищет облака, но их нет, нет их на западе и юге, а на востоке ярко, до боли в глазах, светит солнце. "Солнце"-вот ответ на вопрос. Батя резко изменяет курс и ведет группу на юг. Ведомые не поняли решения командира и по разному расценивали этот поворот. Одни предполагали, что мы идем на Сувалки, другие, что мы идем на шоссе от Инстенбурга на Каунас, по которому, согласно разведке, двигались танки противника. Группа, набирая высоту за 40 минут полета, достигла 7500 мт. Термометр показывал-32°. На самолетах чувствовалось оживление. Члены экипажа спрашивали друг друга о самочувствии, как они привыкли в тренировочных полетах. На самолете № 6, на вызов летчика Артюхова и штурмана Корнеева, радист не отвечает. Снижаться-позор. Снижаться нельзя. Самолет-ведущий в звене, да и до цели осталось 10-15 минут. Решили-летим. Справа по борту серой лентой вьется Неман. Самолеты летят по границе. Под нами, в огне большое село и дальше на Восток, загорается деревня. От нее через час останется черное пятно. Так вот что значит война, -это пожары, вытоптанные поля и смерть и хочется быстрее сбросить смертоносный груз на головы поджигателей войны. Угадывая наши желания, ведущий резко разворачивается вправо, увеличивая скорость. Группа летит над Германией. Так же спокоен воздух, не видно букетов зенитки, а истребителей не должно быть, так как немчура не любит холода. Нет никакого страха и только желание отомстить заполняет мысли и руководит действиями. В последний раз проверяю ЭСБР-2, прицел с проводкой. Вот впереди показался город, по форме и цвету он напоминает котлету. Это Тильзит. Пристально, до боли в глазах, ищу вокзал, но его не вижу, все здания одинаково малы, да притом еще дымка скрывает очертания, ищу ж.д. Вот они ниточки, идущие к юго-западной части города, сливаясь с постройками. Рассматриваю концы ниточек, они соединяются на квадратном темном пятне, с одиноким длинным зданием. Это и есть вокзал. Ведущий открыл люки и снова медленно закрывает. Что такое? -мы не понимаем. Люки ведущего снова открыты. Нажим вниз и рывок на себя-открываю люки, чувствую слабый толчок-люки открылись, а теперь, не мигая, все внимание на бомбы ведущего! Палец на кнопке сбрасывания начинает мерзнуть. Еще первая бомба не успела полностью показаться из люка ведущего, а я уж нажимаю на кнопку и кричу: "Пошел". Самолет немного подбрасывает вверх, значит бомбы упали. Группа разворачивается вправо и в то же время на уровне полета слева появляются сразу 12-15 клубов черного дыма. Еще доворот вправо, со снижением, разрывы зенитки остаются позади, их очень много и с каждой секундой их число становится больше. Но любопытство побороло страх: разворачиваю прицел, ищу вокзал, его нет. Дым застилает не только площадь, но так же и здание вокзала. Разрывы зениток остались далеко позади, но опасность быть сбитым еще не миновала, не лишена возможность встречи с истребителями.

Полого планируя, группа идет на северо-восток. Снова Неман, мы уже над Литвой. Внизу видны горящие деревни, а на западе горизонт закрыт черным дымом, -горит Таураген. С потерей высоты становится теплее, кислородная маска давно снята. Вызываю радиста, но он не отвечает. Что с ним, убит или замерз? По лицу летчика вижу, что он тоже беспокоится за судьбу радиста. На малой высоте пролетаем над Поневежем, людей не видно, движения никакого. Только на вокзале видна толпа, осаждающая поезд. Аэродром мертв, нет посадочных знаков, нет самолетов, только на КП развевается красный флаг.

Самолеты отлично совершают посадку, но ни один самолет не идет на стоянку. Точно из-под земли появляются техники, но им не дают проделать послеполетный осмотр. По взмаху руки командира полка, самолеты снова в воздухе. Почти касаясь верхушек деревьев самолеты уходят на оперативный аэродром. После посадки, без всякой команды, все собрались у кучи валунов, на границе площадки. Там Саша Крылов угощал прилетевших холодным завтраком, одновременно расспрашивая нас о виденном, тут же записывал все нами сказанное.

Выяснились все неясности полета. Оказывается, что перед самой целью была получена радиограмма: "Не бомбить, воротиться назад". Вот почему ведущий два раза открывал люки. Радист Евстафьев, по своей небрежности, перекрутил кислородный шланг и впал в обморочное состояние. Теперь он стоял сконфуженным с отмороженными, растопыренными пальцами. Батя любовно опрашивал летчиков, подбадривая словами: "Начало есть, а дальше будет легче, труден первый полет, а последующие все равно как по учебной программе".

На самолетах снова закипела работа, они заряжались горючим, подвешивались бомбы. Эскадрилья снова готовилась к вылету.

A page from the history of the 9th High-Speed Bomber Air Regiment with a description of the first combat sortie.

An aerial photograph of the station at Tilsit taken in 1944. It is likely that some of these buildings were destroyed by bombing raid back in 1941.

The Commander of the 3rd Squadron, 9th High-Speed Bomber Air Regiment Ivan Petrovich Korotkov, who participated in a raid in the area around Tilsit at approximately 0700 hrs on 22 June 1941.

The moment Captain Korotkov was taken prisoner. He had managed to bail out of his downed aircraft by parachute.

The Commander of the 2nd Squadron, 46th High-Speed Bomber Air Regiment Captain Vasiliy Ivanovich Gryzlov, who led a group of nine SB aircraft that bombed a river crossing close to Vishvill on 22 June.

Commander of the II./JG 53 *Hauptmann* Heinz Bretnütz who was shot down by the guns of an SB from the 2nd Squadron, 46th High-Speed Bomber Air Regiment at approximately 0700 hrs on 22 June 1941.

Aircraft Heinz Bretnütz that was discovered on the site where it made its emergency landing in the area around Erzvilkas.

An SB bearing the tactical No. 7, presumably this is an aircraft from the 2nd Squadron, 46th High-Speed Bomber Air Regiment that made an emergency landing on 22 June following combat with Messerschmitts from II./JG 53 in the area around Vishvill.

The Commander of the 3rd Squadron, 46th High-Speed Bomber Air Regiment Captain Vladimir Yakovlevich Gavrilov, 46th High-Speed Bomber Air Regiment, who led a group of nine SB bombers, which bombed the railway station at Eydtkau.

An officer of the Headquarters of I./JG 54 *Hauptmann* Reinhard Seiler who attained victories over three SBs from the 3rd Squadron, 46th High-Speed Bomber Air Regiment at approximately 0700 hrs on 22 June 1941 in the area around Eydtkau.

The Commander of the 5th Squadron, 46th High-Speed Bomber Air Regiment Captain Nikolai Romanovich Bugay, who led a group of nine SB aircraft, and who halted his combat sortie by order of Command.

Officers of the third group, 3rd Bomber Wing rest in the shade of a Do 17Z. Thanks to the refusal by Soviet Command to bomb German airfields on 22 June, the German units could rest in a calm atmosphere between carrying out their combat sorties.

4.4 The Third Raid by Luftwaffe Aircraft on Soviet Airfields

At approximately 0800 hrs in the morning there was a short pause in the skies over the Baltic region. There had been no large-scale German raids since 0500 hrs but this did nothing to quell the fears of Air Force Command. In anticipation of new, powerful attacks General Ionov, who was very far-sighted gave the units under him an order to prepare for decisive action to counter forthcoming attacks by the enemy. At 0810 hrs order No. 2 came through to the headquarters of the various formations from the headquarters of the Air Forces of the North-Western Front: 'Fighter aviation is to be used sparingly in preparation for an enemy air attack. It is anticipated that this raid will be formed of large groups. Fighters are not to be scrambled for individual aircraft.'

At the same time the Commander of the Air Forces of the North-Western Front was attempting to collate intelligence on the advance made by enemy forces and on the actions of his own air forces. As a consequence of this, the 312th Reconnaissance Air Regiment did not succeed in training the required number of crews prior to the outbreak of war and the orders for reconnaissance were issued to fighter pilots.

At 0730 hrs a flight of I-16s from the 10th Fighter Air Regiment carried out reconnaissance on a route from Siauliai–Taurage–Silute, landing at 0827 hrs. On the front line from Shaki–Vilkavishkis–Mariumpole, and Kalvarija reconnaissance was carried out by aircraft from the 15th and 31st Fighter Air Regiments, while I-153 aircraft from the 42nd Fighter Air Regiment carried out reconnaissance along the line from Mariumpole, to Kalvarija–Druskinikai.

At around 0900 hrs Moscow finally awoke. After receiving back at 0530 hrs from the German ambassador to the USSR Friedrich-Werner von Schulenberg notification of the outbreak of war with Germany, Soviet command chose not to make any announcement about this and after holding a meeting lasting for approximately one hour, they issued the so-called Directive No. 2.

Why the country's leadership did not announce to the troops and to the people that war had broken out and why they did not issue specific orders on the implementation of the plan for the provision of cover remains a mystery to this day.

> DIRECTIVE No. 2:
> On 22 June 1941 at 0400 hrs and for no reason German aircraft carried out raids on our airfields and cities along our western border and they were subjected to bombing. At the same time at various locations German forces opened fire with artillery and crossed our border.
>
> In connection with this invasion, which is unprecedented in its audacity, I HEREBY ORDER:
>
> 1 All troops to descend upon the enemy forces with everything they have and to destroy them in those areas in which they have violated the Soviet border.
> 2. Reconnaissance and combat aviation are ordered to locate the areas in which enemy aviation is being concentrated, as well as establishing the alignments of their forces. Enemy aircraft are to be destroyed on enemy airfields using powerful attacks from bomber, and ground attack aviation and the alignments of enemy ground troops are to be bombed. The attacks are to be conducted to a depth of between 100–150 km inside German territory.
>
> Königsberg and Klaipeda are to be bombed to destruction. No air attacks are to be conducted on Finnish, and Romanian territory without specific instructions.

This directive was less complicated than the first one but for some reason along with a concise allocation of the various tasks there were open-ended instructions contained within its text, which would be very difficult to carry out in a rapidly changing situation. The commanders of the air forces and Air Force headquarters would need to come up with plans for forthcoming operations on the move. It was much easier to invoke the plans for the provision of cover using special signals, even more so in the context of the orders issued by the air forces, which actually reiterated the fundamental provisions of pre-war plans.

Apart from that in Directive No. 2 there was no mention at all of the word 'WAR' which again did nothing to assist in the comprehension of the situation, and many of the cautious commanders who had had already received this document continued to hold back on any decisive action.

This however was not even the main problem. The situation was exacerbated by the fact that the text of the directive was only sent to the headquarters of the North-Western Front at 0815 hrs(!) that is to say one hour after it had been drawn up and by then time was already being measured literally in seconds.

After the morning reprimand even the commanders of the North-Western Front and the commanders of the front line air forces, by all accounts, were attempting to follow the orders that came from 'on high' and the text of Directive No. 3, which arrived at the headquarters of the Air Forces of the North-Western Front was even more cautious than Directive No. 2. General Ionov did not decide to go on the attack, merely enabling a counter-attack against the enemy: 'Bombing of enemy aircraft is permitted up to 100 km inside German territory. During mass enemy raids the fighters can be repelled but the bombers should be escorted to a convenient location and enemy aviation is to be forced to land, after first withdrawing our aviation from any attack.'

No matter how annoying this was, the Air Forces of the North-Western Front lost three precious hours in lingering anticipation of an order from Moscow between 0600–0900 hrs, and failed to take advantage of the enemy's mistakes, which the 'arbitrary' raids by the 9th and 46th High-Speed Bomber Air Regiments took to be the start of a Soviet retaliatory strike. Thus even this Directive No. 2 was late in coming. Specific orders were not issued and while the commander and the headquarters procrastinated, making sense of the directive and working on the orders they were to pass onto the units and formations, the initiative again passed into the hands of the *Luftwaffe*.

Naturally the enemy did not delay in using the gift that Soviet command had passed to them, and after recovering from their fright they responded to Soviet 'kindness' with a series of subsequent raids, which began between 0830–0900 hrs in the morning. The majority of Soviet airfields had been reconnoitred and in contrast to previous raids this time the *Luftwaffe* attacked the materiel belonging to Soviet regiments, therefore the losses in terms of Soviet aircraft were much higher in comparison with those incurred earlier on that morning.

The first aircraft to attack this time were those belonging to VIII. *Fliegerkorps* and the principal attack by German pilots was against the airfields of Alytus, Varena, and Perloja, which were already well known to them. As a result of the previous raids and of the aerial reconnaissance on these airfields the concentration of Soviet fighter aviation units had already been revealed, and evidently the locations of the aircraft hard standings, and other structures had already been established. However the resistance offered by the aircraft of the 236th, 42nd, and 237th Fighter Air Regiments gave rise to a significant increase in the consist of the attacking groups, and now the enemy was acting in large formations and whole groups of German fighters attacked the Soviet airfields. Apart from that these raids were conducted within a short space of time.

Thus at 0815 hrs some 17 German bombers bombed Alytus, and at 0915 hrs this raid was repeated by 20 Bf 109Es from II./JG 27, which not only dropped SD-2 bombs but strafed the runway with machine gun fire. By all accounts it was these raids that put a full stop to the existence of the 236th

Fighter Air Regiment. All the 'Chaikas' belonging to this regiment had been destroyed or damaged on the ground although owing to a lack of detail in Soviet documents it is impossible to establish how many were damaged, or destroyed in the first, second, and third raids.

During the course of this raid pilots of the II./JG 27 were engaged in air combat, or even in combat, as a result of which *Oberfeldwebel* Otto Schultz from 4 *Staffel* at 0920 hrs, and *Feldwebel* Herbert Krenz from 6 *Staffel* at 0925 hrs claimed they had shot down two I-15s. It is likely that pilots from the 2nd Squadron, 15th Fighter Air Regiment, who at that moment evidently were conducting reconnaissance on a route from Kalvarija–Mariumpole had engaged the Germans in combat. No description of this battle or battles exists from either side. The only thing that can be said is that the 2nd Squadron, 15th Fighter Air Regiment lost four I-153s and four pilots on 22 June so the German claims for the aircraft they shot down are quite plausible.

The reader would recall that the only combat capable fighter unit in the Vilnius direction was the 42nd Fighter Air Regiment. As was the case with the 236th Fighter Air Regiment in Alytus during the course of the first raids and the many reconnaissance flights the Germans established the disposition of the regiment's formations on Varena and Perloja airfields. Obviously however they had not taken into account the number of aircraft on these airfields and the training of Soviet pilots.

The third raid on Varena and Perloja airfields took place at 0900 hrs, and aircraft from III./JG 53 participated in it. Naturally there was no chance of an element of surprise. The Commander of the 42nd Fighter Air Regiment kept all the crews at state of readiness No. 1 and according to reports issued by the aerial reconnaissance posts each time an enemy aircraft would approach Soviet aircraft managed to get airborne to intercept it. This was what happened on this occasion. The only minus was that Soviet pilots took off from both airfields and were formally divided up amongst themselves. The first aircraft to take off were those belonging to the 1st, and 4th Air Squadrons.

According to operations report No. 1 written by the headquarters of the 57th Mixed Air Division: 'At 0900 hrs some 12 I-153s in the area around Varena at an altitude of 800 m engaged five Me-109s in combat that tried to attack Varena airfield. The enemy broke off combat and departed back towards their own territory, and neither side incurred any losses. A single I-153 aircraft has sustained bullet holes.'

Senior Political Instructor Smirnov noted that the German fighters managed, despite the resistance, to strafe Perloja airfield, but it was true, without much success: 'Fifteen I-153 aircraft took off after the Me-109s' second approach and attempted to drag the aircraft into combat. The Me-109s did not engage them in combat and departed in the direction of Perloja airfield, where they strafed the materiel that was standing on the ground.'

The fact that Soviet pilots succeeded in beating back the first attack was nevertheless of no consequence, and that morning the Germans employed a tactical approach along the entire length of the front line, which enabled them to almost always secure a victory. This was expressed in terms of an attack that took place between 10 and 15 mins after the attack by the first group that was conducted as the aircraft of the second wave were already approaching the Soviet airfield. This second attack beat the airfield's defence personnel, who by that time had ran out of ammunition, destroying Soviet aircraft on the ground. However, this time around the German approach did not work, and a repeat attack was repelled by just three I-153s from the 2nd or 3rd Squadrons of the 42nd Fighter Air Regiment that had taken off from Perloja. The fortune of war was evidently with the pilots, who after a battle with a group of Messerschmitts were able to claim a victory. In the Combat Journal of the 57th Mixed Air Regiment this episode is described as follows: 'At 0920 hrs three I-153s in the area around Varena attacked 10 Me-109s. A single Me-109 departed towards its own territory, descending as it did so.' It was true that the operations report No. 1 the number of German aircraft is up to half of what it was, but nevertheless both accounts do describe one and the same battle: 'At 0930 hrs three I-153s attacked two Me-109s that had attempted to attack Varena airfield. A single Me-109 departed back towards its own territory at low level, while it is possible to suggest that a second made an emergency landing.'

It has to be said that Soviet pilots definitely did not make any mistakes, since Bf 109F-2 W.Nr. 5523 No. 2 'Black' flown by experienced pilot *Oberfeldwebel* Eduard Koslowski had been seriously damaged. By 22 June Koslowski had amassed four victories on his tally that he attained on the Western Front. As a result of battle damage the German pilot made an emergency landing in the area around Merkine and moreover his aircraft was completely destroyed, according to German classifications 100 percent destroyed, but the pilot was uninjured and the following day he returned to his unit. Interestingly Koslowski also claimed he had shot down an I-153 at 0910 hrs. Evidently, since the pilot had vanished without trace it was decided to make him an ace 'posthumously'. In reality not one aircraft from the 42nd Fighter Air Regiment was lost, but Koslowski's downed aircraft became the first German fighter to be shot down by the pilots of the Air Forces of the North-Western Front.

This round of confrontations for once belonged to the pilots of the 42nd Fighter Air Regiment: they had countered an attack on their airfields and shot down a German aircraft. Unfortunately it has not been possible to establish the surname of the pilot who claimed this victory.

The crews of the I. *Fliegerkorps* were attacking Soviet airfields at almost the same time as the aircraft of the VIII. *Fliegerkorps*. A few Soviet documents dryly record the statistics of the German attacks.

> The attack commenced at 0930 hrs, which was when Gruzdziai airfield was attacked. The 46th High-Speed Bomber Air Regiment that was based there lost nine SBs and one Ar-2 that caught fire, and nine which had been seriously damaged. Two men were killed and six were injured.
>
> At 1005 hrs according to information from the aerial reconnaissance posts 48 German aircraft bombed the city of Kaunas, and the airfield.
>
> At 1010 hrs a group of nine Bf 109s tried to attack Panevezys airfield but were intercepted by two flights of 'Chaikas' from the 238th Fighter Air Regiment. As a result of the air battle Soviet pilots prevented German aircraft from reaching their airfield, no losses or victories were recorded.
>
> At 1000 hrs seven Heinkel 111s (this was the aircraft type that was indicated in the documents, but they were actually Ju-88s) bombed Ventspils airfield (the 40th High-Speed Bomber Air Regiment lost four SBs destroyed, and six damaged on 22 June).
>
> At 1030 hrs a group of 12 He 111s (the aircraft type given in the documents were actually Ju-88s) from an altitude of between 1,400–2,000 m dropped 250 kg bombs on Karmelava airfield.
>
> At 1035 hrs there was a raid by 12 enemy bombers on Siauliai airfield.
>
> At 1050 hrs six enemy bombers bombed Liepaja airfield, at an altitude of +3,000 m.

Unfortunately far from all the Soviet documents confirm the losses incurred by Soviet units, so we shall again return to the recollections of the participants in these events.

A pilot who served in the 31st Fighter Air Regiment, B.V. Veselovskiy, recalled that the raid on Karmelava airfield led to heavy losses and explained how this happened:

> In the first state of readiness the watch was carried out by the squadrons in rotation. The first group that would have scrambled as the alarm was raised would patrol the area around the airfield. At this time German soldiers had yet to appear. As the squadron was coming in to

> land, a large group of enemy bombers appeared accompanied by fighters. The bombs ripped the runway open. And fighters attacked ground targets, strafing the taxiiing MiGs.
> A flight of our fighters that were in the air attacked these bombers but after the first short bursts of fire their machine guns failed.

The reader would recall from previous chapters that the personnel of the 31st Fighter Air Regiment had never tried to fire the machine guns in their new fighters until 22 June 1941 owing to rehearsals for the May Day parade in Moscow, and also owing to the large number of defects in the MiG-1/3 aircraft. The pilots only realised the reason why these synchronised machine guns were failing en masse in their first air battle, but it happened during the course of the second raid by German aircraft on the regiment's airfield:

> The three machine guns in the MiGs fired through the plane of rotation of the propeller, and a special mechanism would ensure that the bullets would pass between the propeller blades. This system had yet to be adjusted. The wing-mounted large-calibre Beryozkin machine guns, as well as the ammunition boxes had been removed from all the aircraft, since their considerable weight would cause the aircraft to slip into a stall that would develop from a simple spin to a flat spin, which would be unrecoverable. This was proven when Yevtushenko's flight entered a spin, and he himself was killed. Now after the weapons had failed in the air the technicians and armament specialists removed the cowling from the engine and were trying to eradicate the defect. Taking into consideration the fact that it was easy to remove the cowling but replacing it was difficult owing to the old 'ramrod' structure [the veteran is getting confused, this refers to Dzus fasteners] considerable time was spent eradicating this defect.

The same thing happened in other regiments and squadrons as well, pilots A.E. Shvarev and V.I. Klimenko recall mass failures in machine guns in MiG-1/3s in their memoirs.

Aleksandr Yefimovich Shvarev, describing the combat activity above Kaunas airfield recalled: 'We approached the airfield and fired but as luck would have it the 12.7-mm calibre BS machine guns on the MiG-3s, which would often jam, ceased and we could not fire any further.'

Vitaliy Ivanovich Klimenko, in his description of the combat activity of the 10th Fighter Air Regiment, noted:

> After midday one of the squadron commanders, who had succeeded in assimilating the aircraft, took off in the only MiG-1 serving in the regiment. Then a German reconnaissance aircraft appeared and he fell in behind this aircraft but did not open fire. I thought to myself: 'What are you doing?' He broke away and got on the aircraft's tail again, but still did not fire. When he landed we went up to him to find out what went wrong. He said: 'The firing button does not work.'*

In fact the pilots of the 31st Fighter Air Regiment were left completely unarmed since the technicians in the regiment had not been able to solve the problem with the normal operation of the machine guns on the first day of the war. It was for this reason that the regiment did not attain a single victory on 22 June 1941.

---

* On Siauliai airfield there were 19 MiG-3s, and one MiG-1. The 19 MiG-3s had been allocated to the 42nd Fighter Air Regiment, and the pilots in this unit were undergoing conversion at that time at the study centre airfield. There was however just one MiG-1 in the 10th Fighter Air Regiment, and as such the veteran mentioned just this one aircraft in his memoirs.

Very few details remain in the documents concerning the combat operations of the 15th Fighter Air Regiment but it is doubtful that the machine guns on the MiG-3s in the 15th Fighter Air Regiment fired any better than those in the 31st Fighter Air Regiment.

The 10th Fighter Air Regiment that operated the 'elderly' type 5 I-16s was scarcely in the best of shape but at least the machine guns in the 'Ishaki' could actually fire bullets. The Germans did not succeed in catching the Soviet pilots unawares, and during the course of the second raid a group of 18 I-16s encountered enemy aircraft as they approached the airfield. The air battle took place in the area around Siauliai–Kurtuvenai and the regiment's pilots provided reliable cover for their own airfield, although they did not manage to attain any victories.

The memoirs of the Squadron Commander of the 10th Fighter Air Regiment V.P. Borovogo contains a description of one of these battles, which is very useful in terms of its chronology:

> On 22 June 1941 the Flight Commander of the 10th Fighter Air Regiment Lieutenant V.S. Loboda took off for the second time in a day at 0630 hrs in an I-16 aircraft as part of a squadron. Close to Siauliai (in Lithuania) at an altitude of 2,000 m our fighters discovered a group of Ju-88 enemy bombers escorted by Me-109 fighters. Loboda led his flight in to attack the escorting fighters. He shot down a single Messerschmitt in his first attack. In his second attack he rammed a second enemy fighter in defence of his colleague, and in doing so he was killed.

The second sortie for this regiment took place not at 0630 hrs, but at 1030 hrs so there is a high probability that he is actually describing this battle. This also correlates with German data, in accordance with which at 1050 hrs a single I-16 was shot down by *Leutnant* Hans Beisswenger from 6./JG 54. Information however on the ramming by a Soviet pilot is not confirmed in German, nor even in Soviet documents.

A group of six Ju-88s appeared over Liepaja at 1050 hrs and this time none of the pilots from the 148th Fighter Air Regiment were kept back from the battle and 18 I-153s took off. However, the German bombers were already over the airfield and were able to drop their bombs with precision on the regiment's aircraft that were taking off. This sudden attack was successful because the Germans approached from the sea and the aerial reconnaissance posts were very late in detecting the enemy aircraft.

The Flight Commander, Political Instructor I.I. Milovanov, was injured by shrapnel from a bomb on take-off, his aircraft ground looped and was beyond economical repair. In an attempt to catch up with a departing Ju-88 the I-153 flown by Junior Lieutenant P.K. Chepur caught fire and crashed into a lake, the pilot was killed. The reason for this loss was fire from the gunners in the bombers, or alternatively the Soviets' own anti-aircraft artillery, which at that moment was firing intensively at the Junkers bombers. A further four 'Chaikas' sustained varying degrees of damage on the ground.

According to documents and the multitude of memoirs, the enemy lost one or maybe even two aircraft. For example the history of the 148th Fighter Air Regiment indicates that the Commander of the 4th Squadron Ya.E. Titayev and the Deputy Political Instructor of the 1st Squadron Senior Political Instructor V.V. Kudryavtsev shot down one German bomber each. The details in a political report written by Commissar Golovachev concern solely Titayev's victory. The former regimental pilot A.P. Degtyarev mentions in his memoirs a group victory over one enemy aircraft: 'During the course of the second attack we still managed to get airborne and we shot down a single Junkers in a group attack, which crashed into the sea.'

However, German information this time does not confirm a single victory. The pilots of the Junkers were most likely not planning in getting into an air battle. After dropping their bombs on the airfield they broke away into a dive, which their altitude of 3,000 m allowed them to do, and departed towards the sea. By all accounts Soviet pilots were able to get within firing range and mistook the diving aircraft for those that had been shot down. This was probably the most widely used approach to escape from a pursuit in the Second World War but Soviet pilots were not yet sufficiently skilled at these nuances, as they lacked experience.

As is evident from the combat chronicle, far from all the attacks on Soviet airfields reached their target and some of the raids were even countered by Soviet forces. However, the enemy that the Air Forces of the North-Western Front had been incumbent with was very tenacious and consistent in achieving their goals. By way of an example the headquarters of the VIII. *Fliegerkorps* reacted very quickly to their failure at Varena. In order that they turn the situation to their advantage it was decided that the allocation of forces for the new attack would be increased. Almost all the combat capable aircraft in the II./JG 52 were sent into battle. The German group intended to attack the airfields belonging to the 42nd Fighter Air Regiment were again divided into two echelons.

The first to approach at approximately 1045 hrs were the Bf 109Fs of the Stab 4./JG 52, led by experienced aces: Group Commander Captain *Hauptmann* Erich Woitke (who had amassed 11 victories during the course of preceding campaigns), and Commander 4./JG 52 *Oberleutnant* Johannes Steinhoff (who had amassed eight victories in the West). Despite the fact that Soviet fighters again managed to encounter the enemy in the air, this time success was on the *Luftwaffe's* side.

Senior Political Instructor Smirnov describes the twists and turns of the air battle that took place over the airfield:

> The aircraft on Varena and Perloja airfields were scrambled as Me-109s appeared overhead for a third time, in total approximately 20 aircraft. They engaged the Germans in combat at an altitude of 3,000–3,500 m. As a result of this battle two I-153s were set on fire in the air. The pilots Junior Lieutenant Karyukin, and Junior Lieutenant Antonov [this was most probably Antipov, since no pilot with the surname of Antonov was found in the nomenclature of the 42nd Fighter Air Regiment], luckily managed to bail out by parachute. Flight Commander Karyukin was injured in the left leg in the air and in the left side [he had been strafed by a Messerschmitt as he descended on his parachute[.
>
> During the course of the battle Me-109 aircraft that had broken formation descended and strafed the aircraft standing on the ground as well as the ditches where the personnel had sought shelter. Six I-153 aircraft were set on fire. No losses were incurred amongst the personnel.

The fact that the battle was a tense one and that it continued for around 15 minutes is visible both in Soviet documents, and in the claims submitted by German pilots concerning victories. The pilots of Stab 4./JG 52 in the period from 1048 hrs to 1100 hrs claimed seven I-15s shot down.

> *Oberfahnrich* Waldemar Semelka, 4./JG 52: an I-15 at 0948 hrs;
> *Feldwebel* Georg Mayr, 4./JG 52: and I-15 at 0950 hrs;
> *Oberleutnant* Carl Hartmann, Stab II./JG 52: an I-15 at 0950 hrs;
> *Unteroffizier* Bernhard Wilskiy, Stab II./JG 52: an I-15 at 0952 hrs;
> *Hauptmann* Erich Woitke, Stab II./JG 52: an I-15 at 0953 hrs south of Varena;
> *Oberleutnant* Johannes Steinhoff, 4./JG 52: an I-15 at 1000 hrs Varena;
> *Oberleutnant* Siegfried Simsch, 4./JG 52: an I-15 at 1000 hrs west of Varena.
> [The above times are Berlin time].

Despite the losses, Soviet fighters remained in the skies over the airfield while the German pilots broke off combat since their fuel and ammunition had run out. However, almost immediately after the first group had departed, aircraft from 5. and 6./JG 52 approached the airfield and the German pilots engaged the Soviet pilots in battle without delay, after replacing their exhausted colleagues. After this there was a break in the fighting, and the Germans claimed a further three victories over I-15s in the course of just four minutes from 1107 hrs to 1111 hrs. *Unteroffizier* Albrecht Hanika, who shot down an I-15 at 1107 hrs over Varena airfield, *Unteroffizier* Franz Gilhaus, who shot down an I-15 at 1108 hrs, and *Unteroffizier* Hermann Spengler, who shot down an I-15 at 1111 hrs over Varena airfield, all of whom were from 5./JG 52, stood out in this episode of air combat.

Senior Political Instructor Smirnov indicated that as a matter of fact the Germans did not manage to shoot down a single Soviet aircraft but a great number of I-153s were seriously damaged and at least one pilot made an emergency wheels-up landing, luckily the airfield was to hand so to speak. A further I-153 ground looped on landing due to battle damage and several pilots were injured in the course of air combat, and their aircraft were seriously damaged:

> One of the Me-109s engaged us in combat on a fourth approach, although no losses were incurred as a result with the exception of the two lower spars on Senior Lieutenant Likin's aircraft being penetrated with a round as well as the contours of other locations on Junior Lieutenant Mitin's aircraft having been shot through. On landing Junior Lieutenant Artemyev's aircraft ground looped, and Artemyev sustained some light bruising. On Junior Lieutenant Mitin's aircraft the undercarriage could not be lowered because the canopy and the air pipes had been shot through. He landed the aircraft successfully on its belly.

Soviet pilots fought desperately despite these most difficult of circumstances, as a result of which one Messerschmitt was shot down and crashed in the area around Perloja. Bf 109F-2 W.Nr.5780 was completely destroyed, and the extent of the damage this aircraft sustained according to the German classification was 100 percent. Interestingly in the losses listed by II./JG 52 there is no mention of which formation this aircraft had come from, or who was flying it. Naturally there is no way of telling from this at what point in the battle this took place and correspondingly who was the author of this victory from the Soviet side.

In a report written by the headquarters of the 57th Mixed Air Division concerning the results of the battle, a moment is described in which the Soviet pilots attempted to break off combat and land on the airfield, since by that time their fuel was running out. The German pilots took this as an opportunity to deal the enemy a decisive blow:

> The enemy subsequently continued its raids on these two airfields over the course of 20–40 mins, employing the following tactics: the Me-109s would not play an active role in the actual battle but would attempt to draw our I-153s up to a higher altitude. They would then bank away from them, and using their advantage in speed, they would then enter a dive and attack the aircraft that had landed in order to refuel.

Undoubtedly one of the factors behind the enemy's success was that despite the many enemy raids Soviet pilots had remained on one and the same airfields up until 1400 hrs. It has to be said that the Commander of the 57th Mixed Air Division Colonel Katichev back at 0910 hrs, that is to say immediately after the start of the third raid, put the question to the commanders of the Air Forces of the North-Western Front concerning the redeployment of the 42nd and 237th Fighter Air Regiments to other airfields. He however only received permission for the redeployment at 1400 hrs and by that time the 42nd Fighter Air Regiment had to a large extent lost its potential and had lost the majority of its aircraft.

Colonel Katichev, who had not received permission to redeploy the 42nd and the 237th Fighter Air Regiments tried to respond to the enemy's action using a clever tactic. The Commander of the 57th Mixed Air Division decided to act in accordance with Directive No. 3 written by the headquarters of the Air Forces of the North-Western Front, and one squadron from the 54th High-Speed Bomber Air Regiment received an order to prepare for a retaliatory strike on German airfields. Moreover for some reason it was thought that the enemy was operating from Gumbinnen. The following is taken from the operations report No. 1 written by the headquarters of the 57th Mixed Air Regiment: 'Ten aircraft from the 54th High-Speed Bomber Air Regiment departed to the holding area at 1020 hrs with subsequent orders to follow behind the enemy aircraft and to bomb them as they come into land at their airfields. THREE squadrons consisting of 19 aircraft are at combat readiness on operational airfields.'

Even this concept however was never to be realised, the Combat Journal of the 57th Mixed Air Division noted dryly: 'This order was not carried out owing to significant resistance.'

The enemy, who had mounted a 'significant' resistance to the crews of the 54th High-Speed Bomber Air Regiment were those same pilots of 5. and 6./JG 52. Evidently the Germans attacked as a squadron while the Soviet bombers were still in the 'holding area'. Thus instead of following the German aircraft from Stab II. 4./JG 52 and 'attacking them from behind as they landed on the airfields', the Soviet bombers themselves had to repel attacks by German fighters. The Commander of 5./JG 52 *Uberleutnant* August-Willhelm Schumann claimed two victories over DB-3s at 111 hrs and 1115 hrs. At 1115 hrs a further victory over a DB-3 was claimed by *Unteroffizie*r Alfred Lehrmann from 6./JG 52. Apart from that *Unteroffizier* Hermann Spengler claimed another victory over an SB although the time he gave of 1032 hrs does not correspond to the chronology of events, but it is possible that this is a strange typographical error and the victory was attained at 1132 hrs.

Soviet data confirms that as a result of this battle the 5th Squadron, 54th High-Speed Bomber Air Regiment lost three SB aircraft along with their crews.

Unfortunately this theoretically sound concept drawn up by the Commander of the 57th Mixed Air Division proved in practice to be easily broken down by the second wave of German fighters, and the Soviet bombers were not able to even begin to suppress the German aircraft, since they themselves were coming under attack from the enemy. Thus no retaliatory strike on a German airfield took place, although of course it could be said that in this case Colonel Katayev was very unlucky.

The air battle, which lasted for approximately 30 mins, culminated in a victory for the pilots of the *Luftwaffe* who were able to attack Varena and Perloja airfields despite the significant resistance mounted by the escorting fighters. Apart from that the Germans called off a retaliatory strike on their own base by Soviet strike aircraft.

Moreover it was likely that the losses incurred by the 42nd Fighter Air Regiment in the air were even more significant. Senior Political Instructor Smirnov only indicated in his report the losses incurred by the 1st and 4th Squadrons, and he did not have any information concerning the aircraft of the 2nd and 3rd Squadrons that were located on the neighbouring airfield. From an operational report 4/OP written by the headquarters of the Air Forces of the North-Western Front it is known that in the course of these air battles three I-153s from the 57th Mixed Air Division had been shot down. Apart from that, a report on the combat activities of the 57th Mixed Air Division between 22 June and 30 July 1941 the 42nd Fighter Air Regiment listed eight I-153s shot down in air combat and a further four that had failed to return from their combat sortie. Considering the fact that after 22 June the regiment all but withdrew from engaging in combat activity it is reasonable to suggest that the biggest proportion of these losses fell on the first day of the war itself, and specifically in this battle. A further confirmation of more significant losses for the 42nd Fighter Air Regiment was the information concerning the losses among the personnel of the 57th Mixed Air Division for 22 June. Aside from those pilots mentioned above it was recorded that pilots Junior Lieutenants A.A. Matyanov, N.A. Eliseyev, and V.I. Antipov were injured in the course of air combat. Thus the claims by German pilots of 11 I-15 aircraft shot down could have some actual basis in fact and the real losses in air combat were five to six I-153s, of which three were shot down, and a further two to three were damaged or were destroyed in emergency landings.

However it is impossible to establish who out of these Soviet pilots was shot down by the Germans and in what order due to a lack of detailed descriptions of this battle.

Soviet pilots were not sparing with the aircraft they shot down either, although it was true that their appetites were slightly more modest: according to the results of the battle the 42nd Fighter Air Regiment recorded two Bf 109s shot down, while in reality just a single Messerschmitt had been shot down. Once again establishing which of the Soviet pilots personally shot a German aircraft down, has not been possible using the documents, and only the list of commendations mentions a victory attained by Deputy Squadron Commander Lieutenant Fyodor Semyonovich Lyapin. Therefore this could be considered a group victory. According to a report written by Senior Political Instructor Smirnov, the following pilots excelled themselves in the course of the air battles: 'Senior Lieutenant Likin, Senior Lieutenant Malyakin, and Junior Lieutenants Karyukin, Yeliseyev, Martyanov, Antipov, and Mitin.'

Jumping forwards we note that this was in essence the first and only clash between Soviet and German fighters that could be called an air battle. Subsequent events unfolded in such a way that no other similar clashes took place in the skies over the Baltic region on the first day of the war.

Let us dwell on the reasons behind the events leading to the defeat of the 42nd Fighter Air Regiment. First and foremost the Germans outmanoeuvred the commanders of the regiment in a tactical sense, the last strikes had been inflicted by the *Luftwaffe* using large groups of between 12–20 Bf 109 aircraft each, separated by short time intervals. As a result there was neither the time, nor the possibility for the commanders or the pilots of the 42nd Fighter Air Regiment to find a way to counter this method of waging war. By 1000 hrs 21 serviceable I-153 aircraft remained on on Varena and Perloja airfields.

Secondly in a manoeuvring, group air battle the German aces of II./JG 52 had proved that an experienced pilot in a Bf 109 was very capable of outmanoeuvring an I-153, and moreover for a moment the Germans lost their quantitative advantage. The advantage that the enemy aircraft had, along with the pilot training, was enough to thin out the ranks of those defending the airfields in the air, if only to attack the aircraft themselves on the ground. Naturally German pilots did not attempt to out-turn the pilots of the 42nd Fighter Air Regiment but as the headquarters of the 57th Mixed Air Division noted so accurately: 'The Me-109s did not play an active part in the fighting but tried to draw our I-153s up to altitude, to then break away from them, and enter a dive using their advantage in terms of speed', that is to say they employed vertical combat tactics, attaining a convincing victory.

Summing up this chapter:

As a result of the third wave of raids on Soviet airfields the pilots of the *Luftwaffe* had overall gained air superiority in the Baltic direction. Alytus airfield had been attacked using mass raids and aircraft from the 236th Fighter Air Regiment, and the 42nd and 237th Fighter Air Regiments incurred significant losses on the ground and in the air, and their potential was reduced to just one squadron. Taking into consideration that the MiG-3 aircraft serving in the 15th Fighter Air Regiment had serious problems in terms of the operation of their armament, it can be said that the Soviet aircraft in the Alytus–Vilnius direction were in no position to put up any kind of adequate resistance at all by midday.

In the zone of responsibility of I. *Fliegerkorps* things for the Germans were not looking so rosy. Owing to a lack of fighters in the second wave of attacks the Soviet airfields in this direction suffered less of an impact. Nevertheless the pilots of I. *Fliegerkorps* possessed some good prerequisites for success. In fact, owing to the losses incurred by the 31st Fighter Air Regiment and the problems with the armament on the MiG-3s serving in the regiment, only aircraft from the 10th,

148th, and 238th Fighter Air Regiments were able to counter the German raids. However owing to the fact that all these units were based on airfields that the enemy had already reconnoitred well at Siauliai, Liepaja, Karmelava, Panevezys, and Kaunas and that these airfields had not been evacuated, the enemy had a superb opportunity to continue to inflict attacks on the targets they had studied so well.

Overall, however, it has to be said that despite the enemy's successes, the units and formations of the Air Forces of the North-Western Front still retained a very significant potential. Many of the airfields had still not been subjected to German attacks, and the units based on them had not incurred any losses and were ready to go into battle.

The I-153s from the 236th Fighter Air Regiment, on Alytus airfield, one of these photos was published in the German journal *Signal* in June 1941.

The I-153s from the 236th Fighter Air Regiment, on Alytus airfield, one of these photos was published in the German journal *Signal* in June 1941.

The pilot of a mixed group from the 2nd Squadron, 15th Fighter Air Regiment, and the 236th Fighter Air Regiment Senior Lieutenant Ivan Iosifovich Podolyanchik and Junior Lieutenants Dmitriy Savich Pashuk, and Pytor Mikhaylovich Koshelev, who failed to return from combat sorties to strafe German motorised columns in the area around Kalvarija.

Deputy Commander of the 4th Squadron, 42nd Fighter Air Regiment Senior Lieutenant Avenir Maksimovich Smirnov. Thanks to his report the details of the air battles over Orany airfield on 22 June 1941 became known.

German soldiers pose on the remains of an SB from the 46th High-Speed Bomber Air Regiment on Gruzdziai, June 1941.

SB and USB aircraft from the 40th High-Speed Bomber Air Regiment, which had been destroyed by German aircraft on Ventspils airfield, between 22–23 June 1941.

SB and USB aircraft from the 40th High-Speed Bomber Air Regiment, which had been destroyed by German aircraft on Ventspils airfield, between 22–23 June 1941.

SB and USB aircraft from the 40th High-Speed Bomber Air Regiment, which had been destroyed by German aircraft on Ventspils airfield, between 22–23 June 1941.

Pilot of the 10th Fighter Air Regiment Junior Lieutenant Vasiliy Sergeyevich Loboda, who was killed in air combat over Siauliai airfield.

An I-16 from the 10th Fighter Air Regiment shot down in the area around Siauliai.

A MiG-3, which had been transferred from the 42nd Fighter Air Regiment to the personnel of the 10th Fighter Air Regiment on 22 June on Siauliai airfield. Owing to structural defects with the weaponry these aircraft were not able to use their machine guns in combat, and were in fact not combat capable.

Pilot of the 148th Fighter Air Regiment Senior Political Instructor Ivan Ivanovich Milovanov, he was shot down on take-off from Liepaja airfield.

Pilot of the 148th Fighter Air Regiment Junior Lieutenant Pyotr Karpovich Chepur, he was killed in air combat over Liepaja airfield.

Captain Yakov Egorovich Titayev and Senior Political Instructor Viktor Vasilyevich Kudryavtsev, who claimed victories in air combat over Liepaja airfield, these however are not confirmed by German data.

An I-153 No. 69 from the 4th Squadron, 148th Fighter Air Regiment he made an emergency landing on Liepaja airfield on 22 June 1941, alongside him is an unserviceable U-2 liaison aircraft.

An I-153 from the 148th Fighter Air Regiment. These are aircraft from the list of unserviceable machines that had stood in a line together; also destroyed and damaged Ju-88 bombers from KG I on 22 June 1941.

Pilots of the 42nd Fighter Air Regiment who had distinguished themselves in air battles above Orany airfield on 22 June 1941. Flight Commander, Junior Lieutenant Nikolai Aleksandrovich Karyukin.

Junior Lieutenant Vladimir Ilyich Antipov.

Junior Lieutenant Aleksey Ivanovich Artemyev

Junior Lieutenant Mikhail Fedotovich Mitin.

Junior Lieutenant Aleksandr Amirovich Martyanov.

Deputy Squadron Commander Lieutenant Fyodor Semyonovich Lyapin, the only pilot in the 42nd Fighter Air Regiment to have a Me-109 downed on 22 June 1941 written into his documents relating to the conference of an award.

Deputy Squadron Commander Senior Lieutenant Nikolai Aleksandrovich Malyakin.

Flight Commander Lieutenant Aleksey Ivanovich Koltsvo, who subsequently became a Hero of the Soviet Union.

Junior Lieutenant Nikolai Andreyevich Yeliseyev.

An I-153 bearing the tactical No. 8 white from the 4th Squadron, 42nd Fighter Air Regiment, he made an emergency landing following a battle with Messerschmitts from II./JG 52 on 22 June. This is a later series aircraft, with one BS, and two ShKAS machine guns.

Commander of II./JG 52 *Hauptmann* Erich Woitke accepts congratulations after a successful combat sortie.

Commander of 4/JG 52 *Oberleutnant* Johannes Steinhoff.

Aircraft of the 42nd Fighter Air Regiment that were destroyed, and damaged on Orany and Perloja airfields on 22 June 1941.

Aircraft of the 42nd Fighter Air Regiment that were destroyed, and damaged on Orany and Perloja airfields on 22 June 1941.

Aircraft of the 42nd Fighter Air Regiment that were destroyed, and damaged on Orany and Perloja airfields on 22 June 1941.

4.5 The actions of the Air Forces of the North-Western Front on the Attacking Forces of the Wehrmacht and the Fourth Raid on the Soviet Airfields

Soviet losses in the course of the third wave were in the main predetermined by the circumstance that despite the enemy's morning attacks, the units of the Air Forces of the North-Western Front nevertheless remained at their pre-war bases. The only Soviet regiment that changed their place of deployment immediately after the first air attack was the 9th High-Speed Bomber Air Regiment, which was re-deployed from Panevezys to Skvarbai airfield, avoiding any subsequent losses on the ground.

It is hard to say now what reasoning the leadership of the Air Forces of the North-Western Front employed in continuing to base their aircraft on bases that had already been attacked once, but judging by documents that have survived, there were at least three factors at play here.

The first was that German aircraft had been active in small groups for the entire morning and did not inflict any significant losses on Soviet aviation units in the course of the first attacks. Intelligence report No. 3 written by the Headquarters of the Air Forces of the North-Western Front and timed at 1200 hrs states unambiguously: 'The enemy has still not introduced its air forces into the battle in any great numbers, and action is limited to individual groups and individual aircraft.'

Reports of losses in the first attacks on Soviet airfields were not so terrible, and what is more they arrived at Air Force headquarters late and incomplete. By way of an example even in operations report No. 4/OP written by the headquarters of the Air Forces of the Baltic Special Military District timed at a1900 hrs losses among the front line units for 22 June were given as just 35 bombers, and 30 fighters. Moreover data from all the units was included in this summary but it was just that the information was transmitted at different times and there were discrepancies in terms of how complete the information was. Thus in the information concerning the 6th Mixed Air Division only the losses incurred in the first raids on Liepaja and Ventspils and the four I-153s and four SBs that were destroyed in that raid were included, along with the 11 I-153s, and six SBs that were damaged. In terms of the 7th, 8th, and 57th Mixed Air Divisions only the data concerning the losses in the air were included in the operations report. In terms of the 8th Mixed Air Division the summary included data on the six I-153s from the 61st Ground Attack Air Regiment that were shot down. As far as the 7th Mixed Air Division was concerned 19 SBs and one I-153 is recorded as having been destroyed in air combat and not having retuned from their combat sorties. The data concerning the units of the 57th mixed Air Division the losses incurred in the first half of the day were taken into consideration; namely three I-153s from the 42nd Fighter Air Regiment, and 10 SBs from the 54th High-Speed Bomber Air Regiment.*

The second factor was undoubtedly the very complicated situation with respect to the operational airfields.

The construction of the majority of the airfields in the border zone was either unfinished or concrete runways had not been built on these airfields, which meant that aircraft from the bases that had been attacked could not be redeployed there. Behind the lines however there were a limited number of airfields and as such a retreat to the Western Dvina line would have put the units of the front line Air Forces in an even more difficult position and would force them to base either two to three or even four regiments on a single airbase.

The third, and most likely the most important factor was that the reserve units of the Red Army Air Forces were not mobilised and were at a standard peacetime strength. Moreover they were in the process of a reorganisation. In the overwhelming majority of the airfield servicing battalions

* Some of these aircraft subsequently returned to their airfields.

the materiel was at no more than a third of their wartime strength. By way of an example there were between fix to six refuelling tankers in each airfield servicing battalion while according to the standard there should have been 15. It is not hard to imagine how this could have influenced the situation on the first day of the war. After the redeployment of the air regiments to the second line airfields the airfield servicing battalions naturally followed suit but they were not able to move as quickly, which put the aviation units in a difficult position in terms of their supplies of fuel, and ammunition. The airfield servicing battalions located on the second line airfields were forced to service not one, but two, three, and even four regiments, which was absolutely impossible since these units had not been mobilised either.

Apart from that, on forward airfields large reserves of ammunition were amassed as well as fuel and lubrication supplies and the redeployment on the morning of 22 June from forward airfields, even to nearby airfields, automatically meant that over the next few hours aircraft at these airfields were left without their standard supplies. The reason for this was that the airfield servicing battalions were only supplied with one third the number of lorries and trailers and were not able to transport the required tonnage of cargo rapidly. Correspondingly, and as subsequent events were to prove, the majority of the reserves were destroyed or were left at the forward airfields.

Undoubtedly these circumstances also influenced the decision made by the front line air forces to leave their units on these airfields up to the very last moment.

After the enemy had inflicted the next series of raids it would appear that there was nothing to prevent the Air Forces of the North-Western Front from implementing Order No. 3 with immediate effect: 'Bombers are to proceed to the location of the enemy airfields and to bomb enemy aircraft as they come in to land.' However, front line command interfered in this process.

Colonel-General Kuznetsov had every reason, up until that moment, to suppose that the principal danger for the front line forces was not the *Luftwaffe* aircraft but the German tank groups, which by that time had broken through the thin alignment of front line forces on the border and which were heading in the direction of Siauliai and Vilnius at some speed. Thus at around 0830 hrs the 1st Panzer Division of the 4th Panzer Group was engaged in the fighting for Taurage and an hour earlier, at around 0730 hrs, German units of the 7th Panzer Division, 3rd Panzer Group had already seen fighting on the approaches to Kalvarija.

After receipt of the intelligence data, including that from aviation, the Commander of the North-Western Front took the decision to commence the concentration of forces, first and foremost the mechanised corps, in order to effect a counter-attack. It was not possible to do this quickly, owing to the considerable distance between the forces themselves and the theatre of operations. It was crucial to gain time, and for this to happen the enemy's onslaught had to be, if not stopped, then slowed. At that time only the Air Forces were capable of accomplishing this task.

The decisions that were taken were realised in the 'Directive of the Command of the North-Western Front, the Commander of the 8th and 11th Armies, the Commander of the 3rd and 12th Mechanised Corps on inflicting an attack on the enemy, that have broken through in the area around Taurage on 22 June 1941 at 0945 hrs.'

In the section relating to the actions of the air forces, the directive states: 'The Commander of Air Forces is to hit the Tilsit and Kalvarija enemy troop alignments with powerful attacks.'

The headquarters of the Air Forces of the North-Western Front in turn issued combat order No. 01/OP, in which the following orders were issued:

> Third. The Air Forces of the Baltic Special Military District over the course of 22 June 1941 are to destroy the enemy's ground forces in the areas around Klaipeda, Tilsit, Stallupönen, and Insterburg.

a) The 6th Mixed Air Division (minus the 40th Bomber Air Regiment) under the cover of the 15th Fighter Air Regiment and the 31st Fighter Air Regiment, 8th Mixed Air Division is to destroy [ground units and enemy aviation on the airfields] [the words in square brackets that have been crossed out, and the word 'tanks' is written in black ink] in the area around [Taurage, Tilsit, and Ragnit] [the words in square brackets are crossed out, and the words 'Kalvarija, Ladzijai, and Seree' are written in black ink. The 40th Bomber Air Regiment is to destroy enemy aviation as well as the enemy alignment in the area around Taurage, Tilsit, and Ragnit.
b) The 57th Mixed Air Division is to destroy [ground units and enemy aviation on the airfields] [the words in square brackets have been crossed out and the word: 'tanks' is written in black ink] in the area around [Bazdennen, and Pilkallen] [the words in the square brackets have been crossed out and the words: 'Lazdijai, and Seree' are written in black ink].
c) The 15th Fighter Air Regiment and the 31st Fighter Air Regiment are to provide cover for the actions of the 31st Bomber Air Regiment in the area around [Taurage, Tilsit, and Ragnit] [the words in square brackets have been crossed out, and the words 'Lazdijai, and Seree' have been written in black ink].
d) The 4th Mixed Air Division by 1200 hrs on 22 June 1941 are to redeploy to the following airfields: The 50th Bomber Air Regiment is to redeploy to Riga, the 63rd Bomber Air Group is to redeploy to Jelgava, and the 35th Bomber Air Regiment is to redeploy to Platone and be at readiness to go into action to destroy ground forces as well as enemy aviation in the area around Taurage, Tilsit, and Ragnit.
e) The other units in the 7th and 8th Mixed Air Divisions are to act in accordance with the plans put forward by the army commanders.
f) The 31st Bomber Air Regiment and the 31st Fighter Air Regiment are to meet above Kaunas at an altitude of 4,000 m.

Fourth. The first attack is to be carried out by: the 6th Mixed Air Division at 1200 hrs and the 7th Mixed Air Division at 1230 hrs on 22 June 1941.

The combat intensity is as follows: fighters and ground attack aircraft— three sorties a day as a regiment, while for the bombers this is to be two sorties as a regiment each day.

Sixth. The night crews in the bomber regiments are to prepare for night sorties in the area around Königsberg.

Seventh: The command post is to be located at Panevezys.

Thus the high command, this time the front line commander ordered General Ionov for the second time that morning to refuse to attack the German airfields. In the corresponding points in the order these tasks had been crossed out, and in their place were written orders to attack the enemy's mechanised units.

We are not in a position today to debate, or criticise Colonel-General Kuznetsov but we nevertheless note that if in the first instance he had brought a halt to Air Force operations in accordance with the decision from Moscow then any continuation of the decision to refuse to engage in combat for air superiority would have been entirely his decision. This decision, which finally put the Air Forces of the North-Western Front in a passive stance, played a fateful role and actually preordained the enemy victory as well as that of the *Luftwaffe* pilots in gaining air superiority by the end of the first day of the war.

A.G. Rytov in his memoirs notes that this order arrived at 6th Army Headquarters at around 1000 hrs and this haste can be explained by the fact that a preprepared order to attack the enemy airfields had actually been used as 'raw material', and this is confirmed by the hand-written corrections in the text of the printed order.

Aside from the 4th, 6th, 7th bomber regiments and the 57th Mixed Air Divisions mentioned in the order, 'Chaikas' from the 42nd and 148th Fighter Air Regiments also took part in the attacks on the advancing enemy columns, as well as a composite group from the 236th Fighter Air Regiment and the 2nd Squadron of the 15th Fighter Air Regiment, and the 61st Ground Attack Air Regiment. The first to take off at approximately 1000 hrs were the aircraft from the 61st Ground Attack Air Regiment.

Since the 4th and 5th Squadrons were yet to return from their raids, and moreover, time was needed to restore the runway that had been damaged by bombs the order for the first combat sortie was received by the 1st and the 2nd Squadrons in Risgonis. According to the 'History of the Regiment', in the first combat order (unfortunately the full text has not survived) an order was issued to attack enemy units in the area around Mariampol–Kalvarija–Lyubavas.

In the absence of squadron commanders the squadrons were led by their deputies: Senior Lieutenants M.R. Lebede, and T.A. Ryzhkin. It was they who were to become the leaders in the first combat sortie performed by ground attack aircraft belonging to the Red Army Air Force on German troops in the Great Patriotic War.

> The composition of the 2nd Squadron was as follows: M.R. Lebede, I.A. Dombrovskiy, L.N. Nikolayenko, M.V. Zabolotskiy, V.S. Soldatyenko, A.M. Miroshkin, A.M. Pleskach, N.A. Konstantinov, I.I. Khulap.
>
> The composition of the 1st Squadron was as follows: T.A. Ryzhkin, K.I. Yakovlev, I.E. Smyslov, P.I. Belyaev, A.R. Moskalenko, M.M. Martynov, P.I. Cherniy, Romanov, V.E. Nedelko (according to other data the third flight was made up of Senior Political Instructor A.M. Latugin, Senior Lieutenant G.S. Yenakev, and Junior Lieutenant V.I. Podlegayev).

Flying along a route from Risgonis–Kaunas–Mariampol–Kalvarija a group of nine aircraft led by Senior Lieutenant Lebed crossed the border in the area over the border town of Lyubavas (Lyubovo) and after flying deeper inside German territory, attacked concentrations of enemy forces. Apart from that, according to a report written by Soviet pilots it was a German field airfield that came under attack in this same area. The Soviet fighters came under fire from enemy anti-aircraft artillery over the target and the group were attacked on their way back by German fighters. Three 'Chaikas' were shot down by enemy anti-aircraft artillery as well as in the course of aerial combat and Junior Lieutenants N.A. Konstaninov, I.I. Khulap, and A.M. Pleskach went missing without trace. ('According to the political report only two I-153s were lost and Lieutenant Pleskach does not figure among the losses. Even if he was shot down he subsequently returned to his unit.') German pilots from III./JG 53 claimed victories in the area in which the 61st Ground Attack Air Regiment was active. At 1038 hrs south-west of Kalvarija an I-153 (identified as a DJ-6) was shot down by *Feldwebel* Hermann Neuhoff of 7./JG 53, while at 1044 hrs north of Kalvarija another 'Chaika' fell victim to *Leutnant* Herbert Schramm of 8./JG 53.

The 1st Squadron, which was led by Senior Lieutenant Ryzhkin attacked a column of enemy vehicles, which were moving in the direction of Mariampol. Despite the thick anti-aircraft fire all the pilots worked the target and according to the report up to 30 percent of the vehicles were destroyed. According to different sources one or two Soviet aircraft were shot down but the pilots were able to return to their airfields.

The principal strike force was to have been the bomber air regiments. This was how the assignment of these tasks for the units of the 6th Mixed Air Division was described by A.G. Rytov:

> This was the directive from the People's Commissariat for Defence [this relates to Directive No. 2 written by this same commissariat]. We are ordered to commence active combat operations. Fyodorov got up from the table—'Go on Commissar.'
>
> 'I have familiarised myself with the document and I am relieved: at last the ban had been lifted that had stifled the initiative of the commanders and cooled the enthusiasm for combat among our pilots.'
>
> The Staff Officer came in with a new order: to attack Königsberg, Klaipeda, and Taurage [this refers to the directive timed at 0945 hrs mentioned above].
>
> 'This means business!' Fyodorov's eyes were burning with the thrill of combat—'let's call Mogilevskiy.'
>
> The telephone operator put him through to Jelgava:
>
> 'Mogilevskiy? How are you? Is everything okay? Take the package out of the safe, open it, and do as it says.'
>
> At 1002 hrs our red star bombers set course for the west.

Memoirs are almost always a subjective thing, people are often inaccurate about the details owing to the passing of the years and the scale of the events that were unfolding at the time, and the memoirs of General Rytov are no exception. Let us not discuss the whole cosmic storyline of how the tasks were allocated to the Commander of the 40th High-Speed Bomber Air Regiment Major Mogilevskiy, and all the discussions that are described around it, suffice it to say that they could not have taken place on 22 June.

> ('The point being that Major Mogilevskiy as the head of the technicians component within the regiment was at that time on a refresher course at the Air Force Scientific Research Institute in Moscow and had not yet returned to his regiment(!) He was killed on his way back from Moscow, leading a group of Pe-2s, which were directly subordinate to the headquarters of the Air Forces of the North-Western Front.')

The main thing is that A.G. Rytov describes the chronology of the directives and orders in some detail, his only omission being that he mixes up the tasks from Directive No. 2 (which stated: 'Königsberg and Klaipeda are to be flattened') and the order issued by the Chief of Staff of the Air Forces of the North-Western Front No. 1/OP, which stated: 'Destroy enemy aviation and the enemy alignment around Taurage.' The advantage with his memoirs is that he mentions another waypoint: 'At 1002 hrs'. These words undoubtedly correspond to the events that were taking place and this is confirmed by the documents, albeit of course, with small corrections. Firstly, there is every chance that 1002 hrs was the time that the 'Directive issued at 0945 hrs' either arrived from the headquarters of the Air Forces of the North-Western Front at the headquarters of the 6th Mixed Air Division, or when the order left divisional headquarters for regimental headquarters. Secondly, as has been noted above, it could only have mentioned attacking enemy troops in the area around Tilsit (Taurage) and Kalvarija, without mentioning the fighting around Königsberg, and Klaipeda at all. Regimental documents confirm this hypothesis:

> Combat order No. 1 written by the headquarters of the 31st High-Speed Bomber Air Regiment 1030 hrs 22 June 1941. Jelgava...
>
> The enemy occupied the area around Kalvarija, concentrating a large number of tanks in this area.

The weather is clear.

2. The 31st High-Speed Bomber Air Regiment is to bomb the concentration of tanks in Kalvarija in two groups.
   a) The 1st group: 1st, 2nd, and 3rd Air Squadrons at 1245 hrs is to bomb concentrations of enemy tanks in the area around Kalvarija, the commander of the group is myself.
   b) The 2nd group: the 4th and 5th Air Squadrons at 1245 hrs are to bomb concentrations of tanks in the area around Kalvarija, the commander is Captain Petrov.
3. The route for the flight: The starting point of the route: Seduva–Kruki–Pilviskiai–on to the target. Kaunas–Sheduva–on to the end of the route.
4. The payload is made up of FAB-100 and FAB-250 bombs.
5. The formation is to comprise a column of nine aircraft, forming up in the area over Jelgava.
6. Subsequently the readiness level is to change to level 2 at 1545 hrs.
7. My command post in the air is as the leader of the first group, with Captain Vildyaskiy as Deputy.

The Commander of the 31st High-Speed Bomber Air Regiment Lieutenant-Colonel Dobysh.

Thus events were unfolding into a relatively logical plan: at 0945 hrs the headquarters of the North-Western Front sent a directive to the formations, at 1002 the headquarters of the 6th Mixed Air Division either received order No. 1/OP, or transferred on to the units within the division, and at 1003 hrs the headquarters of the 31st High-Speed Bomber Air Regiment signed the order for a combat sortie.

The crews of the 31st High-Speed Bomber Air Regiment were the first to act. According to operations report No. 2 and combat report No. 1 written by regimental headquarters the aircraft began to take-off at 1110 hrs.

A group of 38 SB aircraft was led personally by Regimental Commander Lieutenant-Colonel F.I. Dobysh, At 1220 hrs the aircraft were some six to seven kilometres south of Kalvarija and crews bombed concentrations of enemy tanks from an altitude of 2,000 metres. The regiment's aircraft were fired upon by small-calibre anti-aircraft artillery. Crews from the 1st and 3rd Air Squadrons recorded direct hits on enemy tanks, in total 18 FAB-250s and 174 FAB-100s were dropped. No losses and no bullet holes were incurred.

This raid was noted in a report written by the 84th Light Motorised Anti-Aircraft Artillery Battalion, which was providing cover for units of the 7th Panzer Division in the area around Kalvarija. According to data from German anti-aircraft artillery crews, a group of Soviet bombers attacked German forces at 1120 hrs Berlin time.

The 40th High-Speed Bomber Air Regiment commenced their action a little later and it is likely that this happened because of the lack of a regimental commander, and his deputy. According to the regimental Combat Journal the 18 SBs only took off at 1140 hrs from Piltene. The three groups of six—from the 3rd, 4th, and 5th Air Squadrons respectively—were led by the Commander of the 5th Air Squadron Captain Pankov. At 1250 hrs from an altitude of 2,500 metres the group bombed the concentration of German forces on the road between Taurage–Tilsit. The crews recorded direct hits. In the area around the target the aircraft were fired upon by anti-aircraft artillery, but without success. The only loss was navigator Lieutenant Popovich, who for reasons that are unclear baled out by parachute close to the target. The other aircraft came into land at 1412 hrs on Piltene airfield.

Meanwhile from Riga airfield at 1200 hrs nine SBs took off, they were led by the Deputy Commander of the Regiment Captain Lavrentsov. The group of nine aircraft comprised crews from the 1st and 2nd Air Squadrons of the 40th High-Speed Bomber Air Regiment and the Flight Commander's Courses from the 6th Mixed Air Division. The aircraft in the group from an altitude of 1,700 m bombed concentrations of German forces in the area around Tilsit. Despite the fact that in the area around the target the aircraft were fired upon by anti-aircraft artillery and were attacked by enemy fighters, crews recorded direct hits and returned without incurring losses. They landed back on Riga airfield at 1450 hrs.

At around this same time (at 1140 hrs) the commanders of the 57th Mixed Air Division sent eight SBs from the 54th High-Speed Bomber Air Regiment on a combat mission. Judging by order 01/OP, this was to bomb 'tanks' in the area around 'Ladzijai and Seree'. There is no reflection of this raid in Soviet documents.

The sortie by aircraft from the fighter regiments was delayed by the third wave of German raids. Nevertheless immediately after the units had pulled themselves together and had fuelled, and armed the aircraft, Soviet fighters began to participate in the battle.

According to the Combat Journal of the 57th Mixed Air Division at 1240 hrs 'Chaikas' from the 42nd Fighter Air Regiment attacked a German mechanised column. At around this same time pilots from the 2nd Squadron of the 15th Fighter Air Regiment and the 148th Fighter Air Regiment took off to fulfil their combat objective.

The Deputy Political Instructor of the 148th Fighter Air Regiment Golovachev confirms the times of these departures in his memoirs. He testifies to the fact that regimental command were finally convinced that the war had started after listening to a speech given by Molotov on the radio at 1200 hrs. It was after this speech that the aircraft took off to bomb German columns that were advancing towards Liepaja:

> At 1200 hrs, really after sensing that this was no 'provocation' but an actual war, we heard the voice of our Chairman of the Sovnarkom [this was how it was written in the original, but this refers to the Deputy Chairman of the Council of People's Commissars of the USSR V.M. Molotov] on the radio. He announced that as a result of the treacherous invasion by fascist Germany the Great Patriotic War had begun.
>
> After radio communications had been restored with divisional headquarters the regiment received an order: to be ready to attack the fascist columns that were moving along the roads, and to counter raids by fascist aircraft, and at the same time to strengthen ground defences on the airfield using the manpower and resources they had to hand, as well as envisaging the possibility of a rapid redeployment for combat operations from other airfields on the instructions of divisional headquarters.

The details of the sorties to attack the advancing German columns by aircraft from the 148th and 42nd Fighter Air Regiments and by the 2nd Air Squadrons of the 15th Fighter Air Regiment are absent from the archive documents. Therefore one has to be guided by the memoirs of the personnel themselves, and by German sources.

From the memoirs of the Commander of the 148th Fighter Air Regiment Zaystev: 'We made approximately six combat sorties in the course of the day on 22 June 1941 to bomb advancing mechanised columns but we of course did not succeed in stopping the Germans. We did however inflict sufficient losses on them since the columns were moving very fast, but were not camouflaged.'

A pilot from this same regiment, A.P. Degtyarev, adds more detail to the words of his commander: 'That day we succeeded in flying three to six combat sorties each either to intercept aircraft, or to carry out ground attacks.'

Nothing has yet been found concerning the actions of the 2nd Squadron of the 15th Fighter Air Regiment, not even memoirs, and what is clear is simply that the squadron was active around the Mariampol–Kalvarija area along with the 61st Ground Attack Air Regiment. This is confirmed circumstantially by the fact that a pilot from this squadron, Lieutenant V.S. Sharonov, was shot down directly over the Mariampol region and was taken prisoner. According to German data *Leutnant* Erich Schmidt from 9./JG 53 recorded one I-153 shot down at 1235 hrs.

The actions undertaken by Soviet fighters and ground attack aircraft are mentioned several times in German documents. Thus the history of the *Wehrmacht's* 6th Infantry Division notes that at around midday a large group of Soviet aircraft attacked a column of this division. The division was advancing towards Kalvarija so it was possible that the aircraft that attacked the Germans could have been 'Chaikas' from the 61st Ground Attack Air Regiment, or from the 15th Fighter Air Regiment unless of course the times have been mixed up:

> At midday the division was attacked by 20 Russian aircraft, that broke off from their combat formation when they were attacked by five German fighters. In the space of five minutes five Russian aircraft had been shot down, while the others had vanished. Unfortunately one Russian aircraft crashed next to one of the division's marching columns, exploded and drenched the artillery battalion headquarters located there in burning aviation fuel.

According to the memoirs of the divisional doctor 15 men lost their lives, while reports of five Soviet aircraft having been shot down are obviously exaggerated.

The Germans meanwhile continued their military activity in accordance with their plan. *Luftwaffe* raids had already taken on the form of a 'carousel' and it was easy to nominally draw a line between the end of the third raid and the start of the fourth raid. This time around the aircraft of the I. and VIII. *Fliegerkorps* began to act almost in synclwith one another, raids began at 1130 hrs Moscow time at the same time as some of the aircraft that had taken part in the preceding wave of attacks had just come into land.

The first to come under attack again at 1130 hrs was Alytus airfield. According to Soviet information it was attacked by a large group of 25 German aircraft.

Significant resistance, of the type that the German aircraft encountered in the area around Siauliai, forced the commanders of the I. *Fliegerkorps* to undertake a series of attacks that were similar to those that the VIII. *Fliegerkorps* had undertaken an hour earlier on Orany and Perloja airfields.

At 1201 hrs some 16 I-16s from the 10th Fighter Air Regiment took off to intercept the first group of German aircraft but the enemy managed to evade them. The 'Ishaks' did manage to counter the next attack however, which was carried out by 12 Ju-88s at 1240 hrs. A pair of German bombers only succeeded in dropping two bombs on the airfield at 1300 hrs, when the Soviet aircraft had broken off to land. ('The time of their landing according to the Combat Journal of the 7th Mixed Air Division was noted as 1305 hrs.')

According to a report written by the headquarters of the II./KG 76 dated 22 June 1941, two Ju-88s conducted a combat sortie between 1044–1232 hrs Berlin time. As a result of the bombing of the airfield in Siauliai five single-engine and one four-engine aircraft were destroyed.

The Germans of course exaggerated their figures to some extent, from the combat journal of the 7th Mixed Air Divison we know that: 'Two bombers dropped around eight bombs in the vicinity of the airfield.' There is no information concerning losses, although of course there is a possibility that the Germans bombed the old, Latvian aircraft on the edge of the airfield.

No sooner had the technicians finished fuelling the aircraft than another group of bombers appeared over Siauliai at 1335 hrs.

This time it was aircraft from the II./KG 76, a sortie conducted by a pair of Ju-88s from the 6./KG 76 between 1138–1325 hrs Berlin time. A report on this group indicates: 'A raid on Siualiai airfield. No results of the raid have been recorded owing to an attack by fighters.'

In this attack the Germans evidently did not go near the airfield, at least, in Soviet documents there is no mention of this at all. This is not surprising, however, since 19 I-16s were scrambled to counter the raid (this amounted to the entire complement of serviceable aircraft in the regiment). They took off at 1341 hrs. Evidently the German crews were not up to reviewing the results of this bombing raid. Soviet fighters pursued them and attacked the Junkers aircraft right up to the border, one of the German aircraft was hit and only the gunner/radio-operator was killed.

Nevertheless the Germans succeeded in breaking away and returning to their own airfield. According to German information, as a result of the attack in the area around Siauliai Ju-88A-5 W.Nr.2277 bearing the number F1+EP was damaged. Moreover the gunner who was killed, *Bordschutze Feldwebel* E. Markl was an experienced aviator, and had won awards, including the Iron Cross 1st Class.

One Soviet fighter was shot down by anti-aircraft artillery in the area around Taurage and the pilot managed to bale out of the aircraft by parachute.

In contrast to Orany airfield, which was attacked by the newest Bf 109F fighters, it was Ju-88s from 76 KG that were active against the 10th Fighter Air Regiment in Siauliai without fighter cover, and it was this that enabled Soviet pilots to beat back practically all the enemy attacks, whilst incurring minimal losses.

Things were much more difficult for the personnel of the 31st Fighter Air Regiment. According to the memoirs of Boris Vladimirovich Veselovskiy the Germans attacked Karmelava airfleld once again at around midday, and mixed groups of bombers or fighters attacked the airfield within short bursts of time. Since the guns on the MiG-1/3s did not work, however, there was no possibility of countering these raids:

> Right at the critical moment the regiment found itself unarmed. Sensing the impunity, the enemy aircraft became more aggressive. The bombers came towards us group after group. In the intervals between the bombs exploding the fighters would attack any target they could find on the airfield. They literally went after each of us individually.
>
> The airfield was completely covered in craters and upturned boulders. Losses among personnel turned out to be high. The dead were lying next to the aircraft hard standings here and there in pools of clotted blood.
>
> At around 1200 hrs a horse appeared with a cart from the direction of a neighbouring village.
>
> This was our catering staff bringing our lunch to the airfield. They were dressed in floral pattern dresses and small scarves. Our squadron was the first one they had come to. Almost everyone, apart from me, had lost their appetite. I quickly ate a few portions of seconds and some compot. The girls had not yet left the airfield, when enemy bombers appeared. It was likely that they could easily see the floral dresses the girls were wearing.
>
> Their entire cargo of bombs was emptied onto our squadron. The excavated earth trench ended up chock full of people. The earth shuddered and shook as though it were alive. Suddenly a silence came over us.
>
> I was not able to get out from under the weight of the people lying on top of me straight away. Flight Commander Kurovskiy ended up on the top. Evidently he had not managed to get fully into the trench, and his body was cut all over with shrapnel. Not far from the trench a wheel from the cart was sticking up out of the ground. The horse had vanished. Fragments of women's clothing could be seen, white with dark blue spots.

> The starboard undercarriage leg of my aircraft had been broken and the aircraft lay on its wing, oil leaked out of a bullet hole in the engine in black streaks.

After Veselovskiy's memoirs were published one popular author proposed that the veteran had simply made up this episode for a witticism so to speak. However in the documents that were maintained by the 213th Airbase, which served the 31st Fighter Air Regiment, these events are recorded, and amongst other losses the loss of catering workers was noted. Although this was written relatively dryly, specifically as befits similar documents:

> On 22 June 1941 by the end of the day the following had dropped out of the formation following raids by enemy aircraft: four people had been killed, of whom two chauffeurs were killed as they were carrying out their duties servicing the flights, the Head of the Red Army Canteen as they were giving out lunches to the pilots, and one gunner was killed in the line of duty. Two people were wounded. Vehicles were destroyed as a result of the bombing of the airfield, these were: a BZ, a BMZ, a BP, and a wheeled tractor, a BZ was damaged and required an intermediate repair.

At around 1230 hrs 23 Bf 109Es from II./JG 27 attacked Vilnius airfield using SD-2 bombs ('the time of the raid was between 1155–1310 hrs.') Unfortunately the documents of the 57th Mixed Air Division did not record the time or the outcome of the raid. However the availability of a large number of German photographs taken after the capture of Vilnius and which show dozens of Soviet aircraft damaged and destroyed leaves no doubt that the majority of them were destroyed by these same SD-2 bombs that were carried by the Bf 109Es.

While the *Luftwaffe* aircraft methodically worked on the Soviet airfields, a start was made on realising the directives issues by the Commander of the North-Western Front at 0945 hrs using three bomber regiments of the 6th and 57th Mixed Air Divisions ('regiments under the 4th and 7th Divisions were still not yet ready to undertake combat sorties by that time.') Despite the fact that the task had been formally carried out by Soviet bombers, it has to be said that the small number of aircraft that had been mobilised for these raids, and the raid was conducted by 73 bombers, and more than likely, the same number of I-153s carrying bombs themselves, were not able to inflict any kind of significant damage on the advancing German forces.

German Air Defences missed a whole series of attacks and did not pose any kind of a threat to Soviet attack aircraft. Losses of several I-153s occurred as a result of random collisions as the German fighters were taking off on other missions.

It has to be said that in accordance with the order issued by the Commander of the Air Forces attack groups of Soviet bombers should have had a fighter escort but for various reasons these plans were never realised. The majority of the fighters in the Air Forces of the North-Western Front were engaged in countering German raids on their own airfields and the *Wehrmacht*'s attack forces, but even this did not pass without its share of curious incidents. Thus the 4th Squadron of the 21st Fighter Air Regiment took off at 1200 hrs to escort a group of nine SB aircraft made up of crews from the 40th High-Speed Bomber Air Regiment and the Flight Commander's Courses from the 6th Mixed Air Division, which were supposed to attack German forces in the area around Tilsit. Owing to poor navigational training among Soviet pilots, however, 10 type 17/28 I-16s led by Squadron Leader Captain Nestayanov managed to get themselves lost over their own territory. While the leader found the airfield some of the aircraft used up all their fuel and five I-16s made emergency landings. As a result two aircraft were completely destroyed, while a further two were damaged, which required repairs in stationary workshops to put right. Considering the difficulties with the evacuation of damaged aircraft it is not hard to suppose that in fact all four aircraft were lost.

The crews in the SB aircraft and the I-153s bombed the *Wehrmacht* columns almost without losses, since the majority of German fighters at that time, having attacked Soviet airbases, were either undergoing technical ground servicing or were heading back to their home bases. Considering that at around this same time aircraft from the 125th and 128th High-Speed Bomber Air Regiments on the Western Front were working targets in the area around Suwalki, including German airfields, also without losses, a bold conclusion can be made that if strike aircraft from the Air Forces of the North-Western Front had attacked German airfields at that time, the resistance would also have been minimal.

The following should be noted in summing up this chapter.

The actions of the Soviet bombers that were unopposed in the areas close to the German airbases provides a basis to affirm that the decision taken by the commanders of the North-Western Front to strike the advancing enemy troops using all of their Air Forces and the refusal to attack German airfields was, at the very least, reckless. The enemy was very vulnerable right at that moment. After subsequent attacks on Soviet bases *Luftwaffe* aircraft were located on their airfields, and were being refuelled, rearmed, and were undergoing servicing. It is also obvious that in the situation that had unfolded the decision to use what was by no means a small number of fighters for ground attack sorties on German troops was an irrational one. Moreover that the Commander of the Air Forces of the North-Western Front had only just issued a warning in his order: 'Fighter aviation should be used sparingly to counter raids by enemy aircraft.'

It should also be pointed out that the Commanders of the *Luftwaffe* despite the fulfilment of the principal task on the neutralisation of Soviet aviation, could have divided their forces so that some of them would be used against Soviet ground targets and logistic targets. Moreover aside from the dive bomber squadrons specialising in this field, individual bomber squadrons would periodically operate the same combat sorties, along with fighter units. By way of an example according to the testimony of Heinz Knoke, 6./JG 52 Red Army forces were engaged in low level attacks for the entire day. Apart from that the German headquarters held a proportion of their forces in reserve. Thus the crews of the II./KG 76 from the I. *Fliegerkorps* conducted just six combat sorties in the first half of the day and began to become actively involved only after 1500 hrs Moscow time.

The Commander of the Air Forces of the North-Western Front did not, it would appear, have the required experience to be able to take a similar decision, nor did General Ionov want to disperse his own forces to perform different tasks. Apart from that the Commander of the Air Forces could simply have ordered the directive written by the front line commander be carried out with all available forces. One way or another, or to all intents and purposes, for the second time that morning owing to the instructions issued by higher levels of command General Ionov could not have used the advantageous circumstances to try and turn this situation to his advantage.

By midday the air war over the Baltic region had turned into an 'open conflict' in which the enemies attacked each other, all but forgetting about the need for defence. However the *Luftwaffe* units were not capable of inflicting significant losses on the Air Forces of the North-Western Front in the course of the constant raids on Soviet airfields. The refusal, however, to conduct retaliatory attacks on enemy airbases enabled the Germans to carry out their work calmly and methodically.

Deputy squadron commanders of the 61st Ground Attack Air Regiment Senior Lieutenants Mikhail Romanovich Lebed, and Timofey Andreyevich Ryzhkin. It was these commanders who were to become the leaders of the first combat sortie for Red Army Air Force ground attack aviation in the Great Patriotic War.

Pilots of the 2nd Squadron, 61st Ground Attack Air Regiment who perished in a combat sortie: Lieutenant Ivan Ivanovich Khulan, and Junior Lieutenant Nikolai Alekseyevich Konstantinov.

Commander of the 5th Squadron, 40th High-Speed Bomber Air Regiment Vasiiliy Alekseyevich Pankov, he led a sortie by a composite group of the regiment's aircraft from Piltene airfield to bomb German motorised columns on the road between Taurage–Tilsit.

Deputy Commander of the 40th High-Speed Bomber Air Regiment Captain Illarion Fyodorovich Lavrentsov. He led a sortie from Riga airfield by a composite group of aircraft from the 40th High-Speed Bomber Air Regiment and from the flight commander's courses from the 6th Mixed Air Division, to bomb a concentration of German forces in the area around Tilsit.

An I-153 that has been shot down and which made an emergency landing in the area around Mariampole. Judging by the markings on the aircraft this machine belonged to the composite group from the line-up of the 236th Fighter Air Regiment and the 2nd Squadron, 15th Fighter Air Regiment, this group operated from Vincai airfield.

The Commander of the 236th Fighter Air Regiment Lieutenant Vasiliy Semyonovich Sharonov, and was shot down and ended up as a prisoner of war on 22 June in the area around Mariampole.

An aerial photograph of the Karmelava airfield, which was taken by as German reconnaissance aircraft on the evening of 22 June 1941. Some 36 MiG-1/3 and I-16 aircraft from the 31st Fighter Air Regiment that were either destroyed, or damaged are visible on the airfield, these aircraft were abandoned during the evacuation.

An aerial photograph of Vilnius airfield taken by a German reconnaissance aircraft on 22 June 1941. The aircraft hard standings are visible in the photograph, as well as the construction work to build a standard concrete runway.

I-153 and I-15bis aircraft of the 42nd Fighter Air Regiment and Ar-2s and SBs from the 54th High-Speed Bomber Air Regiment, which were destroyed, and damaged on Vilnius airfield on 22 June 1941.

I-153 and I-15bis aircraft of the 42nd Fighter Air Regiment and Ar-2s and SBs from the 54th High-Speed Bomber Air Regiment, which were destroyed, and damaged on Vilnius airfield on 22 June 1941.

I-153 and I-15bis aircraft of the 42nd Fighter Air Regiment and Ar-2s and SBs from the 54th High-Speed Bomber Air Regiment, which were destroyed, and damaged on Vilnius airfield on 22 June 1941.

Commander of the 4th Squadron, 21st Fighter Air Regiment Captain Ivan Mikhaylovich Nestoyanov.

MiG-3s bearing the tactical Nos. 2 and 13 red from the 1st Squadron of the 15th Fighter Air Regiment, which were abandoned on Potsunai airfield due to damage and the absence of trained crews.

Pilots of the 15th Fighter Air Regiment, which were shot down in air combat over Potsunai airfield on 22 June 1941. Deputy Regimental Commander Captain Ivan Alekseyevich Dolzhenko was killed in combat.

Commander of the 1st Squadron Senior Lieutenant Nikolai Nikolayevich Boyarshinov, who was killed in combat.

Flight Commander Lieutenant Ivan Ivanovic Shultz, who was killed in combat.

Flight Commander Lieutenant Mikhail Mikhaylovich Kardenov, who was killed in combat.

Squadron Adjutant Senior Lieutenant Viktor Sergeyevich Martynenko, who was killed in combat.

Flight Commander Lieutenant Ivan Ivanovich Matveyev, he was shot down in combat.

Commander of the II./JG 53 *Hauptmann* Wolf-Dietrich Wilcke, who was the leader of the Headquarters Flight from III./JG 53, in air combat over Potsunai airfield, he attained one victory.

The Technical Officer of the III./JG 53 Headquarters *Leutnant* Jurgen Harder in air combat over Potsunai airfield, he attained one victory.

Headquarters Officer from III./JG 53 Oberleutnant Friedrich Klauss Kleist-Füssen in air combat over Potsunai airfield, he attained two victories.

Headquarters officer of the III./JG 53 *Oberleutnant* Friedrich Karl-Muller in air combat over Potsunai, he attained two victories.

A SB bearing the tactical No. 9 from the 40th High-Speed Bomber Air Regiment, which made an emergency landing owing to combat damage, June 1941. The emblem of the 40th High-Speed Bomber Air Regiment a small, stylised lightning symbol has been applied to the upper section of the rudder.

Major Trautloft who made an emergency landing following a battle with an SB from the 40th High-Speed Bomber Air Regiment.

An SB from the 4th Squadron, 40th High-Speed Bomber Air Regiment the pilot was Junior Lieutenant Aleksandr Vasilyevich Antiforov, the navigator was Junior Lieutenant Ryzhkov, and the gunner/radio-operator was Junior Sergeant Ryzhkov. He made an emergency landing as a result of the direct hit from an anti-aircraft shell in the starboard engine, on Siauliai airfield on 22 June 1941.

Another SB bearing the tactical No. 2 from the 40th High-Speed Bomber Air Regiment, which made an emergency landing as a result of battle damage, in June 1941.

Pilots of the 42nd Fighter Air Regiment who attained an aerial victory over an Me-109 on the evening of 22 June 1941 over Vilnius. Flight Commander Junior Lieutenant Ivan Sergeyevich Zudilov and Squadron Adjutant Senior Lieutenant Nikolai Yefimovich Linchevskiy.

A Bf 109F from II./JG 52 in June 1941.

Oberfeldwebel Josef Kronschnabel tells his comrades about the circumstances of an air battle.

4.6 The Redeployment of the Air Forces of the North-Western Front to the Second Line Airfields, the Subsequent Action Against the Forces of the Wehrmacht, and the Afternoon Raids by the Luftwaffe on Soviet Airfields

It should not go unnoticed that on the first day of the war the commanders of the *Luftwaffe* air corps and the air fleets were active in a way that enabled flexibility from a tactically perspective, and depending on how the environment changed, would introduce changes into the plans with efficiency and responded suitably to emerging threats. After a series of Soviet attacks in the middle of the day on *Wehrmacht* forces, German airfields, and logistics units *Luftwaffe* command retained their presence of mind and did not shy away from the next wave of attacks on Soviet airfields. The rest of the tasks also remained unchanged and some of the sub-divisions continued their attacks on the Red Army's logistics assets and their close support of troops on the battlefield. In response to Soviet raids a decision was taken to allocate several squadrons of Bf 109F interceptors, which immediately began to fly patrols over the *Wehrmacht's* forward columns.

One of the few mistakes the Germans made was their delayed reaction to the withdrawal of Soviet aviation from forward bases to airfields behind the lines. General Ionov had already proved his unusual capabilities by his previous actions and subsequently he was to continue to take sensible decisions, which corresponded to the environment that was unfolding. Aleksey Pavlovich understood very well that any subsequent basing on forward airfields would in the end lead to a loss of the combat capabilities of the units in the first echelon. Therefore despite all the negative aspects of this decision, immediately after the ground attacks had been undertaken against German columns the commanders of the Soviet divisions and regiments based on 'first line' airfields were given an order to redeploy to the 'second line' airfields; Riga, Jelgava, Platone, Risgonis, Markshtava, Daugavpils, and so on.

The permission to evacuate the aircraft of the 42nd and 237th Fighter Air Regiments from Orany and Perloja airfields was received, according to various sources, between 1300–1400 hrs. According to a report written by Senior Political Instructor Smirnov this order reached his squadron at 1500 hrs: 'At 1500 hrs an order came through to redeploy to the Jonava landing site, which was located some 30 km to the north-east of Kaunas [this refers to Risgonis, and Markshtava airfields]. Six serviceable aircraft made the redeployment, the rest remained on the airfield. The remaining personnel began to prepare for the redeployment.'

In total 13 I-153s were capable of departing on the redeployment from Orany and Perloja airfields, which represented the last serviceable examples from both regiments. Unfortunately as it came into land in Risgonis airfield an I-153 flown by the Commander of the 42nd Fighter Air Regiment Major Belousov crashed. It is possible that fatigue and stress from 10 hrs of almost continuous combat had taken its toll. The aircraft was destroyed and Konstantin Emelyanovich was seriously injured. ('Owing to a tragic confluence of circumstances Major K.E. Belousov was taken prisoner in hospital in Daugavpils by German forces. As a result of which he made several escape attempts, but was unsuccessful. He died in captivity.')

At around that same time at approximately 1500 hrs the 148th Fighter Air Regiment was redeployed to Riga. Technician S.A. Ovchinnikov recalls how even the technicians in the regiment left Liepaja airfield between 1600 hrs and 1700 hrs on 22 June:

> The Regimental Commander Comrade Zaitsev issued an order following his return from a combat sortie [this refers to the first attack sortie]: the rest of the aircraft were to land, be primed, inspected, refuelled, and rearmed with ammunition. They are to depart and land in Riga and we ourselves are to depart for Riga once we have sent all the aircraft there, the redeployment is to take place today. Our 148th Fighter Air Regiment has fought very

> courageously with the enemy for the entire first day, and only on receipt of an order from above did we depart our home base.
>
> The regiment's technical personnel were sent in groups from the airfield to Riga. Our group—which consisted of 15 men—left the airfield at approximately 1600–1700 hrs that day, the first day of the war, after all the aircraft that could be readied for take-off had departed. Only then did we leave our airfield.

According to Battalion Commissar Golovachev's memoirs 40 I-153 aircraft were able to fly from Liepaja to Riga.

At the same time at around 1500 hrs the 10th Fighter Air Regiment was evacuated from Siauliai to Platone airfield. In total 25 serviceable aircraft were successfully ferried: 22 I-16s and three MiG-3s [the latter were from a total of 19 aircraft allocated to the 42nd Fighter Air Regiment].

The 238th Fighter Air Regiment redeployed to Skverbai airfield with six I-153s. Seven I-15bis aircraft from the 240th Fighter Air Regiment transferred to Daugavpils.

It should be noted that the stories that have wandered from publication to publication since the 1990s, that German soldiers forced their way onto Alytus and Orany airfields in the middle of the day on 22 June, destroying Soviet aircraft based there, do not correspond to reality.

By way of an example the forward columns of the *Wehrmacht*'s German 7th Panzer Division hurried along the road past Alytus airfield, which means they did it very quickly and without making any unnecessary noise, in approximately three hours. Thus a report written by the 128th Airfield Servicing Battalion indicates that the personnel calmly observed the German armoured vehicles passing the airfield, and completely genuinely mistook them for Soviet vehicles!

Interestingly a German forward detachment, that had captured the 'northern' bridge across the River Neman, which was within visual range of the airfield, went further east, and having captured a commanding height, dug themselves in at this location and awaited the approach of the main forces. Apart from that the Germans did not have anything specifically to do on the airfield, since by the afternoon in Alytus out of the 24 I-153s based there two were shot down in air combat, one was destroyed on landing as a result of battle damage, while the rest were destroyed or were seriously damaged as a result of 10 raids by the *Luftwaffe* [this refers to all the attacks on the airfield, including those conducted in the course of one raid].

The Germans appeared on Alytus airfield after 1500 hrs, when a considerable proportion of the materiel and the personnel in the 128th Airfield Servicing Battalion had already set off in formation towards Kaunas. In the area around the airfield the enemy succeeded in firing on the last vehicles as they left: a fire engine and a battery charging station.

The personnel of the 42nd and 237th Fighter Air Regiments and the airfield servicing battalions evacuated Orany and Perloja airfields completely, without any problems, when the Germans were still some distance away. Moreover after around 1500 hrs when the serviceable aircraft left Oran and Perloja, the Germans flew another three raids against the airfield. From a report written by Senior Political Instructor Smirnov:

> The remaining personnel began to prepare for the redeployment and another three raids were directed against the airfield during this preparatory period by Me-109s and Me-110s. As a result all the remaining aircraft on this airfield were set on fire. The fuel storage depot, which held around 140 tonnes of fuel was set ablaze by Military Technician 2nd class Kharchenko as he left the airfield.
>
> Owing to a lack of organisation, the personnel who did not have access to vehicles were forced to walk to the station at Varena II, a distance of 13 km, and they were strafed more than once on the journey. The personnel did not incur any losses. From Varena II to Vilno is

a distance of 120 km and the personnel covered this distance on foot and only two or three men each were able to gain access to the vehicles belonging to the units departing Alytus.

As a result of the receipt of the order to redeploy to second line airfields the aircraft from the 21st and 49th Fighter Air Regiments were not able to engage in combat, although it was decided that these units would be used in combat activity.

Thus according to the Combat Journal of the 57th Mixed Air Division at 1330 hrs two squadrons in the 49th Fighter Air Regiment were redeployed to Vilnius airfield. However just half an hour later the Commander of the Air Forces sanctioned the withdrawal of forces and the pilots of the 49th Fighter Air Regiment returned to Daugavpils without having fought in a single air battle.

While the German pilots were resting and eating and the technical specialists were preparing their aircraft for the next sortie, the flywheel of the Soviet air attacks continued to turn.

At 1500 hrs 18 SBs from the 9th High-Speed Bomber Air Regiment took off to carry out their second bombing raid of the day. This day the targets for the crews were the outskirts of Tilsit, but more specifically the concentrations of German forces. Owing to the fact that the regiment's flight echelon differed from that of regimental headquarters because of the redeployment to Skverbai, very few details about this raid have survived. In a short report written by the Deputy Commander of the regiment's political section Battalion Commissar Dorofeyev records only that the missions was carried out successfully, for which he received the thanks from the Commander of the North-Western Front Colonel-General Kuznetsov. In the area around the target anti-aircraft artillery shot down the Commander of the 1st Squadron Captain Lukin's and Flight Commander Lieutenant Kormakov's aircraft (with the exception of the navigator from Kormakov's crew Lieutenant G.S. Turukhin, who was killed whilst still in the air, all the rest of the crew members returned to their regiment successfully).

Immediate cover for Tilsit was provided by the 272nd Stationary Anti-Aircraft Artillery Battalion, and apart from that in the area around the concentration of forces from the XXXXI Tank Corps (close to Tilsit–Taurage) the following were located: the 1st Battalion of the 3rd Anti-Aircraft Artillery Regiment, 2nd Battalion of the 23rd Anti-Aircraft Artillery Regiment, and the 92nd Light Anti-Aircraft Artillery Battalion. It was these same anti-aircraft artillery that, according to the results of the 22 June quite simply became the bane of the crews of the 9th High-Speed Bomber Air Regiment. Over the course of the day German anti-aircraft crews shot down five of the regiment's aircraft, and these results do command respect even for an enemy. The quality of the training German Air Defence System crews was excellent.

At around 1530 hrs a group of nine DB-3Fs from the 207th Long-Range Bomber Air Regiment, 3rd Long-Range Bomber Air Corps bombed columns of vehicles belonging to the 3rd Panzer Group in the area around Merkine–Leptuny, and in this case no resistance was encountered in the air. German technicians and mechanics still required time to prepare the aircraft for a sortie. *Luftwaffe* units would be ready by approximately 1530–1600 hrs, and at that time the first aircraft began to start up and by 1600–1630 hrs groups of German fighters and bombers once again attacked Soviet airfields.

At 1610 hrs a group of four Bf 109s tried to attack Panevezys airfield. This time the pilots of the 238th Fighter Air Regiment were able to interrupt the enemy, and the Germans were not able to drop their bombs accurately. Not a single aircraft was damaged on the ground, but the Germans settled the score in the air. Junior Lieutenant K.P. Velikanskiy was injured in the skies above the airfield, and although the pilot was able to land in the conventional way and save his aircraft.

Soviet documents and memoirs record the time of the bombing, thus according to the Combat Journal of the 57th Mixed Air Division at 1630 hrs Vilnius airfield was attacked by 12 Bf 109s. As a result structures and aircraft were set on fire, four Red Army soldiers were killed and four injured. According to German information 23 Bf 109s from II./JG 27 participated in this raid.

At 1710 hrs 12 Do 17s escorted by Bf 109s bombed the Orany station as well as the airfield.

At 1730 hrs another raid took place on Vilnius airfield.

At 1736 hrs a Do 17 and 12 Bf 109s again bombed and strafed Orany and Perloja.

At 1835 hrs according to a report from an aerial reconnaissance post a large group of German aircraft were active above Kaunas.

As is evident from the chronicle of events the majority of the air raids took place against airfields form which all the aircraft had already been evacuated that were capable of getting airborne. *Luftwaffe* crews on 22 June for the most part carried out raids on those aircraft that remained on the ground as a result of previous attacks, as well as on damaged, and unserviceable Soviet aircraft.

There were however exceptions. Thus at around 1600 hrs a large group of Junkers aircraft escorted by Messerschmitts attacked Karmelava airfield. The majority of the aircraft belonging to the 31st Fighter Air Regiment were either destroyed or damaged. From the memoirs of N.I. Petrov:

> Later at 1600 hrs everything was calm, for the most part aircraft were taking off in pairs to patrol their own airfield as well as the railway junction at Kaunas. We heard the hum of aircraft engines and the command from the command post: 'Squadron Flight scramble!' Lieutenant Smyslov, Akimov, and I quickly got into our aircraft [Flight Commander Sergey Sergeyevich, born 1913, was killed in a crash on 18 September 1941]. We started our engines and taxied away from the command post, then red flares were fired and we were not given clearance to take off. Two pairs of Me-109s appeared at an altitude of 800–1,000 m and passed over the airfield, two groups of nine Heinkel 111s were approaching. The explosions from bombs could be heard some distance away from the airfield, and evidently they were being dropped on the road. Bombs began to fall on the edge of the airfield, and individual bombs were being dropped. We were lying next to our aircraft, the explosions were coming closer and the bombs were whistling. Where were they going to fall? They were falling a short hop away from our aircraft, and we were next to these aircraft, almost in the middle of the airfield. A large group of aircraft flew over us and dropped just a few bombs. They were probably playing a psychological game, flying out to a number of targets. As they approached our own airfield it would appear that there was no getting away from this group of bombers. Three pairs of Me-109s passed over the airfield at an altitude of 1,000 m. They had switched to a more drawn out echelon, as if they were over a range and began to attack each aircraft with concentrated fire. In addition they were firing first and foremost at our flight of aircraft that were in the middle of the airfield without camouflage. We managed to run to the edge of the airfield, where there was a dried up well, the water had been drained out of this well at some point and now after being splayed, it lay like a breeding pig with her piglets. We took shelter next to it, where the ground was a little drier. Enemy aircraft flew over the airfield unopposed since there was not a single anti-aircraft machine gun on the airfield at all. I approached my aircraft after the ground attacks by the enemy had passed. Oil was leaking from under the cowling, the engine crankcase had been ruptured and a shell had passed through the dive flap and half of the outer skin was missing from the control surface (it was made of percale). The aircraft that stood nearby incurred a greater degree of damage. Only around eight aircraft were capable of taking off. By evening an order had come through to get into the transports, and the aircraft that were not capable of flight were to be burned, if I am not mistaken.

No explanation is provided as to why the aircraft of the 31st Fighter Air Regiment were not transferred from Karmelava airfield ahead of the next enemy raid, not in the regiment's, or the 8th Mixed Air Division's documents or in the memoirs of the participants. It is possible that the reason was a temporary loss of communication between divisional and regimental headquarters or even an innocuous delay caused by the materiel being prepared for a sortie. One way or another, but because of this lapse, the 31st Fighter Air Regiment incurred heavy losses, and all but around a dozen serviceable aircraft remained in its line-up. These data are confirmed by the 61st Ground Attack Air Regiment, where the transfer of seven MiG-3s on the evening of 22 June from the 31st Fighter Air Regiment to the ground attack aircraft bases at Kedainiai is recorded.

The delay in evacuating aircraft from the 15th Fighter Air Regiment from Potsunai led to even worse consequences. It is not possible at this time to establish why this happened, but whatever the reason, the 15th Fighter Air Regiment paid a very high price for this sluggishness.

At around 1740 hrs a headquarters flight from III./JG 53, which was conducting a 'fighter sweep' spotted MiG-3 aircraft taking off from Potsunai airfield from the 1st Squadron and from the directorate of the 15th Fighter Air Regiment.

In the course of a short battle, which was more akin to a shooting in a shooting gallery than an air battle, four German pilots managed to shoot down five MiG-3s as they were taking off without incurring losses on their side. A further aircraft was able to break away from the attacking enemy aircraft and almost reached Jonava, where it crashed. All these victories were recorded by German pilots as having occurred between 1743 hrs and 1748 hrs. The Commander of the group *Hauptmann* Wolf-Dietrich Wilcke (at 1743 hrs) and the group's technical officer *Leutnant* Jurgen Harder (at 1645 hrs) claimed one I-17 each (the I-17 was a German designation for the MiG-3 at the beginning of the war). *Oberleutnant* Friedrich-Karl Muller (between 1645–1647 hrs) and *Oberleutnant* Klaus Quaet-Faslem (between 1645–1647 hrs) claimed two Soviet fighters each. Documents produced by the 15th Fighter Air Regiment confirm all the German claims for the victories. Five MiG aircraft crashed in the immediate vicinity of the airfield, three pilots were killed, and Senior Lieutenants I.I. Matveyev, and V.S. Martynenko were able to bale out of their stricken aircraft by parachute.

The only pilot who was able to escape from this German persecution was the Commander of the 1st Squadron Senior Lieutenant N.N. Boyarshinov, he was most likely injured or his aircraft had sustained serious damage, or something else happened. His MiG-3 crashed close to the village of Perelazai in the Jonava region. The pilot's body was found and buried alongside his crashed aircraft by local people.

The loss of six MiG-3s was of course as nothing compared to the death of four experienced pilots. Those who had been lost, the Deputy Commander of the 15th Fighter Air Regiment Captain I.A. Dolzhenko, the Commander of the 1st Squadron Senior Lieutenant N.N. Boyarshinov, and the Flight Commanders Lieutenants M.M. Kradenov, and I.I. Shultz were among the few pilots in the regiment who had managed to assimilate the newest aircraft.

Another unfortunate consequence of this battle was that having been evidently influenced by what he saw, the commander of the regiment decided against ordering his younger pilots to take to the skies to ferry the MiG-3 aircraft. In total 13 serviceable, new fighter aircraft were subsequently abandoned during the withdrawal from Potsunai airfield.

The battle continued head on at dinner time and into the evening. Soviet fighters, ground attack aircraft, and bombers attacked *Wehrmacht* units and *Luftwaffe* aircraft at the same time were striking Soviet airfields as well as attacking Red Army units, and fighters were still beating back attacks by Soviet attack aircraft.

The 148th Fighter Air Regiment at around 1630 hrs attacked German forces that were attacking Liepaja. The aircraft landed in Riga. Subsequently aircraft belonging to this regiment repeated the attack at 1800 hrs, this time operating from Riga airfield. According to operations report No.1/OP written by the headquarters of the Air Forces of the North-Western Front by 1700 hrs on 22 June 1941: 'The 148th Fighter Air Regiment in the period between 1630–1809 hrs attacked a motor-cycle column in two attacks on the road from Palanga–Polukne.' After the attack on German forces the aircraft landed at Liepaja for refuelling.

There is little reference to the chronology of the evening combat activities of the 61st Ground Attack Air Regiment in the documents of the 61st Ground Attack Air Regiment. The regiment's crews were very active and conducted 35 attack sorties. Aside from the area around Mariampol–Kalvarija that was attacked again, enemy units were subject to attacks in the areas around Pilviskiai, and Vilkavishkis. Apart from that crews were very active in conducting reconnaissance, and sorties were recorded in the direction of Vilkavishkis, Shaki, Yurbarkas, and Taurage.

The pilots of the 42nd and 15th Fighter Air Regiment most likely, conducted several ground attacks missions in the evening against enemy troops although there is no description of these battles in the documents.

The bomber regiments in the Air Forces of the North-Western Front also continued to fulfil the directive issued by the front line commander, according to which they were required to conduct two combat sorties as a regiment. At 1630 hrs aircraft took off from Piltene airfield from the 40th High-Speed Bomber Air Regiment with the task of: 'Bombing concentrations of enemy tanks that were moving along the road between Mariampol–Suwalki.' According to the regiment's Combat Journal 17 SB aircraft (from the 3rd, 4th, and 5th Squadrons, lead by Captain Pankov) at approximately 1730 hrs bombed a concentration of tanks from an altitude of 2,500 m on the road between Mariampol–Suwalki, in the area around Kalvarija. Now the 'Jagdflieger' were on their guard and Soviet bombers were subject to attacks from several groups of German fighters at once. Seven aircraft were lost in combat along with their crews, and apart from that Captain Pankov made an emergency, wheels-up landing in his own territory.

Eleven SB aircraft, led by Captain Lavrentsov from the 1st and 2nd Squadrons as well as the Flight Commander's Courses from the 6th Mixed Air Division that took off from Riga airfield were operating in accordance with this same task, in addition to Pankov's group. In the area around Mariampol they bombed a concentration of German forces. Crews noticed that enemy fighters were very active over this area and it was as a result of attacks from these same fighters that three aircraft were lost along with their crews. According to a report by Lavrentsov the gunner/radio-operator Sergeant Nikitin shot down a single Bf 109.

According to German data, in the course of the air battles with the Soviet bombers pilots from 7. and 8./JG 53, who claimed five victories between 1730–1740 hrs, excelled themselves, correspondingly 4./JG 54 pilots claimed three victories, while those from Stab 6./JG 52 claimed two victories. The Commander of JG 54 *Major* Hannes Trautloft claimed another victory according to the results of the battle. According to his report at 1748 hrs he shot down a bomber. He became the only German pilot to become a victim of the battle. As a result of retaliatory fire from the gunners in the 40th High-Speed Bomber Air Regiment Bf 109F-2 W.Nr.5761 flown by Trautloft was damaged and the German ace was forced to make an emergency landing on the airfield, without lowering the undercarriage (evidently Sergeant Nikitin's report was accurate). As in the majority of what, for the fighters of the *Luftwaffe*, were successful battles that occurred on 22 June, Soviet bombers lacked fighter cover and as such their chances of survival were not great.

Thus the 10 SBs that were shot down and the single example that were damaged as well as the claims of 11 victories from the enemy's side was a very just result from this uneven battle.

The German pilots who claimed victories in combat with the crews of the 40th High-Speed Bomber Air Regiment:

Feldwebel Hans Ochler, 8./JG 53: SB-3, 1730 hrs.
Feldwebel Hermann Neuhoff, 7./JG 53: DB-3, 1735 hrs.
Oberleutnant Heinz Altendorf, 7./JG 53: DB-3, 1735 hrs.
Unteroffizier Otto Wegener, 7./JG 53: DB-3, 1735 hrs.
Leutnant Herbert Schramm, 8./JG 53; DB-3, 1740 hrs.
Feldwebel Rudolf Hager, 4./JG 54; SB-2, 1745 hrs.

Oberleutnant Hans Philipp, 4./JG 54: SB-2, 1745 hrs.
Oberleutnant Carl Sattig, 4./JG 54: SB-2, 1747 hrs.
Hauptmann Erich Woitke, Stab II./JG 52: SB-2, 1748 hrs.
Major Hannes Trautloft, Stab/JG 54: DB-3, 1748 hrs.
Oberleutnant Rudolf Resch, 6./JG 52: SB-2, 1750 hrs.

The 31st High-Speed Bomber Air Regiment was a little late in this respect, although the regiment's combat order No. 1 set out the following order: 'Be prepared for a repeat sortie at 1545 hrs.' By all accounts the reason for the delay to this sortie was the 35th and 50th High-Speed Bomber Air Regiments, 4th Mixed Air Division's transfer to Jelgava and Platone, which naturally complicated the situation with respect to the servicing, and preparation of the aircraft for the sortie.

The regiment acted in accordance with combat order No. 2:

> Combat order No. 2 written by the headquarters of the 31st High-Speed Bomber Air Regiment on 22 June 1941. Jelgava.
>
> 1. The enemy continues to build up tanks and in the area around Suwalki–Kalvarija, Kalvarija–Simno.
>   The weather is clear
> 2. The 31st High-Speed Bomber Air Regiment is to bomb concentrations of tanks around Kalvarija–Simno.
>   I will lead this regiment.
> 3. The route for the flight is to be as follows: Starting point for the route–Sheduva–Kruki–Pilviskiai –then on to the target.
> 4. The payload is to be FAB-100, and FAB-250 bombs
> 5. The combat formation is to be a group of nine, forming up over Jelgava
> 6. My airborne command post is at the head of the column, the ground bases command post is to be manned by my Deputy Major Shafranskiy.
>
> The Commander of the 31st High-Speed Bomber Air Regiment is to be Lieutenant-Colonel Dobysh.
>
> The Chief of Staff of the 31st High-Speed Bomber Air Regiment is to be Captain Semyonov.

A second sortie by the 31st High-Speed Bomber Air Regiment was overall just as successful as the first, although this time round it did not pass without losses. According to combat report No. 2 written by the regimental headquarters at 1755 hrs the regiment comprising 37 aircraft bombed an enemy column in the area around Lyudvinov (13 km north-east of Kalvarija) from an altitude of 2,000 m. According to the crew's observations direct hits were recorded and in total 17 FAB-250 and 120 FAB-100 bombs were dropped. The crews noted, in addition to the direct hits, intensive anti-aircraft artillery fire in the area around the target as well as an attack by six enemy fighters in the area around Mariampol. The regiment's losses as a result of the attack by Messerschmitts comprised three SB aircraft and their crews. According to a report by the navigators and gunner/radio-operators four Bf 109s were shot down in air combat.

According to German information the aircraft that carried out this attack on the bombers, which were Bf 109Fs from 7./JG 53 actually claimed three victories in this battle but without incurring any losses themselves in terms of aircraft or personnel. *Leutnant* Siegmund Hosnedl claimed one SB at 1820 hrs (this was identified as a DB-3), and *Feldwebel* Werner Stumpf claimed two SBs shot down at 1820 hrs and 1823 hrs (these were actually DB-3s).

Unfortunately this was not the final loss that the 31st High-Speed Bomber Air Regiment incurred. On the way back in the area around Daugavpils the aircraft flown by Deputy Squadron Commander Captain B.A. Beryozin was shot down by 'friendly fire' by fighters from the 49th Fighter Air Regiment.

The last to conduct any combat sorties that evening were three squadrons from the 50th High-Speed Bomber Air Regiment. In the period between 1841–1858 hrs some 24 SB aircraft dropped bombs on German forces in the area around Taurage. For this the 50th High-Speed Bomber Air Regiment transferred to Jelgava airfield from Estonia at around 1700 hrs. A single SB was forced to make an emergency landing during the course of this ferry flight for non-combat reasons.

The details of this combat activity are reflected in operations report No. 1 written by the headquarters of the 50th High-Speed Bomber Air Regiment.

> The first group consisting of nine SB aircraft from the 2nd Squadron bombed a concentration of tanks as well as enemy armoured vehicles at 1841 hrs from an altitude of 3,200 m in the town of Taurage. Some 54 FAB-100 and eight ZAB-50 bombs were dropped. According to the crew's observations the bombs hit the concentrations of materiel and the aircraft were strafed by anti-aircraft artillery in the target area. Two fighters also attacked the bombers. As a result four aircraft sustained between 12–15 bullet holes. On the road from Taurage to Skaudvile some 15–18 tanks were noted as well as concentrations of motorised and mechanised units on the sides of the roads. Lieutenant Ivanov's crew, Observer Vasilyevskiy, and Gunner/Radio-operator Prikhodko made an emergency belly landing in the area around Kurshanta (west of Shavli). The gunner had sustained 11 injuries from bullets.
>
> The second group of nine SB aircraft bombed a concentration of vehicles in Taurage from an altitude of 3,000 m. Some 54 FAB-100s were dropped as well as 12 ZAB-50s. According to the crew's observations the bombs fell on a concentration of vehicles and the bombers were attacked close to the target by 10 Me-109 fighters, two aircraft sustained bullet holes...
>
> Gunners Sokolovskiy, and Shandonovyn shot down one Me-109. On the way back in the area around Shavli the aircraft were fired upon by anti-aircraft artillery.
>
> The third group comprising six SB aircraft bombed Taurage at 1858 hrs from an altitude of 3,400 m. Some 36 FAB-100 and four ZAB-50 bombs were dropped. According to the crew's observations a number of fires broke out in Taurage, and heavy anti-aircraft artillery fire was noted in the area over the target, attacks by pairs of Me-109s were also noted and three aircraft sustained between two to five bullet holes.

Soviet aircraft were attacked by pilots from 5./JG 53, led by *Oberleutnant* Kurt Brandle, however this time the crews in the SB aircraft turned out to be tough nuts to crack. Despite the three victories that were claimed in the air in reality not one aircraft was shot down and only one bomber made an emergency landing on its own territory after the gunner had been injured.

The victories claimed by the pilots of 5./JG 53, although they are not confirmed by Soviet documents, were as follows:

Feldwebel Jusef Wurmheller: one SB to the north of Taurage at an altitude of 3,200 m at 1901 hrs

Oberleutnant Kurt Brandle: one SB to the north of Taurage, at 1903 hrs.

Unteroffizier Manfred Reipert: one SB in the area around Siauliai at an altitude of 3,000 m at 1912 hrs.

Aircraft from the 35th High-Speed Bomber Air Regiment were also supposed to take part in the evening raids. For this to happen in the second half of the day the regiment was redeployed to Platone airfield but the raid did not go ahead. First and foremost this was due to complications linked to the servicing of the aircraft on their new airfield.

At the same time as the raids by German aircraft were taking place to counter Soviet attack aviation raids by German bombers and fighter-bombers on Soviet airfields continued.

On one of these raids the Germans caught 11 I-153 aircraft from the 1st Squadron, 148th Fighter Air Regiment on Liepaja unawares at 1945 hrs as they were being refuelled following a raid on German troops ahead of their departure to Riga. According to a political report as a result of the bombing, three 'Chaikas' caught fire and a further five were seriously damaged. This episode found its way into a radiogram prepared by the Liepaja Military Base.

Received at 2000 hrs: 'Nine German aircraft at an altitude of 4,000 m bombed the southern section of the city of Liepaja as well as the airfield. There are casualties, but an accurate figure has yet to be established. The duty operations officer at the headquarters of the Liepaja naval base.'

Received at 2135 hrs: 'At 1945 hrs nine enemy bomber aircraft bombed Liepaja. According to preliminary data three aircraft have been destroyed on the airfield. The Commander of the Liepaja naval base.'

After this the dreadful episode the 148th Fighter Air Regiment was finally redeployed to Riga, but eight I-153s were to become the last aviation losses in the Air Forces of the North-Western Front on the first day of the war.

Soviet fighters attempted to mount a resistance to these raids, but the Air Forces of the North-Western Front had by this time already attained their final two victories, these were secured by pilots from the 42nd Fighter Air Regiment.

At 1750 hrs three 'Chaikas' from this same regiment engaged a pair of German fighters in combat and as a result of a successful battle, *Oberfeldwebel* Josef Kronschnabel's Bf 109F from 9./JG 53 was shot down. The German pilot reached territory that was in the hands of *Wehrmacht* front line units but his aircraft was destroyed during an emergency landing to the north of Leipalingis (a town situated 30 km south of Alytus). This victory was claimed jointly by Junior Lieutenant I.S. Zudilov and Senior Lieutenant N.E. Linchevskiy.

The final victory of the first day of the war was attained at 1846 hrs Moscow time.

According to the Combat Journal of the 57th Mixed Air Regiment a pair of our fighters overwhelmed a single aircraft over Orany, which was identified as a Do 17. In reality the victim of the pilots from the 42nd Fighter Air Regiment was Bf 110 reconnaissance aircraft W.Nr.2333, bearing the code 8H+DK from 2.(F)/ 33, which made an emergency landing close to the village of Puvociai ('20 km west of Orany'). The aircraft sustained 100 percent damage and one of the crew members was injured. If the heroes of the previous episode were unknown, it has not proved possible to establish who was behind the victory in this instance unfortunately.

Aside from the attacks on the airfields, *Luftwaffe* command in the second half of the day intensified their attacks on the forces of the North-Western Front. Thus the command of I. *Fliegerkorps* activated II./KG 76 which had been idle for almost the entire day. The Junkers aircraft in this group from 1530 hrs onwards conducted four combat sorties to strike marching columns from the 28th Tank Division in the area around Siauliai, that had advanced for a counter-attack in accordance with a directive issued by General Kuznetsov. The following provides a chronology of these raids and an evaluation of their effectiveness and is taken from a report written by the headquarters of II./KG 76.

1. Between 1416–1618 hrs three aircraft.
   Target: to attack a column around Siauliai.
   Result: A direct hit on the columns and strafing with onboard armament. Heavy smoke.

2) Three aircraft.

Target: An attack on columns in the area around Siauliai. Result: An attack on columns of tanks to the west of Siauliai. Two tanks were turned upside down. No further results were visible owing to a rising cloud of dust.

3) Between 1715–1907 hrs five aircraft.
Target: An attack on tanks.
Result: An attack on columns of tanks. Observations revealed the outcome of the attack, namely that out of the 50 advancing tanks approximately half were taken out of action.

4) Between 1942–2136 hrs 16 aircraft.
Target: Combating tanks.
Result: An attack using a large group of aircraft (in pairs and in echelon) on columns of tanks (approximately 150 tanks). A great number of direct hits were observed as well as tanks that had been turned upside down. Forty tanks were taken out of action as well as 10 trucks.

Thus the German crews announced that they had taken around 65–70 tanks out of action, which is a simply phenomenal success. Naturally when this information is compared to the Soviet documents, the German claims are amended significantly downwards. According to the Combat Journal of the 12th Mechanised Corps, significant raids by enemy aircraft were noted on the divisions' marching tanks, which were advancing on a route from Gruzdziai–Czeksi. As a result of the bombing 10 combat and six wheeled vehicles were taken out of action. Nevertheless the destruction of 10 tanks is an excellent result, especially when the fact that Soviet bombers, despite the great number of raids conducted over the course of the day as whole, did not succeed in taking one German tank out of action.

The final raids by the *Luftwaffe* only concluded at 2300 hrs Moscow time, and at this time the German pilots were the only ones left in the air. Owing to the redeployment to second line airfields of the Air Force units in the North-Western Front there was no possibility of preparing the aircraft for a sortie efficiently, and the distance of 200 km from Jelgava and Daugavpils to the areas in which the border battles were taking place was at the limits of the Soviet fighters' performance. Soviet pilots who were left without aircraft departed the beaten up airfields in road transport, and sometimes on foot. German aces in their Junkers and Messerschmitts passed overhead while endless *Wehrmacht* columns marched eastwards as if on a victory lap. From H. Trautloft's diary:

> We had been in the air for the whole of this long day and each pilot had flown between five to seven combat sorties. The backbone and the spine were very painful. Bomber escort sorties were replaced by 'fighter sweeps' or sorties to attack ground targets. We enjoyed complete air superiority and we did not encounter any Russian fighters… An hour later we were in the air again.*

* 'In the course of the evening sorties we did not encounter a single Russian aircraft. We would fly over columns of our own infantry at low level. As was the case in September 1939 in Poland thick clouds of dust showed us in which direction each column was moving. Wherever we saw any flames, entire villages were on fire.' [this refers to the final sortie].

Final Results and Conclusions

Combat activity by the Air Forces of the North-Western Front and the *Luftwaffe* formations that opposed them on 22 June 1941 in the context of the decisions taken by both sides, along with their realisation, appears to the author to be an undoubted fusion of the intellectual might, resolution, and willpower of the commanders.

There is no doubt that victory in this battle lay with the commanders and pilots of the *Luftwaffe*, this can be deduced from the ratio of victories to losses and from the fact that the 'battlefield' remained the preserve of the German pilots, who with their constant attacks forced Soviet units to pull back to second line airfields. The actions of the German commanders on 22 June 1941 were exclusively flexible, resolute, and most importantly, committed to achieving their objectives.

As previously discussed in the actions of the I. *Fliegerkorps'* command there was just one controversial point when the Germans, who were being overcautious, carried out an airfield manoeuvre with their own fighter aviation, actually circumventing their second raid on Soviet airfields. This action can be understood from another perspective. At that time nobody could have vouched that a few minutes later Soviet bombers would not appear over this airfield. Leaving the fighters in reserve at that moment therefore was a relatively logical decision.

The sensible reaction to Soviet daylight raids is also worthy of high praise. *Luftwaffe* command were not going to repeat the mistakes they had made in the morning and having allocated some of their fighters to provide an escort, the rest continued their raids on Soviet airfields.

An additional plus was the determination and tactical expertise with which the result was achieved. German units bombed and attacked the airfields belonging to the Air Forces of the North-Western Front constantly for almost eighteen hours in a row. The pilots in several of the *Luftwaffe's* fighter units flew seven combat sorties per day. If organised resistance was encountered then as a rule the raids would begin to be repeated again after short periods of time using large formations of aircraft and this almost always led to a routing of the aviation units based there. This was the case in Alytus, Orany, and Karmelava.

Apart from that even if no particular resistance was encountered the raids continued right up until the evening. As the reader will recall in the case of the routing of the 1st Squadron, 148th Fighter Air Regiment this was absolutely the right decision. If the materiel in the 15th, 31st, and the 42nd Fighter Air Regiments and the 54th High-Speed Bomber Air Regiment were not destroyed then Soviet pilots that had been redeployed from other airfields could have made use of them later and these aircraft would have been utilised in combat activity, enhancing the strength of the Soviet alignment.

German fighters, aside from conducting their own fighter attacks acted as fighter-bombers and ground attack aircraft. For almost the entire day Soviet bombers conducted bombing raids on German troops, logistics units, infrastructure, as well as *Luftwaffe* airfields. Moreover many groups of Soviet aircraft did not encounter any resistance from German fighter aviation at all. They nevertheless successfully bombed and attacked Soviet airfields and troops, escorted their attack aircraft, acted as air defence fighters, and as air superiority fighters.

Among the shortcomings it should be noted that German pilots did not succeed in neutralising the actions of Soviet bomber aviation fully. For almost the entire day Soviet bombers conducted bombing raids on German troops, logistic units, infrastructure, and *Luftwaffe* airfields. Moreover many of the groups of Soviet aircraft did not encounter any resistance from German fighter aviation at all.

Bomber units in I. *Fliegerkorps* and VIII. *Fliegerkorps* acted exclusively in an aggressive manner, and moreover often without fighter cover. Thanks, however, to the implementation of sensible tactics, the Air Forces of the North-Western Front were able to inflict significant damage, incurring what is more, minimal losses.

Reconnaissance aviation is worthy of separate high praise since they were able to continue the efficient work that was begun in the winter. In the course of the day on 22 June reconnaissance aircraft crews continued to discover new targets and carried out aerial photography, monitoring the results of the air attacks. Among the shortcomings we note that right up until the evening the Germans were still not able to discover where the field airfields were: Raseiniai, Postunai, Vincai, Kryzhaki, Kivishki, Markshtava, and Risgonis, despite the fact Soviet units that occupied these airfields were operating combat sorties from there for the entire day. The biggest failure, however, was that the German reconnaissance in a literal sense missed the general redeployment of Soviet aircraft from forward airfields, as a result of which the final German raids were for the most part made against airfields that the Soviet units had already abandoned.

Without a doubt the greatest gift for the *Luftwaffe* commanders was the Soviet's refusal to undertake retaliatory strikes on German airbases. This enabled German aviation units to prepare for combat sorties practically in the absence of any resistance, which gave the German side an enormous head start.

However despite these comfortable conditions on the first day of the operation, the Germans did not succeed in destroying or even inflicting fatal losses on the alignment of the Air Forces of the North-Western Front. Even after five or six waves of raids on the airfields Soviet aviation units, in spite of the heavy losses, retained their combat capability and right up until the evening they continued to fulfil their allotted tasks.

Nevertheless the tactical measures that were taken in truth did drive the Air Forces of the North-Western Front away from the forward airfields. Not only did this ensure full air superiority over the arena of the enormous battle that was unfolding on the ground, but enabled on subsequent days attempts to be made to rout the Soviet aviation units huddled on the few airfields along the Western Dvina.

Two factors had an influence on the actions taken by the Soviet side:

The first was the delayed reaction on the part of the Soviet military and political leadership to the aggression, which meant that a retaliatory strike against the German airfields, logistics units, and infrastructure that had been organised by General Ionov and was to be carried out by the bombers serving in the Air Forces of the North-Western Front, was stopped. This was to have been a response to the first raids on Soviet airfields that took place early on the morning of 22 June. The orders that had been given by the Commander of the Air Forces of the North-Western Front were cancelled and instead of undertaking energetic counter-attacking strikes, an order came through to pull back passively within the Soviets' own territory.

The second was the successful raid by the 3rd and 4th Panzer Groups which from 0800 hrs in the morning drew all the attention of the Air Forces of the North-Western Front away like a magnet. This action forced General Kuznetsov, who had ignored the orders from Moscow concerning retaliatory action against the *Luftwaffe* alignment, to send all his front line strike aircraft up to combat the advancing *Wehrmacht* motorised columns. This, in accordance with the directive issued at 0945 hrs, became the main task for front line aviation for the entire first day of the war.

However, despite the fact that the crews serving in the Air Forces of the North-Western Front flew around 1,100 combat sorties in the course of one day, only around a third of that number comprised actions by strike aircraft against enemy forces ('it has not been possible to establish the exact figures owing to the fact that many units destroyed their documents.') Of these 173 were carried out by bombers ('a further 38 combat sorties were carried out by crews from the 207th, and 96th Long-Range Bomber Air Regiments, 3rd Long-Range Bomber Air Corps,') and approximately 100–110 fighters and bombers ('between 50–70 were conducted by fighters and ground attack aircraft in the region around Mariampol–Kalvarija and between 30–40 on the German infantry advancing towards Liepaja.')

Apart from that, 43 combat sorties were conducted by bombers on logistics targets in the territory of East Prussia: railway stations, bridges, and concentrations of troops in response to the first raid by the *Luftwaffe*. This was in addition to 10 sorties by SBs from the 54th High-Speed Bomber Air Regiment during the course of an unsuccessful attempt to counterattack German fighters after the latter had attacked Orany and Perloja airfields.

Table 12 Bomber Aviation activities in the Air Forces of the North-Western Front on 22 June 1941

Area in which the action took place	The number of combat sorties		
	Up to 1400 hrs	After 1400 hrs	Total
Tilsit–Taurage	27	42	71
Mariampol–Kalvarija	46	65	111

Naturally there is no question of such a small number of combat sorties, which moreover were carried out in three different directions having any kind of a serious effect. Periodical horizontal bombing attacks by bombers on different *Wehrmacht* units from a relatively high altitude (between 1,700–2,500 m) were not capable of inflicting any serious damage or of halting the German advance.

German reports mention attacks by Soviet aircraft periodically but no mention is made at all of having experienced any difficulties as a result of this activity. Thus the Air Forces of the North-Western Front were not able to cope with the task that had been put before them by front line command.

The enemy made use of the passive stance that Soviet Air Forces had adopted and for the whole day they pursued their own interests by attacking the airfields belonging to the Air Forces of the North-Western Front. It was for this reason that the vast majority of the sorties carried out by fighter aircraft serving in the Air Forces of the North-Western Front were to fulfil the requirements of the air defence system. Of these more than half were aimed at countering raids by German strike aircraft on their airfields on which the Soviet aircraft were based. A further 150 meanwhile were carried out by pilots of the 21st, 38th, and 49th Fighter Air Regiments, deep behind enemy lines. The rest of the sorties were conducted during the course of the first German attacks without putting up any resistance to the enemy.

Despite this however it would appear that in the course of an enormous number of raids to provide cover Soviet fighter pilots were not capable of covering even their own bases. The enemy was often successful in completely destroying aircraft on forward airfields without incurring any losses in doing so. This is not surprising considering the generally unsatisfactory condition of the aircraft serving in the air Ffrces, as well as the anti-aircraft artillery units in the air defence system and the air force aerial reconnaissance posts on the eve of the invasion.

As far as the confrontation in the air was concerned there was no full-scale air battle between fighter aircraft on the first day of the war over the Baltic region as such, with the exception of the battle between the 42nd Fighter Air Regiment and II./JG 52. Nevertheless several German documents record resistance on the part of Soviet fighters. Thus from the daily report written by the headquarters of the 4th Panzer Group dated 22 June 1941 it is known that there was: 'Significant fighter cover near Kedainiai, Panevezys, Siauliai, and and Ocikiai (seven kilometres east of Skaudvile).'

As a result of the events described above the operation that was developed within the confines of the plan for the provision of cover to gain air superiority was never realised. In fact not one sortie was carried out to attack *Luftwaffe* airfields over the course of the entire day and as such there was no point in aiming for air superiority using such a passive defensive tactic.

Nevertheless it should be emphasised that the commanders of the Air Forces of the North-Western Front did try to turn the course of events their way twice, and to commence activities to gain air superiority and strike German airfields. Apart from that as soon as the opportunity arose Major-General A.P. Ionov immediately withdrew his units from the forward airfields that were constantly under attack. It is not possible now to determine where Aleksey Pavlovich was coming from in his decision-making. He did, however, think one step ahead of the actions of his German enemy and moreover he did this in a very far-sighted way. Especially given the fact that he had very little information on which to make his analysis and objective intelligence on the condition and the actions of the *Luftwaffe* was constantly delayed along with information on the movements undertaken by his own forces.

Thus it is highly likely that what in life is known as intuition played a role, although in the case of a military leader this is known as military cunning. Specifically, moves of this nature made by a commander in a critical situation could be described as military cunning.

The question arises of what would have been the effect of these hypothetical attacks on *Luftwaffe* airfields, given that Soviet plans were based on reconnaissance data that was a long way from reflecting the real situation, and that the majority of the airfields on which the German aircraft were concentrated were unknown to Soviet pilots? More than likely the successes would have been moderate but in themselves the raids on the airfields, even those occupied by second line forces, as well as the action against the railway junctions, bridges, and so on would nevertheless have drawn significant German fighter aviation forces away from the Soviet airbases. Apart from that, during the course of this action a realistic opportunity to reconnoitre targets and to have located the German field airfields would have presented itself, which would subsequently have meant that more effective attacks could have been carried out.

From another perspective it would appear that what seemed to have been well-timed and easy attacks on advancing *Wehrmacht* units using attack aircraft, on closer approximation were in fact no trivial matter. Soviet bombers and ground attack aircraft were only able to carry out these attacks by virtue of a specific plan for the raids, as well as specific tactical approaches and special weaponry. For instance, by conducting dive bombing raids or indeed attacking from low level using a large number of high explosive fragmentation bombs, even those of a small calibre. Ideally however the attacks were to be carried out by combining these approaches with machine gun and RS rocket attacks on ground targets. Apart from that the most important prerequisite would be persistent attacks on a small area occupied by the German advanced guard. This in turn would require constant and effective reconnaissance since the German motorised forward detachments were constantly moving eastwards, as well as uninterrupted patrols over this area by Soviet fighters to provide timely cover for the actions of the attack aircraft.

There was not one of the abovementioned components in the arsenal of the Air Forces of the North-Western Front (or in the Air Forces of the Red Army as a whole). Dive bombers were still crude and were available in minimal quantities, and the personnel had still not been able to develop dive bombing techniques. There was an insufficient number of container-type attachments such as the Onisko buckets for low-level attacks, and even if they were available their fitting would require the efforts of a significant number of armourers, who were absent from the front line units. There was a miserly number of fighters in the Air Forces of the North-Western Front that were fitted with cannons, and prior to the outbreak of war the pilots had not fired a single shot from the aircraft these units had available that had RS rocket strakes fitted. The absence of reconnaissance aircraft has already been described above, and the tactical approaches that link the actions of all types of aviation required protracted development. The units and formations of the Red Army Air

Force were only able to acquire these skills by the second half of the war after having come a long way, which cost many lives.

Whatever the reasons for the refusal to conduct operations to gain air superiority, it was these same decisions that became one of the fundamental errors made by the People's Commissar for Defence Marshall S.K. Timoshenko and the Commander of the North-Western Front Colonel-General F.I. Kuznetsov on 22 June 1941.

Many Soviet commanders of a lower rank were of the opposite opinion and felt that time and effort were being wasted on attacking the *Wehrmacht*'s advancing forces, and that it made sense to concentrate all the resources on combating enemy aviation on their own airfields. Thus a report on these combat activities written by the 57th Mixed Air Division notes: 'We needed to keep attacking the enemy airfields, without letting any difficulties get in our way, before we had destroyed their last aircraft. The enemy would have been taken out of action rapidly and would not have been able to beat a path forwards for their infantry and their motorised and mechanised forces.'

There is no doubt that the Commander of the Air Forces of the North-Western Front held the self same opinion as his subordinates. Major-General A.P. Ionov evidently was an advocate of fighting for air superiority by attacking the enemy's airbases and as soon as he had an opportunity to arrange attacks on German airfields he actually began to realise this. The bombers had yet to return from their final attack on German forces when front line headquarters prepared combat order No. 2/OP timed at 2000 hrs on 22 June.

1. The enemy, in overcoming the resistance of our own forces continues to build on their successes with their tanks and motorised and mechanised units in the direction of Kvedarna–Skaudas, Tilsit–Taurage, Suwalki–Alytus. Enemy aviation has systematically attacked our airfields over the course of 22 June.

   The weather conditions: up to 5 oktas of cumulus cloud, visibility is 15–20 km, the wind is light and variable.
2. Our ground units on 23 June will continue to destroy the enemy's Taurage alignment whilst continuing to hold back the enemy's onslaught in the southern sector.
3. The Air Forces of the Baltic Special Military District over the course of 23 June are to fight for air superiority in the area where the attack alignment of the 8th Army are engaged in combat and are to assist in the destruction of the Taurage alignment.
4. The 6th Mixed Air Division under the cover of the 15th and 31st Fighter Air Regiment over the course of 23 June is to destroy enemy aviation on airfields in the area around: Klaipeda, Nida, Tilsit, and is to assist the 8th Army in the routing of the Taurage alignment.
5. The 7th Mixed Air Division is from dawn on 23 June to destroy the enemy aviation alignment in the area around Dobrovolsk, Insterburg, and Gumbinnen, and is subsequently to operate in accordance with the 8th Army's plans.
6. The 57th Mixed Air Division and the 61st Ground Attack Air Division, 8th Mixed Air Division are to act in accordance with the 11th Army's plans.
7. The first echelon are to strike enemy aviation on the airfields at 0400 hrs on 23 June, a subsequent powerful attack is to be carried out at 0700 hrs on 23 June.
8. The loading for this combat activity: the fighters and ground attack aircraft are to fly three sorties each, while the bombers are to fly two each.
9. My command post is Panevezys.

The Commander of the Air Forces of the Baltic Special Military District Major-General of Aviation Ionov.

The Chief of Staff of the Air Forces of the Baltic Special Military District

Brigade Commander Krupin.

As the author noted above, the manpower and the technology were more than adequate to fulfil this concept, and the Soviet units that had already departed for second line airfields still retained a relatively high strike potential:

The 148th Fighter Air Regiment: 27 I-153s along with their crews on Riga airfield.
The 10th Fighter Air Regiment: 22 I-16s and three MiG-3s along with their crews on Platone airfield.
The 15th Fighter Air Regiment: 22 MiG-3s and four I-153s along with their crews on Jelgava airfield.
The 31st Fighter Air Regiment: approximately 10–12 MiG-3s and one to three I-16s along with their crews on Risgonis and Riga airfields (precise data is not available, but on the morning of 25 June 10 MiG-1/3s and one I-16 remained in the regiment, moreover no data is available concerning losses for 23–24 June).
The 42nd and 237th Fighter Air Regiments: 12 I-153s along with their crews on Markshtava and Risgonis airfields.
The 238th Fighter Air Regiment: five I-153s along with their crews on Panevezys airfield.
The 21st Fighter Air Regiment: 51 I-16s, one MiG-3, one MiG-3, and one I-153 along with their crews on Riga airfield (a further nine were unserviceable and were in the workshops).
The 49th Fighter Air Regiment: 22 I-16s and three I-153s along with their crews on Dvinsk airfield, 34 I-153s along with their crews on Liksna airfield.
The 61st Ground Attack Air Regiment: 35 I-153s, and three I-15bis aircraft along with their crews on Risgonis and Markshtava airfields.
The 241st Ground Attack Air Regiment: 27 I-15bis aircraft (15 crews) on Rumbula airfield).
The 9th High-Speed Bomber Air Regiment: 24 SB aircraft on Skvarbai airfield (a further six SBs were unserviceable).
The 46th High-Speed Bomber Air Regiment: by the evening this regiment had 20 serviceable SBs and Ar-2s on Rumbula airfield.*
The 31st High-Speed Bomber Air Regiment: 42 SBs on Jelgava airfield (a further 14 were unserviceable).
The 40th High-Speed Bomber Air Regiment: 43 SBs, of which 13 SBs were on Riga airfield (four SBs were from the Commander's Flight Courses, 6th Mixed Air Division,) 30 SBs were at Piltene (five of these were unserviceable).
The 54th High-Speed Bomber Air Regiment: 32 SBs and seven Ar-2s on Kivishki and Kryzhaki airfields.
The 35th High-Speed Bomber Air Regiment: 39 SBs on Platone airfield.
The 50th High-Speed Bomber Air Regiment: 32 SBs and five Pe-2s on Jelgava airfield.
The 63rd High-Speed Bomber Air Regiment: 40 SB aircraft on Kuusiku airfield.

Almost all the units in the Air Forces of the North-Western Front with the exception of the 38th Fighter Air Regiment and the 63rd High-Speed Bomber Air Regiment, 4th Mixed Air Division were concentrated densely among the second line airfields. In total the combat capable aircraft

* However on the morning of 23 June the regiment was augmented owing to the materiel that had transferred from the 312th Reconnaissance Air Regiment, in total there were 30 SBs and five Ar-2s (a further three were unserviceable).

along with their crews numbered more than 500 of which there were approximately 240 bombers, 220 fighters, and 65 ground attack aircraft.

> (Apart from that the 63rd High-Speed Bomber Air Regiment was able to operate from its own home base in Estonia. On 22 June the regiment did not incur any losses and in a combat capable condition the regiment had 40 SBs along with their crews. The 38th Fighter Air Regiment was very capable of being redeployed closer to the front line, and this would provide a further 60 I-153s, and an I-16).

Thus on the evening of the first day of the war it was still unclear who would emerge from this clash as the victor, and the entire battle was still to be fought.

The Germans understood this too. It was likely, considering the heightened activity among Soviet attack aviation in the second half of the day, and thanks to the actions of the reconnaissance crews, who had identified the principal concentration of the Air Forces of the North-Western Front in two regions: Jelgava–Riga and Ionava–Daugavpils, that *Luftwaffe* command also drew reliable conclusions. The first raids on Soviet airfields on 23 June 1941 were even planned in advance of 22 June, and were to commence in twilight between 0200–0300 hrs.

Losses and victories

Given the lack of a large array of both Soviet and German documents it is not possible to carry out a comparison of the qualitative indicators of the outcomes of the combat activity among the warring sides—such as the exact number of combat sorties, bombs dropped, and shells and rockets fired. Therefore a comparison has to be made based on disparate data of the individual units, and of the ratio of losses to victories.

German fighter aviation pilots carried out on average between five to seven combat sorties each on 22 June and claimed that they had destroyed in the North-Western Front line zone 93 Soviet aircraft in air combat.* The claims for these victories were spread as follows:

Stab/JG 54: 1 victory
I./JG 54: 12 victories
II./JG 54: 15 victories
III./JG 54: six victories. In total JG 54 Squadron scored 34 victories in the air and 35 on the ground.
II./JG 53: 11 victories
II./JG 27: five victories and a further 80 aircraft were destroyed by strafing on the ground (some of these were aircraft that belonged to the Air Forces of the North-Western Front), and apart from that a further five victories were attained in the Western Front zone.
III./JG 27: two victories
II./JG 52: 16 victories
III./JG 53: 25 victories in the air and a further 28 aircraft destroyed by strafing on the ground (apart from that a further 11 victories were attained in the air in the Western Front zone).

* The number of claims for victories submitted by Luftwaffe pilots are to a great extent confirmed by Soviet documents and on average the ratio is at 1:1.5. In total the Air Forces of the North-Western Front lost 80 aircraft that were either shot down or made emergency landings. Apart from that a further nine DB-3s from the 96th Long-Range Bomber Air Regiment were lost on 22 June to German anti-aircraft fire and fighters in the area around Suwalki–Merkine.

The total number of combat sorties flown by German bomber and reconnaissance aviation is not known.

Luftwaffe losses on 22 June on the North-Western Front zone comprised seven aircraft destroyed and 19 damaged. Moreover of those that were damaged five may have sustained this damage in the Western Front zone.*

German fighters lost four Bf 109F aircraft destroyed (according to the German classification of a 100 percent loss).† Apart from that a further four Bf 109Fs were damaged.‡

Bomber losses comprised seven aircraft, of which two were unrecoverable losses.§

Reconnaissance crews incurred the loss of a single Bf 110 in air combat with the aircraft from the 42nd Fighter Air Regiment. Apart from that a further eight aircraft were damaged in a range of different circumstances and it has not proved possible to tie this figure down at present owing to a lack of documents.

The number of Soviet aircraft lost exceeds those of the enemy by a multiple of two, and in total the Air Forces of the North-Western Front lost around 480 aircraft. Of those 70 aircraft were lost in battle and to anti-aircraft artillery, a further 380 were destroyed on the airfields or sustained damage or were abandoned during withdrawal, and 30 were lost to other reasons (for the most part for technical reasons and due to pilot error).

Table 13 Aircraft losses in the Air Forces of the North-Western Front on 22 June 1941

	Shot down in air combat and by anti-aircraft artillery	Made an emergency landing due to battle damage	Destroyed on the ground, or abandoned due to combat or non-combat damage	For other reasons	For all reasons
Fighters	17	8	277	22	324
Bombers	29	8	60	1	98
Ground attack aircraft	8	1	6	6	21
Reconnaissance aircraft	–	–	36	–	36
Total:	54	17	379	29	479

For many specialists and history enthusiasts the high losses sustained by Soviet aviation on 22 June are a source of doubt. For the most part this has happened due to the loss of a whole raft of Soviet documents and the superficial nature of research dedicated to the events of the first day of the Great Patriotic War. Nevertheless it is clear that many of the claims made by *Luftwaffe* aces of victories in the air are fully confirmed by Soviet documents detailing losses.

* Two Do 17Zs from KG 2, two Bf 110s from ZG 26 and the headquarters of Stg1, and also one Bf 109F from JG 52.

† One of these aircraft was shot down in air combat with bombers from the 46th High-Speed Bomber Air Regiment and three were shot down in air combat with aircraft from the 42nd Fighter Air Regiment.

‡ One of these was shot down in air combat with bombers from the 40th High-Speed Bomber Air Regiment, while a second was most likely shot down in combat with an SB from the 50th High-Speed Bomber Air Regiment.

§ Two Ju-88s from KG 77 were unrecoverable losses, they were shot down in air combat with aircraft from the 15th Fighter Air Regiment and the 61st Ground Attack Air Regiment; two Ju-88s from KG 76 were damaged in combat with aircraft from the 10th and 238th Fighter Air Regiments.

To use the example of several units in the Air Forces of the North-Western Front, for which the documents have survived, it is easy to ascertain whether the losses from ground attacks by German aircraft correlated fully with the successes put forward by the *Luftwaffe*.

Thus for example the losses incurred by the 148th Fighter Air Regiment comprised 41 I-153s. Their distribution is as follows:

12 I-153s were lost on the ground due to bombing raids;
21 I-153s were damaged as a result of these bombing raids and were abandoned during the withdrawal from Liepaja airfield;
One I-153 was shot down in air combat (or by friendly anti-aircraft artillery fire);
One I-153 was destroyed on take-off after sustaining battle damage from shrapnel;
Two I-153s made emergency landings due to battle damage and were not repaired;
Four I-153s were destroyed on take-off and landing due to pilot error, technical reasons and so on.

The 15th Fighter Air Regiment lost 62 aircraft, of those**:**
Eight MiG-3s were destroyed during the bombing of Kaunas airfield;
11 MiG-3s were set alight during the evacuation from Kaunas;
13 MiG-3s were abandoned on Potsunai airfield;
Five MiG-3s were shot down in air combat;
Two MiG-3s were destroyed in accidents;
Three I-153s were destroyed during bombing on Kaunas airfield;
One I-153 was set alight during the evacuation from Kaunas;
One I-153 was set alight during the evacuation from Potsunai airfield;
Four I-153s were shot down in air combat;
Three I-153s were lost in accidents during landing or take-off (it is possible these were not necessarily on 22 June);
Six I-16s were destroyed on Kaunas airfield;
Four I-15bis aircraft were destroyed on Kaunas airfield.

The 236th Fighter Air Regiment lost 24 aircraft, of those:
'21 I-153s were destroyed as a result of ground attacks on their airfield;
One I-153 was destroyed on landing due to combat damage;
Two I-153s were shot down in air combat;'

The 238th Fighter Air Regiment lost 25 aircraft, of those:
'18 I-153s were destroyed as a result of ground attacks on their airfield;
Three I-153s were destroyed on take-off or landing due to pilot error
Four I-153s were unserviceable and were abandoned during withdrawal.'

The 61st Ground Attack Air Regiment lost 21 aircraft, of those:
Eight I-153s were shot down in air combat or by anti-aircraft artillery fire, four pilots ('according to other sources the figure was put at three') were killed and a further pilot later died of his injuries.
One I-153 made an emergency landing due to battle damage and was destroyed as it was not possible to evacuate this aircraft;
One I-153 was shot down by friendly anti-aircraft artillery fire, made an emergency landing and was subsequently destroyed;
Three I-153s sustained damage and were destroyed as it was not possible to evacuate them;

Five I-153s made emergency landings due to pilot error and the aircraft were destroyed
Three I-153s were destroyed during bombing of Kedainiai airfield.

The 46th High-Speed Bomber Air Regiment lost 41 aircraft, of which:
Seven were shot down in air combat;
Five were shot down in air combat, made emergency landings and were subsequently abandoned during the withdrawal;
Nine SB aircraft and one Ar-2 were destroyed on the ground during the course of bombing raids.
Nine SB aircraft and one Ar-2 were damaged in an air raid. ('Evidently several aircraft were subsequently repaired.')
Apart from that a further five SBs and five Ar-2s were abandoned on Siauliai airfield since they were unserviceable and there was a lack of available crews.

The final results from the operations conducted by Soviet aviation units on 22 June 1941.

The 31st Fighter Air Regiment
The pilots of this regiment flew 120 combat sorties, first and foremost to intercept enemy aircraft as well as on patrol, as well as flying some reconnaissance sorties.

In total the 31st Fighter Air Regiment lost around 50 aircraft. Accurate data concerning losses on 22 June is not available. According to data for the period between 22–29 June 1941 some 37 MiG-1/3s and 12 I-16s were destroyed on the ground in bombing raids and enemy ground attacks. Considering that practically 100 percent of the regiment's materiel was destroyed during the bombing raids on the first day of the war in Kaunas and Karmelava or were abandoned on the airfield, the majority of the aircraft indicated above relate to losses incurred on the first day of the war. ('By way of an example an aerial photograph taken on the evening of 22 June of Karmelava airfield, no less than 36 of the regiment's aircraft can be seen that were abandoned during the redeployment. There are no less than 15 MiG-1/3s and I-16s visible in photographs depicting Kaunas airfield.')

The 10th Fighter Air Regiment
In total the pilots of the 10th Fighter Air Regiment conducted 91 combat sorties, of these 88 were interception and patrol sorties and three were reconnaissance sorties, up until 1400 hrs on 22 June. 'Evidently in the second half of the day a few further sorties were flown.' First and foremost on one of these flights an I-16 was lost that was flown by Lieutenant G.M. Yakovlev. For example, according to the journal of the orders issued by the 7th Mixed Air Division at 1425 hrs a pair of I-16s from the 10th Fighter Air Regiment were due to carry out a reconnaissance sortie of the area around Kelme–Skaudvile. No details of this sortie are available but from German sources it is known that at 1445 hrs one I-16 was shot down by *Oberleutnant* Adolf-Waldemar Kinzinger from 1./JG 54.

It would have been a great deal to expect victories from the ranks of the worn out type 5 I-16s that were fitted with two ShKAS machine guns, but the regiment countered the raids on Siauliai rather well, and even though they did not shoot down a single enemy aircraft they did prevent a total routing of their airfield.

'The regiment's fighters recorded a victory against a Ju-88 from 6./KG 76.'

In total the 10th Fighter Air Regiment lost 13 aircraft, of these: two were I-16s shot down in air combat, one was an I-16 shot down by anti-aircraft artillery and two were I-16s that were lost to landing accidents. Eight I-16s were destroyed on the ground ('they were unserviceable and were abandoned on the airfield during the withdrawal from Siauliai'). Apart from that a further 17

MiG-3s from those that had been transferred to the 42nd Fighter Air Regiment were unserviceable and were abandoned during the withdrawal from Siauliai airfield.

The 148th Fighter Air Regiment

The regiment's pilots flew 162 combat sorties and this is possibly the best result to come out of 22 June.

Undoubtedly the feather in the regiment's cap was the combat activity against the German units advancing on Liepaja. Evidently it was this regiment that conducted the most ground attack combat sorties. The history of the 29th Panzer Division records combat activity by small groups of aircraft in the second half of the day, which they fought with the help of machine gun fire.

The regiment's pilots did not succeed in beating back the raids on Liepaja airfield, as a result of which the 148th Fighter Air Regiment lost 41 I-153s, which were either destroyed or damaged.

The 15th Fighter Air Regiment

In total the 15th Fighter Air Regiment flew 202 combat sorties on the first day of the war.*

The regiment incurred heavy losses—62 aircraft and was not capable of defending its own airfield.

The pilots claimed nine victories: three Ju-86s (evidently this should read Ju-88), five He 111s, and one Me-109. The unit's operational documents are missing and as such it is difficult to compare these results to German data. In historical literature a relatively large number of victories were attributed to the pilots of the 15th Fighter Air Regiment, and moreover those same pilots who perished:

> The 'Dzerzhintsy' were given their baptism of fire on 22 June. The first day of the war brought combat victories and combat losses. On that day the regiment's pilots destroyed nine fascist vultures.
>
> The Squadron Commander Ivan Alekseyevich Dolzhenko [he had been made Deputy Squadron Commander at the beginning of June] flew six combat sorties and shot down four enemy aircraft. On his seventh combat sortie the courageous pilot was killed.
>
> The other Squadron Commander Nikolay Boyarshinov shot down three enemy aircraft in his first five combat sorties. After getting airborne a sixth time over Jonava railway station near Kaunas he engaged three enemy aircraft in combat. He confidently went on the attack, manoeuvring successfully and evaded gunfire from the enemy fighters. Boyarshinov shot down one aircraft and continued to engage the others in an uneven fight. The fascists set the courageous pilot's aircraft alight.
>
> In the course of a single day pilot Lieutenant I.I. Schultz had shot down three aircraft.†

It is possible that it was these same pilots who were behind the above mentioned victories over German bombers recorded in the 15th Fighter Air Regiment's documents. It is however completely obvious that the victories recorded by this regiment are exaggerated at least four times over. The regiment's pilots can lay claim to one Ju-88 destroyed and one damaged.

* It is more than likely that this is taking into account the redeployment and the flights undertaken by the young pilots to assimilate landing and take-off in UTI-4s, I-16s, and MiG-3s.

† A.N. Sitkovskiy *Falcons in the Skies: A Documentary Story (A Literary Record by A.E. Chernatkina)* (Makhachkala, 1990).

In the area around Kaunas two Ju-88s from 6./KG 76, Stab/KG 76 were damaged. Moreover in the cockpit of the headquarters Ju-88 was the Commander of KG 76 *Oberstleutnant* Raithel, he was in the navigator's position. This aircraft made an emergency landing on its own territory in the area around Bartenstein. On landing this Junkers aircraft was put out of action completely, and all the crew members were seriously injured, the second Junkers managed to return to its home base.

The 42nd Fighter Air Regiment

The regiment's pilots flew no less than 60 combat sorties and shot down three Bf 109Fs and one Bf 110. This was the best result of all the fighter regiments in the Air Forces of the North-Western Front on 22 June 1941. Nevertheless the pilots did not succeed in defending their own airfield and the regiment incurred heavy losses in the air and on the ground.

According to a report written by the 57th Mixed Air Division between 22 June 1941–30 July 1941 the regiment flew 115 combat sorties.

Taking into consideration that after 22 June the number of aircraft in the regiment dropped dramatically, and it is highly likely that more than half of the sorties were flown on the first day.

In total on 22 June 1941 the 42nd Fighter Air Regiment lost 67 aircraft, of which three I-153s were shot down in air combat and no less than four flew emergency landings due to battle damage. According to a report written by the headquarters of the 57th Mixed Air Division the regiment in total lost 78 aircraft in total in the period between 22 June 1941 to 30 July 1941. Of these 27 I-153s were destroyed, 12 I-153s were damaged and were abandoned on the airfield during the withdrawal. Eight I-153s were shot down in air combat, four I-153s failed to return from a combat sortie, and four I-153s made emergency landings, while 21 I-15bis and two I-16s were destroyed, damaged or abandoned on Orany and Vilnius airfields during the withdrawal.

The 236th Fighter Air Regiment

This regiment flew three combat sorties and lost 24 I-153s, of those: 21 I-153s were destroyed on Alytus airfield, two were shot down in air combat and one was destroyed on landing as a result of battle damage. Some of the personnel served as part of the 15th Fighter Air Regiment.

The 238th Fighter Air Regiment

This regiment flew 23 combat sorties, it is possible that the regiment's pilots succeeded in shooting down a Ju-88 from 1./KG 76 (in German documents the location of the attack is identified as Skvarbai).

The losses amounted to 21 I-153s. Of those: three I-153s were destroyed during a bombing raid on Panevezys airfield, 11 I-153s were damaged during a bombing raid on Panevezys airfield, seven I-153s were taken out of action on take-off and landing for non-combat reasons. A further three unserviceable I-153s were abandoned on Panevezys airfield during the withdrawal.

The 237th Fighter Air Regiment

The number of sorties is not known. In total the regiment lost 10 I-153s. Of those, eight I-153s were destroyed on the ground and two were abandoned during the withdrawal.*

* According to a report written by the headquarters of the 57th Mixed Air Division, these losses were for the period between 22 June–30 July 1941 but taking into account the events of 22 June it is more likely that these aircraft were lost on the first day of the war.

The 240th Fighter Air Regiment

This regiment flew 22 combat sorties, losing six I-15bis aircraft, which were abandoned on Raseiniai due to a lack of crews.

The 21st Fighter Air Regiment

This regiment preliminarily carried out around 50 sorties providing air cover over Riga. The regiment lost four I-16s, of which two I-16s were destroyed during an emergency landing, and two I-16s were damaged during an emergency landing.

The 49th Fighter Air Regiment

This regiment preliminarily carried out around 50 sorties providing air cover over Daugavpils and Vilnius. The regiment lost one I-16 as a result of a crash caused by a manufacturing defect in the engine. The pilot was killed.

The 38th Fighter Air Regiment

This regiment flew 57 sorties to provide air cover for the airfield and the city of Tallinn. They did not encounter the enemy.

The 9th High-Speed Bomber Air Regiment

This regiment flew 44 combat sorties, losing five SBs shot down by anti-aircraft artillery, seven were destroyed on the ground, while 10 were damaged as a result of them being abandoned during the withdrawal.

The 46th High-Speed Bomber Air Regiment

This regiment flew 18 combat sorties, dropping the following quantity of bombs: 72 FAB-100s, and 36 FAB-50s. Their losses amounted to 12 SB aircraft lost in air combat (seven were shot down and five were damaged, made emergency landings and as a result were abandoned during the withdrawal) and nine SBs and one Ar-2 were destroyed on the ground. Nine SB aircraft and Ar-2s damaged as a result of the raid were subsequently abandoned during the withdrawal, and five SBs and Ar-2s were abandoned on Siauliai airfield due to technical problems.

The 31st High-Speed Bomber Air Regiment

This regiment flew 75 combat sorties, This was the best result of all the bomber regiments in the Red Army Air Force on the first day of the war. The regiment dropped the following quantity of bombs: 35 FAB-250s and 294 FAB-100s. Losses amounted to three SBs shot down in air combat and one shot down by a fighter from the 49th Fighter Air Regiment in the area around Daugavpils. A further six SBs were abandoned on Vaijnode airfield owing to technical problems.

The 40th High-Speed Bomber Air Regiment

This regiment flew 45 combat sorties. Losses amounted to 10 SBs lost in air combat, a further aircraft was damaged, made an emergency landing on Piltene airfield and was subsequently abandoned during the withdrawal. Six SBs were destroyed on the ground, while a further four were damaged as a result of a raid and were subsequently abandoned during the withdrawal.

The 50th High-Speed Bomber Air Regiment

This regiment flew 24 combat sorties, dropping the following quantity of bombs: 144 FAB-100s and 22 FAB-50. Losses amounted to two SB aircraft destroyed as a result of emergency landings. One was damaged in air combat by fighters and another was lost to a technical problem.

The 54th High-Speed Bomber Air Regiment

This regiment flew no less than 22 combat sorties, of which four were reconnaissance sorties ('owing to the fact that the regiment's operational documents are missing along with those of the 57th Mixed Air Division the exact number of sorties is not known'). Losses amounted to three SBs lost in air combat, one SB lost in an emergency landing (which was subsequently abandoned during the withdrawal). Four SBs and five Ar-2s were destroyed on Vilnius airfield.

The 61st Ground Attack Air Regiment

This regiment flew 53 ground attack combat sorties.* The total number of sorties flown that day is not known.

The regiment's pilots claimed three victories in air combat:

> Junior Lieutenant V.I. Podlegayev claimed a victory in the area around Shaki, and moreover the aircraft was identified as an ANBO-4 (what is meant here cannot be discerned from the archives, but by all accounts this was a victory over an Hs 126 short-range reconnaissance aircraft, since the Lithuanian ANBO-4 is very similar to the Heinkel 126).
> Junior Lieutenant P.I. Chyorniy claimed a victory over an Me-110 in the area around Pilviskiai;
> Junior Lieutenant P.G. Borovik claimed a victory over an He 111 in the area around Kedainiai.

The first two claims are not confirmed in the German data although it is perfectly plausible that the Soviet pilots were able to damage a Bf 110 from 4./(F)33 and an Hs 126 close to these locations.

The victory claimed by Junior Lieutenant P.G. Borovik is confirmed by German data. I./KG 77 lost Ju-88A-5 W.Nr.3432, bearing the code 3Z+EH in the area around Kedainiai and the aircraft was a 100 percent loss.

The 241st Ground Attack Air Regiment

Flew 22 combat sorties to provide cover for Rumbula airfield. They did not encounter the enemy.

In total the pilots of the Air Forces of the North-Western Front flew around 1,100 combat sorties.† Of those bomber aviation flew 228 combat sorties, ground attack flew 100, and fighter aviation flew around 800.‡

---

* In total up until 26 June 1941 some 123 combat sorties were carried out, of which 17 were reconnaissance sorties and 53 were to provide cover for airfields or close support for ground troops.

† These are calculated figures.

‡ It is possible this is somewhat higher since no accurate data is available on the activities of the 54th High-Speed Bomber Air Regiment.

German officers accompany the Japanese military attache during his visit to Daugavpils airfield in July 1941. The arrows show General Hiroshi Oshima and the Commander of KG 77 Colonel Raithel, the photo shows the bandage of Raithel's right arm, which had been broken as a result of an emergency landing on 22 June 1941.

Unserviceable I-16, UTI-4, and MiG-1/3 aircraft from the 31st Fighter Air Regiment and R-5s, and U-2s from the 2nd Aerial Photographic Detachment, which had been left on the northern part of Kaunas airfield on 22 June 1941.

Unserviceable I-16, UTI-4, and MiG-1/3 aircraft from the 31st Fighter Air Regiment and R-5s, and U-2s from the 2nd Aerial Photographic Detachment, which had been left on the northern part of Kaunas airfield on 22 June 1941.

An I-153 bearing the tactical No. 2 red, the pilot of this aircraft was Deputy Commander of the 1st Squadron, 61st Ground Attack Air Regiment Senior Political instructor Lagutin, the aircraft made an emergency landing on Kaunas airfield following an attack by German forces in the area around Mariampole–Kalvarija on 22 June 1941.

Unserviceable-15bis, I-153, I-16, UTI-4, MiG-3, and 15th Fighter Aviation, which were left on the southern part of Kaunas airfield on 22 June 1941.

Unserviceable-15bis, I-153, I-16, UTI-4, MiG-3, and 15th Fighter Aviation, which were left on the southern part of Kaunas airfield on 22 June 1941.

An I-153 bearing the tactical No. 4 white from the 4th Squadron, 61st Fighter Air Regiment, this aircraft ground looped on Kedainiai airfield.

A MiG-3 from the line-up of the 31st Fighter Air Regiment that was abandoned due to non-combat damage on Kedainiai.

Unserviceable aircraft which were abandoned on Siauliai airfield.

Unserviceable aircraft which were abandoned on Siauliai airfield.

Ar-2 dive-bombers from the 46th High-Speed Bomber Air Regiment at Siauliai airfield, the tactical numbers 2, 3, and 4 are clearly visible.

Ar-2 dive-bombers from the 46th High-Speed Bomber Air Regiment at Siauliai airfield, the tactical numbers 2, 3, and 4 are clearly visible.

An early series SB at Siauliai airfield bearing the tactical No. 2 from the 46th High-Speed Bomber Air Regiment.

R-5SSS aircraft from the 11th Air Observation Squadron at Siauliai airfield bearing the tactical Nos. 2 and 5, these aircraft previously belonged to the 61st Ground Attack Air Regiment.

Type 5 I-16 fighters from the 10th Fighter Air Regiment at Siauliai airfield, bearing the tactical Nos 2, 9, 10, and 13.

Unserviceable aircraft left on Vilnius airfield: I-153s, I-15bis, I-16, and UT-1 aircraft from the 42nd Fighter Air Regiment.

Unserviceable aircraft left on Vilnius airfield: I-153s, I-15bis, I-16, and UT-1 aircraft from the 42nd Fighter Air Regiment.

Unserviceable aircraft left on Vilnius airfield: I-153s, I-15bis, I-16, and UT-1 aircraft from the 42nd Fighter Air Regiment.

Unserviceable aircraft left on Vilnius airfield: I-153s, I-15bis, I-16, and UT-1 aircraft from the 42nd Fighter Air Regiment.

Il-2 aircraft from the 61st Ground Attack Air Regiment at Vilnius airfield.

SB aircraft from the 54th High-Speed Bomber Air Regiment at Vilnius airfield.

A rare example of a PR-ZET from the Civilian Air Fleet at Vilnius airfield.

Unserviceable aircraft abandoned on Riga airfield, at the beginning of June 1941. Amongst the later series I-16s from the 21st Fighter Air Regiment type 5 I-16s from the 10th Fighter Air Regiment are clearly visible. These aircraft were transferred between 22–23 June from Siauliai and Jelgava and became unserviceable due to a lack of required maintenance.

An I-153 bearing the tactical No. 55 from the 148th Fighter Air Regiment at Riga airfield.

A MiG-1 bearing the tactical No. 7 from the 31st Fighter Air Regiment at Riga airfield.

A UT-1 from an unknown unit and a USB bearing the tactical No. 4 from the 40th High-Speed Bomber Air Regiment at Riga airfield.

Unserviceable aircraft, which were abandoned at Daugavpils airfield at the beginning of June 1941. The Ar-2 bears the tactical No. 2 and is from the 46th High-Speed Bomber Air Regiment.

SB bombers from the 54th High-Speed Bomber Air Regiment at Daugavpils airfield, the aircraft in the foreground bears the tactical No. 5.

An I-16 bearing the tactical No. 14 from the 49th Fighter Air Regiment, in the background is a Bf 109F from the II/JG 54 Headquarters. Daugavpils airfield.

I-153 fighters at Daugavpils airfield bearing the tactical Nos. 15 and 8 from the 49th Fighter Air Regiment.

Unserviceable SB aircraft from the 50th High-Speed Bomber Air Regiment that were abandoned on Jelgava airfield, July 1941.

A series of photographs taken in Riga at the end of June 1941 by Soviet military correspondents. A type 24 I-16 bearing the tactical No. 2 from the 21st Fighter Air Regiment is taking off, this aircraft is fitted with underslung fuel tanks.

Commander of the 148th Fighter Air Regiment Captain Ya.E. Titayev prepares to take his place in the cockpit.

Flight Commander of the 15th Fighter Air Regiment Lieutenant Fyodor Andreyevich Smyshlyaev posing next to a 'Chaika'.

Another series of photographs illustrating the pilots of the 38th Fighter Air Regiment, these photographs were taken by Soviet military correspondents at the end of July 1941. The comrades are congratulating the Deputy Commander of the Regiment Captain Vasiliy Grigoryevich Kashtanov after the completion of a successful combat sortie.

Flight Commander of the 38th Fighter Air Regiment Lieutenant Ivan Fyodorovich Balyuk gives orders to his subordinate lieutenants Ivan Semyonovich Bakal, and Mikhail Nikitovich Zhukov.

Détruits au sol...

Six photos entre cent et qui établissent documentairement l'œuvre de destruction accomplie contre l'aviation soviétique

Le 22 juin à l'aube, la campagne contre les soviets commençait, et aussitôt l'aviation allemande entreprit son œuvre de destruction contre les avions et les aérodromes ennemis. Au soir du premier jour de cette guerre, il y avait déjà 1811 avions soviétiques de détruits. Trois semaines ne s'étaient pas écoulées que, le 11 juillet, le Haut Commandement allemand était en mesure d'annoncer qu'à cette date, l'aviation soviétique avait perdu 6233 appareils. Ces chiffres ont de quoi étonner. Mais ils sont aussi exacts que tous les chiffres communiqués précédemment dans les bulletins du Haut Commandement et que les adversaires commençaient toujours par contester

Des centaines de photos prises dans de nombreux aérodromes soviétiques, « Signal » en a choisi une demi-douzaine. Elles représentent des documents de la gigantesque œuvre de destruction que l'aviation allemande a su accomplir avec une précision et une sûreté inquiétantes à l'égard de plus de 900 aérodromes soviétiques. En peu de jours, on envoya à la ferraille la masse énorme de bombardiers et d'avions de chasse qui devaient déferler sur l'Allemagne par l'est. Cette destruction fut aussi celle des plans d'attaque des ennemis de l'Europe

Clichés Freytag (PK) (1) ; Huffzy (PK) (1) ; Meyer (PK) (2) ; Speck (PK) (1), Melichar (PK) (1)

A page from the German journal *Signal* on which the captured airfields of Alytus, Kaunas, and Kedainiai are shown.

Soviet aircraft that were captured in the Baltic region subsequently became exhibits at exhibitions in towns across Germany. The Germans inspect I-153 No. 3 from the 238th Fighter Air Regiment.

A German soldier poses for a photo next to a MiG-3 from the 15th Fighter Air Regiment.

An I-153 bearing the tactical No. 21 from the line-up of the 238th Fighter Air Regiment, which was captured on Panevezys airfield. In this photo the aircraft has been loaded onto a railway wagon for transportation to Germany.

This aircraft was repaired with the help of components from other I-153s and served in various training units in the *Luftwaffe,* between 1942–1945. It was subsequently abandoned by the Germans in France, where it remained after the war, it was placed in a French aviation museum in Le Bourget. This is the only I-153 to remain absolutely original. At the present time the aircraft is undergoing restoration.

A plan of the disposition of aircraft of the warring sides on the morning of 22 June 1941.

Appendix I

Luftwaffe aircraft losses in the North-Western Front zone on 22 June 1941

	Unit	Range of operation or losses	Reason	Aircraft type	Aircraft number / registration	% of damage	Fate of the crew
1	1.(H)/11	Dubovo-Nord	Ground fire (*Infanteriebeschuss*)	Go 145			Pilot (*Flugzeugführer*) was injured *Unteroffizier* W. Pinhack
2	4.(H)/10	Ladzijai	Damage caused by enemy action (*Feindbeschuss*)	Hs 126B	T1 + DM		Observer (*Beobachter*) *Oberleutnant* G. Aus dem Bruch was injured
3	7.(H)/21		Damage caused by enemy action (*Feindbeschuss*)	Hs 126B			Observer (*Beobachter*) *Leutnant* A.W. Schulte injured
4	2.(H)/32	Near Kulanec	Damage caused by enemy action (*Feindbeschuss*)	Hs 126B			Observer (*Beobachter*) *Oberleutnant* R. Mentzel was injured
5	2.(H)/23	Near Taurage	Fighter attack (*Luftkampf*)	Hs 126B			Observer (*Beobachter*) *Feldwebel* Fischer was injured
6	4.(H)/41	Tilsit	Damage caused by enemy action (*Feindbeschuss*)	Fw-189A		10%	
7	3.(H)/41	Lindengarten	Enemy artillery fire (*Flakbeschuss*)	Hs 126B	W.Nr. 3167	40%	
8	4.(F)/33	Tilsit	Emergency landing (*Bruchlandung*)	Bf. 110E-3	W.Nr. 2325	20%	
9	2.(F)/33	5 km south of Mordasorowa near Puchacze (south-east of Suwalki). More than likely close to the village of Puvociai (20 km west of Orany)[1]	The reason is unknown (*Unbekkant*)	Bf 110E-3	W.Nr. 2333 8H+DK DB601 engines W.Nr. 65620 and 65617	100%	Pilot (*flugzeugführer*) *Unteroffizier* E.H. Martin and the observer (*Beobachter*) *Oberleutnant* A. Nocke disappeared, and radio-operator (*Bordfunker*) *Unteroffizier* P. Ogorzelski
10	Stab/ StG 1	Thorn	Emergency landing (*Bruchlandung*)	Bf 110-3	W.Nr. 2402	60%	

	Unit	Range of operation or losses	Reason	Aircraft type	Aircraft number / registration	% of damage	Fate of the crew
11	8./KG 2	Near Wilna	Damage caused by enemy action (*Feindbeschuss bei Tiefangriff*, 17.45)	Do 17Z	W.Nr. 3466 U5+GS		Squadron Commander pilot (*flugzeugführer*) *Oberleutnant* E. von Loudon and radio-operator (*bordfunker*) *Unteroffizier* R. Prade were injured
12	8./KG 2	Near Wilna	Damage caused by enemy activity (*Feindbeschuss bei Tiefangriff*, 17.45)	Do 17Z	W.Nr. 2556 U5+1S		Pilot (*flugzeugführer*) *Unteroffizier* E. Schmoormanns, and the observer (*beobachter*) *Gefreiter* K. Kohler were injured
13	1./KG 76	Skworby	Damage caused by enemy activity (*Feindbeschuss*)	Ju 88A-5	W.Nr. 5191		Observer (beobachter) *Unteroffizier* S. Quenstedt was injured
14	6./KG 76	Near Schaulen	Fighter attack (*Luftkampf*)	Ju 88A-5	W.Nr. 2277 F1+EP		Radio-operator (*bortfunker*) *Feldwebel* E. Markl was fatally injured
15	Stab/KG 77	Near Breitenstein	Emergency landing facilitated by damage caused by enemy activity (*Feindbeschuss, Notlandung*)	Ju 88A-6	W.Nr. 2331	100%	Pilot (*flugzeugführer) Oberleutnant* H. Buchs and Colonel *Oberstleutnant* H. Raithel were injured
16	1./KG77	Kedainiai	Aircraft was destroyed and caught fire (*Absturz, Aufschlagbrand*)	Ju 88A-5	W.Nr. 3422 EZ+EH	100%	Pilot (*flugzeugführer) Feldwebel*. R. Meene, and observer (*beobachter*) *Unteroffizier* P. Scharmach both disappeared without a trace. The radio-operator (*bortfunker*) *Oberfeldwebel* R. Geihard, and gunner (*bordschutze*) *Unteroffizier* W. Enderle were killed.
17	6./KG 77		Damage caused by enemy activity (*Feindbeschuss*)	Ju 88A			Gunner (*bordschutze*) *Gefrehter* A. Schweiger was injured
18	2./ZG 26	Rosten	Emergency landing facilitated by damage sustained as a result of enemy activity *(Bruchlandung inf. Feindbeschluss*)	Bf 110E-2	W.Nr. 2933	20%	
19	II./JG 52	Perloja	Engine damage, emergency landing *(Motorschaden, Notlandung*)	Bf 109F-2	W.Nr. 5780	100%	
20	6./JG 52	Augustowo	Anti-aircraft artillery, emergency landing (*Flak, Notlandung, Sobolewo*)	Bf 109F-2	W.Nr. 5460	Less than 10%	*Gefreiter* Walter Kohne was injured

	Unit	Range of operation or losses	Reason	Aircraft type	Aircraft number / registration	% of damage	Fate of the crew
21	8./JG 53	Merkina	Shot down in air combat, emergency landing (*Luftkampf, Notlandung*)	Bf 109F-2	W.Nr. 5523	100%	*Oberfeldwebel* Eduard Koslowski was shot down. He returned on 23 June 1941
22	9./JG 53	20 km north of Leipalingis	Emergency landing, caused by engine failure (*Notlandung inf* Motorstörung)	Bf 109F-2	WNr. 6698	100%	*Oberfeldwebel* Josef Kronschnabel was unhurt
23	Stab II/ JG 53	Between Erzvilkas and Nemakscinai	Shot down in air combat, landed on 'Bryukho' airfield *(Luftkampf Bomber, Bauchlandung)*	Bf 109F-2	W.Nr. 6674	100%	*Hauptmann* Heinz Bretnütz was injured, he died on 27 June 1941
24	Stab/JG 54	Trakehnen	Shot down in air combat, landed on 'Bryukho' airfield (Luftkampf)	Bf 109F-2	W.Nr. 5761	20%	*Major* Hannes Trautloft
25	1./JG 54	Near Allenburg	Emergency landing after running out of fuel (*Notlandung, Brennstoffmangel*)	Bf 109F-2	W.Nr. 12638	50%	
26	7./JG 54	Litzmannstadt (?)	Landed in 'Bryukho' airfield (*Bauchlandung*)	Bf 109F-2	W.Nr. 8230	20%	*Oberleutnant* Gerhard Koall

Notes
This data concerning the reasons for the losses is provided based on the reports written by the *Generalquartermeister* (Gen. Qu. 6. Abt.)

1 This data was provided by the Lithuanian historian A. Novichenko.

Appendix II

Claims by Luftwaffe fighter units for aircraft shot down in the North-Western Front zone on 22 June 1941

Rank	Surname	Name	Unit	Type	Time	Location	No. of kills in personal tally
Oberleutnant	Kinzinger	Adolf-Waldemar	1./JG 54	DJ-6	0330	–	9
Oberleutnant	Kinzinger	Adolf-Waldemar	1./JG 54	DJ-6	0330	–	10
Oberleutnant	Kinzinger	Adolf-Waldemar	1./JG 54	DJ-6	0551	–	11
Hauptmann	Seiler	Reinhard	Stab 1./JG 54	SB-2	0555	North-east of Kowno	4
Unteroffizier	Siegler	Peter	2./JG 54	SB-2	0555	–	1
Leutnant	Raub	Günther	2./JG 54	SB-2	0557	–	1
Hauptmann	Seiler	Reinhard	Stab I./JG 54	SB-2	0557	North of Kowno	5
Leutnant	Raub	Günther	2./JG 54	SB-2	0558	–	2
Hauptmann	Seiler	Reinhard	Stab I./JG 54	SB-2	0558	West of Kowno: at an altitude of 3,500m	6
Oberleutnant	Kinzinger	Adolf-Waldemar	I./JG 54	I-16	0558	–	12
	Possible claims: 2./JG 54 *Oberfeldwebel* Fricke, *Oberleutnant* Hein, 1./JG 54 *Feldwebel* Quack, *Unteroffizier* Bruhn		I./JG 54	SB-2	-	–	-
	Possible claims: 2./JG54 *Oberfeldwebel* Fricke, *Oberleutnant* Hein I./JG 54 *Feldwebel* Quack, *Unteroffizier* Bruhn		I./JG 54	SB-2	-	–	-
Leutnant	Witzel	Hans	5./JG 27	I-15	0354	North east of Alytus	4
Hauptmann	Lippert	Wolfgang	Stab II./JG 27	I-15	0415	South of Knysyyn	17
Hauptmann	Lippert	Wolfgang	Stab II./ JG 27	I-17	0418	North east of Wizna	18
Oberleutnant	Wiesinger	Willhelm	4./JG 27	I-17	0420	North of Zambrow	10
Oberfeldwebel	Schulz	Otto	4./JG 27	I-15 (Curtiss &)	0820	N. Alytus	7
Feldwebel	Krenz	Herbert	6./JG 27	I-15	0825	North-east of Alytus	5
Unteroffizier	Walchhofer	Johann	6./JG 27	SB-2	1500	South of Wilna	1
Leutnant	Witzel	Hans	5./JG 27	*Doppeldecker (Schuflzg.)*	1525	Dogai	5
Leutnant	Schacht	Arthur	4./JG 27	DB-3	1623	South of Berzniki	2

Rank	Surname	Name	Unit	Type	Time	Location	No. of kills in personal tally
Leutnant	Witzel	Hans	5./JG 27	I-15	1815	West of Bialystok	6
Unteroffizier	Spengler	Hermann	5./JG 52	DB-3	0932	–	1
Oberfahnrich	Semelka	Waldemar	4./JG 52	I-15	0948	–	1
Oberleutnant	Hartmann	Carl	Stab II./JG 52	I-15	0950	–	3
Feldwebel	Mayr	Georg	4./JG 52	I-15	0950	–	3
Unteroffizier	Wilsky	Bernhard	Stab II./JG 52	I-15	0952	–	2
Hauptmann	Woitke	Erich	Stab II./JG 52	I-15	0953	South of Varena	12
Oberleutnant	Simsch	Siegfried	4./JG 52	I-15	1000	West of Varena: 1,000m	1
Oberleutnant	Steinhoff	Johannes	4./JG 52	I-15	1000	Varena	9
Unteroffizier	Hanika	Albrecht	5./JG 52	I-15	1007	FL.PL. Orany: 800m	1
Unteroffizier	Gilhaus	Franz	5./JG 52	I-15	1008	–	1
Oberleutnant	Schumann	August-Willhelm	5./JG 52	DB-3	1011	–	4
Unteroffizier	Spengler	Hermann	5./JG 52	I-15	1011	FL.PL. Orany: 800m	2
Unteroffizier	Lehmann	Alfred	5./JG 52	DB-3	1015	–	1
Oberleutnant	Schumann	August-Willhelm	5./JG 52	DB-3	1015	–	5
Hauptmann	Woitke	Erich	Stab II./JG 52	SB-2	1648	North of Marknie	13
Oberleutnant	Resch	Rudolf	6./JG 52	SB-2	1650	–	1
Hauptmann	Spies	Walter	Stab II./JG 53	SB-2	0552	–	1
Hauptmann	Spies	Walter	Stab II./JG 53	SB-2	0554	–	2
Oberfeldwebel	Litjens	Stefan	4./JG 53	SB-2	0556	–	7
Unteroffizier	Rollwage	Herbert	4./JG 53	SB-2	0557	North of Raseiniai	1
Oberfeldwebel	Litjens	Stefan	4./JG 53	SB-2	0558	–	8
Oberfeldwebel	Margstein	Walter	4./JG 53	SB-2	0554	Bedanciai: 2500m	3
Feldwebel	Wurmheller	Josef	5./JG 53	SB-2	1801	North of Taurage: 3,200m	11
Oberleutnant	Brändle	Kurt	5./JG 53	SB-3	1803	North of Taurage	8
Unteroffizier	Reipert	Manfred	5./JG 53	SB-3	1812	South of a lake close to Siauliai: 3,000m	1
Hauptmann	Bretnütz	Heinz	Stab II ./JG 53	SB-2	-	–	32
Leutnant	Stengel	Gerhard	4./JG 53	DB-3	-	–	1
Leutnant	Beißwenger	Hans	6./JG 54	I-16	0950	–	2
Feldwebel	Hager	Rudolf	4./JG 54	SB-2	1645	North-west of Kowno: 2,000m	6
Oberleutnant	Philipp	Hans	4./JG 54	SB-2	1645	North-west of Kowno: 3,000m	26
Oberleutnant	Sattig	Carl	4./JG 54	SB-2	1647	North-west of Kowno: 2,800m	2
Gefreiter	Bartling	Günther	5./JG 54	SB-2	1715	–	1
Leutnant	Pöhs	Josef	5./JG 54	SB-2	1715	–	10
Oberleutnant	Mütherich	Hubert	5./JG 54	SB-2	1720	–	11
Leutnant	Pöhs	Josef	5./JG 54	SB-2	1720	–	11
Gefreiter	Bartling	Günther	5./JG 54	SB-2	1723	–	2
Oberfeldwebel	Kiening	Georg	5./JG 54	SB-2	1725	–	4
Leutnant	Hannig	Horst	6./JG 54	SB-2	1727	–	1
Leutnant	Schreiterer	Günther	6./JG 54	SB-2	1727	–	1
Hauptmann	Eckerle	Franz	6./JG 54	SB-2	1730	–	5
Gefreiter	Zander	Friedrich	5./JG 54	SB-2	1730	–	1
Oberleutnant	Schultz	Karl-Heinz	Stab II.//JG 53	SB-2	1740	–	1
Oberleutnant	Kagenek Graf Von	Erbo	9./JG 27	SB-2	1850	South of Vilna	18

Rank	Surname	Name	Unit	Type	Time	Location	No. of kills in personal tally
Unteroffizier	Riepe	Ernst	9./JG 27	SB-2	1850	South of Vilna	1
Hauptmann	Wilcke	Wolf-Dietrich	Stab III./JG 53	I-15	0400	–	14
Feldwebel	Stumpf	Werner	7./JG 53	DJ-6	0405	–	3
Hauptmann	Wilcke	Wolf-Dietrich	Stab III./JG 53	I-15	0405	–	15
Hauptmann	Wilcke	Wolf-Dietrich	Stab III./JG 53	I-16	0410	–	16
Oberleutnant	Altendorf	Heinz	7./JG 53	I-16	0540	–	8
Feldwebel	Stumpf	Werner	7./JG 53	I-16	0635	–	4
Hauptmann	Wilcke	Wolf-Dietrich	Stab III/JG 53	I-153	0705	–	17
Leutnant	Schmidt	Erich	9./JG 53	I-16	0715	–	18
Oberfeldwebel	Kronschnabel	Josef	9./JG 53	I-16	0718	–	1
Leutnant	Schaller	Wolf	9./JG 53	I-16	0720	–	1
Oberfeldwebel	Koslowski	Eduard	8./JG 53	I-153	0810	–	5
Unteroffizier	Wegener	Otto	7./JG 53	I-16	0935	–	1
Feldwebel	Neuhoff	Hermann	7./JG 53	DJ-6	0938	South west of Kalvarija	11
Leutnant	Schramm	Herbert	8./JG 53	DJ-6	0944	North of Kalvarija	9
Leutnant	Schmidt	Erich	9./JG 53	DJ-6	1135	–	19
Feldwebel	Sauer	Kurt	9./JG 53	I-17	1525	–	4
Feldwebel	Öchler	Hans	8./JG 53	SB-3	1630	–	2
Oberleutnant	Altendorf	Heinz	7./JG 53	DB-3	1635	–	9
Feldwebel	Neuhoff	Hermann	7./JG 53	DB-3	1635	–	12
Unteroffizier	Wegener	Otto	7./JG 53	DB-3	1635	–	2
Leutnant	Schramm	Herbert	8./JG 53	DB-3	1640	–	10
Hauptmann	Wilcke	Wolf-Dietrich	Stab III./JG 53	I-17	1643	–	18
Leutnant	Harder	Jürgen	Stab III./JG 53	I-17	1645	–	1
Oberleutnant	Müller	Freidrich-Karl	Stab III./JG 53	I-17	1645	–	11
Oberleutnant	Quaet-Faslem	Klaus	Stab III./JG 53	I-17	1645	–	2
Oberluetnant	Quaet-Faslem	Klaus	Stab III./JG 53	I-17	1647	–	3
Oberleutnant	Müller	Friedrich-Karl	Stab III./JG 53	I-17	1648	–	12
Leutnant	Hosnedl	Siegmund	7./JG 53	DB-3	1720	–	1
Feldwebel	Stumpf	Werner	7./JG 53	DB-3	1720	–	5
Feldwebel	Stumpf	Werner	7./JG 53	DB-3	1723	–	6
Feldwebel	Klippgen	Rolf	9./JG 53	I-17	1745	–	3
Leutnant	Schmidt	Erich	9./JG 53	I-16	1825	–	20
Oberleutnant	Götz	Franz	9./JG 53	DJ-6	1828	–	11
Leutnant	Klager	Ernst	7./JG 53	DJ-6	2045	–	1
Leutnant	Schmidt	Erich	9./JG 53	DJ-6	2045	–	21
Leutnant	Wiegend	Gustav	9./JG 53	DJ-6	2045	–	1
Unteroffizier	Damoser	Rudolf	9./JG 54	SB-3	0640	–	1
Leutnant	Wübke	Waldemar	9./JG 54	SB-3	0640	–	6
Leutnant	Wübke	Waldemar	9./JG 54	SB-3	0643	–	7
Unteroffizier	Zweigart	Eugen Ludwig	9./JG 54	I-153	1425	–	2
Leutnant	Wübke	Waldemar	9./JG 54	SB-2	1727	–	8
Leutnant	Heyer	Hans-Joachim	8./JG 54	I-15	2035	–	1
Major	Trautloft	Hannes	Stab/JG 54	DB-3	1648	North-west of Mariampol	9

Appendix III

The availability of fuel and lubricants in the airfield servicing battalions

The 8th Mixed Air Division	Available on 22 June 1941 (kg)	Destroyed during the evacuation (kg)	Abandoned during the evacuation (kg)
The 188th Airfield Servicing Battalion (61st Ground Attack Air Regiment)			
B-80 aviation fuel	6,600	6,600	–
B-74 aviation fuel	45,000	45,000	–
B-70 aviation fuel	106,000	106,000	–
Starter fuel	2,500	2,500	–
B-59 aviation fuel	380,000	380,000	–
Fuel for road vehicles	10,000	10,000	–
Diesel fuel	20,700	20,700	–
Aviation oil	23, 416	23,416	–
Product R-9	6,000	6,000	–
The 128th Airfield Servicing Battalion (236th Fighter Air Regiment)			
B-74 aviation fuel	89,764	–	89,764
B-70 aviation fuel	10,457	–	10,457
Fuel for road vehicles	1,000	–	1,000
Aviation oil	3,110	–	3,110
Product R-9	385	–	385
The 129th Airfield Servicing Battalion (31st Fighter Air Regiment)			
B-78 aviation fuel	168,000	124,000	44,000
B-74 aviation fuel	138,000	138,000	–
B-80 aviation fuel	23,000	1,000	22,000
Aviation starter fuel	7,000	7,000	–
Fuel for road vehicles	29,000	5,000	24,000
Aviation oil	22,500	22,500	–
Product R-9	4,500	4,500	–
The 130th Airfield Servicing Battalion (15th Fighter Air Regiment)			
B-78 aviation fuel	330,000	330,000	–
B-74 aviation fuel	30,000	30,000	–
Fuel for road vehicles	2,000	2,000	–
Aviation oil	24,913	24,913	–
Product R-9	800	800	–
The 117th Airfield Servicing Battalion (240th Fighter Air Regiment)			
B-70 aviation fuel	4,050	–	4,050
Aviation oil	350	–	350
Product R-9	260	–	260

The 57th Mixed Air Division	Available on 22 June 1941 (kg)	Destroyed during the evacuation (kg)	Abandoned during the evacuation (kg)
The 125th Airfield Servicing Battalion (54th High-Speed Bomber Air Regiment)			
B-78 aviation fuel	65,000	65,000	–
B-74 aviation fuel	335,000	335,000	–
Aviation oil	21,000	21,000	–
Product R-9	6,000	6,000	–
The 126th Airfield Servicing Battalion (42nd Fighter Air Regiment)			
B-78 aviation fuel	31,260	31,260	–
B-74 aviation fuel	185,740	83,740	90,000
B-70 aviation fuel	10,000	10,000	–
Fuel for road vehicles	2,000	2,000	–
Aviation oil	17,000	16,000	–
Product R-9	2,100	1,900	–
127th Airfield Servicing Battalion (237th Fighter Air Regiment)			
B-74 aviation fuel	15,799	–	15,799
B-70 aviation fuel	35,500	–	–
Fuel for road vehicles	10,000	–	3,000
Aviation oil	–	–	–
Product R-9	–	–	–
The 107th Airfield Servicing Battalion (49th High-Speed Bomber Air Regiment)			
B-78 aviation fuel	164,490		–
B-74 aviation fuel	174,368		
B-70 aviation fuel	190,000		
2nd grade fuel	17,726		
Aviation oil	20,800		–
Product R-9	4,978		–

This only applies to equipment that was evacuated.

The 7th Mixed Air Division	Available on 22 June 1941 (kg)	Destroyed during the evacuation (kg)	Abandoned during the evacuation (kg)
The 100th Airfield Servicing Battalion (9th High-Speed Bomber Air Regiment)			
B-74 aviation fuel	145,000		
B-70 aviation fuel	30,000		
2nd grade fuel	521,500[1]		
Aviation oil	20,000		
Product R-9	2,900		
The 111th Airfield Servicing Battalion (46th High-Speed Bomber Air Regiment)			
B-78 Aviation fuel	125,000	50,000	75,000
B-74 aviation fuel	85,460	25,000	
B-80 aviation fuel	177,470	40,000	35,000
Aviation starter fuel	9,000	9,000	–
B-59 aviation fuel	2,000	2,000	–
Fuel for road vehicles	3,000	3,000	–
Aviation oil	27,000	20,000	7,000
Product R-9	7,300	7,000	300
The 112th Airfield Servicing Battalion (10th Fighter Air Regiment)			
B-78 aviation fuel	26,000	26,000	–
B-74 aviation fuel	37,000	37,000	–
B-70 aviation fuel	58,000	58,000	–
Aviation oil	30,000	30,000	–

Note
1 Of those 500,000 kg represented the Baltic Special Military District's reserve.

The 6th Mixed Air Division	Available on 22 June 1941 (kg)	Destroyed during the evacuation (kg)	Abandoned during the evacuation (kg)
The 100th Airfield Servicing Battalion (21st Fighter Air Regiment)			
B-78 aviation fuel	43,500	–	4,500
B-74 aviation fuel	14,000	–	2,400
B-70 aviation fuel	79,500[1]	–	–
B-59 aviation fuel	750	–	750
Fuel for road vehicles	16,000	–	–
Aviation oil	22,700	–	9,500
Product R-9	5,700	–	2,100
The 101st Airfield Servicing Battalion (148th Fighter Air Regiment)			
B-80 aviation fuel	27,000	27,000	–
B-78 aviation fuel	60,000	60,000	–
B-74 aviation fuel	65,000	58,000	–
B-70 aviation fuel	60,000	60,000	–
Fuel for road vehicles	30,000	30,000	–
Aviation oil	20,000	20,000	–
Product R-9	3,000	3,000	–
The 102nd Airfield Servicing Battalion (239th Fighter Air Regiment)			
B-74 aviation fuel	38,000	38,000	–
Fuel for road vehicles	8,500	8,500	–
Aviation oil	2,500	2,500	–
Product R-9	580	580	–
103rd Airfield Servicing Battalion (40th High-Speed Bomber Air Regiment)			
B-74 aviation fuel	21,000	–	10,000
B-70 aviation fuel	15,000	–	5,000
B-59 aviation fuel	8,000	–	5,000
Diesel fuel	4,000	–	4,000
Aviation oil	28,000	–	28,000
Product R-9	1,000	–	–

Note

1 This was destroyed during a bombing raid.

Appendix IV

The availability of ammunition in the Airfield Servicing Battalions (in terms of pieces of ammunition)

The 8th Mixed Air Division	Available on 22 June 1941	Destroyed during the evacuation	Abandoned during the evacuation	Spent
The 188th Airfield Servicing Battalion (61st Ground Attack Air Regiment)				
AF–70	100	100		
FAB–50	876	500	–	176
AO–25	470	250	50	170
AO–15	200	200	–	–
AO–10	3,189	3,189	–	–
AO–8	1,210	1,210	–	–
ZAB–50	100	100	–	–
ZAB–10	500	500	–	–
SAB–3	156	156	–	–
Synchronised B–32 ShKAS shells	786,000	767,500	–	18,500[1]
Synchronised 3B–46 ShKAS shells	1,329,000	1,314,000	–	15,000[1]
Synchronised P3 shells	624,000	609,000	–	15,000[1]
ShKAS shells both standard and turret mounted	174,000	174,000	–	–
BS 12.7mm and B–32 shells	55,000	55,000	–	–
BS 12.7mm and B3T shells	43,000	43,000	–	–
129th Airfield Servicing Battalion (31st Fighter Air Regiment)				
FAB–50m2	1,210	1,210	–	–
FAB–50	271	271	–	–
AO–8	120	120	–	–
ShVAK shells	1,730	1,730	–	–
ShKAS shells	9,275,000	9,275,000	–	–
BS shells	24,500	24,500	–	–
ShKAS links[2]	2,275,000	2,275,000	–	–
BS links[2]	24,500	24,500	–	–
ShVAK links	3,000	3,000	–	–
The 130th Airfield Servicing Battalion (15th Fighter Air Regiment)				
FAB-50	714	598	116	-
ZAB-50	295	224	71	–
AO-25	1,476	1,316	160	–

The 8th Mixed Air Division	Available on 22 June 1941	Destroyed during the evacuation	Abandoned during the evacuation	Spent
AO-15	420	20	400	–
AO-10	126	126	–	–
AO-8	252	246	6	–
ZAB-10	500	500	–	–
ZAB-1e	960	960	–	–
SAB-3m	156	156	–	–
AO-2.5	980	980	–	–
Synchronised B-32 ShKAS shells	449,290	348,232	–	52,354[3]
Synchronised 3B-46 ShKAS shells	874,630	680,819	97,408	98,333[3]
Synchronised P3 ShKAS shells	458,137	260,721	97,408	100,008[3]
Synchronised T-46 ShKAS shells	91,835	86,217	–	5,618[3]
Standard ShKAS shells	231,395	214,536	–	15,141[3]
ShKAS links[2]	2,132,922	1,607,581	243,520	279,871[4]
12.7mm B-32 BS shells	74,388	60945	–	13,437[4]
12.7mm B3T shells	33,139	21,027	–	12,112[4]

Notes
1 Recovered during the evacuation, the number of shells actually used is not known.
2 This relates to ammunition that has been packed into ammunition belts.
3 Destroyed during a bombing raid.
4 Destroyed during a bombing raid.

The 57th Mixed Air Division	Available on 22 June 1941	Destroyed during the evacuation	Abandoned during the evacuation	Spent
The 107th Airfield Servicing Battalion (49th Fighter Air Regiment)				
FAB-50	1,310	1,310	–	–
AO-25m2	1,000	1,000	–	–
AO-25m1	320	320	–	–
AO-15	392	392	–	–
AO-10	400	400	–	–
AF-16	96	96	–	–
AF-32	50	50	–	–
SAB-15	52	52	–	–
SAB-15m3	504	504	–	–
Synchronised B-32 ShKAS shells	567,014	567,014	–	–
Synchronised 3B-46 ShKAS shells	1,038,400	1,038,400	–	–
Synchronised P3 ShKAS shells	473,520	473,520	–	–
Synchronised T-46 ShKAS shells	471,445	471,445	–	–
Synchronised ShKAS shells both standard and turret mounted	706,546	706,546	–	–
ShKAS links[1]	3,471,000	3,471,000	–	–
The 126th Airfield Servicing Battalion (42nd High-Speed Bomber Air Regiment)				
FAB-50	913	913	–	–
AO-25	500	500	–	–
AO-15	510	510	–	–
AO-10	110	110	–	–
AO-8	504	504	–	–

The 57th Mixed Air Division	Available on 22 June 1941	Destroyed during the evacuation	Abandoned during the evacuation	Spent
ShKAS shells	3,700,000	3,700,000	–	–
PV shells	310,000	310,000	–	–
BS shells	40,000	40,000	–	–
The 125th Airfield Servicing Battalion (54th High-Speed Bomber Air Regiment)				
FAB-500	15	15	–	–
FAB-250	848	848	–	–
FAB-100	4,231	4,231	–	–
FAB-50	1,932	1,932	–	–
AO-25m1	1,806	1,806	–	–
AO-20	180	180	–	–
AO-15	1,050	1,050	–	–
AO-10	1,000	1,000	–	–
AO-2.5	14,000	14,000	–	–
ZAB-50tg	380	380	–	–
ZAB-1ae	2,015	2,015	–	–
RRAB-3	200	200	–	–
SAB-3	560	560	–	–
RS-132	76	76	–	–
B-32 ShKAS shells	264,800	268,400	–	–
3B-46 ShKAS shells	1,225,900	1,225,900	–	–
P3 ShKAS shells	1,011,440	1,011,440	–	–
T-46 ShKAS shells	428,961	428,961	–	–
T-30 ShKAS shells	154,819	154,819	–	–
Standard ShKAS shells	302,349	302,349	–	–
ShKAS links[1]	4,240,000	4,240,000	–	–

Note
1 This relates to shells that have been packed into ammunition belts.

The 7th Mixed Air Division	Available on 22 June 1941	Destroyed during the evacuation	Abandoned during the evacuation	Spent
The 112th Airfield Servicing Battalion (10th Fighter Air Regiment)				
AO-25	700	700[1]	–	–
AO-10	126	126	–	–
AOKh-10	168	168	–	–
AO-8	384	384	–	–
SAB-3m2	70	70	–	–
VAP-6	10	10	–	–
Synchronised ShKAS shells	2,000,000	2,000,000	–	–
ShKAS shells both standard and turret mounted	320,000	320,000	–	–
PV-1 shells	320,000	320,000	–	–
BS shells	70,000	70,000	–	–
ShVAK shells	100,000	100,000	–	–
BS links	70,000	70,000	–	–
ShVAK links	100,000	100,000	–	–
The 111th Airfield Servicing Battalion (46th High-Speed Bomber Air Regiment)				

The 7th Mixed Air Division	Available on 22 June 1941	Destroyed during the evacuation	Abandoned during the evacuation	Spent
FAB-250	110	110	–	–
FAB-100	1,901	1,901	–	–
AO-20	300	300	–	–
AO-215	700	700	–	–
AO-2.5	2,000	2,000	–	–
ZAB-50	120	120	–	–
ZAB-10	280	280	–	–
B-32 ShKAS shells	125,840	125,840	–	–
3B-46 ShKAS shells	250,800	250,800	–	–
P3 ShKAS shells	1,251,360	1,251,360	–	–
ShKAS links[2]	1,625,000	1,625,000	–	–
The 110th Airfield Servicing Battalion (9th High-Speed Bomber Air Regiment)				
FAB-500	30	30[3]	–	–
BRAB-500	15	15	–	–
FAB-250	390	390	–	–
FAB-100	1,989	1,989	–	–
FAB-50	1,125	1,125	–	–
AO-25m1	200	200	–	–
AO-15	3,230	3,230	–	–
AO-10	1,000	1,000	–	–
AO-8	3,000	3,000	–	–
AO-2.5	8,000	8,000	–	–
ZAB-50tg	240	240	–	–
ZAB-10tg	500	500	–	–
ZAB-2.5t	3,000	3,000	–	–
RRAB--3sps	217	217	–	–
SAB-3-m	684	684	–	–
AZh-2	5,000	5,000	–	–
B-32 ShKAS shells	153,894	153,894	–	–
3B-46 ShKAS shells	911,652	911,652	–	–
P3 ShKAS shells	94,298	94,298	–	–
T-46 ShKAS shells	101,200	101,2000	–	–
T-30 ShKAS shells	265,620	265,620	–	–
Standard ShKAS shells	940,848	940,848	–	–
Synchronised B-32 ShKAS shells	250,800	250,800	–	–
Synchronised 3B-46 ShKAS shells	554,400	554,400	–	–
Synchronised P3 ShKAS shells	500,720	500,720	–	–
Standard synchronised ShKAS shells	69,240	69,240	–	–

Notes
1 Recovered during the evacuation, the number of shells used is not known.
2 This relates to shells that have been packed into ammunition belts.
2 It has not been possibly to establish how many were destroyed during the bombing, and how many were destroyed during the evacuation.

The 6th Mixed Air Division	Available on 22 June 1941	Destroyed during the evacuation	Abandoned during the evacuation	Spent
The 100th Airfield Servicing Battalion (21st Fighter Air Regiment)				
FAB-1000	2	–	2	
FAB-500	15	–	15	
FAB-250	178	–	166	12
FAB-100	2,581	–	2,481	100
FAB-50	981	–	969	12
AO-20	416	–	416	
AO-15	288	–	288	–
AO-8	300	–	300	–
RRAB-3	6	–	6	–
ZAB-1e	48	–	48	–
SAB-5	71	–	71	–
The 101st Airfield Servicing Battalion (148th Fighter Air Regiment)				
FAB-100	32	32	–	–
AO-25	1,000	1,000	–	–
AO-8	968	868	–	100
ZAB-50	120	120	–	–
ZAB-10	650	650	–	–
Synchronised ShKAS shells	14[1]	13[1]	–	–
The 103rd Airfield Servicing Battalion (40th High-Speed Bomber Air Regiment)				
FAB-500	15	–	–	–
BRAB-500	15	–	–	–
FAB-250	518	–	–	13
FAB-1000	3,113	–	–	440
FAB-50	1,593		–	96
AO-25m1	920	180	–	–
AO-20	734	–	–	–
AO-15	629	–	–	–
AO-10	400	–	–	–
AO-8	5,543	900	–	–
AO-2.5	8,000	2,000	–	–
ZAB-50tg	120	20	100	–
ZAB1e	4,000	200	–	–
RRAB-3	235	–	235	–
SAB-15	52	–	–	–
SAB-3-m	704	–	–	–
RS-132	76	–	–	–
B-32 ShKAS shells	318,921	–	–	–
3B-46 ShKAS shells	101,572	–	–	–
P3 ShKAS shells	181,152	–	–	–
T-46 ShKAS shells	100,650	–	–	–
T-30 ShKAS shells	105,696	105,696	–	–
Synchronised B-32 ShKAS shells	742,720	–	–	–
Synchronised 3B-46 ShKAS shells	507,760	–	–	–
Synchronised P3 ShKAS shells	500,720	–	–	–
Synchronised T-46 ShKAS shells	249,920	–	–	–

Note

1 Ammunition packs

The 4th Mixed Air Division	Available on 22 June 1941	Destroyed during the evacuation	Abandoned during the evacuation	Spent
The 96th Airfield Servicing Battalion (38th Fighter Air Regiment)				
FAB-50	457	–	–	117
AO-25	1,172	–	–	56
AO-15	401	–	–	–
AO-10	125	–	–	–
AO-8	250	–	–	–
ZAB-50	262	–	–	–
ZAB-10	500	–	–	–
SAB-3	156	–	–	–
AEF-16	120	–	–	–
Synchronised P3 ShKAS shells	519,200	–	–	36,000
Synchronised T-46 ShKAS shells	1,661,000	–	–	–
Synchronised B-32 ShKAS shells	308,760	–	–	18,000
Synchronised 3B-46 ShKAS shells	1,362,000	–	–	36,000
Standard ShKAS shells	1,697,000	–	–	–
PV-1 shells	97,680	–	–	–
Turret mounted B-32 ShKAS shells	242,000	–	–	–
Turret mounted 3B-46 ShKAS shells	366,000	–	–	–
The 90th Airfield Servicing Battalion (50th High-Speed Bomber Air Regiment)				
FAB-500	15	–	–	–
FAB-250	730	30	–	–
FAB-100	2,211	159	–	–
FAB-50	925	200	–	–
AO-20	870	–	–	–
AO-15	1,080	832	–	–
AO-10	1,000	104	–	–
AO-8	1,858	–	–	–
AO-2.5	5,000	–	–	–
ZAB-50tg	250	3	–	–
ZAB-10	500	–	–	–
ZAB-1e	1,008	105	–	–
SAB-25	500	244	–	–
SAB-3m	196	196	–	–
RRAB-3	190	–	–	–
RS-132	226	120	–	–
RS-82	1,000	–	–	–
VAP-500	124	124	–	–
Anisko buckets	250	250	–	–
ShKAS shells	2,602,613	–	44,000	73,800

Index

Index of People – Soviet

Index of People – German

Index of Places – Soviet Zone

Index of Places – German Zone

Index of Soviet Military Formations & Units

Squadrons:

Index of German Military Formations & Units

Air Forces:

Index of Aircraft in Soviet Service

Index of Aircraft in German Service

Index of Aviation Engines

Index of Miscellaneous & General Terms